THE COMPLETE POEMS

OF

LOUIS DANIEL

BRODSKY

VOLUME THREE, 1976–1980

**Missouri Center
for the Book**

ಜಜಜ

Missouri Authors
Collection

Books by LOUIS DANIEL BRODSKY

Poetry

Five Facets of Myself   (1967)* (1995)

The Easy Philosopher   (1967)* (1995)

"A Hard Coming of It" and Other Poems   (1967)* (1995)

The Foul Rag-and-Bone Shop   (1967)* (1969, exp.)* (1995, exp.)

Points in Time   (1971)* (1995) (1996)

Taking the Back Road Home   (1972)* (1997) (2000)

Trip to Tipton and Other Compulsions   (1973)* (1997)

"The Talking Machine" and Other Poems   (1974)* (1997)

Tiffany Shade   (1974)* (1997)

Trilogy: A Birth Cycle   (1974) (1998)

Cold Companionable Streams   (1975)* (1999)

Monday's Child   (1975) (1998)

Preparing for Incarnations   (1975)* (1976, exp.) (1999) (1999, exp.)

The Kingdom of Gewgaw   (1976) (2000)

Point of Americas II   (1976) (1998)

La Preciosa   (1977) (2001)

Stranded in the Land of Transients   (1978) (2000)

The Uncelebrated Ceremony of Pants-Factory Fatso   (1978) (2001)

Birds in Passage   (1980) (2001)

Résumé of a Scrapegoat   (1980) (2001)

Mississippi Vistas: Volume One of A Mississippi Trilogy   (1983) (1990)

You Can't Go Back, Exactly   (1988, two eds.) (1989) (2003, exp.)

The Thorough Earth   (1989)

Four and Twenty Blackbirds Soaring   (1989)

Falling from Heaven: Holocaust Poems of a Jew and a Gentile
   (with William Heyen)   (1991)

Forever, for Now: Poems for a Later Love   (1991)

Mistress Mississippi: Volume Three of A Mississippi Trilogy   (1992)

A Gleam in the Eye: Poems for a First Baby   (1992)

Gestapo Crows: Holocaust Poems   (1992)

The Capital Café: Poems of Redneck, U.S.A.   (1993)

Disappearing in Mississippi Latitudes: Volume Two of A Mississippi Trilogy   (1994)

A Mississippi Trilogy: A Poetic Saga of the South   (1995)*

Paper-Whites for Lady Jane: Poems of a Midlife Love Affair   (1995)

The Complete Poems of Louis Daniel Brodsky: Volume One, 1963–1967
   (edited by Sheri L. Vandermolen)   (1996)

Three Early Books of Poems by Louis Daniel Brodsky, 1967–1969:
   The Easy Philosopher, "A Hard Coming of It" and Other Poems, and
   The Foul Rag-and-Bone Shop (edited by Sheri L. Vandermolen)   (1997)

The Eleventh Lost Tribe: Poems of the Holocaust   (1998)

Toward the Torah, Soaring: Poems of the Renascence of Faith   (1998)

Voice Within the Void: Poems of Homo supinus   (2000)

Rabbi Auschwitz: Poems Touching the Shoah   (2000)*

The Swastika Clock: Endlösung Poems   (2001)*

Shadow War: A Poetic Chronicle of September 11 and Beyond, Volume One   (2001) (2004)
The Complete Poems of Louis Daniel Brodsky: Volume Two, 1967–1976
   (edited by Sheri L. Vandermolen)   (2002)
Shadow War: A Poetic Chronicle of September 11 and Beyond, Volume Two   (2002) (2004)
Shadow War: A Poetic Chronicle of September 11 and Beyond, Volume Three   (2002) (2004)
Shadow War: A Poetic Chronicle of September 11 and Beyond, Volume Four   (2002) (2004)
Shadow War: A Poetic Chronicle of September 11 and Beyond, Volume Five   (2002) (2004)
Heavenward   (2003)*
Regime Change: Poems of America's Showdown with Iraq, Volume One   (2003)*
Regime Change: Poems of America's Showdown with Iraq, Volume Two   (2003)*
Regime Change: Poems of America's Showdown with Iraq, Volume Three   (2003)*
The Complete Poems of Louis Daniel Brodsky: Volume Three, 1976–1980
   (edited by Sheri L. Vandermolen)   (2004)

Bibliography *(coedited with Robert Hamblin)*

Selections from the William Faulkner Collection of Louis Daniel Brodsky:
   A Descriptive Catalogue   (1979)
Faulkner: A Comprehensive Guide to the Brodsky Collection
   Volume I: The Bibliography   (1982)
   Volume II: The Letters   (1984)
   Volume III: *The De Gaulle Story*   (1984)
   Volume IV: *Battle Cry*   (1985)
   Volume V: Manuscripts and Documents   (1989)
Country Lawyer and Other Stories for the Screen by William Faulkner   (1987)
Stallion Road: A Screenplay by William Faulkner   (1989)

Biography

William Faulkner, Life Glimpses   (1990)

Fiction

Between Grief and Nothing *(novel)*   (1964)*
Between the Heron and the Wren *(novel)*   (1965)*
"Dink Phlager's Alligator" and Other Stories   (1966)*
The Drift of Things *(novel)*   (1966)*
Vineyard's Toys *(novel)*   (1967)*
The Bindle Stiffs *(novel)*   (1968)*
Yellow Bricks *(short fictions)*   (1999)
Catchin' the Drift o' the Draft *(short fictions)*   (1999)
This Here's a Merica *(short fictions)*   (1999)
Leaky Tubs *(short fictions)*   (2001)
Rated Xmas *(short fictions)*   (2003)
Nuts to You! *(short fictions)*   (2004)

Memoir

The Adventures of the Night Riders, Better Known as the Terrible Trio
   (with Richard Milsten)   (1961)*

* *Unpublished*

Louis Daniel Brodsky
(with his daughter, Trilogy, circa 1978)

Louis Daniel Brodsky
12/30/07
St. Louis, M

The Complete Poems

of

Louis Daniel

BRODSKY

Volume Three, 1976–1980

Edited by

Sheri L. Vandermolen

TIME BEING BOOKS
POETRY IN SIGHT AND SOUND

An imprint of Time Being Press
St. Louis, Missouri

Time Being Books® is an imprint of Time Being Press®, St. Louis, Missouri.

Time Being Press® is a 501(c)(3) not-for-profit corporation.

Time Being Books® volumes are printed on acid-free paper, and binding materials
are chosen for strength and durability.

ISBN 1-56809-101-X (Hardcover)
ISBN 1-56809-102-8 (Paperback)

Library of Congress Cataloging-in-Publication Data:

Brodsky, Louis Daniel.
    The complete poems of Louis Daniel Brodsky / edited by Sheri L.
Vandermolen.
    [Poems]
    St. Louis, Mo. : Time Being Books, c1996–<c2002>
    Related Names: Vandermolen, Sheri L.
        v. <1–2> : ill. ; 24 cm.
    ISBN 1-56809-019-6 (v. 1); 1-56809-020-X (v. 1 : pbk.); 1-56809-073-0
(v. 2); 1-56809-074-9 (v. 2 : pbk.)
    Incomplete Contents: v. 1. 1963–1967 — v. 2. 1967–1976
    Includes index.
PS3552.R623A17   1996
811'.54—dc20   96017149

Cover photo (of Brodsky and his son, Troika, circa 1978) and frontispiece
    photo (of Brodsky and his daughter, Trilogy, circa 1978) provided by the
    Brodsky family
Cover design by Jeff Hirsch and Sheri L. Vandermolen
Book design and typesetting by Sheri L. Vandermolen
Manufactured in the United States of America

First Edition, first printing (2004)

ACKNOWLEDGMENTS

I am indebted to Sheri L. Vandermolen, Editor in Chief of Time Being Books, who has, with skill and discernment, methodically prepared each of the poems in this volume. Were it not for her commitment to presenting the material in its most complete and correct form, this part of my poetic record would not exist. Her standards of excellence continue to inspire me.

Jerry Call, Managing Editor of Time Being Books, has brought to this project his matchless intellect and editorial abilities, without which my critical judgment would have been less well-informed.

I wish to give due mention to the following publications, in which certain of my poems from July 1976 through December 1980 were published, some in different forms: *Aabye* ("Welding a Sunset"); *Ariel* ("The Ghost of San Clemente"); *Big Muddy* ("Kudzu"); *Bitterroot Poetry Magazine* ("Ossuary"); *Chaminade Literary Review* ("Resurrection" [2/11/77 — (3)]); *The Farmington Press* ("An Elegy"); *First Time* ("Early-Morning Distractions"); *Forum* ("Émigré in the Promised Land"); *Hampden-Sydney Poetry Review* ("Enchantment," as "Gowan's Enchantment"); *The Hollins Critic* ("Pecan Grove"); *Kansas Quarterly* ("An Autumnal" [9/8/79] and "Parachutes"); *Kentucky Poetry Review* ("The Outlander"); *The Literary Review* ("An Accompaniment to the Rain"); *Midwest Poetry Review* ("O, I Sing Ye, Eidolons"); *Negative Capability* ("Oxford Nocturne"); *Parnassus Literary Journal* ("Composing the Garden Book of Verse," as "Composing a Garden Book of Verse"); *Prism International* ("*La primavera*" [4/5/77]); *Roanoke Review* ("Porch People," as "Delta Porch People"); *The Round Table* ("Visitation Rites"); *St. Andrews Review* ("College Town, Friday Night"); *St. Louis Country Day School Magazine* ("Balloons"); *South Carolina Review* ("The Ghosts of Rowan Oak," "Making a Settlement," "Miss Emily," and "The Trysting Place"); *Whetstone* ("The Music of Ancient Pompeii," "THC," and "Voices in the Band"); *Whole Notes* ("Wind-Flowers"); *Wisconsin Review* ("Trial by Fire and Water: After Reading *The Arrowhead*," as "Trial by Fire and Water"); *Women's Studies* ("Miss Emily"); and *Zillah* ("Lament," as "Faulkner and Yoknapatawpha Conference 1979").

Several poems in this volume appear, in different forms, in the two editions of my book *La Preciosa* (Farmington Press, 1977; Time Being Books, 2001): "After Disney World," "Bad Words," "Beachcombers," "Budding Poetess," "Catching Snowflakes," "Easter Sunday: The Hunt," "Full Circle," "The Intruder," "Little Party People," "The Macaws," "Trilogy's Song," "The Typist," and "Zooperstitions."

"Chiaroscuro" appears in the unpublished pamphlet *The Ashkeeper's Everlasting Passion Week* (1986).

The following poems appear in the unpublished pamphlet *Mississippi Vistas: 5 Poems by Louis Daniel Brodsky* (1980): "The Griots of Rowan Oak," "Kudzu," "Miss Emily," "The Outlander," and "Oxford Nocturne."

These poems appear in the unpublished pamphlet *Mississippi Vistas* (1980): "An Accompaniment to the Rain," "A Country Boy's Summer-Afternoon Idyll" (as "Summer-Afternoon Idyll"), "Enchantment" (as "Gowan's Enchantment"), "The Ghosts of Rowan Oak," "The Griots of Rowan Oak" (as "Genealogists"), "The Joggers," "Kudzu," "Miss Emily," "The Outlander," "Oxford Nocturne," "The Passing of Orders," "Pilgrimage in Harvest Time," "Porch People" (as "Delta Porch People"), "Shall Inherit," "Signs of the Times," "Slaves," and "Space and Time" (as "Guest Lecturer").

"Arcady in Tipton (as "Arcady in Laputa"), "The Harvesters," "In the Last Stages" (as "Moe's Bone of Contention"), "'Lions Meet Here'," "Moped," and "Vigilantes" appear in *The Capital Café: Poems of Redneck, U.S.A.* (Time Being Books, 1993).

The following poems appear in *Mississippi Vistas: Volume One of A Mississippi Trilogy*, which was originally published as a first edition, with no subtitle, by the University Press of Mississippi, in 1983, and was then issued as a second, revised edition by Timeless Press (now Time Being Books), in 1990; the poems also appear in the compilation translation of the Time Being Books text (Paris: Éditions Gallimard, 1994) and in the unpublished book *A Mississippi Trilogy: A Poetic Saga of the South* (1995): "Accepting the Call" (as "Quentin at Ole Miss"), "An Accompaniment to the Rain," "Addie's Agony," "As I Lay Sleeping," "As the Crow Flies," "Chiaroscuro," "College Town, Friday Night," "A Country Boy's Summer-Afternoon Idyll" (as "Quentin's Summer-Afternoon Idyll"), "Delta Planter" (as "A Delta Planter Returns Home"), "Drought in the Mid-South," "Enchantment" (as "Gowan's Enchantment"), "The Ghosts of Rowan Oak," "The Griots of Rowan Oak" (as "Genealogists"), "Held Fast to the Past," "The Joggers" (as "Runners"), "Kudzu," "Miss Emily," "The Outlander," "Oxford Nocturne," "The Passing of Orders" (as "Dilsey," in the second and third editions of *Mississippi Vistas*, in the Gallimard text, and in *A Mississippi Trilogy*), "Pecan Grove," "Pilgrimage in Harvest Time," "Porch People" (as "Delta Porch People"), "Shall Inherit," "Signs of the Times," "Slaves," "Space and Time" (as "A Guest Lecturer Rehearses"), "Trying to Conceive," "The Trysting Place," "Visitation Rites," and "Writer in Flight."

"Bud" (as "Freedom Seeker") and "Trial by Fire and Water: After Reading *The Arrowhead*" (as "Trial by Fire and Water") appear in *You Can't Go Back, Exactly*, released as first and second editions, by Timeless Press, in 1988 and 1989, and as a third edition, by Time Being Books, in 2003; they also appear in a compilation translation of that text (Paris: Éditions Gallimard, 1994).

"The Auction," "An Autumnal" (9/8/79), "Balloons," "Composing the Garden Book of Verse" (as "Composing a Garden Book of Verse") "The Drift of Things," "I Am the Egg Man," "*In absentia*: A Panegyric" (as "*In absentia*"), "Jan's Panegyric" (as "A Jan-egyric"), "On the Origin of Mordecai Darwin," "Parachutes," and "The Poet Admonishes Himself" appear in *Four and Twenty Blackbirds Soaring*, published by Timeless Press, in 1989, and in a compilation translation of that text (Paris: Éditions Gallimard, 1993).

"Émigré in the Promised Land" and "Ossuary" appear in *The Thorough Earth*, published by Timeless Press, in 1989, and in a compilation translation of that text (Paris: Éditions Gallimard, 1992).

"Lament" (as "Faulkner and Yoknapatawpha Conference 1979") and "[The rains complain; they groan.]" (as "Ghost Writer") appear in *Disappearing in Mississippi Latitudes: Volume Two of A Mississippi Trilogy* (Time Being Books, 1994) and in the unpublished book *A Mississippi Trilogy: A Poetic Saga of the South* (1995).

"Belinda, Lady of Fiesole" (as "Lady of Fiesole"), "Guilt-Throes," and "Jongleur: Initiation Rites" appear in *Mistress Mississippi: Volume Three of A Mississippi Trilogy* (Time Being Books, 1992) and in the unpublished book *A Mississippi Trilogy: A Poetic Saga of the South* (1995).

"The Pawnbroker's Second Generation" (as "A Second-Generation 'Survivor'"), "Revisiting the Old Home" (as "Revisiting Childhood Haunts"), and "[The days have eyes, have teeth.]" (as "Kafkaesque Vestiges, Germany, 1941") appear in *Gestapo Crows: Holocaust Poems* (Time Being Books, 1992).

"Herr Clement of Buenos Aires," "Patriarch of the Seder," and "[Was it apathy or fear]" (as "The Master Gardeners") appear in *The Eleventh Lost Tribe: Poems of the Holocaust* (Time Being Books, 1998).

"The Rehabilitation of a War Criminal" and "Warehouse of Mannequins" appear as short fictions in *Catchin' the Drift o' the Draft* (Time Being Books, 1999).

"Scroll of a Dead Sea Survivor" and "Sunday-Morning Service" (as "Shabbat") appear in *Toward the Torah, Soaring: Poems of the Renascence of Faith* (Time Being Books, 1998).

"The Rehabilitation of a War Criminal" appears in the unpublished book *Rabbi Auschwitz: Poems Touching the Shoah* (2000).

"The Energy Crunch," "Magi: Fall Sales Meeting '79" (as "Fall/Winter Sales Meeting: Magi"), "Sportscoat Presentation" (as "Spring/Summer Sales Meeting: Sportscoat Presentation"), and "Willy Propositions Beatrice" appear in the book *Peddler on the Road: The Life in a Day of Willy Sypher* (scheduled for publication in 2005).

"Antiphons Sung Among the Dead," "Autumnal Awareness," "The Daydream Tree," "*La primavera*" (4/5/77), " A Morning Valedictory," "Narcissistic Visions," "The Raker," "Rising to the Surface," "Runaway Child," "Sleeping Spider," and "A Taste for Life" appear in the book *A Transcendental Almanac: Poems of Nature* (scheduled for publication in 2005).

---

*Because two or more poems bear this title within volume three, the date of creation is listed, to indicate the appropriate text.

For my daughter, Trilogy,
who will always be the gleam in my eye,

and

for my son, Troika,
in whom I see myself unfolding

The friends that have it I do wrong
When ever I remake a song,
Should know what issue is at stake:
It is myself that I remake.
  — William Butler Yeats, epigraph to his *Collected Works
  in Verse and Prose, Volume Two*

His was a love of Eden's innocent creatures,
Its sky and trees and spices,
A pristine wonderment of its undefiled silence,

Which was the stream that flowed through his head,
Beside whose gently riffled waters
He meditated away his days, years, his life.

His was a child's amazement,
Which gave to his poetry an enchanting purity,
Transformed all who heard it into devotees

Long after he was gone.
And no one ever learned who he was, or cared.
He was his music, and it was theirs.
  — Louis Daniel Brodsky, from "His Music and Theirs"

Contents

EDITOR'S GUIDE TO VOLUME THREE OF THE COMPLETE POEMS SERIES

"Husband," "father," "William Faulkner scholar," "collector," "businessman" — all of these titles applied to Louis Daniel Brodsky, in the 1970s. But by the summer of 1976, his most prominent role was as a "poet in flight," willing to pursue his true calling, as a composer of verse, on a daily basis, no matter his location, even as his thriving manufacturing career exacted further sacrifice from him.

Having seen his outlet stores flourish in Farmington, Tipton, Salisbury, and Sullivan, Missouri, as well as in New Athens, Illinois, Brodsky proposed extending the chain beyond the Midwest, when his father's company, Biltwell, purchased a garment factory in West Helena, Arkansas, in the summer of 1976. While, in part, Brodsky was scouting entrepreneurial prospects in a fledgling industry, the town's proximity to Oxford, Mississippi, was certainly not lost on this consummate Faulkner enthusiast, who knew the additional managerial duties would be a perfect excuse for him to head south, drawn, as he was, to Faulkner's Rowan Oak estate and the University of Mississippi campus.

Consumed with augmenting his Faulkner collection and locked into making rounds, to the Midwest and now the South as well, in order to oversee the stores, Brodsky found himself spending several days on the road, each week, his trips increasing in both frequency and duration. But he never stopped writing. As the demands on his time amplified, so too did his desire to get the poems down on paper, even if it meant he might never return to them, to apply revision, as he had typically done with new work in the 1960s and early '70s.

Compelled, the self-proclaimed "itinerant limner" often penned several pieces per day, and no setting was off-limits; now that he habitually carried a notebook in his attaché case, he could create poems wherever he was, whether in the car, a restaurant, his motel room, or the nearest lounge. Although he still used the typewriter when at home and occasionally jotted on place mats or napkins when at local cafés, the notebook became his tool of choice. Its easy access and numbered, blue-ruled pages reinforced his disciplined routine, offering a ready "blank canvas" at any hour.

Brodsky became ever more adept at writing while driving, and as a result, any given leg of a journey could yield a poem or portion of a poem, to be modified or completed later. However, subjecting the creative process to such stops and starts had its drawbacks. Since he might begin a piece in the morning, on the way from Farmington to another town, and then not finish it until that afternoon (on his way to another destination), that night, or even the next morning (upon his return home), he had to strive continually to retain his initial train of thought, not succumb to fatigue or lose interest in the piece.

Likewise, writing in such sporadic intervals sometimes caused Brodsky's verse to suffer from knotty rhythms, which he had little, if any, chance to recast. Previously he had smoothed ragged lines by retooling the poem, through several sheets of drafts; now his editing was swiftly funneled into each piece via handwritten changes inserted directly on the page of original composition. To compensate, Brodsky attempted to retain fluidity by brainstorming more actively and developing malleable concepts and constructions that he could shape mentally, as they flowed from his pen.

This filtering mechanism enhanced the quality of his writing — a freshly finished poem in the notebook, from the mid 1970s, was equivalent to those, from years prior, having two or three rounds of typewritten corrections. Brodsky had gained confidence and thus composed with greater authority, so the newer pieces held their own, stylistically, despite being slightly less polished. While he never considered these later poems truly "finished," since after-the-fact revision was not taking place, he was accomplishing his more immediate goal of committing them to the page, to document a time and a place, as a "snapshot" of sorts.

While he had originally intended for the production of his books to keep pace with his writing, Brodsky soon faced a backlog of work from the early to mid 1970s and recognized he had few options but to set aside the new poems, editing only those pieces of particular interest to him, like those composed for special occasions, such as holidays or poetry readings. Instead of perfecting his current material for publication, he felt it more methodical to chip away at his previous accumulation and continue formulating his chronologically arranged "white books" (paperback volumes of Brodsky's verse, printed by Farmington Press in limited runs, with white covers bearing reproductions of artwork by his wife, Jan). He revised these poem groupings during days spent in Farmington and during vacations in Fort Lauderdale.

Having tinkered with his latest collection, *Point of Americas II*, for more than two years, to refine its forty-one poems (from March through July 1974) as well as its overall thematic Florida–Farmington–Florida structure, he finally sent the book to Farmington Press in July 1976, releasing it as a signed, limited edition of four hundred copies. He then turned his attentions to two other unpublished manuscripts: *Preparing for Incarnations* (with forty-four pieces, from July through September 1974) and *Cold Companionable Streams* (with thirty-eight pieces, from September 1974 through January 1975). Adjusting wording and lineation for all the poems and removing just two ("New Year's Eve" and "Orange Bowl," from January 1975), Brodsky combined both texts into a single, expanded book, also titled *Preparing for Incarnations*, which he edited for months and would eventually have published, by Farmington Press, in December 1976, as a signed, limited edition of five hundred copies.

Squeezing in revision of this early work as his schedule allowed, Brodsky kept his primary focus on conceiving new, more innovative poems. The flexibility he had achieved as a "road poet" enabled him to branch out artistically, exploring varied forms and voices, with much of the impetus for the most radical experimentation coming from his welling internal chaos. At home, he was beleaguered by marital conflict, as feelings of frustrations and resentment intensified between him and Jan, who had spent so many nights alone, in Farmington, and borne the responsibility of caring for their daughter, Trilogy, while he was away. But out on the highway, he experienced catharsis. Paradoxically, the travel that stoked the tensions also brought relief, by allowing Brodsky to indulge his creative impulses, regain both control and independence. The writing was, at once, a private refuge and a place to soar, lift the poems to daring new heights of sentience, imagination, and fantasy.

Profound themes and characters materialized from his emotional discord as well, including Willy Sypher, a downtrodden but perseverant salesman for the fictional company Acme-Zenith Clothing, who was a composite of generations of Brodsky ragmen, many Biltwell salesmen, and Brodsky himself. The pieces declared Willy's, and the poet's own, loneliness, dejection, and Quixote-inspired determination, as recorded in "Odometer" (July 1976), "Willy, Knight of the Breakfast Table" (September 1976), and "Willy Dines Out" (December 1976). Brodsky also channeled his negative energies into what would become some of his earliest Holocaust and diaspora poems, such as "Émigré in the Promised Land" (July 1976), "Warehouse of Mannequins" (September 1976), "The Rehabilitation of a War Criminal," "Smothered in Christmas," and "The Wandering Jew" (all from December 1976), "Overexposure" (January 1977), and "Patriarch of the Seder" (February 1977).

These darker elements of his imagination were brought into balance with the emergence of a gentler character: the idealistic, if naive, Northern outlander/apologist, a man hoping to right society's inequities by exposing the South's lingering racial biases and highlighting the integrity all people share. Like Brodsky, who had attended his first Faulkner and Yoknapatawpha Conference in August 1976 and was delving ever deeper into Mississippi's mystique, this autobiographical counterpart was an ardent Faulkner novitiate, come to worship at Oxford's literary altar, in the name of scholarship and passion.

Having fashioned various paeans and reflections on Faulkner, the town, and its people ("Chiaroscuro," "The Ghosts of Rowan Oak," "Accepting the Call," "As I Lay Sleeping," and "The Trysting Place"), during the conference, Brodsky steeped himself in the local culture and returned to Oxford as frequently as possible. Whether relaxing on campus, sitting in a bar, meditating at Rowan Oak, or jogging through the shady purlieus of Bailey's Woods, Brodsky was entranced. Even West Helena, Arkansas, though only three hundred miles from his home, felt an entire world away, and he captured the land's tantalizing but sad, even brooding, essence in poems such as "Pecan Grove," "Porch People," and "Drought in the Mid-South" (all from August 1976), "The Outlander" (April 1977), and "Slaves" (August 1977).

In time, Brodsky became so comfortable in that region, it transformed into his home away from home. While Farmington appreciated Biltwell as a major supplier of jobs and respected Brodsky, as assistant plant manager, his occupation was his only true link to the community. But in Oxford, he and the townspeople shared the bond of Faulkner, who had touched all their lives, and he developed strong friendships with many of the residents. Through his participation at the conferences and due to his resolution to meet those who might help cultivate his private collection and broaden his historical knowledge, Brodsky also became acquainted with Faulkner's daughter, Jill, his step-granddaughter, Victoria, and his nephews Jimmy and "Chooky," as well as certain Faulkner friends, business associates, and mistresses. And he came to know fellow historians, writers, and scholars, including Robert Penn Warren, Lewis P. Simpson, Malcolm Cowley, Cleanth Brooks, Joseph Blotner, and James Meriwether, to whom he was introduced in 1977, along with Robert Hamblin, professor of English, from Southeast Missouri State University, whom he met in 1978.

With his Faulkner acquisitions accumulating quickly, thanks to invaluable advice from Meriwether and others, Brodsky realized the need to organize his prodigious holdings and soon partnered with Hamblin, to research and systematize bibliographic data. They spent countless hours poring over notes and files, comparing paper stocks and handwriting samples, and prioritizing stacks of annotated index cards, in a spirit of true camaraderie. Fortified by the satisfaction inherent in the work, Brodsky and Hamblin escalated their efforts, eventually rendering, from their "project," the full-scale text *Selections from the William Faulkner Collection of Louis Daniel Brodsky: A Descriptive Catalogue* (which would be published by University Press of Virginia, in 1979, and, in due course, lead to their multivolume series *Faulkner: A Comprehensive Guide to the Brodsky Collection*, issued by University Press of Mississippi). It was yet another enormous undertaking requiring Brodsky's attention, and even in Farmington, he preoccupied himself with the task, frequently inviting Hamblin to his home and collaborating with him, at the dining-room table, to develop the manuscript.

When not consumed with that endeavor, he pressed ahead in developing new poetry books. With Trilogy having turned three in May 1977 and Jan due to give birth to their second child that fall, Brodsky decided to craft a gift for his wife and little girl, gathering thirty-three pieces he had composed about his daughter since his first "baby books," *Trilogy: A Birth Cycle* (1974) and *Monday's Child* (1975). Tenderly celebrating her growth, as in the poems "Retrieving Leaves" (October 1975) and "Trilogy's Song" (January 1977), and humorously commemorating her daily explorations, as in "Her First Playmate" (June 1976) and "Bad Words" (February 1977), *La Preciosa*, a signed, limited edition of five hundred copies, was published in October 1977, the same month that Jan gave birth to their son, Louis Daniel Brodsky III, whom they nicknamed "Troika" (a term, of Russian origin, for a three-horse vehicle or for a threesome of equal power).

But generating another book did little to decrease the amassing batches of his poems still waiting to be put into print. For the sake of efficiency, Brodsky veered away from complex thematic structuring and opted to sequence his next white books solely by chronology. He apportioned his rapidly diminishing free time into revision sessions for two additional manuscripts: *Stranded in the Land of Transients* (with forty-seven poems, from June 1975 through October 1975), issued by Farmington Press in May 1978, and *The Uncelebrated Ceremony of Pants-Factory Fatso* (with forty-six poems, from December 1975 through March 1976), released in December 1978, both of which were published as signed, limited editions of five hundred copies.

Despite his surging interest in publishing Faulkner bibliography and the white books, Brodsky — always, foremost, a poet — knew his chief priority was composing new verse, much of which now emanated from utter heartache. What had begun as a simple lack of romance and intimacy, between him and his wife, soon ruptured into a chasm of distress, after Troika's birth. Acutely aware of Jan's disappointment in him, as a husband, father, and provider, and beginning to admit his own misgivings about their relationship, Brodsky felt plagued by his failures, both as a family man and a poet. With this turmoil seething just beneath the surface, Brodsky's writing took on a new depth, spawning longer, stream-of-consciousness compositions and confessional pieces, such as "The Wayfarer" (March 1978), "Confessions of a Former Magna Cum Laude" (December 1978), "Looking for Homes" (March 1979), "Skinner Box" (April 1979), "The Father in Us All" (June 1979), and "Returning to Port" (July 1979). Further blurring the line between fiction and reality, he would occasionally pour his desperation into his established characters, especially Willy Sypher, as recorded in "Willy: The Great Wall of China" (November 1978) and "Willy Agonistes" (June 1979).

For all the acclaim his bibliographic work had garnered, success as a poet continued to elude Brodsky. Lecturing and writing about what had become the premier private Faulkner collection in the country had brought him instant gratification, a touch of celebrity. He had maintained contacts with Cleanth Brooks and Lewis P. Simpson, editor of *The Southern Review*, who would later publish not only Brodsky's critical and biographical essays on Faulkner but also a number of his poems, including several about traveling salesman Willy Sypher, and he had come to know Hayden Carruth, the poetry editor at *Harper's*, who evaluated selected Brodsky pieces and accepted two ("Death Comes to the Salesman," from September 1975, and "Rearview Mirror," from December 1975) for the March 1980 issue. But earning the respect of these distinguished men of letters and having selections published in such prestigious literary magazines still brought Brodsky little recognition. In terms of achieving fame, his two worlds — studying Faulkner and composing verse — were mutually exclusive.

Exasperated by the rejection he had come to expect at home and sensing he had lapsed into obscurity as a poet, Brodsky sought yet another outlet for his boundless energy and another diversion from his deep-seated grief: teaching creative-writing and short-story courses, one night a week, at Mineral Area College, just miles from Farmington. While the pursuit brought him joy, by allowing him to give back to his community and reacquaint himself with his roots as a fictionist, it did not lift Brodsky from his despondency, and he continued to express his discontent in pieces such as "Buzzed Confession" (March 1980), "Lament for Paul Gauguin, Who Died in the Marquesas, Bereft" (April 1980), "Tonya" (May 1980), "The Man Who Knew Too Much Too Soon," "[Greed, perfidy, capriciousness, and despair]," and "The Children of the Children" (all from June 1980), "Escaping the Castle's Dungeon" and "Part-Time Poet" (both from July 1980), and "A Call to All Poets and Other Laity and Gentymen" and "Thus Spake Kilroy" (both from August 1980). They were the earliest cries of a man subjugated by desolation, teetering at the brink of a midlife crisis.

It was while caught in this downward spiral that Brodsky committed his first marital infidelity, just weeks after his tenth wedding anniversary. But instead of bolstering his ego, the breach, which occurred during the 1980 Faulkner and Yoknapatawpha Conference, the day before his rousing "The Collector as Sleuthsayer" presentation, fueled his guilt, anxiety, and feelings of inadequacy. Pondering his indiscretion, detailed in "Jongleur: Initiation Rites," "Belinda, Lady of Fiesole," and "Guilt-Throes" (all from August 1980), he vowed, in the months ahead, to rededicate himself to Jan, in an effort to save their marriage. However, the reality of their sundered union continued to manifest itself in poems like *"Los desesperados"* (September 1980), "The Incredible Disappearing Man" (November 1980), and "Down and Out at Forty" (December 1980).

Needing to distract himself, Brodsky set his sights on revising and expanding a small collection of Southern poems he had pulled together, that summer, for Ben Wasson, Faulkner's first agent and editor as well as lifelong friend. To fill out the pamphlet, originally titled *Mississippi Vistas: 5 Poems by Louis Daniel Brodsky*, he chose twelve more Southern pieces from his *oeuvre* and distributed the signed, limited run of fifty copies at a poetry reading on the University of Mississippi campus, in November 1980. More important, the core was now in place for what would become the first edition of *Mississippi Vistas* (published by University Press of Mississippi in 1983) and, ultimately, the first volume of *A Mississippi Trilogy: A Poetic Saga of the South* (unpublished).

During this volatile period, Brodsky also compiled two new white books. He designed the first, *Birds in Passage*, as a gathering of his best work — twenty-seven pieces that had appeared in a variety of anthologies and literary journals (including *The American Scholar*, Ball State University's *Forum*, *Four Quarters*, and *The Literary Review*) as well as in Brodsky's unpublished manuscripts and his prior white books. The volume, he envisioned, would serve as a calling card, of sorts, at literary functions and other events. Because these were favorite pieces that had already appeared in print, he felt no need to alter them significantly or configure the text thematically. Instead, he made only slight corrections, ordered the poems by the journals' dates of publication, and had the book in production by October 1980, creating a signed, limited edition of five hundred copies.

Résumé of a Scrapegoat, on the other hand, received an inordinate amount of preparation. Convinced that writing new poems must take precedence over publishing the old, Brodsky resigned himself to the fact that *Résumé* would, necessarily, constitute the final volume of his white-books series. Thus, throughout 1979 and 1980, he devoted himself to editing the manuscript's forty-seven pieces, composed from March through July 1976. Once he had finished rewording and relineating nearly every poem, he then sent the book to Farmington Press, in December 1980, to print a signed, limited edition of five hundred copies.

Since the white books reached their conclusion in 1980, *The Complete Poems, Volume Three* ends there as well. The pieces in this book have been organized by their dates of creation, which represent the time of their original composition, not their revision. If a poem has more than one creation date (i.e., if it was started on one day and not finished until another, with extra stanzas, closure, or the title coming at that later time), it is situated by its first date, in this book, because Brodsky's poems typically have their intent, as well as the majority of their content, in place at that point. All creation dates are listed at the end of each piece (with bracketed numerals indicating sequence of composition, if two or more poems were produced in one day), and the tracking number assigned to the poem in the Time Being Books database is included there as well.

If a creation date could not be verified, a question mark follows the unconfirmed portion, which may be the month, the day, or the year. On rare occasions, the entire date is in doubt (in which case it is bracketed and followed by a question mark), indicating either that it may represent revision instead of composition or that the drafts were undated but were found near other material written at that time. Likewise, the date may appear twice for the same poem, once with a question mark and once without, signifying that it is accurate for at least a portion of the text but may or may not apply to the whole piece.

The dates and tracking numbers will eventually serve as cross references between the standard *Complete Poems* volumes and the two concluding books of this series: the index of Time Being Books' database records and the volume of ultimate, later revised versions. The index, to be arranged chronologically, will detail where each poem was composed and provide its publication data. This information, in turn, will link the standard set with the final volume, which will show the corrected, most recent version of every poem drastically revised years after its original composition date, often for a new publication. Any poem in this volume that will have its later form printed in the concluding book (either because it has already undergone such revision or because it has been assigned to a future publication and will, presumably, undergo such revision) bears a delta symbol (Δ) after its title.

Thus, in the *Complete Poems* set, the standard volumes will present the text of each poem in its corrected original form, the penultimate volume will chronicle its creation and its publishing history, and the final volume will show its subsequent, revised version, if applicable.

To retain the poems' original authorial voice from the period of composition, the editorial staff of Time Being Books has not fully revised any of the pieces in this volume (except when creating later versions of those poems that have been culled for new publications). Even pieces in undeveloped form have not been edited stylistically, because they illustrate the evolution of Brodsky's writing, in juxtaposition with his more advanced works. To alert the reader, fragmental pieces carry a dagger symbol (†) after the title, and incomplete poems bear a double-dagger symbol (‡).

Brodsky did, however, revise the majority of his poems, after writing them, with the intention of refining their grammatical form. To help him achieve that goal, the editorial staff has worked with Brodsky to make all pieces in this series meet Time Being Books' current guidelines for language usage and mechanics, correcting spelling, punctuation, grammar, and syntax as needed, in accordance with *The Chicago Manual of Style* and Edward D. Johnson's *Handbook of Good English*. Bold and italic typefaces have also been applied as appropriate, and preferred spellings (in accordance with *Random House Unabridged*) have been utilized as well. While Brodsky's use of neologisms and compound words has been preserved throughout, hyphens have frequently been inserted in them, in this volume (unlike volume one), to prevent ambiguity and make the usage more uniform.

These editorial changes are meant to standardize the work and enhance its readability, without any relineation or substantive revision, and they have been made only under Brodsky's direct supervision, bringing clarity and order to the pieces presented here, in volume three of *The Complete Poems of Louis Daniel Brodsky*.

Sheri L. Vandermolen
7/2/2004
St. Louis, Missouri

INTRODUCTION

For me, the last half of the 1970s and the first half of the '80s belonged to William Faulkner.

My odyssey in the South began in late July and early August of 1976, when I attended my first Faulkner and Yoknapatawpha Conference, hosted by the University of Mississippi, in Oxford. Although my admiration for Faulkner's fiction had been ignited during my freshman year at Yale, in 1959–1960, I had, with two brief exceptions, never spent time in that land, to which, for all my sojourns in his novels and short stories, I felt so akin.

In subsequent years, I would lose my social uneasiness at the conferences and become so familiar with Oxford and its environs, so friendly with a multitude of its residents, that I would come to consider the town, and especially the Ole Miss campus, my home away from home. But at that first conference, I kept to myself, remained painfully aloof, taking in the scene as an outsider, a Northern outlander.

That summer, Biltwell, my father's trouser-manufacturing company, had purchased a garment factory in West Helena, Arkansas, sixty-five miles due west of Oxford, in the heart of the Delta. I quickly took the initiative to open up another outlet store. It would add to my successful chain and give me an excuse to spend more time in Oxford, just an hour's drive away. Of course, this could only diminish the time my wife, Jan, and I would have together in Farmington, Missouri.

Always when I was away from home, I desperately missed Jan and my daughter, Trilogy, and couldn't wait to return to them and to our home in Farmington. But once there, I fell right back into the bramble of our disagreements, our growing friction. This paradox is mirrored in poems such as "Mariner's Lament: A Nocturne" and "Outrunning the Snowstorm."

And now, Jan was pregnant with our second child, who would be born in late October 1977, a boy we'd name Louis Daniel Brodsky III, after my paternal grandfather and me, and nickname "Troika" — if Trilogy, his sister, could boast a reference to "three" in her name, so could he. ("Troika" is a word, borrowed from Russian, denoting a three-horse sleigh as well as a triumvirate.)

Troika's birth, like Trilogy's, was a red-letter day for us, an occasion for immense rejoicing. But I found that the spell cast by his arrival didn't elicit much of an artistic response in me. I was as proud as any dad on earth, but "baby poems" refused to take fire with the same frequency as before. The rapture of encountering something for the first time, which transports the creative spirit, just wasn't there.

Despite her great love for Troika, Jan was not at all happy about the prospect of having to do most of the parenting for two children, now, knowing that my travel schedule was even more rigorous than it had been when Trilogy was born. Neither Jan nor I was prepared for the competing needs of two little ones, which would short-circuit our passion for each other, rob us, out of fatigue and frustration, of our intimacies. Gentleness and tenderness had their moments, but as the days evolved, our affections for each other diminished and were replaced by bickering and nagging, followed by bouts of guilt and shame and fear over our impatience, our antagonism. Anger, short tempers, and distrust darkened our hearts.

Jan found herself tethered to the endless responsibilities of motherhood; I seemed, more often than not, to be in the way, clumsy at changing diapers, heating formula, giving baths. The tasks were tedious and wearisome for Jan, who was frequently up all night, nursing and soothing our newborn. As difficult as work was for me, it didn't carry with it the same emotional weight, and I could escape from home by returning to work or driving off to the other Biltwell factories, across the Midwest.

Still, I was responsible for a wife, daughter, and son, along with a large house and the dual roles of assistant plant manager and manager of outlet stores for the company. Also, I was continually impelled to write poetry. This was an act for a circus juggler. I was going in many too many directions for my own good. Jan knew it; my parents knew it; my two young children sensed as much. Only I failed to see that I was, regardless of my boundless energy, vitiating my spirit. Moreover, for the sake of making a name for myself, I was expanding my overly ambitious résumé yet again, hoping to become a premier Faulkner collector/bibliographer/biographer.

Late in the summer of 1977, just before Troika's birth, I had met Professor James B. Meriwether at that year's Faulkner and Yoknapatawpha Conference. He and I became instant friends. As a graduate student at Princeton, he'd known Faulkner's Random House editor, Saxe Commins, and been responsible for assembling the first extensive exhibition of Faulkner materials since Robert Daniel's initial display at Yale University, in 1942. For that major retrospective, at Princeton's Firestone Library, in 1957, he authored a detailed catalog that was published and widely circulated. When Saxe Commins died, in 1958, Random House asked Professor Meriwether to assist Albert Erskine in editing Faulkner's 1959 novel, *The Mansion.* As well as being an authority on Faulkner's fiction, he knew many of Faulkner's family members and friends.

Impressed with the scope of my collection and with my poetry, he was eager to direct me to people with important Faulkner holdings and was directly responsible for my being able to procure three vastly significant archives: those of Phil Stone, Saxe Commins, and Malcolm Franklin. (Stone, a lawyer, had been Faulkner's early literary mentor and closest friend in Oxford; Commins, as editor in chief at Random House, had been Faulkner's trusted editor and confidante from 1936 until his death, in 1958; Franklin was Faulkner's stepson.) Jim Meriwether opened my eyes to possibilities, in the realm of collecting, I'd not dreamed existed. And as an editor of the *Mississippi Quarterly*, he urged me to put some of my newly acquired materials, many of which had never been published, into print and assisted me with my first fumbling scholarly articles, ushering them into several issues of that journal.

In late 1978, I got a phone call from a professor of English at

Southeast Missouri State University, Robert W. Hamblin, who had heard of my collection. He was a former Mississippian who had earned his Ph.D. from Ole Miss, writing his dissertation on William Faulkner. Not long afterward, he drove to Farmington to meet me and view my holdings, which I was keeping in numerous safe-deposit boxes at a local bank. This visit began a wondrous collaboration of intellect and friendship that continues to this day. After seeing my treasures, all Bob had to ask to spark my imagination was, "What are you going to do with all these things?" For a moment, I was speechless. Over the next few weeks, I formulated what I believed to be a judicious response: "I want to make my collection available to scholarship."

From that inspired beginning, I started canvassing America for others who had known Faulkner, to obtain books and manuscripts he'd given, and letters he'd sent, to them. Bob's excitement had compelled me to uncover items that would fill out the collection. He, as professor, and I, as enthusiast, made a powerful team.

In 1979, the University Press of Virginia published the first of eight books Bob and I would coauthor, *Selections from the William Faulkner Collection of Louis Daniel Brodsky: A Descriptive Catalogue*, showcasing highlights from the Stone and Franklin manuscripts, letters, and inscribed editions, which I had acquired over the previous two years, as well as listing all of the other items in an exhibit that Bob and I were responsible for organizing at Southeast Missouri State University earlier in '79. The book filled the two of us with visions of great things. We were embarking on a project, fueled by mutual respect and friendship, that would test our ambitiousness, tenacity, and energy.

But this constant flurry of activity exacted its toll. My family now suffered my being away even when I was home, because much of the work Bob and I did was conducted at our dining-room table. Jan came to believe that she was competing with Faulkner for my affections. Though I denied this from my heart, I could never convince her that she had nothing to worry about. In truth, I was the one who needed convincing. My obsession was keeping me away from my family. And Jan was pushing me away.

Nonetheless, my poetry writing continued to flourish throughout this period, revitalized by my travels, which had become more frequent and much longer, now that Biltwell's outlet stores were in three states — Missouri, Illinois, and Arkansas. The poems were serious and intense, almost always humorless. Some expressed my love for Jan, my hope that we might repair the rift between us, as in "Touching" and "All in a Fog: A Love Poem"; others focused on the increasing tension between us and our resignation to feelings of guilt and unhappiness, including "Leave-Takings," "Looking for Homes," "Separated," and "Peddler on the Road."

Perhaps the strangest poem in this genre, one which I should have been able to use to gain personal insight into our widening separation, is "Returning to Troy." In this piece, the couple keeps up "pretenses of sadness" as the husband leaves home again, prepares to assume "the many disguises / My frequent escapes begged me undertake / For the sake of survival." The husband admits that his is a "restless questing" to "Fashion, in verse form, the heart's dilemma." The view of the land he travels is registered "Through these disillusioned eyes of mine." Finally, he sees himself "Fading out of sight of my wife, / Adrift in an ocean empty of water," and frightened for his life, he turns his car around and flees for home. Unlike the protagonist of this poem, I kept propelling myself farther away.

This poem echoes the theme of desolation first posited in "The Martyrs," in which the husband is depicted as a gallant conquistador unknown to his children, for his extended expeditions to his "mind's concupiscent Spice Islands." From stories told them by their mother, they believe in his "incredible infallibility." The truth is, he doesn't want to return to them. The wife maintains her faith that he will be redeemed one day. Ultimately, his children go off, "Roaming in search of their fatherless past" and discover, on "a tiny island" in an "inaccessible land, / . . . a gaunt man / With glazed eyes, stranded and alone." They transport him, their father, to "the time before their birth, / East of dawn, where their mother waits / To salve his lacerations, slake his thirst, / And succor his broken heart on the journey home."

To counter such desolate views of the future and attempt to ignite some passion in our lives, I composed Marvell-inspired persuasion-to-love poems, such as "Points in Time" and "In absentia: A Panegyric," in which I argue that there must be a design to and a justification for my absences. In the latter, at least, I pose the possibility that each separation is a dress rehearsal for death's separating of our loving hearts, our souls, and I conclude that "Eternity might require of us / Loving that leaps eons and galaxies." Other hyperbolic poems like this one are more overt in their invitation to make love. These poems were hardly satisfactory to Jan, and they did little to assuage my frustration with our sexually impoverished relationship. These persuasions and their justifications were poor substitutes for communication between Jan and me.

Scattered among these were other, more mystical, love poems similar to those that had flowed so effortlessly in that perceived halcyon period preceding the birth of our children. They tend to be sentimental, inclined to bathos, such as "The Opal" and "Wind-Flowers."

Preoccupied with my itinerant lifestyle, I also wrote many poems about traveling salesmen, especially a character named Willy Sypher, a composite of my great-grandfather, my grandfather, my father, myself, and various members of Biltwell's national sales force, whom I'd gotten to know at the company's semiannual sales meetings in St. Louis, schleppers who plied the highways, hawking men's dress trousers to mom-and-pop shops, department stores, and everything in between. Also, I wrote often about nature and the characters who inhabit small-town America. During my stays away from home, I composed poems about the vagabond I'd become, frequenting hotel bars and lounges, bedding down in smoke-soiled motel rooms.

Wanting to enhance these poems and others, I had also been corresponding with Hayden Carruth, writer and poetry editor of *Harper's,* who offered critiques on my submissions to the magazine and accepted two of my older poems ("Death Comes to the Salesman" and "Rearview Mirror," both from 1975) for the March 1980 issue.

When they were published, Ron Short, owner/pharmacist of Dicus Drugs, in Farmington, purchased a hundred copies of the issue from his distributor and set up a card table in front of his store, on West Columbia Street. I signed copies for the fifty or so customers who bought them. While I was certain that my rise to stardom had begun and other journals and anthologies did print my work, the public failed to take note of my auspicious *Harper's* debut.

Unfazed, I continued revising my work for publication, and in 1980, the last two of my ten signed, limited-edition poetry books, *Birds in Passage* and *Résumé of a Scrapegoat*, were published by the Farmington Press. Though I never allowed myself to stop composing poems every chance I had, whether in my writing office at home, in Farmington cafés, or on the road (in the car, at motels, and in restaurants, bars, and diners), I finally realized that trying to keep up with revising them was impossible if I wanted to continue my Faulkner pursuits with Bob Hamblin.

Meanwhile, my relationship with Jan had grown into one of constant confrontation, despite the occasional pleasant times we shared at home with our children. Strangely, both of us grew highly adapted to this contentiousness, so much so that we didn't even realize we were engaged in an ongoing battle of wills. But people around us saw it and found us difficult to be around. The only way I could handle the tension was to turn my back on it. I continued escaping into my work, taking solace in being alone. And the pace kept growing more furious. In any given week, I might be in the Missouri towns of Farmington, Tipton, Salisbury, Rolla, Sullivan, or Jefferson City, in New Athens, Illinois, or in West Helena, Arkansas — places where I would light for a few hours or overnight or a few days, to tend to what had now become a multimillion-dollar factory-outlet business. Or I might land in Cape Girardeau, at Southeast Missouri State University, where I had temporarily deposited my Faulkner collection, in the rare-book room of the Kent Library. Bob Hamblin and I would spend the afternoon cataloging its vast contents and putting together materials for our first volume of *Faulkner: A Comprehensive Guide to the Brodsky Collection*, which the University Press of Mississippi would publish in 1982. On many of these trips, Bob and his wife, Kaye, would invite me to stay with them. After dinner, Bob and I would retire to his downstairs study and resume our endeavors, picking up where we'd left off at the library. These sessions would continue until one or two in the morning, ending only when fatigue would vanquish enthusiasm.

The closest I ever came to relaxing was when Jan, the kids, and I would take off to St. Louis, for a day's entertainment, returning to Farmington late the same night, or when we would visit her parents, in Jacksonville, Illinois, or fly to Fort Lauderdale for a family vacation, at my parents' condominium. However, even there, I never completely unwound, since I devoted the mornings to composing "Florida poems" or revising existing work, often several years old, poems that otherwise would have stayed buried in my blue-ruled notebooks or piles of old typescripts.

Those vacations were never long enough. Once home, I would fling myself right back into the cyclone of my ambitions, poet first, then assistant plant manager, manager of outlet stores, road peddler, and Faulkner collector, with a raging drive to be the best.

By 1980, I realized that my poems were disclosing yet another semi-autobiographical character, one with a darker, more self-destructive mentality: a straying husband, a lonely alcoholic, wandering away from his once-happy home, abandoning his wife and kids, drifting perilously toward the precipice of his soul. "We Are the People We Deemed So Sad," "Buzzed Confession," "Tonya," "The Man Who Knew Too Much Too Soon," and "The Children of the Children" document this decline.

Perhaps the forces that drew me toward Oxford for the first Faulkner and Yoknapatawpha Conference I attended, in 1976, and then beguiled me back in subsequent years, were motivated by my disintegrating relationship with Jan and by a pervasive sense of loneliness.

We marked our first decade together in July 1980, and I wrote the poem "The Tenth Anniversary" to commemorate the occasion. In it, I propose that Jan and I reenact our Sutro Park wedding, "celebrate our second efflorescing of vows," in Manhattan. I predict that the second ten-year growth of our marriage will come from the gorgeous flowers we planted in the seventies — Trilogy and Troika: "No matter how far we travel from now, / Their garden will flourish; it's rooted in our hearts." What neither Jan nor I may have intuited was that this noble and altogether hopeful expectation was not much more than that and relying on our children to supply the glue to mend our fractured marriage was neither fair nor realistic, especially since rearing children demands so many sacrifices.

It was with this delusion that I drove down to Oxford, in early August of 1980, to attend my fifth Faulkner and Yoknapatawpha Conference. I'd taken the 333-mile trip many times before, and I'd formed memorable friendships with scholars who'd made a difference in the appreciation of Faulkner as a sardonic genius of lyrical stream-of-consciousness prose, luminaries of literary criticism, such as Malcolm Cowley, Cleanth Brooks, Lewis P. Simpson, Robert Penn Warren, Joseph Blotner, Michael Millgate, Noel Polk, Thomas McHaney, James Carothers, Judith Wittenburg, and James G. Watson. And with James B. Meriwether's advice and Bob Hamblin's steady collaborative support, I'd established an impressive reputation for myself as the world's premier Faulkner collector.

I had been doing my journeyman's work, biding my time, keeping a low profile, amassing marvelous Faulkner artifacts from all parts of the country, as well as writing my "Southern poems," on business trips to West Helena and Oxford. In fact, during this period, I wrote twenty-nine of the thirty-nine poems that would eventually shape *Mississippi*

Vistas, which would be published by the University Press of Mississippi in 1983.

One part of my soul was a Northern apologist's, who naively hoped to right the wrongs of Mississippi, its fierce, despicable discrimination and bigotry toward "Negroes." In my innocence, I was going to write poems that would expose man's intolerance and thereby redress civil depredations, moral desecrations. Among the pieces I composed at that time were "Chiaroscuro" (about a bib-overalled black sharecropper sitting on the same Oxford-square bench with a Midwestern Jew — two pariahs staring at each other just long enough to understand the common humanity of their smiles), "Porch People" (about poor blacks enduring a blistering hundred-degree night in West Helena, dreaming the same dreams as others but knowing no way of escaping their poverty), "Drought in the Mid-South" and "Slaves" (dealing with white plantation owners and black tenant farmers contending together against cruel nature), and "Shall Inherit" (about dispossessed blacks being the beneficiaries of heaven's treasures, the truly blessed).

A less idealistic facet of my outlander's soul was that of spectator to the cult of youth at Ole Miss. The campus was so crowded with beautiful young ladies that it was impossible for me not to take notice. Before long, I began to fantasize about making love to a "Southern belle." As my relationship with Jan continued to fail, the fantasy demanded to be made reality, as foreshadowed in the poems "College Town, Friday Night" and "Enchantment."

My arrival at the conference caught me at this pivotal juncture. I was anxious, knowing that I was to be one of the presenters, lecturing on "The Collector as Sleuthsayer," describing my recent acquisitions as well as how I'd come to revere Faulkner's fiction during my days at Yale. It would be a different bill of fare, light entertainment, a break from all the intense scholarship. Because I was so nervous and feeling vulnerable, in need of nurturing, I was primed for compromise.

The day before I gave my speech, I was relaxing at the Alumni House's swimming pool and became smitten by a coed assisting at the conference. In the span of an afternoon and evening, I was beguiled, mystified, subdued, and destroyed. All the vows of spiritual love I'd made to Jan, in San Francisco's Sutro Park, dissolved. The sacredness in our marriage evaporated. I'd forfeited my faithfulness.

I wrote three poems about my adultery, ranging from unbridled eroticism to inutterable shame: "Jongleur: Initiation Rites," "Belinda, Lady of Fiesole," and "Guilt-Throes."

The next morning, I picked Jan up at the Memphis airport, and we drove back to Oxford, in silence. She was suffering from a raging head cold, and I couldn't look her in the eye, knowing that I had committed a moral crime against her. That night, I delivered my lecture, and the audience gave me a standing ovation, asking questions for almost a half-hour after I'd concluded. I was elated.

But melancholy, misery, and deep sorrow following my act of infidelity overwhelmed my spirit, disgusted, repulsed, and sundered me. I knew that what I had done was irrevocable. I was so devastated, bedeviled, for having sullied my union with my wife that I withdrew from society, into myself, my family, my work, my writing. I refused to answer the young lady's calls and letters. To save my soul, I had to make myself believe that none of it had happened. I promised myself that I would never let it happen again.

For almost a year, until the 1981 Faulkner and Yoknapatawpha Conference, I kept that vow.

Louis Daniel Brodsky
5/1–2/2000
Fort Lauderdale, Florida

4/23 . . . 7/3/01
St. Louis, Missouri

THE COMPLETE POEMS

OF

LOUIS DANIEL

BRODSKY

VOLUME THREE, 1976–1980

Odometer

The endlessly revolving odometer
Registers the amount of my blood
That passes through miles of tubing,
To the heart, from every cellular particle
Connected electrically to the sinoatrial node.
Recalibrating tenths and integers
Into hours and wear on the engine
Is easily done by dividing income
Into time spent on myself, whose quotient
Equals the buying power my isolation commands
In a market where I'm not in demand.

Once a month, someone dressed in white
Comes inconspicuously inside
To write in a log the degree of change
The dials unquestionably reflect.
Distance becomes an empirical state of mind
Binding me to my past. The numbers
Are faces and junctions hesitating briefly
Before being transformed, forever,
Into history. The configurations linger,
Then shift like slot-machine reels
Without hitting a single rewarding combination.

Soon, the digits lock in an eerie line
Of five 9's linked tightly
As though bound by a steel shaft.
Together, in a monolithic surge,
They turn over, exposing a block of all zeros,
Purging every old mile from sight.
The very notion of purification,
A clean start, rebirth, charges the veins
With new blood. For a moment,
I trick my equilibrium; my senses
Rejoice as they did on reaching puberty.

What if it were possible to disconnect
And reset at will the cable stretching from coccyx,
Through vertebrae, to cerebral base,
Deceive fate, and coax this vehicle, once more,
Over the mountains, down to Yerba Buena,
Where people cash in their blue-chip dreams
*

And retire, before parts become obsolete?
Or if not, what about freewheeling
Or running in reverse to get to my destination
Without accumulating additional mileage?
I'm not too old a dog to be taught new tricks!

Whatever, at sixty, could have caused youth
To tantalize a traveling salesman
Ensconced in his ways is unexplainable to me
As mere epiphany. Perhaps, like Willy,
I've just realized that once the third
Hundred thousand dreams come around,
Any hour might clot the stream with embolisms.
Maybe I've accepted that living
Nailed to a shaft of spinning ciphers,
With all its fantasies and forgetting,
Is far better than parking the car forever.

7/6/76   (02214)

Spiritus mundi

*For my loving Janny,
on our anniversary*

Directions are the clothes we choose to wear
Each new morning,
Fresh and frozen foods we select
Each new afternoon,
Quotes we lift fastidiously from the newspaper
Each new evening
To satisfy our cellular thirsts for rumor.

The quest is Moses' robe, which we mend
Each midmorning,
Manna nourishing without touching our stomachs
Each midafternoon,
The promise that God is growing in size
Each mid-evening,
While our lives diminish in time's eyes.

Destinations are the naked shapes we share
Each old morning,
Evacuated bowels and fluids micturated
Each old afternoon,
*

Conclusions we collect like antique furniture
Each old evening
To use as collateral when borrowing opinions.

The rest is what's left showing
The last morning,
Bones, stark flesh, shadows
The last afternoon,
Truth of the human condition exposed
The last evening
As dust and dreams and sweet amnesias.

7/8/76   (02189)

Émigré in the Promised Land △

Warsaw looms cold and ghetto-gaunt
As a naked, fleshed effigy of David
Dangling from gallows my memory constructs
Whenever I sift through the dust
That hovers acrid and musty in my nostrils.

The odors that own my breathing soul
Are no sweet Proustian teacakes,
Rather stale bread loaves and bones
Smuggled in through holes in the SS net
And rat leavings festering into plague.

Images of naked women and men emasculated,
Screwed to concentration-camp gates,
Oven doors, and occasional coffin lids
As human hinges for all death's portals,
Aggravate my ulcerated stomach linings,

And I puke dry guts instead of saliva.
I wish I knew why my intellect
Has never been able to remove the tattoo
From its mind, erase the *J*
From my psyche's identification papers,

Or accept, without losing control of my bowels,
The fate that differentiated the Jew
From all other humans, labeled him
Scapegoat, and hatcheted his testicles
To fatten him for the Nazi butcher shops.

In my ears, sometimes, late at night,
I hear them chanting, "Jude . . . Jude,"
And I fear my own dreams might make me strip,
Shoot me and, with the thrust of a bootheel,
Mule-kick me into a pit knotted with swastikas,

From which awakening will be my only escape
And day a mere perpetuation of the malaise
That has circumcised my brain. Maybe Madagascar
Would have been a kind of Canaan. Perhaps Israel
Is Hitler's vision come to fruition after all.

7/15/76 — [1] (00091)

Arcadia

On dreaming George Inness
to the surface

My eyes are man-made lakes,
In which ivory cows wade;
While irises and pupils are opaque,
The whites are cattle grazing.

Everywhere, the hazy air is ashimmer
With timid eyes staring at me,
As if I might be seeing myself
In the way that I judge others.

Only, no identifiable feature
Of these bovine, speechless creatures
Binds us in sympathy, except one:
We view each other with dumb mistrust.

7/15/76 — [2] (02190)

When Metaphors Are Born

For Charlotte, my mother,
whose inspirational legacy to me
is a "continuing and awesome need
and ability to express" myself
through words more than by deeds,
I made this birthday poem.

Have you ever seen a skyrocket
Whose flinty sparks, nervous as BB's,
*

Seed color into night's deepest furrows,
Then, against the eyes' expectations,
Refuse to dissolve, rather hang there
On the mind, friezelike, indentured
To a slavery the frenzied senses crave,
Only to outlast the blackest hours
And grow into focus, in bright daylight,
More dazzling and mind-blown than ever?

Last night, as I sat in my poetry room,
Musing out across the greater studio
Twilight was illuminating, illusory clues,
More fragrant bouquet than bloom,
Lingered, suggesting the mimosa's pink beauty.
Yet, on waking, their outrageous hues
Forced me to choose metaphor, not adjectives,
In order for my mind to grasp and contain
The insatiable tendency of its imagination
To heighten innocence beyond description.

7/17/76   (02191)

The Inconsiderations of Preparing Obituaries

Recently, during an abortive interview,
Her heart declined to make comment
On the alleged separation from her soul mate
Or the actual status of their relationship.

Incensed by such blatant invasion
Of her private life, she refused unequivocally
Even the slightest sigh or half-truth
To voracious media hiding beneath their curiosity,

Who, on two previous occasions,
Had misconstrued her fears of his stroke
And hopes for his complete recovery
Into rumors of paralysis and incompatibility.

Her silence froze them into a solitary block
Of self-conscious persiflage,
In which they stayed locked for days,
Like cut beans rotting in an unlacquered can.

Then, when their interest waned,
She entered into conversation with her mate,
*

The faithful soul of her body's years,
And, alone at last, bid him a loving farewell.

7/20/76 — [1] (02192)

Kilroy the Poet

Lately, differentiating left arm from right,
Telling the heart's time accurately,
Reading the body's disease by degrees
Assume a routine that buckles his mind.
He stretches to reach ultimate release,
By deviating from the cloned blueprint
Through whose billion cells he's floated
Since birth. He crawls on tadpole knees,
Scurries like a nervy cat burglar
Across the caul's rough-hewed roof.

Under extreme pressure, he loses his footing
Where pitched gable and porch converge,
Slips, and lands in an abrasive knot of hands
Waiting in the shadows for one such mistake
To bring his escaped spirit back to earth.
Returned to his senses, he weeps at his failure,
Then begins again, with nail-bitten fingers,
The tedious scratching into the coarse years.
The poetry of his scrawl recalls graffiti
He's been writing on dream-walls for centuries.

7/20/76 — [2] (02193)

Tied, by a Kite String, to Earth and to Heaven

I hold the music by its kite string,
Feel its strident tug at my spine,
Reel it out a knotted chord at a time
To keep from letting it get completely away,
Then listen to its images swish violently
Against the breeze, shredding everything in my brain
To tatters. The music maintains its integrity,
While my entire inspired body quivers
To the electricity racing down the line —
St. Elmo's fire lights my mind's mast.

Now, the melodies stutter, the tempo slows,
And somewhere above me, sailing in skies
Drugged with poppied sounds, the kite flies
By itself, having come enigmatically unfettered.
Without its play, I slump into a dull lethargy
No winy bouquet can revive. The earth
Absorbs me like so much dirt; I smother.
Suddenly, the fingers, the spine are reunited
At the base of a taut series of reverberations
That lift me up still holding the kite string.

Out of such an abrupt awakening, I fail,
At first, to fathom the nature of the line
That has involuntarily taken me away
And made of me a piece of the funnel
Through whose eye the elusive kite tunnels.
As I reach up to grasp its fragile fabric,
And succeed, the music I hold in my mind
Becomes more than overtones of a metaphor
That carried me aloft all night — a shape
Of poetry hung, forever, against my memory.

7/20/76 — [3] (00251)

Wine Revivifies a Dry Garden

For flowering Jan

As though focusing on the fragrance
Of one rose posing in a distant garden,
I hold a delicate sip of wine
In the cave my lips enclose
And let its taste seep into my brain.

The flower that blooms in my mind
Is you, Jan, my delicately petaled wife,
Growing absolutely alone.
Your slender shape draws me down
To touch you into being. Your perfume

Floats me over crazy pollen-oceans,
To seed you into the fertile earth
We cultivate while growing in regions
Decidedly apart. I lift my glass
To sniff your variegated bouquet,

And fields of grapes explode whole,
Like souls sparked into existence at birth.
Your face hovers in the gentle breeze,
Sways beneath the shimmering patina
I dream alive by tasting your image.

In my inebriation, you remain safe,
This evening, isolated from energies
That would see you clipped, depetaled
Or placed in a fine Imari vase
To be politely neglected. The wine

Reminds me you need a slow mistral,
Heated at night, cool in the afternoon,
To ensure your ripe, mature flavor.
My enduring love guarantees your harvest
Will be the sweetest blooms ever produced.

It only remains for me to gather your fruit,
Yet everywhere I stare, you are flower
Lifting toward a perfection I hesitate to pick.
I kiss the vision of you I perpetuate intact,
And you stay immaculate, forever, in my garden.

7/20/76 — [4] (02194)

Civilization and Its Discontents △

At times, a part of my essence
Harks back almost naturally
To the age of invading Visigoths
Outrageously void of inhibitions
And Vandals trammeling lands unchecked.

At times, I'm almost positive,
By the way my eyes linger
On tiny breasts and crease lines
Supplely inscribed on female flesh,
That they are ancestors of my instincts.

Yet never have I allowed my actions
The freedom of their lascivious passion
Or sanctioned the public rape
My eyes commit in private every time
They fasten on an image they've undressed.

Just once, when my nerves swerve
To avoid a spontaneous response
Generating from the glands, I wish the object
Of my salaciousness would kick me
In my civilized prick and make me scream.

7/21/76   (02195)

[It's strange not to hear any more trains] †

It's strange not to hear any more trains
Chugging through the ears' convolutions
And Horseshoe Bends of the heart and head.
It's peculiar to awaken in a new bed
Every second night and not be able to reach
And raise a shade, to wave to the changing landscape
Of a nation's roadways behind it

7/22/76 — [1]   (00300)

Spider in the Sky

The hundred-degree sun
Is a tarantula crawling across my shoulders,
Making me sweat profusely
Without moving or even breathing.

Although it's weightless, its eight legs
Penetrate the membranous flesh
That protects my neck and skull
From external infection. I wince;

The pain scalds my flinching brain.
In fright, I fantasize a shade tree
Growing in my mind, to climb under
To avoid an actual mandibular bite

From the excited spider descending
The undulant thread of my imagination.
Only, there's no surcease from the heat.
Even in sleep, I feel the creature's hairs

Bristling across my irritated dreams.
I toss, listening for the distant dawn
*

To crawl up the sheets and overtake me again
At the webbed edges of another fetid day.

7/22/76 — [2] (02196)

Absentee Landlord

My expectations,
As if connected to a light switch,
Wait for any stranger
To enter their dark room
And illuminate their invisible design.

My ideas, as if cast in brass
Around the empty centers
Of Oriental coins
Tied slightly to a chime,
Await the wind's kiss to release them,
Send their timbres flying
To higher frequencies,
Lower overtones
Close to the original notes
Registered by God's first breaths.

Even my caffeined dreams
Are obliged to wait on sleep
To unlock the secrets they keep
And consummate the marriage of shadows
With shapes that define the depth of my insanity.

Only my poetry
Depends on nothing extrinsic
For its motivational thrust.
Whatever metaphors
Await my silent arrival
Do so at their own risk.
Docile and benign, I rule
Each line of verse
Thriving in the mind's precincts,
As though my fiefdom controlled
The lives of yet-unmartyred saints.

7/26/76 (02197)

Alexeyev and Comaneci

A giant and a tiny adolescent
Dominate my awe-stricken mind,
As though the tableaux they've created
Behind the TV screen, this July,
Go deeper than electronic phosphorescences
Perceived by the unbelieving eyes,
From the gestalt of athletic perfection.

I don't see Alexeyev the Great
Breathing the monstrous weights
Rapidly past his protruded belly,
To his clavicle, above his rounded shoulders,
Into a zone where no man has traveled,
To be commended, like Antaeus, into legend
Before releasing his godlike posture to the floor.

I don't see Comaneci the Petite
Weaving her slender body,
With the speed of a computerized shuttle,
Through the twin-harnessed loom
Of uneven bars, on which she produces
A tapestry of movement more beautiful
Than a Gobelin cartooned by Raffaello.

Instead, I see two human beings
Whose ironic contradiction in size
Reminds me how dissimilar to us they must be
In their susceptibility to anemia, fear, lust,
Yet how alike. By extending their thresholds
And achieving distinction for themselves,
They've elevated our collective self-respect.

7/29/76 (02198)

The Closing of Sorrill's Elm City Café ᐃ

Painted red and purple
On white freezer paper,
In quasi-professional calligraphy,
With 3' x 8' boundaries,
Taped to an immense plate-glass window,
*

The obituary reads,
"Restaurant For Sale,
Building For Immediate Lease."

The café's last offerings
Are emblazoned on its front window
For saddened patrons to ponder.
They can order plate-lunch special,
Homemade pie and coffee,
Fresh memories, stale regrets,
And pay their last respects
With silent tips, unsaid good-byes.

7/31/76   (02199)

Sunday-Morning Service ^Δ

The whole road owns me alone.
No one else has even entered Sunday
Or dreamed this sunny, tasseled morning
Into being. I am the breeze,
Widowered, childless, pariah,
Slowing only for an occasional hamlet
Sleeping inconspicuously amidst the corn.

I am the shadow off to my right,
Running parallel, forcing the pace,
Refusing to be outdistanced or buried
Here in this vast, tractor-dappled prairie.
I am the voice Moses perceived
In the wilderness, high atop Mount Sinai,
And down in Egypt, deeply entranced.

Its Talmudic accent remembers my throat
From a thousand passages I've previously made
And commends me to Libra's light side.
The words that speak to me now
Are the same ones that ordained Creation.
They sing themselves free from my imagination,
Like winged hues breaking from prisms,

And urge me on toward a consummation
Of the love relationship I have with life.
Yet as I drive, this seventh day,
*

My soul commands me to retreat and rest
Out of respect. I obey its ancient poetry
By changing to a westerly direction home.
Affectionate tomorrows wait with open arms.

8/1 & 10/22/76 — [1] (02200)

Chiaroscuro ^Δ

For Toby Holtzman and Lisa Paddock

Faulkner and Yoknapatawpha Conference
August 1–6, 1976
Oxford, Miss.

Such vast academic fuss has been made
Over the land, its people, and their past
As fundamental pedantic criteria
In understanding William Faulkner's fiction

That as I sit beside a black man
In bibs, breathing his gentle stench
In the bench-strewn shadows
Beneath Oxford's squatty courthouse,

Catching glimpses of dogtrot dreams
He shades from the blazing sun,
Behind glassy, leonine eyes,
And balances, from tight-lipped conditioning,

On the tip of his tongue, I'm reminded
How elemental we all really are,
Just how consummately incidental
All the skillfully ingenious criticism becomes

Both for the writer, too obsessed by creation
To ponder the implications of his symbols,
And for the Ethiop, who, having inherited
The family crest, refuses to question his flesh.

As unknown "Jew poet" and "useless nigger,"
Unwilling to admit that failure owns us
And insistent on acquitting each other's guilt,
We seal our consanguineous ties with a smile.

8/2 & 10/22/76 — [2] (00055)

The Ghosts of Rowan Oak $^\Delta$

For Eva Miller

The kept lawn is alive with tiny ants,
Following, in systematic single file,
A million tangential Roman roads,
Crossing a hundred blady aqueducts,
Assaulting myriad overgrown Thermopylaes,
To reach the citadel of my seated being.

Cedars inspired by Old Ionic breezes
Acknowledge these presences far below,
Sing a Greek chorus for Agamemnon
And abandoned Odysseus I alone can hear
For their unheeded roistering at Rowan Oak.
A voice is weeping in the nearby woods.

Perhaps the shadows are practicing elocution
Or the temple's pillared portico
Is creaking under the weight of my gaze.
Possibly, the ghost of the writer shuffles still,
In a labyrinthine somnambulism,
Through the convoluted syntax of visions

That linger, indistinguishable from kudzu,
Magnolia, and interwoven vines
Insulating this private place from Oxford
And the world. Maybe that sound
Is the reverberation of urgent ant feet
Racing to overtake me before I escape,

Enthrall me in memory's half-light,
And keep me from making my own achievements,
By chaining my metered mind to this lawn,
Feeding me quotations the wind whispers
Through tedious, empty afternoons,
Gnawing the bones of a poet caught in the shadows.

8/4/76   (00065)

Accepting the Call $^\Delta$

For Father Tom Cademartrie

Each morning for a week now,
I've awakened, at twilight, to the cosmic sounds
*

Of education being constructed
From the ground up by blacks and whites:

Air compressors, cryptic shouting,
The complaint of dropped objects, pounding.
Hard-hatted men in T-shirts
Hack away at what never existed,

To complete the reinforced-concrete
Tinkertoy before the start of classes
Here at the University of Mississippi.
A ubiquitous crane takes my gaze,

Turns my attention in every direction
It moves, as if its skeletal anatomy,
Broken unevenly by a control room,
Were a mildly provoked queen bee

Threatening to penetrate my inviolability.
My mind eludes its slow-moving arc,
Emerges from within its dim nimbus,
Like Jonah climbing out of Leviathan,

Into the pulverized luminosity of August.
Only, today, a Sabbatical quietude
Pervades this academic environment,
Contains it inside a wide sleep

My ears and eyes can't differentiate
From deathly numbness. My whereabouts
Baffle me with weary stupefaction.
I lack insight and initiative to grope

For the exact location of my stymied soul.
Whether at the precipice of an old epoch
Or new, ready to soar or plunge,
Remains for the next few hours to decide.

Meanwhile, I listen for the slightest evidence
That life exists yet on this campus,
Where my solitary, unendowed intellect
Has spent its best years seeking refuge

From the pestilential rigors of society.
Suddenly, my mind identifies the silence
As the kiss God gives His ministers
Prior to sending them into the heart's wilderness.

8/5/76 (00049)

[For a week now, I've heard nothing but praise] †

For a week now, I've heard nothing but praise
Heaped upon the literary achievements

8/6/76 — [1] (06769)

As I Lay Sleeping △

For Dr. James Webb,
who has saved Faulkner's home
from neglect and decay

Although sleep still shoulders my dreams,
Visions of the path salvation takes
Through Bailey's Woods, to Rowan Oak,
Awaken my restless spirit. It flies
Like a biplane crop duster
Maneuvering through Delta planting time.

Deliberately, it twists, spirals, climbs
Over nerve wires strung taut
Along my mind's communicative highways.
It dives recklessly as a wounded duck,
Recovers just prior to its own crushing destruction,
To spray my blighted fields with insecticides.

My drowsy body shudders, lingers
On the brink of consciousness, sinks again
Beneath deeply dug cerebrations
That might have been disked by machines
Guided by latter-day "darkies," and seeded
With cotton. Their reverberations disturb me.

The soul within my soul recoils
At the dust-parched images of black men
Seated in feeble triumvirate, on the frames
Of tractors, spraying plants by hand,
From "cain't see" to collied "cain't see."
My weevily self-esteem wilts in their wake.

Yet, in a matter of unrecorded steps,
My spirit climbs up out of the shadows
Fastened to kudzu and honeysuckle vines,
Arrives at the start of Old Taylor Road,
*

Slips through an opening in Rowan Oak's
Magnolia'd silence, and surrenders to its solitude.

Out of sleep's ruins, this peacefulness
Lifts my being to a new appreciation
For the spotty deposits history leaves
In the form of geniuses who exorcise demons
Threatening the rest of us with uncertainty
About man outlasting his own martyrdom.

8/6/76 — [2] (00059)

The Trysting Place ^Δ

*For blessed Jan, my love,
in our brief separation*

William Cuthbert Faulkner	Estelle Oldham Faulkner
Born Sept. 25, 1897	Born Feb. 19, 1897
Died July 6, 1962	Died May 11, 1972
Beloved	
Go With God	

Seated beneath three white pines,
In the presence of two lesser cedars
Filled with the breeze's suspirations,
My being settles into peaceable repose.

The quietude, absolved of human voices,
Releases me from all earthly ties,
Allows my eyes to follow grave tracery
Horizontally incised in both stones

Lying side by side at the base
Of my reverential gaze. The letters
Come alive one by one
By one, like oviparous minnows from slime,

And swim into the unfocused ocean
Of my most sublimely emotional insight.
Anonymous at first, solitary, scattered,
Grouping finally into a common school,

The individual granite monograms coalesce,
Announce themselves as kindred elements,
Namesakes of the two souls rendezvoused
By time in this timeless trysting place.

A man and lady, writer and wife,
Sepulchered only of bone and hair,
Touch me, share with me their heritage
Of privacy, modesty, and staunch forbearance.

I, in turn, speak to them in verse,
As though poetry were the one language,
Translatable into all human tongues,
That might communicate my heart's need

To love someone transcendent, worthy of worship.
The combined chorus of our silent minds
Revives the vital dialogue between God
And man, which endows survival with hope

And allows us speculation of someday knowing
The communal origins of our brotherhood.
For now, I leave you, sleepy William,
Sweet Estelle. Please wait for me.

8/6/76 — [3] (00066)

Letting Go of Balloons ^Δ

Accidentally cut loose from its stays,
The balloon my imagination keeps inflated
Soars toward a galaxy of metaphors,
Strays off course, before leaving
The mind's inner stratosphere,
And is carried away on thermals,
Toward a scudding cloud-forest
Crowded with crystal distillations.

Trapped below, in the floating basket,
Where operating manuals are stored,
My muse and I comfort each other
By searching for an appropriate rhyme scheme
To guide us out of this maelstrom.
*

Only, the readings we take are misleading,
For misty vapors enveloping our vessel,
Threatening to shred the very image we cast

Against the traditional past, which we remember
Like the backyard of our childhood,
Into unidentifiable pieces of brain dust.
Having lost all touch with the known world,
We rush each other, grope for faith.
To save me, my lady leaps overboard.
The vehicle surges vertiginously upward,
Reaching apotheosis in the completion of its poem.

8/7/76   (01040)

Mosquitoes

Until this morning, I'd almost forgotten
How wet death can be, how stealthily
It creeps underneath the skin
At the least expected instance
And lays its eggs. I'd forgotten the twitch,
So imperceptible on initial penetration,
The symptomatic, telltale itching
That arouses the mind to fits of discontent
And restless scratching at its corporeal cell.
I'd completely forgotten the paradoxical pleasure
Of not being able to stop lacerating the flesh
Despite the growing flow of blood, forgotten
How much pain a body can endure
Before temporarily numbing the source
Of those bothersome, oscillating sensations,
To which mortality has always been susceptible.
Until this morning, when I entered a fog
While driving just beyond dawn
And was blinded as if being bitten
In both eyes by a swarm of anopheles mosquitoes,
I'd not been reminded since my last passage
How near the stagnant breeding grounds are
That surround my days with their inevitable stench.

8/17/76   (05472)

Maidenhead

The Friday-night sky
My eyes wipe dry
And dust away with a swipe
Is absorbed by my moist, crumpled mind.

Along the space vacated by dusk,
Charladies, kneeling on pads, in pain,
Beside sudsy buckets and sponges,
Scrub their complaints into my face.

Instinctively, the eyes blink,
Erase their seemingly ineradicable shadows,
Dripping like fluffy rain clouds,
With their lash-cluttered fluttering,

And make the void filling my gaze
With stray images liquefy again
Into Friday night, then solidify,
While a nubile ivory moon

Inclines slightly toward my pupils
To be kissed before undoing her clothes.
The crying my eyes wiped dry
Was the hymenal urgings of a virgin sky.

8/20/76 — [1] (05473)

Headlights

My departure, this dark morning, was so quiet
No one except the ubiquitous solitude
Could possibly have heard my car start
Or deduced from the complaint of highway tires
That I was leaving, yet something alerted them,
Caused the carbon-arc searchlights to penetrate
The darkness, in whose ambiguous terrain
I'd hoped to camouflage myself until dawn.
Now, they strafe low to the ground,
Almost like fog, in twos for protection,
Snapping militarily straight, out of unseen curves,
Like frog legs galvanized, then bending again
Into another doomed socket of five o'clock.
*

From in front and behind, they blind my mind.
They've mistaken me for enemy craft
Flying underneath their radar screens. They've sensed my presence
And mean, somehow, to annihilate me from the skyways
This highway has provided without incident so many days.
I grasp at explanations, stare blankly
At the illuminated panel of seemingly useless gadgets,
Whose reciprocated gaze is the Sphinx's answer
To all who seek solutions to its riddled enigma.

Suddenly, the arrases hanging from the retinal walls,
On which new cartoons are sketched as perceptions
And stitched, quit shivering, and the headlights
Cease their insistent needling through the eyes' tapestries.
I can see daylight actually erasing their whiteness,
Forcing their narrow shafts back into their reflections
Like echoes finally catching up with their source
Inside the throats of unprojecting silence.
What creatures or mythological embodiments
My passage this morning may have disturbed from rest,
Or whether by sheer circumstantial accident
I happened to threaten the nefarious undertakings
Of a satanic crew pressured into premature escape,
I'll never determine. Yet by some ironic phenomenon,
As the dawn's rheostat systematically lightens the horizon
And cars merge, converge, becoming a solitary watchband
About the wrist of the waking city, my pursuers lose sight of me.

8/23/76 — [1] (05474)

The Regenerate

I used to mix a heated honey-licorice draught
With elixirs of Kickapoo Juice and Dr. Good-God
To lubricate the demons swarming about my sleep
Like manure-flies and flush my tubes of them
At least five times each insomnious night.

You might say inebriation was my only salvation,
The one saving grace in my life's constellation
Comprised of lambent, starlike stations of the cross,
Stark against the soul's perpetually dark night —
Crucifixions consisting of seizures, croup, and diarrhea.

You might say essence and existence got mixed,
So that no one knew whether egg laid chicken
Or chicken hatched in the first place, immaculately.
You might even say that, for a time, time erased me
Like chalky scribblings on a physics-class slate,

Sent me free-falling through an absolutely black lacuna
In space, where Nowhere was the only destination
For my exiled psyche, the blasted halfway house
Where it might rest and recuperate before returning
To live among the quick without getting sick unto death.

Now, if I try to recall my past, oblivion
Sets up a horned barrier, assaults retrospection,
Refuses to release me from the peaceful catatonia
In which my truncated intellect basks. It won't let me
Enter the gates where touch and taste approximate God

And equate man, through Him, to the paradoxical poetry
Of broken bones, sprained toes, frayed nerves,
Exploded kidneys and livers associated with survival,
Nor will it allow me a solitary sip of honey-licorice
To mix with the paraldehyde that still filters my insides.

8/23/76 — [2] (05475)

Pecan Grove △

As I drove past illimitable fields
Of prebolled August-flowering cotton,
Inactive gins, yellow-leafed soybeans,
And idle radial-engine biplane dusters,
I noticed, to one side, an isolated pecan grove.

Juxtaposed to all this bright, inexorable dying
Growing rife at the mercy of unpropitiated gods,
It instantly became a Gothic cathedral
Set against a shimmering thirteenth-century plain
Stranded in Provence, lost as obedient Moses.

Its shaded clearing, a robe draped beneath the trees,
Invited my curious, inarticulate eyes to stop,
Repair from the repetitious glare for a while,
Come inside, and lie quietly in Delta sleep
Before resuming my chase after the elusive miles.

I'd never seen the ceiling of Above from underneath,
Like doves flying upside down or rain-bodies
Looking over their shoulders, on their journey earthward,
Nor ever weaved the sun's rays into macramé,
As do the lithe maidens of Helios for daily exercise.

I'd not dreamed a mere clearing in Mississippi
Could ever be a cool-breathing cave,
Heated deep-sea grot, or reachable mirage.
Yet, as I rested, lulled by speeding vehicles
Into mystical distillations of this anomalous place,

I began to understand and appreciate the relationship
Between impalpable oasis and blistering desert —
That the truest distance between incongruities
In the figmental mind is simply the time it takes
To recognize divine design in both death and in life.

8/24/76   (00041)

The Itinerant Limner

THE ARGUMENT

*The poet, having breakfast at the Crossroads Café in Helena,
Arkansas, is flushed from cover and held under suspicion by
the regulars. His existence is severely intimidated; he questions
the essence of his decision to write and decides belatedly
that, at times, the courage and risk involved aren't worth the
loss of life.*

Time was, when each of us,
Seated in an alien café,
Emasculated of preconceptions
And viable biases, naked
As Juden lined up communally,
Waiting for the delousing showers,
Would just peer at each other
Out of inaudible curiosity,
Not vicious suspiciousness.

Or do I have memory confused,
The sequence reversed, we people
Characterized by a docility unknown
In this universe? Perhaps a shadow
*

From a former era seeded my brain
With poppied hallucinations in which men
Appreciated, rather than feared, differences,
Praised beard and wife and peace
Above the hedonistic pursuit of egohood.

I'm no longer certain, seated here,
What position my existence maintains
Among these cryptic, quizzical faces,
Whether the cliché of safety in numbers
Pertains or if the danger I sense
In their quick-shifting registrations
Means the insights allowed me are numbered.
Without chancing extinction, I close
My poetry notebook and run for cover again.

8/25/76 — [1] (00599)

Porch People △

There's no one particular time of the day
That can be isolated positively from the rest
To suggest the heat has reached its apogee.
Afternoon bubbles up from morning's cauldron;
Night is poured slowly into dusk's molds.
The Delta furnace fires are never banked.

No one escapes the heavy, heaving drafts
That neutralize, assimilate whatever breezes
Lift cautiously off the imperturbable river
Beyond the levee, like mischievous children
Sneaking out of school, into their superintendent's grin.
Breathing smells of the leper's deathly flesh.

Lethargy's leopard-gait crawls to a halt,
Deviates from street to sidewalk to ramshackle porch,
To wait for its human surrogates to catch up.
Everywhere, blank black faces congregate.
Wizened patriarchs and obese Dilseys dominate
Their pigtailed, barefoot novitiates,

Who play mumbletypeg all day long
With dust motes, empty dreams and hopes
Lying on a dry well floor, echoless.
Their dull stares into space are the knives
*

They throw; their stretching legs are shadows
That fail to reach beyond the blades, to freedom.

Day fades into another changeless generation
Each night, as the cicadas' wingy monotones
Unloose turgid air in thermal eddies,
Miragelike, trivial, toward an unnecessary star.
The old people sleep outside in their rocking chairs,
Watching for the elusive moondog to presage autumn,

While their moneyless offspring, unable to wait,
Go crazy from the spider bites of adolescence,
Come home on hands and knees, diseased,
And lie down in a bed of splinters at their feet.
Even undreamed babies, never to be conceived,
Know the omen of creaking porch floorboards.

8/25/76 — [2]   (00042)

Drought in the Mid-South ^Δ

They wait inexorably, exasperatingly,
All day long, for the slightest sign of rain.
They awaken, each hazy dawn,
To make sacrificial oblations to Demeter,
Beg for any talismanic recognition
That might lead them to suspect rain.
Reluctantly, they take afternoon naps,
Afraid they might be leaving to nature
Something within their power to eventuate.
But praying won't inflate stunted stalks
Of runt-sized cotton or straighten drooping beans,
Nor can it persuade an intractable sky
To let rain penetrate its blue membrane.
Supper they eat tastes like pulverized soil.
Their minds can't dissociate from the plight
That plagues enemy and friendly neighbor alike.
From July 4 to this late-August date,
The only construable rain has been the chemicals
They've paid to have sprayed from biplanes.
Even sleep is merely an uncertain prolongation
Of demonized consternation and fear
That the next hour will render the crop
Irreversibly doomed. There's no repose,
*

No hidden path over which to escape fate,
As the moribund cotton grows in six directions,
Choking all hope for keeping alive the promise
Of abundance. In this land of unrained tributaries,
Each planter is inundated by his silent weeping.

8/26/76   (00058)

Sunrise ^Δ

Against the sky's gessoed cloud-fabric,
As if cut out with scissors,
Is the space your two shapes vacated.
Now, the black, faceless, amorphous hole
Begins to float earthward.
It fills my gaze with gossamer lace,
In which my eyes are gently caught.
Visions of you, my wife and tiny daughter,
Circumscribe my mind like a halo
Hovering above a Flemish Madonna and Child,
And I'm contained within a painted circle
That grows, each minute, less ineffable,
More palpably into morning's orange sun.
Despite all my concentrated force,
I'm unable to make your twin images
Stay in place. The earth's entire weight
Is attached to the other end of the chain
Of a clock's mainspring, from which you hang.
As you inch higher, out of sight,
Into daylight's gessoed haze, toward night,
I calculate the hours still separating us
By the elongation of my shadow behind me.
By the time it has completely disappeared,
We three will have reunited, a family
Imprismed in God's diurnally cycling lights.

8/31/76   (01446)

Growing into Identities ^Δ

Like a slow-swirling Tyrian dye
Dropped into a clear solution,
*

Her sweet, docile disposition, in maturing,
Has diluted the translucent vessel of days,
Containing her fluid spirit, with moodiness.

Instantaneous, seemingly unpremeditated
Temper tantrums, which dissipate
With equally unpredictable spontaneity,
Register a jagged, staccato claw mark
On the graph being drawn across her waking hours.

Intractable, vindictive, at times tenacious,
She defies the familiar tone of disapproval,
Takes perilous flight, circles rooms,
With pen, scissors, or knife in hand,
And refuses to surrender without a fight.

Frequently, we eavesdrop on conversations
Between our baby and her tiny baby doll,
Whom she chides, admonishes not to choke,
Advises when it's time to eat and sleep,
And invites to accompany her to the potty to watch.

We're astonished by her emulation of our training,
The thorough, maternal concern she displays
For her dependent. Even her mother's high heels,
In which she shuffles like a string puppet,
Confirm her attachment to a distaff universe.

Once, her dad could elevate her to heights
Above the Wurlitzer's "wonder light,"
Transport her to stained-glass ecstasies,
Through dance. Now, a miniature Isadora,
She's ravaged by the music of her own soaring soul.

9/1/76 (00252)

Song of the Open Road △

I

I leave so early this morning
That even the mercury-vapor streetlights,
Lambent, like quavering distant stars,
From the shadowy bombardment of spastic insects,
Don't suspect night's gradual evanescence.

Like a voice flowing inside telephone wires,
I slide along downtown's East Columbia,
Unnoticed by the bespectacled "residents,"
Whose weak inner illuminations fail them,
Who lean slightly, as if hard of hearing —

Grocery store, post office, courthouse,
Clothing emporium, local bank
Offering free handouts of "Time and Temp,"
Stand at palsied, rubber-kneed review
As I move through their cataracted stares.

Only the newspaper building seems alive.
My eyes recognize the anonymous face inside,
Behind a typewriter, as that of another human
Stranded in this desolated time warp.
He might be Anderson's George Willard,

Exposing exploded truths to the masses,
Or just another picaresque grotesque on the loose.
I don't linger to resolve the distinctions,
Rather disappear again into the Kingdom of Dawn,
On the orange-tinged wings of a lifting fog.

II

The highway down which I soar south
Is a thick, white, fibrous umbilicus
Attached to the earth somewhere behind my flight.
I am its other end, dragging my cord,
Like a diver his air hose, as I go forward.

A persistent desire to clip the supportive bond
And fly free of life's encumbrances
Finally persuades me to deviate from I-55,
Take up unauthorized side roads,
And fend for myself in an endless cottony maze.

Soon, the luminous haze hypnotizes my eyes.
It changes entirely the direction of days remaining,
By releasing spirits the years have held captive,
To pioneer ravines, gorges, and forests
In a land without settlements, unpeopled, clean.

Memory reminds me I've been in this eternity
At least once before, at birth,
Maybe more frequently, during the soul's prehistory.
*

Unfamiliar roads recognize me, tell my time,
Measure the beats left in my pendular heart,

Gently unwind my apparatus. They lead me back
Through the highest, narrowest passes in the mind,
Until I'm free, at last, of my own volition, to roam
The westernmost approaches to my past and answer
"Now" to the patient voice petitioning me home.

9/7/76 (05468)

Slings and Arrows ^Δ

My pen is never still.
It quivers perpetually,
Like an arrow shot into the hard bark
Of a pithy patrician oak
Frozen in a shrill vacuum.

The quill's feathered shaft
Reverberates between my fingers
And hand, head and heart.
I place each overtone
In the spine's slingshot

And catapult its echoes at giants
Waiting behind the glass dome
To crash through, sack my intellect,
Grab the arrow from the tree,
And snap its magic in two.

Now that I've stood guard myriad years,
Hand, heart, shaft, and oak
Have fused into the bow
Poetry loads with metaphors
And shoots perpetually into my soul.

9/8/76 (05476)

Thunderstorm

The thunder in my heart is a rainstorm.
My head is a watershed
For eyes etched with beaded moisture
Collecting on the retinas' cold screens.

Everywhere I look, everything that was
Is wet and shimmery as eels.
Oil slicks seduce me, like Portuguese men-of-war,
With their hallucinogenic hues,

And I step directly into thick pools
Instead of hunting uninundated surfaces
Of pavement to take me under the roof
Quietude erected to protect wayfarers.

Fog, hung from the sky's purlins,
Is fed by sweaty pipes, clogged gutters
Running wild as stallions in a corral
One horse wide, and vomiting downspouts,

Which channel my juices gratuitously
Into tributaries refusing to drain them away.
Zeus unlooses tongues of lightning,
Which strike my mind like vituperative slander,

Then sends pieces of rough-edged thunder
He's ripped from rusty sheet metal,
To patch the holes burned in my brain.
My heart's pain is the rain's reason for grieving.

She knows no other way to show her emotions
Than by crying, and I've never been able
To conceal from myself her undeniable surmise
That I've been dying since leaving the womb.

9/9/76 (05477)

[At the outer grassy entrance,] †

At the outer grassy entrance,
Where the catacomb still smiles,

9/10/76 — [1] (01378)

Warehouse of Mannequins △

In various dark areas of the warehouse,
Filled to its dust-breathing, rusty gills
*

With office equipment and marred furniture
From defunct emporiums, exist graveyards
Exposed to all who rummage its five floors
For bargains among others' fated cargoes.

In these makeshift, accidental cemeteries,
Developed over time whenever a load
Would arrive unannounced and get dumped
Wherever a few cubic feet
Could be forced to absorb more debris,
Repose bodies in suspended animation.

Dead, to be sure, yet undecayed,
These corpses form a chorus
Of incomplete voices, a prism of missing hues,
In their haphazard assemblage of scattered limbs,
Piled in disquieting riot as if a tornado
Had sucked an entire town inside out.

Maimed bodies — bloodless amputations,
Cracks in the wrong places, mixed pigments
Where hands, head, and feet were exchanged
In previous incarnations, unslitted vaginas,
Breasts without nipples, hairless groins
Devoid of penis — belong to the anonymous occupants

Of these unacknowledged burial grounds,
Who, without being consulted,
Have seemingly been made the objects of experimentation in euthanasia,
Then relegated to Bergen-Belsen-like trenches.
They lie in mute, amorphous confusion,
Like millions of newly hatching snakes in a nest,

Waiting for neither death nor reassignment,
Although many will return from beyond the grave
And be sent out on location as useful citizens
In the state's exchange pogrom-program,
Instituted years ago in place of abstractions
Like transubstantiation of souls.

Yet, from these zones of clones, no one
Has ever lifted a voice in complaint;
No protestations against stirpiculture,
Trafficking in white slavery, or transgressions
By avowed rapists have been formally lodged.
The warehouse management is proud of its reputation

For nondiscrimination, avoidance of racist overtones,
Acceptance of progressive female expression of rights.
The directors regard their calling as indispensable
To the continuation of regulated supply and demand
In the land of mannequins, distinctly threatened
On both hands by overpopulation and extinction.

9/10 — [2] & 9/12/76 — [2] (00874)

Zooperstitions ᐃ

I leave unnoticed, this Sunday morning,
Through the cornucopia's slender end
And take to the highway home, alone.
My portmanteau is empty save for sounds
Of trapped memories of yesterday afternoon
At the Children's Zoo with my wife and child.
Visions locked inside my contemplative trance
Rise like medusas as I unloosen the straps
And open wide my traveling bag.
One by one, they escape and pass in review:

Fruit bat; baby spider monkey
The shape of a hairy husked coconut;
Albino raccoon; freakish squirrel
Hued black; nine-foot python;
Variegated eggs in an incubator;
Cavies sharing the domesticated fate
Of being baited, handled, and heaved back
Into limbo a thousand times daily.
The zone in which these creatures float
Closes like a window on my mind's hands.

I can't drive, or revive the ecstasy we shared
Riding behind the miniature locomotive,
Or easily evoke the docile mountain goats
Trilogy and I hugged and sluggish elephants
That excited us equally. Nothing seems
To exorcise the horrific silhouette the bat,
Eating cantaloupe, upside down,
With saber-toothed-tiger teeth,
Flapping its veined wings, cast at me
As we were leaving the Children's Zoo.

I question yet whether those creatures
Were really nature's grotesque throwbacks,
Hallucinatory stowaways
In my lifeboat on its voyage home, or both,
Especially since the only anomaly
Frightening enough to make Trilogy cry
Was the man-made corrugated tunnel
The train threaded like a needle's eye,
With outrageous chaos spewing diesel exhaust,
In cauterizing her fantasy that spectacular day.

9/12/76 — [1] (00771)

Intercourse

The climax of arriving after a five-hour drive
Takes the delirious shape of a reclining nude
Waiting without cessation on a bed of succulent spines.
Something about pain being pleasure's stepchild
Makes self-flagellation of the defenseless psyche
Defensibly tempting, and my mind enters in
By stimulating its flaccid imagination with auto-
Erotic gratifications. As if my body were Aladdin's
Phallic lamp, the jinn-muse inside comes loose
From my brain, and I slide through her vapors,
Collide with semen-boats gliding invisibly

Toward a dividing horizon. Where the ocean opens,

I hang in its crosscut wash, grasping at bubbles
Exploding to the surface like inchoate poems
Breaching at feeding time. I offer myself
In naked oblation, cling to the spongy walls
Of the oceanic placenta forming about my being.
Slowly, sleep drags me down; the waters close.
My baptized soul drowns in the sac of creation.
Nine months contract into eight hours, and I awaken,
Progenitor and child alike of a fertile mind,
Whose procreative urges turn mere words to metaphor
And poems into the immaculate conceptions of my life.

9/12 — [3] & 9/13/76 — [1] (05478)

Harpsichord

I gaze into the notes of an ancient harpsichord,
Floating over a decayed Piranesian vault,
And see trapped voices escaping tight throats
Like house burglars climbing down ropes,
Recapitulating melancholy *carceri* chants,
Undoing their draped disguises as church hymns,
And running stair-scales ascending from Earth
To balconies ending in airy nowheres; spires
Carry them up from depths, into new valleys
Connected to newer depths by frescoed cloisters.

What imminent foreshadowing of apocalypse,
What omniscient conscience hovering nearby,
What gorgon chewing itself to death for food
Has directed the paranoia sensors in my ears
To isolate and focus on the harpsichord's notes?
What agent has singled me out to perceive
The music of the spheres being created originally
From the inviolate instrument Lucifer plays to seduce
The muse of hamartial artists, poets, composers?
Taken in by inordinate self-esteem, deceived,

I've allowed alien chimeras to penetrate the core,
Where my imagination manufactures its visions,
Prepares its flights of fancy for distant trips
To the soul's desolated flats and crystal palaces.
In stretching out to net the tantalizing notes
And free their prisoners by forcing them to o'erleap the gorge
Between metaphorical art and metaphysical death,
My mind has overstepped its delicate threshold.
In the inner ear, I can clearly discern my own voice
Being transposed into the harpsichord's infernal key.

9/13/76 — [2] (05479)

Unwed Black Lady and Child

Tonight, alone in a restaurant filled with lives
At quiet repast, I'm reminded how my eyes
Are the perplexed spectators of a naive heart.
Unable to regain control over the gaze
That's settled on a bereft young black lady
*

And her smiling, pigtailed five-year-old,
I allow a pervasive choir of crying voices to erupt.
A resonant cantor standing in my mind's chancel
Revives the ancient lamentations.
Passages from the Bible inundate my brain
With the awful immediacy of unaging wisdom,
As I watch motherhood first select sustenance
For its dear offspring, lead the way to a table,
Cut its baby's meat, dab the dirty cheek
Before giving a single indication of beginning to eat.
Through the shimmering blur that connects lands
Separating our dissimilar latitudes like an ocean
Waved with weeping, I see her and the child
Turned into tiny, chirping, fledgling birds,
Safe as fate allows in their precarious nest,
Helpless before the slightest malevolence, hungry
For the grubs and morsels rationed by stingy survival.
Scriptural elegies tell me we're all God's children,
Each and every blessed one among our number,
Yet I wonder why, if this is unequivocal,
We deny so many of our own children sympathy
Equal to that which He bequeathed His creatures
Despite disapprobation and outraged patience.
Tonight, I take this young black lady
For my wife and adopt her child as my own baby
In a silent ceremony attended by devout scribes
Waiting to write an extended appendix to Revelation.

9/14/76   (05401)

Willy, Knight of the Breakfast Table

From his polished, brass-flecked black strollers,
Up his clinging knee-high socks,
Through a tailored, wide-plaid business suit,
To his manicured fingernails and short, neat toupee,
He is Sir Satisfied, First Earl of Arrived.

Only, the newspaper he clings to for security,
Like a baby's ragged blanket, hides his stained tie,
His widening girth, the gold-rimmed bifocals
That guide his entire mind, like twin-traced mules
Dragging a plow, through rows of facile print.

The flimsy broadside he ponders assiduously,
As though it might be an authentic Dead Sea Scroll,
Distracts him from ordering breakfast. A short stack,
Steaming beneath a lopsided iceberg of butter,
Arrives without him even seeing a waitress materialize

Or dissolve, into the rug, like the butter
Dripping languidly off the drooping side
Of the rubberized pancakes patiently awaiting his kiss.
Although he continues to peer dead ahead,
They disappear, as if by osmotic assimilation,

Along with coffee and juice. Robotlike,
He shoves the world aside, rises renewed,
Armed with chain mail, heavy metal gauntlets,
Lance, and heads toward his restless mount,
To assault old clothing accounts full tilt.

9/15/76 — [1] (02420)

The Macaws △

I hear the paradoxically beautiful macaws
Screeching hysterically into the air I breathe
Three hundred miles south. My ears associate
Their unbearably penetrative timbre with the crying
Our baby makes whenever fever lands in branches
Outside her window sill and refuses to leave.

The birds' flapping wings stir a whirlwind
Within my skull that unlooses nervous energies,
Cerebral debris, and psychic detritus from moorings,
Which bruise linings of my mind's memory apparatus,
Pock it with fissures and lacunae that allow amnesia
To ooze in from the slimy edges of insensitivity.

For a moment, I forget about my wife and child
And why I'm driving this speeding vehicle
Toward wherever it's taking whoever I am.
Suddenly, my neck is a swollen hunk of meat
Punctured and bloodied by crude, scalding talons
That corkscrew into the spine. My head pulsates

Like the death-rattled chest of a tubercular patient.
My nose recognizes the stench. My lips know
*

The salty, acrid odor that lifts from the blood
As the spectral macaws fly me over, past death,
Then back, and drop me just behind the lines
Where fighting goes on in the zone of her crying.

Her room is a cage crowded with coughs and sneezes.
My gaze wanders from Trilogy's glazed recognition of me,
Through the window, to see, one by one,
The febrile birds of prey take spontaneous flight,
While the prismatic macaws, who brought me home,
Strut peacock haughty in the purgative sun.

9/15/76 — [2] (00770)

Autumnal Awareness △

As I drive through the country, in quietude,
My eyes invite me to sit down and imbibe
The fall leaves' first turning draughts.
One taste makes me dizzy; I swoon,
In a Van Winkle daze, beneath the shade
Of a million autumnal trees. Lazy as a bear
Laired for an endless winter, I prepare my spirit
To enter a cavelike hiatus in the seasons.

God, the body aches with the impending change!
How strange it seems to be taken by surprise
After all these years of conditioned anticipations
And ebulliently hued arrivals I've poeticized.
Yet, once again, my mind is awakened
From its soporific odyssey, as if caught escaping
A perfectly executed crime, while age erases
Another layer of the design that decorates my life.

9/21/76 — [1] (05480)

Deus in machina

The skull, filigreed and truncated
With uneven steeples, dormers protruding
Like eyes, and tiled, tangled angles,
Contains a brain whose Grand Central Station
*

Serves a nation of peripatetic strangers.
The spine is the mind's main line,
Over which flow electric vocabularies
Controlling the body's ceaseless rolling stock.
The veins and arteries are tracks
Molecular trains, painted red and white,
Use to transport their oxygenated freight
And dispose of their carbonaceous wastes.
The arms and legs are trestles and bridges
Connecting one country to another,
Earth to air, depot to whistle stop,
Soul to soul, in a network of railroads
Humans board at birth and ride a lifetime,
Rarely pausing to ascertain the powers behind
The corporate name that subsidizes all operations.

9/21/76 — [2] (05481)

The Glory Train ^Δ

How like a steaming locomotive approaching a station
Has my shuddering psyche come, finally, to rest
On these green, weathered bleachers!
How unlike a machine is my reluctance to resume
Routines that perpetuate the illusory heroic notion
That dreams are destinations to be reached in time!
I've transported my poetic express a million meters
And yet never arrived at the soul's depot,
Where earthly verse is unloaded and exchanged
For the immemorial odes angels recite by heart.

Now, the massive driving wheels are locked.
The colossal length of train is gradually lost
In profuse sumac, elephantine underbrush,
And rust flaking off the sullen creature.
Since I've engineered the vehicle twenty years,
Stepping down from the cab is like inviting death
To invade my bones. After wandering for days,
I turn to gaze at the distant landscape
And see, in gleaming reverie, the sound and shape
Of my failed psyche steaming into Oblivion.

9/24/76 (05482)

Oedipal Complexes in Autumn

I enter the day through an opening
In the raging colors layered in strata
Late September exposes in naked orgasm.
Such lovemaking comes twice, maybe,
Each year, leaving the ravaged mind
Flaccid and feeble afterwards, weak-kneed,
Overshadowed by the absence of leaves
In winter and summer's monochromatic green.

Only during this in-between season,
When rebirth and death converge
And the procreative spirit goes into heat,
Does the regenerative urge of man's soul
Come close to learning the inmost secret
Nature, with rare exceptions, keeps to herself.

By the freshness of her fragrant body
And the brilliant gestures of her émigrés,
I conjecture she's the ageless, immaculate Virgin —
God's perfectly untainted legacy to earth,
Mistress to the generations, herself a helpmate,
Fecund Phoenix-mother of the child I am.

9/29/76 — [1] (05483)

[I descend the past quarter century] ‡

I descend the past quarter century
As though each year were a steep stair
Connecting my memories of adolescence
With my present level of vertiginous existence.
On finally reaching the last step,
I leap off the palpable edge, into blackness,
Fall to my knees, and crawl like a mole.

The senses no longer suffice for survival.
My ears fail to acquaint me with poltergeists
And nightmares swarming around the mind's hive,
Whose stings anesthetize all sentience
And slow breathing to an inaudible beat.
In this self-imposed claustrophobia,
I become, like Lot's wife, a pillar of salt.

Whatever occurred in childhood to divert the psyche
From sending out a normal root system
Isn't discernible, yet the net it's set up
To detect intruders has successfully kept me
From learning the nature of the evil-tree,
Whose fruit has been the sins of my seasons.
Now, even

9/29/76 — [2] (05484)

The Ancient Mariner

Driving through this bleak 5 a.m.,
I hear the distant, loony wail of shofars
And sight watch fires on the lambent horizon's
Outlying perimeters. I might be David,
Loading my mind's slingshot, one tiny insult
At a time, for the final assault on Goliath
And his city of Philistines, or Odysseus,
Hurling scalding anathemas from a fiery cauldron
Aboard ship, toward outraged Cyclops.

Above my vision, the dumb walls of history
Wield their starry weight without noticing me.
Perhaps my passage is that of a ghost ship
Floating on a vast, phosphorescent Sargasso ocean,
And I'm its entire crew, doomed to navigate
Sea lanes beyond Mappa Mundi forever,
As punishment for having abandoned my home.
The only consolation for penetrating the unknown alone
Is in being the first to step foot on the shores of my soul.

Yet now that I've apparently arrived,
The gossamer landscape, planted with red locusts
Swarming with webs and dormant hornets' nests,
Neither revives recollections of childhood haunts
Nor evokes the slightest desire on my part to remain
As the ordained progenitor of a race of beings
Not yet conceived. Suddenly, the vehicle
That has transported me, these many light years,
Sputters in a hideous stiffening like rigor mortis,

And I am left stranded somewhere in the mind's predawn,
Bereft of everything except my desiccated flesh.
*

All directions radiating from the point where I stand,
Unable to move, seem the same. They beckon me
Like friendly, waving hands. I recognize them as impostors.
Within reach, the alabaster moon teeters past.
Frightened, I look down in time to see Earth
Sliding slowly away on the galactic ocean I sailed,
Only yesterday, in quest of a lasting escape from death.

10/11/76 — [1] (05485)

Log Notations from an Agent for the State

The landscape of my travels
Is populated with the haggard faces of waitresses
And cashiers, planted with mechanical slaves
Peddling strumpetlike French ticklers and gewgaws
Fashioned out of chrome, plastic, and air.

It's plastered rainbow-wide,
Across the dingy horizon, with posters
Advertising the shirt off America's back
At factory-outlet prices
And autos below manufacturers' wholesale.

Every front yard and fifty-starred flag
Is a "For Sale" sign
Nailed to the mind's peripatetic eye.
Moving vans, U-Hauls, Winnebagos
Ferry the nation's heritage across Styx

And back, in a ceaseless ritual of bequeathment,
As the generations devour each other alive.
Children roaming the streets during school
Are the aging spirit's hand-me-downs,
Runaways from the family of man,

Truants from the roles endowed out of guilt
With Guggenheims, food stamps, and coupons
For blue-chip stocks requiring signatures.
Their own babies spawn in brief encounters
Like flies springing to life spontaneously

In this landscape where my travels have taken me,
On assignment with an agency for the state.
*

In passing, I might note that, for decades,
The vessel's changing shape and its souring taste
Have allowed my superiors to savor the sweetest bouquet.

10/11/76 — [2] (05486)

Luminaries, or A Sky Composed of Internal Rhymes △

I awaken, millenniums before daybreak,
In time to see Betelgeuse, Cassiopeia,
And the two consanguineous Dippers
Kindled by the lamplighter living in my eyes.

Ineffable specters loiter in the sky,
As if waiting for a vehicle to transport them
Across a bridge whose spans and cables are hours
Wound and riveted to history's mystical columns,

Sunk in caissons buried in man's speculations.
I acknowledge their presence by echoing the names
Navigators gave them to make their astrolabes function.
They speak to me in subtle, fluctuating magnitudes,

Tapping out, in light-year soliloquies,
A poetry reminiscent of Periclean Greece
And Elizabethan New Jerusalem, and I realize
Where Homer and blind Milton walked

When they sought repose for their distraught souls.
Gazing at the vast, rotating mass of *astra*,
I imagine hearing the voice from an invisible, new flame
Whispering refrains of verses I myself have made.

10/12/76 (05487)

Exercise △

Slowly, the rink fills up with colors.
Beautifully hued images
And metaphors, dancing in tandem, race by
Like painted carousel horses.
They prance in leggy merriment, gambol, blur.
*

Soon, my entranced spirit
Infers empathy from their urgent, whirling circles.

Amazed, I watch my hand skate with abandon
Across the frozen page,
Above whose banks, in a most serene trance,
My eyes spectate,
Witnessing a million mystical configurations
Etched in invisible ice
Come alive beneath my pen's blade.

As day descends, fatigue sets in,
And one by one,
Visions leave the arena. Endless revolving
Has finally dissolved the ice.
The rink dissipates into freezing lake,
Lake telescopes into page.
Pens unlaced, I'm the last to leave my trance.

10/14/76 — [1] (05488)

Commutation

"Now that I've arrived,"
Said the flier to the sky,
"What do you have in mind?"

"Now that you're mine,"
Cried the spider to the fly,
"I think I've got an idea:

"Let's dismantle the web
Connecting our lives
And imagine a new conclusion!

"You be wind; I'll be time.
Let the space in between
Be our destination.

"We'll float on a sea
Of wings, fins, and dreams.
Things that soar freely

"Will guide our journeys
To an eternity we'll share
Through separate eyes.

"Once there, we can discuss
The cruelty of earthly appetites
And review our mutual commutation."

10/14–15/76 — [2] on 10/14 & [1?] on 10/15   (02231)

The Scavengers [Δ]

Together, they walk along the beach,
Hand in hand,
Just outside Eden's forbidden purlieus,
Searching for recognizable objects
To remind them of paradisiacal precincts
No longer open to their philandering,

One with stomach plump as Gautama's,
Underneath a bathing suit
Stretched about her resilient body,
The other grown somewhat squatty
With accreted years around his waist,
Like a life buoy tied permanently in place.

They meander erratically through seaweed
Festooned with fetid, sleeping fish
And abandoned calcareous cell-shells
Obsoleted by escaped creatures.
Their feet disturb busy fiddler crabs
Fastidiously sifting desiccated granules,

Send them scurrying into sandy camouflage,
Like dancers doing the Peabody on stage.
The two taunt them with rocks
Aimed at their blatant hiding, laugh
As they surge up in six-legged urgency
And race to caves saved for emergencies.

Yet for all their feigned amusement,
Tumescent Eve and lackluster Adam
Wander absent-mindedly beside the waters.
They gaze at the mutating surface,
Trying to discern the original swell,
As if discovering the ocean's source

Might enlighten them about the force
That ejected them from their extravagance.
*

Brown pelicans distract their concentration;
Sandpipers briefly undo their fixity;
The unamused sun hurls parabolas
That confuse vision; the horizon dilates,

Sending forth, to do battle with their eyes,
Countless multiplying Hydras.
Frightened by such poltergeists,
They leave off their airy speculations,
Retreat to the makeshift shelter
Beneath a caliginous cypress tree

Growing at the base of their awareness,
And weep. They realize, now, that generations
Flying toward them, inside their hopes,
Will never differentiate the old sweet land,
So close at hand, so inaccessible,
From this, which they'll call Florida.

10/15–16/76 — [2?] on 10/15   (02230)

After Disney World △

For fully two days and nights,
Unabatingly,
I've encircled my waking world
Below the cosmos of fantasies.

Like a gold-glowing moon around Jupiter,
My mind, in wobbly ellipse,
Ensconced within the fiberglass belly
Of an ear-winged elephant,

Has orbited itself a thousand times
And still shows no sign
Of dissolving. Quite the contrary,
It seems to soar more vigorously

Whenever I conjure that carousel
And the brass-poled, cigar-store horse
Atop whose hand-carved saddle,
Locked in each other's death grip,

We rode above Peter Pan's London,
Swooped low over Nemo's sub,
*

Revolved through cotton-candy clouds
While gliding, with calliope strides,

Inside a halo of shared excitement
Suspended above our bobbing heads.
Even now, without knowing how,
Cathexis attaches me to its sounds,

Confuses its bellowed air with vapor
Spewing from magical running gear,
Blasting, in spastic escape,
From a screaming steam whistle

Mounted, like a volcanic cigarette,
Atop the plangent Baldwin locomotive
We rode from Main Street Station
To afternoon's exotic depots.

My eyes still wince from grit
Thrown up off the track and cinders
Blown back from its outsize stack.
My ears are filled with its ululations.

Memory retains the ecstatic blur
Of the eternally out-of-focus world
We celebrated, those two days,
In an ageless communion of happiness,

Before boarding the fleet monorail
That transported our fatigued spirits
Over concrete trestles, toward now.
Even the effluvia refuses to fade.

Today, locating the proper doors
To fit my keys, the perfect shadows
To superimpose on urgent routines,
Seems more important than ever before.

Concentrating on baby Trilogy
As she cavorts naked, in high heels,
Clopping across the terrazzo floor,
Purse draped over her shoulder,

In a frozen Vaudevillian two-step,
I'm suddenly reminded of the relationship
Of all things outrageous and sublime,
The nature of memory and time arrived,

And I realize that Disney World
Will stay poignant and alive
Whenever I gaze into our baby's eyes.
She holds the keys to my fantasies.

10/21/76 & 1/2–3/77 — [2] on 1/2   (00775)

[For three days now, we've watched,] ‡

For three days now, we've watched,
With a keen eye, for the slightest change
In the wind-whipped ocean. All that motion
Without noticeable advancement toward a goal
Makes those of us who define progress
By dividends yielded, services rendered,
Grades earned toward a degree
A bit edgy. Perhaps it's the consistency,
Without apparent intention to break its routine,
That tantalizes our sense of expectations:

10/24/76 — [1]   (02500)

Tempus fugit

A solitary crack in the exhaust stack,
Hairline yet visible to a mechanic
Doing his routine preflight inspection,
Has successfully brought time up short.
Schedules blanch. Transient passengers
Step briefly off the moving walkway
They use in passing from dawn through dusk
And back, each waking/sleeping breath.
Their complaints are wet match heads,
Failing to ignite the slightest sympathy
From pilots used to overcaution
And deviation from standard flight plans.

Two hours stratify into drinks
And sandwiches distributed gratis,
Extraordinary courtesies, spoken amenities
Between those who fly the machine
*

And those who say their Ave Marias,
Pray to Elohim in silent Hebraic chants,
Pour salt on the tail of their atheism.
To most, the uncommitted waiting time,
When set against the two eternities
Through which they pass, seems so brief
That the alternative of a potential crash
Is as anathematic as suicide.

For the intransigent few who can't establish
A practical acceptance of "inexcusable delays"
Or commute their indictment against fate
For causing these unpredicted inconveniences,
There's neither elixir nor mystical faith
To abrogate the doom inexorably settling over them.
Without their awareness, renegade tribes of time
Have already been assigned to follow their souls
To their graves, then fly beside them, into space,
As unrelenting, conscious-enervating reminders
That every solitary second, minute, and hour
Is theirs to schedule throughout Limbo's sweep.

10/24/76 — [2] (05489)

Passing the Midpoint

"Midway on my journey through life,"
I write, caught in a strange trance,
Quaking as if shades of the poet Dante
Were breathing over my shoulder,
Trembling as my fingers metamorphose
From puffy stumps into fleshless bones,
"I find myself in a shadowy woods."

These lines remember me from ancient times,
Remind me of escapes into the soul,
Isolation self-imposed when the intellect,
At an early age, sought its own voice
From out of all those echoing sycophants
Seeking recognition by being loud
Inside the cave where Christ lay drowsing.

Only, now, my mind has lost its blaze.
Flames that licked the air as songs,
*

Leaping out of life's inspired fires
Like snake tongues, extinguish themselves,
As though each passing year were oxygen
Leaving the brain as it disintegrates
Slowly, irreversibly — the curse from within.

10/26/76 (05490)

Leave-Takings

In my frequent leave-takings,
I seem to find myself,
As though the textured sheet of frost
And random smoke hovering above water holes,
Escaping stacks scattered along the countryside,
Ballooning from my mouth, outdoors,
Were my identity. I climb inside the smoke,
Rise naked, evaporate into the air
After walking barefoot over the cold ground,
Embroidering footprints where heel and toes
Melt their impressions into the grass
Before the morning sun dissolves both of us.

10/29/76 — [1] (05491)

Détente

In these predawn hours,
Going nowhere except to my occupation,
I approximate a mitigable peace with demons
Who would keep me incarcerated in sleep.
We've made a tacit agreement
That my psyche can investigate and assimilate
Anything its eyes might define by memory
And conclude its own egotistical philosophies,
Providing nothing it deduces interferes
With the year-gears that rotate my arms and legs
Around the face of a masterful apparatus
They've wound to an indeterminate tightness.

10/29/76 — [2] (05492)

The Lake Takes a Bride [Δ]

For my grandmother, Dorothy Malter,
who loved me so much I cry . . .
God bless your spirit, dear "Nonnie";
its love and its splendor abide with us.

Although six concrete stories high
Above Lake Michigan, insulated behind plate glass,
Safe from all elements except our fantasies,
By midday, when the entire family assembled,
We actually began to speculate that the waves,
Breaking with such tempestuous regularity,
Might overtake the outer lane of Lake Shore Drive

And, if left unchecked, gain the threshold
Through whose portals Nonnie had come to stay out
Her denouement. It almost seemed as though,
For all their anthropomorphic prescience,
They'd assumed, mistakenly, she still remained
Here, in this efflorescing apartment, and that,
For all her wasting away, she was yet alive

And that they might yet claim her for the lake,
Beside which she'd thrived since 1894.
Despite our lugubrious gestures to the contrary,
Something depending from the biting October chill
Was driving them on in blind unenlightenment.
Perhaps after she'd lived that many years near water,
The prospect of being cuckolded by the earth

And having to contend with the undying awareness
That Nonnie might sleep with another lover
Somewhere other than where its waves
Could touch her ears, insinuate their song
In the prolonged minuet that swayed the dance of days
Stirring constantly inside her mind's odeon,
Was more than the lake could graciously accept.

At the appointed hour, we were taken by limousine
To the funeral parlor. Gliding along the outer drive,
We witnessed the moiling water turn to hands
Pawing at our vehicle, beseeching us to stop.
Going slowly, we watched it become tongues
And listened to its eloquent whimperings of silent sympathy
Plead with us to release Nonnie unto its keeping.

By the time the cortège arrived at the cemetery,
Twenty miles from downtown, sleet was kicking its feet
Over the freshly dug grave just beyond the canopy.
As blessed Nonnie's casket was being lowered away,
The warming air changed into a finely granulated rain
That fought with every shovelful of dirt for space
In the grave. We knew the lake would somehow get its way.

10/29/76 — [3] (03857)

Red Candle in a Black Room

How is it possible that my ears
Can actually translate the candle's flame,
Speaking to me, in lambent cadences,
Through frosted cranberry glass?

Perhaps it's just my mind's expertise
In eavesdropping on the universe
And reading meanings between strata
Of its most recondite pictographs.

Possibly, the skittish tongue,
Precariously contained beneath my gaze
And aware that its existence
Depends on the benevolence of my breath,

Is cautious in articulating its thoughts,
Conscious of not offending sensibilities
While exposing shadows within its halo,
Heating frozen shafts of incandescence.

Whatever the real reason might be,
Its voice possesses an eloquence,
In its flowing, glowing poetry,
Few humans have approximated,

And when people fail to mollify
My solitude, I seek companionship
In the expressive silence of candlelight.
Its enigmatic divinity is beyond reproach.

10/29/76 — [4] (05493)

Halloween Unleashes Her Specters

Evanescence is the specter we rarely see
Yet hear, rattling chains in our lonely sleep
Even after we've long since awakened.
He's the snowman dressed in suspicions
We know will come to fruition when the first sun
Sends him running to avoid exposing his bones.

His clothes are sewn of diaphanous flesh
Chosen by the archgrand wizard himself,
From among exotic stock in the realm of Necropolis.
And although the philosophy of *carpe diem*,
By which he exists, was recycled from a dead language,
It's surprisingly vital in modern guise.

Last night, while I was standing in my backyard,
Admiring the glyceric horizon, a hitchhiker
Stepped down from the sky, on a ladder
Whose rungs were clouds, and begged a ride westward,
Toward a destination he confided was identical to mine.
I declined yet knew I'd finally seen the specter.

10/31/76   (05494)

Catching Snowflakes △

The entire still, shrill sky
Is a spillway
Of goose-down pillow feathers,
A sluice spume-white
With opiate water-shapes
Changing, as they cascade through space,
Into geodesic flakes,
A millrace
Containing, by gravitational persuasion,
The tumbling columnar spray
Of the whole universe
In an unintentionally chaotic plunge,

At whose base we stand,
Repeatedly trying
To grasp with our bare hands
*

Just one crystal
And have it outlast our fascination
Of having captured it,
If only momentarily intact,
On its passage back
To atmosphere, via ocean and sky,
Before the heat of our flesh
Relieves us of the flake's virginity
And it of our fragile innocence.

11/4/76   (00772)

Untoward Incursions

It grabs my vena cava
Tightly between a jaw full of incisors
And bites down like a giant brake
Shaping steel into an intricate template.
Suddenly, the veins spasm, deflate,
Go flaccid as dehydrated nematodes
Within the consanguineous vascular system,
Which previously functioned with fail-safe regularity.

My alien blood floods the creature's mouth,
As it gushes from throbbing gashes
In my chest and neck. My buzzing ears
Hear every undivided cell
Screaming as it leaves my distressed vessel,
Yelling out life histories,
In fleet seconds, to the bilious winds,
Before spilling irretrievably beneath the dust.

What strange form of corporeal metaphor
Or fate delivered of ancient oracles
Is impossible to fathom merely by peering
Into the amorphous, inscrutable face
Leering down over my prostrate body.
Yet as night's dreams sift slowly,
Cooling, as they go, with rigor mortis,
A vast image rises above my dying ashes,

And I awaken, disoriented, to find
That sleep, by subtle bribery,
*

Has allowed suicide to disguise itself,
Judas-like, as familiar nightmare.
Urgently, I race to the medicine cabinet
And grab a handful of sleeping pills,
Hoping to placate Thanatos this time,
Before his demon surfaces into daytime, beside me.

11/5/76 (05495)

The Decline and Fall of Civilizations

By slow degrees,
All my previous incarnations compact
Behind the reinforced dam consciousness built
To keep history from interceding
Inopportunely on the soul's cycling liaison with life.

The slender, hymenlike membrane
Containing memory disintegrates.
The brain is deluged
With a seething moil of thoughts and ideas,
Faces, codicils, wills, and fears,

Which age has allowed to accumulate
On the banks of its stagnant, man-made reservoir.
Once unleashed, the eviscerate waters,
Draining through every convolution and fissure,
Sweep away my entire existence indiscriminately.

For a brief sequence, the body is held aloft,
Atop a cresting wave, deceived, by such heights,
Into believing it comprehends the nature of catastrophe,
Before being dashed mercilessly
Into the belly of a leviathan-sized trough

And spewed out again, into a tidal basin
Strewn with shriveled vellum illuminations,
Cimabues, splintered della Robbias,
Swollen Gobelins, crucifixes, triptychs —
Salubrious mud glues all objects into One.

I've become a thrashing, Arno-ravaged humanist,
Floating in debris up to my freezing neck.
Crowds lining the shores, wearing raincoats,
Throw blood-soaked bouquets
To see me maneuver futilely to save myself.

Submerging for the third time, I hear voices
Proclaiming my victimization a natural disaster,
Speculating that the knowledge assimilated
Through various phases of my personal evolution
Has outgrown my capacity to order it and exploded.

Beneath the surface, blunt shapes invade
Or leave me, going slowly away. Suddenly,
I realize that all my parts and pieces
Are returning to their Source for redistribution
To new beings waiting at the beginning of Creation.

11/10/76 — [1] (05496)

Welding a Sunset

The 5 p.m. sun,
Balancing on November's cold shoulder,
Resembles the garrulous acetylene point
Of a welding torch brazing two plates
Painted ocher and terra cotta,
Whose union connects dusk with night.

Cloud striations, adhering to the horizon
Like flies to offal, might be beading
Released from filler rods.
Their smeary appearance keeps the job
From being cleanly accomplished.
The object continues to glow red

Long after headlights load the highway
With artificial light. As I drive west,
My eyes try to conceive, through alchemy,
Some measure by which to arrest
The ineluctable sunset
And enter its swirling, purple eternity.

Yet within minutes, without a snap,
The gaseous synapse is gently extinguished.
Black seconds erase the last traces
Of refracting space-sands of time.
Later, tenacious irritants tear my eyes,
And I wipe away day's remaining granules.

11/10/76 — [2] (05497)

Willy Propositions Beatrice ^Δ

Through the stupor brought on
By driving twice two hundred miles today,
Willy finally arrives at his familiar destination,
Away from wife, hometown, known faces,
And, as if penetrating a Dalmatian fog,
Is assimilated into the thick cigarette smoke,
Then lost beneath the polygamous percussion
And lusty brass of another itinerant band.

Just another unproclaimed, drunk salesman,
He realizes the need to break from anonymity,
Shout his credentials, boast his line
Of nationally advertised fine men's clothing.
He takes the waitress's delicate wrist,
Draws his entire weight up her slender arm,
As if to reach the citadel of her charms,
Orders a glass of house wine, asks her

To make change for a five-dollar bill,
Then implores her to keep four dollars,
Promises her more if she'll reach his door
After closing. Later, a quiet rap awakens him,
Retrieves him from facing his salaciousness alone.
Naked, she enters his life, the waitress
Whose nudity he craved earlier this night
Despite the image of his wife hovering nearby.

In fear, he appears at the door, slips her
Ten dollars as token payment to free him
From imminent enslavement to his intentions.
She acquiesces hastily, like a bellboy
Accepting a tip for delivering baggage, retreats.
Willy stumbles to his bed, hurls himself
Headlong into a cool pool of wrinkled sheets,
Tucks his lust into bed again,

As he has for the last twenty-five years.

11/10/76 — [3] (01305)

Dagon

Organ, flute, bass guitar, traps
Fling me over the castle walls.
*

I fall headlong, like rain, to earth
And assume my calling gracefully.
Voices herald me as I enter the city,
Wearing the victory wreath,
Dragging, in cages, the vanquished
As visual displays of our armies'
Expertise in the martial arts.
I myself remain tented with ladies
Who make up my doting harem.

The music sings steeples alive;
Church bells swing wild as trees
In deep breezes. Even owls blink
As daytime proclaims my presence
In the ancient city of Poetry.
Virgins weep at not being invited
To the coronation of a new queen.
I remain within the regal tents,
Entertained by the visceral music
Emanating from saxophone bell,
Flute hole, metal fret, taut string
Touched by the music of the spheres.

Defeating the enemy, comprised of demons
Organized against the sane forces of love,
Doesn't satisfy the seeds that nourish lust.
The thrust of my continued battle is aimed
At enemies hiding behind their naked bodies.
It's the golden calves writhing at the altars,
Manifesting the greatest dissatisfaction,
That drive my mind into death-moth frenzy.
My patience breaks. Outraged, I insist
That my people retreat to the ghettos
To rewrite the Scriptures, reconceive their mission.

Now, after all the celebrations have wound down
And the town has drowned in inebriated stupors,
I walk alone through its deserted alleys
And abandoned purlieus. Strewn haphazardly,
Copulating bodies and exhausted ladies leaking semen
Clutter my vigil. My mind reels
Like a jinn's apprentice pulling the undone souls.
Visions of alien dead left ungraved at Dunsinane
And the Plain of Jezreel unseat my restive quietude.
*

I raise my hands and pray to YHWH,
Begging divine exemption from my sins of haughtiness.

Morning is a nubile, striated sunrise, whorelike,
Touching me in the kidneys. I awaken to fifes
And drums, the dumb, inheriting son of Mars,
An emperor of Rome — Hadrian, Caligula, Nero —
Brokenhearted, startled by the rabble-rousing,
Crying out the name "Christ, Son of God, Christ."
Without advice, quietly, I realize the end is at hand,
The beginning imminent. A baby stirs in a manger.
My scepter dissolves; the diadem melts on my head.
The crown is changing hands. The music stops.
An entire civilization joins hands without knowing why.

Such a stillness as in the Kingdom of Gewgaw
Never existed settles over the castellated realm,
That lamplighter, jailer, jester
Require the emperor to announce his intentions.
An age of interregnum has begun to descend
Over the known world. Changes sail forward,
Toward ancient dominions. Icons and idols
Teeter on their podiums, shatter, as Chaldea
Breaks its sacred cuneiform over its knees.
A rough beast, untried, without credentials,
Rises meekly, preaching nothing other than brotherly love.

Now, years have passed through oblivion's portcullis.
The gates have closed with emphatic finality. The people
Bend on humble knees. Nothing has changed. The rules
Resist amendments. The king recoils in exile,
Remembering his days of glory. Sedentary ghosts
Rarely fly into the night, after aliens, anymore.
Even the moon refuses to exhibit its phases.
Dagon waits for the perfect moment to invade
The kingdom again. He watches the Thorny Man,
Hoping for one mistake, knowing his reign will return
When sleeping armies awaken to clash with lurking Beelzebub.

Dagon: alias of Gerry Ford, an incumbent President of the U.S. of A.,
unseated for strictly subjective reasons

11/10/76 — [4] (01306)

La luna de miel

I wonder what the moon intends
By staying out, this bright morning,
Refusing to disappear in night's wake,
Pretending that by burying her white face
In cloud-wisps, ostrichlike, no eyes
Will recognize her capricious existence.
Is she secretly courting a suitor
Or eavesdropping on people she saw
Last evening? Possibly, she forgot the direction home
Or dropped an heirloom in the sands of earthly time
And has lingered to sift them and find it
Before galactic storms
Fling it into eternity's greedy keeping.

Whatever the reason, her unexpected presence
Distracts me from my mercantilistic focus.
My concentration on the highway ahead,
The day's business calls, my suitcases
Crammed with swatch cards and sample pants
Pales each time I gaze up at her,
Sailing in lustrous juxtaposition
To an invisible sun trapped in sulfurous,
Snow-laden haze somewhere behind me.
Whether pursued by or pursuing *la luna*
Is ultimately immaterial to my decision
To abandon all prior plans and commitments
And proclaim this day our honeymoon.

11/11/76 — [1] (02419)

Plant Manager

Fifteen minutes ago, at 12:30,
This vacated café was trammeled
With the cicada-chaos of my factory ladies.
Now, silence is a tacit suzerain,
Sitting heavily on its vinyl throne,
In a kingdom where I'm the only
Paying customer. My eyes scurry,
Like minnows, across the empty expanse,
*

Fasten on three teenage waitresses
Eating leftovers, and are trapped
In lobster nets draped, for effect,
Down the walls, across the ceiling.
Shells suspended by macramé,
Paintings of oceangoing fishing boats,
And bobbers, poles, starfish, conchs,
Horseshoe crabs almost persuade me
That, any moment, Harry Morgan
Will swagger through the front door
Of Key West to trade insults
With Hemingway. But the freight
From K.C., laden with tottering cars —
Grain and lumber for St. Louis —
Collides head-on with my own train
Of expatiating daydreams. I pay and leave,
Yet all the way up Main Street,
As I freeze beneath a late-November sun,
A persisting vision pins me to an image
In which Bogey, with native mistress,
Swills bootlegged whiskey daily,
Beneath a squeaking, four-blade fan.
Only, once indoors, I'm completely absorbed
By the roaring, piranha-like sewing machines,
For whose order I'm solely responsible,
From morning to 4:30, weekdays,
In a masochistic romance of routine chores.

11/11/76 — [2] (00598)

Rosy-Fingered Dawn

The dazed soul of my splayed existence
Awakens early enough to hear the sands of time
Rushing away from an unseen eastern sun,
Fleeing through space, straight toward my eyes,
As though a horrific specter were chasing behind.

The horizon is a roseate cyclotron
Erupting with enucleating atoms
Living out their half-lives with outrageous haste.
I sit behind cold café glass,
Spectating in puny, quizzical silence,

Listening to the distant, whispering roar,
Imagining its voice growing in pitch,
As it gathers in a final, shimmering boast,
Then dissipates the design of sound and light,
Through myriad holes in my eyes and ears.

When I look again, not a trace
Of dawn's cataclysmic dust storm remains.
Only a Canaletto-shimmer pervades the sky,
And a vague tingling, like bees swarming,
Lingers on the peripheries, where metaphors sing.

11/12/76 — [1] (05498)

The Dispossessed ^Δ

I follow the train tracks
Out of Tipton, slow, dip,
Turn north, where overpass
And spiderlike grain elevator converge
At my pinnacled focal point,
This frost-cursed, glistening morning.

Brindled, pinto, and piebald cows,
Mingled with pervasive Charolais,
Graze ineffectually on stubble
And short-clipped, crystallized hay.
The bent-necked shadows they cast
Fast, as their twins fight for survival,

While all the way up County 5,
To Interstate 70, I fly by them
In heated privacy, unsympathetic
To their plight. Their deprivation
Doesn't seem to affect me directly,
Except, perhaps, in a philosophic context,

Whose unfenced frames of reference
Never could keep my atheistic disrespect
In check anyway. Yet now,
For some unexplainably ethical reason,
My direction changes 180 degrees,
And I stop by the roadside to watch them feed.

Something about the solitudinous quality
Of dreamlike lethargy and simple timorousness
*

These defenseless cows possess
Obsesses me with very personal grief,
Almost as though a lowing from a previous incarnation
Were reminding me that the meek inherit eternity.

Briefly, I weep for dispossessed Edens,
Then proceed, realizing that evolution
Does with us as she pleases,
Regardless of our outraged protestations.
Still, as I track my course, going north,
The lump in my throat continues to grow.

11/12/76 — [2] (05433)

[As has been my habit] †

As has been my habit
These last twelve years

11/13/76 — [1] (01784)

The Old Lady on the Square △

Having outlasted three referendums,
Two bond issues,
And one emphatic municipal decree
Assigning contracts for urban renewal
To certain city fathers
With suspicious conflicts of interest,

The old Square finally succumbed
To its face-lift,
Reluctantly accepted "Central Plaza"
As its new name. Only Liberty
Remains inviolate, virginal
As the day she was set in place

On a plot seven feet east
Of the site of the city's original survey,
Made in 1825,
To commemorate and dignify
*

The brave patriots of Morgan County
Who gave away their lives in war.

Yet even her supplely sculpted limbs,
Shivering invisibly in the wind,
Beneath the draped outlines of sheer robes,
Show signs of corruption.
Her once lustrous, brown/jet flesh,
Though resisting rust, is patinated,

Complains of neglect. In places,
She wears the emblazoned graffiti
Youth, in hasty passage, deposits,
As if leaving a cuneiform record
Close to the surface, for the future to decipher
And decide if their civilization shall be preserved.

Erasure spots and pigeon guano
Also pock her graceful stasis,
Try to reclaim her as nature's surrogate
Through the slow, yearly deteriorations
Of snow, rain, and hundred-degree heat.
Despite daily metaphysical rapings,

She stands untainted in the sight of man,
The one symbol left intact
Above his ever-rearranging,
Ever-dismantling hands, in this land
Where the evangelists plant soybeans
And corn, pray like pagans to Demeter,

Pledge their souls and owe their lives
To those who hold first mortgages,
Deeds and quitclaims, second liens
On seeding machines and air-conditioned gleaners.
Recently, a few inveterate townspeople
Have noticed that the gleam in her eyes

And the marbleized Mona Lisa smile
She always displayed seem to have died.
They speculate sardonically among themselves
That the "old lady" may have finally realized
She could no longer recognize her neighbors
Or simply has grown tired of trying

To make excuses for their greedy presumptions,
Vile public disruptions, and alterations
Of ancient truths to suit their private needs.
Possibly, they err in their conjecture.
Hopefully, Liberty has merely taken notice
Of winter and begun her hibernation early.

11/13/76 — [2] (05499)

First Blood ^Δ

Through the kitchen windows' glass,
Whose sills are strewn with cactus plants
Rooted in close-packed plastic pots,
My eyes watch every moving object
Fluting beneath a blue November ocean.

Two mimosas, dormant as snoring bears
In hibernal comas, cling, like parents,
To their brittle, shivering pods. Their bare limbs
Are catacombs scattered with desiccated bones,
Miles of corridors lined with potted ashes.

A sinister wind winnows wormlike
Through their corrugated husks, bristles,
Plucks a few each hour, inconsistently,
As if composing, on an ancient crowd, ode notes
For winter's poetry, which my ears hear forming

As whispers in distant, invisible snow clouds.
Vicious blue jays, ubiquitous crows
Dismantle day's uneasy equilibrium
By forming a Zorba-like witches' chorus,
Whose taloned screeching scratches my irises.

Leaving the table still cluttered with lunch
Uneaten, silverware bunched like bones
Undone, cup smoking, I run
Toward the back door, throw it open
Just in time to witness the source of the ruckus,

Captured nesting in its heated innocence,
Being lifted swiftly aloft,
Transported with obscene violence, engorged.
*

At dusk, tinges of the baby rabbit's blood
Still drip from winter's steely beak.

11/18 & 11/22/76 — [2] (05467)

Deer Season ^Δ

All the way across country,
My cautious eyes were accosted by hunters
Dressed, like sunsets, in phosphorescent reds
Glowing against a branch-scratched horizon.

Threatened by their blued gun barrels
Glinting militaristically in the sun,
Frightened by the prospect of death's specters
Beating the bushes so close to the road,

I sped ahead, hoping to outdistance
A forest filled with crimson tinges
And the rife odor of distressed flesh
Lifting, like smoke, into the cohesive air.

Yet men gathered around fires
At highway's edge, passing bottles,
Shaking their heads with anxious laughter,
Refused to let me forget the season at hand

Or escape the immediate reality of annihilation
And my slightly diminished possibilities for survival
In a land swarming, like mackereled seas,
With bloodletters obsessed by their own expertise.

For days after I left the forest,
Every car that entered my focus
Seemed draped with splayed limbs,
A scarred hulk tied to its roof;

The rear glass of every truck cab,
Racked with imaginary pistols and rifles,
Glared at me like a witch's toothless smile,
Rekindled a paranoia of being blindfolded

And dying without knowing why.
Months later, I drove across country
*

To locate the remains of my soul's carcass.
The snows had buried it for another year.

11/19/76 (05432)

O, I Sing Ye, Eidolons

I enter the outside, moony morning
Through luminous clouds my breathing detonates
Against cohesive legions of twenty-degree air.
Inside my exhalations, all objects crystallize,
Age in a matter of heartbeats. My slow eyes,
Groping as if to penetrate an iceberg from within,
See themselves reflected on their retinal linings —
Ghosts addressing ghosts in a sunless desert.

In this region, cacti, statues, the frozen sands
Cease to exist. My soul's cargo floats away,
As its listing vessel shifts precipitously,
Then sinks in a sea of radioactive haze
Drifting out of control, overhead.
The stuff that once comprised cortical fibers
My brain electrified dissolves in that ocean,
Whose tides wash my shores with moon dust.

A galactic windstorm scatters my ashes
Through the aperture of an invisible black hole.
Massive magnets, strengthened by whirring dynamos,
Attract my remains. Jupiter and Saturn
Shadow my reformulating psyche as though each
Might be taking turns hatching a universal egg.
Suddenly, my shell cracks. I deviate from the ellipse
My spirit has tracked through space, emerge intact,

A newer being come back from the region
Where life, seething in amniotic solitude,
Awaits generational reassignment.
Awakened to the fact that death is a daily task
To be mastered, not a vast, amorphous hiatus
We cause to metastasize in the imagination, from birth,
By fearing the immaterial enigma of nonexistence,
I rejoice in this total poetical *now* of my life.

11/22/76 — [1] (05500)

The Cradle of Civilization △

If Interstate 70,
Cluttered like plains covered with grazing buffalo herds,
With its daily, four-lane mullet rush,
Pay-toilet truck stops,
Weigh stations, fast-food chains,
And cross-reader billboards,
Were the flood-suckled Tigris of Mesopotamia

And Lake of the Ozarks, near Gravois Mill,
Clotted on its banks with rotting mobile homes,
City doctors' million-dollar "cottages,"
Docks like rows of barracuda teeth,
And self-contained recreation centers
With prepaid package weekends,
Were the fertile-verdant Euphrates River Valley,

Then Tipton, like blind, senile Oedipus,
Seated in tattered robes at the crossroads
Where B and 50 accidentally converge,
Leaning on a broken staff, groping in the dust,
Should actually be a dispossessed king
Waiting for a favorable oracle to dispel doubts
About his patrimony and tell him the direction home.

11/23/76 — [1] (05431)

Sounds on a Snowy Drive Home

The backwash sound of radial tires
Hovering just above the snow-glazed road
Is that of sea waves repeatedly breaking
Against the eardrum, from within the chambers
Of a winged conch. The intermittent squeak
Made by windshield wipers on dry glass,
As ricelike flakes vary in intensity
Mile by mile, is that of caged mice
Frightened by their own hysteria, begging release.
Even my smooth-moving lungs,
Normally accompanied by soothing inspirations
To the brain and susurrant exhalations,
Have been impaired by the heater's aridity;
Breathing wheezes through constricted nostrils.

All the sounds vibrating my mind's tines
Have become victims irretrievably imprisoned
In cells imagination has compelled them to inhabit.
Lacking evidentiary support to the contrary
That the lonely poet who guards their incarceration
Is temporarily demented, they languish darkly
In a dank dungeon beneath a gray sky
Castellated with snow clouds blowing metaphors.

11/23/76 — [2] (05501)

A Postlude to Thanksgiving

Eleven plangent chimes knife the silence
That encapsulates me this Friday morning,
Arouse my drowsing mind to explore
The unfamiliar shore on which I've been washed,
Out of last night's horned sea of plenty.

In their first deliberate act of liberation,
The eyes search for time's source,
Find it contained in a brass-and-glass case
And fix on the solipsistic involvement of its pendulum
And exposed escapement keeping the same pace,

Hoping to discover a secret dimension
To the heart's confused sense of historicity.
Dissatisfied, the wandering eyes flounder,
Get tangled in the voile sheers,
Which restrict daylight's admittance.

Locked within this lugubrious gloom,
Gazing in exultant solitude from the far end
Of a drop-leaf table fully extended
The vacant dining room's dark length,
They survey memory's unloaded holds

For a clue to dream-cargoes once transported
By crews bound for the New World,
Navigating routes past Blefuscu,
Beyond the sweet Moluccas, to Massachusetts.
Finally, they sight the inhospitable coast

And recognize this providential place
As a modern-day Plymouth Rock.
*

The table at which I sit is the original stockade.
The clock's tockings are the names of settlers
Taking turns chopping logs for winter.

The curtains' diaphanous folds are snow
Sloping to the frozen inland stream,
Smoke lifting, in threnodies of hope,
From souls holed up against a cosmos
Relentlessly bent on ending their inchoate adventure.

Although only fifty-one Pilgrims
Saw spring's thaw, my two eyes
Have survived the rugged years by predestination
And managed to keep the enterprise alive
Through centuries the eleven chimes have revived.

Now, I rise from my silence, reinspired,
And step out on the wet lawn to stretch.
In the distance, I hear excited shouts
Beseeching me to return in person, to share
In their first Thanksgiving feast.

11/26/76   (02222)

The Song of Wandering Oisin

The miles I drive are the promises I've made
Being consummated.
Winds whispering against the cataract
Dividing my eyes from outside zones
Are obligations being blown toward fulfillment,
Schemes begging to succeed
As visionary delights I might reach and possess
Just above the roof,
Where my ears, caressing the unknown,
Pierce the sound barrier and touch bottom.

Pinned in a freewheeling vehicle
Streamlining over concrete, alone,
My entire body vibrates, tingles,
Sings a sensual paramnesia
Whose notes are composed of blood and bones
Flowing in a cardiovascular ocean
Synthesized with all my cloned identities.
*

I dip into my life-waters with a dream-net
And catch notions of freedom swimming in close
To shoals supporting the road that owns my soul.

Regardless of how I try to change my ways,
Each diurnal leg of the journey
Discloses the same ancient destination.
The place from which I came alone,
Toward which I daily go, has one gate,
Which swings both open and closed;
It hangs ajar. I try to anticipate,
With absolute precision, the perfect instant
When I might enter of my own volition.
Only, I'm either premature or late.

By evening, I can't even remember my name
Or recite a satisfactory incantation
To assuage the pain of sexual deprivation.
Sleep and forgetting take my whole being,
Control my breathing; they demand my surrender
To the unmapped miles that connect each dream
Dotting night's diameter with dead cities.
Penetrating the gate, I drive into a kingdom
Populated by demons waiting to feast on my brain
And hoping to get a free ride home.

11/30/76 — [1] (05502)

The Priest Leaves Off His Secret Calling

With visions of Gerard Manley Hopkins

Deliberately, he ponders canonical thoughts,
Imagines himself a Savonarola,
Then reaches decisively for a string of litanies
To weave through his teeth like sacred beads.

His speculations warm the dank air,
Which haloes his egotistical spirit,
With tender articulation that amazes even him.
Pontifical broadsides proclaiming him pope

Over the tiny, walled Vatican
His abstruse poetry has maintained
*

Like a nearly invisible rathole
Cut at the base of a vast universe

Become the blessed messages he propagates
To a nonexistent audience he envisions
Kneeling at his throne, listening to him;
They take the form of ecumenical appeal

For world peace and repudiation
Of personal greed and individual self-esteem.
On the surface, there's little to suggest
This minister of the Lord has excommunicated himself,

Yet to the holier congregation
That still lives in stifled cloisters
Inside the cathedral his youthful soul
Constructed, then let go to dust

As word of his poetic talent spread,
A certain hope-filled resurgence
Circulates through the dark, Gothic vaults,
Echoing a renaissance of his old holiness.

Excitedly, they wait while he recites
The final antiphon, lifts his robed arms
To sanctify the conclusion of their mass,
Then retires to his rectory and cries aloud.

From among exegetical texts, hymnals,
Private diocesan publications
On window ledges and warped closet shelves,
In desk drawers, oak bookcases,

He methodically picks the notebooks
Containing three decades of his poems,
Throws them into the fireplace
Without opening the flue, and lights a match.

Soon, the room congests with smoke,
Through whose black vapors he sees
The charred bits and pieces of his poetry
Floating like skittish, delicate butterflies.

Again he cries, as the unmemorized lines
He agonized to resurrect from nothingness
All his adult life, with secret designs
Of achieving public acclaim, immortality,

Rise toward the smudged ceiling,
Flatten out, and dissolve. Eviscerate
Momentarily, evanescently bereft,
As though his mesentery has been excised,

He loosens his collar, removes vestments,
And steps outside his sacred confines,
Into the sunlight. For the first time
In more years than remembering can glimpse,

He's aware of trees, squirrels, people,
Not as coincidental, mind-divined similes
And symbolic objects juxtaposed to his intellect
Nor as barriers between him and God,

Simply as trees, squirrels, and people
Proclaiming themselves cohabitants with him
In a colossal Vatican without walls,
Where all creatures and objects,

Alive and inanimate, are unequivocally
Incapable of being either inflated
Or diminished in stature and size,
Despite his self-induced delusions to the contrary.

In a garden in the nearby public park,
Where the aging priest has come to repose
Beneath Chinese elms, honeysuckles,
And leafy sweet gums, children gather

To watch him hold peanuts in his bare hand
And have wild squirrels and wiry chipmunks
Climb his fat legs, one at a time,
To retrieve the feed untimorously in their cheeks,

Then light. Their mesmerized gazes
Recall his first readings of Moses and Christ.
Into each tiny hand, he places a portion
Of the remaining food and revels in their enlightenment.

11/30/76 — [2] (05503)

Voices in the Band

The flute's tender whisperings in my ears
Are fingers slowly rubbing,
*

In a sensual surrender of the intellect,
Convoluted folds of rabbit fur.
Cochlea hairs stand erect
With each lingering stroked note.

The clarinet is slightly lustier,
More authoritative. It trips,
With sharper certainty, over cartilage,
Up to the cranial membranes,
As if racing to elude the musician
Forcing its nasal sounds with his lips.

The haughty trumpet boasts,
Knowing its only substantial competition
Might come from a stray baritone sax
Or slow-moving valve trombone.
It cauterizes open-ended thoughts,
Is King Leo's roar in the forest.

The electric organ and taut traps
Are frenetic, slapping pistons
Sliding inside slender cylinder sleeves,
Compressing and expanding, reaching climax
In the throbbing engine my heart regulates.
The entire body rides their flights.

Only the human voice is its own metaphor.
It alone desires no counterparts,
Invites no likeness, proclaims itself
Sole progenitor of its potential ranges
And variable limitations. Only it knows
It needs nothing extrinsic to touch the soul.

11/30/76 — [3] (01307)

The Intruder ^Δ

The baby lapses into febrile wheezing
In her restive sleep.
Fever creeps into her heated breathing
Stealthily as a house thief,
Preparing to reive her health
Right out from under our eyes.
We stand by helplessly,
*

As if showing a felon the hiding place
Where we keep the keys
To our precious child's sacred precincts.

Her interrupted dreams collapse
Like shattered pieces of Tiffany glass.
We enter her tremulous Golgotha,
Stoop through plaintive inarticulations
To decipher the nature of grief,
Then offer to transfer her demon's pain
To our breasts. Only, no alchemy
Can put the magical rabbit back
In its hat. Screams stay muffled
Within her rattling chest cavity.

Gently, I lift her from the cribbed nimbus
That failed to guard her from intruders,
And deposit her body in our bed,
Like a seed in annealing earth.
She lies quietly in the furrow between us,
Above the sheets, as we administer
Phenobarbital to free her head
Of chimerical wild cells.
Night closes its door on her breathing.
The thief leaves. We pray for her recovery.

11/30/76 — [4] (00773)

Willy Dines Out

The corridor he uses
In moving from his very temporary cubicle,
To the dining room, and back
Is the spongy, acrid wrapper
Of a perpetually burning cigar.

Invisible smoke,
Permeating the worn shag carpet
And hunched against baseboards like drunks
Slumped irredeemably at a curb,
Chokes his nose, burns his throat
With a sour aftertaste
That explodes the indecisive appetite.
*

Cheap house wine he imbibes
Dissolves traces of nicotine stains
Lingering, like little death-whiffs, on his breath.

Fatigued, he lifts the menu slowly,
Holds it, with quavering thumbs,
Close to his eyes. In myopic light,
The printed descriptions begin to shimmer.
Hallucinogenic butterflies light.
Images of exotic dishes sift by,
Pass into oblivion, as he mimes,
In primerlike rote, the tired equation
Composed of Kansas City strip,
Baked potato, rice slightly dry.

Inside his anesthetized ears,
The silence is so severely austere
He can hear the bites descending, unchewed,
Through lubricous pipes, thumping bluntly
To the stomach's peristaltic hunting grounds.
He assumes the food will find its way,
Despite its formidable integrity,
Into his addicted, protozoan cells.
Distant chatter and intermittent laughter
Complicate his self-conscious digestion.

Finally, he is what his plate contained.
His expansive belly complains
Within its glove-leather confines.
He strains painfully to liberate its burden.
In salacious nakedness, inane fantasies
Of making love to a lady waiting in his room
Crowd the dazed eyes, as he leaves a tip,
Disappears inconspicuously into anonymity,
And is assimilated, with the invisible smoke,
Into the stimulated lungs of passing years.

12/1/76 — [1] (02418)

Survivor of the Diaspora

Tonight comes around only twice
Each eternity: once right now
*

(Like molecules expanding in a tire
Wildly revolving, it pressures my desire
To write creatively) and once, again,
When death sets in and requires
A final review of life's exercises
Before retiring with its prize victim.

For the moment, I satisfy myself
Speculating on images I'll most likely
Conjure with imprecision in the end,
Visions of an implausible fame
Surrounding me like a Persian halo.
I see myself as a light-toed phoenix,
A disciplined Elizabethan poet
Eternally rhymed into imperishable verse.

Meanwhile, I can't deny or elude
The immediate need
That obsesses my moody solitude
This evening, the urgent imperative
To purge myself of excrescent words
Regardless of their inherent meanings
Or lack of classical background —
A feckless peddler of excremental conceits.

12/1/76 — [2] (01308)

The Ghost of San Clemente

The mausoleum he shoulders,
In which his head rests inoffensively,
Six feet above the ground,
Is a cicatrix scarring the earth,
A visible reminder he has died,
Despite rumors that he lives yet,
A gossamer monument
To the persistence of human delusion.

The name, etched in grimaces
Across his stained-glass facade,
And the dates, reclaiming him
From desolated nonexistence,
Comprise the only information
*

Available to the generation of men
Among whom, in flustered utterances,
He still proclaims himself president.

Before the sun's rise and after its set,
He paces the beach, walks memories
On a leash, gropes in the half-light
For "Deep Throat" or agents of news media
Who might disclose clues to the holocaust
His "omissions" caused him to maliciously commit.
Only the gulls recognize his stooped shoulders
And phlebitic gait — the ghost of Nero in retreat.

12/1/76 — [3] (01309)

Premature Forecast of Snow

As I leave town, this luminous morning,
The air is so appallingly cold and clear,
So still, I know God's emissary
Must be here, in Midamerica, nearby,
Waiting to apprise me of imminent intruders.
I wince with quincuncial visions of doom.

Maybe today, Birnam Wood
Has begun moving, a tree at a time,
And the Bastille has given way again.
Perhaps El Alcázar and El Escorial
Are crumbling to a pile of rubble,
Versailles is catching fire, rising in ash,

While invisible, primordial stimuli,
Slithering from phenomena's eggs,
Drag themselves out of tepid quags,
On amphibious, finned legs,
Then fly, like frenzied, swarm-torn bees,
Beyond insight's audiovisual limens.

I grimace before the mind's images
Like a blindfolded prisoner of the state
Kneeling beneath a squeaky guillotine.
Something undisclosed hovers above my eyes,
Just outside my sealed windows.
Its amorphous, see-through shape

Eludes me, exhorts me to believe
That excessive paranoia is merely the way
Boredom fascinates itself when it fails
To entrap the weary, leery traveler.
I'm not easily deceived by invisibility
Or distracted by an overactive imagination.

Show your faces, you wily bastards!
I damn well know you're out there,
Dying to consume my entire mind
By tying me down with spinnerets
That weave hallucinatory threads
You personally design into lethal patterns.

Yet silence remains the silhouettes
A gesturing mime projects in suggesting
The intangible presence of God's breath.
In the distance, white, flickering tongues,
Clicking impatiently like fingernails
On marble tables, wait to have their say.

12/2/76　(05504)

On Reading Milton's "On His Blindness"

Driving into a Guardi-bright horizon,
This snowy afternoon,
The skin around my eyes wrinkling,
Like a wizened widow, from squinting,
I'm reminded that my entire existence
Conforms to the polished optometry
My gold-rimmed frames circumscribe.

They contain the visual hunks and grains
From which my lucid imagination
Obtains its clairvoyance. Their focusing agents
Regulate the degree of tree, the depth
And shape reds, whites, and greens achieve
As they accommodate constantly, chameleon-like,
To what the mind perceives as reality

At any isolated moment in time.
Although the pieces through which I view the world
Are mute and nearly weightless,
*

They remain indispensable tools,
Without which all my attitudes and postures,
Endeavors to order an enigmatic universe,
Would be vain and foolish exercises in futility.

The pair of spectacles resting in place
Is a horizontal hourglass with equal amounts
Of future sifting past an invisible neck
Below the gold bridge. As I drive on,
Between snow-ridged irises, through pupils,
Into visions of existences not yet lived,
I recognize my visage in the rearview mirror.

The eyes within my wincing, constricted eyes,
While trying to decipher the hieroglyphics of captivity,
Acknowledge their indebtedness to artificial lenses
By inscribing Milton's lamentation
Of blindness in free-flowing calligraphy
Behind their blinking lids. All night,
I recite his sonnet in the light of my augmented sight.

12/7/76 (05505)

Jonah

Before liquid light can lift
Over night's smooth edges
And drip into dawn's pool,
Slices of mica begin skittering
Through my eyes. The headlights,
Fidgety as a blind man's cane
Or a liar's tongue, try to penetrate
Shreds congesting immediately ahead,
Without measurable success.

The numb whir of rubber hovering
Just above the earth
Disturbs my cursive balance.
My hands overreact to each curve
In the salamandrine road.
The edge, keeping pace with me
Over the entire countryside,
Persistently nibbles at my tires,
Bites their treads like a school of piranhas,

Sending tremors to the nerve ends.
The mind hyperventilates. Fear
Nearly paralyzes my sentient engine,
Almost shatters the accurate instruments
Which monitor speed, pressure, and fuel.
Soon, snow and horizon change places,
Become one and the same, inviting me
To relax, extinguish my lights, doze,
And relinquish all distinctions I might think

Differentiate the snow from the white of my soul.
Spores resembling uncut diamonds
Pour through orifices in dream-regions
Over which the machine has no control.
Amnesia requests my deathbed wishes
To surrender the spirit, let it depart
Without a struggle. The spores metamorphose
Into sperm whales floating in my oceanic eyes.
I dive in and am swallowed alive.

12/8/76 — [1] (05506)

Mariner's Lament: A Nocturne

For my one love, Jan

Another departure, another trip on which
I stow you into my mind's hip pocket,
Hoping to keep you safe and unnoticed
Until my vessel makes berth, again,
In the harbor that buffers, from dark, rough seas,
The city our love populates.

Meanwhile, we negotiate alone, together,
Swollen ocean lanes, whose woven waves
Are plaintive notes in a rhapsody we wrote
During the last days before my sailing.
Like flying fish in a floating mirage,
Memories of you keep leaping into view.

Overtones of your lingering voice,
Beseeching me to steer a careful course,
Drip from their sleek shapes as they breach,
*

Rising from the deep, silent forests below,
Then flip back. Their halos on the surface
Are your gentle lips kissing my loneliness.

My ears dive through each ring,
Trying to divine the source of your voice,
As it disappears a thought at a time.
After dusk, my eyes continue to trace
The fishes' graceful, persisting trajectories,
As if one might be a golden rainbow,

At whose base you sit, waiting for me.
Only, my ship slips into the distance
Without sighting detritus redolent of land
And comes up safely in irons,
Becalmed, balanced in sleep's palm —
One less night away from you, Jan.

12/8/76 — [2] (04190)

The Rehabilitation of a War Criminal △

On a civil-service application,
He listed his birthplace
As "Holofernes, Germany,"
His age "ancient,"
Marital status "implausible."

He signified his race and faith
As "atheist/Aryan/caucasian,"
With a strain of Teutonic consanguinity
Dating back to Leif the Lucky,
By dotting his anonymous name with swastikas.

The history of his previous occupations
Included systematic extermination,
Sadistic sperm surgery, stirpiculture,
Theoretical recolonization of aliens,
The obliteration of ethics and education.

To the month and day, he was able to recall
Start and **Finish** for each phase
Of his job experience, explaining below,
In the space reserved for **Further Remarks**,
The reason he was presently seeking work:

"I need the job, bad, to survive;
Will report seven days a week,
Sabbath, all holidays; will stay late,
Stand eight hours, if required,
Change locations, salute the clock,

"Inform on neighbors, watch acquaintances —
In short, perform improprieties
Others might consider demeaning.
Self-abasement is a quality with which
I'm more conversant than most people."

On the line beneath the printed inquiry
Friends — Recommendations,
He inserted the terse non sequitur
"Inconceivable,"
Hoping to reassure his potential superiors

That they need not worry he might act
Out of personal concern or with compassion.
Finally, he scribbled his illegible signature,
Authenticating his statements as true
And, to the best of his knowledge, sane.

A month later, out of a thousand candidates,
He was selected and, pledging his allegiance to the flag,
Assigned the rank of itinerant state referee
In cases of unemployment-benefits claims,
Malpractice, and racial discrimination.

12/9/76   (00873)

Nightmares: Surveying a Fine Line

With a single, sharp, stark spasm,
I awaken at 3:00 this dark morning,
Resist sleep's subornations,
Stay unexplainably alert,
Assaying the shape of my naked body.

Against the dimly coruscated sheets,
My disembodied physique is a mummy
Recently deceased, cleanly embalmed,
Lying in cinder-block state,
Waiting for final interment.

My frightened eyes watch the dissolution.
They concentrate, from the waist down,
On limbs and flesh falling away
Like papers strewn in a cyclone,
Lashes plucked easily with tweezers

By an omniscient seer in an invisible mirror.
Sporadic ants, presaging the decay,
Boldly traverse my cold face
Before hesitating at the base of my imposing nose —
I'm anxious Gulliver among the Lilliputians —

Then proceed to enter the nasal caves,
Leading to the skull's rancid sweetmeat,
On their endless pilgrimage to New Jerusalem.
Now, my eyes cease floating, blinking.
They open wide as opaque full moons,

Receive all stimuli on their smooth surfaces,
Reverse each, letting them ricochet back
At unpredictable angles, into space,
Like pool balls accidentally tapped.
Their reflections bypass my dry brain.

Finally, the sheet, wet as toad flesh,
Slips completely away from my bed,
As though pulled off by hidden fingers,
Exposing the horny, shriveled toes,
The torso's whole bony raison d'être

Silhouetted against the sheer scrim curtain
Of nightmares staged and backlighted
By a mind dismantled in sleep by insidious demons.
I leap up, grab viciously at my soul
Being carried aloft by drone angels,

And retrieve the fractionated spirit,
A jigsaw piece at a time,
From insomnia's morgue of bad dreams.
By 5:00, my sheeted corpse is breathing again,
Sleeping peacefully as a fetus,

Its lungs pumping my slumberous engine
Forward, out of the slime, toward dawn,
One more night overcome,
*

One less treacherous Armageddon
To survive. I yawn, and death subsides.

12/10/76 — [1] (05507)

Voyaging to Remote Regions

The lining of the giant's greatcoat
Is a gray horizon. I ride
Inside a blind-stitched pocket
Fastened to afternoon's outer garment,
Hiding from bemused intruders
Who would crush my skull unintentionally
Just for a touch of the grotesque.

My speech patterns and size isolate me
In this land beyond fantasy,
Render my pariahhood elite
And paradoxically acceptable to people
Accustomed to hundred-foot trees,
Elephantine monkeys, and behemoth fleas.
My very feebleness is a protective sheath.

Compromise and conformity excuse me from duties
Expected of the king's vassals and handmaidens.
My disciplined tricks, occasional panegyrics
On the advancement of scientific principles,
The decay of theological ethics, homiletics,
And politics misconstrued to suit specific groups
In the dominion from which I recently emigrated

Give me enduring favor within the court.
Yet for all their endeavors to provide me comforts
And amenities commensurate with my requirements,
Consonant with my obviously gnomic proportions,
I've never relinquished the hope of someday
Gaining my liberty, returning intact
To my previous anonymity in the Kingdom of Gewgaw,

If for no other reason than to record
Comparisons collected, like seashore shells,
On my journeys to remote, poetic regions of the soul.
These uncontrollable flights of mine
Compel me to define, in writing, the furthest limits
*

I've reached in my visionary Terra Incognita,
So that when I'm sedentary and decrepit in Redriff,
I'll still be able to set sail at will.

12/10/76 — [2] (05508)

Smothered in Christmas ‡

With the conspicuously ceremonial Magi
Barely a week away
From repeating their singular journey,
Chanukah, like wizened Caddy Compson
Returning unannounced to Jefferson,
Slips invisibly through the media
To catch a glimpse of its sequestered progeny.

No one bothers to herald its arrival
With flügelhorns and shofars.
Even the ancient Orthodox Jews
From the tribes of Ladue and Highland Park
And the smooth-chinned future rabbinate,
Attending Hebrew school out of duty
To grandparents, refuse to raise their voices.

In this land made prosperous to a degree
By Wolfsheim and Guggenheim,
Harry Houdini, né Ehrich Weiss,
Self-conscious silence is the unifying trait,
Suppression of birthright a universal rule
Established to deceive *Bürgermeisteren*,
Bank presidents, and corporate heads.

During this season, baby Jesus
Is born a thousand times daily
In crèches placed, like fire hydrants,
In the mind's sacrosanct landscape.
Only an occasional nine-fingered menorah,
Paltry, lighted in dim isolation,
And a fistful of desiccated Torahs,

Huddling together inside a dark ark
Like children hiding, in a gutted dwelling,
From inexorable panzer tentacles,
*

Speak their peace in sibilant whispers.
Because gifts are withheld until Christmas morning,
The ubiquitous myth of St. Nick
Sticks to kids' lips like frozen windowpanes,

While we adults, regardless of faith,
Disguise our intentions behind fake whiskers,
Spectacles, and overstuffed red plush
To make symbol and metaphor
Stand up on hind legs and shake hands
With religious allegory. Whether for military victory
Or the miracle of virgin birth,

The celebrations of Temple rededication
And the nativity of God,
Although occurring almost simultaneously,
Make little headway in linking people
In a chain of common

12/18/76   (00872)

The Wandering Jew △

Whispered by goliards and jongleurs,
Solemnized by stentorian bishops,
Dated, with Ptolemaic inaccuracy,
By apocryphal pagan agents,
And perpetuated by Talmudic historians
Of Judeo-lyrico-mystico persuasion,
Christmas imperturbably persists.

Hesitantly, my prescient eyes
Scrutinize the future for a new myth,
Original and pristine,
To substitute for the Nativity
This year-weary play
Has postulated, in stylized dramaturgy,
For endless generations of celebrants.

Reaching, my ears perceive
The sweet timpani-roar of stars colliding
In the distance. *El sonido y la luz*
Whisper a vocabulary composed of death,
Life eternal and finite, hate,
*

Ineffable love, and salvation achieved
By dreaming the eons awake.

They speak to me of touching souls
Floating in intermediate spheres
Between incarnations, remind me
Of ancient, nameless cities
Shimmering beneath the eyes' oceans,
Civilizations buried
Under the mind's shifting Saharas.

Suddenly, I've become the one son
Born of all men
Who ever accidentally wandered
From the path girding heaven
And stumbled to earth
Haphazardly as milkweed seeds
Blown free by an oblivious butterfly.

Birth is the tribe of my forebears.
Sleep's villanelles set the meter
My heart keeps beating
Without forgetting a solitary verse
Uttered during the Creation.
The origin of metaphor is the death
Of breath, sunsets, consciousness,

Yet I'm alive this Christmas,
Thriving inside the body of myths
My poetry sustains. It surrounds my soul
Like smooth flesh. My bones are years
Stretched over the space
Blood has irrigated, brain maintained.
The echo of my voice guides me home.

12/27/76   (02223)

Trilogy's Song △

Day to day, the proverbial pond
Reverberates
From the world's verbal lexicon
Falling, like stones,
From myriad lips to its surface.

Her alert mind
Absorbs their concentricities
As if each halo were a note
Articulated against the membranes
Located deep in her ears.

She imitates the tympanums
By immersing herself
In the effervescent liquescence
Of cohesive syllables,
Letting them kiss her naked brain,

Then swims within an ecstasy
She contrives orally
By squeezing the nubile air
Circulating dizzily around her tongue
Into the shape of communicable speech.

Allowed fleet insights,
She sees herself beneath the surface
Of her own echoed words,
Neither overly decorous
Nor composed of conceited intellect,

Rather growing unpretentiously,
Dressed in natural kindness
And sweet, simple innocence
Reminiscent of puppies and linnets.
Her merriment is a father's prayer.

Yet each new acquisition
For her increasing vocabulary
Is both tiny defeat of silence
And further clue to the truth
Of life's final vanquishment by time.

And too soon,
Her own inchoate voice
Will be confounding the pond
With doom-fugues and lamentations,
Whose tears will fall like stones.

For now, then,
Beautiful muselike child,
Sole perpetuating link
With our immemorial past,
At least while you're still able,

Speak to us your heavenly thoughts
Of gentle memories
So recently relinquished,
And we'll teach you to dream,
In earthly terms, of eternity.

1/2/77 — [1] (00774)

[After a day protracted like windy conversation,] †

After a day protracted like windy conversation,
Snowflakes, fluffy as ladybugs
Buoyed on cluttered air,
Spill over into our

1/6/77 — [1] (02491)

Stroboscopic Effects

The raised shade
Is the brain's lens cover
Removed for investigative viewing
By a lonely scientist
Hiding quietly behind his instrument.

Blue Battenberg-lace curtains,
Draping the sides of the optic glass
Through which he reflects,
Act as blinders
Diffusing the snow's luminosity,

Which otherwise would make vision
A solid mass of alabaster.
They set a frame
Around the minute universe
In which he chooses to operate.

He blinks, as if each retreat
From the window, to his notes, and back
Were a focal adjustment
To his range finder,
A twist to a higher magnifying power,

Rather than a necessary interruption
For studying the successive phases
*

Of the flakes' varying motion.
Each renewed examination
Reveals a metaphorical wavering

That alters his a priori notions
On the nature of snowfall.
A phantasmagory
Laden with constantly changing shapes
Pervades his unimagistic world,

Persuades him to reevaluate
The phenomenology
On which he's always depended
To corroborate his existence
Among visible physical objects.

He winces quizzically,
Watching the dizzy crystals
Metamorphose, first into virgins
Curtsying in white folds
Before sifting slowly to earth,

Then into sawdust
Cut from virgin white pines
And blown, in a fine chaos,
From a planing mill
Above the planet's timberline,

Finally into viral coruscations
And bacterial scintillas
Swimming in oil immersions
Between paper-thin slides
Parenthesizing dawn and night.

In deep disbelief,
He retreats from his eyepiece,
Draws back into the office
Reserved for private research,
Filing aborted dreams

Of discovering new molecules
And working up pertinent data
From interviews and consultations
With victims of his stifled psyche
And egocentric libido.

Slowly, he lowers the shade,
As though not to disturb motes
*

Swirling in the window.
Only, the persistent snow
Follows his purblind gaze,

And he wonders who really belongs
To the identity he's occupied,
All these years,
In convincing himself that things
Retain their basic design

And people their facial profiles
Without radical deviation.
He hesitates to speculate
On the vast miscalculation he's made
Concerning his humanity,

While intuiting the redemptive value
Of admitting his mistake.
Now, he knows without doubt
That the soul within his soul
Demands his confession of apostasy,

Requires complete submission
To the poetry that suffuses the mind
With life, waiting to be harvested
From silent skies, by a mystical eye,
And consumed by a musical ear.

When finally the scientist
Raises the shade again
And peers through his instrument
Without blinking,
He finds that the storm has abated.

Gazing down in amazing ecstasy,
He sees the corpse
Of his previous, unimaginative existence
Buried in the wintry ground,
Under a solid mass of alabaster,

And in place of the fallen virgins,
Angelic surrogates kneel by his grave,
In a sawdust sea of lilies,
Extracting from the bacterial effluvia
Soothing unguents to anoint his memory.

1/6–7/77 — [2] on 1/6 & 1/7 (02224)

Macbeth to His Coy Lady

As Morpheus's anesthesia dissipates,
I tremble from a sinister presence
Lying beside me in my bed:
An anthropomorphic nightmare,
Whose features resemble those of Momus
Reincarnated. My flesh sweats
From the offal-drenched stench
The creature breathes my way.
Slime putrefies the dark silence,
Surrounds me with anxieties of drowning
In my sleep. My quicksand dreams
Are the Chimera's perverse caresses,
Its suffocating persuasions to foreplay.
Lovemaking consists of convincing me,
From the depths of depressed desperation,
To stroke its scraggly, leonine mane,
Mount its scruffy goat's body,
And penetrate the feculent, oozing anus
Beneath its scaly, reptilian tail.

After writhing and hunching
Without surcease, through the night,
I'm aroused, with a start, from darkness
By dawn entering our chamber cautiously
To avoid disturbing us from ecstasies.
She illuminates, with a drowsy amber yawn,
My spent, naked self and the vacancy
Where, until moments ago,
An intractable pariah resided.
As I grope for my clothes, dress slowly
To pursue my inexhaustible solitude,
I glimpse a skeletal shadow
Dissolving from night's residue
And recognize in it the felonious ghost
Of my crazed wife stalking dementia,
Fleeing the murder she reenacts
From habit, each night, in my coffin.
I pray fate will dispose of her fairly
And exonerate us both of her madness.

1/7/77 — [1] (02225)

Blizzard

So silently into the atmosphere
Surrounding my peaceful sleep
Did it creep, hiding its whiteness
So completely in the dark night,
That, at first, on waking,
I never even noticed the snow
Inundating me on all sides
Like a vast Antarctic Ocean.

Nor did I realize for a long while
That it was holding me prisoner
In my own home,
Without having issued a subpoena,
Or that I was fighting for my life,
Floating up to my eyes aimlessly,
Without feeling bone-cold or wet,
In a blinding claustrophobia.

Yet beyond the window glass,
Ashen drifts and swirling whorls
Hurled themselves contemptuously
Against the crystalline lenses
Of my horizon, like opaque cataracts
Layered with dizzying translucence,
Until I became irremediably lost
Within the drowsy contours of a yawn.

Caught beyond the limits to which
My naked vision had ever ventured
And entranced by the necromantic image
Of a stately, stupid, beautiful face
Cruelly etched against the flakes
To make me seek an easy escape
Through fantasy's salubrious teasing,

I threw myself into the storm's eye,
To be consumed by a white vagina
And reconceived immaculately
By an ancient pagan queen of virginity.
Once the snow mass began to melt,
I found myself lying beside the poem
*

That had disguised itself as a blizzard,
Thawing from my drifted imagination.

1/9/77 (02215)

"Lasting Peace and Stability"

Sequestered in echoes of esoteric rhetoric
From homiletics by Heinrich Kissinger
And "Tricky Dick" Nixon, I stagger in a ghetto
My mind has erected like a hasty Hooverville.

Visions of maimed spirits and disabled souls,
Transmigrated from Laos, Vietnam, Cambodia,
Populate vandalized federal housing projects
I pass on my way home from the Wailing Walls.

In the settling dust of another dying dusk,
My eyes gradually decipher the graffiti
Etched in brick, like fragile pictograms
At Altamira, strokes on the Dead Sea Scrolls,

And I realize these are the severed tongues
Of misfits, college graduates, ex-convicts,
Twitching like freshly electrocuted frogs,
Articulating, with a fifth-grade education,

The sad, simple, elegiac lyrics of "Lycidas."
They're also hind legs eaten in half
And left behind in traps by rabid creatures
Trying feverishly to regain natural freedom.

Finally, emerging from the blighted precincts,
I pause to collect my thoughts. As I turn
To look back, my reflective brain vaporizes,
As if seeing Lot's wife fleeing Sodom.

I can't ever recall having viewed a horizon
Totally composed of active smokestacks,
Belching fluffy white statistical facts,
Or a sky so polluted with flying figures.

Majority votes, laundered bank notes,
Death tolls, mounting counts of wounded,
Grain, by the ton, shipped to Russia,
Hundreds of expletives deleted from tapes

Soar as if they were birds of prey
Waiting for the same hour, to swoop down
In a secret, elitist, paranoid seizure
And claim the United States as their victim.

Now, as I move away, day to day,
The diminished city takes on the visage
Of a shimmering landfill haloed in ashes —
An eternally burning commemorative flame

Set in place, in time, in space, to remind
Travelers from every succeeding generation
Of the devastation wrought by those who thought
History was shaped by a few great men.

1/11/77 (02216)

Obsequies in Winter

In memory of Harry Martin

If there is an inherent cliché
In the phrase we've repeated today —
That he died like he lived,
With dignity — then let the cliché
Reinforce his simplicity of being
(Not a mediocrity of substance),
Which gave his loving life meaning.

To die with grace, not in pain,
Neither distorted by disease
Nor protracted in passing uneasily,
Rather with perfect equanimity
And sweet repose suffusing the face,
Is surely God's chief blessing
For the meek among His children.

Our tears are emollients we smear
Gently into the open wounds
That appeared before his spirit
Began to abandon its tiny shell.
Too well our senses knew
What the head couldn't yet intuit
Regarding the onset of death.

Without breathing even a word,
Our hearts started moving furniture
To make room for memories
That would mollify today's grief,
Abrogate tonight's empty gloom,
And substitute images of "Smokey"
For future looming solitudes.

Now, as we gaze at spider mums,
Roses, gladiolas, carnation sprays,
They seem to droop, lose their hues
So brilliant minutes ago.
Maybe he's taken them home with him
As shimmering reminders of faces
He left behind in his wake.

1/12/77   (02217)

Elegy for Sylvia ^Δ

> *Dying*
> *Is an art, like everything else.*
> *I do it exceptionally well.*
>   — Sylvia Plath, "Lady Lazarus"

Intrusive future symposiums
Will undoubtedly impose on truth
The fact that the hibernation
My body and soul went through
These last two weeks of life
Was actually a premeditated escape
Into psychic seclusion,
To elude storm troops
Trying to occupy my neutral state of mind,

Rather than a scientifically explained
Physical cessation
Of all normal outdoor activities,
Occasioned by an eerie series of blizzards
That occurred circumstantially,
By sheer coincidence,
While I was contemplating annihilation
Of my sycophantical identity,
Just beyond Hölle's outer gates.

But then, that's mere speculation,
And I've no reason to assume
My audience will ever question
Or give second thought to the possibility
I might have deviated
From pursuing, in solitude,
My ruminative craft.

Even if they were able to penetrate
To the core of the poems
Composed during my sequestration
And force the door
Leading to secrets
Stored in oblique chambers
Beneath the arachnoid brain,

I doubt they would notice
The tiny vermiculations
Redolent of earth
Or interpret the obvious chaos
In verse order

As reflections of anything other
Than confusions excusable
For their excruciating leap,
Transmigratory hallucinations,
And accidental lapses into lunacy,

Not coruscations of foreign light
Translated and shaped by me
While already in flight,

Certainly not poetry scribed,
After I died,
From the other side of the grave

And left behind as a token

Of the broken spirit's tenaciousness.

1/13/77   (02218)

Trapped in the Blizzard's Aftermath

As he hastens to outdistance himself,
Fleshy facial layers rip away
*

Like the sheets of ice pried loose
From his car hood and hurled backward
By vicious, onrushing winds,
Until nothing remains for his eyes
To identify in the rearview mirror,

Not even his own desiccated skull,
Which time has quietly anesthetized,
Then emptied, by skillful trepanning,
To resemble the bleached landscape
And blend invisibly with his self-image.
When next he passes this way,
His existence will have completely melted.

1/14/77 — [1]   (05509)

Beelzebub

I am Carrie's Hurstwood,
Bowery-bound, purblind, tubercular,
Searching for alternatives to burial,
In bread lines and scurvy beds.
I am dirty, fly-bitten Odysseus
Scratching the dusty earth
For oracular visions and insights,
To better recognize my detractors.
My surname is Ray, Oswald,
Sirhan, my alias Ahab,
And I am hatred personified,
The cleft-hoofed, horned Lucifer,
Draco, Gorgon, chimerical goat,
Pestilential, many-tentacled Hydra,
Bilious Machiavelli.
My breath putrefies the air.
The words I spew burn holes
In the inner ear of all those
Who get close enough to hear me
Curse the haughty Jew Moses,
Muhammad — that Arab! —
Gautama Buddha, sweet Jesus,
Who compete with me for preeminence
Among the generations of man.
*

Look out! I'm the shapes
Into which I change at will.
Run me through with your silver stakes,
I'll dematerialize; spill wine
All over my ermines,
And I'll explode your old notions
Of Ecclesiastes and Deuteronomy.
I'm the wren, the bleeding heart,
Successively, a fraud, confidant,
Friend, enemy, lover, misanthrope.
I'm hope, faith, wellspring
Of every decent dream, the architect
Of Hades, pimp of all succubi
Residing in sleep, whore
Named Lilith, Mary Magdalene,
Cleopatra, Mata Hari,
Tokyo Rose — hi, Joe!
My disguises all belong to death;
In fact, good buddy,
Some folks even say we're twins —
Negatory! Negatory!
Just for the record,
We were born spontaneously
In different rooms of the mind,
At two different times,
Yet our subversive ends
Are identical, you might say.
Just now, I hear a baby
Crying, from the womb,
To be released on her own recognizance.
Excuse me while I bite her free
From that damned placenta.

1/14/77 — [2] (05510)

Crossing Guard ^Δ

The retired mailman
Arrives punctually at 8 a.m.,
Again before 3:00,
Every weekday, regardless of the weather,
*

In a litany of mornings and afternoons
That sing a worshipful service
Through his constricted arteries.

Holding loneliness at bay
Is a matter of raising his hand
In the traffic's face,
Escorting the world's hopes
Over a slender footbridge he weaves
From their smiles and dancing eyes
As he leads them across the street.

When not piping on his susurrant flute,
This gentle servant
Gazes deeply into a perpetual coffee cup,
Trying to penetrate secrets
Swimming in an elusive parallax behind his eyes.
Always, his children rise to the surface,
Calling him to their crossing.

Nights, his brittle dreams
Are wind chimes,
Whose glinting shapes,
Suspended from filamentous brain-strands
In his empty auditorium of years,
Resemble the endless procession of kids
Passing into and out of his life.

Eddies swirling through memory
Stir the fragile brass pieces
To breezy melodies,
Whose titles are his deceased wife
And three scattered offspring.
Sleep deprives him of a reunion;
Waking confirms their insubstantiality.

To avoid exposure to the elements
Reality threatens to impose on his old age,
He rushes into his clothes,
Shoulders the white strap
That holds his patrol badge in place —
Don Quixote, with shield and whistle,
Sallies out on another mission of glory.

1/15/77 (05466)

Overexposure

The air his collapsing lungs gasp
Is pulverized glass
Rasping the tracheal passageway.
Each exhalation
Is a death rattle projecting
From a heart out of its element,
Isolated in an environment
Frigid as ten miles high.

The only noises his ears inhale
Are the echoes of fear
Leaping, like northern lights,
From premonition to premonition.
Even his ponderous boots,
Squeaking out sounds from the snow
As though stepping on white mice,
As they go from island of silence
To island in the mind's Klondike,
Fail to orchestrate the below-zero
With familiar themes and hopes
Of thawing his freezing composition.

Now, his lips, swollen half-moons
Counterposed in frozen parentheses
Over and under a gaping O,
Signal his soul's rigor mortis.
The eyes, like Meissen blanks,
Wait to receive their details
And final glaze. He lies still,
A marble effigy atop a sarcophagus.

Soon, only his stiff nose
Sticks above drifts
Insinuating themselves into a shape
Barely maintaining his human outline.
Within hours, not even the coat
Or shoes, caught in antic postures,
Disclose the body of Jonas Carp,
Who, unable to locate an incinerator
By which to huddle with his wine,
Tried to believe he might curl up
*

Inside his lonely tent of being
And survive the century's coldest night.

1/18/77 — [1] (00871)

[Spanning the horizons] †

Spanning the horizons
On both sides of the highway

1/18/77 — [2] (06877)

Cogito, ergo sum

I am the Midwest covered in snow,
The raspy corn stubble.
My blood is the Missouri River
Clotted with ice floes.

The air at ten below zero
Spins my cranial dynamo
At its minimum capacity.
My gasping lungs collapse
From vapors escaping perniciously
The vital circulating turbines
That work my sinoatrial node.

And I think my ears hear
A being beneath the creature
Wearing my features, screaming
To be released, to soar free:
A brute eagle, a hooting owl,
My sweet stepsoul, homunculus,
Whom I've never even seen.

Time nudges me curiously.
I step off the edge of sunset,
Burn the bottoms of my feet,
Retreating into night's splayed Himalayas.

One minute, I'm among the quick,
The next, diminished into chemistry,
The magic trick and the magician
*

Indissolubly mixed, metaphor and image
Coalesced in a million visions
That compose the bone shop's marrow
And oxygenate the poetry I breathe.

I emerge from the previous day's creativity,
Growing forward in 360 degrees.
Each spoke on the great wheel is me
Reaching to touch the circumference of my being,
Which contracts with dying night,
Widens with sunrays bisecting the land.
I perceive all objects in cross section.

The bleeding earth leaves a white scab.
Stubble, air, ice, eagle, owl, my heart
Beg me to heal the wound with verse.
Only, my words are five months away.

1/18–19/77 — [3] on 1/18 & [1] on 1/19 (05511)

Outrunning the Snowstorm

For beautiful Jan

With severe concentration,
My eyes try to penetrate the veil
Of opaque, crenellated lace
Snow drapes from the sky.
My mind begins to carve the horizon.
Supple, scintillating flakes
Chip away, as a cameo relief
Bearing the shell-glazed profile
Of your delicate face emerges
From the storm's diaphanous core.

Your image stays fixed before me,
A fragile guidepost,
Lodestone coercing me home,
Through the blinding lines of force.
Yet drifts cutting a swirling bias
Across the highway are invading hordes
That threaten to detain me,
Rape my vision of you
Waiting anxiously for my safe return,
And sack our sacred city of poetry.

But while I grope, a strange light,
Imprismed in a van Gogh halo,
Attaches me to its hypnotic glow,
Clears an inviolable path in the snow.
I follow without knowing who leads —
You, my muse, or an optical illusion.
Soon, my vehicle is through the gloom,
Into miles and miles of unobscured sky,
And doom lifts clear of the mirrored room
In which my wife and I caress reflections of our love.

1/19/77 — [2] (04189)

Kunta Kinte Runs in Blizzard Time

*Lillie Mae and Henry Shell,
LaDoris and Charlie Jones:
their blood suffused my youth
with quietude and humility.*

Jesus . . . Allah . . . Allah!
The ferocious wind at my back
Is a paroxysmal pack
Of forty-mile-per-hour hound dogs.
My escape has been discovered
Too soon. Even now,
As this straining vehicle
Weaves the highway into a lanyard
That chokes my neck tighter
Each receding mile,
I see the foaming, gnashing teeth
The gusting sounds bare,
As they prepare to slash me to pieces.

The pervasive clouds
Haloed above the dawning horizon,
Toward which, purblind, I aim,
Are laden with Gothic iconography.
They wait in my knotted bowels
To explode my notions of freedom
And keep me a slave to pagan destiny.
Already, I feel them stretching
Across this new day,
*

In the shape of a snake,
A whip with a frayed tongue,
Slung by the Overseer
To lacerate my naked soul.

Beneath an anachronistic papaya tree,
My fatigued mind collapses.
It becomes a plangent African drum
Beating out the meaningless rhythms of defeat
From a numb heart. I crawl
Through my dusty, punctured lungs,
Across the landscape of years,
Back to the first Virginia plantation,
Back to Annapolis to be unbought,
Unauctioned, reloaded onto the ship,
Lord Ligonier, to be refloated
Over the "river without banks,"
Uncaught again by the Kamby Bolongo,

Where I went so long ago
To choose wood for the drum
That would sound my manhood.
Only, the geography of my vagaries
Is a blizzard spitting chimeras.
Time measures the distance I've come,
With Toby's simple grave marker
And with you, Kizzy, my new dream,
Child of my fetters. You remain
With a handful of my old word-seeds,
Melt the frozen earth with your breath,
Plow the wind, plant your hopes in progeny.
Someday, they'll harvest the ancient bones.

1/28/77 — [1] (00794)

[The potentates from every city-state] ‡

The potentates from every city-state
Gather in the City of Flowers
To represent their respective guilds
In the flourishing wool trade.
Father's Day promotional surplus
*

Is the main topic of discussion.
Excess leisure combinations
For at-once delivery
Dominate the conversational badinage,
Which spatters, like paint brushed sloppily,
Off their fast-stroking tongues.

1/28 — [2] & 2/11/77 — [1] (05512)

Buffalo, New York, Winter '77

An open-jawed vision of frozen persons
Caught in an ice-clogged river
Gnaws at my exposed brainstem,
Causes me to reinterpret first conclusions
Drawn from the superimposition of doom
On my self-assumed unassailability.

Prior to the cold, the snow-blown blizzards,
The reptilian slowing of the blood,
And this inexorable, involuntary narcolepsy
The mind is resigned to accept
Without defined time limits, I believed
That the human spirit was inevictable,

Capable of inventing sufficient alternatives
By which to escape nature's fists,
Miss being hit by her coma-thrown blows.
Only, as I stand above Styx,
On an ice-covered bluff, the bubbles
That once pocked its lava surface

Have metamorphosed into solidified corpses,
As though the world below the earth
Has grown bloated with overpopulated souls
And regurgitated them in a vast contraction.
Even Charon's boat lies broken —
An exploded weapon in an opaque desert.

In catastrophic dismay, alienated, alone,
I grope for survivors, walk across the water,
And enter the frostbitten desolation,
Which, in the past, has only landscaped
*

Nightmares from which I've always awakened.
Now, the open-jawed vision devours me.

2/1/77 — [1] (05513)

[The dwindling echo of my heartbeat] †

The dwindling echo of my heartbeat
Seeks refuge in the soul's cold stronghold.
Its hibernating a cappella quavers,
Resonating the cave-brain's walls
Like the ocean trying to escape a conch.
Such futility only aggravates the demise
Myopic eyes witness

2/1/77 — [2] (01381)

The New Humanism

For Jerry Walters,
art instructor
and
artist,
whose woodcuts
kiss the eyes of sleeping Dürer

Unexpectedly, my hibernating soul awakens
From its cold nest at the adobe-like base of doldrums,
Formed by inordinate snowdrifts.
A Pompeiian sun purges the heartland
Of its white mantle, chips away at the earth
Like a sculptor burrowing into layered travertine
To free its trapped victim. I emerge intact,
Astounded by the heat on my naked shoulders and back.

Michelangelo whispers the disappeared years alive,
Inside my hollowed eyes. I recognize David
Rising fearlessly, behemoth yet sensual,
In my constricting veins. My flexing muscles
Feel him running across their striated tissue,
Twitching nimbly over soggy plains,
Pressing for a position from which to annihilate
Goliath-like chimeras prowling just outside my cave.

Yet on bending down to scour the ground
For the right-sized slingshot stones,
I find the melting snow has polished them so fine
That only minute, ineffectual sand grains
Remain to fill hourglasses tilted sideways,
Through whose lenses doomsayers view the future.
The bright sky blinds me, as I grope for truth
That used to work. Savonorola looms, icy.

Repeated praying, flaying the haughty spirit
To the bone, begging to reenter the stone-cave
Through sleep's opening only exacerbate
The task I've asked to complete, without knowing why.
Night slows the blood. A full moon,
In paradoxical mockery, underscores
My godless, unillumined imperfection,
Tantalizes me with inappropriate hopes for immortality.

Now, privy to intimations of imminent blizzards
Written in the distant stars' lambent Sanskrit,
I will my arteries to harden, my heart to cease,
Rather than freeze, when this false spring
Snaps closed again on my premature dreams
For another supple, green-breathing season.
Alone, I compose the heroics of my own defeat,
By refusing to let death know my reason for leaving.

2/9/77 — [1]   (00738)

Word-Birds △

As if by immaculate conception,
Words constantly emerge in the head's nest
And ask to be fed serpentine ideas
Gathered from the earth, with birdlike persistence,
By a brain devoted to nurturing its offspring.

The words make such awkward squawks
At first. They barely shake the limbs
That contain and guard their kindergarten.
Their beaks, unable to take in whole thoughts,
Regurgitate tiny pieces of rote memory,

Chew, over and over, the same fodder,
Until their featherless bodies
*

Surround the material in an irreversible synthesis
Learning devours in the still hours
Between feedings and infrequent sleep.

Soon, their size requires more room.
Movement away from the base realities
Everyday needs impose,
To conceptualized visions of flying unconstrained,
Like their parents, makes them irritable.

Their complaints grow sophisticated,
Leap to speculative conclusions about the universe
Permutating beyond nest's edge.
One day, a complicated creature
Dares mount its uncertain legs,

Shouts an outrageously feeble profundity,
As it flutters hysterically, jumps into a tub
Filled with rough air, then lifts
On the sheer strength of untried convictions,
Aware, at last, of freedom's perilousness.

Touch-and-go mornings, soaring noons
Finally tune the words' voices
To verse composed of emotive moods
And controlled innuendos. They become
Beautiful songs floating above the trees,

Fugues hopping through luxuriant grass.
The mind watches them pass its windows,
Listens to their music, reaches to grasp,
Without touching, their rhythmic trill,
Records them as poetry, sets them free

To always be God's illusive aviators,
Capable of graceful symmetry,
And remain man's inspirational messengers,
Whose existence confirms His creativity.
They keep the Covenant between heaven and earth.

2/9/77 — [2] (05514)

After the Reformation

The cortical fibers lose their elasticity,
Begin to stretch. Thoughts droop;
*

Ideas wilt. The entire garden is desiccated
Within a matter of lapsed breaths.
A godly, Gothic effluvium
Floats over the deteriorating cathedral,
In which penitential spirits kneel.
The dome within the dome relaxes,
Covers stunned confessions
In sundering rubble. Priestly robes
Rise from the blood-soaked dust,
Clothe invisible supplications
In a ritualistic litany.
Myth lifts, dissipates. The debris
Evaporates. The cathedral is erased
From memory, replaced by a garden
Blossoming thickly with censers
Clinging to vines, rosaries growing
From stalks erect as steeples,
And chalices lifting from mounds.
Off by themselves, wizened ministers
Hoe weeds, turn stubborn clods
With blunt shovels, rake the earth,
As though preparing to replant a crop
Lost in a recent late freeze.
Only, the seeds they take in hand
Won't germinate, have remained
Too long in the dank basement
Of their brains. The earth regurgitates
Its old bones. The cathedral rises
On its ancient foundations, trembles
As forgotten congregations file in,
Genuflect to a stillborn image hanging in space.

2/9/77 — [3] (01310)

Being Saved

For Unauthorized Personnel:
Ted, Tony, John, Peppy,
and
Debbie

Strangers enter my house,
Announcing themselves as electric sounds
*

Sent as emissaries from the Temple of Harmonies.
I let them in, imbibe their gospel
Without questioning their integrity
Or inquiring about the basis for their blind faith.
They speak, in tongues, the language
Exercised in distant caliphates.
I listen to their drums bite the air,
Their guitars and organ snort like Dagon
Decrying God's celestial whiteness.
Soon, their vocabulary vibrates
My legs, hands; my face contorts
With theirs, winces at intervals.
Religion must be taking hold.
I rise out of silence, into violence.

They show signs of being pleased
With my easy conversion, by refusing
To take a break. Soon, epilepsy
Surrenders me to their music.
Satan grabs my hand, drags me
Along taut strings. I am fingers
Manipulating demonic instruments,
Flagellating my nervous vertebrae,
Making a painful complaint
They've never heard. They stop,
Leave me playing solo,
Singing, a cappella, nonexistent lyrics,
From some unknown, bedeviled region,
I keep hearing — an eerie weeping,
A death knell of whispering bells
Reciting Revelation repeatedly in my ears.

When I revive, the room is night,
And on the ground, at my side, are pages
Of a Bible ripped maliciously, as if
By a sick victim of a mind-trick
Or a maniacal prophet disenchanted by existence.
My thick fingers reach to pick them up;
Only, static electricity keeps the pieces
Sticking magically to the slick floor.
In a sinister corner by the open door
Leading from my Eustachian tubes
To the brain, instrument cases wait
*

For an unknown owner to claim them.
Their identification tags bear my name.
Unable to resist a fierce curiosity,
I grip the bags and let them take me
To their whisperous destination, without a whimper.

2/9–10/77 — [4] on 2/9 (02145)

The Universal Man

Leaving Tipton is a matter of blinking,
As two new subdivisions, the country club,
Pool-table factory, Twin Pine Motel
(Boasting cable TV and air-conditioning —
Window units in every room), and myriad gas stations
Pass in review like a ritualistic High Mass
Floating in robes of haze, this February dawn,
Down Highway 50's macadam nave.

This Christian ceremony in which I participate
Is steeped in pagan superstitions.
The seething earth lies dormant as snakes
Sleeping in unincubated eggs. Farmers drowse
In a litany of antiphonal responses to boredom
By attending auctions of field equipment
Recently repossessed by the local bank.
They meet in the Crystal Café, all day,

To edit an authorized Douay almanac
And debate appropriate sacrifices to nature.
Their voices are a censer's acrid odor
Still hanging beneath my cathedraled skull,
As I deposit time-flaked space between us
On my way to a rival neighboring city-state
To assume my next commission from Cosimo,
Who desires to patronize my composing of paeans.

He demands of me terza-rima verse
That will seal his immortality, elevate the halo
He imagines above his ecclesiastical head,
Construct his bier with ethereal materials
Gathered from the airy realms itinerant poets
*

Inhabit in conjunction with comets and angels.
I oblige by complying with his stipulation
That he be marked and set apart from mankind.

O great and sovereign ruler of peasants
And priests, layers of brick, blowers of glass,
Makers of churches, baptisteries, bell towers,
Leaders of armies, readers, scribes, limners,
Praise be thy glory, thy sanctified life,
Thy piety, charity, thy Solomonic insight!
May your blessed City of Flowers, Firenze,
Achieve victory over Siena and Venice

And dominate the Renaissance forever!
Your humble servant Lorenzo da Castagno
Della Robbia Michelozzo Alberti
Da Vinci Masaccio requests, in exchange
For a thousand odes to your perfection,
One favor: anonymity, that no one
Should know the Tiptonian poet defected for money
In the last twenty years of his lonely exile.

2/11/77 — [2] (00697)

Tentacles

For my lawyerly little sister, Dale

After K. had been completely exonerated
From charges of first-degree freedom
And possessing inordinate personal liberties
Typified by speech, mobility, and innocence
Until decree of guilt, the judge, in chambers,
Admitted he should never have been arraigned,
His case never placed on the docket —
An egregious example of mistaken identity.

In the meantime, dazed Joseph K.,
Weak-legged, standing between two men
Appointed by the state to defend him
Without fee, reacted to his acquittal
With a quite uncharacteristic outburst,
Consisting of a grisly, cynical attack
*

Against the system, which, one fine morning,
Dragged him, without warning, from his ennui

To confront an inquisitorial jury of peers
Wearing masks resembling his own face.
In stunned double take, the courtroom
Quaked into silence, waited for the judge
To resume his canonical stasis and pontificate
On this sensational, unexpected change of events.
Fearing he might have jeopardized his commutation
By revealing an antagonism disguised for years,

K. dropped to his knees in feigned collapse,
As if a plague had suddenly penetrated his brain
And relieved him of responsibility for behavior
Unbefitting a citizen of the silent majority.
Assessing his untimely impropriety, the judge
Reversed his decision and sentenced K.
To endless plea bargaining and detention
In holding cells for an indeterminate hell.

2/11/77 — [3] (02286)

Resurrection

A black silence impacts this lonely night.
Strange, sourceless, excruciating pains
Shoot the gap, reach my imagination,
Tremor the brain to vital nightmares,
And reduce the distance between life
And death to steppingstone yawns
Resurrected from depthless depression.

Somewhere in this vast blind eye,
The scattered bones I left behind,
Generations back, wait to reclothe themselves
In my passing shadows. They expose me
An incarnation at a time, layer by layer,
To their devastating scrutiny. My existence
Seeks its primordial globular form,

And the soul seems to be reaching back
To climb out again from the slime
*

That spawned, in spastic saurian ecstasy,
Civilization's first awkward being.
The bones assume my invisible flesh,
Walk my tired, expiring body
Up out of its putrescent desert grave,

Into unexplored caves where dreams
Are stalactites dripping from the brain.
I snap them delicately, taste the future
In their seeping, flamelike drops.
The liquid days ahead fill a stream
That floats me home. My bones decompose
And are inhaled by a universal nose.

2/11/77 — [4] (01312)

Lunar Bodies

My ears kiss your distant whispers.
Lovers hear me weeping beyond oceans
Tilting into Elysian neverlessness.
The irretrievable simplicities sifting away
Color every sunset separating us.
Dusk is a cruel manuscript fading
Inexorably beneath the mind's ink.

My eyes perform a futile exercise,
Trying to read the sky's hieroglyphs
For renewed life on planets we visited
In our scintillating passage through galaxies
Our original excitement inspired.
Desiccated "I love you"s are nebulae
Swirling, in wobbly whorls, around my pupils.

My nose detects love's decomposed dust
Lifting, smoke-cold, in a heliotropic bending,
Toward remorseful dissolve. I sneeze
From inhaling the whole freezing universe
In a final, urgent attempt to catch a scent
Of your perfume. The earth explodes.
Diametrically opposed, we float forever.

2/11/77 — [5] (01313)

The Farmington Altarpiece: A Renaissance Triptych

For Jerry Walters,
art instructor and artist,
whose woodcuts kiss the eyes
of sleeping Dürer

Introduction: The Heroics of Failure

Like Dante, Leonardo da Vinci spent the last twenty years of his life wandering in self-imposed exile. Within the vast frozen ocean of notes Leonardo wrote in his eccentric right-to-left manuscript were many cursive waves he stirred up, whose plaintive, recurring refrain still laps the shores of our ears. Aware that his studies, sketches, and completed drawings of war engines, anatomy, and flying machines were apparently for naught and despairing that his endless exploration of human knowledge had been purposeless, he scribbled over and again, "Tell me if anything ever was done. . . . Tell me if anything ever was done."

What marked Leonardo's cosmic disappointment was his personal sense of failure in accomplishing definite goals, transforming dreams into reality, executing a substantive change in the way men did things and thought. What most obsessed him was an inability to achieve communion with nature, by learning to adapt himself to its modes of freedom, and his apparent failure to incise on man's collective tabula rasa a personal epitaph announcing to future generations that he passed here and laid claim briefly to an eternally finite piece of infinity.

Ironically, with the distinct advantage of historical hindsight, we judge this Renaissance man a genius. We tend to forget his desperation, his obsessive feelings of inadequacy and neglect, or rationalize and justify them as the necessary constituents for intellectual immortality, lacking which man merely recedes into the anonymity out of which he is born.

I: The Universal Man

Leaving Tipton is a matter of blinking,
As two new subdivisions, the country club,
Pool-table factory, Twin Pine Motel
(Boasting cable TV, window air conditioners,
And phones in every room), and myriad gas stations
*

Pass in review like a ritualistic High Mass
Floating in robes of haze, this February dawn,
Down Highway 50's barb-arcaded macadam nave.

This Christian ceremony in which I participate
Is steeped in pagan superstitions.
The seething earth lies dormant as snakes
Sleeping in unincubated eggs. Farmers drowse
In a litany of antiphonal responses to boredom
By attending auctions of field equipment
Recently repossessed by the local bank.
They meet in the Crystal Café, all day,

To edit an authorized Douay almanac
And to debate appropriate sacrifices to nature.
Their voices are a censer's acrid odor
Still hanging heavily beneath my cathedraled skull,
As I deposit time-flaked space between us
On my way to a rival neighboring city-state
To assume my next commission from Cosimo,
Who desires to patronize my composing of paeans.

He demands of me terza-rima verse
That will seal his immortality, elevate the halo
He imagines above his ecclesiastical head,
And construct his bier with ethereal materials
Gathered from the airy realms itinerant poets
Inhabit in conjunction with comets and angels.
I oblige by complying with his stipulation
That he be marked and set apart from mankind.

O great and sovereign ruler of peasants
And priests, layers of stone, blowers of glass,
Makers of churches, baptisteries, bell towers,
Leaders of armies, readers, scribes, limners,
Praise be thy glory, thy sanctified life,
Thy piety, charity, thy Solomonic insight!
May your blessed City of Flowers, Firenze,
Achieve victory over Siena, Venice, Tipton

And dominate the Renaissance forever!
Your humble servant Lorenzo da Castagno
Della Robbia Michelozzo Alberti
Da Vinci Masaccio e Giotto requests, in exchange
For a thousand odes to your perfection,
*

One tiny favor: anonymity, that no one should know
The Tiptonian poet defected for money
In the last twenty years of his lonely exile.

II: The New Humanism

Unexpectedly, my hibernating soul awakens
From its cold nest at the adobe-like base of doldrums,
Formed by inordinate snowdrifts.
A Pompeiian sun purges the heartland
Of its white mantle, chips away at the earth
Like a sculptor burrowing into layered travertine
To free its trapped victim. I emerge intact,
Astounded by the heat on my naked shoulders and back.

Michelangelo whispers the disappeared years alive,
Inside my hollowed eyes. I recognize David
Rising fearlessly, behemoth yet sensual,
In my constricting veins. My flexing muscles
Feel him running across their striated tissues,
Twitching nimbly over soggy plains,
Pressing for a position from which to annihilate
Goliath-like chimeras prowling just outside my cave.

Yet on bending down to scour the ground
For the right-sized slingshot stones,
I find the melting snow has polished them so fine
That only minute, ineffectual sand grains
Remain to fill hourglasses tilted sideways,
Through whose lenses doomsayers view the future.
The bright sky blinds me, as I grope for truth
That used to work. Savonarola looms, icy.

Repeated praying, flaying the haughty spirit
To the bone, begging to reenter the stone-cave
Through sleep's opening only exacerbate
The task I've asked to complete, without knowing why.
Night slows the blood. A full moon,
In paradoxical mockery, underscores
My godless, unillumined imperfection,
Tantalizes me with inappropriate hopes for immortality.

Now, privy to intimations of imminent blizzards
Written in the distant stars' lambent Sanskrit,
I will my arteries to harden, my heart to cease,
*

Rather than freeze, when this false spring
Snaps closed again on my premature dreams
For another supple, green-breathing season.
Alone, I compose the heroics of my own defeat,
By refusing to let death know my reason for leaving.

III: Being Saved

Strangers enter my house,
Announcing themselves as electric sounds
Sent as emissaries from the Temple of Harmonies.
I let them in, imbibe their gospel
Without questioning their integrity
Or inquiring about the basis for their blind faith.
They speak, in tongues, the language
Exercised in distant caliphates.
I listen to their drums bite the air,
Their guitars and organ snort like Moloch
Decrying God's celestial whiteness.
Soon, their vocabulary vibrates
My legs, hands; my face contorts
With theirs, winces at intervals.
Religion must be taking hold.
I rise out of silence, into violence.

They show signs of being pleased
With my easy conversion, by refusing
To take a break. Soon, epilepsy
Surrenders me to their music.
Satan grabs my hand, drags me
Along taut strings. I am fingers
Manipulating demonic instruments,
Flagellating my nervous vertebrae,
Making a painful, outrageous complaint
They've never heard before. They stop,
Leave me playing solo,
Singing, a cappella, the nonexistent lyrics
From some unknown, bedeviled region.
I keep hearing an eerie weeping,
A death knell of whispering bells
That recites Revelation repeatedly in my ears.

When I revive, the room is night,
And on the ground, at my side, are pages
*

Of a Bible ripped maliciously, as if
By a sick victim of a mind-trick
Or a maniacal prophet disenchanted by existence.
My thick fingers reach to pick them up;
Only, static electricity keeps the pieces
Sticking magically to the slick floor.
In a sinister corner by the open door
Leading from my Eustachian tubes
To the brain, instrument cases wait
For an unknown owner to claim them.
Their identification tags bear my name.
Unable to resist a fierce curiosity,
I grip the bags and let them take me
To their whisperous destination, without a whimper.

2/11–13?/77 (date for piece as a whole) (03251)

Colón

Via Fray Luis de León,
E. A. Poe,
Geisel Hippoheimer

Early this morning, I lean out
Over sleep's crow's-nest edge
To discern, through diaphanous crystals
Floating on a sea of tinted windshield,
The nearly invisible concrete ocean lane
I've trained my eye to follow sans charts,
Stars, regardless of weather or destination.

Within minutes, the detritus disappears,
As if a sinister fog has lifted;
The horizon clears itself of old ciphers,
Waits for vision to inscribe new ideas
On a sky made aware of my circumnavigations,
By a ubiquitous intuition paralleling this voyage,
Before my mind can conceptualize its destiny.

Soon, even the prow releases its freeze.
Inland gulls screeching paternosters
Sweep over the bow like flying fish,
Low enough for me to identify their plumage
*

As that of species from Laputa and Balnibarbi.
Undulating currents beneath the smooth surface
Urge me on, in a southwesterly heading.

Penetration is determined by softer winds,
Ever more tepid, shallower waves,
Increasingly tentacled seaweed nets.
Finally, steamy bubbles erupt in a halo
About the ship, becalmed in a shimmering mirage
Ignited by an icy midnight sun.
Celestial time bisects my temporal flight;

I awaken arrived at the Isle of Enlightenment,
A solitary wayfarer facing nature naked.
In this New World, the shimmering breeze
Is a hyacinth inviting me to leap into fragrances
Beyond the future that unlived history shapes
For the unborn memory of generations waiting to sail
From the mind's Genoas whenever the soul prevails.

2/16/77 — [1] (05515)

The Monk of Castle Gewgaw

Unpredictably frequent chills spill over
Within his spasmodic stomach cavity.
An invisible sickness threatens the citadel
In which, for sixty years, he's lived
Without ever once venturing outside.

Disease, encapsulated in pernicious silence,
Penetrates the rough-dressed stones.
It stalks the mazy corridors with precision,
As if its tiny microbes have visited before
Or memorized the castle's complicated floor plan.

Drafts insinuate his sleep, caress his neck,
Burrow, blind as moles, into his chest muscles.
The body convulses without alerting his brain,
Stirs puissantly. Dream-arrases
Ripple and quiver on his bedchamber walls.

He awakens repeatedly, in shallow seas,
Surfaces briefly, then dives deep,
*

Free-falling, for miles, in a black vacuum
Pocked with blastulas and virulents
Contagious as a medieval plague.

Somehow, he escapes their lethal fangs,
Remains stable in his palatial surroundings,
Neither devastated nor left completely unscathed
By invading barbarians that never bothered
To knock or wait at the portcullis gate.

Rather, teased by disease, touched by bacteria
That churns his stomach, shivers his bones,
He awakens at daybreak, sweaty and rank
Yet ready to bathe in the arcade fountain,
Anxious to take vows of renewed faith,

Then administer High Mass to his liege
And the peasants of his demesne, as he's done
For three decades, with undeviable energy.
Only, no familiar faces attend
His vigorous exhortations. The chapel resonates,

From nave to tracery, with conspicuous emptiness.
Decaying flesh subordinates the censer's pungence
To inconsequentiality. He recognizes death
Genuflecting irreverently, drops his psalter,
And runs outside, released, saved at last.

2/16–17/77 — [2] on 2/16 & [1] on 2/17 (05516)

Patriarch of the Seder ^Δ

For Julius, Joanie,
and "Aunt" Lassie Frager,
in remembrance of blessed Joey

Despite his reputation as a tired Job,
A regenerated scapegoat, all-forgiving,
He's still haunted by Third Reich apparitions
Ferreting Juden, by specters of Torquemada,
And by arcane, anti-Semitic, Eliotic poets
Disguised as any generation's laureates.
He hides his anxiety well, bites his tongue
*

When he stares at the bright eyes and smiles
Of the children singing "Two *Zuzim*."

He cries beyond ranges his wife can perceive
In her most sensitive intuitional penetrations
Of moody, inscrutable daydream gazes
That descend on his face like stalactites in his cave of days.
He weeps in his sleep, squirms in his chair at work,
As if he were burning in a Belzec furnace,
Exuding putrid odors at a flaming stake
Witnessed by gaping medieval *Madrileños*,
Twitching in Robert Cohn's Princetonian clothes.

Yet he still believes that God's eye
Lies at the moral core of the universe's Horeb
And that the most direct way to arrive there
Is by chairing the patriarch's place at the Seder table,
Saying the Kiddush, recounting Yiddish fables,
Eating horseradish and bitter herbs
Without visibly gritting his gold teeth.
He toasts the sacramental fruit of the vine
By reciting the lyrical *"Borei P'ri Ha-gafen."*

He keeps the mythic Mosaical covenant alive
By lighting candles, reading Scripture from the Torah
Every Friday night, to an empty temple,
Refuses to violate Saturday's sacred Sabbath
Making business calls, eats kosher.
He decries Volkswagens and Leica cameras.
Once a year, he achieves consolation
From the children's excitement on opening the door
Through which Elijah slips unnoticed,

And he fantasizes escaping, alongside the prophet,
All the ethnic biases and xenophobias
Bigots have loaded unmercifully on the feeble years.
He dreams of outracing Treblinka trains
And blowing their tracks, dismantling Herr Krupp
One precise breech and muzzle at a time.
Only, a real hero he'll never be,
Rather patriarch of the Seder, filled with guilt
And cosmic fear, for his unassailed abundance.

2/17/77 — [2] (02219)

Bad Words ^Δ

For John and Mary Gulla,
Trilogy's dear godparents

With just a trinity of months remaining
Until Trilogy's third birthday,
She displays a sophisticated lady's
Moral indignation over blasphemies
And ill-countenanced vulgarisms in speech.

Each time we beseech God,
Take His name in vain to reinforce
Our disappointment or loss of patience
Engendered by her inappropriate behavior,
She reprimands us, demands immediate retraction,

Rejecting completely the expletive *God*.
"*God*'s a bad word, Dad,
And *shit* and *damn* and *stupid*, too."
"I'm sorry, baby! I made a mistake."
"Gosh! Gosh darnit!" I repeat aloud

After Trilogy, as if reciting antiphons
With a priestess or alternating lines
In a responsive reading after a female rabbi.
Not a solitary infelicitous word
Escapes our lips that her inquisitorial ears

Fail to pounce on it with the instantaneousness
Of a sagacious owl in pursuit of prey.
Yet lately, her mother and I have discovered
A potential dilemma arising, cloudlike,
To obfuscate our child's ethical training.

With Calvinistic rigidity, our little Jewess
Refuses to make a distinction between the god
Moses inherited from Abraham and the archrival
Fiendish Satan held liable for his woes.
She requires a substitute for "*God* Bless America,"

Won't allow us to allude to John and Mary
As her *godparents*. An uneasiness hovers
Between our eyes when we silently question
Our arrival at this theological impasse
And what it will take to divide the firmaments.

For now, *stupid* is spelled or whispered;
Trilogy remains the Gulla's *goshchild*;
*Damn*s become holy stockings we *darn*;
Shit is euphemistically consigned to *shoot*;
And we exist as students of a pedagogical issue.

2/18/77   (00776)

Little Party People ^Δ

> *For Cathy and Julius Frager*
> *and Joshua,*
> *on his fourth birthday*

All in a costume of cottony blue fluff,
His two eggshell-white eyes aflutter,
Cookie Monster flew through the door
Subtly as a fox infiltrating a chicken coop
And announced himself with a mystical hand swoosh.

Startled, distracted from Dixie cups and cake,
The precious little painted-china faces
Gazed at the real-life Sesame effigy
With amazing perplexity. They'd not imagined
Such monumental iconography

Could be translated from a TV screen,
Into their living room, or expected to speak
Individually to them by their first names.
Some of the children rushed under his spell;
Trilogy and others shrank into uncertainty.

Our frightened child curled felinelike at my side
As if to transfer her anxiety, desiring to hide
Beneath a rock, out of the giant's sight,
Avoid reprisals her mind must have fantasized
As inherent in a creature of his outsize physique.

"He's an ugly old monster," she whispered.
An older girl frenetically repeated,
"I know there's a real person in there,"
Pointing at the mask contoured cavernously
Around protruding lips and glistening eyes.

Neither my amused assurances nor the group
Encircling the blue cloud with voluble glee
*

Could unloosen Trilogy's steady grip on me.
Even his offering of chocolate-chip cookies
Was accepted with reticence and timidity, hastily,

As though he might bait her with sweet enticements,
Lure her away from the sofa, take her from Daddy,
And fly to a Brobdingnagian videoscape
Where Oscar and Ernie, Grover and Bert
Exist in the flesh. Yet, with presence of mind,

She grabbed one cookie to sate her craving
And another as a bribe to try and keep me satisfied
As her personal bodyguard. After a time,
The china faces began to dissolve, thin
Into dusk. Strewn piñata stuffings,

Presents, and toys became overtones
From the birthday party, waiting for Joshua
To recompose them in his altered cosmos.
Preparing to leave, I turned to see Trilogy
Wading through the oceanic debris, searching

For some object she must have seen earlier,
Then abandoned when the monster arrived.
Excitedly, she exhumed a stuffed Snuffleupagus
From a pile of rubble and raised it triumphantly,
Proclaiming her mastery over the unimagined.

2/24/77 — [1]   (00777)

Pariah

Floating in a dislocating limbo
Created by opposing mirrors appraising my face
In inebriated volleys of graceless eavesdropping,
I realize how deranged my echoing reflection
Has grown, how far from its original silhouette
My features have ranged, over the changeless years.

Methuselah leers from the mirror
As if superimposed on my catatonic visage
Peering out of an opaque, smoky stupor
This room grips in its sweaty fist,
*

To remind me how viciously time can behave
When provoked to show its true strength.

Bereft of child, a widower whose wife died
In unattended solitude, from a broken heart,
Beside a tideless ocean, in a dry season,
I run wild, uncivilized, through a jungle
That chokes my heart with overgrown regrets
And camouflages my identity in forgetfulness.

I track Adam's footprints back to Eden,
Linger at the distant watch fires to inquire
Whether he and Eve are still alive and, if so,
Where we might rendezvous to discuss our fate
And plot against a mutual enemy, Satan.
Only, no one's heard another word from them

Since the day they were expelled by God, in disgrace,
For disobeying the dictates of their basic humanity.
Discouraged, I grovel in the earth for a sign
Of ancestral bones, sacrificial talismans, coins,
Familiar objects of life once assigned to souls,
Binding mankind in tribes, for sheer survival.

Only, the soil draws blood from my fingers,
Reminds me that a thin-skinned old man
Inhabits my flesh. A pain kisses my vertebrae,
Like a breeze whispering plaintive odes in trees
Waiting for autumnal sleep. I slip slowly
Into deep narcosis, sink in cold seas,

And float alone in a dislocating limbo
Of shimmering mirrors. In the dark, stars appear.
They illumine, with subtle chiaroscuro, the cicatrix
That marks all my memories, every youthful hope,
With the unhealed wound I incurred at birth
By trying to escape, through prenatal suicide,

The grotesque parturition of body from hot body.
Obsessions of protracted death threaten to undo me.
Lunacy bleaches my face. I rush to touch the glass
Formulating my existence and discover an endless space
Proliferating in 180 degrees. The used spirit
Is cut loose. Infinity adopts a new orphan.

2/24/77 — [2] (05517)

Seeing Eye to Eye ^Δ

As I rush homeward, this Sunday morn,
White scintillas fly at my eyes
Like darts completing the martyrdom of St. Sebastian.
Invisible irritants pierce the brain's silence,
Penetrate corridors leading to the heart,
Invade my drowsy equanimity with doubts
Of being saved or blessed with a graceful escape
From the godless atrocities of illogical fate.

The intimidating sky descends, absorbs my passage,
Predominates vision in a sulfurous purple-gray.
Focus bends away in an endless parallax
Perforated by distorted road signs and billboards
Proclaiming a stupendous man-mazed hoax.
The soul's only hope is in reaching the depot
That lies steeped in the valley between sense and memory,
Where my wife and child await my annunciation.

Semiconscious, breathing slowly, totally alone,
I follow the snow to its source, in their remorseful eyes.

2/27/77   (01402)

[The days have eyes, have teeth.] ^{† Δ}

The days have eyes, have teeth.
They see the flesh I leave behind.
They eat the guts of memories
Leaking from shallow lacunae
The brain's alluvial river deposits in caves
Containing stalactites fashioned from blood

3/9/77   (00479)

Resurrection

The head makes one last surge,
Contracts, compacts all its energy
Into a massive flurry of mad intent,
Then takes off into the endless air
*

And is lost in a black, abstract vacuum
That bends, in all directions, around the sun.

The heart follows, with sad despair,
The useless path her soul mate sets
As he flies toward final judgment.
She's been there so many times before
That achieving ecstasy is a boring task
She'd rather forgo; only, death says no.

3/10/77 (02220)

Malignancy

For a solitary, hourless week,
I've known the presentient tumescence
A blooming lady flowering a baby feels.
Only, that pulpy substance
Has chosen to grow, oblique and unconstrained,
Not in my belly but in my pulsing brain.
The uterine, ever-expanding pain
Blurs the printed words I try to write,
Fragments the visual symbols that fly
Toward my adamantine mind,
Seeking refuge from their base creation.

In this paralysis, I'm unable to repulse
Fantasies entering my psyche unfiltered.
With unutterable fear, I become the vessel
That transports the world's illusory graffiti
Across wet-shale cave walls, become one
With wisdom emanating humanely yet deviating
Toward death's dripping, come-hither lips.
Such forced lovemaking distorts my dreams
Of reaching a viable peace with myself.
Soon, the machinery that keeps poetry ovulating
Will cease turning, reach inertia, go cold,

And I'll be left with this breathless child
Metastasizing in swollen, uncontrolled growth
Within my placental lobes. Giving birth
By such a gratuitous impregnation of my soul
Can only result in a stillborn metaphor,
*

Whose removal by Cesarean section will void me
Of all hope for projecting my tiny voice
Through the echoing tube connecting life with Life.
Just now, massive, spastic contractions
Dilate the cranial opening, explode my brain.
I emerge, strangled by my own umbilical verse.

3/13 & 3/17/77　(05518)

Beachcombers △

Every tempestuous wave reaching the shore
Lays down a shadowy swath before our feet.
Each begs us to enter, running, its brief ellipse,
Immerse ourselves ankle-deep, and surrender
To its atomistic mysticism, before it retreats
Into the timeless parabola that completes destiny,
Returning it to the ocean's soul, the sky's mind.

As crest after serpentine crest arrives,
We dive through a continuous pipeline.
Spray creates a polychromatic halo we balance
On the tightwire we trace between beach and sea.
Hand in hand, splendid in suspended laughter,
Ecstatic with our own motion, dad and daughter
Are metamorphosed, by water, sand, and sound,

Into identical interlocking halves of a shell
Recently washed up out of the nervous waves,
Forged by more than blood or the moment.
Suddenly, we realize the need to seek repose,
Regather our energies for the return journey.
Love primeval has touched, kissed, shaped us
With oceanic tongues. Toward eternity we rush.

3/26/77　(00779)

Landlocked △

Even though the beach is a desert's edge,
The eyes won't desert their secure head
*

To set out over the deceivingly depthless
Reaches of ocean. They prefer to remain stationary,

Leaving the distances in between zones
Hued emerald, green-blue sapphire
For the imagination's deep-sea craft
To navigate, speculating on what constitutes truth.

The eyes breathe into sharp focus.
Plangent, fulminating waves slap their irises.
The entire universe shakes violently
With the unmistakably final reverberation

Of the desert's edge pivoting on an oceanic plate
Shifting, inexorably as a polar ice floe,
Toward a new location below the mass
On which I stand. The end is at hand.

Soon, the wet sands engulf my body,
Transform the bones to pulverized silica.
My soul is lost in the lunar-blown motion
It uses to move itself through space.

Dust or water, the particles effervesce
As if capped too long under pressure.
The horizon explodes. The desert slowly advances.
I ooze below its rolling surface, older

For having resisted going to sea, yet
No wiser for having denied myself
The poetry of the unknown. The necropolis
Above me is awash with whitecapped pyramids.

3/28/77   (02287)

Pyramus and Thisbe ^Δ

Hovering like dragonflies above a sluggish pond,
The silver, single-engine planes,
Branded conspicuously with a circled A,
Enter desultorily, then leave the stretch of beach
We occupy. Advertising they drag behind them
Is a leash attaching our eyes to ideas
Calculated to make us indulge appetites —
"PURITAN — ADULT AMERICAN DREAM BOOK."

Long after each lumbering passage,
Their images persist as if etched into
The intermittent clouds by a wood-burning tool.
Their staccato, ear-chopping vibrato,
Exhausted against an intractable breeze,
Remains like a many-stitched wound,
Marring an otherwise unscarred horizon —
"DEEP THROAT OPENS TONITE   GAMECOCK THEATER."

Enfeebled by the mind-blinding sun,
We fail to realize how orgasmic we've become,
How excitedly we lie in salacious anticipation
Of being wantonly violated by the next installment
Of these updated Burma Shave commercials
While bathing in an ocean of inane fantasies,
Drowsing dispassionately as fatting cows —
"'OUCH' YOU LOOK BURNED — COOL IT WITH NOXZEMA."

One by one by one by one,
The combusting drones implant their seeds,
Until our uterine minds fill dizzily with blood
And climactic life-juices spill and dry
Like jellyfish slime in the sand.
Between flights, lust arrives stillborn.
Our deaths are a marriage of desiccated intellects —
"GET OUT OF THE HOT SUN AND INTO A CUERVO SUNRISE."

3/31/77 (02221)

[One by one, then in twos, regimentally,] †

One by one, then in twos, regimentally,
The letters parade across the platen,
In dress uniform. She salutes them
As they march proudly across the page, in review,
Knowing that her efforts have given them
This opportunity to rise from silence.
They respond with rigid visibility
She alone can decipher, for the highly classified
Word order they display as they make their way

3–4?/77 (06721)

Budding Poetess ^Δ

Conversations
That, not long ago,
Were staccato notes,
Truncated as Gothic cathedral facades,
Unsatisfactorily brief,
Like paid stays with courtesans,
Lengthen. They're characterized
By prolixity and weightiness.
Each becomes a debate
In which Trilogy asserts her autonomy,
Has her way,
Confirms emphatically
That she's attained complete mastery
Of her twenty-six-letter inheritance.

Her tongue magnetizes germane words;
Idioms and streetwise apothegms
Surface without coercion.
She rules ideational seas
Like a Renaissance queen.
Free association sets the meter
For her wingless, bardic songs of ecstasy.
Speech is the orgasmic release
Of the collective unconscious
Reaching generatively
To leap all synaptic gaps.
Chromosomes and their genes
Color her fanciful language with designs
Pristine in their simple complexities.

We listen to her voice
Free cathedral bells
And marvel at the purity of their timbre.
The sonorous legato she's achieved
In moving from sign language,
Through obstinate syllables,
To the sound of the centuries
Astounds us with its euphony.
Embedded in her ABC's
Are the keys to the kingdom
Where profundities undreamed sleep
*

And poetry never spoken
Waits to be aroused.
Someday, she'll unlock the fortress gate.

4/1/77   (00778)

The Vanity of Human Wishes: On Mortality

Sometimes, with inutterable puzzlement,
I wonder how our particular predicaments
Pick us out, attach us to the body of a lifetime
By such a frangible umbilicus, and sate our requirements,
Regardless of what our better judgment prescribes.

So many clouds intercede, so many Y's
Loom unpredictably, so few grand sweepstakes
Arrive when we most need something with which
To bridge the unnavigable gap between our dire straits,
Such paltry few endowments sweeten our sour intellects

That it staggers the imagination to conceive
How the spirit even survives, weighted under the detritus
Of its own bodily impedimenta. And yet it does,
On a day-to-day basis, gravitating, like an oscillating fan,
From death to life, sleep to waking, infirmity to health.

Maybe it's sheer inertia that keeps the gyros spinning,
The fleshed skeleton pressing forward, against the headwind;
Maybe it's gravity reversing its magnetic directions constantly
That permits the blood to pass from visceral bed to brain,
Artery to vein, lung to capillary, uterus to placenta to fetus.

We neither choose birth nor acquiesce to eventual decay,
Rather lean out over a balcony and scan the landscape —
Wars, the seasons, progeny, brief flights to paradises,
Passages connecting mammalian routines. The days wear faces
We take off at night or throw away out of impatience.

When the ineluctable announcement does finally come,
We refuse to accept its stark inevitability. We cringe
In disbelief that anonymity could be so presumptuous
As to insist that we go, uproot ourselves from the illusion
That time is our vassal, life our impregnable castle.

So we fight for the right to die with dignity,
As if it mattered that suicide, euthanasia, genocide,
*

And "natural causes" all wear the same solemn profile
On both sides of the coin. Being, one minute,
Nonexisting, the next instant, is the enigmatic condition

Under which we labor, waiting etherized, etherealized,
To pass, from one state to the next, with anticipations
Of beginning again, ever renewed in faith —
Deluded, ultimately trapped in the universal whirlpool,
Swirling toward dissolution, sucked into oblivion.

The earth's inner core roars. Its horrible fires
Send out tendrils that reach upward, through light-years,
Toward the surface, where life thrives in generational seizures.
All elements conform to its force: iron returns to rust,
To ore, bones and shells to dust; flesh, leaves, mud

Rearrange their molecules to fuse with the planet's crust,
Until infinity's cauldron is a fractious volcano
Surging out of control. Its lava, composed of all gone souls,
Flows over the invisible edge, cools, slowly,
Into an ontological progression of fish, bird, snake, and

Two-legged human, perceiving his distinctiveness, fearing himself.

4/2/77 — [1] (05519)

The Typist △

After almost three years,
I've nearly succeeded in teaching my daughter
To write poetry. She sits on my knees,
Naked as a baby just delivered,
And, while reciting her ABC's,
Bangs whatever keys her mind dictates.

I sit back and watch the process evolve:
Hyphen, Return, Shift, Margin Release,
Followed by a Gatling volley of consonants
And indiscriminate, free-sprung vowels
Chosen to depict a specific image
She alone knows. Morphemes and semantemes

Lift like butterflies from her fingertips,
Quick as frogs' tongues gigging insects,
As she weaves her way through a maze
*

Partly intuitional, mostly emotional,
Always electric in her task of creating
Each new untranslatable foot.

Whether through imitation or conditioning,
She's developed a penchant that impels her
To get certain messages off her chest.
Whenever I dissolve into my study
To compose thoughts, she senses my absence,
Realizes where I'm quietly hiding,

And invades my privacy, usually au naturel,
With her perfectly absurd desire to type.
Immobile, I'm unable to refuse her enthusiasm,
Despite the fact that her raw distraction
Will doubtless cost me the elusive great line
That distinguishes Whitman from Whitcomb Riley.

Clearly, she's my monster, a sorcerer's apprentice
For whose eccentricities I'm responsible.
She's an exact facsimile of her impatient dad,
A miniature neurotic artiste whose fingertips
Are masts alive with St. Elmo's fire,
Whose eyes penetrate the soul's blind caves.

I gaze at her nape — the blond curls
Unfurling like sails from a graceful clipper —
And experience salvation's amazing awakening.
At three, she's already been called, elected,
Doomed to the task of creating masterpieces,
Fashioning from the effete a new music.

I sense her fingers hunting the inscrutable,
Attempting to expose the ineffable cause,
Taunting the unspeakable out of hiding,
Daring the unknown to take flight,
Like flushing a covey of unsuspecting quail,
To be replaced by the unimagined. She's stunning

Yet possessed by an obsession that compels her
To disentangle inessential drivel
From the intelligible combinations that appear
On stark paper as she manipulates the machine
To conform to her obscure psychic desires.
Her mode of selection remains unexplained.

Oddly, it seems that whenever I have doubts
About her direction, she gets my vibrations
And jumps off my lap, disappears fast,
As if to reassure me her senses are intact,
Her intrinsic meanings not so profound
That I should continue wrinkling my brow.

Still, I've retained all the fragments
As visible proof for future semanticists,
Hagiographers, and dissertation makers,
Who may someday express doubts
That Trilogy Maya was actually at work
On her *Divina commedia* when barely three.

My archives are brimming with her work sheets.
She's entrusted me as her executor, custodian,
Legal guardian, editor, and agent
Without her knowing it. I, in turn,
Have bequeathed her my familial birthright,
Comprised of diligence, discipline, sacrifice:

A love affair with words, a marriage,
A lexical honeymoon, on a star-blanket,
Through a vers libre galaxy,
With neither beginning, resting point,
Nor terminus, a journey to the soul,
A lifelong purgation by writing verse.

Together, we've begun to gain respect
And mutual awareness of the outer reaches
Of each other's consanguineous identities.
As days pass and pages accumulate,
We find deeper reason for accepting on faith
The creative spark that marks our genes.

4/2/77 — [2] (00780)

La primavera ^Δ

In every direction, swarms of green bees
Have attached themselves to trees,
Forming variegated, pointillistic halos.
The hymeneal season's warmth gushes
*

With menstrual redbuds, flowering crabs,
Lilacs, violets, forsythias. Winter's coarse habit
Drops slowly to the ground around spring's feet,
Leaving her naked in pubescent luxuriance.
My transfixed eyes scurry along the nerves.
Blood surges. My oxygenated mind stirs,
Awakens within its hibernal lung-caves.
The perfume of egg and sperm in thick suspension
Converges on my palpitant senses, hangs awash
In the breeze, as though the air were placental,
Capable of giving birth by sheer suspiration.
Everything is conjugating, being pollinated,
Regenerating spontaneously, and I, once again,
Having impregnated my fertile imagination,
Stand witness to the parturition of this year's issue.
Mild April baptizes her child in my waiting eyes.

4/5/77   (05520)

The Moon and the Felon ^Δ

For flowering Jan,
mientras agoniza

As I take flight, the rising sun
Has already leapt from hiding
And begun stippling the morning lilac.
High above my left shoulder,
A homuncular moon, my distaff running mate,
Refuses to be erased, insists on being taken
Wherever inertia's burrowing mole tunnels me.

Visions of my sleeping wife, breathing unevenly
Inside a caul of bad dreams and nausea,
Haunt me. Her early pregnancy is a demon
Throwing nets and bolas over her sleek loins.
I've watched her freedom of movement dissipate,
Dissolve anemically, the cougar in her subdued,
Her litmus moods altered to a washed-out pink.

The moon illumines her molested silhouette
Like a fluoroscope bones through shoes.
My transfixed eyes witness her helplessness
*

Without blinking. As I put distance between us,
She gains a lunar pallor my senses confuse
With moribund hues the uxorial moon exudes,

And I fantasize her great bodily changes
Erupting from a volcano, whose furious fission
Is being generated by a tiny fetal core
Attached to her cervical roof. She spews moon dust
That leaves a crusty residue in the corners of my eyes.
Whether metaphor or physical embodiment
Of mystical union is unimportant. My mind is buried alive,

Under tons of ash-white guilt and remorse
For having subjected my wife to such upheaval,
Then left her, weakened, to survive by herself.
By noon, there are no traces of the moon;
Only frivolous, snail-glazed contrails
And a haughty April sun congest the sky.
Night appears to be nine months away.

4/7/77 — [1] (01401)

Taking the Back Roads Home

Once again, the purgative search for words
Occurs. My driven mind, fearing itself lost,
Stretches for its first steps, trips, stutters,
Recoils around itself like caducean snakes,
Then breaks through the impregnable silence
To lay down its first, tentative stanzaic verse.

The incredible shock on emerging into a world
Covered in dust, weightless as dragonfly wings
Yet dense as Kilimanjaro's snowy peaks
Seen through crenelated lace, sharpens blades
Oscillating through the pulsing brain's mountain chain,
Awakens the hibernating spirit from its dumbness.

Thinly sliced similes and alliterative onomatopoeias
Fly off the spinning dermatome; ideas catch fire.
The strange landscape through which I journey
Is a rain forest teeming with behemoth creatures
Waiting to be named, defined, and given immortality
In the Great Chain of Being; tarpits seethe.

Darkness barely squeezes its body into the interstices
Equinoctial light maintains all day and night.
Sun and moon stay mated in perpetual eclipse.
Path leads on to path. Rough terrain gives way to plain
Pocked occasionally with caesuras, commas, parentheses.
Metered feet run out behind me in the sand.

Finally, the climactic edge gets closer.
Ten potential endings open before my eyes,
Like fun-house mirrors begging my soul to enter
And immerse itself in their cold, illusive oceans.
A tightness in my throat, an exciting lightheadedness
Direct me toward an appropriate denouement,

Through whose hole I go like Alice in reverse,
Soaring on thermals released by burning word-forests.
I rise, a syllable at a time, to touch the final line,
Converge on a whole poem that's grown up
Around my flesh and bones, at journey's end,
And enter its six rooms, home again, at last.

4/7–8/77 — [2] on 4/7 & [1] on 4/8 (01314)

Lester

In this dark room, buffeted by music,
I almost forget his deathly visage,
His sixty-six skeletal years
Shivering imperceptibly under hospital sheets.

The quivering red candles transport me briefly
To the land of the quick, in which youth dances
And touches with its eyes and bodies and futures.
His irreversible sickness stays in abeyance

As long as the sounds jam my frequency,
Intrude their cacophonous static
On my compassionate and piteous suspension of happiness.
When the band breaks, my silent weeping

Overtakes my strength, and I collapse, screaming
Paternosters and Ave Marias and untranslatable exhortations
For that blessed effigy of a man lying so near
Yet so irretrievably distant, in funereal breathing.

Even the ice, constantly reaccommodating its shapes
To my glass, reactivates impressions I made
On my recent visit. I see in this vessel the one
Containing his oxygenated, liquid life, its tubes

Connecting his emphysemic lungs to the few hours
Remaining, his gaunt wrists, peaked feet
Extending from the pallid peripheries of his sheets,
Sunken cheeks recently vacated by false teeth.

Why are the stricken so infrequently the dying,
Rather those left behind to collect the memories,
Make the final arrangements, bind up estrangements
Inevitably forged in the exasperating dissolution?

All I know is that my crying is the diapason
Of a busy signal, an interminable dial tone.
I still feel his frangible hand in mine,
Limp as a dandelion wilting from insecticides.

Only, the wine that swills through my eyes' gills
Threatens to blind me, anesthetize my tired mind
To the excruciating truth of blessed Lester's demise.
I dive into my libation, drown in its chilly silence.

Yet on waking, I sense a presence, an essence
By which, once, I measured my own extremities,
Missing, a friendship, which extended my existence,
Diminished, an inextricable piece of us deceased.

4/8/77 — [2] (01315)

Easter Sunday: The Hunt ᐃ

It's not yet 7:30,
And we're outdoors, savoring this warm morning.
Distant glories, in the form of flowering-crab petals
A pink, tepid breeze releases from their tree,
Twist forward through time, toward our eyes.
Its million depositions gently repeated
Awaken us to the occasion's relevant iconography,
Focus our minds on the task of hiding Easter eggs
The three of us designed with waxy crayons
And dipped meticulously in mystical dyes last night.

Our first, cursory glance is blurred by lilacs,
Whose pervasive scent submerges our senses
In a lavender drowning so cohesive
We're unable to bury the eggs in their cloyed landscape.
One by one, the mosaiclike ovoids are located
In ephemeral nesting spots in terra-cotta pots,
Crotches of redbuds and weeping cherries,
Swing seats, onion clumps, by the anodized slide.
Each is set on a single sheet of Kleenex
To deprive its blending of pristine completeness.

By the time Trilogy enters the arena,
Peter Rabbit has made his inconspicuous retreat.
We don't have to coax her to take up the chase.
After almost three years, she knows the ritual,
Begins immediately the litany of ferreting, grasping,
And adding eggs rapidly to her plastic basket,
As though counting rosary beads. Occasionally,
She encounters a special gift left in his wake:
A package of cupcakes, bags of marshmallows,
A greeting card signed "Mama and Dude,"

Which we stop to read, though its standardized rhyme
Goes unheeded for her greedy impatience;
She prefers to eat while continuing the hunt
For anything resembling the magical rabbit's leavings.
By counting her cache, Jan and I realize
She's suddenly about to reach an impasse.
She retraces the mother-lode territory a hundred times
Without moving, then runs at random,
Hoping to stumble fortuitously on one more egg,
Flush a final unexpected excitement from its lair.

Only, without knowing why, she's exhausted the supply
And accepts the abrupt cessation with perplexity.
Even as she peels her first spoil, she suspects
We're merely delaying the occasion, changing locations
To another moment in her stream of consciousness.
She'll never know how finishing the hunt,
Forcing ourselves to eat potato salad,
Tuna casserole, deviled eggs for a whole week,
Has made salvation all the more immediate,
By evoking, over and over, the sweet Easter
We three shared in our own peaceful Gethsemane.

4/10/77 (00781)

Desastres de la guerra

In the devastated Vichy of my occupied mind,
Anxiety victims still believe they're being invaded
By demons left behind by an invisible enemy
To guard against any resurgence of self-education,
Pride in being alive, the slightest prosperity.
My imagination is a rubbled Coventry.

In their spiritual and material degradation,
The mind's shops are easy prey for looters.
Prostitutes wave like tattered, washed-out flags
From defunct lampposts, waiting for the wind
And irresolute curfew sirens to proposition them
Along empty *vías/Strassen* in the City of Dreams.

Driverless goat carts and drays,
Transporting blasted, ashen, clinkerlike hopes
From boiler works, pollution factories, coal mines
Located on the irritated banks of each eye's lake,
Pass in cortèged solemnity, morning and night,
Partake of a resignation so profound

As to make the transmigration of sinning souls,
Moving inexorably through Limbo's chambered nautilus,
Toward ocherous Hades, seem salvation-oriented.
Agents subsidized by the new government
March in lockstep, naked to their leather boots,
On the brain's parade grounds, for daily exercise,

Below jammed grandstands of dazed spectators,
Who come, in numb droves, to be vicariously raped.
Meticulously disciplined in the propagandistic arts of subterfuge,
Illusion, and usage of vague and obfuscating arcana,
They represent the state's most recently created corps
Of rhetorically elite, war-ready metaphors.

A sweeping sterility blows over the stadium,
Where I go, each evening, to watch them perform.
My speech patterns conform to a few muffled snorts
Into a beer can's sharp-orificed bullhorn.
Severed vocal chords congest my neck,
Make me belch unshaped, tracheal amens,

While I fight not only to stay awake
But to keep from surrendering total control
*

Over my body, in the half-light of bleachers
Fouled by former colleagues and friends and relatives
Micturating, defecating, masturbating each other,
As if in mockery of the Kama Sutra.

In the devastated Vichy of my occupied mind,
We've all been made over in the enemy's image,
Identical in wizened, brown-splotched skin
And arthritic limbs. Even the poetry once recited
By the griot who ruled my country's youth
Is used as wrapping for stored museum artifacts.

In this rotting Byzantium, there are no young,
Only the forgotten, the unaccounted for, and the nonexistent.

4/13/77   (05521)

The Outlander △

All the way past Batesville,
From Oxford, loblolly giants follow me.
Visions of their shingle-barked trunks,
Glimpsed peripherally, in dim contrast
To blue-gray interstices backed by hills
Alive with Mississippi's distant voices,
Remind me of troops, surrendered regiments,
An entire irretrievably doomed army
Of ragged old men conscripted in youth.

Fantasies riddle my mind's tough hide
As though they were double loads of grapeshot
Wadded in an invisible, smokeless charge.
The trees seem to be retreating behind me.
Involuntarily, I've become their drowsy leader,
Mounted on a foundering nag, guiding them home
From that urnlike moment at Gettysburg,
Prior to Pickett's blind rush
From an old order, as if to reverse time.

But the turning point was reached
So long ago, defeat signed
Into treaty, acquiesced to reluctantly,
If never really assimilated in deed,
*

That I can't fathom their hushed design,
This early April morning, their need
To attach themselves, like womb-seeds,
To my imagination's uterine ceiling.
Perhaps they've mistaken me for their messiah.

Possibly they've confused my speeding vehicle
With a bullet shuttle that will pick them up
As individual threads, zoom through a loom,
And weave them into a fine new uniform
To be worn at a future president's inauguration.
Whatever the occasion, their shadowy weight
Has made my passage oppressive.
Maybe by detaining my spirit, these pines
Hope to gain a final shot at the enemy.

4/15/77 — [1]   (00045)

Mr. Fish

Located somewhere between the Gowries and Snopeses,
His genes rooted deeply in the libido,
Mr. Fish creosotes his hopes' foundation
To keep it from rotting in winter's snows.
By whitewashing his fears, he helps them get sold,
Shows a profit before spring rains
Soak them clean, expose their mottled spots.

Texas ponies are his stock in trade,
Bottled Kickapoo Juice and Dr. Good
His hip-flask, heeltap elixir
When a quick sale requires a toast
Or stalled negotiations demand chicanery,
Need the spontaneous fix of his spirits.
In off-seasons, he sells, door to door,

A   Gewgaws, gimcracks, Goldbergian gadgets
B   Dreams, delusions
C   Sewing machines
D   Phony gold salted in greed
E   Ouija boards neutered of rewards
F   Horse and coke cut with pure cane sugar
G   Florida swampland bordering "Lake Everglades"

In his halcyon days of unrestrained labors,
Mr. Fish managed Madam Ruby Lamar's
Memphian bordello, pimped Lady Marmalade
Expressly to Senator Crump, ran for governor
On a no-blue-laws ticket and barely lost
To the deaf-and-dumb incumbent from Toad Suck,
Just beyond the limits of Frog County, Tennessee.

He ran rum from Haiti to Pascagoula
During Prohibition, netted shrimp in the Gulf,
Captained a pleasure yacht that twice sank
On Lake Pontchartrain, with all lives saved.
He hustled pool, poker, pubic hair
Worn by garish cupids and nude seraphim
Nailed to stations of the cross in massage parlors.

And every-standardized-Dolger-like-where
He went on his peripatetica was instant home —
    1   University student-union opium den
    2   Republican National Convention Headquarters
    3   Ladies' restroom at the Schubert Theater
    4   The Gulag Archipelago
    5   Archie Bunker's living room

Even the Lone Ranger's familiar clearing,
In which he and his faithful Indian companion,
Brian Epstein, met to decide the fate
Of ghost towns peopled with movie-studio desperados
And oppressed "Amurcans" dedicated to settling the East
And achieving peace with dignity, no matter the cost,
Was home base for the well-traveled Mr. Fish.

In fact, it wasn't until later that his pace
Started to falter. Not long after that,
He faked a cardiac arrest to test the terms of their agreement.
Mephistopheles paid daily visits,
Thrice recited last rites,
Conceding disappointment each time
The notorious bindle stiff made a spectacular recovery,

Only to relapse, out of reach of the archfiend,
Beelzebub's cohort, Gorgon's crony, Lucifer.
They'd all borne witness when Satan
Outbartered the miniature Prince of Darkness,
Parted Mr. Fish from his once pristine soul
*

With the tritest, most oft-resorted-to promises,
Seductive, cruel-faced, illusory Medusas:

?   The Muses' breathless inspiration
!   Deathless immortality of Zeus
" " The perfections of heavenly lovemaking
*   Celestial light in which to bathe
&   Lunar moon-fruit to consume at will
:   Music of the spheres to quench the ears' thirst
/   Ivory breasts to satisfy the mind's eye

It had been so effortless, at first,
To give away what he never could conceive,
In palpable terms, anyway, for that which
He could possess and easily repossess at will
Merely by the magic stroking of his genie's appetites.
Only of late did it become difficult
To motivate his habits, stimulate his addictions.

Now, in the dying hospital, his hubris used up,
The final hours upon him, he awakens again,
Recognizes with fright the face hovering above him,
And realizes, at once, the nature of this visitation.
Knowing that playing dead won't save him,
Mr. Fish rises, proclaims himself healthy,
Hoping to devise another means of breaching contract:

X   Being held in detention cells indeterminately
Q   Plea-bargaining
Z   Placing oneself in cryogenic sleep
U   Pleading *nolo contendere*
Y   Filibustering under the First Amendment, forever
W   Erasing the incriminating eighteen minutes
A   Donating one's soul to the Kidney Foundation

4/15/77 — [2] (05522)

The Sons of Ishmael

There were Gus and Charlie and Ben
And my dad's dad, Lou, and Sam,
Aunts Mamie and Etta — the Brodsky clan,
Russkies, scions of Kiev peasantry,
*

Who, instead of settling on the Lower East Side —
Delancey and Houston streets — Chicago,
Opted for Los Angeles, Quincy;
Sam ended up in Suite 8-D,
Of the Frontenac Apartments, St. Louis, Missouri,
63108.

Today, the radii retract toward the hub;
The wheel teeters. Four generations
Momentarily roll over each other.
Distant cousins and nephews, uncles, nieces,
People whose tied identities were divided
By the Diaspora, sundered in anonymity
By being haphazardly displaced east of Eden,
Congregate at graveside, like docile cows
Grazing by hay, beneath a gray sky,
Ruminating the Kaddish as though it were kosher food.

Annie Brodsky, née Singer, of Springfield, Illinois,
Married at sixteen, in 1909,
Has finally slipped the shackles Sam's devotion
Forged about her mind's wrists.
His aloneness is cosmic, shattering in its stillness,
A dry Niagara, the Mississippi River
Backed up to Itasca's original spring.
I watch my great-uncle pace at the grave,
Keeping vigil over the penultimate survivor
Of a heritage that, with his demise, will die out,
Weeping violently, "Good-bye, Annie."

They had stayed embraced on the sacred raft
Sixty-seven years, outlasted
Biblical statistics, escaped the malaise of aging
And chronic disease until recently.
Now, at ninety, only Sam remains,
A tiny, white-haired anachronism
Sired in a time of steam, outliving coal,
Coke, gasoline, acutely alive
To comprehend the benefits and fright of the atom —
My father's only link with his own tribe.

He kisses his prayer book, wipes his nose,
Touches her cold, closed casket once,
As if to penetrate her unaccustomed seclusion.
*

He shakes his head, frowns profoundly.
His cries resonate through nine decades,
Like stentorian organ notes in a prolonged dirge.
My eyes fill with his liquescent grief.
I reach into the landscape of his devastated passion
To grasp a last, fleeting piece of his agony,
To retain a keepsake of my ties to Kiev.

Yet something repels my empathy,
Refuses my admittance into his private sorrows.
This is his pinnacle, his Gethsemane,
His arrived tomorrow, not mine,
Despite my physical presence in this cemetery
And our identical surnames. Armageddon
Floods my eyes. Visions of a slain David
Awaken a doomsday clairvoyance,
Through whose cataracts I see patriarchal Sam
At the end of generations, ready to leap.

4/20 & 4/22–23/77 (00475)

Full Circle ^Δ

For my beautiful wife, Jan,
who cried on first reading this one;
I adore you!

Like giddy filly and stallion,
Trilogy and her bare-chested daddy
Lean frivolously into the breeze,
Rush through dusky evening
Without surcease. Lost in play,

We doggedly chase each other,
Escape outreaching hands,
Fall to our backs occasionally,
And lie on the grass, waiting to be tickled
By the self-appointed victor.

Gatsby and Quincy cavort,
Tracing a blurred canine halo
Of dirty fur about our laughter.
Circles within circles converge,
Until we turn on the earth's axis,

While the whirling, leafy sky
Hypnotizes us with its lunar nebulae
Swirling high above,
Glues us to the roof of the universe
By sprinkling moon-dust in our eyes.

Night anoints us with drowsy solemnity,
Reduces our two heartbeats
To a solitary metronome
Counting the bobwhites' stichometry,
The docile robins' fastidious hopping.

Drinking twilight from a single cup,
I see my little baby girl
Through an invisible, vitreous film,
Her lips touching the identical rim
180 degrees from mine,

And at once, we each realize
We're growing up, slowly draining
The admixture of aging innocence
And adolescent ecstasy
That, moments ago, touched the top.

We stop, gaze at each other
In a painful, mutual awareness of change,
And, mindful of a missing essence,
Raise what remains of youth's future
To toast the lady who owns us both.

For the next half-hour,
We ride the squeaky glider in silence,
Assay, with Monet-like assiduousness,
Nightfall's implosive shifts.
I listen for the slightest whisper

From my flowering mistress, resting within,
Who, for the past two months,
Against her will, has resisted
All calls to join our mischievousness
And cast her shadow with our quick spirits.

Trilogy tries to fathom my tacitness,
Arrive, by uncertain deductive logic,
At explanations for her mother's fatigue,
Her seemingly unprovoked weeping,
Erratic lashings out, her impatience.

Even were I to disclose the reason
For Jan's tribulations, I doubt
If either Trilogy or I,
After three years' communicating,
Could grasp its ramifications,

Approximate the nature of fragmentation
That will occur ineluctably in November.
The glider is a smooth half-moon
Shuttling us inexorably
Through a love-loom, weaving us,

From nothingness, into an intricate design
Composed of exquisite blood ties
And bright, fanciful hues.
Seated opposite each other,
We move without moving,

Our distance remaining constant,
Urnlike in our desperation
To possess and be possessed, to touch,
Kiss, comfort, protect, and pedestal.
Briefly, the enchanted arc ceases;

Trilogy leaps from the double swing,
Into the aura her beautiful mother
Brings floating from the house,
As though she's intuited on her own
That a soul mate has been created.

In sleepy embrace, the three of us
Leave April's final hours
For bed, confident that the days ahead
Will partake of the arrested tranquillity
Tonight provided our family cluster.

4/28/77   (00782)

Middle-Aging

Fleet, inconsequent, stuttering,
My shapeless dreams repeat themselves.
They cascade over a precipice
Whose age-worn sedimentary face
*

Vaguely bears your profile, Sphinx-like;
It gazes out at me through layered sleep.
Deep in my ears, I hear their stream.
My amphibious remembrancers crawl back
Piteously, on stone-bruised feet and knees,
To the diaphanous spring rimmed with violets,
Strewn with watercress, back to the pool,
The narcissistic glass beneath whose surface
We kissed each other's goose-fleshed nakedness,
Discovered youth's orgasmic flute and crowd.
But the spring is dry, the stream illusory.
No new conclusions climax my nights.
Each morning is a doorstep on which sits
The same cradled sensation of déjà vu;
And you, my once beautifully amusing lady,
Lie drowned in your lacy peignoir,
Beneath the reflection of my awakened melancholy.

4/29/77 — [1] (05523)

The Rosicrucian

Limbo is a slowly opening rose,
Whose vaginal odors
Disclose the most fantastic embryo,
Promise a birth so profound
In its precocious nonbeing
I shudder to think my genes
Might have fathered this profligacy,
Could have nipped creativity in the bud,
Plucked me from my flowering bed,
In which birds of paradise hover,
To deliver my soul into Satan's grip
And let me slip my earthly bonds
And allow my spirit to float, weightless,
Through eternity's vaporous gates,
Into this everlasting, damnable etherization.

The rose metamorphoses before my eyes.
My nose refuses to admit that its scent
Is indigenous to a geography so sterile
Even my mind doesn't recognize
*

Its own ego identity, yet my blueprints
Are indelibly etched on each petal.
My breath wilts its delicate velvet,
And I am drawn into its deep vortex,
Disrobed completely, from head to toe,
Imploded into oblivion as nectar-atoms
Carried, on bees' thrashing wings,
Toward the hive suspended inside my skull.
I've become the sole source of my immortality.
Survival is a litany of exquisite half-lives,
Bleeding thorns, and seasonal lobotomies.

4/29/77 — [2] (01316)

The Frost-Nixon Interviews

While protestors are arrested
Outside the White House,
Nixon is asphyxiated by his lies;
He dies a thousand deaths
Yet survives his checkered Armageddon.
His demise is more political subterfuge,
His escape an expedient means
Of avoiding complicity, if not in crimes,
At least in doing time in a padded cell.
He chooses, through executive privilege,
San Clemente's well-heeled solitary confinement,
Refuses, for at least two years,
Until, hopefully, all the furor blows over
And the facts are washed back into the sea
Of public apathy, to grant interviews,
Then, with prudent selectivity,
For multimillion-dollar speaker's fees.

Despite previously undisclosed tapes
Of him and his counsel, Dean,
Recorded only three days after
The Watergate break-in, in which "stonewalling"
Took formal precedence in affairs of state,
His familiar, furrowed-brow ghost
Worries, shifty-eyed, through repeated denials
Of guilt. His insistent pleas of innocence
*

Gain little sympathy with sixty million viewers,
Though they do elevate the Nielsen ratings,
Cost his sponsors $150,000
For sixty seconds of cancer-promoting testimonials.

Yet this mothballed chief is legendary,
Living proof that Horatio Alger is relevant
To today's cloned, wine-soaked society.
His presidential pension is our modest way
Of thanking this misunderstood genius
For proving that no amount of slander and scandal
Can quench the fires of pernicious rage
Or douse an Ahab-like megalomania
Once begun, regardless of smoldering, Hitlerian coals,
Overwhelming socialistic votes for high posts
In closely allied nations, and Chinese smiles.
How fortunate for us that just when things
Seem to be losing their luster, patriots rise from the ash heaps.

4/30/77   (05524)

A Painful Awakening

For Lester McConnell;
despite his affliction,
he held himself erect.

I linger, deaf, inarticulate, damned,
Abandoned of family and air to breathe,
Like Lester, inside my own stranded vehicle,
I above and he beneath,
Doomed to inhabit fate's two vast rooms,
Separated by a solitary systole and diastole,
Thrall, both of us, to the elements.

My eyes gasp for words to make my grief
Release itself, free my lungs of their claustrophobia,
Speak elegiac emotion worthy of his being
So recently deceased. The rain is angels' tears,
Too cohesive to permit me access,
Let me trespass cleanly the blotchy window glass.
My fleet penetrations are oblique as a flounder
Undulating through cold seas to elude a predator.

My enemy is sorrow, a painful migraine
That refuses to completely annihilate my awareness
Yet chooses to concentrate all its energies
On my memory. The tinted windshield
Reveals last week's gay-colored funeral bouquets,
Whose plaid ribbons have come unstarched,
Whose many-looped bows are spiders
Lightly squashed, whose mums have joined the rush
Toward oblivion. Even the virginal carnations,
So nicely dyed yellow, green, pink, and coral,
Run, as though someone has slashed their wrists,
Trepanned their fragile skulls, somehow.

The rain changes their multihued spray
To white again, perhaps to blend with Lester,
As he wends his way invisibly through death's maze,
Toward endless twilight. I fight back the tears,
Whose conspiracy of years has suddenly brought me
Nearer, today, than ever before to my own once-distant moment
      of truth.

5/1–2/77   (02256)

[Now, the wet-kissed wind whispers its version] †

Now, the wet-kissed wind whispers its version
Of the Twenty-third Psalm against my glassed-in

5/6/77 — [1]   (07719)

The Commuter

Seventy miles out, the highway
Has already begun to accumulate stragglers,
Strays, waifs emanating sourcelessly
Out of the fog-robed, May, Ozark morning.
Metal filings at impulse's weakest peripheries
Begin lining up along magnetic fields.
Albino and piebald two-eyed mice,
Still on high beam, skitter tentatively
*

Through one of sunrise's mazy corridors,
Toward the Swiss cheese center city,
Where achievements are rewarded with pain,
Daily migraine pain administered inexorably,
Ever so slightly, almost unidentifiably,
For each minute dismantling of the soul,
Where only an occasional headache ball
Penetrates a board-meeting wall
Or rolls through a desk-strewn room,
With its fuse sparking rapidly into ignition,
Where thirty-story window washers
Scrape grit out of the city's eviscerated eyes,
Hang perilously on each intimacy
And confidential aside the androids inside
Deem absolutely necessary to their survival,
Where a nation's tastes are preconceived
For easy manufacture, rapid distribution,
And amazing pretax profits on sales
To multitudes flocking to shopping centers
To hock themselves into voluntary sharecropping
With the solitary wave of a plastic card
And the exchange of a few algebraic equations,
Indentured forever to the tentacled beasts
Thriving on every other street corner,
Eager to make initial contact, gently concealing
The excoriating force of their tenacious suction cups —
Pulpos, calamaries (Captain Nemo's nemesis)
Disguised as lending institutions scrupulous,
Dignified, whose vaults are strengthened with integrity
And circumspect altruism, whose arms
Are wrapped around their sadistic victims' lives
Like professional wrestlers tied in a death grip.
Twenty miles out, and the filings are ants
Colonizing along dense suburban jungle paths.
The mice no longer race in crazed frenzy
Toward a remembered gratification; rather, they slow
In panic, start and break erratically,
As the corridors choke with the overload,
Give way to uncontrolled chaos ten miles out.
Ahead, in the crenelated sunlight, arise the citadels,
Blunt, domed, and spired like the rapier
Of a horseshoe crab, admired for their daring
*

To trespass and squat on the sky's rightful territory.
Drawn in, now, by a colossal vacuum unit,
Each of us is sucked through a corrugated tube
Of cobbled brick or haphazardly paved one-way alley,
Into huge concrete catacombs, each assigned a slab
On which to leave his steely vehicle. We evacuate
The darkness for light, until the subterranean instantaneity
Of neon fluorescence takes hold of the brain,
Gonads, changes us into sinister ghosts, clones,
Whose only excuse for pursuing the routine hours
Is to arrive, again, at quitting time
And fly to pleasures seventy miles out,
Where breathing is still the lungs' chief function
And trees not potted in cement containers
Overhang sleepy, many-eaved Victorian houses,
Beneath whose leafy-boughed arches my car passes
On entering my tiny country town again —
A triumphal Caesar returning from the Peloponnesus.

5/6/77 — [2] (05525)

The Courtesans Are Dead

They used to come in deep
    and sourceless profusion.
Beasts, demons, affinities —
    dreaming's intruders —
Would chew sleep into small pieces
    issuing, eviscerate,
Through breathing's convoluted
    distilling tubes.
Even uneasy silence
    would effervesce,
And the dark would erupt in bubbles,
    like Vesuvius.

Such seething and turmoil
    occurred nightly
From my eighteenth year
    to the thirty-third,
Disturbing the perfect world
    of puerile fantasies
    *

I'd always imagined existing
in female mythology —
Cynthia, Helen, Leda,
Beatrice,
Dulcinea, and Caddy . . .
handmaidens to my naked imagination.

Suddenly, one morning,
a baby was born
Of my surprised, laboring wife.
A shrill trilling
From life's newest voice
drove the demons
Into isolated confinement.
Angst and pain
Forgot the names of their courtesans,
dissolved like ice
In the heated brain, dried into dust
in the arteries and veins,

Where, for so long,
my sanguine heart,
Stirred to sensual lust
at the slightest touch
Of an unattainable passion,
would come to bathe
And soothe its aching scars.
Now, at peace
With the thieves and lunatics of youth,
I see Beatrice
Only as graffiti on the gravestone
of my aging intellect.

5/10/77   (05526)

Adamic Temptations: Illinois College Campus

What other than an absolutely unpremeditated,
Innocent act of faith could have brought me here,
Guided me back to this miniature locust grove
Enchanted with invisible bird-shapes making euphony
*

From such bucolic solitude? What other pursuit
Than that of approximating the elusive scent of Hippocrene
And unicorn would have entranced my highly civilized soul
To seek refuge within this peaceful Xanadu
Of isolated, Saturday-afternoon, end-of-May Academe?

Yet as I sit on a marble bench, intoxicated
With the thick, possessive essences of raining bud-clusters
Maize-colored, shaped like cloves, acrophobic,
My face is gradually violated with etched shadow lines
Made by trespassers dragging their low-flown trajectories
Just overhead and branches scratching my lashes
With the tender, sensual teasing of a mistress's liquid kiss.
My eyes, containing the universal spermatozoa by which
Poetry's seething egg is seized and fertilized, climax.

In this ancient, untainted Delphi, idea and image,
Nature and space become extensions of my imagination.
The elements converge as if immersed in a whirling cyclotron.
They bombard each other's identities and scurry forth
Through a tiny orifice at the base of my vaginal brain.
In one urgent, creative seizure, metaphor is born.
Reality is a finished poem on a page, philologic.
Soon, sirens intrude; warbling fades; the campus
Explodes with lusty students; the locusts refuse me their liquors.

5/14/77 (05527)

[Air that rushes in and out of my head —] ‡

Air that rushes in and out of my head —
Push and pull, give and take —
Is seawater contaminated with toxic jellyfish,
Ancient curses, monsters scaly and gargantuan,
Oil spills filled with _____ .
It slaps the base of angular skull plates,
Penetrates lacunae, fissures, permeates the brain,
Where something terribly sharp, unannounced,
Has trepanned its way into an imagined whale case
Or honeypot.

5/16 & 7/21/77 — [1?] (01382)

G. Samsa Awakens

Slowly, with blind tenacity,
A groggy roach reaches
Sleep's last few feet of tubing.
He navigates, inebriated, the pendulous U
Separating coma and yawn,
Everlasting dawn and enlightenment,
Then draws his awkward husk,
Stiff-legged, sore, stunned
By the unnatural incandescence
Washing hardwood floors
That embrace him like unexplored shores,
Up through morning's drain,
Past kelp beds,
Above eel-nested atolls,
Abalones, and Dungeness crabs,
Awake, shaking, displaced,
Scrambling to surmount the rim
And enter day. He falls onto his back,
Lies still as fear.
Finally, he stretches one leg,
Raises both arms curiously,
As if they may have sustained injury.
The lungs generate pain,
Reluctantly exchange a few breaths.
He muses on spongy layers
Of flabby abdomen, horny thorax,
Unexposed since adolescence,
And marks how unrelated
His parts seem — ancestral vestiges
Emasculated of function, from neglect.
Delirium tremens mesmerizes him,
Whips his muscles and tendons
Into an aching, throbbing knot
That straitjackets his brain,
Short-circuits his nerves.
Motivation dissolves like butter
Left too close to a stove.
He spatters himself with fecal matter.
Sclerotic veins buckle
With pressure from incessant coughing.
*

His penis leaks semen,
Urine, and cancerous strands of blood,
Whose unfertilized, yolklike substance
Glues him into a gelatinous pool
On the floor, by the bed,
Near the double-bolted door
That Red Seas his desired exodus
From the inevictable rituals
Of his mortality. His feeble weeping
Crystallizes the silence. His husk
Provides a convenient mausoleum
For his dusty metamorphosis.

5/18/77 (05528)

The Ghost of Melville Posthumously Exposed

Billy Budd stayed locked
      inside a breadbox,
Cryogenically, until 1924.
      Imagine living alone
Eighty years, in a wide amnesia,
      sleeping in sweet repose,
Then waking to a conspiracy of quaking applause.

      The fright after a solitude
So colossal might be cause indeed
      for abrogating the laws of reason,
Striking society's superior officer,
      retreating from life's steeplechase,
And returning to an Arcadian funny farm
      situated in upstate Hallucination,

Where, with neighbors Ahab, Pip, and Ishmael,
      he might witness two-humped leviathans
Leap and breach the snowy layers
      of a nearby mountain range
While sailing eternally beyond windowpanes
      sheltering his blown brain
From reality's mists and salty spray.

      Only, suppose the same curious hands
Had never dusted
*

the rusty breadbox, ransacked its contents,
Hovered above the sepia manuscript,
    calling forth seaman Budd
From death beneath allegory
    to explain his Nazarene insubordination,

Rather allowed his ghost,
    lingering, inarticulate, in anonymity,
To be disposed of by fire,
    scattered ashes rising invisibly from the dead,
Instead of surviving whole,
    as a glorious, posthumous epitaph for the soul
Who reclaimed his martyrdom from nonexistence.

Then, the legacy of Melville's genius,
Subordinated to financial requirements
    of raising a family, would have endured,
One monument less weighty,
    to glut archives kept by skeptics
And pestersome scholars in search of
    final solutions to his elusive lunacy.

5/24/77   (05529)

Above Seal Rocks

The syncopated waves, gliding in
    one behind one,
        side by side by side,
Remind the sleepy eye of bolts of lace
    being untied and opened,
Rolled down a long countertop,
        by an overanxious custom tailor
        bent on interesting a prospective bride
        in one of the ocean's myriad styles:
    the sea-veil, the sea-gown, to be handmade —
        Cluny,
        Alençon,
        Venetian —
    by the imagination and worn to celebrate the
        marriage of land and the world's
        *

watery parts to the euphoric eye —
An epiphany of spirit and substance, soul, flesh, life.

5/28/77 (00792)

Flying Through the Watery Parts

We relax in patient, unambiguous amity,
Torpid slaves to an early awakening,
And wait for the massive fanjets to yawn,
Intake their first congested breaths,
Then rebel against inertial moorings
That keep steel and soul and dreaming gyved,
In monolithic stasis, to the uxorial mother, Earth.

Within minutes, the smooth grouping of circles
Is a numbing hum to which we succumb,
As though jumping headfirst into a whale's case.
A perpetual reverberation rises, like smoke,
From our bones, lifts, in a shimmering unfocus,
Along the eyes' horizons, becomes airy music.
Distant lutes and strummed lyres accompany the sun,

As it follows us, tropistically, toward the heartland,
Projecting its protean voice across a route
Three hours wide. We're held cleanly aloft
On its cosmic singing recital of vers libre
Springing, unpremeditated, from the Sierra Madre,
Continental Divide, and Kansas flatlands,
Inspired by its subtle interplay of symbol and image,

Mesmerized by the metaphors inherent in flight.
Through the High Eye, the subtly curving surface,
Anchored miles below, is a cloisonné urn,
Slowly turned to show us its intricate mosaic
Of mountain peaks stippled with snow, cratered lakes,
Neatly outlined farms, its seemingly unpeopled plenum
Pristine, spectacular, imbued with galactic virginity.

We chase our ceaseless, unreachable imaginations
Around its rim, victims of the sweetest submission to fate,
This unbelievably vulnerable morning.
Being borne is tantamount to being born again.
*

At 37,000 feet, our untrammeled minds
Make no distinction between earthly parturition
And ethereal renaissance. Euphoria delivers us

From our mundane selves. We come unwombed,
As the minutes, like invisible white corpuscles,
Resist angels of doom that hover about our vessel,
Pass into obscurity behind our annealing swoosh
Through time, and are replaced by newer integers
Rushing up to intercept our easterly procession.
Our passage is a sequence of jettisoned pupae and chrysalises,

An evolutionary climbing toward mutual oneness
With the hand-riveted butterfly-leviathan,
In whose skeletal, roomy aluminum belly we ride.
Soon, the ocean that has buoyed us diminishes,
Grows shallower with our ascending descent.
Its minuscule cities, hidden beneath polluted tides,
Rise like bubbles and are magnified in our eyes,

As we prepare to ferret out a hospitable landing site,
Go ashore, and enter, once more, the forest,
Where our souls' chattel, covered with sheets,
In storerooms memory keeps guarded from vandals
And worms, awaits our routine human unveiling.
Suddenly, the incessant hum of jet engines dies,
And we're left treading for our lives, head-high in silence.

5/29/77   (05530)

The Drummer's Last Run

Chat dumps breach on the horizon like leviathans,
Plunge into memory's slime ponds, and persist,
While I follow, atop the outer layer of intestine
Encased by Highway 67's mesentery,
Remarking all the alienated souls in cars
Going both directions with numb abandonment.
Some are driverless, others impatient
To reach destinations at Land's End,
Where Piranesian hydraulic compressors,
Operated by skeletons wearing bib overalls
And monitored by cancerous engineers carrying clocks
*

Calibrated in milliseconds, wait to clasp
Their arachnoid mandibles about time's prey.
My reason for edging away from home
Is obscure. Logical hypotheses I deduce,
As the miles accumulate in meaningless sums,
Confuse obsolete notions of heroic expeditions
Into aboriginal Cíbolas, to extend God's word,
With missions in search of ladies to save
From rapacious *enfants terribles* and misogynists.
Neither cause surfaces in my eyes' pools,
This cool June morning, as the generative force
Behind my lunatic craving to overcome stasis,
And nothing can assuage the uncertainty of purposes
Cursed by the internal workings of the mind gone mad.
I'm a spastic fly, dashing myself against walls.

Not freedom, not psychic arthritis,
Not even the perversely masochistic urge
To outrun my identity, molt my old flesh,
Stream, naked as the breeze, through space,
And escape the imperative to be constantly aware
Of myself has made me take to the road;
Rather, the dream, gnawing, again, in sleep,
Ringing ominously as obdurate fire sirens
During routine waking, this past week,
Has forced me to leave the security of my family enclave,
The dream, whose visionary illuminations have prophesied
A king, enthroned over an open grave,
Beseeching me to kneel in eternal obeisance, at his feet.

Toward this colossal, spectral simulacrum
I drive, eschewing home, wife, child.
The obsession overwhelms life's passion for peace
And companionship. Totally alone, like a tree,
A stone, undistracted, now, by personal ambition
Or heterosexual desires to satisfy myself in climaxing,
I arrive at the required speed to achieve flight,
Reach a perfectly hermetic state of vacuum.
The plenum containing my brain is complete.
I am my own reliquary. The day accepts
My trepanned offering, as a soft, pelting rain,
Streaking my dust-covered windshield,
Washes my spirit deeper and deeper into the earth.

6/8/77 — [1] (05531)

La primavera

The close-mown grass, through which she traipses
Barefoot, naked to her sweaty breasts,
Takes its last gasps, begs priestly visitation,
Administration of last rites. Her soles bleed
From such frenzied orgy with Clootie,
Just beyond the rough, in the panting woods.
Sybaritic creatures, cloven-hoofed goats, the snake
Lie drugged, enfeebled, covered with sperm
Ejaculated immaculately at her mere passing.
Her endless dancing even arouses Helios
To feline licking with his hectic, heated tongues.
Her saline flesh refreshes his jungle cravings,
Sates his taste for fecund female fluids.

Under summer's heavy persuasion, she drowses,
Writhing sensually into sleep's private grots,
Falling vertiginously from one abductor to another,
Until she becomes sodden, loose-limbed, used,
The object of lechery to every leper
And ghost who chooses to violate her numbness.
Soon, her supple belly thins; the bones appear,
Menacing as rose thorns. Only the blind
Continue to intrude on her hibernation. Eventually,
They find her withered body spiny and brittle.
Her final death within the cave of life,
Cutting in uneven convolutions, from May and June,
Through July and August, comes as no surprise.

Her brief cycle each year delights only those
Who anticipate her urgent coming, her ripening.
Yet once arrived, she entrances everyone,
Entices all with her concupiscent nuances,
Her crisp, cool, lascivious redolences,
Her unspoken promises for blooms and births
And purgative new beginnings. Such a lady
Stays with me each time her season comes round,
Pampers, teases, excites my imagination
To ecstasies I've never found with kindred muses.
Why, then, am I moved to painful bereavement
Each April's end? Perhaps it's that her children,
My poems, need their mother more than I need them.

6/8/77 — [2] (05532)

The Stages of the Lawyer

For sister Dale,
of whose achievements I'm so proud

How proud is their gait,
Those robed recipients of diplomas
Hand-lettered, suitable for framing,
As they endure the awkward processional.
How supercilious the imperious grins
Those weaned of a collegiate education wear
While sharing the podium briefly
With deans, chancellor, president of regents.
How condescending each becomes
On forsaking the ivory tower's
Rarefied air for the smoky cloakroom,
To return his rented gown and mortarboard;
How quizzical, dazed, how impatient
In the maze of swarming parents,
Relatives, and well-wishers come to graduation
With invitation in hand, making the reception a chaos
In which speedy extrication
Becomes the common goal of all in attendance.
How lost the next morning, amnesic
In the wilted afterglow and serpentine;
How inutterably disgusted and humiliated
On being rejected, without a jury of peers,
By the first thirty law firms
Worthy of their hard-fought-for services;
How stupefied, how vastly disillusioned
On achieving the status of waiter
At Cliff House, instead of head of the paraclete,
Tribune, trustee of the law review
Of sweet alma mater, patriarch of the Sanhedrin,
Next in line for nomination as Chief Justice
Of the Supreme Court of the United States;
How appreciative and gratified on being asked
To clerk for Judge Such and Such,
Advancing to do research work for the senior partner
Of a pedigreed office preferred by the wealthy;
Finally, how humble, conservative, circumspect
On being elected to join the prestigious attorneys
Who form the city's most lucrative consortium.
*

How proud is the gait each approximates,
Entering the echoing halls of civil court
To argue an important case for the first time,
On the way up to the ivory tower once more.

6/8/77 — [3] (05533)

Composition △

Soft, mellifluous notes
Soak slowly as rain
Into the parched earth
That contains and nurtures my garden.
I dig handfuls of wet soul-soil
From my revivified brain
And examine each soggy clod
For stray, unused metaphors
That somehow escaped desiccation.

Uncomposed scherzos and villanelles
Reverberate invisibly in my fingers.
My eyes witness the beginnings of vision,
From within. Ears beneath the surface
Listen to inchoate poetics
Breaking from seething moon-seeds.
Beyond night, a sympathetic sun
Rides my mind-tines' vibrations
To their source. My voice inclines toward heaven.

6/8/77 — [4] (01317)

Rites de passage △

To get here as dusk arrives,
    one must pass through twenty-six miles
Of undulant wheat tinged with sun —
    an ocean on a slow tilt, aflame,
Constantly groaning in motionless pantomime,
    its watery verdure composed of wheat-waves,
Soy-tides, corn leaves borne back on the breeze
    like sea spray, conspiring to extinguish
The listing horizon, bank its fires.

To get here as dusk arrives,
One must trust his life to eyesight
   incapable of differentiating curve
From straight line, precipitous dip
   from undeviating series of myriad inclines.
He must submit to this foreplay
   spidery twilight has designed to entice,
Tantalize, and ensnare the unwary waif,
   straying off main roads, into her web.

He must somehow survive these trials
   before bedding down in blankets
Stuffed with moony dust and shooting stars,
   must first immerse himself, volitionless,
Within the disappearing hues, choose refraction,
   fragmentation, diurnal self-destruction
Over safer, alternative avenues (major highways
   in place of state roads craving repair),
If he is to taste the heartland's lips,

   run his senses' fingers through her pubes,
Lie down in naked silence, astride
   her blond-fuzzed, writhing thighs . . . writhing,
Leaking summer semen, releasing eggs,
   in ecstatic, hermaphroditic spasms.
Finally, he must whisper the crickets asleep,
   hum the lumbering freight train's elusive fugue,
In soothing accompaniment to his dreaming soul,
   as it slides down night's occidental slope.

6/9/77   (05430)

The Harvesters ᐃ

The men compare makes of hay rakes
And balers, the agonies of cutting fescue
And wheat in rough, heavy pastures,
The urgency of doing so before the rains
Brush them back, comb them down slick
On the land's scalp. With indolent vigor,
They discuss next week's harvest,
Moisture counts reaching 12 to 14,
*

The imperative to dry it before storing
In silos. They deviate momentarily.
Someone mentions fishing and hunting,
Leaving Tipton, in September, for Alaska,
Where caribou and ptarmigan abound;
Flying into no-man's-land in style,
Inside an air-conditioned combine
Fitted with deicer leading edges,
Flexible wings, and demountable pontoons.

Clootie laughs loudest of all, guffaws,
As their incandescent fancy expands
About the breakfast table, hovers,
Colors the air obscenely as nicotine.
They reminisce, these young bucks,
About relatives fifty years predeceased.
Each reasons simultaneously that the past
Was somehow pristine, if not easier,
At least laissez-faired, uninflationary.
Yet Mamon reminds them that success
Breeds success, profit increases
With each machine-made swath.
"Eleven hundred bales from one field
Ain't hay." They all agree enviously.

Clootie muses to himself; his eyes smile:
"Who would ever have dreamed
That a humble wheat farmer
Could own a hundred-thousand-dollar home
And drive a Designer Series Lincoln
The five miles from county road B
Into the Crystal Café, each morning,
And back, change from Dacron slacks
To denim haying overalls, boots,
And billed cap with 'Funk's' insignia
On the front, 'Tipton Country Club' on the back?
Who would have ever believed he might
Accomplish his toil, cool as branch water,
In a cab alive with music and news,
Instead of crawling, sweaty, on his belly?"

Beelzebub appreciates their childlike delight
In themselves. He squeals his approval,
Patiently waits for one among them,
*

The obese, most affluent, least modest,
The preacher's son, "Big Jim" Lapedes,
Who will be leaving his elite group
Unexpectedly, this coming September,
After completing his most successful harvest,
Just at the height of ptarmigan season.

6/10/77 (00596)

Mr. Alighieri

The concrete I drive, this morning,
Is pachydermal gray, lachrymal.
Rain lifting behind my tires,
In tongued vapors, hymns threnodies
Reminiscent of Gothic cathedrals.
A very fourteenth-century Fiesole,
Sleeping on the edge of history,
Opens one eye wearily,
Focuses opaque cataracts on my passage,
As though I were the vagabond
Rather than she the lithe Beatrice,
Naked beneath my imagination's sheets.

Valleys I thread on my journey
Are soaked with low fog,
Ghostly in their immateriality.
My eyes strike *fósforos*
Inside their white caves,
Yet the flames flicker and die
Without revealing deeper chambers,
Exciting my mind to blind fantasies.
Can it be that the rain is semen
Swimming, evanescently as flagella,
Across my wind-screen, and its moaning
Time's grieving maiden, begging me
To awaken from the Dark Ages again,
Shed my deaf and dumb intellect,
Lie down between her fecund legs,
And forget the most recent generations,
Whose ameboid procreations have fathered me,
The androgynous product of machines
And electronics — modernity's computer?

Perhaps I'm still dreaming midnight
To elusive conclusions against its will
Instead of accepting its tantalizing amnesias.
Whatever the reason, I seem trapped,
At impasse within this abstract evocation
Of the past. Just up ahead,
The spires and parapets of the city
By the river rise castellated, real —
Arno or Mississippi, uncertain.
Its spectral, boalike flow
Attaches my freewheeling boat
To its glassy back, delivers my shadow
To the desk where, for thirty years,
With businesslike stichomythias,
Employing, always, terza-rima verse,
I've written invoices, shipping tickets,
A hundred discarded resignations
On check stubs and deposit slips —
The cantos of my *Divine Comedy*.

6/22/77   (05534)

Herzog the Jobber

Inside his automobile crammed with clothing,
He's oblivious as a decayed tree
To the landscape cycloning by his eyes.
He intones simple melodies from memory,
Resurrects irrelevant lyrics from ads
That have bombarded his intellect's heart
Like nicotine emphysemic lungs and watches them
As if completing an eight-piece puzzle
Of a misregistered-color pizza or burlesque queen.
One would never suspect from his easy demeanor
And equanimity that he harbors deep doubts
About prospects of jobbing his carload
Of unbranded, off-season "dogs."
Yet he's always subscribed to his own advice —
"For the right price, anything will sell" —
And eked out a decent livelihood.

Seemingly satisfied with his musical selection,
He hymns himself, with Bartokian illogic,
*

Into a trance, through whose golden portals
He flees majestically into the last century.
In the distance, a steam calliope wheezes,
Perforates the air with triumphal strains,
Announces the legendary Herzog's return
As Grand Imperial Potentate and Wizard,
The Emperor of Seconds and Rejects
(No holes barred), dressed in flesh,
With epaulets, medals suspended from ribbons
Pinned to his bare, curly-haired chest,
Naked to the townspeople crowding the streets
To view his hand-lettered dray wagon,
Which he likes to regard as his winged chariot.

Within minutes, children and spinsters,
Crotchety shopkeepers, vested attorneys,
The inebriated doctor, livery hands
Stop, as if carved, that moment, in a frieze,
Out of the day's houred entablature,
And watch him begin his center-ring act:
"Madras woven by hand, in Senegal,"
He whispers, wide-eyed, letting the fabric
Drape from his swaying hand like a snake
Being charmed into an outrageous docility;
"Tattersalls, hound's-tooth checks, tweeds,
All of the finest imported worsted blends,
Flannels, gabardines, military twills
Manufactured in Brooklyn's finest mills,
Silks and velvets and cashmeres
Gathered in Persia and Turkey and Bruges."

Mesmerized, one at a time, weak-kneed,
They rise to his exhortations, come forward,
Toward the platform, as if to take communion.
The Jewish eucharist he performs is ludicrous
Only in that he's never been able to justify
Hawking snakebite remedy with his goods,
As a substitute for the sacred-wine ichor.
Clothe the body of Christ, he thinks.
"Suit yourself!" he shouts. "Go in peace,"
He repeats, as he clasps their greenbacks
And gold certificates and sweaty change,
Until his shelves are empty as damned souls,
His wagon haughty atop its leather springs.
*

Only then does he revert to silence,
Resume his ruse as pariah of the Diaspora —
Lowly Herzog, purveyor of off-priced goods.

A car speeds by him on the right side.
Herzog shakes his head, realizes with fright
That daydreaming has got the upper hand.
Unable to use the rearview mirror,
For the clutter sardined into his station wagon,
He inches over slowly, blind, hoping
Salvation will be waiting in the next lane.
Only, as if in a last-ditch effort
To avoid their fate, the distressed coats and pants
Shift, avalanche over his shoulders and head.
Panicked, he swerves, plummets down an embankment.
Thrown from the burning car, he comes to rest
At the edge of a cornfield, unscratched.
As spectators gather, standing in stunned awe
At his amazing survival, he smiles to himself,
Imagining how a claims adjuster will, perforce,
Award his misfortune the highest insurance
Or risk the pernicious "whiplash" suit.

6/29/77 — [1] (02417)

Kinetic Reincarnation

The whole notion of motion
Pure and untrammeled
Has been blown totally out of proportion
By those who, having lost their spontaneity,
Are stuck with undefined lust
And, as such, are forced to accept stasis
As the only alternative to death.
To some, flight is the one romantic quest
Left to inspire life. To others,
Escape is the required vaccine for ennui;
Some still believe it's the panacea
Poets and children are bequeathed by their muse,
Athletes and movie stars consciously pursue,
And absent-minded Einsteins choose
Without a choice, being doomed
To an ever-expanding, atomistic freedom of will.

For me, motion is the soul's fuel,
Its plutonium, whose dynamics are blueprinted
At genetic birth. I'm ever modified
By it, it by my refusal to cease.
Inextricably, we spin inward,
Continuously rushing from breath to breath,
Convinced that somewhere in the distance,
An invisible vehicle is moored in port,
Near a shore washing a celestial city,
Waiting to transport our spirits
To the source of all empyreal energy.

Meanwhile, my twisting existence
Emits its scintillating crystals like sparks
Scattered by a grinder's wafer disk
Biting insistently into tempered steel.
Each faceted chip of jettisoned ego
Reflects the past, as it falls away,
Illuminating the future, just clearing the horizon,
Reminds me how controlled by half-lives
My peripatetic mind has been through the ages.
The prospect of being present to witness
Armageddon's last sunset is incredible
Yet conceivable. I accept my immortality
As one more natural force in the universe.
Birth and death are mere human postulates.

6/29–30/77 — [2] on 6/29 (05535)

The Last Supper

The men preside behind swatch cards
Stacked in fabric-content categories
And rubber-banded by range and lot number.
Attentive, solemn, glassy-eyed,
Cauterized by cigar smoke, invisible tars,
At the U-shaped, satin-draped table,
As if painted by a da Vinci–ed imagination,
They shimmer as quizzically as Biblical disciples
Confronting premonitions of demise,
Wondering whether Judas-like fashion
Will exercise his greedy passion this season
Or suspend his zealot's insensitivity
*

For another year. Each questions the other,
Through endless disputation,
On color and model changes, price structures,
Territorial and proprietary rights.
They don't know for certain what fate
Their new line will encounter next week,
When they journey away to proselytize,
Or what reception they'll get from buyers
Still smarting from late deliveries,
Broken sizes, and goods substituted
Despite written instructions to the contrary.

The cyclical nature of the rag business,
Bombarded by endless trendy philosophies
And the uncertain worship of personal tastes,
Makes these men's lives vulnerable.
One among them will forfeit his loyalties;
One will be crucified on a worsted cross;
A third will find friendly audiences
Gathered to receive his subtle Hebraicisms;
The rest, with ineffable complaisance,
Will pace inflationary deserts and marketplaces,
Confident that a messianic age will dawn,
While their weekly draws against commissions
Dwindle at a steady rate. As sales reps,
They all agree that penury and affluence
Alternate almost like prophesied plagues.
Home and motel room, swimming pool
And toilet are interchangeable euphemisms.
Just now, their patriarchal leader
Declares the meeting briefly adjourned for supper.
Praising their patient, steadfast devotion
During the tedious afternoon, he exhorts them
To be prepared to resume prayers after repast.
A matter of extreme urgency has still to be aired.

7/1 & 7/20/77 — [2] (02416)

Jonas Messias

Out of the entire, wide,
    early-morning, superheated sky,
    *

An inverted air mass,
    indurate as scybala,
Attaches its cosmic sucker
    to the dusty windshield and roof
Of my speeding vehicle and lifts me,
    like a gigantic electromagnet
Grasping a jagged chunk of scrap
    from a junk pile. The earth
Disconnects from my eyes. The highway,
    receding below, invisibly, as I rise,
Is adhesive tape being painfully ripped
    from my mind. Equilibrium
Becomes a wounded bull
    struggling to gore death in the groin
Before the final *"olé!"*

Slowly, I dissolve in blindness
And am assimilated by the horizon.
    As I ride its dimensionless swath
Through oblivion, as if underwater,
    blunt objects jut, froth,
Then retract phantasmagorically.
    Perhaps they're memories, succubi,
Actual faces swimming in this ocean
    of lost souls I've entered
Against my consent. There's my Madonnaed wife,
    crying; my child, clutching her breast;
My blessed mother, witnessing my passage
    with sad eyes; ancient, sainted lovers,
Listening attentively to my lips,
    as if old poetries I've written for them
Might still be lingering like spice odors,
    ready to slip from my numb tongue
And enter their nipped-in-the-bud vaginas.

In the July-fired landscape,
Where this drawn-out day
    is a leviathan beached gravidly
On the heartland and I've been led to believe
    that Jonas Messias in the flesh
Has made me his surrogate slave
    interred in the infernal belly
Of the earth, for an indeterminate span,
*

I strain at the slightest flicker of light
From the outside, climb time's vertebrae,
    clutch the nightmare's ivory teeth,
In hope of latching onto diatoms
    floating back out of its mouth.
Suddenly, the sky shimmers.
    A mystical blue liquid, like mercury
Set loose from a tube, rolls over me,
    and I escape on a prolonged yawn,
Just as morning tide releases the whale.

7/13/77   (05536)

The Art of Courtly Love

Alone as righteous Alighieri
Assigned to float in his own limbo,
By an invisible Torquemada
Looming ubiquitously over his soul,
I curse the viscid sky
That haloes every bit of distance
Between my squinting eyes and the life,
Loaded up with pleasures and hopes
For a languorous, slowly unfolding demise,
I so abruptly left behind
When I rushed outside,
This morning, to keep the sun
From seizing, undressing, and enrapturing Diana.

Perhaps a *recherché*
Du temps perdu, déjà vu,
Or a chivalrous sixth sense
Made me feel I might save the moon
From Helios's voracious rays
By following quixotically their recessional path
Across prolonged afternoon,
Through the crepuscular forest
Edging night's foothills,
And into the obscurely illumined thicket,
Where, in orgiastic absorption,
Those two heavenly bodies
Fused with a shuddering lunar climax.

Doomed for presuming to intrude
On the universal harmonies and isolated
From my loved ones, in a kind of death,
For attempting to arbitrate immoralities
I assumed nature must abhor
And would indeed desire rectified
Through poetic adjudication
Consonant with my understanding
Of statutory rape, I curse the notion
That drove me to involve my soul
In such sublime affairs of the heart.
In exile, I weep for Beatrice.
She sleeps on the dark side of my lunacy.

7/20/77 — [1]   (05537)

Legendary Lady

Her lips were tinged
With the brilliant shrill of salvia.
Her eyelids were shadowed
With a wisteria-and-cherry mascara
That dramatized their dripping lashes
Of weeping willow and flowering crab.

Even her slender nose
And her convoluted ears,
Pierced with the jewelry of undergrowth,
Were mere pieces of topiary
Sculpted from the dense sensuality
That gardened her lush face.

Chin, cheeks, and forehead
All conformed to the sweeping contours
Her body's nubile breasts
Projected against the fecund landscape
As knoll, gentle slope, rolling dissolve
Drifting invisibly into naked reverie.

Her honeysuckle hair
Saturated the air haloing her head
With a sweet bumblebee ambrosia
No human, once exposed,
*

Could long endure without drowning
Or briefly escape unchanged.

She remained the jasmined wilderness,
Inviolate, untrespassed, serene,
All during youth and adolescence.
Her unquestioned perfection
Was never defiled or molested
But respected, above all virtues, by man,

Until complacence got an advantage
On his senses and demanded her surrender.
Slowly, the days and hours and months,
In ruthless conjunction, forced her decay,
Clearing, grading, vitiating her features
Into unregenerating subdivisions.

Finally, the land's beautiful lady
Lay buried in dank concrete basements
Identical and myriad as catacombs
Containing nature's displaced bones.
Above ground, not a lawn or yard
Retained a trace of her devastated loveliness.

7/20/77 — [3] (05538)

Quotes from My Soul △

Poems attributed to my signature
Are, figuratively speaking, only quotes
My memory seizes eclectically
From the soul's vast, inexorable past,
Lean translations from an ancient language,
Comet sparks, infinitesimal twigs,
From individual trees in boundless forests,
My senses bend down to pick up
And arrange with dried grasses,
And leaves pressed between pages
To fill the mind's translucent vases
With pleasing, lifelong designs.

If, in a weak moment, I postulate
Immodestly their imagistic significance
Or expropriate their scintillating profundity,
*

Forgive me my insecure braggadocio,
My hubris, my puny *orgullo*.
I am merely an amanuensis,
Sensitive to a more intense pulse,
Driven by an invisible alchemical force
To communicate with the ineffable source
From which all music emanates
And every tender mentality derives
To color our intellects with love.

Nothing I create belongs to me.
The imagination upon which I heavily rely
For my "inspirations" is merely on loan.
Its complex gadgetry has been revised
Millions of times, passed down to me
From ancestors even my genes have forgotten,
And requires a Galilean respect
For the celestial laws that keep it alive
Despite all my tendencies toward pride,
Pleasures of the flesh, and laziness,
Which might otherwise explode
Or arrest a man-made machine.

And yet I've been elected, somehow,
Out of our earthly crowd, to perpetuate
The silence by making its hidden voice
Loud enough for newer Moseses to hear,
Through constant repetition of the quotes
That appear, in tyrannous fugues and trances,
For my ever-perceptive ears to identify
And write down before they disappear.
The poems I sing, then, though incomplete,
Excite me beyond belief, because they ring
With whispers of life's original idea,
In godly overtones that vibrate the bones.

7/20/77 — [4] (05539)

Lazarus the Tatterdemalion

His eyes twitch like a son-of-a-bitch.
Like a dog lifting its leg on a tree
At every corner down an endless street,
*

He raises his disheveled brows
In feigned amazement each time
Someone lingers on his motley visage
As he loiters in empty daydreams.
He coughs and wheezes beneath his breath,
Muffles the ague that inhabits his head
As if it were a sublet cold-water flat.
He blows his guts out of his nose,
Into a soiled handkerchief,
Hoping to stay the overflow, conceal
His uneasiness. He scratches his whiskers,
Out of habit, is oblivious to the ticks
That, consuming him like maggots,
Burrow deeper into his psyche each year,
Until they've left him eviscerated,
Rusted, and pitted from within,
Like an old boiler subdued by scale,
Whose handhole covers threaten to give way
At any moment. He expectorates
A scrofulous phlegm in public places,
Without warning, trying ineffectually
To eradicate the acrid taste of wine
Mixed with coffee, tars, barbiturates
Never completely dissolved. His mouth
Is a pit of restless bullsnakes
Biting themselves in relentless pain.
He belches the unmistakable gas
Sewers and cracking plants emit,
Passes sulfurous flatuses aloud,
Without concern for those around him,
On buses, in parks, outside stadiums,
Where he rifles waste containers,
Stuffed with beer cans, for heeltaps,
Collected like ambrosial rosary beads
In the tin, cylindrical cathedrals
He holds up to his lips with votive hands.
Curiously, graffiti has never excited him.
He neither reads nor writes the incunabula
Society Kilroys on its most convenient walls;
Rather, he prefers the oratorical frenzy
Extemporaneous speaking requires him to exercise
For relieving his cosmic grunts and groans.
*

Something about the loudness he generates
Stimulates his blood, temporarily unblocks
The clotting islets in his veined archipelago,
Allows his system to flush trapped poisons.
His voice, once unloosed, is a loon's
Or wolf's ululation, a sad, strange wail
Flying away from his vocal chords,
On human slingshots, searching the throat
Like a boomerang wheeling back
To its home source. Only, his voice
Fails to connect with invisible audiences
He imagines gathered below his eminence.
It trails off into inconsequential slobber
And epileptic froth that stain his raiment,
Gets confused with the useless existence
His flesh and bones, by sheer persistence,
Accumulate like calcium deposits.
At night, his glazed eyes are mesmerized
By the delicate engraving of revenue stamps
Stuck to slender necks his hands caress.
They vaguely remind him of Gideon Bibles.
He recites their sacred Deuteronomys
By heart, as though he were the prophet
Who composed their logos so long ago,
Until he lulls himself into a pungent drowse
Which no amount of raucous snoring
Or cold rain and snow can dismantle.
Between the last, long-drawn yawn
And dawn's strong radiance, he malingers
In Satan's basement, waits on cold steps
Below death's brownstone-tenement entrance,
A waif, a tatterdemalion, named Lazarus,
Who, praying to be admitted without waking,
Daily exemplifies God's greatest miracle,
By returning to earth's squalid alleyways
With a smile frozen to his face and eyes
Vacant yet alive to survival's alternatives
And possibilities. Each new day
Is another handout to spend
On an endlessly extended busman's holiday,
Paradoxical delay of his welfare check.

7/21/77 — [2?] (05540)

Slaves ^Δ

Still they're slaves, all of them,
Black and white alike,
To the fields, potential mildew,
Rust and blight, beneficial bugs
Too early exposed to insecticides
That might offset nature's metabolism . . .
Slaves to rainfall, "harmfuls,"
Slaves to their own paranoias,
Extravagant financial anxieties,
Ghosts of older plantation owners,
And vagaries of being shipped back,
White and black alike,
The one race to Gambia,
The other, rascally descendants of Byrd
And Oglethorpe, to Old Bailey,
Once crops fail to mature,
Futures bankrupt their guarantors,
Notes on loans come due,
And farm machinery is coldly repossessed.
Slaves subordinated to their king,
Cotton, swelter in their vassalage,
All classes one under a common fate
Despite the ramshackle abode
Or lordly prefabricated manor home
To which each retires at day's edge,
Bordered on all horizons by plants
Stranded in elongated, leafy verdure
So endlessly green as to be confused
With the world's watery Caribbean.
Men become indistinguishable from trees,
In their erect pacing over the land.
Vehicles that pass by are ants
On their way to oblivion beneath the haze,
Make no noticeable impression
On the growing going on in their wake,
Disturb no sleeping souls from dreams
They keep alive, through every season,
Of one day being shot of their dependence
On such a delicate crop for livelihood —
Black hand, white landowner
*

Alike. Yet, one more time,
Compresses, gins, combines, and tractors
Begin to whine. Their reiterations
Fill the air with the ancient call to unite
That almost every inhabitant of this South
Has responded to an entire lifetime,
Despite laziness, insurmountable hatreds,
Physical pain, and psychic abomination.
A sibilant excitement is abroad,
Silent, coming slowly alive, like a bear
Abandoning hibernation. Soon, the land
Will exact its annual tithes in sweat
And fatigue, "from can't see to can't see,"
Require each family to submit itself
To a communal allegiance to duties done
For the sake of an obsolete monarchy,
Until even the slaves lose their accents
And the countries from which they came
Lie as fallow as other cradles of civilization.

7/22/77 — [1] (00040)

Splenetic Curse: Ishmael's Endless Quest

Having traversed, nearly a dozen years,
Over concrete sea lanes
In oceans washing his peripatetic soul,
Ever in desultory motion,
As though his destiny were to locate
The Holy Grail
Instead of an undisclosed identity,
Needing clarification,
He abandoned in early manhood,
Before its voice had a chance to change,
The moon-crazed mariner
Sets a guesswork course in the direction
He suspects will whisk his vessel home.

Yet it's been so many typhoons ago,
So many inestimable trips around Cape Hatteras
And the Horn, so many forlorn days
Alone, aboard his oft-quarantined ship,
*

And myriad layovers in disease-ridden ports,
That he's not even able to motivate memory
To conceive mental images of his house,
Its spacious lawns and lovely trees,
Neighboring forests, ancient cemetery,
Where his parents, his three children
And wife lie buried in cypressed silence.
The constant bombardment of salt mists
Has rotted his living cortical pith.

Passing the Farallons and dropping anchor in the bay
Manacled to the land below Yerba Buena,
He rows ashore, mounts a rickety wharf,
And stares, for a frightened, frozen moment,
In utter disbelief at the human bees
Swarming the blighted Barbary Coast.
The holocaust of a recent earthquake
Has left buildings gutted, cobblestoned streets
Gnawed by gargantuan teeth, the city
A charred, discarded chunk of meat.
As if recognizing a familiar curse in hot pursuit,
The mariner flees without even looking back
To see if the water itself has yet caught fire.

7/22 — [2] & 7/31/77 — [4] (05541)

The Battle of San Romano

The sky that dominates my eyesight
Is a screen drawn down to the treetops,
On a spring-loaded roller.
Hippogriff, ibex, unicorn,
Suspended in furious immobility
As if figments of a Uccello battle scene
Refitted into different altitudes,
Assume the positions clouds once held.
The screen shudders with their restiveness.
Their irascibility threatens vision
By not allowing my mind sufficient time
To locate itself in a changeless design.
I grow anxious, get dizzy
With their ceaseless shifting and feinting.
*

Up ahead, the trees are trampled
Under their kicking hooves.
Reins grasped by invisible equestrians
Snap. Their sounds are drowned out,
Devoured by inaudible thunder.
Lightning spearheads their stampede.
Suddenly, the distance envelops me.
My vehicle is overrun, sundered
By a plundering storm-horde
That frees the screen's taut ratchet,
Sets it spinning upward, inwardly,
Dislocating my being between layers
Of my tightly wound imagination.

7/31/77 — [1] (05542)

[Has ever anything more beautiful] †

Has ever anything more beautiful
Manifested itself to me and you, Jan,
Than Trilogy

7/31/77 — [2] (06931)

Death Wish

I spend this Sunday morning alone,
Templed in my soul's boneyard,
Whose gentle, tremulous odors of ivy
And acanthus, essentially scentless,
Arouse my nostrils, expand my mentality
To encompass and exhume old friends
Decomposed in my memory's cemetery.

Birds hymn threnodies, crickets dirges
That spring alive from the silence
Like shoots from a severed tree's roots.
I stand in awe, as a hundred kas
Come flying back on their music
To animate their wasting bodies
And illuminate their patient eyes,

That we might communicate our adoration
Without reverting to breathless words
And desiccated lips kissing dust.
Whispering reminiscences brighten my solitude
For a few hours. Smiles are gold togas
That clothe my nakedness for a while,
Until the musical tapestry unravels

And I'm left standing outside the tomb,
Within the perimeters my funereal soul
Has paced off and set aside,
Just at the edge of my lifetime,
For the day when survival will free me
From its fleshly, Sisyphean routines.
I beg entry. My reveries desert me.

7/31/77 — [3] (05543)

Kudzu ^Δ

Bilious and livid tongues of kudzu,
Clumped lasciviously over the road's lips,
Wag in the back-blown wash
Of passing cars, like dissolute hitchhikers
Thumbing their drunken way to oblivion
Or slobbering hunchbacks ready to jump
Into my path. I succumb to their jeers,

Envisioning these ostracized pariahs,
Lining the highways at wilderness's edge,
As discarded pieces of decayed wrappings
Fallen in desiccated cascades from mummies
Long interred in nature's tomb.
The remains they once encapsulated
Have molted their carcasses like resurrected Christs,

Abandoned their piny trunks and limbs
Smothered under seething green bindings
And eaten alive by carcinogenic excrescences,
Until, now, no bodies are left
To house the dislocated kas, allow them to find
Their ways home. Only their pungent odors linger —
The stale perfume of senescent flesh —

While the Dionysiac gloom chews the hills
Into food that fills its glutted gut
With useless, ever-accumulating excrement
And has no place to dispose of its waste.
Suddenly, I sense the kudzu lining the road
Assuming the shape of a voracious saurian mouth,
Crouching herbivorously to consume my imagination.

8/2/77 (00031)

The Child Seeks His Source

Out of the formless, primordial order,
Chaos and Proserpina,
Entwined in time's slimy thigh-lock,
Consort with demons dreaming of earth,
And climax. Her unfertilized eggs
Drip, like pulp from a ruptured pumpkin,
Through the cosmos, atrophying millennially,
Shaped, finally, into star-chips
That scratch my glassy cataracts.
As I genuflect at the tower's edge,
Head stretched in astral erectness,
Asking the ancient, sacramental penance
For a bastard's immaculate conception,
I beg deliverance from this awful unknowing,
This unfathomable legacy of illegitimacy,
This orphaned ignorance of my parental ties,
By raking a hand across the horizon,
As if sweeping cigarette ashes off a table.
Not even my frustration is relieved
Nor my ache for primal identity satiated
By my attempt to devastate the wide universe,
Which floats, quietly as a hovering seabird,
Beyond my feeble reach. The same stars
Remain in my gaze, burning painless holes
Through which all my spirit escapes
Like steam rushing from a screaming orifice.
The heart's sad, implacable passion week
Comes round in the moon's gossamer glow,
Sounding the death of an insignificant foe
*

Of Satan. I am ready for death
And anxiously anticipate the transfiguration
My soul senses waiting to take me aloft,
To the land where the family of man began.
Bereft, all that's left is for me to move the rock
That bastions the cave where phantoms
Plaguing my entire existence have been stationed
To make sure no mutiny ever succeeded.
Like crazed bees, they swarm away,
Leaving me totally alone, empty, awash,
Buoyed in an ocean flowing in space,
Forced through an umbilicus, whose fluids
Swoosh me headlong from one tumescence
Into the nexus where Heaven begins
And the mellifluous, extraterrestrial surreal
Stretches forever. Just up ahead,
I envision a man and woman holding hands,
Focusing slowly into my dazed perception
As we approach each other. As they near,
My shadow slips into theirs, fuses,
Disappears within a slim nimbus of remembering.
Eternity obliterates all traces of my shape.
Even the bones exchange their chromosomes
For the dusty vacancy of the deceased
They assume. Yet, within the womb of death,
My eyes come alive, recognize their parents,
Revived by my arrival from earthly exile.
I'm one of the wandering tribe come home,
Son of the gentle moon and the sentient sun.

8/3/77 (05544)

[When I close one eye,] ‡

When I close one eye,
The nose's obtrusive profile
Is automatically exposed to sight.
It becomes an integral part
Of the eye's focus,
Dividing the horizon, diffusing light
Oozing in from the periphery
Despite this arbitrary barrier I impose.

Trees, people walking dogs
On the edge of an undulant golf course,
Martins darting spastically
Through a stark blue Illinois dusk
All lose bulk, fade into flatness,
As if a painted stage backdrop
Had been lowered on cue.
Even their elongated shadows
Are cast loose, dislocated
Like boats floating on an ocean

8/12/77 (05545)

Brief Flight

Set adrift in a spendthrift wind,
My timorous heart fibrillates
Like a frog twitching after death
By electricity. I switch systems,
No longer relying on earthly energy
To power my navigational apparatus,
And soar free of my previous self —
A prisoner released from his chrysalis.

Air tearing past the fuselage
Squeezes my sensitive body cells
Into buoyant, superheated molecules
That course over and beneath
Fancy's leading edges. I float
In a zone I've never before flown,
Through an ocean located between Rhodes
And Areopagus, above and below both.

Time surrounds my streamlined vessel
Like an eternal, crimson anemone
Caressing me with its lubricous tentacles.
The heart constricts; arteries surge
With the endless violation of thermals
And changes in density and pressure,
As I descend from the empyrean to earth —
A shipwrecked victim washed ashore.

8/14/77 (05546)

Each New Day

Each new day dawning
On his soul, fleeing, in retrograde,
Morning's zealots, is a bane,
A poison no palliative can purge,
A brain assailed by migraine lightning,
A star-spangled surrender to insanity,
A fleshy body maimed by piranhas
Swimming in drowsy, patient suspensions,
Circling endlessly in the murky tank
Imagination allows to stagnate
Between hirsute bulrushes
Lining both banks of each eye-pool.

Each new day dawning
Announces another successive death
To which he'll submit his pitiful self-esteem
By clothing his nakedness with guilt
For having made it this far alone;
By washing the flesh off his face,
Exposing the Greco-like, elongated bones;
By brushing blood up from the gums,
Defecating scybala so indurated
As to set pain free along the entire colon,
Like rats pacing with tiger feet;
By burying himself behind an office desk.

Each new day dawning
Is a breach of the sacred Commandments,
By being a harbinger of greed
And lust-troubled covetousness,
Beneath whose golden idol of Helios,
Heated in a universal crucible
And sculpted by penitential senators,
He kneels. His appetites incite him
To riotous idolatries,
Outrageously sterile autoeroticisms,
Wasted dreams of fathering a family
To outshout loudmouth anonymity.

Each new day dawning
Is an essence of the present,
*

A rotten perfume of forgotten bedrooms,
The future dressed in yesterday's hopes,
A knot tied about the spirit's finger
As a reminder that tomorrow is the watched pot
Dreamers and winos and moneymongers
Never see reach boiling point,
For the vaporous steam that fogs vision
And lulls thought into entrapment
By body fat and mental cataracts,
Ever a step closer to the last new day.

8/18/77   (05547)

The Kiss of Death

He squeezes through night's teeth
Precariously as a sparrow
Seeking refuge in a bramble bush
And emerges unscathed on day's lips,
Himself a kiss, a flexing yawn,
An embryo of words
Not yet arrived at full term,
Assuming the soul's earthly disguise,
A poet chasing his Maker's shadow
From sleep, through airy aspiration,
Past caprice, daydream, and reverie,
Back to sleep that approximates death
Without actually severing the knot,
A creature who wakes in dark,
Lies down in broad daylight,
Shouldering the immense weight
Of growing old, inarticulate,
Suffering aphasia, dyslexia,
Without realizing his powers are waning.

Having escaped night's teeth,
The aging child-pariah
Takes up his pad of paper and pen,
Knapsack filled with metaphors
And idioms never before used,
And sets out, fresh and edgy,
*

To record, in his generation's voice,
History's chivalrous resonances,
The ocean's sibilant whispers,
Basaltic groans of volcanoes,
The loon's lonely Adirondack wail,
And the pale moon, forever cameoed
Against an unimpassioned sky,
Keeping pace with his fragile exile.
Only, the images his imagination seizes
Freeze, shatter like unannealed glass
When touched by his shrill artistry.
His vocabulary unlearns its task,
Abandons him in a vast, white silence,

Into whose funereal embrace he blends,
Peaked as antibodies, invisible
Against the stark scintillas of stars
And asteroids wheeling, like gulls,
About his voiceless degeneration.
To what end his vessel is destined,
This day, he can neither intuit
Nor second-guess, since his brain,
Submerged in a nonexistent lake,
Can't differentiate the shapes of sounds
Or the colors shading his path,
As he stumbles over the years,
Strewn, like autumnal leaves, at his feet.
Suddenly, the region in which he drowses
Dissolves into perpetual twilight.
Glowering night gnashes her teeth
In anticipation of his unwary approach
Toward the entrance to her gaping mouth.
She puckers her lips to kiss a ghost.

8/23/77   (05548)

Waiting Area

Dazed faces,
Dissociated from torsos and legs,
Form a crazy-quilt confluence
*

Of black, alluvial tributaries
Emptying into my astonished gaze.
Seated, caught in eddies of talk
Animated by an atavistic lethargy,
They become lowland primates
Telescoped in reverse,
Until evolution urges them
Into an arboretum of elephantine split-leafs
Fanning languidly above my head.
Numbed by this abrupt influx,
I begin to fear the determination
This extended family,
Apparently migrating to other climes,
Might make regarding my intrusion.

Suddenly, the lush savannah
With which imagination has edged the jungle
Of my anxiety about flying,
This morning, is transmuted
Into terrazzo, chrome, and vinyl
Crenelated in cigarette smoke,
And the transient creatures
(Who, I soon realize, as grass eaters,
Can never cannibalize
My unassailably white flesh)
Who've stalked the ghettos
Of my until-now undisclosed bigotry
Become polite teenage blacks,
Dressed without overstating
The essence of their deprivation,
Athletes waiting to change planes,
While my old self-esteem is defeated
And shamed by a profane, rum-gutted slaver.

8/24/77 (05549)

[A wine-tinged ichor] †

A wine-tinged ichor
Soothes my supine brain,

8/26/77 — [1] (06934)

The White Geese

The Golden Gate, Seal Rocks,
Cliff House, Playland at the Beach,
And the Great Highway,
Sparks, Reno, and Sutro Park
Are geese flying in haphazard formation
High above memory,
Fleeing westerly,
On their ancient migration toward the Pacific.

My wife and I observe
Their curiously silent flight,
Remark their serene dissolve,
As if twilight's spectrum
Has refocused their entire V
On the sun's original prismatic facet,
Feasted on their sensual speed,
And erased them with a sepia wash.

Only, neither of us realizes
That these are the same geese
That have passed each night, for decades,
Etched on a Praxinoscope screen
Revolving on an axle of shared years,
Or that they have stayed on the same plane,
Unfaded, three-dimensional, pristine,
Since the day they became our wedding vows.

8/26/77 — [2] (05550)

Cherubim and Seraphim

Flashing on jet planes
before boarding

The undulating roar of soaring machines
Sets my cells quavering,
The spirit on edge.

                    Sinuous premonitions

That, until this most recent eternity,
Lay buried in the intellect's potter's field
Rise from the dead,
Shake the beggar's-lice
From their skeletons.

They awaken me with a start
To breathing ghosts landing and departing
Every few heartbeats,
Coursing casually back and forth
Between now and the hereafter,

And suddenly, I'm convinced,
As each winged vessel gains momentum,
Rotates on my eyes' focal point,
And climbs out to the left,
In a westerly embrace,

That the one on which I'm ticketed today,
Loaded with my overweight imagination,
Is the angel of death,

       waiting to hijack my soul.

9/2–3/77 (02255)

Baptism of a Mystic ^Δ

The ocean's gravitational lope,
Its ebb and recessional undulation
Tonguing my legs and stomach,
Close in against the hot beach,
Is the most dissipated edge
Of Neptune's energies.
His nerve ends are exposed.
It's the arterial and venous extremities
Across which his bloodlike ichor,
Effervescent with salt, flows,
Just beneath the sun's surface.
This narrow zone of ocean,
In which a man can stand
And still breathe without gills,
Amphibious,
Within his feeble anatomy's limits,
Is so far from the heart,
Whose anagogic palpitations
Tremor each beach it washes,
That it never hears the aortal roar
Powering its vast, amebic force.

Ankle-deep, waist-high,
Now up to my neck in detritus,
Gently assailed by sea beans,
Sundered shells, and jellyfish
Inching inexorably shoreward,
I dare bury my entire head
In the element. Silence hides me
Momentarily. Suddenly, the beat
Of a distant sinoatrial node
Explodes my mesmerized ears,
Attaches my pulse to the ocean's,
Worms its way into every pore,
As though I were an assimilable shell
Being peaceably occupied by a parasite.
Eons glow in my heated forehead.
A space in the accommodating ocean
Opens, encapsulates my passage.
I enter its bloodstream,
Emptied of memory, consciousness.
Breathing becomes a series of turbines
Churning, slowing, ceasing completely,
As a primordial current leading out
Toward an ever-retreating horizon
Assumes the task of propelling my soul,
Seeing that my recent shape is changed
From human fetus into mystical fish
As it passes back to the source
From where the ocean's waves emanate.

9/10/77 (05551)

Abortive Attempt

Cement streaked with tar seams
Screams a futile, desperate wail
Only those locked in cerebral catalepsy
Know. I collect the tires' vibrations
In every nucleolus and gene
Constituting my breathing oversensitivity.
My congealed juices are spun
Until they rise involuntarily,
Ooze, in sticky sickness, from my mouth,
*

While I drive this station wagon/hearse
Over this last highway
Before night's guillotine blade drops,
Severing the sun's fibrous spine.
Mile by shattering mile, the nerves,
Inside their myelin sheaths,
Thicken as if the cement were extruded
Through the eyes and wound around them.
Finally, bone, ideation, speech
Succumb to blindness. The vehicle weaves,
Takes my life into its mad deviations,
Commands me to seek safety
By praying for a miraculous absurdity
To intervene and retrieve my soul
From the teethlike guardrails
And parallel traffic speeding past,
Honking like geese frightened by a wolf.
Why I've been visited by pestilence,
This inconsequential afternoon,
When I've merely taken temporary flight
From demons invading my privacy
As I tended to the innocuous occupation
Of painting a self-portrait with daydreams,
I can't say, unless some feature
Of my jostled psyche came loose
And defected to the enemy, reality.
In a flame-out, my senses take leave,
Break into ashes rising above the crash.
Suddenly, space is a red flashing,
Intermittent as heartbeats, demonic,
Anonymous, not quite statistical.
Survival is a Nembutal-faint penumbra
Weighted with the traumatic postponement of failure —
Unsuccessful even at the artifice of suicide.

9/12/77   (05552)

Intimations of Autumn

I step from the porch stairs,
This unusually cool September morning,
*

Like a dory shoving off from shore
To ply unexplored watery territory,
And enter an autumnal current
Scented with summer's last mowed grass,
Dabbed, at eye-line and higher,
With sugary red and yellow impastos,
Where, until just an hour ago,
Chameleon-leaves bathed in disguises
Green as primeval, seething ferns.

The vessel, floated by ecstasy,
Is a child's rocking horse,
Heaving recklessly, threatening to turtle
In the wavy undulations of convex craters
That contain a single aqueous sea
Inside the three-dimensional diameter
Where vision focuses the images of my life.

In the distance, Lugnag and Laputa
Lift, crenellated, against the sun,
Shimmer in the Jupiter-winds of winter.
Phosphorescent flying fish
Breach and dive across my scudding bow,
Almost distract me from my compulsive task
Of discovering the actual time line
Behind which Lucifer-troops are stationed,
Waiting to mount their cold, odorless invasion
Against spirits straying indefensibly
Beyond the threshold of their human limitations.

Only, as day widens, the sea subsides
To a docile channel of sunlight.
Japanese breezes reinspire the lungs
With one more Respighi-like stridency.
Fields twitch; crocus and coleus climax.
Lesbians running naked in my veins
Are paeans that hasten my heart to retreat
Before frozen snows close all openings
Leading out of these oceanic doldrums.
Over my shoulder, I see ancient Janus
Waving me home, waving me away.

9/20/77 — [1] (05553)

[The national cortical landscape] ^Δ

The national cortical landscape
That stretches, three states deep,
Into the continent of my buried imagination,
Is planted in cotton, corn, and soybeans.
It's watched over by an agrarian myth
That still persists on a ramshackle homestead
Granted its forebears
On their merely accepting federal handouts.

The seasons speak an eclectic dialect
Comprised of intellectual drought,
Flash floods that erode the old foundations
Rooted in sweaty, African patois,
Hester Street Yiddish, and Back Bay Mather,
And send it rushing unintelligibly
Into fast-food chains, to disappear forever
Beneath billions of Eucharistic beef patties.

Sun and moon illuminate the solitude
Imposed by flashing neon tubes.
This great nation's reputation
As the melting pot of the world is stained
By grease splattering from chicken thighs
And french fries sizzling in deep-fat vats,
While millions of disaffected illiterates,
Felons, and waifs immigrate to its shores.

Each fresh day is a testimony
To the colonizing spirit of a collective race
Of displaced people motivated by need,
Free enterprise, and personal achievement.
The brain is stunned by massive proliferation
Across its terrain; shopping centers,
Subdivisions, condominiums, and golf resorts,
Tennis and racquet and civil-law courts,

Cantilevered, reinforced-concrete garages
And sports stadiums encroach unchecked.
Ever-new interstate highways
Suture the wounded mind's occipital flesh.
Despite Master Charge and Visa,
Layaways, Christmas plans,
*

Coupons, and food stamps,
The head short-circuits. An acrid burning

Covers the horizon. At first, they name it
Pollution, for fear of alerting the public
To possibilities of congenital cybernetic disease.
One by one, every American
Is immolated in his or her sleep,
Exterminated by the same lack of concern
Their rapacious ancestors manifested,
Murdering the first red man on a bet.

Now, the land reseeds itself,
Each year, without the help of man.
Its crops are yet watched over
By an omniscient agrarian myth
That has lingered in the absence of words
To articulate its basis for existence
And wisdom to assimilate its law,
While the fittest can't survive themselves.

9/20/77 — [2] (05429)

Reunited

The mind's dendrites spark and crackle
Like severed high-tension wires.
Anxieties are northern lights
Forming carbon arcs across the synapses.
Axons draw taut. Atoms collapse,
As elastic bands, expanded
Past breaking, slap the brain
With a pain so outrageous,
Tears race from the eyes in cascades
That displace the grass at his feet,
Erode the entire earth,
Above which he hovers in disbelief,
Wash clean all human colors
That might remind him of home,
Exposing a vast black hole
He gravitates toward without control.

Suddenly, his body is a globe
Reflecting a rainbow along his spine,
*

A sundog haloing his head.
Encapsulated by his own crying,
Speechless as he enters the deep,
He penetrates death's plenum,
Gasps with paramnesic relief
On seeing his wife again,
Dressed in his lacy memories of her radiance,
And reaches through a fluid parallax
To taste her lips with his fingertips.
She swims toward the image of him
That has survived his whisperous trip
To time's beginning and disappears
Inside the fading legacy of his solitude,
To mend dendrites and reconnect their love.

9/20/77 — [3] (01318)

[The day breaks rain-strewn and gray,] ^Δ

The day breaks rain-strewn and gray,
Specked with ineffectual headlights
Feckless as a dying patient's eyes,
As he leaves cigar-stained Kafka Inn.
His brittle chrysalis lies in a pile
With soiled towels, candy wrappers,
And the residue of musty dreams
Ripped into confetti and tossed down
From Olympus, on crowned heads of state.
Only his disguised, Phoenix-rising pupa,
Having emerged from sleep's sheets,
Dares journey onto the highway alone.
No butterfly comes alive,
Rather a torpid caterpillar,
Who almost recalls his name is Gregor,
A millipede, fearfully prehistoric
Even to his own spurious eyes,
An eight-legged brown recluse spider,
An elongated praying mantis.
His mortification claws his face
Beetle-raw from side to side,
As he guides his vehicle blindly,
Rushing from memories of last night
*

That might yet remind him
Of the identity with which he arrived
At the inn. The whine of wet concrete
Is the shriek of the planet at Creation,
Hurling frictioned through space.
Vehicles passing, spewing water
In his glassy face, are asteroids.
Onrushing beams across the lane
Are galactic debris, gaseous bodies
Flaming up and away. He is atomic,
Back again, this antediluvian morning,
To protozoan origins, one with the rain,
The sclerotic sky, green things
Dripping rapidly into autumnal decay.
And at once, he awakens, recreated
In the named image God gave him
To distinguish his individual birthright
From that of fellow manimals —
Drummer, hawker, Diaspora-man,
Hooknose, kike, Jude, *schwein*,
Babbitt, Loman, flabby Prufrock,
Medicine man, carny barker,
Unmodified husband, intransitive father.
The rain-strewn hours gnaw his senses,
As he inches his way, on a thousand legs,
To the drain of day's ringed tub,
Where his first customer probably waits
To paw through his swatch books
And wash him away with cold complaints.

9/21/77 (02415)

The V.F.W. Meets to Break Fast at the Crystal Café

Fat, raspy hands and ringed fingers,
Faded fatigues and limp caps
Reminiscent of Seabees on Guadalcanal,
Muddy boots, faces strewn hirsute,
Blubber slovenly stuffed under waistbands,
T-shirts, and cheeks, lascivious guffaws
Locked deep in thoracic caverns,
Like black leopards pacing in cages . . .

This knot of details collects, like filings,
About my mind's magnet, as description
Rises, gasping, to the surface, inside bubbles
Imagination releases as it descends
Into a steaming ebony patina my hand
Raises to its addicted lips, to taste.
Suddenly, the coffee is awash with my profile,
My toes, flesh, severed features, and bones

Flowing over the tongue, like logs
Unjammed above a falls. My lungs constrict,
As if asphyxia has punctured their plenum
With claws. A bloodless liquid
Oozes out of my mouth. Myriad tight eyes
Drive me back against the beachhead
Paranoia has erected to isolate my presence
And highlight the death of a dreaded enemy.

9/22/77 — [1]   (00597)

Exultations ^Δ

I am milo, endless in vanishing,
Whose bulbous, multifaceted heads,
Cornlike, waxy leaves and stalks
Await the combines' sensual, scythelike blades.

I've become a fake-fronted country store,
A solitary turtle compelled to cross
Highway 5, with only a soft shell
And a legendary reputation to keep me safe.

My heart beats beneath the work shirt
Of every indigent seated on the concrete wall
Of last century's pinnacled courthouse.
My eyes share their imperturbable repose,

As I pass through Boonville, Arrow Rock, Glasgow,
River towns dozing, Van Winkle–warm,
Beneath this last day of summer's sun,
While the Missouri whispers through my veins.

I am the sugary ichor of sweet gum,
Sycamore, black walnut, hard maple,
*

Coursing urgently as racehorses
Through xylem and phloem, my fleshy leaves

Sweat beads beginning their rapid dissolve
From green to gold, purple, tangerine,
To bright, corpuscular bleeding, to brown.
With fierce abnegation, I refuse to release hold

Of limb, of node, branch, trunk, ground
In which my own familial roots are buried,
Upon which silo and barn, windmill
And barbed fence protrude against my mind

As one monolithic tombstone marking a heritage
In whose fluid myths I bathe my soul
And weigh the yield of my mortal patrimony,
In whose Midwestern grips I ever reminisce

Of white clapboards and steeples,
Red-brick chimneys and gingerbread visions,
Black wrought-iron fences and brittle corn.
My dreams are baby's-breath, columbine,

Nights lambent with fireflies, pumpkin lights,
Wing tips blinking, stars enlarging, receding
Against an unscientific, insignificant ignorance
I perpetuate to protect myself from demons

That might otherwise persuade me to leave
This self-created fiefdom I keep in trust,
Without needless deeds, quitclaims, and leases,
For the tiny issue I've been privileged to seed

And breathe, full to bursting, with genetic ecstasy,
A seething excitement about all creatures alive
And about to be that has inspired my hopes, since birth,
With the possibility of outliving my earthly verse.

9/22/77 — [2] (05428)

Yom Kippur Unobserved ^Δ

For Kenny Sinner

Somewhere buried in my dispersed heritage,
A mythical synagogue is draped
With the plaintive, wailing ceremony of atonement.
*

My anguished heart can almost discern it
Through all these years of my abject, impious neglect,
Beating as faintly as the drugged blood in my veins.

Its remains rise like a Loire Valley chateau
Above its own shadow cast over an empty plain.
Memory enters its echoing temple gates, strains
To collect the lyrical faith of a swaying rabbi
Chanting transliterations from the ancient Torah
His shaking hands keep spread apart before the Ark.

The echoic Hebrew he recites bites my dumb ears
With gold-capped teeth. My ahistorical existence
Amidst these outlandish imaginings awakens me
To the chill of being unequivocally naked, fully dressed,
In the smug and sterile complacence comforts have caused
My soul to wear in place of a charitable holiness.

For no convenient reason, my knees buckle
Like a mourning dove unexpectedly shot from flight,
As an invisible audience, consisting of my parents
And every scioned relative they've ever had
Since Abraham, joins in a common exhortation
Spanning Judaic man's oppressive past.

Their responsive prayers choke my throat, close my nose,
Draw me into the sanctuary on all fours —
A sacrificial goat come home to let my blood,
Confess my voluntary disavowal of the laws
Taught and learned in Sunday school and *shul*,
And await the Sanhedrin's disposition of my case.

The entire congregation goes quiet as lightning
Trapped between its conception and thunderclap.
Silence rips through the temple walls with claws
Fitted to superstition. My numinous spirit
Dies under the censure of hypocrites afraid to admit
That my penitence might be their only hope for survival.

9/22/77 — [3] (01319)

Hangover

Mythical alligator lizards, extinct buffaloes,
Dinosaurs, and vampire bats hiding in the morning mist
*

Lifting off a reluctant, autumnal land —
They assault my noisy head, bite it
Into a million pieces of confetti I'll hurl,
All afternoon and evening, on the procession
Of maimed metaphors and dissolute philosophies
My brain will attempt to tame and lead
Through narrow avenues and dead-end streets
Along the unmarked route to the seat of my heart.

The hour that madness came, last night,
And appropriated, for its insane Prince of the Opaque,
My brain's highly polished and balanced apparatus
Is mere conjectural irrelevance. What is clear,
However, is the vast chasm, filled with creatures
Horned, scaly, cleft and clawed and wet,
Left in its backwash, which I have to navigate
Or transcend if ever I intend to return
To my senses. Time pauses. The sky guffaws
At the tininess of my monumental dilemma.

9/23/77 — [1] (05554)

Cancer Comes to a Young Man

For Janet Douglass

Lesions, adhesions, aneurysms, embolisms,
Feckless tests and x-rays,
Sexless respect for checklists
Inspected at specific intervals
Shimmer in the cloyed, antiseptic air
That fills this self-contained cosmos,
In which he exists *in absentia*.
Lifted from all familiar surroundings,
He fears each distant footstep
And intercept of the terrified premonitions
He wears on his bloodless face.
He's terrified by every unannounced intrusion
By the few visitors who dare come
To express their grief and sympathy,
Disguising it with too-obvious silences
And blatant floral arrangements,
Whose rapid decay only highlights
*

His daily deterioration. Promethean,
He waits without being able to see
The green flies and their progeny, maggots,
Gnawing at his imagination,
Eating his intestines, imbibing his bile.
On rare occasions, he questions why
His stout, blessed physique and disciplined mind
Have acquiesced to host such ghostly guests.
Finally, last rites are administered
To deaf ears. In the unventilated vaults
Of ultimate consciousness, he hears a voice,
A whisperous facsimile of his own sibilance, shouting,
"Son-of-a-bitch! Son-of-a-bitch!"

9/23/77 — [2] (05555)

Two Mothers

Oblivion is my one mother,
The earth my other,
Who suckles my lungs with ether
Released from the sun's lungs.
I breathe moon-dreams through a funnel-teat
Protruding from a night-seam. Twilight
Drips its delicious ichor
Intravenously into my mind.
Naked Diana knots my axons.
My blood clots at the tender end of the penis,
Where being and screaming fantasy climax
And creativity sprouts shoots and blooms
For its Venus's-flytraps to assume.
A hundred nubile moons loose me
In their vertiginous proliferation.
The ragged soul, fused with love-spill,
Writhes below, above, and in between
The ginger-dappled, curry-tart thighs
My collective desires invite to their bed.
A delirious asphyxia numbs the senses.
Legs, stomach, back, scrotum, and toes
Cringe under the voluptuousness cessation
Of the bodily functions brings to the weary brain.
Such supple emptiness, such whole pleasure
*

Must be a prologue to metamorphosis.
My heart can't keep pace with itself.
The eyes roll back up under sleep's lids.
Time occupies red cells, crowds out
Ether trapped in earthly sun-lungs.
Oblivion gently soothes her tumescent belly
With effleurage movements. Soon, now,
She'll be giving birth to cold, used bones,
Cradling them in the dark cathedral
Where all her children are mitered and robed
For the ceremonial procession through the years,
Who will grow to be sons and daughters
Of nameless generations removed from humanity,
Shadows delivered from the womb, unbloodied,
Full-bodied, ready for the business of eternity.

9/28/77   (05556)

Raining Cats and Cats: A Prelude to Winter

Invisible, clicking cat paws,
Tracking repetitiously across the glass,
With dazzling irrationality,
Cause me to conjure shapes and patterns,
Transformed implausibly out of the rain,
That claw my face, my brain, my imagination to shreds.

October is a snow leopard more gray-black
Than white — opaque, disturbed, abject —
Whose cage contains my aging spirit.
It paces the highway I drive,
Confined, like me, to the two identical lanes
My days take from bed, to waking monotony, and back.

Each beat of the windshield wipers
Erases its myriad paw prints, replaces them
With teeth, whose scintillating, irregular canines
Seem aimed at maiming my inviolability
By devouring my eyesight, mangling my reflexes,
Gnawing the fibers from my mind's solar plexus.

Intermittently, through the blinding bites,
I snatch glimpses of a light on the distant horizon
And wonder what lands and climate exist
*

Beyond this wet depression in my life
And question why the leopard has fled again
Before reaching Kilimanjaro's snowy heights.

10/7/77 (05557)

They Die, That We Might Live ^Δ

No bereavements, no eulogies
Accompany the irreversible cascade of leaves;
Rather, threnodies of jubilant color
Reach my ears eleemosynaryly,
Beseeching me to heed the death
Of a season, its interment and
Resurrection. Their fading spirit
Seizes my heart, alerts my mind
To search out hibernal refuge
Within the burgeoning word-forest
My verses leave behind like echoes
Endlessly breathing, as autumn's children
Submit willingly to gravity's maternal tug,
Relax their nodal hold on earth,
And vacate, in majestic recession,
Their natural stations of the cross.

10/16/77 (01027)

Water Lilies ^Δ

For my flowering Jan

After our three years of primordial sleep,
Paramnesia shapes us into water lilies
Efflorescing in morning's light,
From out a night of silent hiding.

A subdued, Edenic mood urges us
To renew our acquaintanceship with procreation,
Awakens us to a renaissance of life
Growing inside my ripening wife's calyx.

An aquatic flower waits to embrace us,
Make us custodians for the hopes of a race
Accustomed to plastic nosegays and sprays.

Adrift, we sit alone, shivering, entranced.
Our marriage and friendship undulate
Below the banks of an unfathomable lake
Floated with omens, oracles, and fantasies.

Effacement done, dilatation begun,
We tremble in anticipation of the hour
When processes of eruption and upheaval
Will change forever love's supple crust

And the petaled corolla will bud open,
Exposing a rose-clothed soul
Tenderly scented with our own genes' aroma.

10/17 & 10/24/77   (01408)

Revisiting the Old Home △

Focus is a series of blunt geometric shadows
      cast from shapes in a Sheeler factory scape.
As we drive further away from the city,
      vision's cataracts lose their opacity,
And the past invades with teary familiarity
      the wooded estate where my youth's novitiate
Commenced its intense escape from adolescence
      and the white-columned splendors of innocence.

Suddenly, a hundred crows, like chunks of coal
      or stray clinkers strewn along a track,
Interrupt the dazzlement, divert the sun
      from its surging cascade of ultraviolets.
The pupils contract in fracturing despair,
      fearing for their very existence.
Talons and corny beaks scratch the afternoon
      with crosshatched images of doom.

The eyes search in every direction
      surrounding their sensate apparatus
For carrion, flesh left to November
      for immediate disposal. No recognizable odors
Lift from the furious, cawing congestion of birds,
      yet in a flash, the eyes' miasma
Detects a suggestion of deathly dimension.
      My shouts are rocks dropped to a pool's surface.

The crows scatter with a shattering cacophony,
    as though the infant world's crust
Were splintering into space, and dissolve from sight.
    I enter an unsurmised woods behind my eyes,
Where memory and reveries of childhood nest,
    survive, despite my absence all these years,
And follow to the forest's core, then rest,
    while the eyes refocus on the next few steps,
Waiting for the crows to show me the future.

10/21 & 11/24/77   (02025)

The Last Show of the Season

Just a day ago, or a week or three,
Autumn was a movie marquee
Whose steadily flashing incandescence,
Trapped in spastic, filamentous, colored glass,
Was composed of leaves, each achieving epiphany
At a slightly different moment — transitory

The moment, the shadowed space in between,
Where speculation and memory fester,
Transitory even the dazzling persistence of vision,
The overtones thrown back
By the mind's magic lantern
After rains dissolve their water-soluble colors

Like tears eroding mascara and rouge
Of a lady impassioned by its sad denouement.
Now, a draped fog
Lets fall its curtain. The theater empties,
Leaving the last show's ticket stubs
To molder ubiquitously beneath its killed marquee.

10/25/77 — [1]   (05559)

Ishmael, Again and Again △

Once again, the slender, seminal threads
Bend past snapping, attracted by an egg
Suspended in busy, buzzing blood-buds,
Then recover effortlessly in climax.

Each catapults an encapsulated embryo,
Whose features resemble two beings
It's never seen, through pleasure tunnels,
Toward the fundus, where life takes hold.

Only one or a couple endure the flight,
Arrive at the shore, and go aboard the vessel,
Whose voyage stretches nine months wide
Before its survivor is expelled on dry land.

Attended by its Genius or female counterpart,
A child finally ignites its first cry,
Awakening briefly its sleeping sisters and brothers,
Left forever bereft and unrealized inside.

10/25/77 — [2] (01409)

An Autumnal Birth ^Δ

My wife and I arrive before dawn,
Descend the neon-lighted concrete cavern,
And leave behind the hissing earth.
The elongated tunnel echoes our hesitation,
Magnifies our flight-frightened palpitations,
As we enter the hospital's bowels, possessionless
Except for the unexpelled creature whose birth
We've come to initiate, naked, we three,
Destined to taste the same unfiltered air,
Assimilate identical auditory sensations,
Register visions from one sun and moon.
All that remains is the singular parturition,
The swim to freedom, the labored escape,
The exile's hegira through a uterine wilderness,

And my wife's uncongenial expectation of pain.
Beneath the sheets, her tiny frame
Shapes sand dunes with smooth peaks
That simulate the outline on the graph
Monitoring, in eerie green twitching lines,
A highly audible fetal heartbeat.
The magical, illuminated machine flashes data
In red digital displays. Vibrations
Rise from beneath the ocean floor,
*

Like bubbles from some lung-bearing creature,
Through black tubes, while clear plastic
Carries Ringer's lactate, electrolytes,
And Pit back to an actively stimulated heart
And brain urgently generating contractions.

As we wait (the delay is ink on a blotter),
Fantasies expand to include stillbirth,
Strange aberrations, cerebral defects.
Hours rearrange themselves into integers,
Each minute more severely entwined,
Until, finally, the tenacious cervix yields,
Raises its temple gate one centimeter,
Then another, grudgingly. The bag ruptures;
Flood tide inundates the fecund plain
Our anxieties have disked and drilled with pain
All morning wide. Up ahead,
Armageddon looms, yet the delivery room
Invites us to disentomb our tiny, vital messiah
And rejoice in his momentary triumph over doom.

10/26 & 10/31/77 (01410)

[Beyond my immediate reach,] ‡ ∆

Beyond my immediate reach,
Russet and amber leaves
Rush into the lush traps
Vision sets with ear- and eye-nets.
An autumnal rhapsody spirals and tunnels,
Serpentine, scented gently with decay
Yet seething to rise above the cooling sun,
And materializes in the shape of a baby boy.

I stir from my hibernal hermitage
And acknowledge a child newly arrived,
A paradoxical life-sign in a time of dying,
A son, come to me out of the tumbling cascade.
I sing the season green again with my pride.
Each note foliates an entire forest;

10/29/77 (01411)

The Open Road Closes

A glassy opacity intervenes between me
And a completely porous gray sky.
Space on each plane of the mottled windshield —
That outside, running ever ahead,
And that enveloping my coffee-spotted breath —
Comprises the two distinct focal zones
In which the mind and its mindless disciples,
The eyes, attempt to differentiate and define life.

Within this floating, temperature-controlled environment,
I am actually aware of and can scientifically verify
My existence, my very mortality, by running my finger
Through the moisture and filmy millimeter
Breathing deposits as its by-products of escape.
How easy it is to redesign or erase the evidence.

Beyond is silence, a plenum filled with migraine-rain,
The imagination's broom closet, a vast drain
Sucking down, every second, resolute vows
Left untouched or incomplete by a mediocre brain,
As I penetrate deeper, each hour, the piece of future
Allotted me for the plot of being my body occupies.

Suddenly, the maelstrom dissolves. A dry, white clearing
Materializes. Horizon and concrete enter each other
In my rearview mirror, rising high above
A lushy, lilac-pocked valley, in which memory
Discerns all my old incarnations waving me home.
In a moment, I see the whole road — a circle closing.

11/5/77 — [1] (05560)

Final Recognition

When threatened by brain waves,
His mind hisses like an aroused alligator.
It refuses to cooperate,
                    much less
Respond to memory's sensual proddings.
Even nymphs yet swimming at the sedgy edges
            of an aging man's fantasies
      *

Fail to stimulate his atrophied thought-buds.
    Outraged by such disturbances,
No matter how infrequent, these days,
    when even reading the *Sunday Magazine*
And *TV Guide* requires total concentration,
    he retaliates by entrancing himself,
Pretending alien creatures have invaded
                                    his psyche,
Changed him into an all-knowing toad,
And commanded him to observe silence.
    Old friends, remembering when his eyes
Spoke five languages and his hands
    juggled divining rods and magicians' wands,
Plant ivy on the plot in their gossip-cemetery
They've reserved for him and his senile ways.
    He remains caged, crotchety, odorous.
The medicinal scent of decaying membranes
            and desiccated glands expands gaseously,
Until the rooms through which his abolished existence paces
            reject any more breath. He gasps,
Grasps his throat. The lungs collapse,
            thrust him into one last, paroxysmic spasm.
As images vanish from his cataracts,
                            he cries dry tears,
Whose invisible grief exonerates him from anonymity
    by allowing angels somewhere to detect his withered soul
    and scatter his wisdom among the earth's
                                    crepuscular dust.

11/5/77 — [2] (05561)

Mrs. Boswell △

She'd not disinherited herself
But of her own volition relinquished hold
Of the Steamboat Gothic manse,
That we might reinvest her eclipsed dream
With new music, youth's exuberance,
Set new roots, perpetuate the beauty
That had endeared her to this small town.
One April day, she moved out
And into a small house behind the fence,
*

Through whose caliginous overgrowth
She might still dream her mazy reveries
By staring at the ice-white diamond
Mounted in her memory's most expensive setting.

For nearly five years, we would wave
And lean across the fence, exchange cakes
And smiles, delicate irrelevancies,
Until Trilogy arrived. Then we three
Would venture through the dense brush,
Which I purposely never cut, to allow ambiguities
To thrive. Neither we nor Mrs. Boswell
Could ever quite clearly discern
The other's activities without spying
Or seeking out a mythical route to China
Through the rotted fence. We might accidentally
Catch glimpses of her entertaining guests
On the screened back porch or bird-watching,
Feeding the nearly domesticated squirrels
She'd call by name. She always knew
When we were away, out of town,
By the silence — no mower snorting uproariously,
No smoke lifting sinuously through oaks,
From the barbecue, no caged dogs barking,
No baby girl cavorting after rabbits and shadows
All spring and summer. She knew we were gone,
Other seasons, by our doused lights.
Perhaps the echo of our spirits
During those brief hiatuses merely ceased.

Yet we thrived, each in our repose.
Then her legs began their awful deterioration.
The clotting, the invidious clotting,
The exposed sores, the pain, whose complaint
She could no longer contain, changed everything.
The sweet, bucolic design of our years
Became tainted. Her pain contaminated us,
Made us self-conscious of our robust existence.
Yet imperceptibly at first, then slowly, noticeably,
My wife began to engender a new life
Within her fecund body. We rejoiced,
Wasted little time in telling our neighbor
Of our good fortune. Summer ripened with us,
Harvested its fruits, readied itself for autumn.
*

Together, we watched the leaves twitch,
Shiver, change pigments, slither away,
Acorns and walnuts drop, unpicked tomatoes
And pumpkins and squash decay to seeds,
Until October rains washed away the sun.

Two Sundays ago, we went to the hospital
To visit Mrs. Boswell. She seemed well enough,
Heady with new hopes that the pain
Would dissipate once her leg was amputated.
She took from her purse a dog-eared packet
Containing pictures of our house
The way she'd always remember it,
Furnished with her earthly possessions,
And two portraits of her adopted son, Robbie,
Waving good-bye with more finality
Than she'd realized at the time she snapped him
Mounting the airplane stairs, for Hawaii.
We celebrated, with her, two births that afternoon:
The imminent rejuvenescence of her spirit
And a baby, soon to be delivered to us, in St. Louis.

But when we came home with our new charge,
Two weeks later, and returned to the hospital room
Where we'd last seen Mrs. Boswell lively
And indomitable, we could only sense fatality.
Even the bouquets sought the shadows
Emanating from her whisperous intoxication.
We had not expected such a metamorphosis.
Her short breaths and absented, fathomless gaze,
The flat sheet, where her leg had been
And had never healed, the skeletal face
Claiming no relation to the eyes inside
Or the barely oxygenated brain behind them
All bore witness to a passing of orders.
We retreated into speechlessness. Aghast,
We backed away, into a sadness so devastating
Nothing could erase that last image of her
Lying there, voided of strength, wasted.
She would never see our little baby boy
Or hear the mower snorting or the dogs.

My stomach knotted with thoughts of her leaving,
This woman we'd grown to love for loving's sake,
*

With whom we'd associated intimately,
As though she'd somehow come with our house
When we moved in. "You'll be fine,"
I said, squeezing lightly her flaccid wrist.
"Is that the new little baby?" she murmured,
Eyeing my wife's purse at her side.
"No," Jan smiled, "but you'll be out in a while.
We'll bring him over in a few days."
Mrs. Boswell paused before slipping into the gloom
And, as if dredging up the last bit of lucidity
From the drugged pool in which she floated,
Said, "I guess we'll be fence-climbing soon."
Then she slumped from us, into numbness.

11/7/77 (02024)

The Birth of Time $^\Delta$

For LDB III;
my first poem for him

Two weeks have now transpired,
Breathed their shallow sighs across creation's breast.
Their chapped lips bear evidence of the tit,
Toward which their earthly instincts gravitate,
As they feed their wizened existence
Growing not in inches, rather by minutes,

Until their contracted limbs straighten slightly,
Begin coordinating with the rhythms
Light, sound, and temperature engender in space.
The days stretch like resilient flesh
To accommodate to their perpetuating shape.
Already, a lifetime's schedule is being registered.

Time's child is embraced in a crocheted bunting
Interlaced with hours unwound from skeins
Spinning around fate's spindled regulator.
The newborn's tiny, twisting fingers and toes,
Its smiles and frowns, metamorphosing inconsistently,
Remind us of our own outgrown origins,

Confound our speculative senses with nostalgia
And regret for an innocence at whose breast we suckled
When time first released us from immortality.
*

Now, we receive the blessing and accept responsibility
For seeing that these first few weeks flourish
And the years ahead mercifully nourish their progeny.

11/10/77 (01412)

Thirty-Second Spots: My Program, Breakfast Table † △

My family really takes it to school —
    it's new cholesterol!
Put a handle on it, and take it to school with you!
It's good for all the kids and for my family — bran cereal
                                   with strawberries.

Blue vanilla chocolate — it's in the mix!
    Get any kind of Fruit Loops for your children.
        They're new!
If you turn it over, it slides down,
        and if you turn it again, it comes downer!
It comes with milk.
        I love 'em!

Forty pounds-dollars.
    This is foamy medicine.
    It is medicine-krink.

11/30/77 (00699)

Apidae

Headlong, invisibly leashed, buzzed,
The servile workers focus on the hive.
They hover above concrete, nervously alert,
In an endless procession, like grackles
Clotting a summer's night with moony peripatetics.

Each evening, these same wearied creatures,
Embalmed in their bug-eyed vehicles,
Retreat from six-sided city routines
*

And reenter the caked air, like vapors
Escaping a superheated meerschaum bowl.

Somewhere in between arrival and flight,
Life's futile fight for survival is suspended.
Work ethics, myopic hype, delusions
Outrageously conceived to bear sweet fruit
Yield unknowingly to Mammon's stroking hands.

Laundered mornings tainted with aftershave
And barbed repartee wilt by noon
And fade into the jaded aroma of semen
Wasted in too hasty orgasm.
By three, all tired identities are fused;

Organs, faces, legs are fastened with screws
And glued to each other's boring chores.
Excess honey clogs the body's pores.
Wings droop from the day's mindless activities.
Antennae attract fatuous static and garble.

Finally away from the hive, at five,
Flying homeward, through the needle's eye,
Like driver ants lining the entire route
Between two distant colonies, they pause,
Awed by the heat or cold, the preemptory dusk

That enfolds their brittle, overly delicate husks.
At once, the future responds to their knocking,
Unlocks the garage door, to let them enter
Their own four-walled microcosm,
Where the actual rigors of living commence.

Prayers and lullabies and television's persiflage
Comprise the litanies they weave into sleep
They submit to without considering how or when
Their release from death will eventually come about.
Each mate masturbates the other's dreams,

While their issue commit premarital incest —
Sister with brother, unmarried mother
With undiscovered husband/child/lover.
The buzzing turns to groaning moans and snoring.
Midnight drugs the senses. Silence ensues.

Ultimately, life awakens in every shoebox
Where the resting insects have chosen to nest.
*

Yawning wings and clicking heels reverberate,
As swarms lift and merge with morning's traffic,
While the recurrence of resurrection goes unnoticed.

12/1/77 — [1] (05562)

Divine Inspiration

His two flounder-white eyes
Are Eucharistic wafers he offers the day,
Which kneels above him in penitential supplication
For having dawned unannounced
        And interrupted his reverential occupations.
His profound forgiveness, although presumptuous,
        Sings through the frozen twilight,
        Like fingers plucking Celtic harp strings.
Something about his absolute Mosaical command
        Demands the senses' attention.
Grass thatched with snow, trees unfleshed,
Convolvuluses of clouds and cows
        Connecting the frozen ground with the Absolute,
        In a kinship of ever-changing shapes,
All awaken to the touch of his fingers on their tongues.
        His entries on the page of their existence
Assure them a decent and lasting place
In a civilization's heritage he's been asked,
        By his Maker, to perpetuate in verse.
Having accomplished his Communion,
        The robed poet lifts his golden chalice
To the Sun, toasts his earthly congregation,
        And retires to his quarters,
Where, in total submissive repose,
        He'll await the next awakening of his mortal soul.

12/1/77 — [2] (05563)

Premature Death by Drowning

Alone, he navigates the mazy sea lanes
Etched in his heart's memory,
        Whose ocean floated, in their youthful days,
        *

A fresh-fleshed son and daughter,
A wife exuberant, Isadora-like in her bare feet,
Lithe and scarved in the wind's colors,
And a sleek-waisted Athenian athlete/poet/lover.

The perpetually foul weathers sour his juices
To bilious melancholia,
Rust his bones with arthritic friction,
Jaundice his eyesight, until flying fish
And invisible manta rays become interchangeable
On a horizon that never rises or sets,
Rather postpones its diurnal actions indefinitely,

As if its silence might be antecedent to all time
And its cosmic mauve tint portending storms
Mariners call galactic typhoons. He shrinks from the glow
Rising to starboard. A silvery-tongued funnel
Points its menacing finger in his face, accusative,
Admonitory, postulating the end of the search
In which he's participated with his grief, all these years.

Stray cormorants wheel in the confused chaos of currents
Converging in tidal waves twenty stories high.
Debris composed of sea urchins, barnacled keels,
Fantasy's half-naked mermaids submerged during adolescence,
And anemones, killer whales, protozoans
Pocks his eyes, while his soaked limbs stiffen
In premature rigor mortis. Tying himself to the mast,

He abdicates all further responsibility for his fate.
Shrill banshee winds rip off his ears and clothing,
Cast his inconsequent body to the howling wolves
Lapping at his scuttled vessel. Numbness overcomes him,
As a hole in the ocean opens slowly to engorge his soul.
His relinquishment is a mere perfunctory motion
Previously guaranteed to Beelzebub in exchange for earthly freedom.

Now, bubbles lift around him like leaves breaking from buds,
As he descends through cold, opaque, fathomless volumes,
Toward his final resting place. In a flash,
The onrushing waves evacuate his remains on a shore
Smooth as porphyry, mottled with exquisite florescences,
Where his lithe, naked wife and two beautiful children
Lie beneath an endless sun, awaiting his return.

12/1/77 — [3] (05564)

Quetzalcoatl

Flute-hues undress before my celibate ears,
In a pleasing striptease tinged with heat
Bubbling my benign blood to a slow seizure.
Percussed cymbals send the skin into shivers.
Drumsticks whip my sex buds; they explode,
Full-blown, into love-leaves blooming under a rain forest
Dripping, from morning-glory horns, felonious bone-tones
That entice the lesbian tendencies inside me
Out of hiding, into the open, for public showing.
    I writhe unself-consciously in my chair,
Drawing off one article of my clothing
With each musical climax, until, completely naked,
I sculpt my clay into a shape the torrid air
Can accommodate to its prearranged design.
    Instantaneously, the strange faces congregate
Before my sinewy yet sensually breasted thorax
To examine the supple, bony chest, which plunges,
    Recovers, as my uncontrollable cunt gesticulates
The inarticulate *langue* of deaf-and-dumb lovemaking.
    At once, the music subdues me. I am seized
In a creamy ecstasy so sourly sweet
    Even the eyes absorb my pleasure in utter blindness.
    Rape is such an unmercifully pure arrangement
Made between the body and its righteous enemy, the mind,
    That nothing, not even total rhythmic cessation,
Can stave off its inevitable undoing. I am ravaged
    By my own escaped inhibitions. In this room,
The gawky spectators, who glare with Grosz-snickers
And mouthfuls of gold fillings, can't defeat me
    In this free flight above the sedgy edges of sexuality.
My soaring is prismatic, outrageous, chaotic as limbo.
    A thousand liberated Phoenixes lift into the air,
Carrying with them platelets, chromosomes, fractured genes
Spraying the stratosphere with my most secret blueprints,
    While what was once a palpable being
Becomes invisible dust dissipating in the estranged sky.
When the lights materialize, my chair is bafflingly empty.
    In its place is a nameless, shapeless silhouette,
A memory, trace, whisperous, nonexistent effluvium
    Of someone who happened on this place accidentally
    *

And was incidentally transformed from a nonentity
    Into a cosmic force absorbed by nature
On the eve of its original and solitary creation
    As an agent of the great god Animacula.
When the lights dim and reappear for a final time
    And all the people dissolve into inebriated oblivions,
A faint suggestion lingers beyond the fading electric echoes:
A fresh breath of dead flesh resurrected from silence.
    Mystic metamorphosis returns me to my senses,
Anesthetized, filled with ageless forgetting, alive,
Covered unexplainably, from toe to face, with ejaculate.
I abandon my hollow shell, regather my energies,
And dissolve through the exit, into a familiar universe,
    To resume my union with Mrs. W. C. Prufrock
Before she misses my perfectly compatible companionship.

12/1/77 — [4] (01320)

Frequenter of Nightspots

In these sleazy nightclubs,
Inebriated by cheap house wine,
Out on the road every other week,
I remind myself in a vaguely literate way
Of Toulouse-Lautrec visiting Parisian haunts,
In quest of illusory May Belforts
And agile Jane Avrils to metamorphose into chalky silhouette.

Suddenly, something intervenes. The distance confronts me.
I see Stephen Crane sleeping in ten-cent tubercular dives,
Reading *Leaves of Grass*, dreaming Henry Fleming and
Maggie alive,
Contracting catarrh, sweaty agues, dying
            in stark anonymity,
And I wonder where the road not taken leads
    whenever I assume quill and plunge headlong
Into the blank pages, to discover what the soul withholds.
    The silence is excruciating.
            Why can't my created words project aloud
To the nightly crowds insulated against scorn
            and inevitable truth, without offense,
Instead of sticking to my intellect's solar plexus?
Is there no music capable of translating me
*

along vertebrae supporting night's spine?
The wine climbs down the nubile sides,
Enters my stem. The need to micturate
   elevates me to higher purposes. My intelligence
Streams out, douses a thousand fires in the queen's abode,
While I watch innocently from the sidelines,
   an unnoticed pyromaniac
Who goes around setting his own fires without getting credit.

Someday, when the juices have all dried
And the veins have constricted to half their size,
   I'll recall in dull reverie the long journeys,
The aimless walks through the heart's Bowery,
In search of the experimental ichor to record life
In the brittle dialect of ritualistic truth,
   and I'll recall the vapid, unconsummated evenings,
Latent yet unrequited, in which ladies of the night
   circled, like death-moths, about my undeviable occupation
   of versifying, trying to penetrate to my glands,
While with unquenchable abandon, I wrote the tones
   that lifted, vapor-soft, to my ears,
   as I dissolved inside the vast earth's stirrings.
Perhaps thirty years hence, the compulsion to speak
   in inky calligraphy will have dissipated,
And I'll be able to direct my cursive urgencies
   through the penis alone.
For now, this sensual pen will have to suffice.

12/1/77 — [5] (01321)

Ozymandias II

Caesars, Pharaohs, *Führers*, mandarins, and czars
Are ghostly nomads traipsing over sands
That expand past the edges of memory
And fill the brain's fissures with irritable fears.

Like preposterous Magi, they arrive mystically,
Materializing unpredictably on gusts of summer wind
Or as whisperous puffs of smoke or aromas
Redolent of sumac, bituminous coal, sewage.

Every so often, my ineffable imagination,
A Gethsemane, Himalayas, Mount Zion,
*

Rises before their ageless, destinationless caravans,
Arrests and invites them to dally beside its oasis.

On nights like those, my mind's demons mutiny,
Seek refuge in the moist, fleshy female folds
That constitute the carnal delights of their harem.
Lethean ladies, shades of Damascus and Lesbos,

Suck the blood from my aorta, drug my soul,
Expose me to humanity's vanities and gross insanities,
Persuade me to put on robes of the Apocalypse,
Make rapine and pillage and rape my main goals.

Comatose, unable to act in my own best interest,
I surrender to their sadomasochistic metamorphosis.
Even charity and faith, yesterday's queens,
Become today's hags, abdicating tomorrow.

On mornings after such unanticipated debaucheries,
Waking is a chaos composed of hardened semen
And menstrual rust strewn like galactic dust
From a cosmic storm accelerating through the universe.

I rise, rub the calcified sleep from my eyes,
And try to focus on the evacuated landscape
Stretching, forsaken and desolate, to the mind's horizon.
Nothing stirs, radiating outward forever.

Finally, as I wander, days, for traces of life,
A solitary, faceless lunar apparition,
Locked in a crater formed by vast, serrated dunes,
Blooms. A looming, Medusa-like, thorny cactus

Fills the flaking, silvered back of vision's mirror
With the jagged, totally effaced image of a man
Doomed to survive shifting oblivions unmoved,
And I recognize myself taking root in the future's sand.

12/3/77   (05565)

Living on the Site of the Old Bailey Estate

December winds dismembered themselves
Against the irregularly shaped eaves
And honed hexagonals of the old, towered house
*

Leaning precariously as a heeling sailboat,
In that first snowy squall of the season.

Inside, all united in a common prayer
That the fiendish elements wouldn't penetrate the dikes.
Objects inanimate and breathing, alike,
Huddled against the steadfast enemy.
Draughts were another generation's laughter.

Suddenly, a report of undetermined scorn
Blasted from basement, through abdomen and thorax,
To attic, in fantastical chain reaction.
Plaster, lathing, wallpaper, and bones
Commingled, undifferentiated with infiltrating flakes,

Until the house dissolved in a hoary fog.
Before morning, the pervasive white invaders
Evacuated their occupied positions without a trace.
Only remnants of the hand-laid stone foundation
Suggest that the place was more than an ossuary

And that, once, a family may have actually disappeared
At the height of a holocaust, as if a sinkhole
Had drawn their entire existence through its wide fissure,
Into depthless silence. Outside, my ears detect snow
Trying to probe my poetic elegy for an opening.

12/6 — [2?] & 12/13/77 — [1] (05566)

Looking for a New Home ᐃ

I leave the three of them sleeping soundly
In 5:30's sea-bound lacunae.
The chambered nautilus in which we exist
Fades into the fog I slip through like sound
Disappearing in deafness. Forgetting chases me out of town.

My serenely blessed, shallow-breathing creatures,
So docile, so totally surrendered to the silence
That subordinates their sweet dreams, in ageless parentheses,
To the actual anatomy of their soon-to-awaken bodies,
Will presently discover me vanished from their routines.

Neither fortune nor cleft-footed fame
Could have gathered my clothing and packed my bags.
*

Only the loneliness of not knowing where to go
Or whether going nowhere was really my elected goal
Made me take to the highway in this unlikely season,

When Christmas beckons us in head and heart
To the tabernacle where atoning for our souls' misdeeds
Is only a matter of holding and kissing each other.
Bereft of children and wife, directionless, aggrieved
By the deathly Mephistophelean suggestion of method

Attending my evanescent yet inexorable madness,
I grope for the reason my rhyming tenaciously withholds,
As though the voiceless, elegiac ode I write to myself
Might contain, in its carefully unlaced analysis,
An explanation for my behavior, redolent of salvation.

The road lengthens as my patience grows short.
Rain disfigures its even concrete patina
With disquieting, misshapen visages that rise up
And assail my eyes with teeth the windshield wipers
Refuse to remove with their half-moon swipes.

Soon, the land over which I travel
Turns to days, to glass cracking under the weight
Of my passage. The years change from cement
To oily macadam to bedrock and chat to dust,
As my shadow fails to keep pace behind me

And finally drops from sight. Still, I inch ever westward,
Toward one frustrating sunset after another,
In an attempt to end the search and return home
By stepping through dusk's dust-clustered prism
And letting its grits erase all memory of my leaving.

Only, the nomad instinct that gnaws my bones
Won't give up until the skeleton is clean.
Night closes in around my cold solitude.
In half-dreams, I watch my boy and girl
Grow up, bury my wife, embrace marriage.

I feel them kneel on a barrier of air,
The earth's numb tympanum, just above us,
And hear their prayers for their parents, who sleep again
In repose. Now, I know they'll move to this house,
Which I first found alone and reserved for our eternity.

12/13/77 — [2] (01413)

The Lecher

Ladies, naked save for lacy peignoirs
That drape languidly over their peaked bodies,
Dance behind fantasy's scrim curtain.
Footlights emanating from his bloodshot eyes
Cauterize these lithe creatures, in half-strides,
Leaping to keep their bare feet from bleeding
On the horned thorns of his erogenous desire.
The ritual they reenact is inspired by the chase
Of Thisbe and Pyramus, Beatrice and Dante.
Their ripe chastity begs to be violated
By anyone capable of climbing on and staying
While the racing crests of their spumy waves,
Threatening to expunge him in a premature ejaculation
All the way in, climax fractiously
Against the endless shore their satisfied forms,
Lying prone in spent, nubile excitement, create.
Fantasy stands before the shadowy stage,
Takes off his shirt and perspiration-stained pants,
And enters the air like the aroma of moistened soap.
One from among the Lethean maidens calls his name,
Waves him back just as his painful genitals
Explode in her face. She submits to his cradling,
Allows him to surround her in his dizzy lovemaking,
Until all that remains is her lacy gown,
Fallen like a solitary feather of a meadowlark
Frightened from her cover by an awkward hawk.
She slumbers inside the cocoon his fire has spun,
Numb, unconcerned that he has turned her life
Outside in or that when she revives,
He will already have left her, forever,
To fend for herself while he locates newer flesh
For his insatiable appetite. Just now,
At midstage in the completely darkened theater,
Naked, barefoot concubines in sheer lust
Pace gracefully over his flaccid manhood.
Although their teasing torments him to rage,
He's unable to recover sufficiently for the blood
To reintoxicate his arteries and enlarged heart.
Holding hands, they weave invisible strands
In a Maypole dance about his deflated spirit,
*

Until he's a tired wasp caught in a web
In which they'll continue their sinuous attack
Without ever once touching his restive flesh,
Until the day he wakes and rips the net to shreds.

12/14/77   (05567)

The Opal

A Christmas gift for Jan

Peering into the world's milky star-shine,
My eyes divine your scintillating features,
Iridescent against night's black velvet,
Draped to highlight dreaming's precious designs.
In your opaline profile, I see the whole lambent sky.

Your tiny face, with its pixie ears
And nose so Rodin-wrought;
Those delicately blown eyes,
Like Christmas ornaments fastidiously decorated
In a quaint, crisp Swiss atelier;
Your glistening lips, reminiscent of pears
More delicious unbitten than kissed;
And fawn-smooth, tawny hair,
Like a halo below which your moods metamorphose . . .
All issue from fissures in a celestial opal.

And if, indeed, these are nature's imperfections
That dynamite my mind with coruscating light rays,
Then I will always choose a fragile, blemished gem
To wear suspended from my marriage-laced chain of years.
You, prized wife, are my life's beautiful jewel.

12/20/77   (02251)

Homo Sapiens

I breathe the new day into being
Long before Morpheus relinquishes his hold
On my cryogenic, dream-drugged sleep.
The brain pulsates on the heart's frequency,
*

Keeping the meter free-flowing and alert
To nuances that every so often arise
As the lungs, in crazy exultation, taste the sun,
Under a million layers of living epidermis.
My veins chart no threnodies this morning,
Rather pound the interstices of their cages,
Setting up a vascular reverberation
Throughout my bones, whose complaint
Escapes as purgative sweat at every pore.
The membranes turn wet as cold rain,
While the senses my ephemeral body houses
Soar from bed, abandon sidereal speculations,
And enter my head, on a yawn's backwash,
Like a child drawn into the ocean's embrace
In the arms of a wave receding from shore.
My eyes flame. My nose invites the air
Into its caves. My ears are aware of hair
And fluid moving sounds along mine shafts,
To synapses, from where they'll be alchemized
In the mind's roaring cauldrons. My teeth
Bite the lips and tongue alive, bathe them
In brine, until the sting is such ecstasy
Saliva refuses to flow from its tiny orifices.
Toes and fingertips and every limb
Twitch, flex, bend, and extend
To the physical extremities within their grasp.
Cobwebs, stretched, like bridgework,
From tendon and ligament and cartilage, endlessly,
To opposite members of their muscular structure,
Snap, float to blood's ocean floor as sediment
To be carried away as the organism gains strength,
Roars forward like a Cyclops
Asserting its ascendancy over its enemies.
Like a full moon, I achieve total control
Of my potential growth before noon is conceived.
My existence is known to me through hunger,
Fierce movements of feces, urine, flatus,
And by the mirror's ritual of expected reflections.
Harmony, symmetry, physical stability,
And an ineffable intuition of being created
For a higher earthly purpose than mere work
In the service of the Devil or for personal aggrandizement
*

Move me, now, through potter's fields, whose urns
Are bumper-locked automobiles, and churches,
Whose sacraments and vestments are three-piece suits
And computerized invoices with terms set
At thirty days net, to the higher elevations of Helicon,
To whose base I come daily to pray for inspiration.
Neither do the ghosts of Moses and Plato stir,
Nor do I know the few contemporary poets
Who languish here, like vagrant bums, with me,
Yet my bones are composed of older songs
Than those in Ecclesiastes and the Greek odes.
They resonate with tones of the great bell
Whose strokes proclaimed the earth's creation.
My wisdom keeps man's history from dying.

1/3/78 — [1]   (05568)

Bagworms △

The eyes gaze opaquely,
In alienated amazement,
As his erratic scrawl
Crawls ferociously from its brain's cocoon,
Across the notebook leaf
                              and,
               backwards, itself rappels
        onto
               the following page,
Where it fastens itself again
And begins eating one horizontal vein
                              after
                              another,
Until all empty space,
Filled with its calligraphic existence,
Is finally rendered vermiculate, spotty,
Devoured by its insatiable appetite
For embodying reality in metaphor.

        Over a period of years,
The tree on which his ideas have thrived
    Has defoliated. Only brief quotations
    Still bother to attack its decayed pith,
While the unnourished worms —
*

The cursive verse in his faded notebooks —
Wither, back in their brittle, obsolete cocoon.

1/3/78 — [2] (05569)

Celibacy: Midwest Cold Snap △

Nature's fenestration is a mezzotint of flakes,
Whose intricate prismatic facets
Glisten in abstraction, with seductive designs
That invigorate the blood, persuade the avid eyes
To run unclothed over a frozen, wintry antipode.

Each crystal is a mystical nightgown,
Through whose diaphanous folds vision slips
Invisibly as ether, glimpsing farmhouses,
Bright-hued implements hibernating outside,
Brittle cornstalks, rivers with stilled tongues.

The land is a fecund lady on birth control,
Who lies perfectly silent while I fondle her tits,
Finger her rigid clitoris with my imagination,
To stimulate the slightest recognition of my existence.
Manipulation fails to arouse her drowsing desire,

Yet my pupils persist in registering images
In snowdrifts, arthritic shivering trees,
Ghost towns along the Mississippi and Illinois,
As if seeds sleeping beneath the surface of verse
Might catch fire, explode in frenzied girandoles,

And inspire my shallow-breathing solitude with child.
Only, no impassioned cries arise from the prairie.
The marriage of poetry and her soul mate, winter,
Is unconsummated. Its postponement until April
Aborts my orbiting the source where flakes are formed.

1/9/78 (05427)

Arriving by Train △

When finally the countryside
Begins inexorably to slide into billboards,
Hillside enclaves of costly suburban housing,
*

Frequent crossing-gate bulbs frenetic as squirrel eyes,
Factories breathing ocherous exhalations
And the train passes raucously by the terminal,
Coming into sight as we go on by it,
The mind is beleaguered with half-doubts
(Perhaps in haste, I boarded the wrong train;
Maybe while I was asleep last night, near Altoona
Or Terre Haute, they changed engines,
Shuffled my car and destination, unannounced),
Until the adrenaline-filled blood stands still,
Runs upstream, the way flooded tributaries
Often do, as forward motion grinds into silence.
At once, my imagination is both control room
And myriad-tracked yard. Switches snap
Open and closed, like lobster claws, behind us.
Lanterns swivel in a green-red blur.
I hold tightly, anticipating the release of brake shoes,
The abrupt jostling of knuckle couplings,
The angry, burning turning of roller bearings,
As a snub-nosed yard switcher grabs hold
Of the observation car, while the streamline
Gulf, Mobile & Ohio diesel is retired.
Somewhere, a smooth whine moves us,
Directs its charge into a stall, crawdadlike,
Inching tailfirst into the vast barn,
Along concrete platforms, toward the lighted bumper
Proclaiming "Ann Rutledge" to the animated people
Waiting behind the glass partition to greet us.
Suddenly, all the friction disappears. Reverberations
Sift into memory's insulation. The security
Of narrow aisles, gray and green enamel paint,
Thick-glass light fixtures, stainless steel,
The musky aroma of dusty, plush-cut fabrics,
Curtains, and pinch-released window shades
Dissipate in the face of daily reality.
And I regret, as always, having reached the station,
Arriving home, leaving the open road
Without knowing when I'll climb the folding stairs
And mount the vestibule again,
Especially since it's now been eighteen years
Since the last passenger train brought me back
From the phasing-out period of my youth's halcyon days.

1/10/78   (05425)

Degrees

For Elaine Wesley

Some come and go and never even wonder
                              why
Cataclysmic silence parenthesized their lives.

Others merely smile the peaceful repose of sleep,
                              on dying,
As though the slightest disapprobation
    might keep them awake through eternity.

A few, like me and you, are always outraged
                              by
Fate's imposition on history, intellect,
    and the body's desire to perpetuate itself forever.

We outdistance time by hiding inside the poetry
                              we write,
Reciting to generations not even conceived.

The rest, with blessed delusions of election and salvation,
                              fly,
In confused spirals, about a distant light,
    until they flip into a bottomless abyss.

Only a handful among the scions of mankind,
                              by denying
Earthly pleasures, possessions, and celebrity,
    ever return to their soul's place of birth.

1/11/78 — [1] (02250)

Sylvia's Husband △

It's not so much the unheroic pain of growing old
That aggravates his equilibrium,
Because he doesn't know it's been going on
Since birth, or that he's grown used to making excuses
For frequent inadequacies and ill-timed truces.
Rather, the drear recognition
That the distinction between decrepitude and youthful flesh
Can no longer be made by his sensibilities
Arises whenever his tired, granulated eyes
*

Arrest the mind from its vacant stare
Long enough to register a fair young barmaid
Dressed in sheer black crepe, curvaceous
Of cheek, buttocks, breasts redolent of erect nipples,
And head encircled in nymph-blond hair
Cascading like water lifting from a fountain,
Only to then find the dulled nerve endings unstimulated,
Completely drugged by the chilled rosé she's served,
His body just another rolled and pleated piece
Of the tufted chair in which he's been seated for hours.

No amount of pseudoengineered sensuality
Driven by musical speakers, coruscated from lights
Concealed in the ceiling and beneath smoky grottoes,
Or absorbed by contact with collegiate couples
Leaking love from their speech and touching cheeks
Can regenerate the age-stretched ecstasies
That once filled his resilient vessels to exuberant overflowing.
Now, loneliness, like a sleazy, flabby, wizened courtesan,
Accompanies him in dreams and waking practicalities.
Her nagging blandishments have convinced him
That what intellect he possessed is nonexistent,
Has given way to getting through each day on a whim,
Void of logic, syntax. He actually grunts and moans
The inarticulate, disowned poetics that rarely flash
Across his memory. Somewhere, buried in the vague scape
That drapes, like scrim curtains, the stage on which
Silhouettes of a faded lady parade before his teary eyes,
He remembers himself as the wide-eyed writer
Who died when his young wife tried to include him in her suicide.

1/11/78 — [2] (02678)

Scroll of a Dead Sea Survivor △

My days are spaces in a ragged sea scroll
Scribbled on at random, unrolling erratically as winds,
Talmudic their message, Mosaic their brittle beauty.
No matter my resolve, they rip like leaves
Breeze-blown, sift inevitably to the dust
That surrounds the tree that owns the family
From which I've sprouted without being discovered.

The poets that etched my genes with verse
Converge on my mind, recall me to the time
When Hasidic scholars would squat all day,
Reciting Judges, Ecclesiastes, and Deuteronomy.
I am their progeny, a doomed soothsayer
Whose task it is to reiterate the old codes
Upon which the law of the land was predicated.

Their wailing, incantatory music
Fills my anonymous soul with hope
Of one day returning to the Dead Sea alive,
To receive YHWH's ordained ablution.
My heart composes heroic lyrics to refit Scripture
With new meters, new humanistic ecumenism
That lifts my spirit to blessed, ineffable ecstasy.

Each morning, my waking turns the scroll
A single notch. I soar on its wisdom,
Shimmer in its revelations of war and famine,
Peace, education's advancement, of disease
Being daily unmasked and eradicated.
Although they're unheard by others, I trust the words
That translate my poems from the dust of ancient sand.

1/11 — [3] & 1/13/78 (02679)

Traveler's Advisory

Last night's light cascade of snow,
Followed by its continuous peppering this morning,
Through which I slip, returning from Tipton,
To Byzantium, makes this highway a stage
For Arthur B. Davies' diaphanous ladies.

Each speeding vehicle levitates their spirits,
Sets them writhing in orgasmic eddies
That tantalize my imagination, invite me
To abandon my fastidious task of driving home
And enter their seasonal celebration.

Everywhere, these voiceless ballerinas
Pirouette in the argentiferous air.
By threes, in pairs, individually,
*

They distract me with their uninhibited gymnastics,
Ask me to suspend my defenses, escape with them

To an isle washed by purple seas,
Seeded with camphor and ilex trees,
By ancient dynasties. My eyes dilate excitedly,
Come unfocused, as a passing tractor-trailer
Wraps my vision, multifold, in mummies' gauze.

When I awaken, the ladies have dematerialized.
The snow has changed componentially, so that sand
Undulates, like thousands of slender water snakes,
Across the gray-white desert before me,
And I am a stranger stranded in an alien land,

Being pelted by tiny, granular stones
As though branded an adulterer from older times.
Now I know I should have genuflected to my senses,
Surrendered my soul when fantasy presented itself
For the asking. I could be basking on a beach

If only I'd have made the necessary leap
From reality's ledge, the deathly plunge upward,
Out of the mind's rigid fundus, into the zone
Where snow, genes, bodily desires, and God
Become the poem that outlives its own victim.

1/12/78   (05570)

Seduced by Sirens

One week ago today, I left my family,
Stepped off the known world's edge
By boarding a vessel headed for Capitalismus
And other navigable Midwest figments,
And disappeared. The rigid transition
From happy, loquacious compatibility
To solipsistic silence, fraught with fears
Of crashing on shoals and reefs at night,
Being torpedoed by anachronistic U-boats,
In broad daylight, dying of scurvy
Or starvation, lasted the entire passage.
Even after I arrived at my destination,
*

Phobias with which I'd never held conversation
Demanded my attention, began shouting out doubt
About my manhood, accusing me of cowardice
For having abandoned my wife and two children.
Nowhere in the foxed copies of Milton,
Shakespeare, Melville, Conrad, and Donne
I'd brought along to comfort me in my exile
Was mention made of a land so unavailing,
So desolate that not even algae, bacteria,
Or primordial cocci spores could vegetate,
Yet on these anfractuous shores
Did I finally come to rest, a skeleton at best,
Destined to watch my body dehydrate,
Wizen to the size of a brittle cornstalk
Crackling in the wind. Only then
Did I realize that the shrill whimpering
That haloed my comatose brain was a dog whistle
My lonely, forfeited desire for my family
Had been blowing just below my ears.
Only then did I recognize that the painful silence
Was meant to accompany my punishment,
Like a mistress paid to listen while I repeat,
To the end of my life, every tender, gentle word
My wife and I ever set free between us.

1/15/78   (05571)

Word-Seeds ^Δ

A bouquet for Jan

My words emit slender tendrils,
Whose subtle bending
Penetrates the dense layers of intimacy
You've neglected tending.
They insinuate your inarticulate resolve,
Dissolve your obdurate fears
Of being touched by gentle flowers
Sprouting in thin air.

Now that your garden is all aroma
Of harvested lilac and clover
*

Tilled under, my hybrid words
Rise, like eager spores,
Toward reincarnation. Entwined
In yours, they search the air
For the mind of an unborn child to inspire
With their slender, bending tendrils.

1/20–21/78 (01047)

Pelicans ^Δ

They strafe and glide close into shore,
By the rocky spit of Port Everglades,
Where invisible mullet by the millions
Await their hot beaks and oblivion.

Hovering like rigid airships docking,
They watch for the perfectly mitered angle,
Then drop like spiders letting go
Or mail passing through a chute

And flawlessly thread the needle's eye
Each time their pterodactylic shapes
Penetrate the impasto surface. The feeding
Goes on, unimpassioned, for hours,

Just within the limits of my vision.
Whatever frenetic screams or fright
Attend the mass annihilation are absorbed
In the roaring hooves of palominos,

Atop whose bare backs the pelicans ride
Like cowboys mounted on rodeo broncos,
As they allow their prey to dissolve,
Their muscles to regain needed resilience.

Repeatedly, they lift, ponderous, controlled,
From the whisperous wave-nests, climb,
And initiate the same predatory ritual,
While I stand here on the beach, amazed,

Meditating on these prehistoric scenes
As though, locked within this tableau,
*

My eyes should be capable of evoking
Meaning relevant to my life's design,

Possibly as an omen of holocaust, plague,
The Apocalypse, the soul's lonely exodus
From the body at death, the plucking of roses
In May. Only, no symbol is manifest,

Nor should it be so merely because
I've been trained to arrest time,
Make slides of elements sliced from nature,
For examination under my poetoscope.

When I look up from my writing tablet,
The ocean is a wide ice floe
Bordered on three sides by a maddening abyss.
The birds have disappeared; silence abides.

1/25/78   (02245)

Airy Pursuits ^Δ

For my blessed charge Trilogy Maya

She calls the sea gulls "eagles," believing them so
Because her dad revels in twisting sounds into pretzels
To be thrown to the wind or eaten for their salty tang.
Although realizing the outrageous beaked creatures
Are more blatantly predatory,
She prefers pelicans to "eagles" and pipers
Because her daddy comes undone with excitement
Each time one dives, from heights, underwater,
To seize from invisibility a shimmering mullet for survival.

Notions of inculcated tastes, brainwashing, dogma
Float like the birds wheeling above the ocean,
Back and again, circling, banking,
Ever eying the changing zones of perspective
Over which they go in search of "total" knowing.
Not beauty of form, symmetry, graceful shape,
Or docility can distract the mind from its fanatical belief
That nothing supersedes prevailing tastes, fashion, fads
Dictated by changing tides, winds aloft, philosophy.

So, hand in hand, like Eve and Milton leaving Eden,
We walk, my three-year-old and I,
Talking of things that exist on this catechism of beach,
Whose future proceeds no further than we can see
And whose past dissolves with our footprints.
We name objects, study functions, memorize sounds,
With thirty-nine combined years of consciousness,
And, sustained by a colossal cosmological delusion,
Claim suzerainty over the Domain of Universal Knowledge.

1/26/78 — [1] (01415)

Troika: His First-Quarter Birthday ^Δ

Plump as summer squash,
Like a ripe, tumescent love apple
Dappled with overstuffed tufting,
Happy, docile, a smooth-skinned pear,
Whether cradled at his mother's breast
Or lying flat on his flabby back,
To whom all come adazzle,
In reverence, Troika is lush fruit
From Jan's garden. He gets tasted by us
Without our fearing violating ancient mandates
And seems so sweet and dulcet
That tongue and ears confuse their senses;
Each hears his cooing,
Both touch his honey-glazed flesh
When our lips fly through the air
To reach his nested shape.

Often, without warning,
The acorn between his legs,
A fuming Vesuvius,
The true Fountain of Youth,
Lets loose a Lilliputian freshet
That catches us off guard,
Inundates the queen's castle with a stream
That carries our laughter past practicality,
To precincts where giddiness
And insanity fuse in spasms of sheer delight.
His eyes merely twinkle, as if,

*

Despite the uncontrollability
He's so conveniently mastered at three months,
Years of disciplined training were required
To achieve such predictable responses.
His satisfaction rewards our frustration.

To commemorate his first-quarter birthday,
We lay a trinket at his feet.
Although the ameba-like hands and fingers
Can't yet grasp the plastic rattle,
Fitted with google-eyes glued to a static face
On one side, mirror on the other,
His fascination attaches us
To eyes sighting eyes, ears retrieving the beat
Of beads speaking, to each other,
Rhythms derived from my wife's pulsations.
Troika is kicky as a chicken
Pecking his way out of an egg, into existence.
He's a babe wearing our name,
On loan from a distant incarnation,
A manifestation of our own innocent faith
In the perpetuation of love greater than ours.

1/26/78 — [2] (01414)

Coconut Grove, 1978 ^Δ

How is it possible that, at three and a half,
Trilogy is able to captivate me?
Does something in the genes
That is uniquely, irrefragably female
Breach all time barriers at birth
And assert its dynamic, sensual hold
Over its host, coerce her, first,
To entrance her father, for practice,
Before stepping off the precipice?

I follow from boutique to shop,
Stopping only when she decides,
Wants to slide through crepe and Helenka,
Linger wistfully at a candy counter
Before entering the flux again,
*

Then pause to assimilate shapes of jade,
Turquoise, Etruscan gold, welded copper,
Pastry, cassette tapes, stuffed ducks,
Prewashed jeans, and proprietors
Tired and unamused by the promenade
Of feckless spectators come to let
The day spume through the Grove's drain.
I acquiesce to her hungry protestations
By locating a table in a gay restaurant.

She laughs from her soul at dogs
Gathered outside the window,
Notices an ambulance, waves at children
Passing in strollers, counts cars.
Her awareness is a bitter reminder to me
Of how life, congested like this,
Automatically becomes hieroglyphics
On my mind's blotter rather than
Reason for wonderment at man's leisure.

"I'm so glad we're together, Dad."
Bridges leading from my heart outward,
In all directions, collapse. I dive
Into her siren-filled sea of smiles
And hide behind her vibrant eyelids,
Safely inside, as though, being close,
We might be protected from interlopers
Called years — life's highwaymen —
Experience, waiting just up ahead.

"I sure like your pretty vest, Daddy,"
She says, pausing between bites
Of french fries and hamburger with bacon.
Trilogy is both mistress and wife,
My blond-headed leprechaun and Veronica,
Rejuvenescence of my spirit, a moon
Reflecting the best of both parents,
My friend, who, on sunny days like this,
Billows my soul with pride, accompanies me
To the other side of my existence,
Where, once again, I am twenty-three,
Unencumbered by familial responsibility,
Freely sprung and uninhibited
As a Faulknerian interior monologue.

"Daddy, if I could just have dessert,
Everything would be perfect."
"What would you covet, my dear love?"
"A cookie — a giant chocolate chip!"
On a park bench, we each sit munching
The delicious minutes of this afternoon,
In vaudevillian silence, savoring the taste
Of our extraordinary relationship,
Until we've devoured the entire sun.

With great haste, we leave the Grove,
As though to keep the coach,
Horses, and glass slippers from metamorphosing.
All the way back, her head on my lap,
She sleeps, while I construct dreams
And tuck them under her twitching lids
Surreptitiously, that she might never know
I was the one who insinuated her psyche
With wishes that we remain soul mates forever.

1/28/78   (01416)

The Kids' Playground, Lago Mar △

Who ever dreamed of being able to climb,
In broad daylight, a giant spider's net
And, on reaching its apogee, see ocean
Dotted with mystical flying fish,
Eternity's shores, and, beyond, azure ramparts
Floated above golden deserts of Byzantium?

Who ever dreamed of being able to climb
Up the side and red-plastic back
Of a grasshopper slanted in the sand
As if ready to hop away to infinity,
And then descend a silvery path, at whose base
Ecstasy awaits the flight through space?

Who ever dreamed of climbing aboard
A horseless carousel spindled invisibly
On the earth's greased axle and spinning
Fast enough to catch up with shadows
Evaporating from the body, before passing the self,
On a course bound through dizziness, to euphoria?

And who ever dreamed of climbing inside
A fiberglass pipe, six feet in diameter,
To reach the moon, hover freely
In a halo with zero gravity, stand on hands
Planted on the edges of a landslide,
And tumble safely from under tons of laughter?

None of us ever dreamed of climbing
Such heights without ever leaving
The earth's sphere. Yet today,
Trilogy and I, on entering the playground
Near the beach, came within earshot
Of gods gaming in the shaded groves of Arcady.

1/30 & 2/4/78 — [1] (01417)

Leave-Takings

A persuasion to love,
for my blessed wife, Jan

Why does leaving imply dying,
Grieving, breathing with difficulty,
Fleeing, in centrifugal ellipses,
From those magnetic beings
Whose lives attract us
Most heliocentrically?

Why are these untimely emigrations
More excruciating than childbirth,
Cataclysmic as fracturing atoms
And quakes the earth makes
Before its plates break apart,
Leaving oceanic scars between desolations?

Why do our good-byes disguise anxiety,
My eyes fixate on your eyes
As if they were cosmic bits
Racing terrifically ablaze across the sky,
Into sidereal evanescence,
And our kisses disappear like liquid ashes

Vaporizing from alchemical fires,
Each time the hour assigned
*

To our final separation groans louder
With its own inherent winding down?
Maybe solitude allows us these previews
To acquaint us with the hazards of life everlasting.

Perhaps these brief preludes are stimuli
By which the ears are cued
To the ultimate atonalities of a universe
Whose music will soon replace the corporeal beat.
Possibly, our passages diverge for the purpose
Of alerting saints and angels to our availability.

Regardless, these leavings are an elemental part
Of the loving two hearts intimately inured
Must endure if they're going to survive
Their interdependencies. While alive,
We must learn to accept these compromises
As providing alternatives to a complacent relationship.

2/4/78 — [2] (04188)

Disconsolate

The day wearies like my interest.
Living is just another chore
To check off of a self-imposed schedule
Before company arrives. Work
Turns on an unoiled axle.
Even the body seems to spoil;
It won't assimilate new food,
Continues to disintegrate
In horrifically rapid half-lives.
Soon, only sleep will consent
To accept my leprous physique,
And the brain will refuse to listen
To excuses for staying awake.
I'll dissolve in an endless coma,
Whose labyrinthine, convoluting dreams
Will bring me back to my senses.
Mortality! Oh, you silly bastard,
You sweet, silly son-of-a-bitch!

2/7/78 (00258)

Ontogeny Recapitulates Phylogeny[*]

The dance I do barefoot
On the frozen snow
Is an extravagant ruse
By which, naked to the bone,
I try to make the gods believe
My soul won't give in
To sidereal intransigence
Without a cosmic confrontation.

A sunrise flecked with spears
Sears my eyes,
While ice, a sheet of adhesive,
Tilts as if lifted by a giant.
I slide out of a yawn,
Into the harsh morning air,
Like a new vessel down bed-ways,
Like a breaching baby being born,

And arrive at the beginning of existence,
Where molecular threads swarm,
Waiting to be assigned to specific organisms.
I cringe on seeing my primordial form
Swimming up through the ice
To enter my next incarnation
And surrender without a fight,
As the future accepts me as a tadpole.

[*]This poem resulted after reading, in utter amazement, the findings of
the following monograph, appearing in the most recent issue of *Ichthy-
ology International*: "Studies on the Recent Unexplained Recurrence
of Regressive Genes Reversing at Birth, or How Lobe-Finned Lungfish
Are Fixating in Human Fetuses and Reaching Maturity in Pregnant
Women over the Age of 75," by Dr. Emanual Gradishar, Dr. Elgin
Emerson Momaday, Louis B. Friend, LL.D., FuBar, D.D.S., Dr. Hymen
Crapper, and Dr. Abner Bunghole.

2/8 — [1] & 2/21/78 — [1?] (05426)

[Why wasn't my dust permitted]

Why wasn't my dust permitted
To maintain its original position
*

Beneath fathomless strata
Rather than to suffer ephemeral resurrection
In this fleshpot containing my waking ashes?
Who asked my personal preference,
Consulted the fates before making plans
For the gross transformation
Of spirit and soul to flesh?
Turn me back to compressed quartz,
Marbleized shale, glistening coal.
Let me pass eternities between layers,
Lying stone cold and silent,
With inarticulate wisdom,
In catacombs where the
Unborn live in peace.

2/8/78 — [2] (00253)

[Each yawn I leave is a memory]

Each yawn I leave is a memory
Of some previous deliquescent happiness.
Smooth, exuberant college *femmes*,
Whose opalescent eyes have youth's gems,
Linger on daydreaming's edges,
Like phantoms, before dematerializing.

Weak-kneed, I chase them,
Fall behind their fleet, lithe shapes,
Breathing harder than a racing engine
At full throttle. My lungs scream
To the numb, fantasy-making machine
That yet sustains my spirit,

Keeps it manufacturing delusions
The body can't possibly maintain.
As the hours pass into shadows,
My mind's focus fractionates.
Images dissolve: Emily and Penny
And Suzie pale, blend into a full moon,

Assume the imprecise outlines
Raised, in a lunar repoussé, against night,
Whose unrevealed forms
*

Grudgingly refuse to illumine my insight.
Suddenly, I'm reminded of old wives' tales,
Greek myths, literary allusions to Hecate

And that region to which all things
Forgotten and lost flock
Like magnetized entities to a lode-rock.
I see Abishag, Brunhild, Griselda —
Immemorial women — plying my body
With emollients, swabbing, massaging me

Along the banks of a Nile-like confluence,
Whose sacred waters bathe our nakedness.
Whether arrived at my fated resting place
Or merely on my way, I feel changes
Investing my being and realize memory
Has finally succeeded in drawing me home.

2/9/78   (02041)

Coal-Burning Furnace

Each being
Is a red-hot clinker
Burning briefly
In the earth's furnace
Before turning to ashes
And entering the stratosphere.

Girandoles
Of exploding comet-wash
Toll the death
And passing of souls.
Generations ago, men and women
Kissed where, now, stars sleep alone.

Eventually,
From coaly regions,
Argosies weighted with diamonds
Escape across celestial oceans,
To safe harbors
In our imaginations,

And stratify.
Over extended periods of time,
*

Survivors are mined
And surface. Ancestors
Of ancestors a million times removed
Are fired in crucibles

Whose expendable fuel
Keeps the planet's halo aflame.
Each depletion of reserves
Is met with reciprocal increase,
As birth and death, fraternal twins,
Regulate the works eternally.

2/16 & 3/2/78 — [2?] (01068)

[Memories are the time you borrow]

Memories are the time you borrow
To spend
When you get to tomorrow.

2/21/78 — [2?] (05392)

Planned Obsolescence

Brief, intermittent, stertorous yawns
Explode invisibly on the rank air
Squared off to form a cubicle
Where sleep has drowned his senses
In an endless schedule of major repairs.

His yawns are unseen exhaust
Escaping painfully from a machine
Irretrievably out of time,
Whose internal parts perdure
Past fatigue, running only from habit.

The two-handed engine awakens,
Shakes as if with perpetual vapor lock,
Not delirium tremens or death-breath.
Only, the shriveled, shivering creature
Can't propel himself from bed,

Lies supine and useless, barely alive,
While his body adjusts to daylight,
*

And urine, saliva, gastric juices
Inch, in lethargic, peristaltic belches,
Through his sclerotic conduits and glands.

In his bay, this obsolete vehicle
Has remained outwardly intact,
Decaying from within, forgetting avenues
He's traveled. Occasionally, his systems
Are energized, his pistons fired by others,

Who have patiently endured
His unpredictably rude temperament
Out of pity and fear that their neglect
Might cause him to commit physical suicide
Before he can dictate his last will.

They wait; he waits. The stalemate
Between "loved ones," sycophantic acquaintances,
Executors for the disposition of his estate,
Former mistresses, and third-party wives
And himself extends over decades

Undistinguished by a changeless stasis,
In which only the horny nails,
On fingers and corny toes, and hair grow
To lengths resembling a Lugosi vampire,
While the fleshy epidermis slowly oxidizes,

Until his visual identity is unrecognizable,
All birthmarks, scars, special features
Are obliterated as though smoothed away
By coarse sandpaper. Suddenly,
Viscid red oil leaks from his lungs,

Drips to the soiled sheets, in streams,
Ceaselessly. He sputters, grasps his stomach,
Throat. His pulsing temples come undone
Under the skull that hoods his mind.
A plangent shattering rises with smoke

That carries his spirit upward, unnoticed,
As the hulk itself rushes to the furnaces
For recycling. The bereaved grieve and cleave
To memories of him they fastidiously manicure
For the church oration and graveside gathering,

Then depart with hearts filled with hatred,
Anticipating the probate of his testamentary predisposition
*

To leave all earthly possessions to a charity
Called the Committee to Reelect the President,
Which he picked from a list submitted by Nixon

And his top aides. Now, new vehicles,
At least ten different models,
Streamlined and speedy as naked satyrs
And nymphs, incorporate his rebuilt parts.
His sidereal presence invests them

With a vengeance they wear like ornaments
Garishly displayed over their bodies.
From the other side of death, he directs
Their hedonistic motions. They spend their energy
Denigrating his dematerialized reputation,

Refusing to consider his existence dismantled,
Until, one day, their bones awaken, stiffly,
To discover youth spattered with stale blood
And old age standing imperiously in its place,
Anxious to drive each of them to the scrap heap.

2/21/78 — [3?] (05558)

Cetology, or On the Elusive Nature of Whales

A white ocean, stretching inexorably away,
In an eye-squinting tidal wave,
Below a Guardi-bright sea
Skying the frozen architecture of Oblivion,
Reaches me way out here in space,
Commingles with my hazy imaginings,
To form a poesy composed of vapors,
Watery distillations, and precious ecstasy.

My spirit is a hulking gray whale
Breaching evanescently,
Hanging in an amazing halo of spray
And monolithic spume
Surfacing through a tiny hole
To make room for my expanding joy.
Grudgingly, the waters let me loose.
Gladly, they embrace my falling weight,

As afternoon shadows radiate from the sun,
Harpooning the massive mammal
*

Reposing in its docile and antic flotation.
My spirit sinks as the rising moon
Draws the rope that closes the curtains
Separating Earth from space. Cold sheets
Keep me beneath dreaming's surface —
An extinct species, sweaty to the bone.

2/21/78 — [4?] (01026)

Seller of Sunday Sundries

His existence consists of ignoble agnosticism,
In which spirituality and daily worship
Orbit and halo a constantly lit cigarette,
Whose smoke is reminiscent of Original chaos.

He chokes on unarticulated insights
That approximate possibilities of an omniscient god
And postulate prospects of life after death.
Skepticism denies him access to the soul's duomo.

Nightly, he stops in sleazy monks' cubicles
With crucifixes bearing the fruit of Mary's womb
Gyved to an eternal optical illusion of Christ
That persists despite his obstinate denial.

By day, he hawks authentic Holy Grails
And gewgaws, blessed by the Magi and pope,
Below wholesale, for promotionals,
To anyone receptive to his anomalous Hebraicisms

And flatulent braggadocio, in a heartland
Unaccustomed to old-country Ethiops and Philistines.
Like the Nazarene, he goes among heathens
And disbelievers, absorbing their vituperations and scorn

With forlorn resignation, occasionally connecting
On a prepaid order for items in his line,
"The Lord's Ornaments," to be drop-shipped
F.O.B. Hoboken, New Jersey,

To a storekeeper who signed away his privilege
Of returning the spurious merchandise,
Without knowing it. More often, however,
He exhausts his monthly draw against commission,

Goes in debt to the company for which he's worked
These last thirty-five years,
Moving their objectionably distressed dross
Not at a loss, rather at a handsome tax advantage.

Lately, with his sixty-fifth birthday
Limping toward him, he's been seized with fears
Of being left bereft, without adequate means
For supporting his frugal but necessary routines.

A nagging, migraine vision of the Red Sea
Closing in on Pharaoh's armies; flying locusts
Swarming the prairie that forms his territory;
The vengeful, contorted faces of Nebuchadnezzar

And wicked Haman all chase him,
Converge on his fleeing spirit in daydreams,
Until these looming fantasies merge in his decision
To quit of his own volition, relinquish his samples,

Retire to the solitary occupations of fishing,
Carpentry, and gardening, contemplation of past
And future. Anxiously, he heads home
For the last time, for the first time inspired.

2/23/78 — [1] (02414)

Magnetic Time ᐃ

Parenthesized by time's half-moons,
My mind's internal windings
Spin forward, then reverse on their axle
Without warning, as though a force
Not wholly magnetic or gravitational,
Rather emanating from a lunar lodestone,
Had assumed total binding control
Over the ineffable poetics of my soul.

In awe, my eyes observe my fingers
Chasing an automatic scrawl
Across a desolate page,
In a futile, urgent rage
To record every alternating impulse
Racing from the brain, to my extremities,
*

Before dissipating like fangs of lightning
Snapped by biting down on insulated rods.

However, no amount of concentration
Can tap the energized momentum my ideas,
Whirling in their self-contained gyrations,
Generate or capture more than a glimpse
Of the actual godly pictograms
Etched on each rapidly passing mind-plate.
Frustrated by their sheer weight of ages,
I buckle in submission to my apocryphal ignorance

And continue tracing the spinning core
Until, finger muscles constricted in agony,
Overheating occurs beneath the cranium
Or a mischievous interloper from Porlock
Knocks at my front door,
Demanding payment for an overdue note.
Only then do time's vise jaws
Relinquish their hold over my motor,

Relax their polarities long enough
For me to crawl out from under
And seek repose in sleep or eating,
By disengaging my plug from the sun's navel.
Yet it's in frictionless moments like these,
Paradoxically, that the helpless psyche,
Realizing it's letting go its sweetest freedom,
Creativity, drops from time's magnets, in silence.

2/23/78 — [2] (05572)

Reflections on a Snowy Day

The white silence outside
Sets up such a ruckus behind my mind,
One might expect to see demons, in sheets,
Stirring through ash heaps,
In search of virgins and deities to scourge
By dematerializing their adamantine spirits
In crucibles where sensuality,
Covetousness, and jealousy, when poured,
Produce a human metal more base
Than any ever known before.

Instead, when I peer through the glass,
An endless procession of robed nuns and priests,
Monks, novitiates, lay brothers,
And self-anointed transcendentalists,
Tonguing Pan pipes and flutes
Singing with their pliant, vibrating breathing,
Strumming lyres and Irish harps
Strung with wired imaginations,
Pass close to the house in which I'm seated
And enter, en masse, my poetic meditations.

Suddenly, I'm no longer certain
Who is outside whom or whether the music
Expanding throughout the room,
Roofed with fantasy and hallucination
I pace beneath, from apse to nave and back,
A thousand times, is that which I make
With words I use to recreate the universe
Or note-flakes falling from the mountain,
In Boeotia, where all pure snow originates.
For a moment, I am echoes within echoes.

I rush from the cathedral that keeps me warm,
To touch the white-bearded faces
Of regenerated men and marmoreal flesh
Of saved women. But when I finally get
To that ineffable spot,
The real, niveous air is wet and cold.
My actual eyes are set upon by demons
Sent to remind me epiphanies are mental
And that the intellect can't even exempt poetry
From the rigors of physical living.

3/2/78 — [1?] (01066)

Prufrockian Observations: On the Essence of Similes

Like croaking amphibious creatures
Concealed, except for their blinking eyes,
In natural camouflage, along a pond bank,
Post office, the *Evening Press* building,
And Brooks Café twinkle in somnolence,
*

Yawn a thousand times, awaken,
This predawn, to mark my passage
Down East Columbia and out of town.

My lame breathing is the only sound
That fills this morning with chamber music.
It accompanies me like overtones
Of the old, woeful Elizabethan motets
That rose, through plangent glissandi,
To periwigged ears sitting in haughty judgment
Over qualities they barely understood,
Undoubtedly appreciated even less.

My lungs' compositions escape unscored,
As I sojourn into the rain-gray day,
Wondering how my unimaginative brain,
So totally dispossessed of poetry and demons,
Could possibly fixate, in metered introspection,
On similes completely ill-conceived
And unrelated. That unseen frogs
Should fuse my ears and eyes to music

I've never heard is not merely surprising,
It's an absurd juxtaposition of contrarieties
The conspiring senses have offered up
To unnerve me, flush me out of my lethargy,
Make me take stock of orbiting opposites
That have commandeered my mind over the years
And rendered it useless for joining revolutions
The future might march past my gates.

Only, at my age, no pretensions to greatness
Motivate my actions. My deeds remain routine,
Easily achieved on a daily basis.
Although there are few cerebral excitements,
Depressions, disappointments, mistakes rarely occur.
Why, then, I should have been inflicted
With a leap of creativity so substantive,
I can only surmise. Speculation is rife,

As I continue my drive away from the house
That has contained my entire adult life
Like stewed tomatoes in a sealed fruit jar.
Apparently, something outside myself,
*

Beyond nightmare, rare theological insight,
Infrequent clairvoyance into mystical phenomena,
Has decided to try my patience, test my aptitude
For these transmutations of *be* and *seem*.

Predictably, I respond by seeking mollification
In literary readings. It's obvious enough
That Main Street can't possibly be misconstrued
As a pond bank or that plate glass
Resembles not at all the viscid eyes of a frog;
Furthermore, its patently ridiculous to link
The congested breathing of a consummate smoker,
Just waking, with lugubrious harpsichord scores.

Yet the solitary image of the house looms.
Its high-ceilinged, dust-laced rooms,
In which my youth settled into gloomy recesses
And faded into its fabric and wallpaper patterns,
Resemble the skeletal quarters my spirit inhabits.
It is the pressurized jar preserving my existence
As pickled gewgaws, photos, clothes in closets.
A vision of blood-ripe objects floats to the surface.

Suddenly, nausea causes me to vomit.
The acrid, acidic taste of stewed tomatoes
Etches disgust across my derisive face,
Burns away death's dusty layers,
Exposing raw dendrites writhing in pain.
Ceaselessly, I drive toward my destination,
Without knowing direction or time of arrival,
Hoping mind-signs will illuminate the way.

3/7/78 — [1] (05573)

The Ethics

The deathly ethics of survival
Defy codification, yet they persist
In demanding complete respect
From the most zealous disbelievers,
Whose haughty attempts to hide behind
Snide remarks and cynical witticisms
Fail to escape their circumspect eye.

Even their worshipful disciples
Confess to anxiety and uncertainty.
The ethics guarantee safe exodus
To no one, despite rigid fidelity,
While requiring absolute honesty
Between blood relations, sincerity
Among business associates, love

That reaches beyond articulation,
Into eternity, for those couples
Who cherish sharing their lives,
And compassion for the oppressed,
Whether alien, pariah, or neighbor.
In the end, all men genuflect,
Surrender to ethical domination,

Submit their souls volitionlessly
To the unerring omniscience of the eons,
In whose chronicle all human deeds
Are cauterized, and are sent into orbit
In the galaxy of exhausted transmigrants,
To pass through desolate portals,
On their way back to rejuvenescence.

No one chooses or eludes their call.
None who requests postponement
Is purposely omitted or exempted by privilege.
Ultimately, every decision is acted upon
By chemical agents sent to catalyze
The mystical essence of birth and renaissance.
History's ancestry is completely interrelated

And consanguineous. Blood-ties unite,
Every living minute, in an extended family
That overrides all languages and pigments,
To find common means for reaching
Peaceful coexistence. Each fresh baby
Is the hope of the ages, pure snow,
A seed dropped from the tree of good,

Not evil, ripe and alive in the earth,
A novitiate ready for ethical initiation
Into survival's frightening *rites de passage*.
No being has ever seen the ethics
Or communicated with them face to face,
*

Yet their mandate to behave righteously
In the sight of man and the imagined alike

Has caused each sentient creature
To come under scrutiny and be judged
By the One whose law is irrefragable
And above reproach. Lonely and alone,
Each approaches the gates with trepidation
And trembling, to receive his new assignment:
Beast again or angel, heron or sterile wren.

3/7/78 — [2] (05574)

Freeing the Marble Faun

For Larry and Dean Wells,
Oxford, Miss.

A harmlessly lethargic rain
Hops sporadically, in silence,
Over the field through which the world,
Hovering in a wispy, argentiferous mist,
Enters my drowsy eyes.

Bucolic reveries crowded with druids,
Brancusi-smooth nymphs and fauns,
Linger where each drop stops
And widens under the wind's pressing thighs,
Forming pools into which I dive.

We enter each other simultaneously,
The world outside and I.
Insight is multiplied a thousand times,
Magnified to reveal trees, sky,
The rain, as they penetrate my brain,

While my imagination arrests them,
Substantiates their right to breathe.
Finally, my blood, as arbiter of fates
For all objects inanimate and carnate,
Becomes the rain, the rain one with blood,

Until even my most dependable senses
Can no longer differentiate
Poetry from the poet, nymphs
*

From their nymphomaniac desires. Only then
Does the universe surrender her virginity.

3/9/78 — [1] (01067)

The Wayfarer

How can ever I let go the hold
My soul has on my precious children
Or interrupt the transcendental spell
Of their helplessness, which begs me stay
Each time I leave for a week?

Perhaps when next I'm home and notice,
I'll discover that my growing absences,
All self-imposed, urgent,
Essential to my own notions of manhood
And survival, are the actual Sorcerer's apprentices,

The poltergeists acting out my tragicomedy
Without wearing masks, invisible
To nobody except me. Maybe
I'll realize the culprit and the crime
Are united in ignorance, like fornicating dogs,

And, as such, all the more insidious.
Possibly, my wife's lustrous hair,
Once a cascade of Niagara splash,
Which seems even thinner since the trip
Last time, tinged with a spider's spinnings,

Might alert me to the inexorable changes
I've apparently failed to put in perspective . . .
Degrees, everything by mere degrees,
Themselves fleas on an elephant's ear,
Until, in staggering agony, one day,

The beast can no longer endure the roar of the pests,
Who, having multiplied, in equatorial heat,
To the size of a gross tumor, over months,
Bring him to his knees, in defeat. I shriek,
As though my nose were a bothersome trunk,

With guilt's contagion. How to relax,
Bring my ambitions into phase with Earth's
*

Rotation on its axis? That's the ultimate question,
Manifesting itself as cosmic dissatisfaction.
How can the quest for feckless fame

Claim me as its victim so easily,
Without so much as allowing me the chase
And ultimate capture by degradation,
Mental collapse, or dismantling by the vanities?
How can she deny me my wife and children,

With such unimpassioned objectivity,
While I burn in an endless rubbish pile
Fed by empty flatteries, vacuous promises,
Hopes for creating poetry for the ages,
Despite knowing it won't get etched on a single page?

Now, I've returned home once again,
Yet try as I might, I can't enter
The smiles, the anxious embraces, the eyes
Exuberant as fresh, ripe robin eggs
Breaking open with squeaking new life.

My senses have rusted shut, corroded
From having been left outdoors
Too long, unpainted. No amount of emotion
Can smooth away the rough surface
Of my inconcealable lack of ease,

My inappropriate show of real love,
The businesslike stiffness of a distant relative
Come to collect possessions left him
By bequest, in a town where he never visited,
My tacit acceptance of their good-night kisses.

Sleep comes slowly to me at home,
As though traveling on a single wave
Across an ocean. Each night, I wait
To be crushed between rocks and beach,
Thrown up, ragged and bruised, beside a dream,

To slip away, leave again unnoticed,
And resume my travels where I left off,
Doomed to the relentless and restless solitude
The quest for Xanadu and delusive Cíbola
Requires of its misguided zealots and dreamers.

3/9/78 — [2] (05575)

Bum Ingenerate

Out of sorts, at his wit's end,
At odds with a universe
Whose surface he's never scratched,
Whose depths he's not plumbed,
For lack of a fine-diamond drilling point
Fastened to his rapidly spinning mind,
A waif amidst cosmic forces
Too great for his resourceful imagination
To flimflam, he slogs through bayous
And back channels lined with cypresses
Constricted with wispy water moccasins,
Wades a million Tallahatchies
And Yoconas, until his shriveled skin
Resembles an amphibian cave creature's
And he shivers at the slightest breeze,
Burns beneath the mildest sunlight.
Nightmares hostel his ragtag body
Each skulking p.m.,
When skunks and wildcats hunt shadows
To feed their gurgling stomachs.
From the Gulf of Mexico, near Pascagoula,
And Bay Saint Louis, near Pontchartrain,
All the way through Mississippi, Tennessee,
Past Hayti, Sikeston, Cape Girardeau,
To Farmington, he's wandered aimlessly,
In search of nothing more consequential
Than the next ride, meal, wine bottle
Littering the highway median, cigarette
To tide him over on his journey home.
That the time in getting the miles
To rewind themselves on the spool
Threaded with his destiny is indecipherable
By recognizable human standards
Bothers him not the slightest.
Years ago, he decided to jettison choices,
Goals, forget to make excuses, explanations,
Or settle on reasons for the prevailing apathy
That attacked him erratically as narcolepsy
Whenever he strayed from day, awake.
Time became not even arbitrary or infinite,
*

Rather an extended, abstracted digression
From one end of night to the next,
Inside which his breathing was contained,
A vacuum, perhaps, in which all his steps
Were measured like words in the ears,
Echoing from some originless source,
Or as scratches across a graph
Monitored by the bones. Not death,
Not the forgotten cemetery of youth
He kneeled in, each weekend, to pray
For the safe passage of both his parents,
Then never exited from, one autumn morn,
When he finally left, the last time,
But the next step in his succession
To Beulahland looms ever before him,
As he stares up the road ever ahead.
The gate separating his earthly oblivion
From a heightened reality, in which living
Consists of touching love by being touched
By others, looms somewhere in the haze
Through which his tatterdemalion vision peers
In hope of reaching the fated terminus.
As he aims homeward, his myriad children,
Fathered like Cadmean seeds sprouting
Wherever he'd scatter his silent musings
In passing over the years, reach out
To shake his hand, kneel to him
In awe of his regal, indomitable shabbiness.
They realize that for all his ignominy,
He's survived his own questionable existence
Without compromising to persistent handouts,
Fixed raffles, glittering quiz games, and charities,
Which would have rejuvenated his spirit
Without his having to surrender more than his will.
He passes with a slow, close-eyed forbearance
Redolent of numb satisfaction and happiness
Born of knowing no one owns his soul.
The multitudes weep. Their flesh palpitates
With heated ecstasy. They know he's a man,
Not a shadow dressed in approximations,
A man nameless, nearly vague as animals
That never leave their subterranean lairs
*

Yet resembling them in straining sinews
And flexing muscles, a man on his way
By virtue of refusing to hear their praise.
Suddenly, the sky absorbs the sun,
Vomits out its reciprocal lunar mate,
And changes the wayfarer into a yew tree
Stirring with congregated songbirds,
Whose music enchants the entire dark woods
Into which he's disappeared without notice.
At the height of the moon's orbit,
Higher than the birds' threnodies can lift,
A scintillating speck, cometlike, nebulous,
Rushes across the Milky Way, as if chased
Or chasing itself in a sweeping, eternal circle,
Then spirals up and out of sight,
While the birds quit their mellifluous chirping
And begin nervously pecking themselves to death.

3/15/78 — [1] (05576)

[His rounded crown] †

His rounded crown
Is smooth as a cue ball,
Perfectly white

3/15/78 — [2] (07058)

Car Clock

At 3:24,
The digital quartz-crystal clock,
Renowned for its accuracy,
Embedded in the immaculately gadgeted dash
Of this Brougham d'Elegance I drive,
Reads 8:03.
The nearly five hours in between
Escape explanation. The absurdity
Inherent in the blatant discrepancy
Is like that of a three-eyed Cyclops
Shrieking outrageously from a cliff
Above my floating boat.
*

The minutes, so totally irrelevant
In relation to the bright afternoon,
Are stones hurled to my vulnerable decks,
As my vessel navigates past the cove
And enters this unknown ocean again.
Surrounded on all sides by time,
Enclosed inside an ever-expanding zone
Toward whose outermost horizons
Each heading necessarily excludes the rest,
I ponder my course, curse myself
For allowing such a hiatus to develop
In the present. Being *now* and *later*
Simultaneously wearies the imagination.
Such pseudoimmortalities are preludes
To the future humans can't comprehend.
The notion of being *now* and *ever*,
At the center, where all loci meet,
Gives rise to speculation as to whether
Living and dying might not have blood ties,
Be coevals tuned to the same reiterating frequency.
Is what I'm passing through at this hour
The same landscape on both my wrist watch
And digital dash clock, or am I trapped
In a DMZ, at eternal impasse?
Is it possible that my entire existence
Is doomed to be ahead and behind, forever,
Without knowing the beginning from the end?
And will my death really arrive on schedule,
At the precisely decided minute, as is written,
Or will I survive for nearly five hours,
With a punishment of having to witness
My own demise in all its minute disintegrations?
Even if I could change the car clock
To the proper setting, who could guarantee
That I'd make the correct adjustment
To the right timepiece and that the new time
Would actually align with the rotating lobe
That shoves the cogs of Earth's escapement
Into the smooth-fitting harmony of the spheres
That ensures it safe passage through our galaxy?
Perhaps two crucifixions,
Two Exoduses from Egypt, two nuclear bombs
At Hiroshima shattered our collective consciences
*

Without notifying history: the one we've recorded
And the other, its echo, its overtone,
Like a sonic boom yet to catch up with us.

3/15 — [3] & 3/18/78 (05577)

The Westminster Chime

I sit in the bowels of this silent house,
Listening to a Seth Thomas Westminster chime
Announce the somber quarter-hours
As if time were a procession of dignitaries
Filing past the casket of an assassinated president
Lying in state; the line has no finality.

Sunday morning is a gray-headed man
Dying interminably, irretrievably sinking away,
Through comatose stupors laced with lucidities
In which seaweed-memories rise to the surface
To bury him before senility draws him down.

The sad, sweet chimes seem so frangible
One would never suspect the gross specters
Hammering away at their invisible ends
To evoke such death-infested notes
Or imagine the sheet music they interpret,
Scored with bass- and treble-clef dust motes.

Suddenly, the clock vomits spasmodically,
Retches eight times without stopping,
Then dissipates into the numinous stasis
Violated by sunrays that embrace me
Like the slimy tentacles of a mind-squid
Cruising in the shallows where my spirit wades.

The relentless pulling apart begins.
From the body, my sensual desires and intellect
Are extruded. The brain relinquishes its fancy.
Imagination breaks away from the forces of reason
That keep it from reaching beyond credibility.
Ultimately, my being is sliced into ticking seconds

That fly off into the air, enter the morning,
And are absorbed by the gray-headed man,
*

Whose breathing has become a labored rattle
Expanding within my own congested chest.
In a rare moment of insight, I recognize myself
As the dressed, sepulchered skeleton the seconds file past.

3/19/78 (05578)

The Degradation of the Democratic Dogma

For Lloyd Krumlauf

The gratuitous dying goes on
Ubiquitously.
We don't even question why
Felons are held in detention cells
Indeterminately,
Arraignments are postponed ad infinitum,
And the grieving families of victims
Are buried under accumulating headlines
Of newer atrocities and forgotten,
As days, in arrested malaise,
Are measured by lawyers' fees
Unpaid and gaining constantly
At 1° percent monthly interest rates.

Nothing changes. Attorneys for the state,
Appointed by the prosecution,
Perfunctorily assume their advocate's task
Of rescuing animals from traps.
In their dubious fiduciary capacity,
They twist and extrude truth
Past its rational threshold,
Until confusion and circumstantial evidence
Dilute all that we consider "inhumane"
And we vacillate and we fabricate
Justifications for pardoning the violators
By reason of unpremeditated insanity,
Self-defense, or plea bargaining.

The needless grieving persists in all quarters,
From Garden City, Kansas, to Indianapolis,
Austin, Houston and Dallas, Los Angeles.
Meanwhile, Speck, Manson, Son of Sam
Languish in commodious incarceration,
*

Heroic for their inverse notoriety,
Free within the prescribed limits
Set by the color-TV screen they watch
With total abandon. Neither income tax
Nor monthly rent distracts them;
No children to clothe or feed or school
Intrude on their easy equanimity,
Cause them to lose a night's sleep.

Relieved of the burdens of being responsible
For their actions, by a society
Convinced that rehabilitation, rather than
Forfeiture of a life for a life,
Is God's fiat, these diabolical creatures
Are merely removed from our sight
For a while, isolated, until influence arrives
By the changing of the two-party guard
Or parole is granted by a relenting people,
Who, by then, have endured so many wars
That monsters of previous generations
Pale in relation, become puny, ragged waifs,
Themselves the seeming victims of a crueler age.

3/29/78 — [1] (05579)

Just Beyond Walden Pond △

Chromolithographed trade cards,
Dated 1880s,
Displaying stove black,
Zephyr Bosom Pads, Pears' Soap,
Ayres Sarsaparilla, Corticelli
And Coats & Clark Spool Thread,
Niagara Starch are autumnal leaves
    F
    l
    u
    t
    t
    e
    r
    i
    ng from Above,
    *

To the base of history's tree,
Beneath which I sit alone,
Musing with reverential curiosity
On obsolete products of gone generations.

I'm entrenched in reveries.
Sun-drenched incantations penetrate
The empty branches, sear my squinting irises,
As, peering skyward, I witness the last glints
Of a passing civilization finally disappearing
Into an argentiferous horizon.
In the distance, car horns guffaw;
Televisions emulate the hyena's shriek;
Shoppers, entreated in a million Wal-Marts,
Over speakers, to worship in peace, squeal.
The tree shivers. I huddle underneath,
Knowing it will never again turn green.

3/29/78 — [2] (05424)

Mamo's Requiem

For Mr. "H," Harry Hofmann, Jr.

Finally, with benign indifference,
She resigns, enters transition, disappears
Into the earth from which her spirit
First appeared. Her roots shrivel.
The slow decomposing begins,
As if in contradiction to this season
Of silent upheavals, in which forsythia
And crocus sprout from winter's womb.

All the scions, magnetized by her demise,
Return to honor her tenacious survival
And recognize her four-score-and-three years
As a godly accomplishment.
Her great-grandchildren, oblivious to the hour,
Are April's blooms, shoots, fecund flowers,
Who, taking their nutrients from her heritage,
Wreathe her grave with youth's fragrant designs,

While her one remaining son,
Grieving yet relieved, mopes in her garden.
She could have died a week ago,
*

When snow, then choking ice,
Glazed every tree and roof and pole
To breaking. Her going out
Might have been marked by mutinous elements
Redolent of violent endings, bereft of gentleness.

Instead, she waited just long enough
For the sun to open its floodgates,
Thaw the frozen stream leading to Paradise.
Perhaps she'd sensed our radical discontent
With such an extended sequence of moribund months,
Our anxiety to step foot outside,
And decided that she would choose the time
To invite us to witness her own rites of spring.

4/1/78 (02277)

Early-Morning Storm

For Roger and Saul,
who share April 5

Just moments ago,
A mild April-morning stasis
Held everything in place.
The gray anvil, shaped like angst,
That subsequently replaced it,
Was just entering mitosis.

Sporadic forsythias,
Dotting my irises an outrageous yellow,
Like incandescent fireflies
Popping on and off in gentle suspensions,
Made no indication that the sun
Would erase their haughty glow,

Nor did the lime-green trees,
Just reaching term, breaching,
Whose tiny scrolls were just opening,
Realize that such a gust
Could distract them from sensualities
They'd anticipated for three seasons.

Even I, sitting quietly in my study,
Gazing through a rimpled pane,
In private amazement,
*

Had no idea, ten minutes before,
That a storm of such evanescent force
Could ravage an entire civilization,

Undo its monuments so impassionately,
Overlay its landscape
In somnolent wash, then retreat,
Allowing the sun to intervene as before,
As though no disturbance had occurred
To change the status quo.

Within minutes, the brute Colossus
Who intruded on my solitude,
Ripping a gap through my imagination
Without leaving a record of its passing
On nature's indifferent existence,
Will have been completely forgotten.

Only my arrested, impermanent words,
Undulating on fast-evaporating rain pools
Among severed forsythia petals,
Redbud blooms, and leaf husks
Pulled loose from burgeoning twigs, remain.
Like the storm, I've changed course.

4/6/78 — [1] (02278)

Paean to Spring

As yet, no bumblebees
Or yellow jackets infest the rose beds,
Which still sleep under cover of leaves.
No *mariposas* waft; no crickets buzz.
The mimosa, patriarch of my memories,
Planted from a solitary sprig,
In 1950, is a skinny bindle stiff
Bumming its vagrant way into spring.
Invisible merriments and throated ecstasies
Bridge the swaying tree limbs
My heart traverses, this sunny day,
On wings of cardinals, starlings, and jays,
Anticipating the onset of germinating things.

My eyes wheel and dive,
Surviving repeated falls from heights
*

Inspiration reaches as it tries to scale
The sky's scaffolding unsuccessfully.
Although earth owns my body,
Its soul knows no restraints
Except those imposed by an imagination
That rarely slows long enough
For time to overtake its leading edge,
Cause it to stall on faulty poetics,
Send it crashing to a thoughtless impasse.
Such soarings occupy my days,
Now that the outdoors is wide awake.

4/6/78 — [2] (05580)

Rituals by Night △

For Trilogy,
approaching four years

When both hands on her timepiece
Reach straight up,
She knows eight o'clock has arrived,
The net has snared her,
And that Cinderella's coach-and-four
Have begun their metamorphosis
Toward lizards, pumpkin, and mice.

Although giving in without a fight,
She still requires "Dude"
To hoist her, fully relaxed,
To his shoulders, traverse the stairs,
As he did when her weight
And shadows were half the size
Her burgeoning shape now supports.

First stop is the bathroom,
Where her dad operates,
With outrageous slapstick imprecision,
On her teeth, chanting, off-key,
Meaningless soliloquies,
Whose rhythms distract her
From a basic impatience with the task:

"Fi fo fe fum,
Brush the teeth, brush the gums.
*

Rinse and spit. Now, let's quit.
Fo fe fum fi,
Uppers and lowers, open wide.
Fi fo fung dung,
Out of the way, you silly tongue!"

The next destination
On her magical path toward sleep
Varies, depending on where the bucket
That contained Kentucky Fried Chicken
Was last left. Once located,
It's only a matter of filling it
With water to load in the vaporizer

She runs winter and summer
So that its companionable motor
Will defend her against sounds
From the outlands,
Bent on entering the apartments
Where she reposes with gentle fantasies,
In a bed of sensual cast-iron roses.

Before another day concludes,
Dude and his *preciosa*
Select, from a babel of scattered books,
Whatever happens to move her
To visible anticipation. Together,
We settle atop her little sleep-boat
And float out on a word-sea,

Whose source, this evening,
Lies between the enchanted covers
Of *Max, the Nosey Bear*.
With inutterable glee, we share
The special smells of Camembert cheese,
Strawberries, peanut butter, buns
Radiating a sweet cinnamon spell,

Which all lift their phoenix identities
Into the air, with a solitary scratch
Of the thumbnail against the camouflaged patch
Attached to each palpable illustration.
Somehow, we escape ethical lessons
And parables hovering just below the surface,
By savoring the scented shape of sounds.

Reluctantly, she turns the last page
And realizes that Max's escapades
Will terminate if she fails to intercede,
Get his sentence commuted. Under duress,
I agree to listen while she rereads
The entire journey from her memory's diary,
With the high seriousness of a Hasidic scholar.

Finally, she clothes her pillow in a blanket,
Takes up the tuck-legged position —
Lying on her side — she's never relinquished,
And begins reciting, line by responsive line
(One night in solemnity, the next
With playful irreverence), to have the last say,
Her sacred "Now I lay me . . ."

I kneel at her bedside, ministerial,
Marveling at how far we've come
In so abbreviated a time, wondering
How ecclesiastical and just how miraculous
Our future together will be, as we share
Each new Blakean grain of sand,
Containing universe after shimmering universe

Brimming with beauty and passion, truth
And grief and satisfactions beyond belief,
The passing of friends, the birth of her children.
With a sad tremulation in my voice,
I begin singing our ritualistic lullaby,
And though it remains essentially the same,
Night after night, it's forever changing,

Like the sky, the ocean, our own lives,
Self-renewing yet hermetic and unviolated,
Belonging to me and my daughter solely.
I sing a slightly wistful, totally melodious
Kol Nidre: "Lul-la-by and good night
To my dear lit-tle Tril-o-gy.
You are love-ly, you are pre-cious,

"You are beau-ti-ful and wise.
In the morn-ing, I'll be here,
Right by your side, so good night,
Nick-e-nick, and sleep ti-ight, my love."
When I look into her smooth face,

*

Quietude and peacefulness have taken their places
At the gates to the fortress I've helped create.

4/10–11/78 — [2] on 4/11   (01418)

The Voices of Spring

Jesus, how the voices sing, in key,
Such sweet mellifluities,
This spring of elegant deliquescence!
Each color, when blended
By my excited eye,
Renders a natural harmony
So transcendent that trees
From which the voices of forsythias,
Redbuds, and flowering crabs issue
Become facets of one vast
Theater-in-the-round,
Haloing my senses with incandescent sound.

I listen, as never before,
To intense pinks, purples, mauves,
Vibrating yellows, and dogwood whites
Coming to climactic ripeness
Within a green overtone
Of dew-glistening grass and supple leaves,
Hoping to discover a new fugue
Or variation on a theme previously missed
That my insight might attach itself to
And be passed through April's musical iris,
Into the land where abandoned dreams
And youth's squandered pursuits await plucking.

4/11/78 — [1]   (05581)

Chariton County Pastoral $^{\Delta}$

American bison, hirsute and motley,
Wade in the shadows they make
While grazing on baled hay.
Their shaggy, anachronistic shapes,
Projected in antic stasis
*

Against late afternoon's scrim curtain,
Are arranged in a strange abstraction
Jackson Pollock might have painted
Except for the fact that the landscape
Containing and framed by their very being
Is illuminated by an actual sun,
Not museum fluorescents or anodized floods.
The amber dusk suffusing the dust
Their languorous shuffling kicks up
Belongs to the generation of Eakins
And Sidney Mount. George Inness
Is seated at his portable easel,
At field's edge, feverishly sketching the scene,
In hopes of capturing the etherized peacefulness
Evoked by the essence of buffaloes at feeding.
For some reason, his brush strokes
Have leaked through time's porous canvas,
Onto my forehead, and etched into my mind
The kind of solitude that typified an era
Undefiled by psychiatry and heroin.
As I pass, the crimson-tinged sun
Stabs my eyes, and as I squint,
The varnished impasto begins flaking,
Until only an insatiable itching remains.

4/11/78 — [3] (05423)

Willy, Knight Errant

Imported musicians traverse back roads,
Finally arrive at the sleazy posada
Where Sancho and I recuperate
From our endless days of wasted gestures
In behalf of disgraced ladies of the night.

The music they make reflects exotic cultures
Whose inhabitants parade naked as chimps,
Dance like fireflies repeatedly igniting,
Then disappearing into the nearest flesh.
They pave the way to our salvation,

By suggesting other neighboring planets
Whirling in spectacular, scintillating flames
Within our same galaxy. We shimmer,
*

As electricity, percussion, and Pan flute
Radiate a sensual fantasy about our stupors.

Suddenly, my trusted companion and I
Leap onto the stage. Dear Sancho
Mistakes an idle saxophone for a *bota de vino*,
While I attempt to mount a female singer
Gyrating, with moon-madness, to bell tones

Emanating from distant, inspired musicians.
In half shadows, I unmask her voice,
Penetrate to the source of her minstrelsy.
Her spurious virtue is lost in the sound —
Dulcinea rises before me like a jinn

Called out of hiding by my Rabelaisian mind.
All my life, I've been searching *calles*
And *rincónes polverosos* for such a queen.
Only, now, her skin is unquestionably leprous;
Scabs, pocks, and pustules dot her face.

And I wonder what agent made me acquiesce
To finally gaining access to the princess
Who has dominated every waking quest
All these ramshackle, unsuccessful years.
I realize now how much more satisfying

The dream, untranslated, was. The dream
At least allowed me a reprieve,
By letting me return to my dusty bookshelves
To reread the romances without knowing
Whether or not the outcomes were relevant to my life.

We slither, twined like mating snakes
Or strands of coarse manila hemp,
Wound about each other in scabrous embrace.
Friend Sancho guffaws to see such pleasures
Concluded on the stage above his slumped body.

Soon, the music slows into blue-black silence.
Applause drowns out our useless groans.
Only our shadows, cast against the curtains,
Reassure me that we are reaching climax;
Otherwise, I feel the loneliness of other nights.

Revived, Sancho grabs me by the mustache,
Dumps my limp and squandered bag of being
*

Into a grocery sack, and transports my spirit
To the unclean bed where, for a week,
I've retired with my fantasies, waiting to sally out.

The mirror into which I peer unimpassionedly
Returns a gruesome leer. A queer premonition
Hovers about me as if to announce the end.
Rigor mortis waves its wand over my bones,
As the Knight of the Doleful Countenance snores.

4/11/78 — [4] (01323)

Los olvidados

> *Anyone who dares to be "different" in our society runs the
> risk of wearing a disguise he might never be able to remove.
> Ultimately, he stands a chance of choking to death inside a mask
> that refuses to give with outside pressures and accommodate
> to those from within.*
> — from "Manifestations of Unfulfilled Accomplishments As
> They Relate to the Pursuit of Unconventional Contrarieties," by
> Lionel Olschwanger, D.D.S., Ff.T., and Myron Oxenhandler,
> Chief of Psychiatric Deviations, Mount Horeb Hospital, Tel Aviv

Stranded in the Land of Transients,
Sentenced to a thousand Dantesque nights
Between soiled sheets and cigar nicotine,
Within isolated, commercial-rate incarceration,
I lose sight of invisible vertical interstices
And black horizontals etched across the flesh
Of all the other prisoners confined, with me,
To ennui, the mind's high-security penitentiary.

We circulate in the yard, exercise, expectorate
With derisive hostility whenever the conversation
Backs up, floods the sedgy edges of animosity
Each of us harbors for the state's legislators,
Who were responsible for dropping justice,
From gray civil buildings, on our heads,
Like rocks crushing unsuspecting tourists
For doing absolutely nothing whatsoever.

Occasional TV, billiards, reading,
Masturbation, bowel movements, urination,
Hebephrenic waking sleep, eating —
*

These are the indulgences we're permitted
By authorities whose sole duty
Is to shelter the wealthy from felons like us,
Convicted of nonviolence, circumstantial anomie,
And conscientious objection to suspected bellicosity.
Aliases of *"faygeleh,"* "schlemiel," "putz,"
"Poet," "pharisee," "jack-off," "fag"
Follow us as reeking feces a wino.
Every politico and pedagogue decries our lethargy
As the ultimate degradation of a classless society,
The bane of free enterprise, freedom, democracy,
The only potential threat to the myth of progress —
Beatnik, hippie, radical, communist.

How I ever arrived at such a stalemate,
Midway on my journey through life's woods,
Not being able either to advance or retreat,
Rather remaining stalled in this quicksand bog
Smothering my brain, restraining its release
From this land where each of us is an epithet,
A cipher by which to identify the photograph
On a driver's license, is unfathomable to me.

I only know, now, that the creature who began
As a promising writer of sentimental verse,
Then reached impasse when endless rejections
Started to filter through his pervious shell,
Shriveled into a silent, dehydrated wreck,
A skeleton holding its own ossified skull
In its bony hand, a dust-filled wilderness
Sifting into time's seams — anonymity personified.

4/12/78 (01324)

The Septuagenarians ^Δ

For Al Martin

Their slow, brittle bones
Rattle and clash beneath the flesh,
Like cold radiator pipes
Coming alive on a wintry night
For the first time. Each is blind
*

To significant degrees of fumbling.
Neither can read newsprint,
Though one holds a lighted magnifier
Between the page and her deteriorated eyes,
In futile exercise, to keep her brain alive.
Their flesh, exposed on the face
And hands alone, is a series of fields
From which harvests have exhausted all growth
Except ocherous stubble and excrescences
That will disappear with the next plowing.
One still lives in town, by himself,
Makes five daily visits to the nursing home,
To comfort his numb, beloved wife,
Reposing in senescence so pronounced
That not even his arrival can stir her
From the final hibernation of her gray decade.
He eats each meal out, in perpetual silence,
As though sentenced to a hunger no food
Could possibly satisfy. The other,
Having bedded her nest years ahead,
In anticipation of the day when old age
Would demand her resignation from duties
That kept her active and alert,
Accepted her premature solitariness,
On the departing of her youthful husband,
As a mandate to prepare herself against boredom,
Courted self-reliance, remarried resourcefulness,
That she might someday outlast her own decrepitude.
Like a miserly exchequer, she counts the hours
Stockpiled in her locked vaults, pays out
With reluctance, is niggardly to the end,
Enjoys the freedom of remaining unattended
And being still capable of doing completely for herself
In the newly built senior-citizens' housing
She rents nominally with a government subsidy.
Both, without ever having known each other,
Have joined the same extended family,
Adopted the names common to all those
Not related by birth but by death:
Waif, pariah, bereaved, elderly, aged.
Both, without their actual awareness,
Have already been shipped, in unsprung vehicles,
*

Over rutted, dusty cuts through the Great Divide,
To internment camps, abandoned airfields
Dotted with gray, corrugated Quonset huts,
Desolate Indian reservations plagued with flies.
Both, although not yet told, have left
The premises where their spirits resided.
They've released their souls like doves
And pigeons, to fly home and announce
The imminence of their long-awaited return.
All that remains now is the final grave
To house the vaulted coffin of earthly vows
They'll take with them and the flowers
That will stay behind to celebrate their triumph
Over escaping Egypt and finding Canaan at last.

4/13/78   (05422)

Becoming Spring

Everywhere, the solitariness of bare trees
Has assumed a sociability
Whose congenial greens speak to us
With ceaseless garrulity. We forget
That only moments ago, earth and space
Were a vast exposed burial mound,
In which bones and inanimate natural objects
Reposed in a stasis embraced by oblivion.

Now, the cosmic nodes reverberate.
The elemental spark throws off scintillas
That glint in the mind's dark compartments,
Illuminating the cobwebs and dust,
The gloomy accumulations the heart suffers
Whenever fall enters sleep's caves.

Every single entity breathes, mingles now,
Sings the silence of nonexistent things
Out of earshot, expels the old air
Trapped in winter's mausoleum, shouts.
My ears and eyes trade places,
Share each exploding girandole,
As the leaves fly to their assigned locations
And grass rises, Phoenix-like, from its nests.

In this season of awakenings, the hours fade.
Preceding generations and those not yet created
Coalesce, accept me as a sacrificial surrogate.
I am the planet's adolescence. My ecstasy
Is its ever-renewing juvenescence, my breath
Every man's evanescent everlasting nay.

4/20/78   (05582)

Writer's Block/Spider's Block

For nearly five months,
The urgent, versifying spinnerets
Of the spiderlike agent that dominates my brain
Have remained idle. Silence fills the void
With a nonexistent lake,
In whose saline liquescence the meninges bathe.

The consistently vertiginous clicking,
Which once fashioned word-webs from suggestions
Lodged deep in the creature's blood,
By isolating insights and shared passions
Floating precariously near its lair,
Then snaring metaphors and slant rhymes
To strengthen the frangible strands
It wove without demanding of itself a rationale,
No longer operates with untrammeled abandon.

Apparently, aliens invaded the brain,
Severed its webs with chain cutters,
Manacled the arachnid's back legs,
To suffocate all future extrusions,
Whose music alone made my spirit forget
That every predator must have victims to exist.

4/28/78 — [1]   (05583)

[Was it apathy or fear] Δ

Was it apathy or fear
That nourished the seeds in the Warsaw garden
Hans Frank tended? Who could have dreamed
*

They would blossom with such motley costumes —
Carmine and rust — suspended in nude humiliation,
On tulip-slender stalks, before the scythe
Cut across the entire plot like a shadow
Cast earthward from a V-2 rocket?

Why weren't the beautiful, supine flowers
At least allowed to mature,
Then be sold from booths on Munich streets,
Into aesthetic servitude, as useless baubles
In the cut-glass universe of Prussian stuffiness,
Instead of being systematically snapped
At the spine by lead shrapnel
Or sprayed for lice, with Zyklon B crystals?

By degrees, tendentious and extravagant ivy
Grew up above healed crevasses
Loaded with the severed stems and petals.
In later years, scientists coming to view
Beds adjacent to the greenhouses at Auschwitz,
Treblinka, Belzec, Chelmno could only speculate
What fertilizers might have been used
To produce so furious and unexpungeable a bloom.

4/28/78 — [2] (00870)

The Raker ^Δ

It's Sunday, and I've taken leave of April.
The terrestrial hours, stretching skyward,
Lure me into a celestial trance I forage
And explore for relaxation, recreation,
And forgetting, perhaps something more.
Oh, such a wondrous escape I've made today!

With rake and a handyman's love of puttering,
I gently sunder choked fence rows,
Unloose intractable caches of matted debris,
Delve under Pfitzer junipers,
Whose mysterious grots yield to my prodding,
And along the barn's rotted baseboards.

The rusty implement I shoulder and wield
Is a staff that refuses to support the weight
*

Of my shadow, attached by my hand's clasp,
To the lawn. It's limp as a windless flag.
My raspy tines finally tatter it,
As they gather up everything in their path.

Each stroke I make through knotted clots
Of last year's castoff leaves
Discloses furious scurrying,
Promotes the season's resurrection
By freeing winter's caves of their barricades.
Even my covert soul shimmers in the sun.

5/3–4/78   (01065)

Willy Fantasizes to the Accompaniment of a Soft-Tone Alarm Clock

Morning dings repeatedly.
Tiny sheep somersault
Across dream sequences,
Alerting the unseen projectionist
To prepare for a reel change.

Suddenly, the darkness parts
Like a Red Sea mirage.
His sleeping image shimmers
In the dim chiaroscuro
Between his seat and the white screen,

As though he were Moses fleeing,
Seeing himself in history's eyes,
Escaping mankind's abominations.
Again, like parted waves
Converging, coercive sounds

Dovetail in his inner ears.
He cringes until, somehow,
The volume is modulated, the picture refocused,
And dreaming makes its final appeal
To keep its victim alive.

Once more, he's caught
Beneath sleep's sweet amnesia,
Between sea and shore,
On desert beds, soaring in space,
Unable to awaken his senses

To the fact that the theater
In which he's passed the night
Is now silent, empty,
Impatient to evacuate his spirit,
That the cleaning up might begin.

He starts. His numb fingertips
Flip the switch to SILENCE.
The ringing in his skull ceases,
As he lifts his sweaty body
And heads stiffly toward the wilderness.

5/5/78 (00254)

At Least He Passed Quietly, in His Sleep

Not sure whether waking
Is sleep's defeat,
A victory for the demons of boredom,
Or merely an exercise in futility,
Calculated to make the ultimate passing
As unobtrusive as possible,
He stretches. The etched amazement
That appeared on his face, at daybreak,
Dissolves as if dipped in Drano.
His body, dotted, from corny toe
To bald pate, with poison ivy,
Itches as though he were isolated
At the epicenter of a thousand-mile-wide
Mosquito-breeding bog.
Unlike other mornings, yawning
Has failed to wash him clean,
Cause yesterday's flesh to molt.
Apparently, leaving sleep
Did not effect the expected escape,
Deaden the tingling epidermis.
Rather, the condition seems to have worsened,
Rendered him without use of his legs,
Erectionless,
Devastated from the waist up.
A catatonic excrescence on the land,
Spewing, inexorably, abdominal gas,
*

Like a spastic volcano,
He grasps the brass headboard,
With feeble fingertips,
In one gasping, last-ditch attempt
To lift himself from the morass
That, during the night, silently,
Must have clawed through its banks,
Inundated the safe high grounds
Where, in past eras,
His better dreams laid a foundation
To support his power station,
And surrounded him with its slime.
Now, neither his own conditioned inclination
To rise into the shafting sunlight
And be speared, another time,
In a godly apotheosis he fantasizes
Each fine new dawn
Nor the brain's claxons
Can rouse his anesthetized spirit.
Immobile, drowsing in a twilight
Pocked with Miró-like specters
Floating in aqueous suspensions
Behind his dilated, blinkless eyes,
He waits in a shameless anonymity
Void of nurses, wife, sirens of Tyre
Or Nineveh, waits for a change,
A transformation, any deterioration
Or ameliorative sign that life will return
To his spent, uncelebrated existence.
He waits like a cancer patient,
Unaware of his constant evacuations,
The vitiated skeleton sleep has fashioned
From his once vital sac of being.
Soon, even the waiting disintegrates
Into a series of labored insights.
He sees his scattered incarnations
Crowding back down through the neck,
Whose constriction is his clogged windpipe,
And he knows the end is close,
Redemption withheld. He spits blood,
As his ghost gets up to get dressed.

5/11/78 (00257)

The Disbelievers

The agonies are out in force.
They bear no malice
Yet devastate their victims mercilessly,
Who expose their vulnerability
Belly up, in a sweat-beaded whiskey glass,
At the bottom of a hundred coffee cups,
By riding inside the arsenic aureole
Of a constantly conflagrating cigarette.

The pandemoniac hysteria
Of their rattled breathing, speaking, actions
Resounds through steamy Hades'
Labyrinthine corridors and mazy pits,
At whose base waits a scaly creature
Too long denied human grief
And passion gone completely lunatic
To refuse the slightest mortal dross.

Tumbling, they come over the world's rim,
In droves, those with emphysemic lungs
Hung, like burned sponges,
In the mucoid ocean of thorax,
Those gerontological oddities
Who defy medical explanation
And modern logic as long as possible
Before voluntarily surrendering,

Those with faultily fused vertebrae,
Transplanted corneas, valves, kidneys,
Colostomied, pacemakered, cancerous,
Bionic, electronic, mechanical,
Each a perfectly imperfect specimen
Of a species addicted to used parts,
Factory rebuilts, junkyard souls,
Recyclable spirits, biodegradable hearts.

Off to one corner, the shadow of a man
Wearing a black patch
Banded across his wizened forehead,
Heavily bearded, holding in his hand
A fanned-out peacock tail,
Fidgets, shimmers back and forth
*

In a nimbus not quite extraterrestrial,
Neither of this earth nor the nether world,

Rather obscure. His diabolical likeness
Strikes fear into those nearby,
Who witness the peacock feathers
Metamorphose into tarot cards
Sliding through his clicking fingers
Like knives in and out of a magician's casket
Loaded with a naked odalisque.
Each one he withdraws has a bloody tip,

Signifying the incipience of an unexpected trip
For a specific victim, as yet unannounced.
Each creature, with haughty indifference,
Saunters past, smiling snidely,
Almost taunting the shade to make a move
In his direction, each moving fast,
Toward the precipice of the vast chasm,
To gain distance on his bleakest disbeliefs.

5/12/78 — [1] (00255)

Between Three and Five ^Δ

For my beloved Trilogy,
on the advent of her fourth birthday

Tomorrow, on waking and all day long,
What we will call her
And officially celebrate with birthday cake,
Invited preschool mates,
Clown, magician, horse rides, balloons,
And souvenir coloring books to take home,
She will have already been becoming
For three hundred and sixty-five days.

Although we shall say she is four,
It will be no beginning at all,
Rather a leaving behind, a completion
Of that which she's been achieving without realizing
Or refused to acknowledge,
Even up to the last possible second,
*

By asserting her seemingly inalienable birthright
To be three, unequivocally three.

How ironic she's waited an entire year
Before claiming sovereignty over the past,
Only to find she's a full season behind.
Tomorrow, she'll open the back door,
Where four lives, fumble around inside
Without recognizing the faint, mazy corridors
As actual days ahead belonging to five,
Then exit by the future's front gate

And enter a warp soaring with pleasures
Winged and singing, insights magnified
Through eyes on fire, flutterbies,
And tiny sensualities, whose antennae
Will forever guide her instinctively
Toward May. Whether merely four
Or in her fifth year, beginning five,
Trilogy thrives in her own timeless sphere.

5/12/78 — [2] (01419)

Balloons

The poem I wrote yesterday
        Was a balloon blown up, knotted,
And tied to a convenient pinnacle,
        Then left overnight.

Today, when I returned
        To admire its sensual design,
Passion that had inflated its shape
        Had escaped. It hung limp,

A victim of intrinsic fissures.
        Its translucent skin
Was opaque, inscrutable, uninviting
        To the eyes' smooth fingertips.

When I tried to revise it
        By unknotting it and blowing new life
Into its stretched recesses,
        The vessel exploded in my face,

Scattering tattered images and symbols
    For me to gather up and throw away.
Oh, to release a balloon
    And be inside as it rises from sight!

5/18/78 (00099)

Addie's Agony ^Δ

6:25 a.m.
Is just another impersonal shape
In night's prolonged mosaic of hours
Waving me off. My escape
Is neither ritual nor sacrament,
Rather a sanctimonious coeval,
The act evacuated,
Empty of all meaning, abstracted
To the point of incomprehensibility.

The green-steamy countryside
Named Ste. Genevieve,
Into whose misty oblivion I slip,
Gives its gifts as unself-consciously
As a sinner, nearing Golgotha,
Emits supplications from moist lips.
It offers me insights into the solemnity
And perpetual happiness of brainless things,
Reinforces my unremitting need for peace.

Cows lolling in stolid muteness
Moo so loudly
Through the verdant, fertile silence,
I fear the slightest move
Might cause them to stampede my cortège.
Spring-fed ponds and creeks,
Whose surfaces are as smooth
As unviolated membranes,
Refuse to reflect my vagrant design

Or accept my Thespian desires
To enter the earth while yet alive,
By being penetrated by poesy
*

Diving deep into my stream of consciousness,
And emerge, purged of a dependency on words,
To fashion truth from its burning crucible.
Even the waxy, umbrageous trees
Remind me how puny I am,
How irremediably human is my destiny.

Just now, a vaguely familiar putrescence
Insinuates this vessel that's coffined me,
All these word-cursed years,
In going from one exit to the next.
Perhaps, on this final occasion,
Anse will take the initiative, respect my wishes
To be transported to the source
Where all dying is a matter
Of getting ready to stay alive forever.

5/24/78 — [1] (00054)

Troika and His Helpmate ^Δ

Troika, our six-month-old
Plump putto,
Wears, from dusk to dusk,
The mask of comedy. His smiles
Radiate from the inside out,
Like the rings of a ripe sapling
Exposed to sunlight.
Regardless of the face he beholds,
His delight is immediate,
Epiphanic, insatiable. He squeals,
Continually gargles saliva
Growing baby teeth cause to flow,
And I, by trilling
Taught in myriad Spanish classes,
Am able to converse in his idiom,
Dovetail our inarticulate patois.

He sits on a fiberglass throne
And surveys our eating habits,
Scoots about the kitchen,
Over frictionless vinyl,
*

In his Supercoupe, like a fiddler crab,
Sideways, unadroit, definite
In his intentions to arrive anywhere.
Atop the bed or on the carpet,
Plush to his supple, nubby touch,
In the front hall, he stretches out,
Rises on his knees, in an effort to crawl,
Rolls from back to belly,
Then reverses without notice,
Like an AT-6
Simulating combat maneuvers;
Inevitably, he comes to rest on my chest.

Of pleasures derived from our second child,
None is so totally gratifying
Or more enlightening than the love
Between four-year-old Trilogy
And Troika, which has grown synergistically.
When they're together, she can do nothing
(Whether inventing strange sounds
To distract him from the bottle,
Yanking his hands and feet,
In keeping beat with music
Groaning from a heated TV,
Or soothing his smooth goose down
With a Madonna-like quietude)
That ever fails to make him gleeful,
Calm an unreasonable crying spell,
Knot him tightly in her blood tie.

Most of all, my wife and I admire
The ineffable closeness that possesses them.
Unlike relationships we've known before,
Theirs is lacking all jealousies.
No rivalry, based on possessions,
Attentions rendered by doting parents,
Dispensations and double standards
Related to age and sex, exists.
Surely, if ever Genesis
Were recreated, even in evanescence,
Before our Earth-weary eyes,
This, where these two revel
And cavort with quintessential innocence,
*

Which we've been privileged
To witness, would be Eden,
Peopled with its prelapsarian deities.

5/24/78 — [2] (01420)

Oxford Nocturne ^Δ

Only last night, we sat outside,
Admiring the giant talisman-moon rising,
Listening to the soft-struck overtones
From the cupolated courthouse dissipating
In the humid gloom embracing midnight,
Then 1 a.m., then two,

And we talked of Aristotle's *Poetics*,
Faulkner's epicene women,
His fascination with hermaphroditism,
Nympholepsy, and notions of romantic chastity,
Nixon's abject abrogation of truth,
Kennedy's mistresses, Tinker Bell.

She dreamed aloud her unfulfilled wishes
To stay awake forever,
Crowd her life with gentle lovers,
And pretend to be crowned queen
Of New Orleans society, "called out"
To dance with every masked Cyrano.

He incorporated, in the chain she wove,
Golden links of his own fancy,
Imagining himself her savior, Lothario,
Capable of containing her urgent desires,
Making her serve his own puissant ends
By genuflecting to her writhing psyche.

I reeled and teetered vertiginously
On my earthly high wire,
Kissing their eyes with my poetical spirit,
Twice missed my footing,
Nearly plunging into the netless abyss
Defining the desolation of our desperate lives.

Now, morning is a painful cranial throbbing.
The sun is a burning rubbish pile
*

Set in the middle of a landfill,
Whose gaseous effluvium suffocates bell notes
Choking in the throat of the courthouse.
Our talk is of coffee, aspirins. Faulkner is dead.

Having resumed our doomed pretenses
And put on our Ku Klux Klan
Suit and shoes, assumed our respectability,
We're ready to teach school, prepare briefs,
Poeticize, and forget how human voices
Nearly waked us from our drowning dreams.

5/26/78   (00060)

[Freedom is the rough brush strokes] ^Δ

Freedom is the rough brush strokes
Van Gogh used to apply impasto to his soul.
It's the fiercely insatiable insanity
That permits the spirit to override inhibition,
Exist in a sphere both outside and within
The psyche's expectations simultaneously,
While rising briefly, before succumbing to fatigue,
To the pinnacle, where the cornered beast,
Gripping survival in one hirsute hand,
The impregnably chaste and perfectly taintless lady
Of all man's dreams in the other,
Contemplates life's self-perpetuating mediocrity,
Then plunges earthward, to his extinction.

5/27/78   (01020)

Iconoclast ^Δ

Rituals haloing Trilogy's living
Might be indigenous jays,
Robins, redbirds, furry squirrels
Perched, one moment, nervous, alert,
Disturbed by their own rapid breathing,
Then dissolved in shadow,
Shifted, changed in coloration and shape,
*

Disappearing forever,
As new habits inhabit the places
They've vacated.

This morning,
Forces which order each week
Into days allotted for work and repose,
Hours segmented into sleep,
Wakefulness, and fleet moments
Given over to my soul for seeing,
Resurrecting, from the numbing ennui of reality,
Bits and pieces of natural piety,
Human beauty, and glimpses into the ethereal,
Embrace me in a blinding silence.

I am neither myself nor the shade
That once resembled my sentient self.
Since I've already gained distance on dawn,
Only my memories will take her to school today,
Sing in preposterously gleeful harmony
As we leave the rutted driveway,
Enter tree-shaded West Columbia,
Pass Chuck's Florist Shop,
Jack and Ann's house, hold hands,
As I relinquish Trilogy for three eternities.

For what conceivable reason
Could the circumstances have diverted me,
Made me miss this last day
Of her first monumental experience?
Is it that I'm overly sentimental,
Burdened by a vulnerable gentleness
That turns even the most mundane activity
I share with my daughter into a sacrament
Invested with godliness? Do I
Make too much of the breaking of ritual,

Or is there inherent in my disappointment
A disparaging sadness that presages death itself,
Adumbrates the almost absurd irrefutability
Of the passing of all things good and decent?
Whatever the explanation, I weep
On missing her graduation from preschool
And pray, with deep, compassionate feeling,
*

That I've not permanently frightened away
The jays and redbirds, robins and squirrels
That populate the places where we've worshiped together.

6/1/78 — [1] (01421)

Fire-Breathing Sky-Dragon

Suddenly, the sky was alive
With a thousand vibrating viper tongues
Sliding out, flickering amphibiously,
Retracting into Leviathan's wide mouth.

Wind-scorned treetops
Were nearly torn loose from moorings,
In the oceanic, black forest
That floated the vast sea-dragon,

As it flapped its massive tail
In spastic, convulsive smacks.
Its anger was white-hot.
Violence rained from its engorged eyes.

Soon, in uncontained frenzy,
Its writhing body loosed a tide
So high as to o'erleap the shores
Separating earth from horizon

And inundated the land with water,
Before it finally swam away.
Now, the sky is a smooth, cerulean hue.
Night invites its frightened navigators inside.

6/1/78 — [2] (05584)

The Operation

Today, traffic is backed up
Half the length of the taxi strip.
Blunt, fleet objects land and rotate
Like nurses, interns, ward orderlies,
Physicians, visitors investing hospital corridors
With the awful, furious finality
*

Of their ephemeral endeavors. They pass by
This stalled stretcher, while I wait
To be wheeled into the operating room.

Suddenly, a terrific whine
Rising from fanjets, a forward surge
And turn onto the runway, the takeoff,
Whose coarse reverberations
Awaken my innards from their corpulent sleep,
Occur with a disturbing simultaneity.
My ears gasp for breath.
Etherized air, forced through menacing nozzles,
Transports my dazed spirit into oblivion.

The severing is neither swift nor smooth.
Being borne aloft
Is radical surgery, whose accompanying flight
Leaves behind, in its slipstream,
An incision that heals immediately. The stitches
That seal the air through which I fly
Are made of wing-tip vortices.
Recovery is a safe flare, touchdown.
Arrival is awakening from restive anesthesia.

6/9 & 6/11/78 (05585)

Intimations of Feeding the Death-Worm

All day, solitude has followed me
Like a boa constrictor stalking a mouse
Within a five-sided house of glass.
Each step I take, every posture,
Facial expression, motion I make,
Gives my position away,
Renders me violable, indefensible prey
To fears of being swallowed alive,
Which slither hysterically, by the millions,
In the dry lacunae of my brain's vipers' pit.

There is no place to hide,
Inside my wakefulness. The resigned mind
Cringes before the design of its fate,
Evacuates its bowels, urinates uncontrollably,
*

As, in a graceful series of daily serpentine contractions
And menstrual relaxations, life's jaws
Fix on my immobile soul, from behind,
And initiate the silent, inextricable digestion,
Whose juices will soon reduce my being
To feces and food for the insatiable death-worm.

6/20/78 — [1] (05586)

Doubly Inspired by the Moondog Mistress

Forty miles out, ranging westerly,
I finally separate from suburbanites
Returning home from work and gain speed.
My eyes become artificers
Trained in maintaining a true magnetic heading
Despite the mind's tendency
To deviate from the salamandrine highway.

Necromancy embraces my dazed intimations
Of one day taking to the road,
Vacant of purpose, destinationless,
To journey, like a migrating butterfly,
Toward a recondite rain forest.
Suddenly, I separate from the vessel
That has so neatly contained my soul
Within its ribbed, fleshy, tumescent cage.

As my spirit soars free,
The skeletal vehicle drops from sight,
Disappears, as whisperous, filamentous clouds
Kiss my winged eyes. The sky
Takes my weight without complaint,
Tightens its smooth, twilighted thighs
About my naive desire, writhing, writhing,
Until, once again, fragmentation climaxes
And the eyes separate from the imagination
That has driven them to see,
In nonexistent intuitions,
The beginnings of ungerminated dreams.

In this boneless, stoneless, primitive place,
Where not even bacterial stirrings
*

Or tornadic dust storms occur,
What remains of my obliterated, displaced selves
Slowly coalesces in a floating halo
That burns ferociously about its edges,
Turning like a dervish pinwheel
Spitting imagistic scintillas.

Now, formless night, like an ocean,
Occupies all space not taken by islands
Flickering, in stippled silence,
High in the galaxy haunted by mankind.
Far below, ranging ever westerly,
A weary driver pulls off the road,
To recuperate from the endless miles
That have lured him on, past endurance,
To discover a new place to worship his muse.

Gazing upward, he sees a ring,
Phosphorescent and shimmering, about the moon,
Fluctuating back and forth, and is mesmerized
By its mystic recognition of his tiny, rising voice
Crying to his distant mistress, Diana,
To return to him once more,
That again he might kiss her eyelids
And lay orchids on her throbbing, naked breasts.

6/20/78 — [2] (05587)

A Summer Affair

This June afternoon,
Through which I leisurely pass,
So seethingly green, so rife
And sweet, so incalculably adolescent,
Is a blond-headed temptress
Undefiled despite repeated seasons
Violating her fleshy abdomen,
Wet vagina,
And breasts barely noticeable
Yet undulant as ocean floors.

My eyes kiss her leafy corn
Luxuriating in its newness,
*

Wheat uncut for grazing,
And subtle bean sprouts
Blading their way toward the light
As though it were pubic hair
Covering the young summer's
Loving source. I'm thrall.
Seldom has a spell taken me
So irresistibly away from myself.

Ultimately, dusk sifts in,
Changing the lusty gradations of love
To sensory fatigue. My psyche
Retires from its rituals,
To bathe the eyes, take leave
Of afternoon's bed. My mistress,
Having robed her satisfied body
In diaphanous shadows, remains silent,
As I whisper a hasty good-bye
And head home to confess my infidelity.

6/20/78 — [3] (05596)

The Music of Ancient Pompeii

For Jon Washington & Company

Two epicene shades,
Mouthing Pompeii's most lustful complaints,
Ran their fingers down my spine,
Bit my ears with their feline screaming.
Flutes, crowds, tambourines,
Skins stretched to reverberate the earth
Catapulted me out of my senses.
My fleshed carapace slumped in its seat,
While my raw, renascent psyche
Soared toward the source of sound,
Penetrated the man-made chords,
To the godly spark, surrounded by the darkness,
From which all inspiration is ignited.

Once arrived, the music and I
Were united in a communion of vibration
So profoundly tactile
*

We were lost in each other's touch.
Caught in a mutual frenzy, rapt,
The two sirens surrendered
To the hot shafts of my imagination,
Running ahead of the scored notes
Flying from their fingers and lips.
For hours, like mating gyrfalcons,
We copulated in the high, thin air,
Until the music stopped and I dropped
Back into my chair, covered with lava.

6/20/78 — [4] (01325)

Willy Experiences a Stroke, at the Wheel

There is heresy in the air this morning.
The moon is still in plain view,
And myriad naked hitchhikers,
Holding signs denoting Hades and Limbo
As their desired destinations,
Line the highway I travel alone.
A drizzle has begun
Despite an inestimably blue sky
For a hundred miles in every direction,
As though someone neglected
Tightening a tub faucet
Or plumbing above has begun to leak.
Squinting upward,
Through the glaring windshield,
I'm unable to detect the actual sun.
I suspect invisible clouds
Of collaborating to form cataracts
Over my eyes, disguising the fact
That all is not as it should be.
Suddenly, my breakfast rebels.
A very hysterical paranoia
Overwhelms me with the realization
That my unsuspecting equanimity
Has been called into question,
Threatened, and that I'm not well.
Suddenly, my routine destination
*

Eludes memory. My body freezes
As if anesthetized with amnesic fluid.
Even my identity, like a boarder
Who's always paid his rent
A year in advance, leaves me
Without notice. Forgetting
Fills the vacancy in my duplex.
In the high grass at the edge,
Past which monstrous vehicles rush,
Throwing back black, catalytic sulfurs
And gravelly tornadoes in my face,
I wait, helplessly paralyzed
From the brain upward
And the nose down, through my legs,
To my toe tips, stiff with rigor mortis.
Only my eyes yet register
A perfectly azure sky,
Moonless, without clouds,
And a sun so bright
No rain could reach the earth,
For evaporating in midair.
There are no hitchhikers now,
Except for me. Patiently, I wait
For some concerned, unhurried soul
To stop and ferry me home.

6/21/78 — [1] (02413)

The First Day of Summer

Central Missouri,
This first, cool, green day of summer,
Is a budding teenage female
Just becoming aware of her breasts,
Pubic hair,
Menstrual seasons,
Callipygian suppleness.

Her burgeoning fields
Invite my eyes to delight their appetite,
Taste of fresh-turned earth,
So rife and redolent of fertilizers,
*

Waiting for its germinating seeds,
Anxious to experience their myriad explosions,
To rise, Phoenix-like, out of the rain.

Yet when I ask her name,
Reach, with my anxious eyes,
To take her slender hand,
Kiss her glistening lips,
Persuade her to allow me
Into the sweet coverts
Of her confidence, she blushes,

Backs away from my imagination,
Retires in shyness
And trepidation,
As though I might be her enemy,
A poet bearing magical philters
Capable of metamorphosing youth,
Aging her prematurely.

With deep disappointment,
I withdraw my sensual evocations
And sink into despondency,
Like a suitor severely refused
For some foolish concupiscence
Or a eunuch cuckolded by his own libido
For trying to conceive preposterous possibilities.

6/21–22/78 — [2] on 6/21 & [1] on 6/22   (05588)

Cosmic Lights

The sky under which I drive, tonight,
Is a forest striated with shadowy mists
Penetrated by a thousand peering eyes.
Coaly pupils, shimmering red and green,
As though they belong to raccoons,
Chipmunks, and porcupines instead of Mars
And gaseous Saturn, attract my gaze
Momentarily. I tremble from fatigue,
And as I pass slower-moving vehicles,
Memory transports me to Lake Superior,
Where my youth waded into the fifties
*

For the first time and drowned
In the sweetest body-lust and love-spill.
Now, a preposterously overripe moon
Rises, solitary, docile, unassailed
By all other creatures, in the vast bowl
Haloing my smooth-floating passage.
Again, the past crosses my vision
Like a lithe deer, then disappears
Into the darkness, but not before
Awakening reminiscences of two o'clocks
Spent racing between Duluth and Minong,
Lake Nebagamon and Brule,
Over sinuous county highways,
In heated quest of female flesh
To devastate. Such a vast eye,
Containing all things lost by man,
Has always watched over my trips.
Yet, tonight, its taciturnity
Whispers, across the immemorial distance
Separating us from each other,
Intimations of solitude and futility,
As if this might be the last time
These eyes will remain uncommitted
While I continue to violate their sanctuary.
Suddenly, the entire welkin goes black,
As an elongated cloud dissolves
Into every lighted fissure above the horizon.
Only head beams, scratching the zinc plate
That ribbons the earth I traverse,
Awaken my sleepy eyes to their destiny,
Crouching just ahead. I press the brakes,
Yet the vessel continues in freewheeling,
Like a friction toy pushed forcefully
By a child at play. Entering the forest
Through an invisible, dilating iris,
I finally arrive, abandon my vehicle,
And lie down in a moon-dust desert
Dotted with tombstones engraved with names
Old friends once owned,
Then traded for unaging anonymity.
With involuntary and effortless expectation,
The inexorable dissolving commences.
*

What was recently my bodily being
Becomes a pulsating, phosphorescent mass,
Whose gyrating incandescence
Begins to expand like spilled paint
Over slick paper. The sky brightens;
Clouds lift, fractionate, scatter
Into bits of bright confetti.
A new moon has just been sighted
Flying in a mad, ecstatic, elliptical frenzy
About haughty, nude Diana,
Once more strutting across the universe.

6/21/78 — [3] (01326)

La Pavilion ∆

Disembodied waifs take their places
At tables in this flickering chiaroscuro
Softened by piped-in music,
Candles, darned linen, chipped crystal,
Catered to by college students
Garbed in starched black-and-white uniforms.
Occasionally, entire families arrive,
Who, during their fleet stays,
Lend a domestic note of tranquillity
To this otherwise gloomy way station
For traveling salesmen and conventioneers.
From my routine corner booth,
I'm able to survey the whole floor.
My eyes witness people seated
In varied degrees of eating,
Speaking conspiratorially, reaching out
To capture an avowed disbeliever
With hyperbole and persuasive prevarication
Emanating from an overinflated ego.
My ears flinch under the inanities
Unleashed by middle-aged ladies
Newly baptized into the faith of real estate,

And district, regional, and national managers
Representing worldwide cartels,
Selling firefighting equipment, tractors,
*

Remaindered designer fashions,
Rain gear, voting machines, ladders,
And plastic phylacteries.
As I swallow some dry baked potato,
Saw a sinewy piece of roast beef
Garnished with wilted parsley,
And nurse the tepid house rosé,
These voices converge on my vulnerability,
And for a moment, I envy
Their strenuous sense of being accepted,
Belonging. I covet their membership
In the sororities and confraternities
Devoted to the furtherance of commerce,
Christian love, and Kiwanian camaraderie.
Bereft of family and group identity,
My shadow is lost in the half-light
That remains unilluminated by their gregariousness.
I, not they, am the real waif
In this motel. I *live* here.

6/22/78 — [2] (02412)

Black Tuesday

Tonight, my heart files for bankruptcy
Under Chapter 11. All creditors
Shed tears for its abrupt collapse.
None suspected that my dreams
Had been hypothecated against loans
On a long-overdue note or my hopes
Turned over to a broker, as collateral
On bonds that would never mature.

Now, all my capital is squandered.
Those who esteemed my dealings
Look askance at my shabby estate,
And I'm no longer allowed to indulge
My most pleasurable avocation
In the company of former associates.
Marriage has constrained, under contract,
The highly speculative nature of my heart's desires.

6/22/78 — [3] (01327)

Paean to Crazy Al

For Al Pethtel

His blood courses across frets,
Through vein-strings,
Toward the mainspring of his inspiration.
Screaming intensity
Escapes from his bones, like steam,
As his brain creates the score he plays,
Within its flaming hemispheres,
By translating, from incandescent air,
Invisible images into harmonies
His fingers fling at eternity's ears.
He is the bass guitar he manipulates.

We mere ungifted novitiates
Sit listening in dazed amazement,
Trying to penetrate his reverberations,
That, in touching their origins,
We might be blessed by his gods.
His flights stimulate desires
To free ourselves from ties
That keep us gyved to our tedious lives.
Ultimately, his picking resurrects us
For our quotidian existence.
He is the high priest of mystic guitars.

6/22/78 — [4] (01303)

[How strange! The dead of night]

How strange! The dead of night
Has come back around
And changed phases with midmorning.
The customary sun has been subjugated,
Billeted in an invisible cave
Behind the tumultuous storm line
That is clawing an awkward path,
Like a maddened crab, across my sight.
A frightening, ocherous striation
Radiates, with Rorschach indecisiveness,
From an indistinct hole in the sky,
*

Projecting its tornado-laden fingers
Through my mind's paranoid stirrings.
Inside the questionable refuge
My car provides in this swelling ocean
Inundating the dry flatlands
Over which I've driven
So many times before without suspecting
That it is a vast seafloor
From antediluvian times, I cringe.
Now, an impenetrable rain-sheet
Cascades in every direction,
As though I were under the full thrust
Of a raging, cresting wave
Just breaking through a splintered dam.
Intermittent lightning is a fluorescent tube
Blinking eerily beneath a bad ballast,
And I am blind Tiresias,
Forced off into the highway's safety lane,
Trying to outlast the outraged elements
Rather than continuing to submit
To the possibility of driving right off
Vision's precipice, into a nether existence,
Or being swallowed alive by the albino leviathan
That swims in this day's opaque, viscid eyes.
For an hour, providence hovers above,
Envelops my stalemated spirit
In this airless compartment,
As though I were being held at bay
By a vicious cougar pacing on my roof,
Stalking a way to gain entrance
Into my fear-weakened sanctuary.
Intimations of tininess and fragility
Slip through the mind's static defenses.
Yet just when I find myself
Doubting the storm's ultimate cessation
And my eventual escape into a universe
Made up of controlled environments,
The clouds and rain fractionate
Like oil spilled in a vat of water.
Light pours through breaking seams,
Until relief comes to the inundated plains,
And I enter traffic's tentative flow again,
*

With head beams glowing white-hot.
As I go forward, it appears that
A vast, insensate creature
Has ravaged the entire countryside
In foraging undiscoverable nourishment.
Limestone boulders broken from cliffs
Litter the highway, at whose sides
Stalled passenger vehicles lay strewn
Like feisty hounds brushed viciously away
By a cornered bear. Three twisted transports,
Each guarded by a state patrol car,
Remain as evidence of the devastation
Attending this most recent upheaval.
Heading home, brooding in silence,
I can't help wondering why
Violence of this kind arises and strikes,
Denying us the right to discuss measures
Calculated to avoid such confrontations,
At least participate in the decision-making process
For their eventual disposition.

6/23/78   (05589)

Encapsulations

Thick, monolithic concrete partitions
Form a shadowy house of cards,
Within whose eerie superstructure
I park and abandon my car.
Burdened by an inconsequent briefcase,
My otherwise sleek shadow
Seeks its way through the maze,
Toward an escape escalator,
Ascends, in a series of smooth squeaks,
To its end, and steps into the terminal,
As the moving stairs descend, again,
Into the darkness.

A voracious light
Devours the last remains of my identity,
Vacuums my expatriate body
Into a vicious, swirling centrifuge,
*

At whose edges millions of transients are collected,
Their faces frozen in cloned, dazed poses,
As though each were the ghost
Each other has seen in a dream
Too recent to be dream, waiting
For some ultimate intimate inspiration
To inform them they have achieved immortality
Rather than the precarious status of "passenger."

By sheer force, I break from the mass
And fly out, like a meteorite,
Toward paranoia's checkpoint,
Where my body is bombarded with x-rays
Before being thrust into another corridor
That leads to destination's boarding gate.
I might be Jonah, swallowed alive
Within a gigantic skeleton
Whose gills are anodized ducts
Moving conditioned air to the extremities,
Whose nerves, arteries, and veins
Are exposed wiring, conduits, tubes, pipes,

Whose bones are steel girders
Supporting the entire length of breached creature
Through whose vast insides I traipse
As if spelunking for the first time.
Ultimately, a recognizable set of shapes,
Numbers, and letters gains my attention,
Beckons me change directions, take heed
That I've reached the place of reckoning
And must surrender my membership
In the race of mortals to unguessed fates
Swarming, just beyond the plate glass,
Like flies attacking a decaying killer whale.

Once more, I submit to encapsulation,
Resign myself to the degradation
Of being flushed through another intestine
Like food decomposing slowly into feces
Or used fluid being drained
By a city's lift station and removed
To a sewage-treatment facility.
The segmented fluke worm that's attached
*

From the main body to the flying machine
Passes my disembodied spirit along.
I am sucked into a seat, shackled,
As if preparing myself for cyanide gas,

And made to listen to echoes of echoes
Emanating, from a source beyond comprehension,
Information relating to emergency exits,
Oxygen masks, measures to take
In the unlikely eventuality of a forced landing
Or crash. Images of a Dantesque world
Crowded with lizards, snakes, and dragons
Swirl in the opiate smoke
Filling the narrow fuselage that holds my life,
Within its thin, membranous embrace,
A sheer half-inch away from extinction.
I pray for the vessel's safe passage,

As it slides through a tunnel in space,
Realizing now that my entire life
Has been a continuous existence within limits
Prescribed by artificial light, walls
Squared off or made cylindrical
To disguise the basic nature of confinement,
And distances to be mastered by wheels,
Fan blades, elevators, and, to a lesser degree,
Feet scratching concrete, fiber, and vinyl.
Canals, conduits, covered aqueducts,
Anal cloacae coalesce. My perspective flows,
And I am drawn headfirst in a birth

That delivers my being back to earth
Intact, ecstatic to have survived the flight,
Whose blessed arrival ensures me
Yet another opportunity to devise a way
To escape the human limitations
That define the scope of my survival
And find an opening that has no strictures,
Leading to a land without borders,
Through which my soul might be transported.
Ah, yes, I've bested the fates again.
Hope begins in locating the poem to write;
Salvation is its long-sought song.

6/26/78 (05590)

Drummer Judas at His Last Sales Meeting

Once again, the men convene
To review offerings for the new spring season.
Three days become an argot
Dotted with side vents, gorges,
Seven-inch-drop suits
Vested, with extra contrasting trousers,
Sportscoats showing the "imported look."

The nomenclature of fibers
Reiterates a xylophonic fugue in their ears —
Tropical, texturized cotton-polyesters,
Solid kettle cloths and oxfords,
Nylon whisper-overchecks,
Pinfeathers, poplins, linen plaids,
Hopsacks, patch madrases, tattersalls.

The disciples make notations on summary sheets,
Intrude occasionally to ascertain a truth
Pertaining to make, availability,
Salesmen's commissions, advertising participation,
Presentation to customers. Despite isolated discord,
A basic agreement that the products are gospel
Shimmers on their da Vinci–ed demeanors.

Only one among the gathered crew
Refuses to be accused, by future inquisitions,
Of sycophantish worship. His hands tremble
Beneath the table as he contemplates his apostasy,
Rallying courage to defect to a competitor
Who's guaranteed him the territories of Purgatory
And Hades. He yearns to make the connection.

6/29–30/78 (02411)

Fugue

Due to rain, an unusually smooth
Race against gravity is concluded.
Peering through superstitious eyes
Filled with fright, I glimpse the windows
Streaking with spermlike vermiculations,
Changing the plastic into sea coral
Pitted with fossils. The waiting clouds
*

Begin their endless, voracious engulfment.
Soon, there is merely a vast morass,
Gray and laden with unexpected grottoes,
Whose denizens claw and buffet the ship
As if to bring it down, subjugate us,
Cannibalize our delicate mechanisms.

Memory bumps into itself
On its way back through the gloom,
Trying to find whatever
It doesn't yet realize it left behind.
Time rewinds itself.
I rush past people rushing, in reverse,
Toward a million entryways,
Toward a million back doors,
Toward a million beds
Empty or filled with the soft sleeping
Of wives, mistresses, odalisques, succubi,
As though a colossal vacuum
Has somehow been attached to my spirit.

Now, this vessel penetrates earth's surface.
The gothic pinnacles of a billion cathedrals
And medieval castles swim below me,
In docile and delicate suspensions,
While we continue our ascent endlessly,
In a mellifluous, mystical thrust,
Pressing ever upward, toward the sun.
Memory and the present coalesce
Like two parallel tracks finally touching
Somewhere beyond invisibility,
And at once, all omens and portents
Fall away in naked abandonment.
The mind floats free in space.

Tumbling through blue ecstasies,
Reckless as a balloon whose nozzle
Has accidentally come unknotted,
It races toward the faces
Love has indelibly etched on perceptions
The saturnine morning gloominess
Has mercilessly disconnected from vision,
As if to arrest my soul,
Incarcerate it in irreversible forgetfulness.
Before my senses, the wide horizon
*

Funnels through day's neck,
Into a perfectly clear, star-faced night
That embraces my safe passage.

Home is the slender, sentimental lady
Whose gentle tears were the rain;
It is the girl and tiny boy-cub
Whose cries and tired exhortations
Were the air shrieking by,
The strange whining of jet engines,
The fitful, hysterical paranoia
That filled my pained ears with vibrations
All day long. Now, I am returned,
Neither conquistador nor victim,
Rather survivor of my own obsessions,
Alive forever in this moment of kissing,
Immortalized by their relieved, extravagant eyes.

7/10/78 — [1] (05591)

En soto voce †

disentangle
exploding girandoles,
mimosa clusters
dissolving into a pink
        extinction
so mortal, so absolutely
female, as to blow the lenses
through a hole in
oblivion's volcano

7/10/78 — [2] (07722)

Bequests △

For my beloved Jan

The earth, this misty morning,
Is a swollen ovum
Growing on the fundus of my poetic soul.
Its children, Troika and Trilogy,
Have not yet reached term,
*

Exploded the mind
That has kept them confined
To creations I've projected on their uninformed psyches,
Or seized the moon,
Eternal creature of amnesic delights,
By her bare-breasted whiteness.

Soon, too soon,
Emergence will occur,
Delivering them from my expectations,
And they will begin the outpouring of words
Their voiceless unconscious absorbed
Before being borne aloft
On inspirations conceived in their own imaginations.
For now, I content myself
With mesmeric pleasures, inventing verse
With which to slow the earth,
Orbiting my future with irreversible determination.

7/13/78   (01422)

On the Dismantling of Obsolete Habitations: Molting

Genes entwined in their own quotidian being
Slip the knot,
Slither free, and begin, in silence,
The inevitable migration out of bondage,
Back to solifidian origins.
The mind-gauges lose pressure,
Register erratic dips
Suggestive of corrupt volcanic eruptions.
Narcoleptic fogs,
Like tapestries hung from cold castle walls,
Line thought-chambers,
At various points along labyrinthine corridors
Forming the way his days progress.
Even the engorged, corpulent physique
Relinquishes its appetites and physiological thirsts.
Hair thins. His nails cease growing.
The flesh whitens, as if his entire body
Were an aborted fetus
*

Suspended in a sealed, formaldehyde-filled beaker.
Even the serpent who guarded the twin gates
To his desires' flaming dominion
Sleeps in an innocuous, shriveled coil,
Dreaming of ancient ravishments.
All along the watchtowers,
Circuit breakers flip switches.
Valves collapse, from ichor escaping veins.
A murmurous dirge reverberates the bones,
As though his grieving, breathing corpse
Were impacted in concrete
Over which a million daily vehicles
Pass on their way to and from oblivion.

Suddenly, morning is a bottomless crevasse
Filled with suffocating sunlight.
His eyes react with violent, burning pain
As he rises to the surface,
Holding both legs with a death-grip,
Reaching the upper edge of nightmare,
In a dead-man's float,
Leaving beneath his upward thrust
A momentary suction-funnel
The remaining hours of his existence
Tunnel back through,
Until all past and future are glued
To an immediacy completely used up.
Slowly, the last clean air,
Hovering in cranial and cortical lacunae,
Surrenders to his urgent, futile suspirations.
Resurrected from the dead,
He exits a protracted waking yawn,
With parasitical succubi and incubi
Still clinging to his ruptured, bloody umbilicus,
And is washed ashore, to be freshly born.

7/18/78 — [1] (05592)

Miss Emily [Δ]

The soul's topiary grows monstrous
With neglect. No one
Appears to live on the grounds any longer
*

Or comes at orderly intervals
To trim, mow, or hoe the formal gardens,
Weed-infested and overgrown
With mimosa seedlings sprouting in grotesque profusion
From every available plot of earth.

It's been ten years at least
Since townspeople have perceived lights
Blinking lambently, at night,
From the old mansion's eyes
Or noticed comings and goings
Of those paying social visits
And making service calls,
Ten years since lightning struck,

Ripping through the attic,
Collapsing the chimney inward,
Brick by brick, setting fire to rooms
In which peacefully sleeping fantasies reposed,
Extinguishing, with incendiary evanescence,
The fragile, passionate desires
Of one who yet hides
In the charred depths of her lingering mortification,

Afraid to come outside,
Actually unable, by now,
For having survived persistent anorexia nervosa,
To admit her brittle memories to fresh air,
For fear of their immediate disintegration.
It's been ten years or more
Since we glimpsed her supple, naked soul
Cavorting in the gardens, under a magnoliaed rain.

7/18/78 — [2] (00061)

Entering the Gone Land

For Joshua and Cheryl Lucenti

Electrified pizzicati stick to my spine
Like suction-tipped arrows
Shot by a thousand ancient Visigoths,
Aimed haphazardly skyward.
The synthesizer's notes are footsteps
Pressing persistently through the solitude,
*

Toward my unlocked fortress.
The sheer abrasion of their driving cacophonies
Releases the hinged inertia of my brain.
They wake me from my aging lethargy,
Invite me to participate in a celebration
For trombones, trumpets, alto saxophones.
Suddenly, all the caged rhythms,
Long confined to the penitentiary for lost souls,
In which my stultified, fetid senses
Have languished, explode in spectacular mutiny.
My bones tingle. An ecstasy
So close to the old erotic climaxing
That occurred involuntarily in youth returns
To remind me how piquant is the urgency to feel,
Be reached, conceive time as nights,
Eye-blinks, knee-taps, kisses,
Not decades or lifetimes squandered
On nonspontaneous, inessential polemics.
The convoluted, fugue-strewn jazz
Discloses to me the truth of my ineptitude,
Exposes my Van Winkled soul as a body
Abandoned, years ago, to impotency.
Now, my shimmering flesh draws tight,
As though an incredible shrinking has begun.
A hole in the swirling ceiling opens
To accept my anonymous spirit,
Like a colossal mouth ingesting a wafer
Offered by the high priest of death wishes.
Over and over, as if rolling up a hill,
I go toward the music's awesome precipice,
Then pass into a happy, passionate trance,
In which my resolve to disappear forever
Is accomplished. I am granted safe passage
To the land of sweet, sensual infinities,
Where mortal ashes assume new shapes,
Change the very nature of metaphysics,
In accommodating to immortality's corporeality.
In dazzling ravishment, I leave myself,
Consumed, dismantled, dissolved,
With the soaring sounds coeval, inextricable —
A gone man gone absolutely mad.

7/18/78 — [3] (01329)

Up from Egypt

I fly across the countryside,
Lightheaded,
Frightened by the vastness of the solitude
That engulfs my psyche in green leaves,
Mesmerized
By the absolutely bucolic cow-scape
And cloud-eyes
That attend my escape like innocents
Made to witness a gratuitous medieval execution.

Suddenly, the serpentine highway
Forgets in which direction its destination lies,
Comes to an abrupt cessation.
I apply my brakes in time to avoid crashing
Into a black cat, or its shadow,
Racing across the blood-rusty dusk
Sifting down like dye in water,
And leap from my paranoia before it explodes,
Fated to go the rest of the way on foot.

7/19/78 — [1] (01330)

The Martyrs

For Jan,
my love

While he circumnavigates the globe,
In quest of a more expeditious shortcut
To the mind's concupiscent Spice Islands,
His two children question his absence,
Establish fantastical images of him
From artist's conceptions their mother renders
From memory. Amerigo Vespucci,
Cristóbal Colón, Fernão de Magalhães,
Vasco da Gama rise, like gallant conquistadors,
From her disquisitions on his great escapades.

And they grow from crawling, into speech,
Toward independent formulations of liberty
And personal freedom,
Believing in his incredible infallibility,
*

While he ranges ever more irretrievably away,
In his disinclination to return to them
And be haunted by such complex responsibilities
As recognizing his children as his
And kissing his wife good evening
Without wishing to consummate his lust.

Despite the extended, letterless gaps
In their marriage, she maintains a faith
That presages his eventual salvation
And the renascence of their once profound communion.
Ultimately, the children, emulating her stoicism,
Edge away from the shore, together,
Roaming in search of their fatherless past,
To recapture the essence of innocence
They never knew, let alone imagined
Should have been a natural adjunct to childhood.

Canvassing land after inaccessible land,
They finally arrive, by chance,
At a tiny island inhabited by a gaunt man
With glazed eyes, stranded and alone.
They carry his limp body to their vessel
And set sail with their shipwrecked heritage,
Ultimately reaching the time before their birth,
East of dawn, where their mother waits
To salve his lacerations, slake his thirst,
And succor his broken heart on the journey home.

7/19/78 — [2] (01423)

Bereft

*For Jerry Walters,
printmaker*

Bereft
Is a state of mind,
Bounded on all eight sides
By scaly chimeras.
It's an incandescent vacuum
Lighted by fire-belching bats
Flying haphazardly into the glass,
As if to shatter the illusion
That survival is sightless.

Bereft
Is a foster home
For souls abandoned by God.
It is lungs gasping for breath,
A tunnel running underneath Styx,
An echo chamber
Loaded with diseased rodents
Screeching hysterically to escape the pain
Of their inescapable complaints.

Bereft
Is a footprint left on the moon,
An electroluminescent glow
Viewed under a raging sun.
It's a space capsule
Whose broken heat shield
Forces it to orbit an unapproachable globe.
It's a vast computer
Lacking a solitary silicon chip.

Bereft
Is, ultimately, this series of metaphors
I've dreamed into existence
To distract myself from the real fact
That other than my verse,
There is nothing in the universe
Worth waking for or disturbing.
And it's sad that even my poetry
Shows no signs of recognizing its master.

7/20/78   (02234)

Sun and Moon ^Δ

If Trilogy be the moon
And eight-month-old Troika the sun,
Then traditional characteristics
Must be forgotten or adjusted
To render this juxtaposition functional.

She is the flaming, radiant source
From which all energies emanate,
He the reflective entity
*

Recycling bright, twinkling smiles
And docility no tempests can fractionate.

Although each is a heavenly body
Orbiting in a galaxy ordered by parents
Whose sympathetic omniscience
Keeps chaotic objects
From crashing through, into their atmosphere,

And fathomless gravities from distracting them
From their balanced gyrations,
Neither logic Copernican
Nor Ptolemaic adequately explains
The nature of their strange rotations.

Whether sun chases moon
Or the reverse obtains remains to be determined
By time alone. Regardless, we assume
That their mutual attraction is godly ordained,
Their light symbiotic, their love universal and enduring.

7/21/78   (01424)

Sudden Cloudburst ^Δ

So spontaneous and uncontained
Is this steaming summer thunderstorm,
Underscoring this lonely dusk,
I'm unable to break from my solitude,
Return home, for fear of being drenched
                    to the bone.

I sit within the sterile skeletal husk
Of America's mastodon,
A fast-food fad-creature,
Tasting of its decaying flesh and mocha blood,
Wincing in ignorant and meek
                    resignation,

Realizing that I am here of my own volition,
Having exercised very scant control
Over the complaining appetites my body preempts
From a brooding, inarticulate soul.
I try twice to counteract my fright
                    of going outside,

While lightning skims across the earth's pond
And thunder undoes its disguises
A few at a time, as though determined
To expose itself, in public, to the elements,
That it might establish, once and for all,
                its masculinity.

Only, the rain forms a barrier of pointed pales
Before my feeble indecisiveness.
I see my elongated face, gaunt and horrified,
Mounted, in grotesque, mimic ridicule,
Atop each shaft. I stay put,
                imbibing coffee,

Until, after an indeterminate period of quietude,
The sky returns, in nocturnal decline,
To its gentle, if imponderable, demeanor,
And I enter the hours, still glistening,
Listen for distant reports, cringe yet
                from my entrapment.

7/24/78 (02266)

Taken Hostage

Never before have I overslept.
Why, then, this bright July morning,
Did my senses stretch past nine,
My eyes wake with slug trails
Designing their retinal tapestries,
My ears twitch uncontrollably
As if their receptors were clogged
With waves of last night's crickets
And rhythmic cicadas? My surmise
Is that something strictly nocturnal,
Like a fleet fantasy or foggy dream,
Perhaps an argentiferous portent
Of eventual plummeting to forgetting's depth,
Lured me into the forest,
From whose bowered desolation
No poor soul leaves unchanged.
I suspect, from my bones arthritic stiffness,
That the place where my transformation occurred
*

Must have been cave-wet and clammy
And cool as smooth eel skin
And, by the way my flesh has dried so,
That demons with eternally burning torches
Must have leapt through dense coverts,
Setting fire to the entire obscurity,
Under whose vast, shadowy canopy
I tried to hide from myself.
Although airy speculations
Are mere approximations of half-truths,
I believe that a stealthy, stalking felon
Wearing striped convict clothes
Must have escaped from the nearby penitentiary,
Where my soul performs guard duty
Over inmates remanded there
By my never-quite-satisfied psyche,
And found his way, somehow,
To this solitary room, where I rest
From the routine brutality of each waking day.

Now, I can't even move.
It's as if I were being held hostage
For an unnegotiable ransom
Consisting of my simple signature
Etched at the bottom of an endless series of mandates
And complaints against me personally.
I squirm. The tourniquets about my arms
And brain contract, as I refuse to acquiesce
To his threats and physical abuse.
Yet no matter the effort expended,
There's no apparent exit from this sequestration.
Frustrated and in extreme pain,
I finally give in to his rigorous insistence
That I submit my resignation
From the institution and exchange places with him,
Go behind bars,
Where I'll be free to pursue my solitude
In peace, relieved of the responsibility
For having to guard the Gates of Id.
When I finally rise from my bunk,
A hundred familiar eyes
Engulf me in their predatory gaze,
Tear the clothes from my body,

*

Make me stand naked before them,
As if they'll evaluate the puny, feeble reality
Of the colossus who not long ago
Made them quake with his sadistic vulgarity.
I tremble in the shimmering sunlight
That penetrates to the courtyard,
Wondering how this could have happened
And why, praying that I might prevail
Beyond the duration of my waking nightmare.

7/26/78 (05593)

St. Jerome

At 6:00 a.m.,
The city teeters on sleep's precipice,
Unable to make a clean break
With gratifying dreams
And the actual stuff from which they're made,
Just below, in morning's canyon.

On my way out of St. Louis,
Toward the country,
Going against clotting termites
Making their pilgrimage downtown,
I nod at hospitals, subdivisions,
Shopping centers not yet aroused

That are lying in last night's dewy grass
Like numerous drowsy lion prides
Waiting silently, patiently,
For their prey to awaken
And seek them out. I shout
As though I were hard of hearing,

Peering almost contemptuously
At the hell-bound innocents,
Contemning their destinies as mindless.
I vilify and excoriate the fate
That has persuaded them to stay there,
At the epicenter of devastation,

Where today, like every day,
A neutron mushroom will rise
*

Above the skyline, mistaken for pollution,
And an entire population
Will be stuffed, like mail, in burlap bags
And shipped home, each afternoon,

To receive a patriot's burial
In plots made for TV,
With microwave solemnity,
All watched over by the dazed eyes
Of eight-year-old children
Reciting Rabelais for nightly prayers.

As I dissolve further and further,
The scurrying termites thin to a trickle.
Billboard displays cease slashing my irises.
The land is all apple orchards
And orchid plants. Gardenia trees
Signal the paradisiacal outskirts I penetrate

Without ever actually realizing
Where the two boundaries fused.
Soon, the highway ends,
And I am arrived home,
Exempted from time's nagging strictures,
Anxious to assume the responsibilities of solitude.

7/27/78 — [1] (05594)

The "Golden Doors" △

For Jack and Ann Clay,
with love

My poems are ornate Ghibertian doors
Leading to the soul's cathedral.
Each frieze portrays a specific scene
From the heart's Passion Week,
Depicts daily agonies
My psyche endures while seeking truth,
Through mere words,
By reciting, in verse litanies,
Mysterious insights whispered by God.

Although the doors are locked,
Whenever the gentle knocking begins,
*

Behind my eyes' mind,
They admit me at worship time,
As if my presence were expected,
And allow me access to their altar,
Where, kneeling, I receive blessings
That emanate from Creation's ineffable lips.
When I leave, they remain forever open.

7/27/78 — [2] (02235)

A Family Man

*For my lady,
Janny*

My words are my children and wife.
My rhymes are their smiles.
Their eyes are my insights.
Their griefs spark my fire.

My dreams are their lips,
Kissing earth and sky.
Their love for each other
Is my flying song.

My audiences are their ears,
Listening to the wind.
Their silence through the years
Is my music of the spheres.

My poems are my family.
My books are their heritage.
Their wisdom is my spirit.
Their lives justify my existence.

7/30/78 (01425)

Delta Planter ^Δ

Pines melt to hot-Delta cotton.
Air alive with dragonflies.
Batesville, Marks, Clarksdale,
Then the Old Man,
*

Torpid as a glutted snake
Sunning on a log.
Ever west,
Past dogtrot hovels
And parked tractors and plows
Inert as obsolete parts
On hardware-store shelves.

Compresses and gins
Galvanized into silence
During this inchoate growing,
Over which crop dusters fly,
With unwieldy contortions,
Between telephone-pole wires
And low-lined fence rows.

Suddenly, my mind is obliterated
By a viscid, hazy spray
Sifting down through brain chambers
Penetrated by sunlight,
Riddled by portentous insights
Into Mississippi pesticides.

Now, the levee washes away,
Taking me with it, as day,
Reaching its apogee, plummets,
And the shimmering, still land
Absorbs my dreams, like seeds,
In its native embrace forever.

8/1/78   (00057)

Cabbages ^Δ

For my most dearly loved,
Trilogy

No human's passing has moved me
To such deep-seated grief, in years,
Or left me with so profound a feeling
Of bereft and incomplete resignation
As has the death of Trilogy's pet, Cabbages.
Surely, this was no mere dog!

Throughout the night, I cried,
Until, finally, the archangel Michael
*

Was awakened and sent to console my anguish.
Not even his pacification of me
Could render bearable the sudden loss
Of a creature so ineffably docile.

Still, Trilogy has been spared the mean
And irreversible certitude of truth.
She yet believes he's being treated
For a "bad cold" at the hospital
And that "Uncle Jack" will make him well.
It's just a matter of time . . .

Just a matter of time, her learning
The disturbing fact of his not returning
Ever again, not being, breathing,
Prancing, sleeping in his raffia basket
Neatly lined with her affection and concern,
Eating, dancing about her knees, in dreams.

It's just a matter of time, perhaps,
Until what she doesn't yet expect
Will have dissolved behind the ebbing waters
Lapping the shores of four and three months,
Been forgotten among the flotsam
Left to witness her disappearing prints.

In the meantime, I contemplate words,
Triangulated half-lies,
Concepts by which men attempt to understand
God's mysterious and ineluctable ways,
That she might comprehend when I tell her
Cabbages will not be back again.

Even as I sit in my silent room,
Tears confound insight.
I can't control my lachrymose emotions,
For visions of his last gasping seizures,
The constriction and release of his thin legs
As life evacuated his vanquished frame.

I weep, wondering to myself what remains,
Just how I might overtake my cowardice
And explain to my unsuspecting daughter
That a natural catastrophe has occurred
In the universe, for the purpose of balancing
The vulnerable equation that maintains life.

I weep tremulously, neither for her
Nor for me alone, rather for both of us
And those who've been abandoned
Abruptly, caught up short,
With sorrow's words stuck in the throat,
Desolate, adrift in space, arrested forever,

With only blurred impressions of memories,
For having not prepared clear negatives
Ahead of time. Now, I go to her,
A day late, to disclose her dog's fate.
Only, as our eyes touch, kiss,
It's as if a mutual intuition persists,

In which our blood already knows
Each other's transcendent woe
And our bones have reconciled the grief
Inherent in the dissolution of friends.
Almost in desperation, she hugs me.
"Daddy, I love you."

"My baby, I love you, too.
You'll always be my favorite."
Suddenly, a fleet vision of little Cabbages,
His tag tinkling like breezed wind chimes,
Jumps at our feet, begs to be petted.
His presence permeates our sad, prolonged embrace.

8/7/78 (01426)

Frangibility $^\Delta$

My little Trilogy
Has absolutely no fear of insects,
Tiny flying ecstasies,
Awkward locusts, lithe chameleons,
Who celebrate their earthliness
In minuscule silence, all day and night,
Without the slightest heresy
Or deviation from convention's paths.

Just last evening, at dusk,
While we played in the churchyard,
*

She spotted a grasshopper
Practicing takeoffs and landings,
Making erratic touch-and-gos
From strips stippling the turf,
And stabbed abortively,
Finally grabbing it by the hind legs.

Tonight, we discovered death
Had delivered her pet frog of breath.
In its vented glass jar,
It rested as though millenniums
Had arrested its shape, in crude paint,
On cave walls. Creation's child
Had returned to its original bed,
Leaving behind only incomprehensible grief.

Trilogy's delicate whimpering
Fills the air with solemnity.
Lugubrious strains swell. The night,
Languorously chained to August,
Assimilates her weeping litany.
All ears listen to her plaint,
As she moans for the loss of her "baby."
She knows what it means to be bereft,

Even at four years of age,
Senses the deprivation parents realize
On the loss of a son at war,
A daughter taken by force, at fifteen,
Into white slavery, a dream
Erased clean by reality's tornadic winds,
The basic beliefs, in Christ
And Moses, eroded by endless hypocrisies.

Her passionate little eyes
And soft, smooth face contain nature.
All creatures are subordinate to her grace,
Her searching gaze, her touch.
They fashion themselves to conform
To the shape of her supple, cupped palms,
Beg to be taken into her sacred keeping,
For hers is a gentleness so pure

And so unadulterated, innocent,
That those deemed ugliest by man —
*

Worms, water striders, locusts, cicadas,
Slugs, beetles, chameleons —
Assume a beauty unexcelled by creatures
More elusive, majestical, godly,
For their winged colorations
And soaring freedom.

What will she next enchant,
Lure from its natural habitat,
Into her delicate, miraculous adoration?
We worry that she'll weary
With disillusionment, as one after another
Escapes from her motherhood,
Weaned prematurely by deathly spirits
She's unable to fathom.

Perhaps discouraging her affections
For undomesticated pets
Might relieve Trilogy of the afflictions
Inherent in adopting wild things.
Yet neither of us has the heart
To deter her curiosity
Or isolate her involuntarily
From an environment strange and exciting,

Whose landscape is teeming with faces
Not encountered elsewhere.
We choose to nurture her unself-consciousness,
Promote her idiosyncratic desire
To "mother" her "baby"
Each time she brings home a new friend.
God knows her maternal instincts
Are ever so delicate.

To deprive her of this compulsion
Would be barbaric.
Through the kitchen window,
I see Trilogy, just now,
Reading her favorite bedtime books
To Cabbages, her constant companion,
Despite the fact that the dog
Is almost three weeks deceased.

8/29/78 (01427)

Roger and Shelley

With all my love

Marriage is the simple, soaring flight
That unites two souls
At heights ne'er before sought
Nor thought attainable.

It's the night before, with its anticipation
Of the day to dawn,
And the morning after, with its reveries
Of the dusk just eclipsed,

That are ecstasies of the highest order.
Their blessed hours will not be forgotten,
Nor will their dreams,
So delicately wrought, so serene,

Be left behind, as their love-seeds
Lift with the breeze,
Like glistening milkweed silks,
Into this twilit evening

And mingle there for us to witness.
Their singular communion,
The simple, soaring flight of man and wife,
Unites us all tonight.

8/30/78 (02236)

Opening and Closing ^Δ

Mother and son slumber
In umber-stippled, twilit shades,
Squeezing the last drops from dreams,
While dad and daughter
Escape through a maze of wakefulness,
Into the Kingdom of Blossoming Hours.

Brushing teeth,
Dressing, eating breakfast,
Leaving for preschool
Are routine seeds thrown
To reassure the keeper of fields
They labor there.

At some gentle juncture,
Morning's sensibilities converge.
Mother and ten-month-old
Rise in fragrant transcendence
And enter the silence left behind
By disappeared husband and daughter.

Son's mellow meekness, mother's warmth,
Extraordinarily inarticulate,
Seek the light, straighten slightly,
Until they blend,
Their frangible shapes becoming petals,
Wings, of a cosmic flower,

Whose hushed floating
Hums the wind the melodies it sings.
At the far end of day's field,
Two inconspicuous toilers,
Bending just above upturned furrows,
Finally perceive their distant whispers,

Follow, as if hypnotized,
Their ears' tingling inspirations,
To the source. Man and wife,
Their children, united again
In loving quiescence, close their eyes.
Their lives fold tightly around themselves.

9/8/78   (01428)

Babbitt Survives a Slight Nightmare

Once again, I enter day's cave,
Hang suspended by a solitary yawn,
And witness my jagged, squirming shadow,
Perforated by serrated shades and shapes,
Wriggle hysterically, like a bleeding worm
Twice run through by the rusted barb
Of a hook tied to invisible line.

Suddenly, I feel myself swallowed alive,
Shadow, fleshy essence, and soul,
By a gigantic imagination
That stalks this dismal abyss
*

To satisfy its insatiable appetite for bait
Meant to lure it from its confines,
Make it surface, fully exposed.

Now, the cord that has kept my mind
Warmly connected to night's placenta,
Feeding a constant stream of dreams
To my head, is completely severed.
I float inside its numbing, rumbling stomach,
Buffeted by specters, chimeras, females
With feline bodies below their breasts.

Slowly, total darkness dissolves,
As though each fantastical creature
Flying past me were a meteoric spark
Transforming blindness to chiaroscuroed insight.
Soon, the subterranean region opens.
Below me, icy diamond slopes
Rise through diaphanous mist, into my eyes.

Instinctively, I step onto a ledge
And begin climbing, climbing ever higher
Out of myself, climbing vertiginously,
Until I sense my spirit exiting the pupils,
Into sunlight. All at once,
The crystal shatters into familiar faces
Reclaimed from yesterday's existence.

Despite the excitement of my fortuitous rescue,
I am left speechless. My numb tongue
And chattering teeth refuse me the pleasure
Of describing my exotic odyssey,
Until, finally, I'm absorbed, once more,
Into the civilized weave of meetings, leases,
Important phone calls, until I even forget
I ever awakened and went spelunking at all.

9/13/78 — [1] (05595)

"Ah So, Fot Fotty" △

Never was there a more exact facsimile
Of the Gautama than squatting Troika Brodsky.
His rounded, glowing cheeks and jowls,
*

The ever-distended belly,
Tumescent as an overripe melon,
His corpulent thighs and biceps,
Rippling with excess fleshy bulk,
Are reminiscent of a full-blown Buddha
Perfectly at peace with his static universe.
Even his smile seems chiseled indelibly
Into the facade of his relaxed happiness.

At times, he shrivels his bulb-nose,
Assumes the pose of a maddened Ming dog
Or spiny Chinese dragon, and snorts,
As if to spray the air with flames and smoke.
And if this fails to communicate his pleasure
With our presence in his outdoor temple,
He brings us to our knees with mimesis:
By quickly flicking his rosy tongue
Against teeth and upper palate,
He achieves a cricket's clicking
That tickles his worshipers to ecstasy.

At eleven months, our tiny Ho Tai
Still prefers crawling, climbing, touching,
Clutching anything he might shove in his mouth,
Consume or just interminably chew,
And I am still obsessed with love for him,
Which manifests itself in rubbing his tummy
Whenever he comes within arm's reach.
Perhaps this ritual presages good fortune.
Hopefully, a lucky Oriental spell
Will guard his health, keep him well ahead
Of demons envious of his holy demeanor.

9/13/78 — [2] (01429)

Freshman-Year Pressure

The New York, New Haven & Hartford
Weaves its unwieldy weight
Through the station's cavernous reaches,
Into the sunlit labyrinthine yard.
Each car, passing across switches,
Elicits a massive grinder's screeching,
*

As if it were a knife blade being sharpened
Instead of two mindless trucks
Being led blindly to endless precipices.
Rolling less slowly once the tunnel
Is mastered, the sooty segments
Stretch out taut and lean, like greyhounds
Chasing each other's drafting shadow,
Linked vestibule to windy vestibule.
Trapped in the dry, drowsy, dusty gloom
Of unvacuumed crushed-velvet recliners
And musty, worn-out mohair pews,
Commuters, distracted by newspapers,
Last night's poker losses, today's gains
On the Big Board, yesterday's aborted deals,
Endure the vertiginous swaying,
The monolithic, standardized anonymity
Of public housing, smoldering landfills,
As prospects of stops at Stamford, Bridgeport,
New Haven loom like dull bulbs,
Suspended by a single frayed cord,
In the men's room of a sleazy greasy spoon.
Only one of the passengers this evening,
Refusing to perpetuate the depressing routine,
Will never ride the train again.
He is a student, who will commit heresy
Before the night concludes its phase,
By committing suicide, taking his life
In a free-fall flight from the heights
Of Sterling Memorial Library's massive stacks.
Just now, he steps down to the platform,
Takes a cab back to Bingham Hall,
Shuts the shiny oak door on his aloneness,
And cries a pained eulogy to sheets
That muffle his desperation.
When he awakens to his two roommates
Shaking him, his head, neck, and chest
Are sweaty. He's been shrieking —
Something about the train, the train,
Being choked to death under tons of dust,
Being burned all over the flesh
By dull, ocherous night lights, being deafened
By the asphyxia of frictioned ticking
*

The old rail joints set up, with arrhythmic clicking,
In his indefensible ears. Shuddering
Like a car engine with retarded spark,
He rushes from their astonishment, in T-shirt,
Bare feet, without shorts, wheels across the campus,
Toward the singular retreat of his solitude,
Sneaks past a guard, finds the stairs
That carry him to the edge of his agony, and leaps.
In the distance, a faint, sibilant train whistle
Blends with his sweet, swift wail,
Then disappears into thin, invisible forgetting.

9/21/78   (05597)

Beyond the World's Rim

It's not even 6:30,
Yet already the earth's red edge
Is surging and pulsating,
Burning a semicircular girdle,
Like a permanent laceration,
About my forehead. Everywhere,
A terrestrial fog bathes the eyes,
As if to anesthetize the pain
Dawn's first light causes its waifs.
It spills onto the road like dry ice,
Parts mystically,
As if identical vaporous halves
Of a monolithic cliff had split in a quake,
Admitting my amazed spirit
To a remote valley far from home.
The deeper my vehicle penetrates,
The more unrecognizable and indescribable
Become the ubiquitous, whisperous fog,
The gnarled, leafless trees,
The sky, floated with sinister fish,
In an environment dramatically emptied of people.
Miles superimposed on hours
Fuse into days misplaced and forgotten,
As the journey lengthens unaccountably,
Until, unable even to recall
The nature of my past
*

Or the original purpose for my journey,
I'm trapped in an amnesic nexus,
Stalled in a cul-de-sac,
With my naked back to night's black wall,
My scalding bowels coming loose,
Numb beyond abominable fear,
Waiting, like a blind beggar,
For absolutely anything at all to happen.
Gradually, ever so gradually,
A scintillant, byzantine glint
Begins to disclose morning's profile.
The earth's red edge,
Surging and pulsating, remembers my shadow
From another incarnation, takes pity on my soul
By warming the solitude from my bones,
Resurrecting my intellect from depths of depression,
Illuminating the nearly invisible pass,
At the base of the split cliffs of treacherous fog,
For me to take in making my escape,
Before the gates forever close.
Suddenly, I awaken with an abrupt shaking.
Nightmares drop from my ears and eyes
Like bagworms sprayed with a pesticide.
The sun tastes sweeter than honeyed fruit.

9/26/78 — [1] (05598)

The Years at Giverny

> *For Jan;*
> *she has learned to endure*
> *my ambitiousness.*

Jesus! He's still painting at eighty!
How can he possibly
Even muster the energy to bend down
And tie his shoelaces,
Let alone prepare pigments,
With mortar and pestle, and place them
In their proper stations on his palette?
And why is he yet concerned
To ponder, labor, contemplate design
*

And composition, when his eyesight
Must rely entirely on inner visions
And sixty years of intuition
Just to recapture mere essences?

Perhaps it's precisely these essences
He still desires, these fleet redolences,
Whose liquescent enticements
Drive him to ecstatic madness,
Demand his full attention span
Despite the lapses of fatigue and blindness
He suffers ever more frequently.
Each day, his brush strokes enlarge,
Resemble less their intended likenesses,
More themselves. His canvases
Grow abstract, assume the attitude
Of the colors he applies. No longer
Does hue introduce change in luminosity,
As it did in his poplars and haystacks,
His myriad facades of Rouen Cathedral;
Rather, it reflects his distracted mind,
At odds with a body frustrated by old age.

Just now, the slow-flowing Seine
Takes him, in a moment of drowsy reverie,
Back to his youth, his Parisian friends,
His bohemian Helicon. He swims in the tears
That silently well up behind his eyes,
Thinking, now, how nothing has changed
Except change itself, how his fervor
For making colors grow and effloresce
In the sunlight he himself made persists
In his ambitious imagination, how life
Still consists of nonexistent images
Needing definition. He weeps in his beard,
Not for his unrecoverable past
But because the impasto on the canvas
Depicting his self-portrait grows heavy,
Stiffens, stretches with each successive decade.
He laments having to confess that, soon,
Time will arrest, forever, the gift
Which has pleasured him, the inspiration
To make the mutable resist decay
By arresting it for the soaring intellect to adore.

Once more, he lifts his long, big brush,
Points it in the direction he wants,
And begins slashing with rapid, accurate passion.

9/26/78 — [2] (05599)

[Factory girls in careless dress,] ‡

Factory girls in careless dress,
Slovenly to a degree of poverty,
Not beyond . . . proud of their strength,
Fortitude, skill, and speed
Against a demonizing piece rate —
The daily race to maintain their integrity
In the face of the inflationary dragon
That chases relentlessly from in front
And behind, simultaneously.
The sewing machine knows no colors,
Bears no grudges, perpetuates no malicious biases.
It relies on its judgment alone,
Counts the needles broken,

9/26/78 — [3] (05600)

Pilgrimage in Harvest Time △

Lining both sides of the highway
I use, passing through the Delta,
From West Helena to Oxford,
Via Clarksdale, Marks, and Batesville,
Is the ubiquitous cotton crop.
Everywhere, biplane dusters
Knot the air in double bow ties.
Their hectic flights are those of bees
Pollinating white dogwood trees,
Leaping hysterically from blossom to leaf.
I turn sideways frequently
And muse on the profusion of acres
Planted in endless clusters. They blur
Into a snowy blizzard, lose depth,
Dimension, perspective, until I blink
And they come back into sync.

This land of compresses, pickers,
Gins, and four-wheel field cages
Strewn with wadded tufts
Looms about me like a padded cell
In a desolate sanitarium
Where I've been left to waste away
In anonymity. I feel crazed,
Stranded, unable to ascertain
How my nomadic soul ever managed
To lure me so totally away
From my family, home, and noble profession
Of educating children to Shakespeare and Milton.
Suddenly, the land to the east expands,
Becomes hills covered in loblollies,
Kudzu, vetch, cedars, and cypresses,
Reminding me of the nature of my quest.

Just ahead, though not yet in sight,
Is the plantation house named Rowan Oak,
Where William Faulkner ate and slept
And wrote with such frantic indignation
And wit that even in death,
He calls to me, possesses my spirit,
Haunts my breathing with awe and inspiration.
So now, I approach the destination
That, for so long, has absorbed my thoughts,
Afraid yet impatient to step foot
Inside the sacred modern potter's field
And satisfy my curiosity about the place
Where genius paced in meditation,
Raised consciousness beyond human limens,
For generations to ponder and emulate.
I kneel, a pilgrim at the Wailing Wall.

9/27/78 (00064)

Tithonus

Why do the children, the students,
The newlyweds seem to grow younger,
Each year? Do they become
Creatures other than themselves
*

When I blink, then look again?
Are they constantly being replaced,
Like worn parts in a generator?
Maybe they are confetti, serpentine
Strewn in a Mardi Gras wake
Each day, in a perpetual celebration of youth.
Or is it that my waning imagination,
My vision, stuttering and dimming
Like trim, incandescent filaments
Vibrating in an unseen wind,
Mistake the longhaired ladies
In sandals and clinging garments
For ageless, naked Naiads
Because they realize some compensation,
At this late date, just must be due
The recluse I so long ago became?

Whatever the ultimate consideration,
If this be my fate, my doom,
To be taunted, waking, in daydreams,
At noonhour lunch, commuting to my room,
Then I surrender to my solitude,
Confess my desperation, my anxiety
About dying in bed, with a strange mistress,
A nameless waitress, a neighbor's wife.
I refuse to allow myself the dubious pleasure
Of ephemeral and uninspired masturbation,
And I reject all notions of stoicism.
Surely, to someone, I must seem young.

9/28/78 — [1] (05601)

Celestial Birds

The dusky sun is a scudding duck
Barely wounded, reluctantly falling,
Whose silent, shrieking pain
Is its blinding light. I gaze westerly
Just as it disappears into a net
Consisting of umbrageous treetops.
To my right, the innocent earth
Converts its memory to shadows,
*

As though death's reflection were expected
To be a reminder, to those left behind,
That nothing escapes the inevitable sleep.

Soon, darkness encapsulates life.
Only a few lambent-luminous stars
And the quartz-mottled moon
Shimmer in my windshield's scope.
At first glance, they are holes
My vision probes for microbial shapes.
Then, as I stare, they begin to move,
Fly wildly, change directions.
They become night birds before my eyes,
Soaring in the sky, like predaceous vultures
Circling a vast and still-warm corpse.

9/28/78 — [2] (05602)

An Autumnal

For Anna Ladd,
who was recently summoned home;
her beautiful memory overshadows my grief.

Once again, the whisperous resurrection,
So long anticipated
Yet arrived with messianic unexpectedness,
Is at hand. Nature's annunciation
Hymns the crisp, thin, autumnal air
A proud, majestic recessional.
Its notes are old and ancient magi,
Draped in robes stained plum and crimson,
Yellow, saffron, ocher,
Who, crucified in brittle postures on their limbs,
Bleed, shiver in the breeze,
Preparing to prostrate themselves
At the foot of each rooted tree.

Soon, all the earth will be teeming
With their self-sacrificial gifts.
Frozen snows will close the opening
To the cave their accumulating flakes make,
And winter's stark dreams will turn gray,
*

Sink into a Dark Age,
Where their collective spirit will slowly rot.
Fetuses, human souls, and seeds
Sleeping in spring's certain chrysalis
Won't even hear the mourners passing
Just beyond their temporary graves.

Ah, while yet one breath remains,
Let me join, in celebration,
The worshipers who gather to exalt nature,
Revel in this simultaneous epiphany of birth,
Renascence, and life eternal.
Let me affirm my own imperfect holiness,
By throwing myself into a pile of leaves
And lying there, in silence, an entire hour,
To remind myself that death is God's kiss.

10/3–4/78 — [1] on 10/3 & 10/4 (05470)

[Day fades like newspaper] †

Day fades like newspaper
Left out in the sun too long.
Spaces yellow momentarily.
Black areas
Become gray rearrangements
Of distilled atoms

10/3/78 — [2] (01383)

Admiral of the Ocean-Sea △

Conquistador de la poesía

I pass the massive smokestacks
Belching gaseous, bituminous stains
Against a painfully blue sky,
Outdistance the shopping center,
Car-rental lots with chivalric pennons
Tattering in the frosty air,
The "family rate" motels,
Cruise unobtrusively by
The Ellis Fischel State Cancer Hospital,
*

Looming beside the highway
Like a maddened Cyclops,
Then shoot free of the rapids
And find smooth open water
In this Midwest Mediterranean I ply.

Now, only an occasional billboard,
Tastelessly decorated with the heraldry
Of traditionless families,
Blurs vision, distracts the alert mind
From its pleasurable disorientations.
Sailing over the fog-mottled Missouri,
Through brittle corn, Octobering leaves,
Past docile, stolid cows, I enter the Provence
Where, for years, my pastoral poems
Have composed themselves into odes,
Villanelles, elegies bucolic and mournful.
Hopefully, this trip will yield insights
Distilled from silence, disclose music
Whose notes are memories rising from graves.

Hopefully, it will bring me closer to my ancestors,
By tuning my senses to rural simplicities,
Like the absence of covetousness, like love,
Respect for sun, rain, and moon,
Parents and children under one roof,
Through crises and exaltations alike,
A lifetime, never moving far from home.
And hopefully, I'll return from my voyage
With cargo, equal to an entire empire,
To spend in my retirement or lend out
To friends deprived of the desire
To seek unknown destinations
Beyond the mind's dark, uncharted regions
And arrive for the first time, each time.

10/4/78 — [2] (05421)

The Magical Pen ^Δ

Once again, the pen holds the key
To my psychic whereabouts.
Whether in Alexandria, Florence, Cairo,

*

Or Illinois depends on which script
My instrument decides to use,
Which mystical calligraphy comes loose
From the jinn's wand-end.

My location is obliquely related
To the ink's hue, the point's edge.
Fine tips slip through complexities,
Like needles probing the cerebellum.
Medium balls roll smoothly as wheels
On a train moving across Utah,
To Colorado, in and out of dreams.

Blunt points evoke hippopotamuses
Wallowing in pools of Whitmanesque ecstasy.
My eyes follow the purgatorial flow
Of red as though it were a stream
In which each letter, every word,
Were a sinner come to purge itself
In a baptismal trial by fire and blood.

Black, green, and blue fuse
Like earth, sea, and sky in a hurricane,
Suck me up, out of my astonishment,
And leave me suspended above the page,
Like a whirling bird anxious to light,
Waiting to witness the natural conclusion
To the unrelaxed imagination's upheaval.

Whenever stranded in a strange land
Or lost in familiar bailiwicks,
I appeal to my magical pen
For proper directions out of the abyss,
Follow to the final stanza's end;
Then, shivering on the airy precipice
Where insight approximates omniscience,

I bend out over a vast metaphor,
Embrace an entire idea dotted with rhymes,
And see, for the last time
Before dematerializing in depression and fatigue,
A pristine revelation of the final moment
When the artist in me climaxed and passed
From nonexistent concept to completed poem.

10/4/78 — [3] (01331)

The Lovemakers

On this beautiful gloomy day,
The fulminating clouds
Crowd out all blue
Save for a few nubile jigsaw pieces
That peer through with tantalizing unpredictability,
Like glimpses of breasts
And supple flesh beneath a sheer celestial dress.

The azure spaces arrest my gaze
As I press ahead toward my destination.
Their expanding and contracting
From moment to moment, opening and closing,
Converging, then separating, as though contained
In an ever-turning collide-o-scope,
Bubble my blood, incite my gonads to riot.

My imagination gasps at such evocations
Of extraterrestrial foreplay
And erotically spasmodic lovemaking.
My eyes become voyeurs impotently excited
By the sky's sexual excesses.
They pulsate vicariously, throb, vibrate
To the intensely aggressive copulation above them,

Until vision blurs from sympathetic wetness,
Which streams across pupils and irises,
And my speed is automatically reduced,
To compensate for psychic fatigue.
Relieved to see our partnership dissolved,
I'm once again able to concentrate
On earthly purposes, forget the mind's caprices.

I drive for hours, without the slightest desire
To revive my fantasy by gazing skyward.
Yet, drawing closer to home,
I sense the autumn afternoon losing its light,
Filling with a chiaroscuro quietude,
As the last tatter of blue
Disappears for good, beyond the horizon.

When I do look again,
The massed clouds are soiled sheets
Rimpled and strewn haphazardly
*

Across a bed recently used and abandoned
By lovers enmeshed in fantastical ecstasy.
Briefly, I grieve for our spent pleasure,
Then cease, knowing tomorrow by name.

10/6/78   (05603)

WJIL Country Music Month Parade ^Δ

In our country, every October Saturday
Is a homecoming parade on a brisk day
Mottled with lusty, striated, sunny skies.
Pumpkins, bats, and ghosts dot the eyes.
It's a quick-paced anticipation
Of last-minute basement cleanings,
Storm-window placements, flue checks,
Exchanges of suits and shirts from attic to closet.
Each Saturday is alive with football games,
And on the air is the smell of snow
Still in the wings, yet accumulating,
In some vast desolation of oblivion, for the hour
When all hatches are battened securely,
All contests are neatly recorded and forgotten
On shelves, trophies, ripped tickets, in books.

Driving toward the Square,
We see the unobtrusive gathering of elements
At West State and Fayette, across from the high school:
Shivering teenagers in silver-and-gold lamé
Practice routines with flags, batons, plastic rifles;
The band from a neighboring community,
Hovering around themselves like a blood clot,
In their tattered crimson worsted-wool outfits;
Radiating out from there, like debris
Floating on endless tributaries after a flood,
Are the constituents of the extravaganza.
Soon, all streams merge into one current,
Which surges ahead erratically, stopping, starting,
Like rats in an electrified maze,
As it rapidly begins to seek its own level.

At the head of the colossal procession,
Its myriad alternating, blinking, and rotating lights
*

Shimmering like an entire galaxy at night,
Is a state-patrol vehicle. From hatted driver
To elaborate pinstriping and paint job,
Its immaculate symbology commands respect,
Announces that substance is about to materialize,
Persist for a short time, then pass into history.
Immediately behind comes the slovenly band,
Out of time, cacophonous, whose standard-bearers
Can't keep the flags from tangling in the breeze,
Whose musicians can't read the tiny music sheets
Refusing to stay still just beneath their eyes,
As they play a Sousa march so fragmented
No one along the curbs might guess its message.

Next, in no particular philosophical arrangement,
Comes America's heritage, modernity at large,
Affluence's mighty issues, indigenous to a time,
If not a specific geographic and demographic population.
Case tractors with air-conditioned cabs,
Six gigantic wheels, capable of supplanting the work
Ten older, smaller machines once accomplished,
Rumble past the Victorian clapboard Baptist church,
Snorting like saurian amphibians landlocked and hungry.
Refurbished Corvettes, customized Fords, Mercuries,
And Overlands from the thirties and forties,
With chrome plating, flaked enamel paint
Twenty coats thick, glistening naugahyde,
Glide past like ducks in a shooting gallery,
Their owners proud as visiting foreign dignitaries,
In their emblemized, red acetate-and-rayon jackets.

A float, thick with banjo and guitar pickers,
Corn shucks fashioned into a hut,
Scattered kids and friends dressed in overalls,
Throwing wrapped caramels and hard candies
To the inspired spectators, drifts past
In precarious, lurching fashion, its sounds
Clogging the air like leaves in a gutter drain.
Soon, ponies, mules, and curried show horses
Come into view, with their riders
Waving to everyone. The bright colors of their habits
Fuse with the manure they conspicuously leave behind,
Through which convertibles carrying local politicos
And their cronies pass, the candidates filling the air
*

With slogans, vituperations against their opponents,
And promises empty as spent rockets.

Roadmasters, Coachmans, Leprechauns, Winnebagos,
Like circus elephants trunk to tail,
Enter focus, followed by lesser-decorated vans
Pulling fiberglass speedboats on trailers.
Heightening the full effect of such magnificence
Is a perfectly anomalous Santa Claus,
Sitting on the rear deck of an expensive rig,
Like an outboard motor, throwing more candy.
Now a news truck, now a traffic car,
Now a gold cart with canopy, conveying disc jockeys
And newscasters from the radio/TV station
Sponsoring this commemoration of Country Music Month,
The bodies and faces of ubiquitous voices
Finally brought to the surface for the purpose
Of alerting the public to their basic humanity.

The parade begins to thin and fade,
Until it climaxes with Nick Nixon
And Tommy Overstreet, dressed in cowboy duds,
Winking indiscreetly to the giddy teenage girls
Standing in ganglia of embarrassed puberty,
Secretly fantasizing being asked to climb aboard
And carried to their motel rooms, where they'll discover
That all that glamour is skin-deep and evanescent.
The parade's caboose is a reclaimed Greyhound bus,
Painted with the insignia of its current owner
Painted over at least three other recent heralds
Of equally brief traveling "shows." It passes
In silence and out of sight, while the crowd
Dissolves, like ice cubes in a heated water glass,
Into the October morning, to shop for bras
And gaskets, microwave ovens and Quarter Pounders,
To complete a perfectly exhilarating Saturday.

10/8/78 (02263)

Resurrections in October

Crisp autumn's victims
Are brittle and stiff with rigor mortis.
Even their crepuscular hues
*

Slip unnoticed from death's lips,
As ironic commentaries on life.

A chill stillness fills the woods,
Tinges sunlight, charges afternoon
With invisible soul-bolts,
Which strike the mind's ground wires.
The moon refuses to leave the execution room.

Box-elder bugs, profuse as tumorous cells,
Swarm in the eyes' fenestration
Like invading Asian-flu strains
Claiming suzerainty, by ukase,
Over every breathing shade in sight.

Only the ancient, coal-black crows
Hold their ground, remain unperturbed
In the face of such blatant hypocrisies
Perpetrated on the universe by strutting summer.
They've known hag death intimately.

Suspended in October's fragile twilight,
Stepping tentatively to avoid corpses
Strewn over the earth, walking the wire
Stretched from snow line to greening ecstasy,
I wait for sleep to sweep away my dust

And scatter my atoms over seas,
Like caravels running, wing and wing,
Toward tomorrow's vernal equinox.
For now, I surrender to the hour's amazing grace
And watch the leaves genuflect in their ageless resurrection.

10/19/78 — [1] (05604)

Emil Nathan Faust, Doctor of Biophonetics

Beelzebub, whose pseudonym is
The Prince of Lies and Darkness,
Backlights vision, from behind my eyes.
He causes insight to be isolated
And divided into primal compliance
To erogenous appetites, on the one side,
Obligatory obeisance to icons, rituals,
And occult sacrificial practices, on the other.
*

All images within my cosmos
Assume a severe spectral unreality,
Consisting of goblins, gremlins, ghouls, ghosts,
And grotesque trolls. I tremble constantly,
Like a junkie deprived of his habit,
Shiver each time the sun disappears,
As if night were a viper's pit
With its gate accidentally left open.
I lose control of my bladder and bowels
Whenever contemplating escape from his clutches,
Yet the devil knows only too well
The perpetual reprisals for bloodletting,
Soul-selling, contractual liens,
And second mortgages on a weakened heart.
His net is securely anchored
By Mephistophelian favors sanctioned and fulfilled.
Long ago, my spirit's enfeebled hands
Quit tugging at its resilient strands of silk
And filaments of fine extruded gold.
No longer do I perpetuate the untruth
That my youthful rectitude
Survived its coming of age, at twenty-two,
When my Alexandrine Library was looted,
Torched, and buried under the onslaught
Of unbridled freedom arrived for the first time
In a life of authoritarian demagoguery.
Now, I die an agonizingly slow death
By satiety. Neither compassion nor sadness
Rises on my dreamless horizon. Regret,
Remorse, jealousy, hatred, love, respect
Are noticeably uninvited guests at a fete
Celebrating the retrospective impressions left on my friends
By a man so totally and methodically anonymous
That not even whores in my mind's bordello
Can distinguish my flesh from the rest of the crowd.
Only one toast and one testimonial
Remain in the echoless chambers of my brain
After sleep finally overtakes
And subdues my mortal charade. Angular praise
Stabs my glands with its empty flattery.
Through the endless caves of Hell I dance,
Reciting the demonic, patronizing verses I've memorized,
Reiterating, forever, the word "Burn!"
*

Until my tongue sets fire to the earthly house
In which I've lived self-satisfied and died.

10/19 — [2] & 10/23/78 — [1] (05605)

Exodus: An Autumnal

The chanting leaves are slaves to a brazen season,
Readying their brittle selves for the exodus.
They change clothes for the journey ahead,
Choose robes of saffron, russet, ocher —
Garments in which to enter memory's mausoleum
And sleep for as long as forgetting exists.

I witness their ritualistic preparations,
The frenetic disarray of their sacred trappings.
Their gentle unattachments, monumental lettings-loose
Are the giddy laughter of four-year-olds
Enraptured by unimagined magical happenings.
Their strewn shapes are wind-hymns and Nile barges

Anchored at the shore while autumn is loaded aboard.
Soon, rain and snow will wash their patinas,
Remove their identities. Storms will force them north,
Then east, toward ever-new Jerusalems,
Until only their bare trees remain,
Like condemned ghetto tenements awaiting demolition.

In this desolate land, abandoned by its oppressed,
The ancient snake will hibernate, time will arrest itself,
While beyond history's sea, anxious ancestors
Will embrace these newly arrived émigrés as scions,
Whispering promises of future civilizations
Born of fecund Aprils mellifluous and Canaan-mild.

10/23/78 — [2] (05606)

[It was just an eye blink or two ago] †

It was just an eye blink or two ago
That you and I said good-bye to three,
Prepared ourselves for the concept of four.

10/25/78 — [1] (07158)

Troika: A Paean Occasioned by His First Birthday ^Δ

As though overseeing an entire lifetime
From a balcony, I gaze on his face,
His sweet, smiling, docile, vulnerable face,
And shoulders, captured like a Copley bust
Of a Cape Cod child in his highchair,
Eating supper. He waits for me to stare,
Make a grimace, put on a mask of comedy,
Play with Falstaffian heartiness,
Laugh us both past oblivion, into the realm
Where amicable spirits cavort and prance.

We share the blood of ghetto ancestors
Raised to the nth power, squared forever
In a geometrical progression worthy of kings
And emperors. His giggling timbre tickles my ears,
Forges new tuning forks, whose tines
Reverberate the essences of my fanciful mind,
And I muse on the truth that one whole year
Has just about expired; one year
Less one day has walked the wire
And survived the passage from birth to maturation.

And I marvel at the notion that I was once
A bum ingenerate, a lusty, aimless bum,
Whose bohemian concepts of freedom consisted of
A jug of cheap Chianti, cheese, and meat
And the most convenient road to Roncevaux,
For whom poems and a diaphanous maiden
Were the modus vivendi. Now, I know better.
A daughter, my slim college-sweetheart wife,
And a blond, cheeky son persuade me I am
The Pied Piper, the Mad Hatter, rolled into one.

I raise my triumphal wings in praise,
Prance like a peacock at St. George's Castle,
Yell, to the starry darkness I traipse beneath
After dinner, this eve of his first anniversary,
The magical dialectic of pride and contentedness,
For I am a father, the father of the boy, Troika,
Father of the man who will one day bear away
Another man's offspring as bride, father, first
*

And last, of the child I left behind with God
When I set out to find my birthright and purpose.

In him, I have been given a second chance
To relive the inexorable and unpredictable ecstasies
Through which I passed without sensing,
The mystical growing from inarticulateness to speech,
The immobility of infancy, which turned, initially,
To crawling, then to walking, finally to soaring.
We own his shadow only. Even his motion
Belongs to a higher divination, a governing force
That leaves us just the most scintillant memories
To savor. Already, I see him approaching our wisdom.

Yet this is the end of his first full year.
Innocence wanes, drains away like lilied waters
From Monet's beautiful pools at Giverny.
For a moment, then, we stop, edge the precipice
With gentle, cautious steps, careful not to slip off,
And look down with inutterable amazement.
The depthless distance to the abyss's base is horrific.
How he scaled such foreboding, craggy cliffs
Is impossible to gauge. Just ahead is Tibet's peak.
The distance in between is his unlived existence.

10/25/78 — [2] (01430)

Troika's First Birthday ^Δ

If ever God's cherubic embodiment
Has been assimilated by one of His minions,
It is surely apotheosized by Troika the Boy,
Whose divinely inspired smile and composure
Disclose a mild and meek holiness
Not even a saint could approximate.

On this first commemoration of his nativity,
We solemnize and consecrate his life
By recapitulating his monumental accomplishments,
As though reciting lines from *Paradise Lost*;
His mastery of crawling, standing, singing, grasping
Is perfectly metered and scanned blank verse.

We remember phases, rather than occasions
Or moments, of our American Beauty rose
*

Opening its 365 petals
To become the celestial flower we worship today.
Now, we hover above his blond halo,
Breathing the pristine fragrance of his hour.

Gazing at the solitary, lambent candle on the cake,
We reiterate the words he's learned to associate
With *doll*, *bug*, *banana*, *daddy*, and *dog*
And watch the sparks of recognition lift
From his eyes' flying grinding wheels,
Until child and flame fuse in a brilliance

That fills the room with wisdom's promise to youth.
The communion of earthly and ethereal spirits
Is consummated in the birthday we observe.
From this point forward, Troika the Boy
Will be the keeper of his dreams, creator
And partner in the covenant of love his deeds engender.

10/26/78 (01431)

An Intimacy with Leaves

I am the autumn leaves, falling forever,
Moribund, brittle, and vulnerable to sun,
Frosty breeze, invisible synesthesia
Tingeing October with rustling, touching hues
Vagrant as hitchhikers heading indefinitely west.
I surrender my lonely, peripatetic soul to the road.

Afternoon's blue, bright, cloudless bowl
Is a celestial flute piping soothing fugues
Just outside my windows, as though velocity
Were the universal inciter, the reed, breath, and tongue
Whose music inspires me to forsake the quick
And seek solace in the darkling night to come.

I succumb to its luscious insinuations. My blood
Palpitates. The highway enters my eyes,
Divides into two streams, behind the chiasma,
Then reunites, as the lungs assimilate its miles
For the heart and arteries to flood my cells.
My imagination is baptized in its own River Jordan.

It swims neither upstream nor with the current,
Rather goes nowhere, stays out of the flow,
*

Between land and sky, above the motion
Yet below the oceanic silence, submerged
And dry at the same time, dead and alive.
The leaves I drive through whisper for me to follow.

10/27/78 — [1] (05607)

Over the Earth's Edge

Soon, now, twilight will toss, spread,
And draw taut its net of shadows over my eyes.
Already, my senses lament the loss
Of all that effervescent brilliance the sun,
In its fantastical blasting ejaculations,
Casts over the lusty earth's seething crust,
From dawn to dusk. Already, I'm caught
In the first tentative crosshatchings, dazed,
Mindful of my partial blindness, as I gaze ahead,
Unable to distinguish where grass and highway meet,
Sky and tree and human eye reach infinity.
Finally, night's black snare completes the task,
And I am trapped midway on my passage
From one day to the next, forced to rest,
For lack of resolution and courage, detained
By a stark, obsessional fear of the dark.
Impatient to locate the nearest stopping-off place,
I race the engine, pray to make an exit,
Hoping that when I do, sleep will come fast
To unravel the strands of the net, free me,
Let the better angels of my being breathe again.

In the distance, neons buzz like bees.
I commit myself to the first "Vacancy" I see,
Like a TB victim seeking relief
In a free clinic. I hide beneath the sheets,
Content to surrender my breathing to strange odors
And the soiled, invisible agonies and deceits
Of the thousand brief ghosts who've preceded me
In this sterile and suicidally silent cubicle.
Dreams refuse to surface; even nightmares
Can't penetrate to the heart of my pariahhood.
In this zone beyond aloneness, I shiver,
Wishing that the ageless mistress of my adolescence
Would at least motivate me to spiritual onanism.

Only the winking light outside my window
Touches the nerves, disturbs the otherwise numb psyche,
Whose dim reverberations do nothing more
Than confuse the somniferous pleas of my fatigued body,
Scrape the bones to a pile of snowy soap shavings.
Across the screen on which my restless soul
Projects its idiosyncratic fetishes and prurient fixations,
Premonitions pass like searchlight beams,
Crisscross, weaving, like maddened bullet shuttles,
An invisible thread that sutures the wound
I received, early this evening, by driving
Headlong into the sunset, getting myself lost.
Now, beyond the glass, dim at first, brighter,
As if connected to a rheostat, the semicircular glow
Pervades collied night, breaks it open,
Holding out the possibility of getting back on course,
Heading home before another lunar windstorm
Blows me out of the safe lanes of daylight,
Onto shoals in the Straits of Dead of Night.
I rush into my weeklong clothes, brush teeth,
And reach for the car keys, as I leave port again.

10/27/78 — [2] (05608)

Homecoming

Homecoming does not exactly evoke
Magi making their sanctified way to Bethlehem,
With gifts to place around a straw-strewn crèche,
In which lies a Messiah-child, meekly mild,
For whom mankind has waited all its existence,
Rather motel rooms, boisterous and rowdy
As mackerel-crowded seas, with refugees
From the postgrad reality of tractor sales,
Advertising, accounting, whole- and term-life
Insurance agencies, swilling whiskey and beer
On Good Friday evening, before Saturday's game,
Reminiscing the same two or three incidents
History has encapsulated, like Proust's teacakes,
To make education's four-year hiatus from life
Easier to exhume, in mackerel-crowded rooms,
Every five years, give or take a decade or two.

It is not an earthly, mystical birth
They've come to celebrate nor a new faith,
Descended from the church, they've come to embrace
But an occasion for embarrassing merriment,
Stuporous bad taste, lusty immoderation,
And the exhibition of Kennicottian mediocrity
That calls them back to this perfectly Missourian,
Mackerel-crowded Midwest Mediterranean,
To participate in a collegiate Passion Week
That arrives, conveniently, once a year,
Each October-ending, to assert its supremacy
Over whichever sacrificial victim
Its wintering Pilates have scandalously arranged
To bring to the stadium, to suffer physical disgrace.

Homecoming does not evoke ultimate transcendence,
The final terrestrial epiphany and apotheosis
Of God's celestial will or His attempt at mercy
And salvation, an eternity of sacred Sundays.
On the contrary, it becomes an arrested breath,
An endless, irritated yawn, a numb sensation
Without recognizable source of final termination,
The classic smoke-reek, the proverbial hangover,
A baseless lip-service series of regrets
For chronic habits and consistent undisciplined acts
That carry in their inherent makeup no hope
For repentance nor any reason for locating a remedy.

To the mackerel-crowded leisure baths they swarm,
Somewhere, weekly, daily, hourly,
To wake momentarily before drowning together, forever.

10/27/78 — [3] (01332)

The Auction △

Tipton's tight-fisted wizards of Wall Street
Confer, early this Sunday morning,
At the Crystal Café, to interpret the implications
Of yesterday's auction of widow Scott's estate.
The Chrysler-Plymouth dealer, as dean emeritus,
Leads the heated debate over devaluation
Of the dollar as seen by the conspicuous consumption
*

Characterizing the sale. He remarks,
"You shoulda seed the prices that damn junk pile
Of rugs brought, even if they was from Persia
And Brussels, seventeenth and eighteenth centuries."

Another intones, "I bid a hundred and forty
On a parlor stove, and it sold for thirty less.
Later, they claimed I'd become the owner
Of a broke TV, and I didn't even bid."
A third exclaims, "I saw sets of dishes
Bring over six hundred each
Just because they had gold rims
And 'Bavaria' and 'Prussia' printed on their backs."
"People are sick," pontificates a retired farmer.
"An inlaid dining-room suit,
Though it was a beautiful piece of equipment,
Went to a young kid I ain't never seen,
For just under thirty and one hundred beans."

"I'll tell you one thing," adds the pharmacist,
"We need to revise our standards and expectations.
Something's wrong when people can clip
Food coupons, draw stay-home pay
Through the week, and come out on the Sabbath
And drop a wad on shit they wouldn't buy
At the dime store. What's the difference
If it says 'Spoede' and 'Sèvres' instead of 'Nippon,'
'Hong Prong,' or 'Korea'? It's all made
By foreign sons-of-bitches anyway."
"All the power to thems what got it,"
Says the cop. "If I was black and sixty-five,
I'd have it made in the shade, wouldn't I?"

"Boys, I've got to get to church; it's late."
Collective voices rise like wood smoke
And gather in a common exhortation: "Pray for us,
Diamond Jim." The Chrysler-Plymouth dealer
Gazes sidelong, his eyes shifty as a snake
Slithering away from danger. He sneers,
"Pray for yourselfs, boys. It's gonna take
All I got just to persuade God
To extend the loan He refinanced, yesterday,
So's I could buy one of those ratty rugs
Eunice just *had* to have for our rathskeller."

10/29/78 — [1] (00120)

Bison, Diesels, and Leaves

Sunday is stillness filled with American bison
Grazing on silence, in my eyes' pastures.
It is three diesel engines, in tandem,
Pulling the weight of its endless freight cars
Along afternoon's shiny parallel T's,
Toward the vanishing point where darkness
Meets track. It is leaves cutting ties,
In a final, frenzied desire to emigrate
From a land watched over by a dying giant.

I can almost hear the rapid snapping
Of each leaf coming undone, the low moans
They evoke, sifting through the air, to earth.
Only, their ephemeral ecstasy
Goes unshared by me. I'm merely a witness,
Aroused to disconsolateness and envy
By their exemption from winter's cruelty.

I can almost feel the coordinated diesels
Reverberating my assaulted mind
Past pain, to numbness, as though my spine
Were the roadbed on a steep uphill grade
Over which the brain is laboring, full throttle,
Pulling itself through every tendon and bone
And into the station, where my loneliness waits for me.

I can almost smell the rank odors
Of the buffaloes' fur, matted with urine and manure,
Almost touch them with my nose's sixth sense
And memory, as if, in a previous existence,
I were no stranger to goatherds,
Feedlots, open plains dotted with horned creatures
Roaming wild, on which I depended for my survival.

Sunday is all these simultaneous evocations
And none of them, until I alone decide
Which configurations of my mind are most appropriate
For relating the design of my living to a poetics
Capable of sustaining me between two worlds.
Bison, leaves, and diesels are only the soul's marrow,
The body's ineffably sublime epiphanies,
Yet they metamorphose and elevate me to godliness
By assuming the shape common to our separate compositions.

10/29/78 — [2] (05609)

[To sift nonexistence] †

To sift nonexistence
   for the paltry few images
   and visions roaming
      free through oblivion
And end up with a sieve full
   of poetic nuggets
   to juggle

10–11?/78   (00746)

[This sunny morning belongs to another epoch.] △

This sunny morning belongs to another epoch.
The castles of Roncevaux, Kenilworth, Carcassonne,
And Segovia glisten, from spires and parapets.
My eyes spark like two chunks of mica,
Enlarge and constrict with the medieval aura.
The minutes scurry backward, down
Spiraled bell-tower stairs, to courtyards
Isolated from the world by portcullises and moats,
Where unspoiled speculations of the future
Neither obtrude on nor threaten, from coverts,
The perfectly virginal, lassitudinous shadows
That have gathered since Eden's creation.
The hours follow a slow metronome's arc
Through the voiceless air, whose blown notes
Lift like doves abandoning a dense copse
One at a time. My ambitionless desires, this day,
Are the birds' haphazard, whisperous feathers
Sifting to earth beneath their disappearance.
Only November's crisp and brittle leaves,
Clinging like burrs as I roll over and over,
Connect me to a specific seasonal geography.
Their pungent aromas resurrect me from a death,
By sensual anesthesia, of complete consciousness.
Suddenly, the city's graffitied water tower
Slips between empty trees. The trouser factory
Materializes. Shoebox houses and used cars,
*

Parked like souls excommunicated from the Church,
To become peasants and ragged shepherds,
For arbitrary heresies, loom in the eyes' myopia.
Patients from the state hospital, taking recreation,
Blur the street with their erratic goose-stepping.
The peaceful medieval reverie tied at mind's edges
Slips its pegs. The threads lose their resilience,
Shrink back into the imagination's skein.
Once again, I'm a victim of circumstance,
Manipulated by the flesh, impotent and inconsequential,
Wishing I might evoke the past, enter its echoes,
Coming up off narrow cobbled streets,
And assume the sacred duties of translator
And illuminator of Scriptural passages on vellum —
A poet of the Dark Ages, exempt from time.

11/4/78   (00256)

Salmon Run

Acquired intelligence,
Without the innate ability to bridge the chasm
Separating madness from imagination,
Is nothing more than an inane peacock's strutting,
Mundane bravura, the Sunday rotogravure
Highlighting a ghost town's blue list.

The Chaplinesque gears of modern times
Spin on academic axles. State universities
And privately endowed colleges churn out,
Every honeysuckled and wisteria-blooming June,
Thousands of summa cum alcoholics
And potheads. Temple Drake is alive and well,

Disguised as Cheryl Tiegs and Farrah Fawcett
On life-size posters, suitable for fucking,
In every Woolworth and Wal-Mart
Lining all the "franchise miles" in the kingdom.
Undergraduates masturbate, deviate,
Fornicate with instructors' wives and lab rats,

While their brains, in standardized tandem,
Pulsate with the ceaseless input of "knowledge,"
Until painting, sociology, business statistics,
*

Western civ, Milton, and American studies
Fuse into Oscar the Grouch's sacred trash,
Lose their majestic, unapproachable essences,

Rise to the surface, white bellies up,
Like electrocuted fish. Tuition increases
In inverse ratio to quality achieved.
Suddenly, another four-year stint finishes
In pharisaical celebrations a summer wide,
Before reality's indifferent maw opens wide

To ingest potential profligates, public defenders,
Perpetual pedagogues and bibliophiles,
Public spectacles, high-wire Wallendas,
And Nixon-like politicos aiming toward immortality
In the nose cone of a Saturn V rocket,
All in a solitary bite, like a whale swallowing diatoms.

Everywhere, on billboards, in the yellow pages,
Buried in local, freely thrown shopper's guides,
On radio and TV spots, humanistic acumen and facts,
Every memorized bit of trivial history and law
Civil, statutory, and contractual break out,
Like chickenpox, to plague an inattentive society.

Dilettante and socialite alike wave credentials
Over lunch, cocktails, motel quickies,
As if lifting a white flag in bovine surrender
To each other's elitist membership. Condescension is rife
Among Shel Silverstein, Leroy Nieman,
And Rod McKuen, our generation's laureates.

Meanwhile, on some humble farm in Iowa
Or Illinois, in a Pruitt-Igoe ghetto complex,
In Marks, Tipton, Brule, an unlikely child
Grows, in relative isolation, to manhood,
In a canning factory by day, reading voraciously
Every afternoon late, through evening,

Until he feels the butterfly inside his chrysalis
Stretching toward independent success. Then,
One night, he steals away from his heritage,
Enters a nearby asylum, passes for deserving,
And matriculates to assume his fate's destiny
As Ishmael, the only poet to survive his age.

11/11/78 (01322)

A Sailor Is Lost While Trying to Discover a Route to the Spice Islands by Sailing Westerly ᐃ

This morning, a heavy chop
Gnaws at the creaky bow gunwales,
As though a malign ocean
Intends to engorge me in its maw,
Keep me from penetrating foggy portals
Beyond dawn, reaching tepid straits
Dotted with tropical, exotic places of refuge.

For thirty years, a recurring dream
Has transported me, aboard a brigantine,
To the Pitcairn Island of my twilight years,
Where indolence and sensual appetites are revered,
Spirit is sacrificed at the vaginal tabernacle,
Immolated in love-spill, and God is benevolent
Despite phallic icons stationed in His temple.

Now that the actual occasion of my transformation
Is near at hand, can it be that the fates
Will conspire against me, doom my passage
To become a silent and futile exercise in dying,
Violent, unwitnessed, anticlimactic
In its stark lack of heroic justification,
Or will I leave behind an eternal flame?

Suddenly, the boat shudders under the impact
Of a raging mouth of irregular wave-fangs,
Which cut my vessel in half. Cast adrift,
I cling to the last pieces of clotting debris
In the veins, hoping to stay afloat
Long enough for the heart to right itself,
Resume its beat, allow me to climb aboard.

Only, there are no more resurrections.
Comatose and frozen, I watch my life's hopes
Spin on an invisible diorama, before my eyes,
As my stiff existence spirals downward,
Toward the floor, where wrecks from every epoch
Are suspended in undulant and harmless lassitude,
And I realize my dream's patron was Prince Satan the Navigator.

11/16/78 (02274)

The Music of the Spheres

I listen to argentiferous articulations
Whispering down like dove feathers fluttering
From the sky. They tickle my eyelike ears,
Whose sensitive antennae peer across the horizon,
As they focus on the locus of November's song,
To hear the sun exploding, the wind undulating
Beneath celestial oceans, the minutes flowing and
Ebbing continuously. Their gentle overtones
Are revolutions of a vast axle controlling a cable
Coordinating the harmonious stellar motions of planets,
Whose orbits form red-hot filaments
That incandesce, in my brain's container, to ecstasy.

Just why I've been invited to share a slice
Of this day's quietude, rather than someone else
With poetic aspirations, capable of describing divinity
In terms of word-sounds and profound rhyme-schemes
Or with the painter's sense of proportion and color
Or the musician's blessed perception of mellifluity,
I cannot define to adequately satisfy my curious mind,
Yet my suspicion is that these ubiquitous articulations
Are voices speaking to me through silvery, ancestral lips
Belonging to dreamers who've witnessed me sitting here
Outdoors, alone, wishing to disappear, forever,
Into the silent inspiration of their angelic chorus.

11/18/78 (05610)

Early Birds △

Box by dusty box,
We retrieve, from the basement, our heritage,
Neatly packed away last January,
Beneath the warped and creaky wooden stairs:
Handblown and painted ornaments
From "Allemagne," frangible as eggs,
Nestled in their cardboard compartments;
Taffeta and calico ribbons; winged doves
Shaped from papier-mâché;
Plaster-of-Paris gingerbread men; from "Nippon,"
*

Sapphire, crystalline, and ruby fireflies
Connected, by green threads, in a blood-tie
That discloses, when electrified, the dark cave
Where Troika's fantasies wait to be born
And Trilogy's soar and twist like energized bats.

Finally, the artificial tree, docile and helpless
Yet undiminished in its essential function,
Is exhumed and resurrected, whose rings
Are the glittering garland memory strings
Around each previous season, whose roots
Are the rituals we bring to the ceremony
Of its majestic efflorescing, whose consecration
Is a family affair, a sharing among spirits
Blithe and jubilant with ignited compassion and love
For each other. With an entire month
Before the blessed celebration of birth occurs,
We revel in our own early yule,
As though the only things that really matter
Are Trilogy's mastery of the occasion, Troika's dazzlement,
And our pride and happiness in providing for both.

11/28/78 — [1] (01432)

Touching

For us, touching was once no mere anodyne
Against incursions from an impersonal universe
Whose sole purpose might have been to discourage
Our inordinate adoration for each other;

Rather, it was a way of seeing beneath the flesh,
Probing the soul, to discover what motivated our love.
It was our halcyon courtship, our passion,
Our kissing, fired by invisible, insatiable flames.

To this day, my fingers retain the impress
Of your delicate erect nipples, your clitoris,
From those spontaneous occasions
When we'd forget the moment, the place, the explanation

For our uninhibited behavior. To this day,
The muscles in my legs and abdomen pain me
When visions of your sensuous thighs and hips
Rise, undulating through tear-seas in my eyes,

Reminding me how late the hour has grown
Since last we chased each other, like Naiads,
Through orchid petals and juicy grapes
And just how alone our togetherness has left us,

Now that the thrill of co-ownership has deteriorated
To gross negligence or, at best, maintenance of basics
For appearance's sake. Oh, my disconsolate lady,
Let's lie side by side, tonight, and touch our silence.

11/28/78 — [2] (04187)

Crew Shells ^Δ

For Malcolm and Muriel Cowley

All up and down the serpentine Housatonic,
This May-warm afternoon,
The crew shells glide like water spiders
Doing eight-legged maneuvers for exercise.

So beautifully fluid and smooth are their movements,
We're beguiled, mesmerized, disillusioned.
They seem to go ahead as if blown from behind
By invisible river nymphs or sensual breezes

Instead of from tremendous energies expended,
Each agonized second, by athletes at practice,
Pressing, with every flex and relaxation of hamstring
And bicep, to achieve the necessary edge of endurance

Required not even for victory but survival,
On race day. Luxuriating in this irony
Distance and lack of experience make possible,
We revel in a wine haze, high above the basin.

Lying together on a blanket woven of romance,
We drowse in our own newness. Inchoate dreams of us
As Keatsian paramours chasing each other,
Remaining inviolate despite our mortal limitations,

Suspend us in the warm, Chablis-tinged air
Above the sleek and slender shells
Taking racing starts, power-twenties
That lengthen into sturdy thirty-twos.

We watch them fade beyond the bend,
As others inch continuously out of the silence,
*

Into view, while the day changes to years,
Then a decade, then two, and again.

And still, whenever our children discuss colleges
Or beg us recollect our courtship,
Visions of those swift vessels, with their oar tips
Etching the air beside them blue and white,

In precision timing, rise to the amber surface
Of our glasses and linger there long enough
To remind us of that easy freedom we knew,
That glittering splendor of youth's final regatta.

11/29/78 — [1] (02257)

Willy: The Great Wall of China

Another vacant and empty evening spent
Huddled against the cold, beneath the shoulder
At the base of the mind's Great Wall of China.
Located somewhere along its undulating expanse,
I slump, after the day's frustrations and failures,
Palms weary from toting leaden cases
Crammed with model garments and swatch cards,
Feet blistered from endless unannounced advances
And unceremonious exits. Which way station
I've arrived at, tonight, remains to be established
By soap wrappers, match packs, the insignia
Embossed on a green, plastic room-key tag.

In the confines of my scabrous disquietude,
I remove from a travel sack antique copies
Of the Upanishads, *I Ching*, and the *Kama Sutra*
And begin frenetically ripping pages from each,
For kindling, to get the dead brain's fire ignited.
Soon, the bones' virulent chill dissipates.
My flesh banishes its vincible goose pimples.
The blood rushes past the astonished valves
As if chased by passion's naked seducers.
I tingle within lucid, self-induced stimulation
Setting up around my meditative shape,
Stranded in this unlikely Lotus paradise.

Images of flaming asteroids with girandoles
Exploding across the entire visible night sky,
*

Babies escaping small, white mouths of maidens
Conceiving by immaculate articulation, rain forests
Profuse with black orchids, and snow leopards
Leaping great chasms of uplifting heat drafts,
In quest of feline ghosts to furiously mount,
Enter my naturally inebriated landscape
And assault my sense of credibility. I surrender
To their surreal superimposition on my senses,
Enter the teachings of Muhammad, Buddha, Christ,
Through the evening's mystical apotheosis, and sleep

Without even breathing, dream without signs
Of rapid eye movements, wet the bed repeatedly
With wasted semen without realizing it.
I stir like a harpooned whale in a mad ocean-sea,
As my body passes from a state of stolid being
To one of suspended, cryogenic euphoria,
In which all memory of past incarnations is jettisoned
And the future awaits choosing by the next soul
To inhabit my relinquished husk. Suddenly, dusk
And dawn are reversed. I awaken in pitch black,
Shaking against cold stones composing the Great Wall.
It calls me to resume my endless quest for failure.

11/29/78 — [2] (01333)

A Question of Time

Now, the countdown for a final annihilation
Has begun. Jonestown, Guyana,
Relinquishes its victims like so much gristle
And bone cut from a vast rump roast
And thrown in the trash, out back of the shop.
Mexico City breaks apart at the seams,
As though grown obese overnight,
Rather than buckling from underneath,
As the earth's bursting appendix screams in pain.
Manson and Speck reject early paroles,
To show a skeptical yet merciful people
That complacency and forgetting are Siamese freaks,
Whose radical grotesqueness only begets violence.

Even Milhous Nixon is asked to visit,
By foreign dignitaries, the world's capitals,
*

To do his celebrated imitation of Rich Little
Impersonating P. T. Barnum,
Making his legendary "eighteen-minute erasure"
And near-sacred "Checkers" speeches,
Accompanied by miscellaneous minor confessions.
His memoirs are printed on recycled paper,
Collected, in the White House basement,
From shredding machines belching like blast furnaces,
And donated in hope of replacing the Gideon Bible
In every delicatessen, nursing home, state asylum,
Church, and castle in Floral Heights and on Ventnor Avenue.

All fail-safe mechanisms have been disconnected.
Every silo, nuclear sub, flying scourge
Is programmed to coincide with the innocuous spark
From the silent, pliant contact points
Of a button inches from a puny, sweating president.
Doctor No, Ernst Stavro Blofeld,
Goldfinger wait, in their impregnable volcanoes
And undersea fortresses, to inherit the whirlwind
Once the ash and radioactive particles
Subside to a fine layer they can burn away
With lasers. For now, we merely wait to see
Who will kill the next mayor of San Francisco
Or assassinate the communist Prince of Sarajevo.

11/30/78   (05611)

Shattered Beakers

Chirping redbirds and foraging squirrels,
Nervously gathering in winter's scattered detritus,
Shatter the silence that contains my desire to create
Within its heated beaker of total recall.

First, it reverberates violently,
Then explodes. Its jagged pieces
Coalesce, for moments, as future daydreams,
Immediate hopes, memories of goals sought,
Caught, framed, and hung, then lost
Among the pack-rat dross stuffed in attics
Of the mind's many homes away from home.

Finally, the sharp, fractured slivers of glass,
Those atomized, invisible components
*

That, whole, constituted the soul's defense against distraction,
Enter the cold, sad, slow November air
Like snow flowing upwards from the frozen earth,
And with them go all potential poems,
One of which I might have chosen to distill,

From the floating, bubbling emotions inside the beaker,
Into something transcendent, lovely, and mild.
And I'm left with the echoes of cardinals and squirrels
Shattering their own tiny vials with elegiac madness.

12/6/78 — [1] (05612)

[A thousand expiations] †

A thousand expiations
    Floating above our marriage
        Like hot-air balloons in gay hues

12/6/78 — [2] (07321)

After the Ice Storm

I

Through two studio windows
Separated by a shimmering, incomplete vacuum,
I peer out on a dazzling desolation
Ignited by an anomalous sun.

Such brittleness deceives; such freezing
Misleads the inner eye, safe in its layers,
To assume that pine needles, limbs,
Telephone wires wear an ethereal glaze

Rather than suffer, in pained silence,
The tenacious weight of rain
Detained midway between its destination
And moon craters, where it originated.

II

Suddenly, vision reels itself in
Like a spring-loaded tape measure
*

Released, focusing for a numb moment
On its readings of distance, depth, dimension.

I begin to wonder, then speculate on,
Just how much distortion is caused
By the thin, rimpled inner window,
Magnified by the flake-etched glass

Flush with the outermost plane of the house,
Which guides my eye to objects outside
I can't touch, feel, hear, or smell,
And how much is a product of vagary and caprice.

III

Ultimately, I question whether the extrinsic
Is actually ever reality or if, instead,
It's not the essence demoted to comprehension
By the soul transmuting it to fit the head.

When I look again through twin windows,
The entire white, icy sky is melting.
Like bubbles slowly rising from ocean depths,
Nature's inexorable unbending has commenced.

In fathomless contemplation, I try to imagine shapes
The trees will take once their halos disintegrate.
When, in spring, I go out to inspect the changes,
It's doubtful I'll know even my own shadow.

12/9–10/78   (02337)

THC

For Mel Curdt

Today's young have been stung
By a malaise seated in the lungs and brain.
They remain strung out, shaking, dazed,
Within a nimbus laced with ecstasy
Tinged with hallucinogenic glazes
That tantalize and stimulate the drowsing cells
To sensual rebellion, orgasmic insurrection,
Without ever even waking them.

Such monumental lethargy is not achieved
Without surrendering the spirit to diabolical apathy,
*

Nor are fancy's appetites rewarded satiety,
Admittance into the region of lotus-eaters,
Or perpetual forgetting, without unlocking its doors.
Existence is a high toward *up*,
At a pace so slow that *down*,
Like lust and death, is nowhere to be found.

And when that exotic, faraway state
Becomes *here*, becomes *now*, forever,
Tomorrow disappears into yesterday
Like a whale being swallowed alive
By a three-inch fire-breathing chimera.
Once inside the cannabic leviathan,
Each innocent, by degrees, is burned out,
Asphyxiated. What dies is only his ghost.

12/12/78 — [1] (05613)

Following a Moonbeam

Twilight, tinged crimson and gunmetal gray
At its extreme edges, drips over me
Like a tepid crystal mist. I run naked
Beneath its scintillant, sensual glow,
A concupiscent sylph dancing, deer-fleet,
Through this forest forever stopped
In an endlessly dissolving five o'clock.
Time kisses my loins. My groin
Groans with the complaint of unconsummated lovers.

Just ahead, eternally ever ahead,
Is winging Diana, singing to herself
The lunatic strains of her cold captivity,
Crying out, from her earthly banishment,
For some fated Sir Galwyn of Arthgyl
To save her from everlasting chastity.
I lean toward her, without gaining,
And all the while, night's feline shape
Creeps up behind me and overtakes my lust.

Suddenly, my blood turns to panic.
It rushes from the heart. My parts go cold,
Turn black, become one with the darkness.
I am consumed in snarling, voracious jaws,
*

My carcass left for gnawing jackals
In the dead, fathomless center of my dazed head.
One by one, the stars enter the clearing,
To remark the bones of the alien who came
To liberate the moon and died in his own solitude.

12/12/78 — [2] (05614)

Confessions of a Former Magna Cum Laude

There was an urgent time
When I fancied myself
A celebrated aesthete, a genius
Necessarily oblivious to the common rush
Toward degrees, local renown,
Petty promotions, and foundation grants,
Postponing the inevitable return
To classrooms, faculty meetings,
Lecture circuits cum honorariums and expenses.
I fantasized that in monastic isolation,
I might produce treatises and tomes
On previously unilluminated poets
And playwrights, create sensational works
From my own imagination
That would be taught future generations,
In the company of Faulkner, Milton, and Donne.
In manic moods, I even envisioned myself
A great debater, a statesman
Whose youthful exuberance
Would elect him to the presidency
And eloquence on crucial matters of state
And national security might sway
Conservative and liberal alike,
Win the nation's commendation.

To this day, I can't explain
Just what happened to change my direction
Or when it first occurred,
Nor can I recall why my passion
For learning and rhetoric stalled in midterm.
All I know for certain
Is that a vast and enigmatic happiness descended,
*

Allaying my adolescent yearnings for fame.
Whether it was Jan,
That lithe, long-legged filly
Who pranced before my fenced stable,
Loosened the gate, and begged me follow,
Or the boy and girl foals
She gave our oneness remains unanswerable.
I do know unequivocally
That an indispensable sense of contentment
Subdued my former beliefs
In the omnipotence of cold intellect.
It subjugated my academic hubris —
Being oblique as an Elizabethan conceit —
To a compassionate deference to people
Who labor daily for an hourly wage
And bring their lunch in a bag.
From them I've gained my greatest education.

12/12/78 — [3] (02094)

Points in Time

For angelic Jan

Each of our waking hours is a precious child,
A delicate violet petal. Each day alive
Inside the backwash of consciousness
Is a flight to the sun's core and back.

Every new year is a youthful explosion,
Whose fallout of poppies and manna
Spreads a ubiquitous white, silent wand
Over our convalescing Earth, commanding growth.

Every minute spent with you, wife,
Every evanescent second alone together,
Is a communion of *now* and *then* lapsed,
A fusion of souls, whose future is absolved of death,

And every millennium is an Edenic reminiscence,
God's supernal kiss, His promise
That life will survive its incessant half-lives.
Eternity is you and I, tied to His omniscience.

12/12/78 — [4] (01334)

Vigilantes ^Δ

Even at this early-morning hour,
As the moon, veiled in smoky gauze
At the western extremity of night, sleeps,

Tipton's dependable vigilantes are awake,
Taking their coffee, sausage, eggs,
And stout conversation at the Crystal Café
Before manning the watchtowers.
Among topics of discussion most pressing
Is the blister-cracking cold weather,
The difficulties it presents to well diggers,
"Power pullers," business in general,
Frightened off the roads by lingering ice.
The thrust shifts to slick fields
Inaccessible to tractor and half-ton,
Frozen ponds withholding their water from cows,
Plows stuck in the earth like obelisks.

As soon as an unusual lull intrudes
Through a space their mutual chewing provides,
One among them lets loose a joke-snake
From its cage of bigotries, into the brief clearing.
"Did you hear about the nigger boy
Who found a gold stone? In shining it,
A genie appeared, who gave him two wishes:
'I's always wanted to be white.' 'Granted!'
'I's always wanted to have a pile of money
Without working for it.' The genie stops,
Thinks awhile, then replies, 'You're black again!'"
The self-deputized P.B.P.C*
Guffaw, nod in all-knowing agreement.

One half-hour dissolves into the next
Like cubes floating in a whiskey glass
Set out and left at room temperature.
The telephone fellow relates, with indignation,
The recent travesty of a local lady
On a two-party line, refusing to relinquish it
To a mother, with a dying son, trying to locate
Anyone to help save him.
"Now, ain't that the worst thing
You've ever heard?" "Sick!" "Unbelievable!"
*

"Disgusting!" rise on the air like clouds
Weighted with black anger. "I mean,
Granted, the boy woulda died anyway," he added.

One by one, they leave and enter December
Pink and chill and moonless, ready to assume
The monumental duties of maintaining Tipton's integrity.

*Protectors of Benevolent & Pious Causes

12/14/78 — [1] (00595)

The Creative Flame

The candle's quavering shadows are voices
Rising out of the silent abyss beneath night,
To kiss my ears. I listen like never before,
As if, in the shifting flame, a prophet in robes
Might be standing atop Sinai, against a sun,
Translating aloud the sacred tablets' sounds.

Only, the lambent candle's slow, shrill glow
Hisses and twists like snakes slithering in a pit.
Visions of diminutive, horned, scaly lizards
Leap into my eyes, biting irises and pupils,
Until sight is a nightmarish Pandemonium
Alive with devils conspiring to overthrow life.

The noisy hours lapse into blind contagion.
Distant thunderclaps suggest worlds colliding
Inside the halo cast against my face
By the candle burning low. My mind is blown
By sourceless tongues. As the light dies,
A thousand resounding echoes from the grave

Seduce me toward amnesic sleep,
By whispering into the vacuum I inhabit
That time has come to take me home again.
Where the candle once burned in pure air,
Ashen wax stands like a cast-bronze statue
Shaped in the image of God's spoken Word.

12/14/78 — [2] (01335)

Getting High with Uncle Funk

For "Crazy Al" Pethtel

I listen to their music and see wine
Cascading over the Housatonic,
In a stream of consciousness so Faulknerian
Even the fish rise to the surface of my eyes
To dance to the jubilant celebration of the spheres.

What I hear is a music so special the angels
Dance naked. Before me, a thousand Eves
Slither toward the apple tree; Adam falls
To the base, in aimless and drowsy sensuality,

Inebriated on the sounds flowing over the falls
Floated by a cold rosé. My head screams
Inside a pure, ignited ecstasy of deliquescence.
The flesh stands up erect as an excited bear

Frightened by the presence of its own stolid shadow.
The blood mixes with the chilled spirits,
Spills into the arterial extremities, escapes
Altogether from the head, into the superheated air,

And hovers, like mist, between the crest and trough.
Now, the melodies fragment, atomize, disintegrate.
My energies follow them to the edge, drop off,
Plummet to the rocky bottom, where ecstasy waits

To take me into its jagged embrace,
Assimilate my pieces one at a time. Dying
Is nothing more than being completely absorbed
By the sounds the earth makes as it turns to dust.

12/14–15/78 — [3] on 12/14 & [1] on 12/15   (01336)

In vincoli

The nonexistent contract
Between his Diaspora-bound heritage
And circumstance stipulates he never stop
Opening up new accounts
In remote regions or eat regular meals
With family and friends. If he could,
He would take his sustenance intravenously,
*

On the go, day after day the same,
Whose very changelessness might eliminate
All delays caused by choosing and chewing.

Like a bullet shuttle, he would ply
The country's highways, from Grover's Corners
To Cannery Row and back, a million times,
Without ever even refueling
Or staying the night in one more stifling motel.
He would take one change of clothing
And a toilet kit containing spare dentures,
Glass eyes, hearing aid, and colostomy bag,
That his requirements would always be confined
To local pharmacies, in case of emergency.

Only, these are vagaries his capricious head
Weaves out of interminable shreds of idle time
He keeps rolling up onto a portable skein.
In nearly half a century on the road,
He's never really discovered a trade route
To the Indies that would circumnavigate
Scraggly seraglios, gulag ice floes,
Jew-baiters, nigger-haters, xenophobes,
Nor has he ever conceived an alternative scheme
By which to repay his ancestors for their tenacious legacy.

12/15/78 — [2] (02410)

The Poet Goes Deaf

Slowly as goose-down snow
Sifting, in akimboed drowsiness,
Through gray-misty hours,
Outside sounds filter to numbness
Before ever reaching my tympanums.

They dissolve in the sweet acoustics
Between formulation and formation,
Metamorphose into unshaped, impotent expectations
My imagination eagerly conjures,
While failing to recognize them as its own,

Until what began as actual patterns
Set to speech, to fashion an environment
*

Capable of sustaining and conveying another's ideation,
Becomes sheer speculative echoes of my soul,
Forever confined in an invisible prison of silence.

12/19/78   (05615)

New Albion ᐃ

Three Victorian floors above the ground,
In warm, soundproof angularity,
We enter the evening hours like Pilgrims
Come to demonstrate our faith in make-believe.

This airy, cathedral-ceilinged attic
Provides all the stimuli imagination requires
To let our antics transform this setting
Into youth's peaceable kingdom,

A refuge where brother and sister,
Mother and father might enact
The blessed sacraments of family worship
Without religious persecution or threat of gaol

For libeling the monarchy. In this New World,
Survival is child's play:
Fantasizing with toys, mounting a spring horse,
Racing after shadows, turning in circles

While dizziness mottles the mind
With polka-dot Kerploppuses and a Spotted Atrocious,
And wrestling with mythic goddesses and gods
Named Trilogy and Troika, invariably.

Neither Dionysian nor Puritanical extremes
Guide us in our labor of love,
Rather the sheer, inevictable conviction
That sharing and laughter and touching, alone,

Provide the mystical, innocent elements
On which colonies are founded and perpetuated,
As parents dissolve and their children grow up
And bring forth descendants of their own.

Eventually, exhausted yawns presage sleep.
Sadly, we leave the silent attic,
*

Knowing that to return, we'll have to navigate, ourselves,
A zone of aging and two vast oceans

Before we spy New Albion's shores again
And that, even then, the land we abandoned
Only a day ago will have measurably changed.
It won't recognize us as its first inhabitants.

12/23/78 & 4/9/79 — [2] (01436)

The Christmas Rose △

*For Lloyd and Mardie Krumlauf,
12/25/78*

Slowly, the things of the Old World,
Luxuriant with ritual and robed ceremony,
Rise to the surface of the eyes' fonts.
Beginning at the outermost edges,
They ripple inward, centering, centering,
Like scattered petals of a supple rose,
Floating back to reattach themselves
To the godly core of their original body.

I linger in their singular fragrance,
Where visions of mercurial children
Opening dazzling, magical sights
And ideas left by itinerant wise men
From the Hesperides and Zion, invisibly arrived,
Fill my breathing with the incense of gold snow.
The afterglow from an incandescent crucifix
Inside the globe of my silence lights this day,

And I'm inspired to reflect on the Covenant
Entered into by each of us and the Igniter of hopes,
Dreams, defeats, deaths, and resurrections.
We reaffirm our belief in the unity of the spirit
By clasping hands in a sacred sharing
Of familial repast and by reciting prayers
Whose heritage binds us for all time.
In unison, we kiss the sacrificial wine,

And as we lift our glasses skyward,
Rays streaming through the hazy, lacy curtains
*

Gather the eight stems in a bouquet,
Fuse them into a crimson rose,
Whose liquid petals fan out above us,
In blessed holiness. One by one by one,
We become this mystical Christmas flower,
Which enriches the soul's soil even as it grows.

12/25/78   (02130)

Trial by Fire and Water: After Reading
The Arrowhead △

For Nardie and Sally Stein

As the past gathers momentum,
Seeing blurs into a misty, reverse myopia,
On whose unfocused lens memories converge.
Images splinter. Accomplishments disintegrate
Like logs cast into a fireplace
And left overnight. Now, I sweep up ashes
The years have created in their unclean burning.

Not even echoes of youth's singing voices
Linger above the regal Norway pines
Or between the dense sumac and third-growth birch,
Nor do the sweet adolescent faces,
Beaming with promise, the lithe, athletic bodies
We each inhabited, the incomplete souls
Impatient to be molded and cast into shapes
Lifted from the rib of Michelangelo's maker
Swell with their original energy and purpose.

They've all become fire bells, on tripods,
Caked with rust, cracked, without clappers,
Whirligigs flaking mercilessly
In a vacuum where no winds stir,
Paddles, oars, and taut, billowed sails
Separated from their canoes, rowboats, yachts
Floating on a lake drained of its waters.

They've become screened-in, rough-framed cabins
Devoid of trunks, bunk beds, laughter,
Inhabited, instead, by skunks, chipmunks, squirrels.
Only their outlines, highlighted by snow
*

And somber summer shadows,
Locate them in the mind's mythical Wisconsin
My glowing spirit knew intimately
Before growing up and going away from home.
Even their flimsy green doors are warped shut.

Blindly, my hands grope among the cobwebs
Lining their rafters, dusty shelves, and ledges.
They stick, like sadness, to the fingertips.
I tug at what remains of frayed bell ropes.
The dull thud of bloodless years
Pulsates my brain. I spin a whirligig's thin propeller;
Limbs shiver in rickety, arthritic imprecision.

Through a mystical, liquidless immersion
Consisting of shifting amnesic images,
I swim toward a golden swath
Splayed across the lake by a gibbous moon
And enter its shimmering, lunatic ebb and flow.
Only, the paddles, oars, and masts I grab
Refuse to keep me afloat. Slowly, all hopes
Of retrieving the gentle moments of a lifetime
Drown. The past is a clammy undertaker.

1/5/79   (00016)

Magi: Fall Sales Meeting '79 △

Once again, the harbingers have returned
To counsel with their supreme leaders,
Regarding next year's fashions,
Whose swatches and models and stock sheets
They'll carry away cautiously as archivists
Guarding recently excavated scrolls.

Only the most recent representatives
Occupy chairs at the sheet-draped tables
Weighted with bulging card lines, ashtrays,
Cigarette packs, water pitchers, and plastic glasses.
Generations of their ghosts, smoky spirits,
Hover in line, behind each animated bust.

The present faces, with few exceptions,
Are imbued with the same sleazy voraciousness
*

As their predecessors. They postulate a baby's need
For spoon feeding, the novitiate's desire
For indoctrination into the creeds of a father figure,
Shylock's incessant obsession with shekels.

And like their forebears, they wear the heritage
Of street peddlers, only slightly glorified
By the advent of the auto and three-piece suit,
On their accented vernacular and aquiline profiles.
They babel in tongues, brief solely for their regions,
As the universal arbiters, sneer, hiss, whisper,

As, range by range, taste is channeled
Into knee, rise, and waistband dimensions
And style is defined for the millions by the line
Each man will carry into his territory.
Finally, all identities, names, and appearances
Merge into the surging whirlpool of collective acquiescence.

They dematerialize through vaporous cigar reek
Deposited by the last three days' vituperations,
Taking the future with them. In their hushed wake,
Voices from the past shimmer in heated debate,
Praising, with envy, the newly introduced raiment,
Grieving their own lack of active participation.

Unheard, invisibly, their ancient lamentations,
Like nebulae shining pervasively in the east,
Infiltrate the marketplace, soften traditional attitudes
Toward change. They light the way for the harbingers
Advancing, by day and by night, with gifts —
Swaddling clothes for the naked children of the Lord.

1/13–14/79 (02285)

Wind-Flowers

On this Lord's-day morning, I soar,
Enter the Mentor's splendid, airy gardens,
Dotted with wind-flowers, exotic flora,
And mottled, thermal orchids gloriously white.

My flight is a gentle swaying, side to side,
A limbo of luminous fusions and silent growth,
An interlude moving, with gliding rotor-motion,
Through fields profuse with blooming poppies.

The wide, slender moment composing its existence
Is a rope bridge connecting invisible oceans
Floated with white-ripening Monet lilies.
Precariously, I inch along its narrow path,

Frightened yet obsessed to pluck one
And take it home with me. I look down
And, leaning, lift a glistening shape from the sky,
A gift for my children and wife: the wind, the wind.

1/28/79 (05623)

Southern Flight #218

I: Montgomery

Just prior to takeoff, the plane trembling on the apron,
I pray that chance and circumstance will keep their distance,
Not intrude or dismantle my Hegira-like mission
To get myself back, safely home, intact.

My bones reverberate like xylophone bars
Coursed lightly over by startled-mice feet.
Even my teeth chatter with nervous uncertainty,
Regarding destiny breathing cold sweat on my neck.

I become an incongruous priest in street clothes,
Called in, by a somnolent echo beneath my soul,
To begin administering last rites, just in case
The chase is preemptively concluded in midflight.

II: Birmingham

Down, now, on the first of three scheduled descents,
I rise, pace as though my anxiety might dissipate
With slight persuasion. Everything is so stable
And silent, I dread the renascence of the rotors' whine.

Then, again, the sleek, full-sheeted caravel
Takes the wind into its twin sails,
Climbs into a shimmering oblivion, with me inside,
A chained slave regurgitating fear in its plush hold.

My prayers become wake-spume trailing off,
Attenuating in the receding slipstream. They dissolve
*

Like bubbles blown in desperation by a drowning sailor.
Slowly, I sink to the bottom of a blood-swollen ocean.

III: Memphis

Distant Memphis looms just up ahead,
Substantiating the reliability of our gadgetry. Dead reckoning
Fidgets hastily with its invisible Kohlsman window,
Brings us narrowly back from death, into the wind.

With half the navigation unequivocally done,
I entertain hallucinations of being boarded by pirates
While moored in irons, exorbitantly skyjacked,
Then cast adrift, five miles high.

Suddenly, my ears detect the reiterating fugue
The susurrant engines, in their ineluctably smooth ignition,
Send into the universe, on mechanical lute strings.
I am helpless in resisting the seducer's fanning fingertips.

IV: St. Louis

Airborne for a final time, I revive my prayer
And ride its frantic, raging, osprey-like trajectory
Toward worship's merciful destination.
Below me, the great undulating snake follows my shadow.

Forty-eight minutes of space separate my family
From their blessed gatekeeper; forty-eight minutes,
Untrammeled by renegade demons and stray shades,
Need merely evaporate into the atmosphere,

And I'll be delivered of fate's awful, taut chains;
Forty-eight minutes distilled from all eternity
Own me. Yet, in their eyes and on their faces,
I see my children and wife praying for my release.

1/29/79   (05616)

No Rest for the Weary

This silent, snow-mottled Sunday morning
Is the destination my nightmares
Try to keep me from reaching, by obliterating sleep,
Annihilating the paltry refuge I seek
From antagonisms, obstacles to my base security.

This Lord's day is a mild oasis connecting deserts
Named for the desperate days of my workweeks.
I throw myself down on my stomach and drink
Until the desiccated mind's raging thirst is slaked,
Then enter a state of shimmering tranquillity.

Vacant of such abrupt uprootedness,
This day of rest becomes a spawning pool
For dreams squandered in perpetual breakings of camp
And directionless wandering. For a moment,
An eon, I almost believe in redemption,

Yet its unexpected arrival has surprised my senses,
Turned them into skeptical scientists
Casting madly about for empirical explanations
To the godly design suggested by its unbroken code.
No amount of forced relaxation will stop the process,

And I am made to watch the gentle tedium of hours
Drain away without releasing a reflection
Or leaving behind a solitary palpable artifact —
Melody, bleeding scratch, villanelle, sketch —
To remind me this Sabbath ever housed my soul.

Only the thick-drifted, imperturbable snow,
Conspicuously placid in its cold aloneness,
Reposes without pain, its fate beyond knowing
Except to me. Already, I hear it melting
Under the sun's gaze — my only witness dying.

2/11/79   (02226)

To Lloyd: A Panegyric

His is a brain trained in retaining universal humor,

A spirit dissatisfied not with existence
But status quo statistics on growing old,

A soul ambitious as a raging Charlemagne's
Yet gently sensitive and sentimental
As a Keatsian ode,

An ego motivated by the essence of the quest
For expeditious perfection,
*

Nothing less than *the* best his being can expect
From its bones and flesh and intellect,

A heart vibrant and driving, whose blood
Pulsates with the moon's tides,
Powering a thousand generations not yet arrived,
Recycling the ichor of a thousand more
Who died before the flood.

2/12/79 — [1] (02228)

Going Forward: Lloyd's Poem

        Tonight, locked tightly inside
The azaleas' amazing pink-petaled bouquet,
        We enact a lay eucharist,
Raise glasses filled with effervescent rosé,
        And pray, in silent, sibilant soliloquies,
For the safe passage of our dear, dear friend,
        Seven hours distant from our immediate world.

His absence is a shimmering meteor shower
        Consisting of images of him.
From such heights, the exploding girandoles
        Scatter pieces of his past over us,
And we are gracefully singed by his radiance.
        The azaleas' sweet, delicate faces
Attract us; we see his laughter in their eyes.

        Later, lying together in bed,
We gather him into our dreams,
        By recollecting track meets, football games,
Apartments decorated with stark inventiveness,
        His wife, Mardie, and recent baby,
His abrupt uprooting, the about-face
        At comfort's front door,

To seek something illusive and abstract,
        Not necessarily fame or affluence,
Rather a name to give his inner self —
        The child of his earthly desires —
A justification for self-actualizing drives
        To reach peace with his aging hopes,
A home wherein he might live with his pride.

By the time morning's light awakens us,
He'll be flashing beyond Oklahoma City,
Past New Mexico, alone, totally alone.
We'll float downstairs on drowsy yawns,
Enter again the fragrance of azaleas,
And, remembering our last night's toast,
Seek redemption in our aching emptiness.

2/12/79 — [2] (02227)

An Aubade △

Troika at sixteen months

Each morning, we reenact a ritualistic aubade,
A celebration of waking, a praise to morning,
In which I gather up my waiting baby, Troika,
Patient in his ammoniac stench. First, my face
Peers in around the doorframe, wide-eyed.
Delight surrounds him with radiance. He stirs
Like a chick breaking from its egg; his shell
Is a wad of soiled blankets he casts aside
To grasp the pull-string on a plastic bee,
Whose wings flap with raucous cacophony
Each time he jerks it into erratic life.
"Pull the bee! *Pull* that bee!" I exclaim,
As his laughter gets tangled up in his pride.

Soon, he is riding my sturdy embrace,
Down the penumbrous corridor, toward the stairs.
We skip over each step like a speeding needle
Not missing a stitch, then pause at the first landing,
To pay allegiance, do daily obeisance,
To the framed engraving of Trilogy's face
And, beside it, the beautifully muted portrait
Of "Mama," arrested forever clutching a single rose.
We both know this moment's lingering
Is inherently sacred. Then, again,
We descend, touching bottom with a shout.
Troika's euphoria, relating to a sitting Nipper,
Mounted on a horn phono, translates into "dog."

As we approach our destination, his head lifts,
His eyes net their expected images,
*

Without a hitch, and he enters the aromatic kitchen
As if arrived in paradise. The sight of his sister
And mother ignites his entire existence. All that remains
Is for him to be willingly secured in his highchair
And to have the lotus-eaters' feast of bananas,
Peaches, raisins, cereal, and milk laid before him.
While waiting, he scans the landscape
Like an oscillating fan, focusing on the bugs —
Trilogy's six-, seven-, and nine-legged spiders —
Taped to the louvered partition beside the refrigerator.
"Bugs! Bugs!" he screams at his favorite playmates.

With one more breakfast soon etched
Into history's glass, we release the boy
And let him begin his own expeditionary trek
To gather Darwinian data. Where he sat,
Scattered debris of cyclonic proportions is left
For us to clean up. On the tip of his nose
Is toast-butter. Each cheek is a painter's palette
Smeared with accidental impasto. His clothes
Are a clown's costume, his hair a nest.
Before I can even grasp my attaché
Or zip my woolly coat, he notices my attitude of haste.
Without protest, he flexes and relaxes his fingers,
Waving good-bye to another blessed aubade.

2/13/79 — [1] (01433)

A Valentine for Jan, 1979

This Valentine's Day, I absolutely refuse
To surrender to recycled sentiments
Rendered fully acceptable by public demand
And to canned, clichéd, bromidic slogans
Beautifully reproduced from colored designs
Endlessly evoked from the four hundred pens
Of surfeited, impersonal women and men
Working for Hallmark and American Greetings.

I abnegate all easy excuses and philosophies
That might send me to the florist's icebox
To choose cymbidiums or sweetheart roses
In coral and muted pinks or persuade me
*

That a certain perfume might suffice
To satisfy a material obligation for the occasion
Or a sheer peignoir might tantalize
My lady's appetite for erotic delights.

I refuse, with all the energy invested in me,
To give in or sell out to the tyranny of hype,
Confectioners of moral marzipan,
And Marjoe-artists pimping words at every turn.
Instead, I come to you, my blessed love,
Unsundered, naked, fresh as a May rainbow,
My flesh throbbing to possess your precious heart.
Let us be valentines, lusting for each other forever!

2/13/79 — [2] (02229)

Comes Creeping In

Somehow, the echoing literary overtones
Of the metaphor "fog-paws"
Seem inappropriate and implausible
In this town of Popeye patois
And Olive Oyl appearances,

Yet this elaborate erudition,
Dripping, like cold cave-water,
Off the hollow bones of Sandburg
And Stearns Eliot mimics me,
Heightens my sense of expatriation.

The thick, opaque, vaporous air
Remains grayly impenetrable.
Even high beams can't disentangle
The morning's matted fur
Or clear a path through the ratted mist.

All streets resist violation.
My eyes strain, in dilated amazement,
To detect strange superstitions
Rising up out of my steamy brain.
Even caffeine charges fantasies with evil.

The lurching, whirring tires purr
As they skip from chuckhole
*

To cicatrix to freshly scratched gash
The snows have opened, with icy claws,
In the town's macadam hide.

Still frozen, the transmission groans.
The entire machine, arching its back
In feeble defiance, hisses at the elements.
It shivers violently, as if hysterically frightened
By the imminent prospect of a fight to the death.

Suddenly, a truck looms up,
Like a giant feline leaping from night,
With a terrific rush. The near impact
Staggers my imagination, stalls my reflexes.
The brakes squeal with a macabre shrill,

And all the silvery light explodes,
Fills with grotesque geometric shapes
Colored by a cyanide-damaged mind.
Shaken, I can almost feel
A scalding, sandpapery, epileptic tongue

Licking away the bleeding hallucinations
That have clung, like bat dung,
To my drowsy waking existence. With a start,
I dash away from the scene of the crash
And rush into my office, to escape a stalking madness.

2/15/79   (00249)

The Children of the Universe

Alcestis, Alcibiades, Nicodemus, and Peter
Rise, like wood smoke, through time's flue.
Their flying sparks singe my dark eyes
With glimmering images. They light the night
I pass slowly through, groping for pathways
And voices to take me back to the ancient womb.

My empty guts gurgle with hypnotic futility,
As though churning food in ecstasy
Instead of uncertainty and abateless fear.
The nearest creature to my aloneness is me,
And even my eyes fail to recognize my face
In their anesthetized gaze. The strange intruder

They arrest in their focus is a naked baby,
Newly spawned, still wet from gestation,
Who bears a nightmarish resemblance to death
Dressed in my features. Its penis, feet, and butt
Are miniatures of my own clothed parts.
Its febrile, hysterical crying reminds me of wind

Whispering through my mind's cypress swamp.
Suddenly, the four specters, robed in fire,
Lift the child high above their heads.
It flickers like the wick of a lambent candle,
Exposing my shadowy presence among the wide silence.
I feel my shivering bones suspended from the stars,

A pendent orb, a coffin, a chrysalis
Spinning dizzily in twisting, invisible fists,
Spiraling upward, into a mystical ellipse,
Until the pallbearing figures disappear from view
And I am thrust outward, adrift
Within the primal realm where souls unite

And spirits commune with their future and past.
Gathered on fine, white, warm shore-sands
Washed by a golden ocean, the children of the universe
Wave to me. They stand silently mesmerized,
Awaiting the arrival of my delicately petaled vessel.
At last, I'm totally unborn. All that remains

Is the sweet, swift dissolution, the elemental alchemy
That changes matter back into recyclable vapors.
Suddenly, a vast, surging hurricane
Sweeps the beach, whipping the seething sands
Into a mass of bees swarming the earth's horizon.
The bees become years seizing me in their frenzied flight.

2/19/79 — [1] (05617)

Tax Collectors, Whores, and Fisher Kings

Visions of tax collectors, whores, and Fisher Kings
Pervade this ecclesiastical day,
When February breaks its icy shackles and glows
Like a glittering, inlaid Byzantine mosaic.
*

Although it's cold enough to change my urine to steam,
Make the norepinephrine in the brain's receptors
Slow to reptilian lethargy, cause Johnny,
The town's resident crazy, to wash cars
In T-shirt, no one minds the frigidity,
For the sun's premature attempt to overcome winter.
Its scintillant fires, burning like a coal mine
Raging out of control underneath oblivion,
Threaten our hibernated souls with an extinction
So blessed and totally weighted with ecstasy,
We share a paranoia that snow creatures will extinguish it
Before it reaches our volatile magazines.

Born again, this afternoon,
I am too soon doomed to be torn
And bent, like crocuses and forsythias in March storms,
Without a moment's notice, destined, by April,
To come to rest in a deathly wasteland
Pervaded by tax collectors, whores, and Fisher Kings.
On this ecclesiastical day, all that's left
Is the uneasy belief in the earth's perpetuity;
Otherwise, even these killing seasons
Would be too final to try surviving.
Just up ahead, the sky shakes its dice,
While moneychangers, shaped like clouds,
Scrape together the last pieces of sunlight
And gather in temples scattered across the horizon,
To gamble away my soul with the flick of a wrist
And a wistful resignation to fate's sacerdotal gaze.

2/19/79 — [2] (05618)

Arcady in Tipton ^Δ

I've watched the sages and philosophers
Of my left-wing generation
Deliberate, speculate, pontificate,
Then deteriorate into sheer rhetoric,
Mere logic, and fearful persiflage.
Now, their names flap in a tattered breeze,
Like pennons flying from flimsy poles
*

In memory's deepest bleachers,
Whose stadium is empty as Jesus' cave.

Only these Tiptonian Aristotles,
These Midwestern Platos,
Six o'clock Socrates, Dracos,
And Alexanders the Great,
Remain pristine and inviolate
In their tenacious opposition to the new humanism,
Which presumes equality of birthright
And freedom of speech and will
As necessary coevals to society's survival.

They've prevailed, despite the winds of change
Washing inland from Montgomery and Selma,
By fervently debating to the death
The two ubiquitous enemies to "truth":
TV and newspapers.
Each persists in his sacred belief
That the former city is celebrated yet
As the Confederacy's first capital,
The latter as the home of Yazoo Brush Hogs.

Never once have they deviated from professing,
Through unadorned bigotry,
Scurrilous calumniation of neighbors,
And expletives carefully selected
To gain the most putrescent public effect,
Their collective allegiance to the supremacy
Of an unadulterated white race.
Like vigilantes, they stand united and ready
To combat all threats to their perpetuation.

Although the Crystal Café, a converted gas station
Located at the only crossroads the town boasts,
Is an unlikely Arcady, it's convenient
To every Periclean Athenian in the community.
In blind retreat they come, each morning;
Enlightened they leave, after an hour's discourse,
To lay pipe, feed livestock,
Curse the weather, contemplate next season's planting,
And pay homage to the gods that be.

2/21/79 — [1] (00600)

Painterly Hallucinations on a Gray Day

On this wet, wintry, snow-strewn day,
Polled Herefords and Charolais
Are splayed over the chaotic landscape
Like erratic jabs on a Seurat painting.
The sky has a Thuringian gray cast.
The dead grass is an unimpassioned Flemish amber.
The air is Sloan's gaseous Manhattan.

Blood-rusted fences and their rotted posts
Sag, like swaybacked nags,
Under the weight of accumulated drifts.
Their stuttering postures are reminiscent
Of flustered redcoats
Dying in ignorant and ignominious formation
At the base of Trumbull's clamorous canvases.

Even the road I travel endlessly, alone,
Is a malign chain in a Piranesi etching,
Stretched from one invisible prison wall,
Through an inscrutable vault, into a windowless chamber
Ominous with unevenly hewed stones
And perspectives diminishing in a distance
Not fit to accommodate human dimensions.

In this desolate Missouri heartland,
There's no Sienese brightness,
No Arno's dancing lights. No Pisano
Or Brunelleschi, no Cimabue
Or Giotto, ornaments the ramshackle silos and barns
With spires, terra-cotta tiles, travertine,
Or quatrefoils to make them come alive.

Nor are there signs of breathtaking grandeur
That an Asher B. Durand, Thomas Cole,
Albert Bierstadt, or Frederick Edwin Church
Might transmute into shimmering beauty.
No Monet haystacks or poplars dot the horizon.
No *grande jattes* or Cézanne-scapes
Undo the gloom, the indomitable gloom,

And as I go ahead, changing directions
At unpredictable intervals, the road I've taken
Becomes a frame around an abstract mass
*

Globbed and knotted, not blended
Into any recognizable shapes. I stop
To contemplate this day's intended design.
Like a loose bristle, I'm trapped in its cold impasto.

2/21/79 — [2] (02253)

Returning from the Dead

For some reason, my leaving, this morning,
Coincides with the little uniformed ladies
Guiding their maintenance carts, from door to door,
Along the smoke-reeking corridor. I'm numb.
My overstuffed, anonymous visage
Stumbles toward the front desk to settle up;
Only, the labyrinth's mouth swallows me,
Dissolving my will to survive in the confusion
It secrets about my unenlightened mind.

My inordinately late waking perplexes me.
Explanations remain vague as sea creatures
Dragging themselves over murky sand-floors,
And as I make my way home, through a fog
So dense its impenetrable shroud
Clouds out even memory, ghostly hallucinations
Begin worming toward the base of my skull.
Again, I surrender to a knee-buckling malaise.
Parasites carry me away a piece at a time.

The jaws of the fog are a spider's fangs
Clawing me apart, ingesting my fleshy meat,
Burying the cleanly gnawed bones and tough carapace
In a series of coffins each second provides
As it arrives, like a bottle on a conveyor belt,
Waiting to be filled, then abruptly departs.
Only my eyes are left unmolested.
They hang behind the windshield, in blind suspension,
Like testicles dangling from a vasectomized giant.

Suddenly, the diaphanous vapors lift,
And I can see my shadow cast against the sun,
As though someone has cut my silhouette
From black asbestos and glued it to its surface.
*

Concentrating with all my energy, I enter myself.
The flames burn away excrescences and tumors
Grown up overnight, purge the malignant parasites,
Reshape my clay into a scintillating spirit
Capable of surviving another day's lifetime.

2/22/79   (05619)

Loose Change

Every new day
Is just more loose change,
Lint-strewn, smudged, and tarnishing,
Which anonymous fingers
Have grasped evanescently
Before relinquishing their claim forever.

Yet each coin
Is individually pinched through a thin slot
In attaché cases, photograph albums,
Laundry hampers, checking accounts, houses,
Families, friendships, deaths,
Where it accumulates in unapprehended solitude.

Frenzied to locate a windfall
For some unexpected crisis,
We might take notice of our makeshift banks;
However, pausing hastily to contemplate
Robbing from the past,
We most often negotiate another approach.

The changing years weight the containers,
Glut their worn passageways.
When the gentle tinkling of days
Becomes a giant's heavy snoring
And no more coins will fit in their space,
We bow to the inevitable opening of molds.

But combinations, scribbled on paper,
And keys aren't where we placed them.
Implements for prying bottom covers
Have disappeared, and the thought
Of marring their carefully guarded finish
With oversize screwdrivers and pliers

Or hammering their delicate shapes
Into a hundred pieces
Staggers the aged intellect,
Which has always relied on wisdom to prevail.
The sad heart pales before the truth
That its imagination can't break the seal.

Suddenly, the long-awaited occasion
For spending the last afternoons
With pleasurable recollections
That formed the savings of a lifetime
Evaporates. Their inaccessible largess
Is the price we pay for forgetfulness.

2/25/79 (02204)

In for Tests ^Δ

How far back do we have to go,
Before we can unmask the ancestral culprit,
The progenitor of the bad seed,
Sower of our small son's petit-mal syndrome?

How deep do we need to probe
Via vinyl-coated, color-coded wires,
Whose electrodes, taped to the head,
End at the sensitive antennas of a Grass electroencephalograph?

How many unrecoverable medical histories,
Lost to silverfish, fires, statutes of limitations,
Must we exhume for the imagination to examine,
Before it can isolate the seizure-prone forebear?

How long does the machine have to function
In its jittery reading between the lines,
While the child sleeps in his mother's arms,
Before the brain's Rosetta stone spills its secrets?

How suspicious do we dare become of our partner,
How sharp in our own self-doubts
About dormant inadequacies, emotional shortcomings,
How malicious toward fate's innocent bystanders?

How certain can we be, when the data is gathered
And all tests prove negative, that no relapses
*

Will creep into the placid afternoons back home,
No more disorders boil portentously beneath the core?

How compassionate and sad and self-pitying
Will we be if, ultimately, we find
That a distinct incompatibility between husband and wife
Tied our son's mind to a wobbly grindstone?

How impotent and empty and defeating will it seem
When we've accepted the machine's prophecy as gospel,
Surrendered to its counsel, and watched the drugged days
Drag into our lives like bears entering their caves?

2/27/79 (01434)

On Paying Last Respects

This day glistens like the mica chips
In the highway I listen to, hour by hour,
Whose miles are fugitive voices
Lost in the backwash of my streaming consciousness.

Deaf to their resonating threnodies, their end rhymes
Connected to unresurrected poems from the past,
And lacking apparatus to amplify cosmic vibrations,
I acquiesce to a narcoleptic discontentedness,

In which dozing and waking are chess moves
Punctuated by disconnected quotations from Donne
And Milton. The zigzag ragtags
Of Roethke and Eliot are a buzzing of bees without stingers.

Even the stressed and unstressed metrics of Brodsky
Are decomposed corpses from wars between Moses,
Zoroaster, and Baal,
Moaning as I drive, in blind defilement, over them.

The mind that once could milk music from sunlight,
Distill unbroken filaments of insight and vision
From the eyes' hallucinatory pools, and undress metaphors
Cavorting restlessly in the virgin moon's bedroom

No longer delights in penetrating the invisible.
Mica chips flashing in my face are gnat bites
Pocking God's flesh, shot perforating the membrane
Conversant with mundane tunes and the breathing of angels.

And as I advance, the voices I knew so well
In youth consume me in their derisive monotony.
I sense my destination just up ahead:
The dead, spent spirit's Westminster Abbey.

3/12/79 — [1] (05620)

The Dancers △

Before, there were just the two of us,
Father and goddess, soaring through the din,
Clear of the uproarious orchestrion,
Into a kind of Doric paradise on earth.

Now, we are a triumvirate,
Ruled by our passion for the stained-glass music
That cascades from its piano strings and pipes
Via bellows, tracker bar, and hoses.

Standing in its golden-oak shadow,
One child cradled in each arm,
I am a Libra, balancing my scales,
As we dance, entranced by its necromancy.

Sister and brother, mounted shoulder-high
On each side of their daddy's smile,
Lean over, kiss in midstride,
And are anesthetized by the opiates of innocence,

Which drug their flight with scintillating love-sparks.
Tune after raucous tune, we cling
To the ring our harmonious gathering provides —
A buoy floating in a vast ocean of sound —

Until my straining biceps, coinciding with the machine's
Prearranged climax, surrender their charges
And the spinning fascinator, winding into darkness,
Suspends them from threads of frustration and dismay.

Reluctantly, we disband and resume the scheme
Of tedious relationships that demand of us
Something less than companionship
And the vulnerability that comes from adoring others.

Hopefully, whenever the silence grows deafening,
We three will always return
*

To the base of Mount Helicon, to embrace as we did
When Terpsichore bore us on winged feet.

3/12/79 — [2] (01435)

The Griots of Rowan Oak △

Once back in my car,
Parked just outside the undefensive gate
Separating Rowan Oak
From Old Taylor Road, Oxford,
And the flock of cosmic pilgrims
Who come to eavesdrop on the gods
And ghosts gossiping ubiquitously
About William's relinquished domain,
I doff my coat, shake the chill
From bones mid-March has filled with stiffness,
And settle down for the long drive home.

But my senses hold me fast to this place,
So isolated and empty and silent
Save for the importunate, predaceous jays,
Docile robins, and sparrows, whose collective chirping
Is a griot's ceaseless recitation of genealogies
Existing yet in Mississippi's record books.
My mind listens assiduously to the birds,
Enters their conversations,
Begs to be heard, to be heard,
Even as the distance I put between them and me
Diminishes their voices to whisperings.

It's my heart, that voluptuous courtesan,
Who's spent so many naked nights
In his bed of metaphors and days dreaming of being kept,
Forever, under the body of his climactic passion,
That desires to remain and confess my presence here,
Not my intellect, which has always rejected excesses of the soul.
I've come back once again, this spring,
To ask the birds if his spirit has changed directions,
That I might fly in search of him, the days of my life.
Their answer is his voice quavering in the elegiac cedars.

3/15/79 — [1] (00068)

Looking for Homes

Each place I go is foreboding,
So that nowhere is there a destination
That comforts my estranged soul.

The weary spirit, long inured
To the implacable forced marches
Imposed by survival, grieves for its freedom,

Prays for relief from its uprootedness
From God. Some evenings,
I can even hear the moon whispering,

Lamenting my wayward condition,
Begging me to cease roaming,
Calm down, and make peace

With the demons that set me fleeing
Originally. Only, I don't know
How to start stopping, to slow down,

Close the opening ever widening,
As I ride from town to town
Like a gear spinning on an axle of years

That transmits power through me,
To a final source of energy,
While I remain perfectly static.

Perhaps one day
The sweet siren of eternal sleep, Lethe,
Will invite me in for the night,

And I will stay on,
At her behest, a permanent guest
In the house kept by Mistress Death.

3/15/79 — [2]   (000869)

All in a Fog: A Love Poem △

A birthday gift
for beloved Jan;
thirty-five years has she!
3/23/79

Last night's fog,
Like minute bits of confetti
*

And shredded dreams, lingers yet
In sleep's streets. It stretches past
The outermost edges of the city
Toward which my waking existence drives,
Greeting my sensitized eyes
With diaphanous knots of morning sky.

I stoop to gather stray serpentine
(The regalia of last evening's lovemaking)
And sweep up the spent shards
Of gentle Yeatsian poesy
We quoted to each other,
Touching, tasting, entering,
In sweet, peaceful solemnity,
The twilight beyond climax.

Now, you and I
Are opaque shadows suspended in the fog,
Clinging still to the spot
Where we dropped off of our gliding float.
As our rising silhouettes dissolve
In a widening sea of sunshine,
We glimpse the parade, just ahead,
Beckoning us to catch up.

3/22/79 (02092)

The Passing of Orders △

This day dawns bleak and chill,
Like Dilsey's vision of the Compson decay.

A gray gloom fills the room
Through which I drag
Benjy's voiceless sperm bag,
Trying to decide which way to turn
The knurled knob that unlocks words
Impounded in cells of slobber and moaning.

Even the humid silence
Absorbs echoes of long-ago nights
When youth climbed down the drainpipe
To rendezvous with its own supple odor
And discovered lust waiting, instead,
To ferry it forever from its safe abode.

This day is Quentin masturbating,
Caddy come home,
Crying on spying her motherless child,
Jason standing outside the hardware store,
Cursing the lightning and thunder of a migraine storm,
Father drowning in his inebriated rhetoric.

And as I traverse my stark hallucinations,
Searching for the proper exit
To escape their hold over me,
I see in the shadowy, swirling sky
These apocalyptic specters
Bearing down on my progress, from above.

Within seconds, my windshield is splattered
With silver blood. The day is grieving my soul's death.

3/28/79 (00036)

The Killing Ground

A vicious wind sharpens itself
On gingerbread whetstones
Formed by eaves of this turn-of-the-century
White-clapboard castle.
It rattles and scratches windowpanes
As it prizes the glass in tight casements
And penetrates the peaked silence
Pervading this attic, in which I relax.

Quietude, surrounding me like a chrysalis,
Bleeds from the wind's quick jabs
And deep stab wounds. My conscience,
Absorbing the blade's full thrust,
Shivers in its last gasp,
As a rusty chill reaches my heart
And spills the soul's innocence
Into death's seething Love Canal.

Soon, my spirit's acid-eaten bones
Will be indistinguishable from dioxin,
Carbon tetrachloride,
Benzene, bubbling, oozing, seeping,
Year by year, through the clay seal
*

Giving way day by day by day.
Their toxins will rise sporelike,
Infect streams and dairy pastures and sties,

Then begin the incubation
Of dreaded carcinogenic mutations
The next generations will be unable to alter:
Damaged livers, malfunctioning kidneys,
Microcephaly, double rows of lower teeth —
Grotesqueries left behind by man
To mark his progress in universal neglect,
Our bequest to the children of the apocalypse.

Suddenly, the crimson wind diminishes,
Leaving a vacuum in the attic,
Where I came to relax before the TV.
Now, the silence isn't a chrysalis
But rather a graveyard I share
With thousands of rotting chemical-waste drums
Indiscriminately dumped on land
Reserved for my fancy's future expansions.

3/30–31/79 (02134)

River Burial

This morning, just before noon, a tow crew assigned to Metropolitan Police dredged up the forty-third vehicle, in less than a month, from the foot of the 9th Street Bridge. A massive auto-theft ring is suspected of stripping vehicles, then disposing of them in what now appears to be a vast underwater graveyard. No clues as to where and how this gang operates have yet surfaced. Baffled by this bizarre case, police refuse to estimate how many cars may yet be submerged or from how far away they may have been brought in and dumped. Salvage operations are scheduled to continue indefinitely.
                              — recap of an April 9, 1979, UPI wire report

As I draw closer and closer
To the vortex at the gray epicenter
Of morning's core, bleeding vehicles,
Speeding like misappropriated spirits
Fleeing River Phlegethon,
Materialize before my eyes. I follow
Like a mole hollowing out a path
*

Below the earth, burrowing blindly
Through the mountain range of 5 a.m.

Trucks transporting balled trees,
Hauling garbage, colossal brakes and mills,
Slaughter-bound hogs and cattle
Crowded, like Juden, in straw-strewn compartments,
Course, in a mystical sibilance,
Before my uninitiated vision.
They metamorphose like fish in a tank,
Twisting from angles of incidence to nonexistence,
As they abruptly change directions.

Up ahead, a grotesque, sulfurous glow,
Yellow as the stench of urine,
Absorbs the flowing traffic,
As though in a gigantic cosmic maw.
Suddenly, my time arrives
To exit the ramp connecting the bridge
With my past. Amnesia takes the wheel,
As my car crashes through the guardrail
And sinks slowly in a graveyard of stolen souls.

4/9/79 — [1] (05621)

Transcending Fevers

Alive inside the flying spores of a contagion
That shows no traces of running its course,
I soar like fever in a child
Susceptible to febrile seizures, reach apogee
At day's end, and explode in myriad pieces,
Which scatter my frothing, exhausted intellect
Over the barren geography of wasted hours,
Like radioactive fallout.

I lie down on a bed of crystal cacti
To recite the Dead Sea Scrolls.
Blood neither clotted nor wholly liquescent
Oozes, like Vesuvian lava,
From my clogged nostrils, transforms the air
Containing my shattered visage into a sacred pool,
In whose stench my senses bathe.
The mirror refuses to return my dumb gaze.

I'm caught in night's witch's broth,
Scalding, while freezing with incandescent sweat,
Stuporous within the hallucinogenic cauldron
Nightmares fire to boiling, for sheer sport.
A shard of floating flesh and bone,
A vessel, omen of disaster, a cataclysm
In human form, alone, nameless, mind-blown,
I'm destined to shipwreck on the reefs beyond madness.

Suddenly, from out of the diaphanous mist
Lifting above the hysterical screeching of moonbeams
Streaking, like death-eyes, across the reeking horizon
Demons, in slithering chaos, have inhabited,
A vast, resonating thunderclap resounds,
As if to call a permanent halt to the universe.
All over, my body succumbs to the twitching
Of a postmortem frog. Death's invisible cicatrix

Itches beneath my trepanned skull.
Life climbs back up a rickety ladder
Anchored in the soggy base of the splintered brain,
Like an arthritic victim of Hiroshima's blast,
And peers out over the lidless rictus of eyes
Focusing on the mirror, in whose cold embrace
My prostrate shadow stirs. The rising sun,
Violating the sleazy curtains, electrifies my heart,

And I rise, like a newly created organism,
From the slime. I'm neither ameba nor paramecium,
Rather a multicellular complexity capable of discerning
Hand from penis from little toe. I'm a breathing being,
Completely clean and anxious to be unleashed
On a waiting Eden, a pristine creature
Absolved of disease, a haughty little yahoo
Ready to assume the responsibilities inherent in Godhead.

4/9/79 — [3] (02560)

Skinner Box

For Joe Geist

Suddenly, the noise of the spheres ceases.
The universal clepsydra no longer spills oceans
From its ticking lips. The muse's voice,
*

Which, for so many years, has whispered in my ears,
Fails to echo the earth's pulsing blood.
Its verses crumble like sandcastles
Before voracious waves, and I lapse
Into a drowsy silence, whose numbness
Rumbles my brain to a bruised disquietude.

In this vast and unrequited void,
Tiny mice feet scamper across the stage
Once inhabited by Hamlet, Falstaff, Romeo,
Odysseus. They race across an electrified grid,
In search of crumbs, stumble in pain
From the cruelty inflicted invisibly from above
By some itinerant god, then crawl toward the gate
Leading to temporary escape. I lift the mesh,
Not expecting a gratuity for my humane consideration

Or a word of thanks for liberating them from fear.
Meanwhile, I sulk in the backwash of dreams
Woven from delusions of greatness, those illusive echoes
That once reiterated promises of fame.
Even now, I'm able to quote entire passages
Of poems I wrote while inebriated and spaced,
Poetry for the ages, never quite materialized,
Which I envisioned transcending Milton's and Shakespeare's.
I'm at sad impasse; the ancient voices shock me to death.

4/9/79 — [4] (02561)

In Camera

For my beloved father, Saul,
king of my heart,
on his seventieth birthday,
4/5/79

Hush, hush — the king draws nigh.
Let silence attend his venerable presence
As he enters the great hall, this evening,
To deliberate on echoes recollected in tranquillity.
Let not even family members
Molest his bittersweet nostalgia,
His mind-sweeping passage backward,
To 1909.
Only his ego, his intractable pride, his vanity
*

Have the right to distract him
From indulging a very rare weakness
For looking back briefly
And lingering on the old passions and griefs
Of the man he became, who began so humbly
And transcended anonymity all by himself.

There should be absolute quiet in the kingdom
As His Highness takes time to contemplate
The nature of conquest and ponder his diminishing goals.
Hush, hush — he enters now,
In periwig and robes brocaded of cold intellect.
Soon, he'll assume his leather-upholstered throne
And recline behind the desk
Over whose bailiwicks he's maintained suzerainty
Half a century. Slowly, he draws near,
Sits and peers at favorite photographs
Of his own revered father, his wife
And four grown children, until tears
Smear his wizened visage. We know
The kind and generous might of our king
Emanates from such private weeping.

4/11/79   (02135)

Sacred Burial Grounds ^Δ

A stark and splendid bronze-green statue of Liberty,
Surmounting quartz-mottled figures
Of a man and a woman, with a child on each side,
Thrusts itself into a prairie sky
So supernally blue that nothing save night
Could possibly diminish its reign over day.

I stare at the silent grouping
Reposed at the center of this busy square,
Trying to share its secrets,
Penetrate the wisdom of its imposed symbolism,
To arrive at its raison d'être,
Explain the anxiety that moved men to place it there

Instead of as a cenotaph in a cemetery
Consecrated to those who gave their lives,
In a long-gone time, that slavery might be abolished.
*

Only, nothing surfaces. My eyes fix
On this lady, dead to the world,
Who gazes at me with implacable serenity,

Refusing, even in the masculine wind
That whispers, in her ears, uneasy lustings,
To bat an eyelid, twitch, lift a hand
In recognition of my transitory existence
In this land strange to my heritage,
And suddenly, I am aroused to undress her,

Remove the terrific, cold weight of the robes
Whose draped folds embrace her anatomy,
Unlatch the breastplates conforming to curves
Sensuous even in their stasis,
Disburden her of shield and sword and garland
Encircling her perfectly sculpted head.

I grow berserk with perverted desire
To breathe my breath into her lungs,
That I might enter her in broad daylight,
Fire her with the poetry of my lonely soul,
And have her reciprocate my aching passion
With movement, the naked fornications of angels.

My entire body, realizing its inherent failure
At transcending physical limens,
Begins to shiver in the duskbound wind.
My mind, disappointed at not being able
To resurrect life from daytime shadows,
Descends into an undisciplined melancholia,

A catacomb crowded with awakened souls,
Whose angry voices, tinged with revenge,
Accuse me of having violated, by my covetousness,
An immortal goddess, protectress of their sanctity.
I cringe as a thousand veterans rise to arms
Behind the lady wielding her shield and unscabbarded sword.

4/14/79 (05420)

Sunday Morning: Easter

This house is silent, save for the clock's pulse
And my pen's point, superimposing its cursive voice
*

Over blue-ruled musical scores
Exhumed from storage rooms deep in memory's vaults.

Whose compositions these were is insignificant.
Their brittle anonymity even enhances their beauty,
Rendering my verses and the accidental combinations of melodies
That fuse with them, past with future, uniquely byzantine.

Neither Easter solemnity nor rituals of Passover,
Resurrection and Exodus coinciding so ironically,
Upstage the gentle obbligatos my heart senses
Hovering on the lips of its lover, death,

Who lusts beneath the sun's pagan feast of April,
Sipping liquors squandered by greedy bees,
Waiting to lock its goat feet, hermaphroditic,
About my liberated spirit and enslave my passions forever.

Rather, to soothe and placate my illusive mistress,
I pipe simple Pan tunes on my pen-flute,
Passed down from flock tenders who once slept
Beneath the stars on the rolling slopes of Arcady.

The soft-uttered lilts and wind-tongued trilling
My words whisper in the ears of invisible goddesses
And gods, this warm morning, fill the silence with reminders
That the dead hymn the living imagination to ecstasy,

Bless its animated speculations of afterlife with hope,
Instill in the dreamer's pantheon subtle fugues and fantasias,
Largess suggestive of immortality. Just now, eternity
Converges in a stirring of twelve o'clock bells.

The poem I was writing finishes itself in a flourish
Of unexplained inspiration. The house revives
From its sleepy reveries. Even the eight-day clock
Rewinds itself for the endless procession of dead to come.

4/15/79 — [1] (05622)

Suffering for Others: An Easter Offering △

Slow, mellow sadness, like drizzle, envelops me,
This afternoon, as I return home, alone,
Through the upturned prairie.
Echoes of our recent togetherness
*

Ride beside me and in the backseat.
Surrogates of Troika and Trilogy
And their Isadora-figured mother, Mistress Jan,
Keep me company, reiterating Easter
Scene by scene, as the lump in my throat expands.

My little girl's new-bought frock
Of yellow gingham check with appliquéd rabbit,
The too-large corduroy shorts my little boy wore,
My wife's sophisticated Parisian taste,
The egg hunt and buffet luncheon at the country club
Speak to me, in eloquent taciturnity,
The nomenclature of life's sweet, blessed pleasures,
Now gone from all save memory,
Like souls rescued from death's hold at the last moment.

And as I veer on a southerly tack,
I can hear their mellifluous whispers
Chasing me, calling me back to chide them
With preposterous nicknames, kiss them
In moments of reckless ecstasy, lift them bodily
Above the lovable giant I become
Whenever their capricious alchemies
Change me from clay. Even at this late hour,
My shape retains traces of their whimsical play.

Only, there's no eluding the lugubriousness
That settles, with twilight, over my eyes
As I drive this familiar route by myself.
There's no escape from the destitution separation engenders
In one grown so used to fatherhood
And the privileges that accrue through responsibilities
Continuously administered to others equally fragile.
I accept my sadness as a natural coeval
Of holiness, one of the hazards of mortal adoration.

4/15/79 — [2] (01437)

Separated

Something about leaving one's family
Terrifies the sensitive psyche to madness,
Invents dread machinations,
Dire fantasies, and hallucinations that rise up,
*

Like Golgotha and Gethsemane, before the innocent eyes
Of itinerant creatures such as I.
The uncertainty of circumstance gnaws clean
The future's bones. The past
Shivers in a drafty corner, like a famished runaway.
At dismal impasse, bereft of everything
My life's become, I succumb to tears
Like a bum without a dime for wine,
A salesman without a line to drum,
A victim without a crime to use for excuse,
A husband moth-dizzy and numb from still circling
A stubby candle whose snubbed wick
Derived its lambency from his incandescent family.

4/15/79 — [3] (01400)

In Search of Immortality ^Δ

In this season of unfolding green scrolls
And exploding nodes, pubescent nature exposes herself
Without modesty. She is a Naiad, a wood nymph,
Unclothed, luxuriating beside the covert pool
Of every poet's lusting eye.

On this day that marks the thirty-eighth
Celebration of my birth,
I set out alone, to seek her retreat
In April's womb and impregnate her
With words, the soul's ejaculate.

In the distance, I glimpse her basking.
Vision burns with envy
To emulate the sun's rays penetrating her,
In every nubile position, without complaint,
To make her desire my pervasive verses over his.

Only, as I approach her with ravishing passion,
My naked, seething meters and rhymes —
The iambs and trochees of the goat-blown mind —
Climax prematurely, like cloudy, wasted semen
Dripping from the heavens, to the grass below me.

She laughs at my adolescent lack of control,
My brittle composure, as I sit beside her,
*

Shivering, tacit, and spent.
Our silence begets a deaf child,
An orphan we name Youth's Lament,

For having its conception in juices squandered
On mutable beauty, April's evanescent blooming.
The illusive muse, who's tempted me again,
At thirty-eight, dissolves, like unwritten poems
The wind, in its passing, grinds to grit.

4/17/79 — [1] (05624)

Footfalls

The years passed
Are footfalls at my back,
Belonging to a masked stranger
Wearing my hand-me-down mannerisms
And obsolete enthusiasms.

They shadow my passage
As I go toward the graveyard
Where I've buried brittle, opaque husks
My psyche has outgrown,
To seek refuge in moments of solitude.

Only, their echoes are the restless dead,
Crunching under my unsteady progress.
I wheel unexpectedly, to catch a glimpse
Of the specter molesting me.
Emptiness is the only face I recognize.

The years ahead
Are footsteps not yet taken
By the Minister of Infinity,
Who beckons me to return from within.
I gasp at the prospect of outliving myself.

4/17/79 — [2] (05625)

In Praise of Quests

How ironic
That what we consider a beginning
*

Is always actually the finish,
Whether referring to birthdays arrived
Or anticipation dissipated
As the long-awaited occasion materializes.

The end of things looms ubiquitously
As carcinogens disguised as vitamins,
Hair dryers, and artificial red dye.
Our starts are mere iceberg tips,
Scientific syntheses, tricks performed
With slick obliviousness.

Something there is about the quest,
Meshing bone and flesh into readiness,
Through grueling exercise
And the agonizing preparation of intellect
By reading and assimilating, en masse,
The world's largess,

That assumes quintessential significance,
Transcends the deed itself
And its concomitant failure or victory.
It's the silent years, whose coevals,
Anonymity and spartan penury,
Provide meaning with its marrow,

That support and sustain us when fame
Fades into framed sepia.
It's dreaming of reaching Helicon's peak
That makes falling down the mountainside
Such a profound achievement
And getting up again so wonderfully presumptuous.

4/18/79   (02136)

Composing the Garden Book of Verse △

The cosmic plowman turns earth
The surging brain keeps heated and moist
Just beneath its cortical surface.
He sprinkles the furrows, its uneven fissures,
With word-seeds pinched through his fingers
One at a time. Coursing back and forth
*

Between sleep and dreaming,
He covers them over with gentle strokes,

Then relaxes, until, at unpredictable intervals,
Tiny shoots break through
And enter the air haloing the garden
That shimmers with the presence of flourishing things.
In such climes, verse-flowers fructify,
And the mind finds a new source of nourishment
To sustain its appetite, as, row by row,
Ears and eyes collaborate in harvesting the soul.

4/20–21/79 — [1] on 4/21 (00102)

Whitecaps △

The ocean, driven to madness by winds
Inciting it to riot, becomes the sky.
Its whitecaps are gulls flying from the horizon,
Toward shore. Millions of aquatic birds,
Like squadrons of warplanes
Winging for Pearl Harbor on a Sunday morning,
Undulate in sun-stippled liquid clouds,
Shift, roll, and dive, as if whipped,
With an invisible switch, from behind.
As they reach the spit, their feathers disintegrate,
Sift viciously in the breeze, as spume,
Before being reabsorbed into the atmosphere.

Two hours later, when I return to the spot
Where this colossal migration
Passed chaotically before my imagination
And entered my eyes, nothing remains,
Except sea beans, shells, skeletons, and glass,
To remind me a disturbance ever occurred.
It's as if the birds flew into a cliff
And dropped stiffly to oblivion's abyss.
As I search the sky for signs of them,
It turns back into ocean, pacific, impersonal,
Mottled with yachts running wing and wing
And pelicans plunging awkwardly from above.

4/21/79 — [2] (02137)

[Saturday, Sunday, Mon-] △

Saturday, Sunday, Mon-
Day, Tues-
Day,
Now Wednesday, it's taken to build
To crescendo,
The wind, of course, the ocean, of
Course,
Whose gray-green rumbling is the throb
Of a monster's arteries,
Whose awful, inexorable threat
Grows, every minute, more palpable,
As we watch, from our lavish glass cells,
The colossal swells eradicate the beach,
Changing the defenseless blue cabanas
To Portuguese men-of-war,
Accordioning back and forth in the gale,
And the anomalous palm trees,
Fronds whipped viciously back like war bonnets
Crowning Indians racing, headlong, toward a cliff,
Chasing mirage-buffaloes.
Five days, the roar has remained in my brain,
As though I were mounted in the cab
Of a straining diesel engine
Dragging two hundred freight cars
Through a tunnel connecting an endless chain of caves;
Five days trapped inside Leviathan's belly,
Outside,
Tremulous, pinioned, totally unable to retreat
Or gather the strength to escape
The morass my pusillanimous spirit,
With unnatural curiosity, has demanded I outlast;
Five days, in growing skepticism,
I've witnessed sky and water conspire
To overturn an empire of concrete, steel, and glass,
Which, until this outrageous 6
A.M., has somehow seemed to maintain its equilibrium.
Now, the condominium in which we've stayed
On our "vacation" is a wino
Stumbling uncontrollably, swaying, bumping into him-
Self beneath a constantly sputtering mer-
*

Cury-vapor light. Its safety-pane plate-glass windows,
Bending at their centers with each unannounced gust,
Are the one eye in Cyclops's forehead,
Are the two eyes belonging to Goliath, vulnerable as hell
To nature's sadism, and as I look out again,
I see the last sliver of beach disappear
Beneath an onslaught of angry waves
Foaming and seizing at the mouth like bulls
Unleashed, in the streets, for a Fiesta de San Fermín.
And at my back door, knocking obnoxiously,
Demanding of me an answer, is the fulminating sky.
Suddenly, I've become the sacrificial victim,
The token poet,
Object of Zeus's offended sensibility,
Who obviously requires of me an oblation
More substantial than mere words
Set to verse and stanzas,
Some act yet more personal,
A physical act of courage to purge my soul,
Set my spirit free at the epicenter
Of this scourge. I hesitate,
As though the survival of an entire civilization
Hinged on my decision, then rise up
And rush out into the howling Charybdis,
Naked to the bone,
Neptune's lone creation, newborn,
Untested, and ignorant. An Adam-atom
Battered in a cyclotron, I inveigh against the storm
With my voice alone, which cuts the wind
Like a greased knife blade,
Until it finally penetrates the ears behind
The eyes that have been watching us
For five prolonged days.
Covered in spume, cut by flying shells and sand,
Shivering from April's coldest blasts,
I finally make myself heard above the din
And come back inside,
Satisfied that the tides will soon recede,
The cat-o'-nine-tails wind,
Which has indiscriminately lashed everything in sight,
Will subside. Within hours, the sound dies
That has kept us awake five nights and days.
*

The ocean draws back its vipers' tongues.
I have spoken with Zeus and survived,
This time.

4/25/79 (00248)

Mai-Kai ^Δ

A constant influx of customers
Feeds the Polynesian deities
The only sacrificial rites
Capable of paying for the gas and lights.

Rum drinks festooned with gardenias,
Maraschino cherries, pineapple slices
Entice the conspicuously affluent
And RV tourists alike.

Busboys, waiters, section managers,
Captains, and maître d' loiter
With the efficient, inconspicuous expertise
Of a Houdini making his tricks happen.

The foliage, so profusely exotic,
Thrives inside and out
Despite air-conditioning and cigarette smoke
Not wholly indigenous to its ports of origin.

Just now, the supple-bellied dancers
Hula their nimble way across the stage,
As native Floridians approximating Tahitians
Assume electric guitar and amplified drums.

Chopped onions, bamboo shoots,
Pea pods, water chestnuts, and lumps of fowl
Begin writhing, like Mexican jumping beans,
In time to the music, as boneless chicken,

At $8.95, exclusive of the fried rice,
Rumbles in the depths of my sensibilities.
As abruptly as the festivities end,
The bill descends out of thin silence,

Neatly itemized by NCR's
Latest computerized register.
*

Seventy-eight dollars for two, less tip,
Gets me right where the Fiji grows.

Even in the half-light, shadowed with masks,
Swords, weird gods, and gaslit torches,
My wife detects me turning white,
Cursing the demons of Samoa and New Guinea,

Tonga, New Zealand, and Tahiti,
As I reach, with injured pride and hostility,
For my wallet. But it's not until
I've paid the porter in the men's room a quarter,

Made an obligatory pass through the gift shop,
Dropped a five-spot on a grass skirt
For Trilogy, at home, sleeping we hope,
And surrendered a valet ticket

And fifty cents to an apathetic attendant
That I'm actually able to finally escape
The South Seas phage, the typhoon,
And head for America again, in my outrigger canoe.

4/29/79 (02138)

Taking Leave of Myself

Once again, I've voluntarily taken leave
Of my earthly senses. Something about the skies,
My being unlatched from landed attachments,
To climb the ladder whose rungs are altitudes
Thinning gradually as oblivion's campanile
Narrows to its inevitable pinnacle,
Reinforces the monasticism I always seek.

Up here, I'm able to lean out
Over the edge of myself and shout
Without being heard below. My words are winds
Returning me, unremarked, to the kingdom of eternity.
They say my name in shapes of clouds
I've never rhymed, in scraps of landscape
No dreams of mine have ever festooned with metaphor.

Time invites me to guess its age.
Hours are civilizations waxing, waning,
*

Regaining their stature through strange incarnations.
My heart is a burning rose, whose wet petals
Open and close as endless day metamorphoses
Into perpetual night each second I breathe.
Light-years are the ichor that makes it grow.

Too soon, I'll be asked to unthink myself back
To the destination I made before boarding the plane.
Maybe memory will refuse to surrender me to my fates.
And since it alone dictates who I was,
When and where, it's just possible
No one will come to claim my baggage
Or page my soul when I fail to appear at the gate.

4/30/79   (05626)

A Rainy Farewell

A voluptuous rain,
Syllabled against May's book of hours,
Fills my eyes with elegiac sibilances.
Invisible noises articulate my vision,
With eloquent melodies
That echo the silent flapping of butterfly wings.

Each nacreous globe that reaches me
Is a kiss you've spoken before,
As I've left your presence.
Now, day's evanescent wetness
Shapes my melancholy with your weeping.
Your voice sees me going out of focus.

5/3/79   (05627)

The Poet Prepares for His First Public Reading

For Joe Geist

For three weeks prior to the reading,
My nervous eyes and tongue
Played hide-and-seek among the words,
Slipping through caesuras and gentler openings
In poetic strophes, chasing inflections
*

And subtle phonetic distinctions,
Until no uncertainties of interpretation
Or stumbling over obstructions remained.

Yet even when oblique metaphors
And recondite sound-chimes
Had surrendered their ultimate coverts
To orderly and reasonable discovery by the intellect,
My adrenaline kept threatening head and mouth
With throbbing ache and dry palate.
By the day I arrived on campus,
Anxiety had become the opposition,

Tracking a half step behind my shadow,
Demanding of my participation
Unmoving and expressionless quietude.
I never even noticed the few students
Or the room in the union or heard the introduction
Expurgating questionable digressions of my odyssey,
Rehearsing in eloquent, extravagant hyperbole
The humanism my work was reputed to possess.

Now that I've resumed my safe vocation
Of being monumentally neglected,
Recording rejection slips, on silicon chips,
And scribbling elegies and odes to my soul,
I can't recollect reading at all,
For the brief and dazed hiatus
That preceded and followed my appearance that evening,
Or seizing my fear, hiding behind its silence.

5/4/79 — [1] (02139)

Raising Statues to the Dead

From this grassy vantage where I sit,
Watching students pass, in twos, threes,
And singly, through lilac and redbud hues,
Like colors escaping a coruscating prism
Or balloons lifting vertiginously,
My shadow casts its stolid mass.

The contrast between its static attitude
And that of the myriad lives filing by,
*

On their way toward formulated destinations,
Persuades me that my motion has ceased,
That old dreams, energies, and hopes
For reaching new plateaus have now exceeded
Their own imposed statute of limitations.

As I gaze, with not-quite-amazement,
At the excited, energized faces, the bodies,
Whose youth outrageously tantalizes my eyes,
I sense, among all their unfamiliar profiles,
One staring at me, preternaturally,
Out of the crowd. His moves coincide with mine.
The fidgeting outlines of his tufted hair
Ride my skull. We share a derelict fate,

As if arrived here, from separate lives,
By a cosmic symmetry foreordained
And irreversible. Why this halcyon place,
This stately, ivory-towered fortress?
Is it possible that in a former incarnation,
We were one fulgent star, not Dioscuri,
Circling this illuminated galaxy of learning?

Or are we mere displaced accidents of nature,
Freaks by virtue of similar shape,
Whose only distinguishing feature is the absence of color
In one, the full spectrum in the other,
Brought together, for the first time
Under the sun, to speculate on eternity's duration?

When I look up, the multitudes passing the library,
Where, for hours, I've drowsed in vagrant suspension,
Have dissipated. The walks and lawns
Show no trace of having been trespassed upon
Or violated, except by me.

I rise, stretch, choose a direction
That might let me elude my second.
Only, no matter which way I turn,
I can neither absorb him nor be penetrated.

It grows late. The air changes its mind,
Refuses to retain day's heat.
It tries to rob me of mine, to stay alive.

Suddenly, I am my shadow, abandoned
And alone on this silent campus,

                    o
                    b
                    e
                    l
                    i
A transplanted s from the land of the dead.
                    k

5/4/79 — [2] (05628)

Drinking Alone

I raise to my lips a wineglass
Filled with a thick, rich, burgundy liquid
And taste its cold aroma. Softly, I'm blown
Across its lake of vapors, on a raft
My imagination fashions from felled memories.

Time is a matter of miles traveled
From one shore toward another, its distance
Measured by the glide achieved in getting there.
Even my arrival is an estimation
Based on recorded high and low tides.

Yet once I'm there, the air is luxuriant as hair
Flowing to the legs of a naked Beardsleyesque lady.
I bury my face in its sensual bouquet,
Allow my knotted body to dissolve
Beneath its voluptuous undulations,

Be enthralled by its tender fingers,
Smoothing the tired eyes' thin skins.
Soon, an effluvial numbness
Overcomes my muscles, begs me sleep
On a gently swelling breast of sandy cove.

I acquiesce, as music insinuates my ears
With sighs of lesbians whispering
Beneath an envious, dripping gibbous moon.
Slumber is something, a dream,
To which I succumb with easy release,

A new world, a peaceable kingdom
Inhabited by friendly adders and tarantulas,
Minotaurs, angels, and satyrs
*

Relieved of their reproductive parts, a zone
In which thought is pristine and invincible,

Able and eager to vindicate human ignorance
By recreating itself as poem,
Concerto, collage springing spontaneously
From nothingness. My drowsy intellect,
Peering through nearsighted lids, shimmers.

The space containing my spirit's preserve
Diverts me toward wakefulness,
Mandates my future, aims my raft back
Across the draining lake that transported my soul
To this place of lotus-eaters thriving on lassitude.

A vague hand holds the wineglass
Containing my existence, this solitudinous trip.
Slowly, I surface out of an aromatic haze,
Climb up the slick sides, and reenter this evening,
Knowing only that the ride is over.

Now, night draws me back, bodily and cold,
Into its procreative embrace, saving me
For tomorrow. I leave the lake
Half-filled, on the table that accommodated me,
Seeking solace in the real lady, who waits at home.

5/4/79 — [3] (02565)

The Pawnbroker's Second Generation △

For Quiet Fire

Music from distant spheres seduces the ears,
As it appears out of the dim night welkin.
The *Zeitgeist* and poltergeists suggest Bergen-Belsen
Flaming in the eyes' nostrils. Thirty-five years
Back up in my mind like bad plumbing.
The pressure exacerbates sensibilities, begs release
From my inhibited hallucinations, as I'm transported
To Hans Frank's Warsaw ghetto, bone-cold
And hungry as dead rats. Why is this night
Different from all other nights? All is gone
From this world of light, in which gentle souls
Once caressed on hills high above the crowd
*

And illuminated hope, by their loving. Now,
An empty and selfish greed converges on me,
A radiated disease, whose spores close in
Slowly, inexorably, until the tumorous flesh
Has no room left for infection to take hold
And flourish. I enter the strange music,
Hoping to find acceptance in its resonation tones;
Only, the echoing notes close their eyes and ears
To my petitions for admittance. I'm left alone,
Out here, within this alien wasteland,
In which bartenders and waitresses pace
Like caged leopards and black zoo panthers.
Nothing registers. No faces beckon to me
With fondness or vague familiarity. I shrink,
Thinking again of the endless procession
Of screeching, straw-strewn boxcars, and weep,
As the floor rumbles with their imminent advent.
Suddenly, in the distance, I perceive the engine,
Plangent and ominous, making its way toward me,
Through a bleak and rain-bled Polish afternoon,
Streaking like Ibáñez's apocalyptic equestrians,
And I realize that my shadow has found me,
All these years after the Holocaust,
Hidden under the decorative academic robes
Of Herr Professor Respectable Venerable,
Doctor of doctrinal liturgy and iconography,
Expert in Hebrew Scripture and exegetical texts.
Under the ultraviolet light, my white armband,
Announcing "Jude" to the entire purblind world,
Comes alive. My breathing subdues the lungs.
I plunge into the underbrush, just as a train
Rushes past, on its way to dump its seedy cargo
At the roaring doors of impatient gas chambers.
For now, this time anyway, I've escaped
Fate's palsied hand. History anguishes
Over its slight mistake, as I race away,
Toward the border separating memory from today.
By sheer luck, the spectral music abates,
And I'm able to feel my way, like a snake,
With my senses alone, toward Canaan's border,
Toward sleep, just beyond the hoary gates
That swing open and shut, like shark jaws,
*

On souls entering this land of transient spirits.
In a matter of moments, my fears explode.
I lie, naked as ancient bones, in my bed,
Waiting for someone to claim me, take me home,
To the Kingdom of God's chosen people, home
Forever, to that land where men and women
Thrive without fear of being subjugated
By fools with Schicklgruber mustaches
Or shriveled noses, who play championship checkers
For a living, home to the seething womb,
Mother Earth, who originally produced my corpse,
Home again, home, one final time,
In a shrill climax worthy of God's finest creation,
Never again to return to this tiny pendent orb.

5/4/79 — [4] (01337)

The Light of the World ^Δ

The pen stutters, sputters like a wet match,
As I draw it across the imagination's flint.
Reluctantly, it throws off ineffectual sparks
While starting over repeatedly.

Finally, the ineffable flame explodes
At its flashing tip, illuminating the universe
My eyes simultaneously hold focused
Before my trembling mind — the metaphor ignited.

5/5/79 — [1] (01338)

The Eyes Grieve for Their Own Demise

Souls scattered for moonless eons
Converge on my earthly eyes
Like innumerable multitudes of migrating birds
Scudding across a postmeridian sky,
Toward memorized preserves. I wince
As if blasted by a blizzard of gritty irritants.
The lids drip profusely. Vision drowns,
As ghosts of ancient generations invade my insight,
Enter my mentality without permission,
*

Reach the source where dreams
And nightmares originate. Suddenly,
Tremors loosen the brain's foundations,
Shake the convoluted storage chambers
To such unprecedented disruption
That *up* changes places with *right*,
Left crosses the chiasma, becomes *down*,
Until the specters force me into submission.
In this position of purblind defeat,
I cease fighting for my present identity
And surrender to the keepers of my heritage,
Who I now realize have arrived
To take me home despite my desperate claim
On life. We leave as they came,
In timeless silence, ageless configurations
Suffusing space with the invisible shimmering of angels.

5/5/79 — [2] (01339)

Scrim Curtains ^Δ

Somewhere behind the obscurity
That obstructs sight, my children cavort
Like loose-jointed foals
Running through the soft May wind.

I can almost hear their sweet laughter,
Almost see their miracled eyes
Loading the redbuds with purple fuzz,
Filling robins' wings with flight.

Yet the barrier between us is a fence
Whose posts are my days away from home
And diaphanous netted mesh
The forgetting that stretches inexorably

As the distance carries me along with it.
If only they knew I were so close,
They'd surely o'erleap their innocence
And caress the wanderer who seeded them

In his own poetical image. If only
They realized that their weeping
Emanated from his adoring broken heart,
They'd undream the obscurity making my eyes tear tonight.

Only, neither I nor my blessed charges
Can intercede for each other. We remain trapped
Between myriad shimmering scrim curtains —
Shadows overlapping without touching.

5/5/79 — [3] (01438)

Limitations

In May's fecund fields,
Ranging orgiastically between Salisbury and Tipton,
Outrageous clumps of goldenrod,
Like millions of fidgeting bumblebees,
Hum my eyes' cones to buzzing ecstasy.
Lilacs' purple, screaming, female scent
Signals spring has come into heat.

Even the smooth, lush voluptuousness
Of greening boughs, ravines, and copses
Tumbling in madcap riot
Provides paltry relief from such urgencies.
This Sunday morning, obsessed with its beauty,
I leap from my words, into God's creation,
To get a yet more immediate gratification.

5/6/79 (05629)

In Rings Begin a Mother's Love

For my mother, Charlotte,
on this special day,
5/13/79

At the start,
When your heart leaped constantly
To the surface of my needs,
Its tight, untried ripples,
Almost superimposed
Like threads on a bolt,
Buoyed me on my adolescent odyssey.

Each ring was a special kindness,
A specific gift
To fit whatever hobby
Most interested me at the time,
*

A love-tear
Filled with perpetual endearment,
An unpremeditated kiss.

One harbored my delicate vessel;
Another slaked and fed
My irrepressible ambition
To succeed at words and athletics,
While a third circle
Clothed my nervous intellect
In Solomon's robes.

Now, those ripples,
Grown fewer and wider apart,
Take longer to reach the edge,
Where I stand
Watching my own children
Grasp with open hands
The undulating waves of my love,

And yet each shimmers
Like a flaming halo
Containing my grateful existence.
Still, my blessed mother,
You touch me with your concentricities
Whenever I return
To bathe in your maternal pool.

5/12/79   (02140)

Highwaymen

Time is a highwayman
Who stops me periodically
To remind me that my possessions
Are obsolete and must be surrendered.

The relinquishment goes on endlessly,
Invisibly, without my awareness,
As new items, ideas, and physiologies
Are gathered from the onrushing future.

Each encounter is as painless
As the lungs exchanging old air
For new, refusing to remain complacent,
At the risk of compromising fate.

I've been detained on myriad occasions,
Made to empty my pockets,
Been subjected to naked frisking,
Taken abusive threats from masked cowards,

Yet the humiliation
Has always seemed so minimal
In relation to safeguarding my integrity
And perpetuating life,

As I've navigated, night and day,
This pike without exits
And accesses, whose weigh stations
Are never closed or open

When I pass, rather stranded
Like shadows on a moonless eve
Or years I've known intimately
Before leaving them behind.

Now, my belongings grow sparse.
The loosely fleshed skeleton
Containing my exhausted chemicals and liquids,
My brain, sexual apparatus,

And cellular makeup, deteriorates
At a rate disproportionate
To former stages in my development.
My existence offers scant enticement

To potential reivers anymore.
Lately, I've noticed an alien odor
Either trailing my motion
Or flowing from unseen coverts,

To engage my frightened curiosity,
As I plod homeward.
It assails me with premonitions of being robbed
Just one more time.

5/14/79   (00246)

Drayage

As I take to the road again,
This perfectly tractable spring day,
*

My overloaded wagon complains
Like a convict being whipped
For picking away at oblivion too slowly.
It's low, moaning groans
Are those of a patrician oak in a tornado.

Because the sixty mythical horses
That power my Diaspora machine
Know my idiosyncrasies at the reins,
They balk inordinately,
As if to warn me I'm not fit
To take the team out
Along its preordained route.

Never have I had such blatant indications
That nature was not with me
On my mission. Superstition dismantles my joy,
Reinforces an ancient, inherited paranoia
That I'm descended of ragmen
From one of the ten lost tribes of Israel,
Meant to contend forever with disaster.

Abruptly, as if struck on the neck
By a brick dropped from Heaven,
I jerk the wagon off the pike,
Climb down, and begin to inspect my goods,
Knotted like a thousand slithering snakes
In a nest. Worn sportscoats, suits
Whose pants are mismatched or shaded,

Trousers with cut belt loops,
Broken zippers, seams too loosely stitched,
And leisure combos five years out of style
All seem to have conspired against me.
They lean precariously to one side,
In an attitude of imminent upheaval.
Envisioning my stock strewn piecemeal

Over six Shylock-baiting counties,
I rearrange the items,
Like meats in a delicatessen display case,
Praying they'll stay in place
Until final distribution is made.
Drawing the sideboards together with ropes,
I shake the reins and resume my schedule.

Soon, the soothing susurrance of highway
Passing beneath my wheels
Transports my mind to its familiar dream
Of dining on shrimp appetizer and prime beef
At Toots Shor's, with the head buyers
Of the May Company chain — Willy Sypher,
Chief supplier of fine men's merchandise.

5/15/79 — [1] (02409)

Parachutes

*For my sister Babs,
on her thirty-fifth birthday*

Words suspended from silk chutes
Repousséed against the sky's smooth sides
Float slowly into my mind.
One at a time, they land,
Each as graceful as a leopard
Leaping a hundred feet to a standing crouch,
Their fragile patterns intact.

From a distant promontory,
Through binoculars, I view them disrobing,
Removing the harnesses of soaring,
Until their sleek suits,
Strewn on the ground, and their slender bodies,
Naked to the cursive bone,
Are all that remain of my euphoric brain shower.

Only then do I descend
To gather their impedimenta
And retrieve them before chill sets in.
Although little is said between us,
I intuit their ecstasy yet regret
I'm left with only a free-fallen vision,
To reconstruct an entire sky.

5/15/79 — [2] (00097)

Inquiring Adam

At this shimmering, homeward-wending hour,
The fulgent sun, dulling subtly,
*

Plummets down time's westernmost edge,
At whose blazing base I stand
Barefoot, haughty, and preposterously naked,
Defying it to annihilate me with its dying heat
As it wades into cold, golden solitude.

The stertorous roar of its gaseous passing
Is that of an elephant herd
Spooked to chaos by a savannah fire.
I cringe as it slips by me. My eyes
Are singed, momentarily blinded;
The tissue-thick lids disappear
Like paper ashes lifting in a chimney.

Suddenly, as though a ghostly insurrection
Had been quelled in Heaven,
Silence assumes the universal throne,
Whose simple mandate commands the opening
Of fortress doors. Mute at first,
Diffident and vaguely opaque, the moon appears.
Her perfume neutralizes the sun's dead scent.

In dazed amazement, my regained sight
Flies me into her luminous gaze.
I'm an autistic dream-child
Banging my head against her breast,
Flailing my arms in spastic inarticulateness,
Until her gibbous tits
Pierce my wrists, nail me to the crimson sky.

My body's juices mingle with night's mauve
And sepia hues dripping into the trees.
I lose consciousness, go comatose
In Hecate's land of lost émigrés,
A sad, baffled soul, who accidentally died
Trying to locate the sun's colossal dynamo
And the moon's inviolable, lace-strewn boudoir.

5/15/79 — [3] (05630)

China Syndrome

Long before the term "China syndrome"
Gained currency in lay circles,
*

My psyche had already experienced
A dozen scrams, and
Notwithstanding minute scrutiny
And removal off line
For months at a time, my brain
Had twice sustained severe meltdowns
Of its reactor cores, explosions
That sent memory flying, in fragments,
Through the skull's spinal base.

Only, when these painful seizures
First began to register on my gauges
As writer's block, depressive fits,
Gross melancholia, paranoia, and loneliness,
I reacted without fear,
Attempted to cancel their detrimental effects
By resorting to safety checks,
Bypasses built into the system's controls.
I'd let vast reserves of wine
Flow into the cooling unit serviced by the blood,
Open valves the mind had never used,

To help speed Librium to the weak parts,
Redirect Valium capsules
To the leaking pump, in a feeble attempt
To contain the hyperactive cells.
My efforts at maintaining a low profile,
Covering up the imminent seriousness
Of jury-rigged danger signals
Calculated to postpone *the* ultimate disaster,
Were successful for nearly ten years.
Lately, though, I've sensed strange reverberations,
Tremors in the veins, inner ears, and heart,

Whenever I wake at odd hours of the night
Or day, on moving away from the table
After surviving another silent gluttony,
Or on slumping into my own corpulent stomach,
On trying to type out love poems
On a typewriter that's lost its tongue.
Something about the sounds' growl,
The quality of ominous hostility in its loud howling,
Alerts me to doom, orders a shutdown
*

Of my life's work. Refusing to comply,
I seal my room and wait for China to arrive.

5/17/79 (05631)

"Fatitia" ^Δ^

At almost twenty months,
Plump Troika has mastered the spring horse
He pumps as if in hot pursuit of desperadoes
Or cattle loose from his herd.
He climbs and dismounts with adroitness
No Wallenda would trust enough
To get him one rung above the sawdust,
Yet his raw awkwardness
Satisfies his inchoate boyish self-image.

When in his familiar outfit,
Consisting of white plastic diaper
Tightly girded about his chunky thighs
And waist, his amazing corpulence exposed,
He resembles a Samoan or Tahitian god,
A gnome, a witch doctor, whose omens
Are first words spoken, chanted, sung.
His dreams and waking center around eating;
He prays to the great god Cake.

The relationship that has steadily developed
Between him and his sister, Trilogy,
Is ineluctably close and beautiful to see.
At play, they are two bear cubs,
Capricious and gentle, whose slow motion
Keeps them constantly floated
In the imagination, like a juggler's bowling pins.
Though different in age, shape, and sensibility,
They know their seeds are from the same tree.

At almost twenty months,
Plump Troika touches us with serenity
And overwhelming joy. His existence speaks
A language only poets, birds,
And eternal creatures still use.
We feel privileged indeed to have received
*

For such humble deeds as ours
The gift of being allowed to witness
His halcyon flowering during the harvest of our marriage.

5/21/79 — [1] (01439)

Obit for St. Jerome

They were forever proclaiming him
One of the finest minds of his time,
A self-taught genius with thoughts
One would surely have supposed inconceivable
For the son of a dockhand to grasp,
Let alone transmute, from raw syllables,
Into syllogistic constructs for the world to ponder.

Only, like Asimov, Hoffer, and Einstein,
He could never gain control
Over the robots who'd commandeered his soul.
Eating was a banal exercise,
Bathing an erratically fatuous chore;
Socializing was unendurable boredom,
And sleep a postponement of his reason for being.

Nor were there ladies to chase him,
Make his incessant coffee,
Empty the ashtrays, change his yellowed sheets,
Distract him from his onanistic tendencies
Long enough to let him discover
That love lay in fields beyond his lust
And that in dreams began lasting passion.

Neither Furies nor demons
Could penetrate the carapace
His calculating intellect draped over his heart.
They couldn't make themselves heard
By yelling just outside the fortress gates,
Where, day and night, he contemplated
The motions of asteroids, the weight of galaxies,

Postulated the density of vacuums,
Mapped black holes, like Henry the Navigator,
And labored over his ultimate obsession:
To invent a singular new vocabulary
*

That would fit the tongue of everyone in the universe.
Only twice a year would he appear
In public, then to visit the cemetery

Where his ancestors were said to be buried
Beneath sandstone cenotaphs
Whose markings had been erased by generations of rain.
At midnight, he'd come, predictably,
When no moon shone and the town was mute,
To strew dried cornflowers
Delicately, as though he were planting seeds.

A caretaker would always confirm his vigil
To members of the council, who, in turn,
Were charged with informing the world
Of their celebrated resident's every maneuver.
But they never learned when he'd first died
Or how many times he'd returned
Before his final, recent demise.

All they had to share with news crews
Sent in to cover his funeral
Were rumors of the solitary, enigmatic bequest
To mankind of his books and papers,
Mentioned in his last will and testament,
With the proviso that his name and dates be recarved
On every erased stone in the graveyard.

5/21/79 — [2] (05632)

Signs of the Times △

> *For Faye Wallace and Nancy Cooper,*
> *West Helena*

No diesel fuel. Too much rain.
Jesus! The fields are still unplowed,
Fallow as vestal virgins,
As May gives way, without complaint,
To doom. Meanwhile, massive tractors,
Frustrated and impatient, remain static.
Folded gangs of ubiquitous disks,
Clinging slavishly to their backs,
Just beneath power takeoffs,
*

Are ominous saurian birds of prey,
Waiting to shred the earth's dead flesh.
Pesticides in drums corrode their containers
From within, beside idle biplanes,
Beneath whose rubber feet runways dissolve.

Nowhere in this plague-ruined cradle
Of mid-Southern civilization
Are there signs of living inhabitants.
Even the snakes flee inundated brakes.
Where, last year, stands of cotton plants
Crowded tenants off the land,
Wayward grasses, oblivious to flooding,
Fill old furrows like indignant sneers.
Up in Memphis, down in New Orleans,
Nervous bankers, brokers, restless investors
Twiddle their thumbs over beers and martinis.
Near Helena, Hughes, and Tunica,
Blacks and whites commune in common fear
Of watching their livelihood disappear without a fight.

5/21/79 — [3] (00043)

Trying to Conceive △

As I veer east at Greenville
And commence the desolate trek across the Delta,
Innumerable looming clouds
Force themselves on my senses,
Like condescending thoughts. At once,
They put my intellect on the defensive.

Images within my newly kindled cauldron
Scuffle over which will gain its freedom,
Whose metaphor will achieve preeminence,
Be chosen today for its originality and relevance.
Their fighting is that of a thousand minnows
All trying to reach the same breadcrumb.

By the time the fittest vision survives the struggle
And rises to the mind's surface
To be festooned and pedestaled, arrested forever
*

By the poet who stirs behind my eyes,
The sky, like a fully dilated cervix,
Has totally effaced. It requires reanalyzing.

Once again, the cauldron roars with metaphors
Giddy and extravagant as adolescents
Just discovering their sexuality
Without knowing what to do with it.
Just as a fresh description
Slips over the edge, rain cancels its appropriateness.

The frustrated brain must reconsider its options.
Only, its fires emit too little heat
To regenerate my poetical sensibilities.
Painfully, I watch the Delta, devoured by rain,
Dissolve into kudzu, as the concrete highway
Transports my aborted brainchildren to the City of the Inane.

5/23/79 — [1] (00972)

Sentenced to Life

I float home, alone and sullied,
Like a bone-white moon seeking dusk,
On its own recognizance. My destination
Is the same as it's always been:
Unknown and ever just ahead of me.

Now, after having been away three days,
I chase the sun, outrun my blood,
In hasty retreat from the wasted hours,
Left behind to find their own graves.
The past sweeps its dust under a drug-rug

Woven and crocheted by crones and hags
Left for dead by rapacious generations.
Forgetting is my sole salvation.
Amnesia refuses to release information
Relating to ladies I've impregnated,

Children my careless and feckless heart
Has manufactured and branded with serial numbers
Traceable to an automatic stamping machine
In my brain, and friends and enemies
I've treated with hatred and disdain, from boredom.

If only memory would bring me to trial
Rather than postponing my sentence,
Perpetuating inexorably this stay of execution,
I believe the future would exonerate me
Once and for all, proclaim me rehabilitatable,

Instead of the present making me play
The gross goat-monster to its demure Isolde.
Only, it won't relent. Repentance
Is out of the question. I remain bereft,
Destined to float home alone, forever,

Whether death approves or rejects the notion
Of my perpetual uprootedness.
Suddenly, the moon, tumescent and bleeding
From her womb, spies me in futile flight,
Beckons me follow her rife translucence

Across the lilac-tainted sky. My heart pulses
In wild response. I take up the chase,
Knowing that once again, tonight,
I'll end up sleeping beside her, on the ground,
Embracing my shadow, beneath her white sheet.

5/23/79 — [2] (05633)

An Ode to Pied Beauty

This lush, supple dusk
Brings my eyes to their knees,
In awe-struck genuflection
To the One who has rendered May
An ecstasy I can actually breathe
As well as see with my senses.

Synesthesia reiterates itself
In sunrays, breeze-flushed trees,
Uncut grasses, just-turned earth.
Love is youth's mystical elixir,
And now that spring clings to me,
I am another year younger.

5/23/79 — [3] (05634)

Meditation

Thanks be to pied beauty
In all things dappled and godly.
How unendurably barren and arrogant
Our lives would be without reminders
From the outside, continually,
That we thrive, despite our dreams
And grieving, simply because we are
Parts encompassed by the breathing whole.

5/23/79 — [4] (04701)

The Last Day △

A deep chill
Fills this shadow-laden May morning.
Clean, shrill volumes of sunlight
Deceive the eye, from inside the house,
Sting the unwary pilgrim
Exiting sleep's cave at an early hour.

A still deeper chill
Infiltrates my drowsy bones,
On leaving home with Trilogy
For her last day of preschool.
I say, as we navigate
Our bumpy driveway, enter West Columbia,

"What a wonderful day this is,
My blessed precious,"
To which she replies with finality,
"No it's not! It's sad."
Remorse courses through my veins.
I've seen her grow up overnight.

The solitary minute it takes
To arrive at her rendezvous place
Elongates in my rearview mirror.
The mind's eyes watch five years
Diminish into destiny's greater gaze,
As we're borne forward.

We are the rites of spring
Our spirits sing, this morning,
Violable and gentle children
Who've surrendered, in total innocence,
Our corporeal souls to the sun,
Novitiates accepting each other's vows.

Now, the iris-tinged playground
Rises up like a rainbow,
To guide us the rest of the way.
Reluctantly, I park the car
And escort my blond, hazel-eyed child
To vaults where the gold is stored.

My tongue wants to weep,
But her excitement silences me.
As she passes through the door
To her sacred classroom,
I feel my body's essence metamorphose
Into shadows absorbed by the corridor.

Our parting devastates my spirit
Momentarily, yet I know
Farewells and first encounters,
Beginnings and finishes, are coevals
Irreversible and absolutely necessary
For life to balance on its slender wire.

I realize, also, that when I return,
At noon, to retrieve the girl
I left earlier, she'll be newer
And wiser, both phantom and seer,
And I wonder if she'll recognize her dad,
Grown older, slower, and vaguely sad.

5/25/79 (01440)

The Body Snatchers

Each evening,
When I leave behind
My waking identity and enter
Sleep's disguise,
I still find words
*

Waiting, lurking like lampreys,
To attach themselves
To the belly of my dreams.

Their convoluted shapes,
Sounds, and dizzy symbolisms
Break into strophes
Separated by breathing's caesuras,
Fragment. Trochees
And iambs become atoms
Colliding violently
In the mind's cyclotron.

Not since I was twelve
Has my slate been erased
And voided of intimations
That I'm the one
Fate's chosen
To doom with great notions,
Presentiments, and precepts
Descended from the empyrean.

Nowhere is there refuge
From the nagging curse,
Demon-conceived and fired.
Silence pierces clouds
Surrounding my imagination
Without dissolving
Or allowing me
To penetrate my own psyche.

Compulsion's pain
Is daily aggravated by guilt,
Whispering, in the brain's ear,
Like queer Lucifer
Scheming against Heaven,
Grandiose delusions,
Disastrous machinations
Incomprehensible and finite.

Despite my efforts
To contain the flood,
Draw tight the locks,
Cease thinking, writing,
The words cascade
*

Up the falls,
Back against the current,
To their inscrutable source,

Where they turn again,
Recycled and energized,
And recommence
Their journey toward birth.
Embryonic mackerels,
Blighting potential moments
Of blessed quietude,
Clog my brain's veins.

I remain a spectator,
Day and night,
A hired amanuensis
Inadequately paid
For services rendered
Against the will,
A recorder of deeds
Metaphorical and sonorous.

Please rescue me
From this scourge!
Let me slip away
Unnoticed and alone.
Anonymity
Seems so sweet,
Right now,
Death so inviting.

I burn
Inside an eternal yearning
For self-expression.
My perpetual flames
Are lampreys, trochees, atoms,
And mackerels, images
Ethereal and terrestrial,
Endlessly evolving.

I'm helpless
At containing or erasing them
From conscious emancipation.
Like souls, they come
And go at their own pace.
*

Not even the grave
Is safe anymore.
My vessel belongs to them.

5/29/79 (00247)

Herr Clement of Buenos Aires [Δ]

You scrawny, gaunt, arrogant bastard!
How dare you flaunt your Aryan polemics
In cold, bold austerity,
Blindfolded, drawn taut at rope's end,
Caught, finally, in the cul-de-sac
Of a labyrinth fifteen years intricate!

Just a cog in a colossal gear,
You reiterate. And it was your doing
That brought about subtle changes
In the carrying out of the Final Solution —
A chocolate for the children,
Before the showers, so they wouldn't fear

What their peristaltic stomachs,
Spastic valves, and pumping hearts
Had already made them privy to,
Out of the ancient, miasmic oppression;
A Strauss waltz improvised by prisoners
Not yet metamorphosed, by the Zyklon alembic,

Into more blanched bones for the smoldering,
To ease the older ones into oblivion.
This was also your contribution to humanity.
How considerate, Herr Monster,
To wear a skin graft under the armpit
Where your SS number once pulsed.

How perfectly sensitive of you, Herr Butt-
Sucker, who said when you die,
You'd leap into your grave,
Taking six million Jews with you.
Well, now the time has finally arrived
To let your prophecy fulfill itself.

Trial is too good, because it's righteous
And moral. Any schoolkid knows
*

You can't add apples and goats,
Let alone crossbreed different species.
Races — ah, yes, they can be exterminated,
Hybridized through stirpiculture;

Even Mendel wouldn't deny the possibilities.
But adjudication of madness
Is delusion, madness of another kind.
Yet we bring you to trial, Herr Eichmann,
For crimes against humanity, genocide.
Your execution is far too lenient for mankind,

Even though we realize the absurdity
Of thinking in terms of reparations.
Neither the total effacement of your indignation
Nor your signed confession of guilt
Can assuage the dead. They still live
In the Mediterranean, to which we'll cast your ashes.

5/30/79 — [1] (00868)

Megapolis

I flee the city
Just as the many-eyed beast
Begins to rattle its bars,
Scream with hyena-like idiocy,
Stomp its clawed paws on the cage pavement.

Its heavy breathing, rank as diesel exhaust,
Suffuses the sky I drive beneath,
For twenty-five miles out,
As though it were a mythic dragon
Singeing the entire environment with its fire,

Instead of a creature we've created
Out of our collective base need
To perpetuate Eden in Gethsemane.
I barely escape its horns and teeth,
Which threaten me with gratuitous extinction.

And even now, nearly an hour
Out of reach, past the imaginary gates
Beyond which it's never strayed,
*

A faint aroma of its wet fur
Permeates the sensory vaults of my memory.

Repeatedly, I check my rearview mirror,
To make certain I'm not being chased,
Knowing it's only a matter of years
Before the gross demon succeeds
In accessioning my territory.

As I enter the sleeping village
Where I've thrived in clean, quiet serenity,
I'm assailed by a minor traffic jam.
The many-eyed beast has arrived,
Embryonic, tractable, yet with gargantuan appetite.

5/30/79 — [2] (05635)

Leaving for Work

As I leave my sleepy self
Standing beneath massive oak trees
In pools of cool June shadows,
Waving farewell to my waking half,
Watching wistfully my unheralded departure,
I detect a sad, slow melancholia
Etched, in retrograde, on my older face.

The further I get from my refuge,
The harder my eyes strain
To maintain my image in the rearview mirror,
Until I exceed the range
Beyond which vision changes from memory
Into landscape and they forget
The features I was born with, this morning.

The miles defile my ancient identity,
While time's thumb,
Using me as a touchstone, to assuage its anxiety,
Rubs off the nubs on my energy-cam,
Smoothes over the brain's convolutions,
Reducing my imagination to a suffocating miner
Trapped in a cave of burning gases.

No matter my efforts at conjuring
Or postulating, by virtue of cryptic logic,
*

The docile fellow who witnessed my exodus
(Whether from necessity or greed
Is not important) for other realms,
I can't possibly evoke his spirit
Or recreate the shadows that enveloped him.

Only his sad, slow melancholia persists.
I catch glimpses of it intermittently,
As I peer into the rearview mirror
And through it, to myself.
Suddenly, I know the meaning of loneliness:
I see two people, who were one,
Separated, sundered, and irrevocably numb.

6/1/79 — [1] (05636)

Ex Post Facto

When the meeting subsequent to meetings
Preceding meetings prior to meetings
Postponed from meetings
Scheduled to convene to discuss meeting
Finally caught up with me,

I'd been exempt from its inevitability
For nearly an entire year,
Without anyone realizing that I'd resigned
Without notice and died
Just two weeks into my unspoken retirement.

Even with my obtrusive absence
From the annual corporate-board meeting,
The directors, in muted striped suits, club ties,
And polished wing-tip shoes,
Failed to enter, in the minutes, anything unusual

Or significantly different about the performance
Their company had again experienced.
It was only when my mandatory donation
To the chairman's favorite charity
Did not appear in its prepaid envelope

That the computer was told
To withhold all further communiqués
*

And bulletins, pending notification
To my associates and underlings
That I'd deviated from policy and been relieved of my post.

6/1/79 — [2] (05637)

The Baptism

I

We arrive as a trifling herd
Scurries from the churchyard,
Not quite stunned, rather empty-faced
And numb from grazing on 5:30 Mass.

No robed shepherd in black
Stands at the door to wave them off;
In fact, he waits impatiently
With the family gathered to witness a baptism,

Near the back entrance, before a chancel
Flickering with lambent candles beside the altar,
To whose right a font squats
Like a hitchhiker by a silent highway.

II

Through the cool obscurity flanked by pews
And statuesque stations of the cross,
Gyved to brick, at various mystical junctures
Within the octagonal space, whose otherworldliness

They penetrate for the moment, images of Lucifer,
The Prince of Darkness and Lies, rise.
The family focuses and holds them in their sights,
Until their vows exorcise his singeing fires

And replace his corrupted and abominating spirit
With its archetypal counterpart,
The love of Christ till the end of the world.
They shimmer, as the priest anoints the tiny head.

III

Suddenly, imperceptibly, all life
Skips a single beat. A child is saved,
*

At the last possible instant,
From plunging over the falls of perdition,

Into Satan's snapping jaws,
Which wait, at the base, to obliterate the unwary.
They congratulate each other
On the miraculous nature of salvation

And give thanks for the amazing grace
God has vouchsafed them, this day,
By reciting from irrefragable memory,
In self-satisfied piety, the Twenty-third Psalm.

IV

Having expressed our modest hopes and prayers,
My wife and I, our two children,
Dissolve into the late afternoon,
Which neither knows religious distinctions nor cares

What faith, if any, its minions choose.
A gray humidity looms over our shadows.
Slowly, a muted sun explodes the gloom,
Letting rain inundate our souls.

By the time we reach our car, we're bone-wet.
Our drenched clothing is a kind of swaddling garment.
Alone, we revel in our own sacrament
Of purification. We've awakened to our blessed selves.

6/10/79   (05638)

Renaissance Man

The 8 a.m. brightness
Bites my eyes, as I drive out of town,
Into the sun. June is bovine,
Sallow. Its days wallow and graze.
The herd they form remarks my passing
With dazed, uncontemplative reflex.
I am an ephemeral aphid
Flashing across their glassy screens,
A shadow emanating from itself.

Why is it that existence concerns me
And that I'm obsessed with history
*

And leaving a continuous slug-slick of verses,
By which the future might trace my progressions?
This season and its verdant land
Have no need for my posturings,
My tiny affirmations of individuality.
Their translations derive from nature,
Not man's paltry art.

Yet we are partners, symbiotic coevals
Requiring each other to survive.
My mind alone postulates their palpability
And my divinity, while essential union
Provides a climate for my growth and dying.
So today, as I drive out of town,
Into the sun, I sing myself awake,
Proclaiming my oneness among the ageless creation,
A Leonardo scribbling his dreams, in exile.

6/15/79 — [1]   (05639)

[Too soon, June loses her virginity,]

Too soon, June loses her virginity,
Forgets her sensual ways,
And surrenders her delicate ripening
To the sere beguilements of her seducer, July.

At his behest, her humid nights
Pace moon-illumined alleys
And cloven-hoofed boulevards,
Like meretricious strumpets. Profusely they sweat,

Assume the rife scent of mimosa blooms
Wilting after a furious adolescence.
Defiled and spent, May's children
Become nature's wizened vagrants and derelicts,

An entire generation accepting annihilation
As a manifestation of God's mercy.
The universal euthanasia September performs
Is a mere prelude to winter's sterility.

December blends into January.
February rises from its frozen embers
*

To tantalize March and April with seeds
Their climaxing sprays into the earth's womb.

In glorious multitudes, youth resumes
Its vertiginous rush toward fruition.
Everywhere, the greening tumescence
Intrudes on the past, reinhabits abandoned spirits,

Until, once again, virgins flourish,
Drowse for their hour of inviolate perfection,
Before succumbing to the July goat,
Who ravages summer moons with mad appetite.

6/15/79 — [2] (05640)

Father's Day ^Δ

All during the June-humid morning,
We made our visitations,
Kept our sweaty vigils at gravesides
In the two old cemeteries
Where our Jewish ancestors from Kiev
And Belfast were buried in the 1920s.

My father's grandfather, Daniel,
The patriarch and progenitor of our line,
His wife, Anne, and her parents,
Sepulchered near a mausoleum
Suggestive of affluence in a past
Otherwise unimbued with echoes,

Their miscellaneous scions prematurely severed
From life by infant mortality, disease,
Undiagnosed pleurisy and catarrh . . .
I witness their carved markers, the dates
Proclaiming their earthly evanescence.
I barely hear my tears crying

Yet realize why they've begun to effervesce,
As we motor a brief three blocks
To the second necropolis, where my grandfather
Waits to take his son's breath away,
Compel him to pick sprigs of grass
And hurl them gently to his ground cover.

I stand in reverential awe
Of my dad's deferential contemplation,
Imagining his saddened thoughts
While he surely reaches back to recapture
The last days of his own sacred youth,
Imagining myself someday standing here,

Just a few yards to the east,
Gazing down, with the same fascination,
On his kingly name: Saul, 1909 to . . .
A date not yet differentiated from the miasma.
Together, we relive random anecdotes he tells
About Lou and his dominating wife, Ruth,

Who, amazingly, at ninety-two,
Still drives, plays cards, curses
Herself and YHWH for the inconveniences
Of old age. The unviolated plot
Beside her long-deceased husband remains silent
And patient. Eternity needn't be hurried.

Over the grave of my father's brother,
We ruminate, until consanguineous eulogies
Drip from our eyes like soft rain.
Those two tiny daughters, flanking Martin,
Are destined to remain, forever, the Christmas gifts
God delivered to all of us, out of the fire
That consumed them December 25, 1970.

We stare — Jeffrey, his only son,
Saved, without explanation, to maintain the line,
And my father and great-uncle and I —
At the senseless atomization of this family,
Struck numb. None of us (Jeff doesn't know)
Can forget the suicide that left them,

From the beginning, without a wife and mother,
That beautiful lady whose features her son shares.
Jeffrey lingers long after we disband
And return to the car, hides his crying
Behind a dense stratum of wounds
And an unevenly healed series of scars.

As we drive home, silence overwhelms us.
At seventy, fifty-nine, thirty-eight,
*

And eighteen, we share a living essence
That emanates from the dead we've visited.
Today, a proud family's blood
Has been made to flow. Its bones have spoken.

6/18/79   (02205)

The Schizophrenic

This morning, he confronts his visage
In the medicine cabinet's glass,
Which surveys his bathroom's desolation,
And is amazed to find it still there,
Intact and unchanged, save for its hair,
In disarray and slightly sparser.

Taciturnity sets the mood for his wakefulness.
Shaving and communication are perfunctory tasks
Four strabismic eyes witness,
Panning the physiognomies' features for creases,
Adventitious ingrown stubble, excrescences,
And traces of melanoma. The scrutiny is cruel

And excessive, to a degree of perversity.
Yet the faces have achieved complete symbiosis.
Neither will act or speak
Without first conferring with and gaining approval
From his subaltern. Their interdependence
Assures the best check against insurrection

From occasional wayward senses
Or an intractable original idea questing freedom,
To defy the stifling hierarchy of mediocrity,
Which suffices to maintain their equilibrium.
Since birth, they've been inseparable,
Like two hermits sharing their solitude.

Yet this day has a strange cast.
His twin is fidgety, displays a tic
Over his right eye, for the first time.
Divergences have never occurred.
Even when he engages his image
In small talk, their words fail to coincide.

Paranoia bolts from his brain's corral
Like a frightened stallion. He concentrates
*

On the insane liturgy being spewed
From his duplicate mouth. It curses him
In an ancient, obfuscating dialect
That bears no relation to reason and truth,

Which he's grown used to expecting from his surrogate.
Suddenly, an abrupt, mirrored hand
Slashes his cheek with the razor.
It bleeds like a snapped milkweed,
Crimson pulsing from the deep gash,
Down his neck and gray-whorled chest,

While the maddened visage in the glass
Laughs with sadomasochistic delight.
The victim, noticing his rival's viciousness,
Smears the mirror with blood,
Obliterating the clear and unfamiliar profile
Leering at him, then disappears

Into a tepid washrag, for relief.
Not until he's administered the styptic stick
To his wound does he look for himself again.
Only, when he wipes away the red,
Nothing remains except a deathly echo
Rising from a silvery screen bereft of reflections.

6/19/79 — [1] (05641)

[All week, I've traversed back roads] †

All week, I've traversed back roads
And highways connecting watchtowers
And sentinels, watched the masses

6/19/79 — [2] (07723)

Peddler on the Road

Each day away is another layer of dust
That buries memory a notch deeper
In numbness and misty sentimentality.
My two tiny children become Naiads
Cavorting naked in an enchanted copse.

My wife is a blessed princess
Dancing behind a prism of dripping flute colors
That change her, each mind-blink,
From melody to pigment, then back.
The song she paints fills my ears with trembling.

I imagine myself in heroic guises,
A crusader, conquistador, astronaut,
In quest of suspected destinations
Unarrived at by twenty centuries of men
Bent on illuminating all God's mysteries.

Only, each night grows older and longer
Than the preceding one. Sleazy motels
Expose my fantasies to cigar reek.
My sloppy signature on the guest card
Proclaims me an imposter to myself.

Even my one indulgence, the phone call
I make every evening, at dinnertime,
Reminds me that necessity binds me to routine
And that mere intercourse with my family
Has its price to exact from my servitude.

Somewhere beyond midnight,
Peace reaches up from a deep wineglass
And seduces me to sleep. Like a monk,
I put myself to bed in my coffin of loneliness,
As dreams of being reborn take me home.

Morning light rips me from bed
By my eyes, flings me into the outside air
Without my consent. Once again,
I enter the groove that tunnels under the dust
One stratum lower than yesterday.

6/19/79 — [3] (02408)

Willy Agonistes

Already, the drifting begins.
Gravity thins at the center,
Over which I pace with nimble indecision.
My mind falls through
*

Even as it elongates in space.
Its movements, both horizontal and vertical,
Are stationary. A cruel stasis
Exchanges its pervasive cells for mine,
Like a terminal carcinoma binding the spirit,

And I dwindle down a deep spiral,
Spinning vertiginously,
Trapped in silence, by a bleeding tongue
Bitten in half by fear's snapping teeth.
Fractured rocks I pass
Scratch my flesh, bruise the bones to throbbing.
My testicles are torn from the groin,
Leaving my flaccid penis intact,
Useless as a eunuch's fatuous apparatus.

Dissolution of the emotions and the intellect
Is such a grisly and protracted death.
How is it that God allows us admittance
To the promontory from which we witness revelations,
Without inviting us to share in Paradise?
"First Cause" and "original sin"
Are mere terms for pedagogues, bullshit,
Claptrap resurrected from metaphysical sermons.
I am the sole reason for my existence.

My descent is measured in heartbeats
Calibrated in years spent, unwisely,
In studious pursuit of universal mysteries
And truths of the human heart
In conflict with its own mortal afflictions.
The death-whiffs I breathe
Are those emanating from the brain's crematorium,
A trained intelligence that finally short-circuited
And burned in its own furnace.

Now, the consequences of failure
Have come 'round, demanding payment in full.
All that remains of my dismantled soul
Is a paltry collection of manuscripts,
Two children, and a wife disconsolate and shattered
By my unconsummated hopes of achieving celebrity
From the words I so fastidiously gathered,
Like delicate and precious shells,
Off the shores of my youthful inspiration.

I am my own dissolve. My demise
Is a bad imitation of dry runs
I performed for selected audiences of my admirers.
Suicide, though never mentioned,
Rises to the surface as Medusa's head.
I kiss her cold lips, embrace her body,
And cling, as she takes me down into solitude
That surpasses silence. The final drowning
Climaxes in a flourish of spurious curse words.

6/19/79 — [4] (02566)

The Father in Us All

As I sit here, sipping chilled rosé,
Repeating to myself the silent litany
That comprises the names of Troika and Trilogy
And Jan, I can't quite imagine myself
Progenitor and father of offspring.

Rather, I see myself as a profligate,
A dissolute and wayward vagrant
Ever searching for new ways of saying
Ancient words and Biblical phrases,
A poet absolved of common responsibilities.

Yet God has predestined me to be guardian
Of two tiny children and an earthly wife,
First and foremost. Whatever pretensions
And intellectual condescensions I may have designed
Are irrelevant to my mortal vocation.

Although I continue to retrieve poems
From oblivion whenever I'm able to escape
The confines of my home, my prime task
Remains the education and socialization of scions
I've procreated out of an overriding desire

To outlast anonymity, outlive death,
By perpetuating my name through them.
I have been entrusted with the well-being
Of two helpless souls, two beautiful babies,
Who know nothing of fame and broad acclaim.

Ultimately, I have no choice except to accept
The finality of my actions. As father
*

And mentor, I must needs relinquish my needs
For self-expression through words linked to words
In verses speaking the gossip of angels and gods.

I am relegated to the mundane task
Of guiding my children in the ways of righteousness
And sensitivity. Whatever I might have achieved
Must be postponed for eternity.
Now, my priorities are foreordained and certain,

And the slightest deviation from this course
Will be interpreted by God
As a gross infraction of celestial mandates,
A transgression against Scripture.
I acquiesce with great reluctance,

Realizing that the seat of God
Resides with my children. My last hope
Rests on their shoulders. With profound remorse,
I pack up my pen and paper and books
And head for home, without looking back,

A sad and broken man, a failure,
Who has succeeded at something admirable
And worthy despite his own inherent dissatisfaction —
Father, husband. Ah, those words!
They bring tears to my eyes. They assuage my regrets.

6/19/79 — [5] (02567)

Erica's Paranoia ^Δ

As I stare at the blank paper before me,
Terrified that neither idea
Nor poetical image will rise, from its grave,
To penetrate and enter my inspiration
And, in doing so, achieve its own liberation
From the awful paralysis of oblivion,
My eyes are invaded by afterimages.

It's as though they've focused too long
On an Albers *Homage* or an incandescent bulb
Or seen a ghost's grossest anatomy
By having accidentally gotten close enough
To recognize its bones as those of my own skeleton.

My endless trembling is the rumbling of a subway
Passing under my feet, a submarine's thrust
Churning my blood. The stunned heart fumbles,
Stutters as if it were tongue-tied,
Then races, in a frenzy, to outrun itself.

Old notions lurking just below the surface,
Verses overworked and inauthentic from the beginning,
And abused word-chimes form the snake heads
Of a grotesque Medusa lifting, from the slime,
To haunt my psyche with reminders of failure.
Yet the gruesome creature resembling my past
Refuses to submit itself to scrutiny.

Instead, it seethes just out of reach,
Taunting me with inaccessible thoughts
And visions. Nothing materializes from the ether.
Neither simile nor cerebral metaphor
Surrenders to my frustrated sensibility.

I'm left with unsuggestive emptiness
To endure, this evening. My breathing tightens,
As invisible vises squeeze the brain's nostrils.
My gelded eyes and vasectomized nerve-ends
Throb, without relief, from the pain
Of unconsummated creativity, as the unretrieved poem
Decomposes beneath the page's white silence.

6/20/79   (02562)

Bacchus, Patron of Poets

Ah, how the grapes' chilled first taste
Liberates the intellect from its day labors,
Makes the soul's watercolors copulate
With invisible bodies hovering above it,
In the energy field haloing my poetry.
I gaze into stained-glass lunettes
Blazing with the sun's amazing coruscations
And am transformed into Rouen Cathedral.

This place is the mystical, musical womb
I left. Surely, this is the dome of Paradise,
*

Where my imagination was spawned, my psyche bathed
In prenatal streams bubbling with opiates
And lotus-ladies giving birth to verse-children
Through God's immaculate perception.

Now, time and silence and death climax
Inside this breathless moment. Interpenetrated,
Married to the air that carries my dreams aloft
On surging word-thermals, I suck deeply,
Through my teeth, all the universe,
Free from having fasted, for weeks, on images,
Similes, and delicious, mellifluous visions.
My exhalations are translations of the long-ago.

The emptying vessel fills my inebriated heart
To intoxication never reached in stupors.
Slowly, the thin, cool, crimson ichor
Floats my tiny boat toward the edge,
Where the vast unknown ripples my existence
And home is the poem that shelters me from loneliness.

6/21/79 — [1] (02563)

Moses in Sodom

Rebekah, Rachel, and Leah
Creep into my hermetic desolation
And seduce me from my stoic ways.
These three mythical Jewesses
Arouse my intellect to erection.
They make my passions ejaculate,
Bring forth poems I've kept secret
Beneath the sensitive priapus of my heart.

Why I've been made to surrender my virginity,
Rise from bondage, and seek refuge
Within this maternal harem,
I'll never know. My only consolation
May be the sensual delight I derive
From the female body. It excites me
To a kind of cerebral climax,
A mind-blowing I'd never conceived.

6/21/79 — [2] (02564)

Return to Rock-'n-Roll

Specters claw my ears to bleeding shreds,
With sound generated in Hell's war shops.
The air blends with Mary Jane and patchouli oil,
To form an elixir the lungs can hardly refuse
Despite all former admonitions. Behind the scrim
Woven of dissonance and sheer decibels,
Shadows gyrate. I've been here before,
In another incarceration; only, the avatar
Escapes my memory. Youth's enemy
Is youth. I'd almost forgotten . . . almost
Forgotten the motorcycles' raucous exhaust,
The driving insanity of the driven body
On edge and spaced out on its own energy . . .
Almost forgotten Hendrix and Joplin and Morrison,
Exploding as fleet ecstasy annihilated them.
Once again, I've entered the loud dungeon
Where libidos of unknown and inessential souls
Writhe like snakes inexorably hatching
From eerie-sounding eggs, for the pure pleasure
Of their uninhibited self-expression.
Jesus, Lord, how could I have forgotten
Such primal concerns? It's not fair
That I've been excommunicated from this universe
Just because aging has blown me past the point
Where return is tantamount to apocalypse.
Why can't everything in life run parallel
Instead of diverging so precipitously?
Let me return, now, without dying
Or suffering everlasting corporeal pain.
Let me remain inside my emotions'
Whirling dynamo for more than minutes
At a time, during the residue of my future.
At least let me revel in *this* escape.

6/21/79 — [3] (01340)

Columbia, Mo., Post 280 Hosts the Statewide V.F.W. Convention, at Ramada Inn

For three days and four nights,
This Midwestern college-town motel
*

Is transformed into a hotbed of patriotism.
In my mind's dreaming corridors,
I hear an endless litany of choruses
From "Columbia, the Gem of the Ocean" being chanted;
Only, on waking, each shaky morning,
I realize just who and what
Is actually responsible for the outrage and corruption.

Men reminiscent of Trova's falling souls,
Without any of their pleasing aesthetics,
Rather bellies distended beyond repair,
Some tattooed, slovenly as old toads,
Totter in anomalous double time,
Loiter in endless backslapping,
Name-calling, handshaking camaraderie.
War is their confraternal denominator,
Yet none has survived the battle of the bulge.

Most escort their ladies-in-waiting,
Who are equally festooned and emblazoned
With mass-produced regalia:
Vests bedizened with fancy appliqués
Announcing hometown and post number,
Ribbons, medallions, lapel pins —
Their visas and identification papers,
Their weekend passes to gain admittance
To the greatest campaign of their careers.

Calling each other "old man,"
Smoking incessantly, loud as athletes
Constantly taking the field somewhere,
They mill and pace, proud of their status
As veterans of foreign wars.
They frown on my hirsute insignificance;
Mustache and gold-rimmed glasses
On a face as diabolical as mine
Automatically place me on trial for war crimes

Against democracy and "the American way."
Conscientious objectors and youthful defectors
Are *personae non gratae*, "degenerates" all.
My eyes watch, through binoculars,
Their arrogant passages. They go by
Like tedious arguments without conclusions.
Only their brown caps and their outfits
*

Remind me that once upon a time,
These people must have been children.

Yet in my mind of minds, I can't define
The force that motivates them to unite,
Bind, and cling, like ivy, to an ideology,
Let alone one so antagonistic
To life and peace and decency.
Isn't our most dread anxiety
That of being captured by the enemy?
If so, then why don't the men recognize
Their interminable herding is the "sleeping giant" stirring?

6/22/79   (05642)

Assimilation

I step outdoors, this cool morning,
To survey my waking prospects.
Lush dew beneath my shoes
Enters, through holes in their soles,
As oozing silence. Shadows, set loose
In random chaos from the sun,
Crawling, spiderlike, across its webbed net,
Shatter the eyes' blurred mirrors,
Which night, in orgiastic abandon,
Scribbled over with slug trails.

Vision's concern turns to the earth,
Whose tumescent, leafy poke
Grows through cracks in the asphalt
And other improbable locations,
As though it were outside of time,
Whose ivy sends out fingers,
Like Visigoth hordes, to subdue
Everything in their imperturbable path,
Whose waxy hollies and vaginal magnolias
Absorb my attention in subtle chiaroscuros.

Involuntarily, I enter their dimensions
And am scratched and bruised and choked
In sadomasochistic confusion.
Who might have abducted my spirit,
*

This seemingly ordinary Tuesday morning,
Escapes me absolutely. Nature's forces
Command my surrender to chance and fancy,
And I acquiesce without vituperation.
By noon, the dew will have evaporated;
The moon will count me among its shadows.

6/25/79 (00245)

Benefactors

Why are we always trying
To substitute words for silent worlds,
Coax meaning from the implied,
Read symbols into the simple truth
And abstract from concrete ideas?

Who determined that poets, painters,
And composers are the chosen few
Endowed with extrasensory powers,
That they alone are privileged
To transmute life into art,

Matter into spirit, endless night
Into the psyche's lunar daylight?
Am I not equally capable
Of entertaining incarnations,
Taming unicorns, soaring with Oisin,

While I sleep, eat, dream of deeds
Requiring my immediate decisions?
Is it not just as possible that God
Allows His creatures to choose how
And to whom each will contribute his dues?

6/26/79 — [1] (00244)

The Rebuff

A sliver of the crescent moon
Shivers my bones, as though it were a shiv
Entering my heart through the eyes.

I grimace as passing clouds
Lend to its stark, elongated shape
The illusion of a moving scimitar.

A hundred times it penetrates, withdraws,
Like a solitary retractable claw
Tightening its grip on a victim.

Bitterness bleeds from my stab wound.
Shame pulsates around the cicatrix,
Until clotting turns to scab,

Entombing, forever, rumors of my failure
To seduce the horned moon
With mad and passionate fornication.

Stumbling against blunt shadows,
I rush to the nearest street lamp
To engage a less demanding courtesan.

6/26/79 — [2] (02141)

Ka

> *For Jerry Walters,*
> *who knows his pyramids*
> *inside out*

Five a.m. breaks apart
As though dropped from a great altitude,
Detonates my listless soul.
The drowsy spirit
Rouses from its body of nocturnal hours
Like a meteor shower.
I awaken in a thousand fragments
And slowly get up and set out,
Gathering myself together
From the cratered surface of my psyche.

Even now, no ghosts are about,
Floating in the air
Separating Sheol from the paradisiacal terminus.
Gently, I fill the contours of fields
Like an ocean, pass through cows
Grazing in docile solitude.
With time no longer
*

Fleshing my bones and the bones
No longer holding my will intact,
Flight is a matter of pure letting-go.

The cool ether that caresses me
Reflects my smiling face
In prismatic angles of coincidence.
The ecstasy of release is enormous,
As I penetrate and reinhabit myself
In anticipation of the long, peaceful sleep
Attended by the sensa of my former existence.
You, blessed wife, and you, my children,
Draw nigh even as I go.
My eyes breathe you alive.

Suddenly, the pyramid-shaped sky
Admits me through an opening
At the base, where I used to pray.
Inscrutable corridors, crowded with toys
And books, poems, clothes, and foods
I once loved, comfort me toward the core,
Where kinesis is the essence of immortality.
In the womb entombed by this endless day,
An embryo grows to fetus and is born anew.
A boy king rises, rubs sleep from his dreams.

6/28/79   (02142)

The Masses' Mass

I

An underlying anxiety shadows the faces
And glass-shrouded eyes of the men
Who've come, once again, to St. Louis,
To take communion from the company priest.

A pervasive and reiterating chant,
Composed of admonition, mixed with exhortation
And panegyric, on pitfalls of social Darwinism
And virtues of the Protestant ethic,

Issues like ritualistic liturgy being whispered
From the altar. God's minister isolates
*

What he sees as the great adversaries
To the continued well-being of his congregation:

Recession, tight credit, low fuel supplies.
The men look inward and upward
For instruction, commiseration, and understanding.
Each realizes the precariousness of the season at hand.

II

Suits, sportscoats, and dress slacks,
Summarized by lot number, model, and price
And reffed on hard swatch cards,
Form the canonized trappings of the trade

They proselytize. Their faith in raiment
Transcends all mortal, corporeal considerations,
Despite the naked truth that man demands,
For survival's sake, a practical application of religion.

Yet in genuflecting to the general consensus
Of imminent Apocalypse, each vows
To carry forth the house image to the outlands
And reestablish their apostolic approach to clothing.

One by one, they leave their seats,
To experience the Eucharist, taking coffee,
Acidic and rich from sitting in an urn all day,
And glazed donuts kept perpetually heated.

III

Silence prevails, as final antiphons are lipped.
"Go — the Mass is ended" sifts down
To the tip of Friday afternoon.
Fatigued, dazed, and relieved, the men disperse

And return to their hotel rooms, to freshen up
Before being transported to the rectory,
For cocktails and catered supper.
Escorted by their wives or alone, they arrive

To socialize and share their immaculate inebriation
As one tight-woven family,
Before scattering to their own parochial locations.
By Monday, the pilgrimage will have commenced

Through cities and hamlets and shadowy valleys.
Next January, they'll be back, to confess
Omissions in sales, shipments missed,
And to pray for redemption through increased commissions.

6/29/79 (02407)

The Peddlers' Grail Quest

The hour is Saturday morning, early.
People sleep, who share no awareness
Of finalizing their lines, making certain
That all offerings have accurate status
On summary sheets; whose guts and intellects
Don't rumble with the premonitory anxiety
Of hovering on the edge of a new season,
Fully armed with the latest hardware
And arsenal of swatched and modeled
Soft goods to take to the "enemy";
Who've never felt the compulsive urge
To seek the limits of the unknown
By searching their own known capacities
And be adjudged worthy by others
Not all that accommodating or intrepid.

People sleep, who need to recuperate
From the malaise of nine-to-five weekdays.
Their easy breathing, this Sabbath morning,
Floated with snoring and vivid fantasies,
Sheds the last vestiges of individuality
They began with in childhood and jettisoned,
Inexorably, as job led to desk job,
Assignments got successively undermined
By hierarchy and distant, invisible decisions
Sifting down, like laughing gas, through speakers
And IBM readouts.
Meanwhile, the zealous clothing peddlers
Twitch urgently to make a selling date
And turn in their first booking today.
Sleep will wait until September 15.

6/30/79 (02406)

Narcissistic Visions △

July's butterflies
Seduce my eyes with hues
Whose fluttering sky-dance
Entrances the torpid spirit.

Musical transmutations
Flute through me like spice scent,
Blowing gentle, sensual halos
Around my impoverished soul.

I am a prisoner of my senses,
Soaring evanescently,
Yet majestically as inspiration,
In gossamer circles,

Without realizing my hours
Are expiring even as the spiral,
Through whose driving pulse
I climb and dive, widens.

July is an eye blink, a sigh
Unconscious, invisible, silent.
I am her sight and sound,
Her earthly articulation.

My blood is her speaking voice,
Whose renewal and release
Are, in my arteries and veins, coeval
And inexhaustible while I suspire.

Now, my visions tire.
July lights in a nearby clearing,
Where butterflies go to die
When their flight finally unwinds,

And drops me to the ground,
By a cress-covered stream.
I plunge through a surface opening
In my own reflection and forget to breathe.

7/4/79 (05643)

Returning to Port

"So we beat on,
Boats against the current . . ."
*

Ah, how Nick Carraway's phrase
Surfaces, this early morning,
Through the sarcomatous haze
Hovering, like a great omniscient conscience,
Over the city and suburbs I flee,
Along an empty highway, heading home.

"Borne back ceaselessly . . ."
Despite my efforts to progress from the depths,
Soar free of the chrysalid,
I regress, with systematic unawareness.
My shadow is a sail flailing above me,
In a squall of screaming energies
That trail off in the wake of my failure,
Taking with them any sense of movement.

For so long, dreams of achieving success
In worldly terms, having my work
Published, discussed in the same breath
With past masters, taught in college classes,
Motivated me to press ahead,
Remain in this Midwestern Dead Sea,
Floated with people whose sandstone faces
And souls are worn smooth as silence.

Only, now the hour is too late.
The green light at dock's end,
Ever elusive, enigmatic, alluring,
Flickers like a victim of delirium tremens,
Then dims into the obscurity
That beckons my vessel. In the distance,
The treacherous shoals speak the idiot's demotic.
I batten my hatches and prepare to crash.

7/10/79 — [1] (05644)

July Demise

The severing is so subtle
Yet inexorable as ice floes.
Before my mind has had time
To know its own tropism,
Fathom predestination,
Prime itself for the death of its soul,
*

It's been overtaken by loneliness,
Sent to the cloakroom,
To ruminate on its isolation, in silence.

Its petals grow desiccated,
Draw up into misshapen attitudes
Of resignation, and drop off.
Salvation is myth
To the wandering Jew
And coast-blown eucalyptus alike.
Neither delicate cymbidiums
Nor intransigent crab grass
Can withstand a blighted heart

Or outlast a spirit gone flaccid
With arrogance and meretricious vanity.
Now, the edgeless garden
Containing the remains of my colors
And scents lapses, lackluster
As a drab fog. My eyes,
Afraid of what they might find,
Sift through the dirt, scratch themselves
On roots and shards of ancient urns.

Slowly, the mind's catacombs
Are inundated with their own dankness.
Memory, like a fastidious bee,
Barricades itself behind a door
It creates between existence and sleep,
Until pollination of all senses ceases.
Above ground, through the weeds,
Hearty acanthuses embrace the surface,
Choking the last breath from my throat.

7/10/79 — [2] (00243)

Marilee

At twenty-nine,
Her identity crisis widens.
The quest becomes congested
With existential questions,
*

While survival goes on, unmolested,
In its protracted patterns.

More often than before,
She catches herself distracted
At work, concerned by whispers
Skipping past her open door,
Annoyed or frustrated
By conversations sifting through the walls.

Lately, she's been prey to strangers
Trespassing on her domain
Not for the sake of gain but rather admittance
Into the sacred, secret sector
Where she keeps her allure
And the accouterment of her illusive beauty.

And she's relinquished her privacy
Twice to promises of security
And trusted friendship. Both occasions,
Like sculpture carved from marble,
Have liberated her from stony isolation,
Only to emphasize her captivity

And vulnerable fragility.
Twice submitting herself bodily,
Twice immolated in lust
To a beastly, irretrievable dream of love,
Twice abandoned to herself,
She no longer believes in gentleness.

Soon, she'll have a yard sale
For her heart, auction off
Her cherished gewgaws,
Accumulated with delicate acquisitiveness
From out of the welter
Of crass kitsch merchandized by minds

Bent on self-aggrandizement.
Then she'll leave town
As she arrived: anonymous,
Insubstantial, and transient
As junk mail or a road peddler
Hoping to open up new accounts.

7/11/79 (02143)

The Rain-Angels of Darkness

Driving westward, ahead of the sun,
I'm assailed by chimeras
Who've possessed the rain clouds
By devouring the sky, with their ominous shapes.

Afternoon's refracting shafts
Are tentacles these grotesque creatures
Send out to snatch me, bodily,
From the peaceful lassitude I seek.

It's as though they've recognized in me
A semblance of Nemo
Or one of his seamen threatening to heave
A harpoon into their collective eye.

Having surrendered to the humid effluvium,
I now pass through a space
That envelops me in oceanic opacity.
My tiny submarine blows its ballast.

My imagination becomes a diving bell,
In which disbelief is suspended.
Around my eyes, weird amphibians
And exotic eels and poisonous fish hover.

Suddenly, as if waking from death,
I discover rain
Inundating the windshield, pelting my brain,
And I wonder about the drowning,

How and when I went down
And where, in relation to known time,
This sand ledge, on which I balance
With such precariousness, might be located.

Even tentative blinking
Threatens to dislodge my teetering vessel.
Just up ahead, a flashing neon
Signals respite and escape from fatigue.

So close is the grottoed sanctuary
Yet so inestimable, I weep,
Knowing the chimeras have succeeded
In keeping me from reaching my destination.

When I look again,
Night has descended over the wilderness.
*

Nearby, a whippoorwill keens,
Calling my soul to come join the migration.

7/17/79 — [1] (05645)

The Poet Locates Himself in the Universe

Slowly, slowly, I dissolve in trance.
My soul soars past earthly encumbrances,
Toward verse shimmering in Elysian trees
Rooted to Mount Helicon. My eyes reach out
To pluck the ripe fruit beautifully pendulous,
Bite, chew, digest, and assimilate
Its sweet flesh. Ah, the taste
Touching insinuates on the mind's tongue!
Ah, the ecstasy of consuming the intellect
Without exhausting its skeletal essence!

God, how absolutely fanatical is my adoration
For words. How completely obsessed I am
With giving birth to the virginal metaphor.
Perhaps this endless parturition
Is God's admission that perfection is myth,
Save for the poet's lowly approximation of Creation.
Possibly, it's Satan's curse, my doom
To illuminate the heart's empty chambers
With tapers that burn without flame.
Regardless, I revel in this syllabled legacy of mine.

No longer does the moon control my tides
Or Hecate gather in my lost thoughts,
Nor do whippoorwills call out my soul
To follow eunuch death to the necropolis
On the earth's dark side. I am godhead
In my own cosmos, master tactician
And strategist, composer who orchestrates
The universal chaos around the tonic key of C.
Each poem that slips, in whispers, from my lips
Is Pan's breath blown across a celestial mouthpiece.

Just now, because of loud voices intruding,
I've become conscious of my pen's movements.
The eyes try to keep pace with its meaning
By trying to translate the cursive shapes
*

Writing inscribes on oblivion's cave walls.
No new language materializes. Only the soul
Reappears, in its lowly role of blessed mime.
The trance is dismantled slowly, slowly,
Until I'm returned to my very first word,
To ponder the distance between then and the end of now.

7/17/79 — [2]   (02546)

Worms and Moles

Despite all my frenetic and importunate efforts
To stop the crimson-bloated worms,
The blind, plodding star-nosed moles, I can't.
They proceed regardless of the years passing,
The energy exerted to control their activities,
Ultimately coming to signify failure of the will.

I've dug yards of garden to eradicate cutworms
And night crawlers, stuck myriad spring traps
Where it appeared the moles' earthly repoussé
Had temporarily ceased its devastation, to rest,
Without success. The inexorable undoing
Commences despite holocaust, apocalypse, death.

In simplest terms, we share a sense of finality.
Our blood runs at the slightest scratch.
Starvation and defecation are inevitabilities.
We are soul mates, cellmates in time's prison,
Whose crime is mere materialization.
Immortality is not a part of our genetic structure;

Rather, we survive by accident, sheer accident
And chance circumstance. Our paths cross
Almost never, and yet we recognize each other
As victim and emblem, symbol and symbolized.
Others' dying reminds us we're alive
For a while; our dying is just a matter of time.

Now, the cold, dank grave looms,
Ubiquitous as decaying rose-blooms in July.
In anticipation, I assume a horizontal memory
Whose geography is a past crowded with worms
And tunneling blind creatures. Nothing new
Confuses the notion of escaping into oblivion.

I prepare to exit the bleak nexus
And have my precious, delicate flesh consumed
By time, assigned to follow me through eternity.
Only, the shame of having to leave
Bereaves my spirit. I cease breathing,
That the silence will listen to my inexhaustible voice

Proclaiming my abhorrence of the nether world.
You sons-of-bitches, serpents of the dirt,
Condemned to crawl on your smooth bellies,
Through eternity! I abjure your existence!
Exit my sight, you motley bastards!
Give me room to soar free of your clutches!

Dreams fall away. Hymns hover
Above the profusely strewn ground cover,
Though no one has come to grieve, now,
For more than a decade. And the nematodes
Thrive on the rich earth embracing my coffin,
Just waiting for its walls to deteriorate.

Like wild asteroids and uncontained comets
Flying through space, moles etch paths
Surrounding the cavern in which I've been buried,
As if they might somehow find an opening
And penetrate the sanctum sanctorum of mortality,
To discover the secret leavings of the heart.

Only, the body is left to its own dissolution.
Its dispersal is slow and lonely, performed alone,
Despite nature's anxious spectators. My death
Remains a private and inviolate celebration.
The moles and worms twitch and squirm,
As their own unconscious demise surprises them from behind.

7/17/79 — [3] (02547)

Changing Territories

The bright sun, this July morning,
Is an irritant, a mica chip,
Whose raw glistening blinds the eyes
With invisible scratches and nicks.
I peer ahead. Vision is a bouillabaisse
Of sinister images from dreams recently abandoned.
Instead of lined highway,
*

A rabbit path, festooned in caliginous grass,
Winds and flattens out interminably,
As if its labyrinth has been calculated
To ensnare the innocent traveler
Rather than transport the wary clairvoyant
To day's end without serious mishap.
I follow its tedious Möbius strip
As though floating, on a roller coaster,
Through space not violated by tracks
Or arachnid framework. I follow,
Unable to force a change on hallucinations
Still emanating after sleep's assassination
By the waking psyche. The highway
Veers, suddenly, through a wilderness
Whose trees are billboards and poles,
Whose living creatures are derelict cars
Parked as a result of the great bloodletting.
Their veins are empty of vital life,
Yet they thrive in silent mummification.
No humans roam the plains with bows
And maces, in search of food and maidens to plunder,
Nor do thunderous herds of star-nosed moles,
Cutworms, garter snakes, gophers
Trouble the landscape with their incessant aloofness.
And as I drive on, toward the precipice,
Ever advancing, my entrancement deepens.
I realize that I reached the edge
Sometime back, beneath sleep, and that this trip,
Recorded, to the letter, on my expense account,
Has been assumed and paid for in full
By my competitor, who, for years,
Has been after me to join his company.
For Mr. Death, it's a perfunctory matter
Of writing me off as the cost of doing business;
For me, the move is not as easy to justify.

7/19/79 — [1] (02405)

Willy: The Energy Crunch ^Δ

Once again, Willy concludes his trip
By floating facedown in a wineglass
*

Filled with the house's chilled rosé.
Survival in the backwoods requires stamina
And a sense of necessity so urgent
That even solitude and desolation
Can't undo his desire to circumvent damnation
By keeping to his ancient sales route.

Yet a nemesis never before encountered
Threatens his redemptive obsession with the Protestant ethic.
Willy, the Jew peddler, child of the Diaspora,
Believer in overstock and flawed merchandise,
Promotional goods, old and undesirable items
At a price enticing enough to snare the skeptic
And iconoclast alike, has no conception
Of how to soft-soap this enigmatic enemy.

All he's been able to ascertain to date
Is that some vast omniscience is vying with him
For his territory, by sabotaging gas stations
He's memorized in every Tipton and Salisbury
Throughout his Hester Street-ed Midwest.
The severe frustration of discovering "CLOSED" signs
Affixed to pumps and the fear of running out
And being stranded in the Land of Transients

Annihilates his ambitiousness, with anxiety.
The cost of waging the battle outrages his pride,
Pressures his resources with impending penury.
Unable to ever engage the beastly creature
In full light of day or under the moon,
He finally resigns himself to accept the fate
Of old oppressions come back around
From the days when pogroms were commonplace.

But he refuses to be frightened away
By alarms and hysterias blowing notices of doom
And economic catastrophe across the nation.
Rather, having submerged himself, temporarily,
In his wine, to achieve a peaceful, inviolate silence,
He beseeches the God of Moses and Jacob and Job,
Who conceived the idea of divine retribution,
To show him a sign, lay down a miracle,

Manifest, before his lambent eyes, a way
To exact an eye for an eye, a heart and brain
*

For a spirit and a soul, that he might go out
And slay the cowardly son-of-a-bitch
Who's been chewing holes in his confidence.
Slowly, he emerges from his turgid stupor,
Staggers back to his room, with an answer from YHWH:
"Liquidate rags! Get into real estate!"

7/19/79 — [2] (01341)

Early-Morning Distractions

I would like to believe
That reincarnation is just a breezy matter
Of climbing the stile between breathing
And oblivion and leaping through fields
Profuse with milkweeds, thistles,
Queen Anne's lace, and narcotic poppies.

Also, it would pleasure me profoundly
To know that my newer shape
Would assume a mesmerical transmutation,
Like that of a phoenix ever renewing
Or a whippoorwill forever entranced
With calling out its own immortal ka.

These vague hallucinations I postulate
And those for which no words
Or images exist haunt my waking spirit,
Taunt me with the beginning of death wishes
I prayed would not intrude, this day,
On the urgent routines begging my attention.

And yet I hear them, the ecstasies,
Playing out their little waiting games
Behind my inner ear, gamboling impatiently,
While I exhaust my remaining energy
On respectability and fading hopes for fame.
They chant my name in an endless roundelay,

Whose contrapuntal harmonics soothe me,
When I should be firing my engines
To cope with imminent imbecilities
Already winging toward convergence with my soul.
*

Slowly, distractedly, I rise from the table
And exit, forgetting to pay my breakfast check.

7/20/79 — [1] (05646)

Charlotte's Roses

For my mother,
on her birthday,
7/17/79

Her years are dew-dappled petals
Enfolding the rose
Whose deliquescent odor encloses her essence
In velvety gentleness,

Whose endless blossoming
Pleasures our senses,
Inspires us to emulate her graceful perfection
By smiling, kissing, touching each other.

Although her seeds
Have thrown blessed familial clusters
That share her earthly garden,
She stands alone, efflorescing in the sun,

Inviolate and unmolested by time,
Which might wish to clip her stem,
Dismember her, defile the features
Bequeathed her by paradisiacal Eve.

Never will she fade.
No sleep-weeds, oblique shadows
At midnight and twilight,
Or accidents of fate will ever eradicate

The shape of the image she's created
During our brief stay
In this phase of the journey from birth
To life after afterlife.

Never will death gain purchase
In the earth where, someday,
Her body will lie, even as now it thrives —
A rose by all names, incarnate: Charlotte.

7/20/79 — [2] (02144)

The Last Days

A copper-hot air mass
Hovers just above the treetops,
Like exhaust snorting from stacks
Fastened to a colossal, diabolical tractor
Reshaping Hell's abysmal swamplands
To make room for an influx of the scandalous
Recently damned in America and Iran.

The taste is acrid and gritty.
Its scabrous odor burns the nostrils,
Makes the nose twitch without relief,
As if a persistent housefly
Were using it for a landing strip,
To make practice touch and gos.
The eyes wilt like dying birds-of-paradise.

The pervasive, ocherous haze limits vision
To premonitions of choking and suffocating
In showers spraying Zyklon B mist.
For weeks, no moon has been sighted
By astronomers, and on good days,
The sun is a runny fried egg
Stuck to the bottom of the sky's greasy pan.

Each dawn is like the preceding one,
Only slightly more soiled
And unenticing. Each is a sortilege
Redolent of irreversible consequences.
This very morning, the copper-hot air
Threatens to detonate the last outposts
Of an experiment set in motion eons ago.

7/21/79 (00867)

Returning to Troy

Once again, the leave-taking occurs
Without fanfare or ceremony
Between us, as if each has reached
The undreamed nexus of resignation
While keeping up pretenses of sadness.

She blends with early morning shadows,
In the doorway, a sensual chiaroscuro
Enveloping her languid good-bye.
My ephemeral gaze becomes tongue-tied,
Refuses to reciprocate the slightest sign,

As I drive away and assume the shape
My hallucinating mind impresses on its intellect.
Suddenly, I am the many disguises
My frequent escapes beg me undertake
For the sake of survival. A tenuous avocation

At best, this restless questing of mine.
The blood that pulses my temples
Compels me to log undefined reflections
On the inexorable unspooling of highway,
Fashion, in verse form, the heart's dilemma.

Am I Quevedo's Buscón, Rasselas,
Tom Jones, a huckleberried incarnation?
Am I Quijote el Magnífico,
Joe Christmas, Holden Caulfield,
Going out in search of Isadora Wing?

Or is that thing which lures me away
Every few weeks less literary,
More quotidian, easier to ascertain
Merely by discarding these masks,
Which transmute the view I get

Through these disillusioned eyes of mine?
In furious abnegation of the past,
I undo vision's occluded cataracts,
Spray a fine rage of forgetting
Over all the pages in my notebook,

And emerge just in time to see myself
Fading out of sight of my wife,
Adrift in an ocean empty of water,
Whose sandy landscape bears traces
Of desolated ancestors, abandoned friends.

Abruptly, I turn the car around
And flee back to the city,
Back to our rented apartment, back
*

To my two tiny children and to the lady
Who alone knows me as their blessed Odysseus.

7/25/79   (05647)

Self-Portrait △

> *For _____,*
> *who is the sum*
> *of all she dreams*
> *of becoming*

The sleuthsayer, purveyor of flaw
And surplus, is a dragon-slayer,
An assayer of pyrite and paste diamonds.
His vision penetrates sortilege,
With soothy clairvoyance,
Explodes the occult,
With tragicomic histrionics
And hyperbole worthy of Adolf Nixon.

He justifies his invisible existence
By weighing himself each hour,
Calculating the gain and loss of ounces
To determine the status quo
Of his quotidian low profile.
When the moon is perfectly tumescent,
In sleet or snow, he sleeps outdoors
And moans like a loon in heat,

Whose eerie ululations
Shiver the universe, to remind himself
That his libido isn't defunct,
His instincts for plundering females
Aren't sunk so deep in depravity
He can't at least approximate passion.
Although never married, he's fathered chimeras,
Phantasms, and Bedlam-bloated creatures,

Who've scattered throughout his imagination
And settled in its craters, to multiply.
Only when people come to him
For advice about what might be done
To efface religion and education
*

From man's curriculum does he respond
With a sibilant benediction or panegyric
On the innate wisdom of the primate *Homo sapiens*.

Otherwise, he merely doodles on menus
And place mats and in notebooks,
Recording his solipsistic data for no one
Except the angels he suspects
Hover just above his paranoid ego.
As poet laureate of his own proprietary cosmos,
He feels entitled to indulge in verse —
His one sin, the curse of his desolation.

7/26/79   (01030)

An Accompaniment to the Rain △

All the way down,
Past Cape, Sikeston, New Madrid,
And Hayti, to Blytheville, through Memphis,
On into Oxford, off I-55,
The rain reiterated its slow, silver grief,
As though someone in the celestial order
Had encountered a reversal of fate and died.

Even the canopy beneath which I drove
Stayed as grayly fragmented
As a cubistic painting by Picasso or Braque.
No blue pools glinting with goldfish
Opened up, the entire afternoon,
While the slick road maneuvered from side to side,
To gain a better foothold on the earth.

By the time I arrived, six hours later,
The sky had cried itself out.
Streets and houses were dry, and lush growth,
Though imperceptibly dripping,
Was already slipping back into July's dryness.
Indeed, by evening, I'd forgotten
The funeral that had taken place,

In which I, as the head of the imagined cortège,
Led the procession that transported my spirit
*

From its sweet retreat among family and friends,
Out of the heart buoyant with ecstasy,
Into a land of strange faces and vacant gazes.
And on waking, I failed to recognize myself
As the dead man, lying in state, in my bed.

Even now, surrounded by white silence,
Rowan Oak's solitude disguises the nature
Of my transfiguration. Slowly, I stroll
Into the caliginous fragrance of Bailey's Woods,
Wading deeper, as into an ocean,
Until sorrow leads me home again,
To my children, my wife, rediscovered, alive.

7/27/79   (00035)

Visitation Rites ^Δ

Each year, the pilgrimage seems to increase.
Those he's touched with mere words
Come to lay praises at his grave site,
Contemplate the simplicity of his final repose,
And be sanctified or redeemed by the quietude
That emanates from this peace-pied cemetery.

Each year, I make the same journey to Oxford,
Alone, to breathe, for a few days,
The breeze and humidity, the birdsongs
And pastoral rhapsodies that still reside
In this isolated settlement
Seventeen years after his death.

It's a humble grail I quest:
To return to his modest resting place,
That I might mingle with his ghost,
Catch vagrant traces of his redolent presence
Among the white oaks standing guard,
Converse with his bones momentarily,

To reteach myself the nature of austerity
And patience, be reminded of the privacy required
For creation. Yet as I sit uncomfortably
On the cement retainer surrounding his plot,
Translating images still white-hot
From God's crucible, a car enters the cemetery,

Breaks my serene concentration. I hesitate,
Praying it will proceed and that my paean
Will be able to move toward its own conclusion,
Without conscious prodding from my intellect.
Two ladies aiming cameras assail the grave
With laughter and vague speculations

Not about eschatology, rather the natal date
Of man and wife clearly emblazoned in marble,
"Eighteen hundred and ninety-seven,"
Common to both. Snapping shutters
Chew the air, riddle the silence like bullets.
I cringe to keep from watching myself shot

And envision my image, in someone's album,
Captioned "Oddity Squatting Beside Grave
Of Celebrated Writer, William Faulkner; Caught
While Photographing Oxford's Scenic Spots."
When I turn back, they've dissolved,
Having taken with them all my poetic resolve.

7/28/79 — [1] (00067)

Thirty-Three Lines on Suicide

*Dis*location and *dis*embodiment —
Wow, how the simple, oblivious prefixes
Make all the difference to my sensibility!

My condition suffers from too-accurate definition
Of the situation that has subdued my spirit.
It's the itinerancy from which it suffers.

Words — ugh! All mere cuckolding words!
They strangle me in their adjuncts,
Tangential ramifications, and inherent symbolisms.

The etiology is easy to diagnose.
Acute pusillanimity and virulent instability
Are the causal elements of my disease.

What I need to discover is a cure
To this vexatious obsession with death,
Which wakes and beds with my restless soul.

Perhaps this is the reason I continue the quest
As a vagrant, nomad, bindle stiff
Disguised in affluent robes of a respected aesthete.

But where is my destination and when?
How much further must the bending continue,
Before the intellect, which initiates it, fragments

And the end rises, upside down,
To engage me bodily in its abysmal crypt?
Dear Mom, send me back to conception,

That forgetting need not even occur
Or my sleep and dreams and breathing
Not trouble the universe with their cursed verse,

Which stirs incessantly as a wide-throttled dynamo.
Mother dear! If you can hear me,
Answer by dematerializing my very essence

With your kiss from the moon's far side,
That I might return to my senses and survive.
Hurry, though! Suicide's dogs are barking outside.

7/28/79 — [2] (05648)

[Deep in Bazarney-Gazurns,] †

Deep in Bazarney-Gazurns,
Harp-twanging snarp
And marsupials take turns
On the belly and back of a spotted bizarrp.

7/30/79 — [1] (07280)

[Word's out that a female deer]

Word's out that a female deer
With venereal disease of the fern
Has been seeking a new career,
Seducing the hunger artist Bob Burns,

Who suffers from gynocentrism.
Such sexual delights, unspurned,
Could indeed relieve the menses
That have kept Burns's bowels in a churn.

But when the deer drew near
And lay down beneath Sir Burnkey,
He refused, in abject fear,
To return to the womb cold turnkey.

7/30/79 — [2] (01386)

Lament ^Δ

For Noel Polk, Tom McHaney, Judy Wittenberg,
Jim Carothers, Jim G. Watson, Michael Millgate

This return journey is especially bereft,
Whose unspectacled exit from Oxford
Was accomplished, like its arrival,
In diametrical aloneness. I grieve,
On taking to the road again.

Dislocated and absolved of the camaraderie
Which, during the week just dissolved,
Grew, like violent ivy,
Out of the fertile minds of disparate lives
Conjoined by a sublimely common passion,

I grieve over the inconstant paradigm
That shapes my clay into unfinished pieces
Displayed day after day.
The constant rearranging of my soul
Has rendered memory prone to forgetting faces,

Gentle sensualities, and intellectual distillations
Molded out of silence and light,
Waiting to reach my ears and eyes,
My entire inspired vitality. I grieve
For the love I've left in my friends' safekeeping,

Not knowing when, if ever again,
We'll gather each other into each
Other's blood, set our beating hearts
In synchronous wonderment, touch the source
Of youth's musical exuberance.

I can only surmise, from our reluctance to part,
Our inchoate yet overt remorse
On witnessing our rosary unbead
A sigh at a time, that joy is infinite
And dying a mere detail for the mind to delegate

To its fleshly subordinates. Still, I weep
As my spirit flies homeward,
Through a quietude suffused with epiphanies,
Knowing that our laughter and ribaldry and pride
Desert us as we return to ourselves.

8/3/79 — [1] (03548)

The Joggers ^Δ

*For Tom McHaney
and Noel Polk*

Not like wild geese
Fleeing their back-winging shadows,
Rather as exhilarated phantoms
Do we soar, in liberated cadence,
Through the heart's Bailey's Woods
Each morning, before the world awakens
To our crazy, insatiable stirrings.

We run as one, we three,
In unassailed camaraderie,
Partaking of the cool, dense-scented solitude,
Whose profuse trees admit the shafted sun,
Like slanted, argentiferous rain,
Through hidden openings. We run
Under a mist of sweat and heated breath

Exiting like ecstasies emanating from heaven,
Our flesh pressed to its limits.
Yet there's no oppressiveness
Where the dialectical essence of friendship
Repulses fatigue's ubiquitous incursions.
The woods' mesmeric sea changes
Anesthetize pain, as we reach into reserves

To rediscover the nature and the depth
Of our volition, until, in luxuriant apotheosis,
Rowan Oak materializes through the cedars
And waxy magnolias. Arrival is sweet cessation.
No matter how transitory, the moment
Satisfies the sum of our individual years.
We revel in the silent Greek edifice,

Before turning and reentering the slumberous aura,
Whose mud-spongy paths are the labyrinth
We must traverse before our day begins.
Deeper and more heavily with each step,
Our bodies wade the leafy ocean
That tugs at us, begs us surrender
To its insinuations. We resist, reminding ourselves

That the finish is just a matter of distance,
While quitting prematurely is the denial of pride
And fidelity to an ideal principle of discipline
We each thrive on and share.
Suddenly, the end invites us into daylight.
Three phantoms, purged and transcendent,
Emerge as one, brothers unto the universe.

8/3/79 — [2] (00062)

In for Tests

Once again, the terrific pace
Dissipates in inexorable, languishing postures.
Sedentary paranoia establishes its grasp
On the immobilized psyche, caught up short
By the nature of impending doom.

In this tiny waiting room,
The ears are assailed by fan motors
From vending machines, migraine humming
Of fluorescent ballasts, and whispers
Sibilant and unceremonious and hysterical.

The possibilities are so palpably exponential.
Our fragile designs, complex and magnificent
As da Vinci sketches, are confined
To a few basic rubrics and paradigms.
Tumors, occlusions, aneurysms have no bounds.

Yet we press ahead hourly, daily,
Until encountering the inescapable essence
Of our mortality. Even then, we vehemently refuse
To be subdued by flying viruses
And malign bacteria. We temporize,

Vacillate, imagine ourselves invincible,
Inaccessible up to the last moment,
*

When the diagnosis is rendered,
The truth deduced beyond doubt's shadow,
And the hourglass is reversed for the final time.

Having submitted to brain scan,
X-rays, blood-taking,
And the giving up of urine samples,
My wife returns from the land
Patrolled and commanded by lunar people.

Like desiccated coleus and dusty miller
Wilting in an outdoor flower bed,
We wait for the results, numb, befuddled,
Fearful of letting our minds run free
Through fantasy's poppied valleys.

The passing hours forget us,
Leave us to console the grieving silence
With our own melancholia.
Word-strands that once supported the bridge
Connecting our thoughts buckle.

Suddenly, a uniform of white nylon and cotton,
White shoes, white socks —
An alabaster statue — materializes before us,
Gestures us to its nearby room,
For consultation with the powers that be.

We pass through the walls,
Following its spectral directions down halls
Without doors or windows, odorless
Except for faint suggestions of Lysol, alcohol,
And death-whiffs filtering down from vents.

My wife chases the gleaming white aura
Until it dissolves into a thin nimbus,
Partaking of outside air
And carbon dioxide hovering at the edges,
Where her lungs do their exchanging.

Without warning, I'm left by myself,
Listening to her gentle suspirations
Grow further and further and further apart,
Until breath is oblivion's echo,
Resonating in my head, and death its pulse.

8/9/79 (02254)

Manic-Depressive

My paradoxical heart
Soars, this rain-misty morning,
When few spirits would dare venture out.
Why it chooses such gloomy weathers
To enact its ritualistic ecstasies
Is inscrutable, yet it's a condor,
Audacious and indomitable,
Wheeling above sleep's lingering yawns,
In smoothly maneuvered Immelmanns
That move, without noticeable volition,
Into hammerhead stalls
Accompanied by earthward plummeting
So preposterous that vision explodes.

Perhaps something its keen sight
Has spotted way out and far below
Motivates its quest, urges flight
Beyond the limits of its own metaphysics.
Suddenly, its wing tips fully extended
Between invisible sun and moon,
Its furious blood surging to the ends
Of every tributary in its system,
The great bird that transports me
In its clutches dives for a final time
And lets me drop out of the sky,
Into a thorny patch of abandoned realities.
Preying on itself, my heart bleeds to death.

8/11/79 — [1] (05649)

The Nixonian Legacy: A Crisis in Confidence

His words go up in a thin line
And diverge like atoms
In a linear accelerator. They explode,
With vicious volatility,
Against vulnerable ears, spray grapeshot
In every direction, penetrating spaces
Shaped like human minds,
Before lies entomb their echoes.

Yet they're pesty flies
Buzzing at the twitching ears of an elephant,
Who hears the universe's pulse
In its pounding footbeats, without fearing
The consequences of morality and consciousness.
Although his contumelious discharges
Scatter and miss the mark,
Their stark reports perforate the air,

Allowing logic and conventional wisdom
To trail off in vaporous convolvuluses
Approximating odorless factory gases.
His exhortations for peace, his pleas
For brotherly love among obdurate peoples
And Arch-ie Bunker enemies dueling in the same house
Are blanks no one heeds. They've caused
Too many false starts already.

8/11/79 — [2] (05650)

Passing Through △

As I pass through this farm country,
Advertisements inscribed on porcelain road signs
And lithographed on trade cards
Made by the firms of Strobridge and Currier & Ives
Surface from the 1880s,
Flooding my anachronistic mind.

I see De Laval cream separators,
Pears' soaps and Castle stove-black images,
Ayer's sarsaparilla slogans, and threads
By Coats & Clark and Corticelli
Converging out of another generation,
Colliding with 1979,

And I gasp from the strange sensation
Of déjà vu that begs me stop,
Take note of changes, progress,
The state of grace a hundred years of solitude
Have preserved for the inhabitants now living
In these same clapboard houses I pass.

I recall how the corn,
In a rife year, would crowd us out,
*

Use up all available space,
Right up to our back door, displace silence
With its own sibilances on windy days,
Speak its private vocabulary of growth,

While all we could do was pray
That its dread coevals —
Storms, flash floods, and droughts —
Would fail to materialize, leave us be,
Yet one more season, before fate
Remembered to include us in its strategy.

I can remember how the beans,
In their infinite, stolid plenitude,
Brooding, like roosting hens,
Under the endless summer suns,
Would yield to the slightest weeds,
Give supplely to our harvest scythes.

Now, as I pass, it seems to me
That people wandering about in yards,
Milling on Main Streets in each town
My journey takes me through,
Are waving to me, inviting me back home,
To a heritage my ancestors knew intimately.

I almost recognize their blank faces,
See myself in their fleeting stares.
Only, my momentum keeps me from lingering
To speak, inquire of my birthright and relatives.
Regrettably, death won't let me get in touch
With my bones. Even my dust belongs to others.

8/15/79   (05419)

Bud △

For my dear friend
Bud Herzog

At thirty-eight ripe years,
I've returned to the silver poplars and birch,
Fleshed white as icicles
Glistering in the sun, and to the pines,
Whose deep-green conical designs
Define my spired reverence toward nature
In this Wisconsin of the mind.

I surrender my citified dissatisfactions,
With happiness, forget my ambitions
And tendentiousness, without argument.
The oak aroma of wood smoke
Lifting into cool, blue evanescence
Takes my spirit beyond its inhibitions.
The exuberant child my heart outgrew emerges,

First as shadow, as breeze, bird,
Chipmunk, then as chubby little boy
Innocent of clichés and franchise mentalities,
Absolved of imperatives to succeed
In material and professional terms.
Youth's untrammeled ignorance
Adopts me, as I sit listening to the sky.

It tempts and taunts me with heady desires
To retire to this sylvan wilderness
For the remainder of my ordained life,
To be a poet of pine needles
And cricket choiring, fate's surrogate,
In charge of changes in the weather,
Mastermind of my own bodily orb.

Only, the realities conspire against my lark,
And it's too far to travel,
To get back to the start before dark.
With words, I pen this gentle lament
For my children to sing to their offspring
When God quits whispering in my ears.
It's the closest thing to freedom I've achieved.

8/19/79   (00017)

[All this August day,] ‡

All this August day,
I've listened to the rain dripping persistently,
In slow, sibilant lisps,
Through the leaves. It speaks to me
An ancient liturgy of lovers trysting
In verdurous gardens dark and deep
And of poets rehearsing a thousand words,
*

To construct the few simple verses
Their breathing starts for their hearts to complete.

Its silver voice is a slender villanelle
Sleeping naked beside the Lethe,
A troubadour performing minstrelsy on panflutes

8/22/79   (05651)

Satan's Expulsion from Heaven

His words pour forth
In boring cascades of commonplace liturgy
Gleaned and memorized from his reading
Of those in vogue. An independent thinker,
He prides himself on ideas
First seen and heard on TV commercials,
Predigested, as it were,
Which his spongelike psyche,
With unerring mastery over phonetics
And syntax, transmutes into new propaganda
For the masses, to whom he preaches.
In his recently anointed position
As leader of his people, he is circumspect,
Deferential, saccharine as marzipan.
He chucks babies' cheeks, works the confessional
Twice a week, at the singles bar
Just down the street, and writes poetry
In the vein of Rod McKuen,
Over whose flimflam stanzas
His entire mind-body apparatus is dismantled.
Only when he returns to his room,
After each day of being listened to
By admirers and sycophants currying his favor,
Does he annihilate the disguise,
By reaching inside the mirror
And wiping away the desiccated facial flesh,
With his preternatural screaming.
Only when the immutable silence of bachelorhood
Absorbs his crying does he find release,
Through gross onanistic manipulation,
Whose hot, brief ejaculate turns to dust
*

Before his eyes. In a final seething,
He dives through sleep's hymen
And lands in the mind's dark recess
Crowded with nameless skeletons.

Slowly, inexorably, a gnashing of gears
Brings down the sun-colored blade
That guillotines night, severs the succubi,
Who have delayed too long
In making their escape from his trepidation.
He wakens like a volcano,
Raging, in shuddering numbness, his name,
As if to resurrect it from forgetting
And have it invite him back inside.
Within a matter of cigarettes and caffeine
Sucked directly out of freeze-dried coffee
He prefers to chew, rather than brew,
To soothe his acute nervous intellect,
He's alive, spewing the mystical ideograms,
Prophetic conundrums, and poeticisms
That have made him famous
In his own frangible estimation.

Only, this morning, no audience arrives,
And he knows in an instant
That the night through which he just passed
Saw him die, cradled him in its shroud,
Without so much as a redolence of death.
With an effort, he begins reciting McKuen,
To see if he might elicit some response
From the ubiquitous silence. But his breath,
Leaking from his self-imposed caesuras,
Inflates the vacuum in which he floats,
As dust begins to collect, like rust, on his bones.

9/7/79   (05652)

An Autumnal

For Hayden Carruth

Like the edges of bird feathers,
This Septembering air
Is tinged with a definite hint of change
And rich mysteriousness.

I sniff its crisp morning chill;
Wisconsin fills my nostrils.
My eyes become chipmunks
Foraging for memories of summer's events,
To hoard against imminent winter,

While the autumnal equinox,
Like a star-crazed tatterdemalion
Hitchhiking into oblivion,
Evanesces in gentle, sugary opaques.

Even my opalescent children
Have exceeded, too quickly,
The velocity of vision and insight,
As though the days passed
Were compressed in a necromancer's wand

Waved over their growth,
To show them the passage back to God.
I turn toward the mirror of my thoughts
For a reflection, an echo, and I balk.

The visage in the glass is the Harpy,
On a fence, stiff and stark black
Except for the edges of its feathers,
Which are tinged with the ocherous scent
Of someone, nearby, waiting to die.

9/8/79 (00113)

Incarnations of the Ancient Mariner

For my blessed, precious Jan,
who dreads every voyage I make

My vessel clears its slip.
As though they were spots in my gaze,
Clothed ghosts, pacing remorsefully
Along the quays, erase themselves
From visibility, by waving to me.

The shore recedes. Sea and sky
Form two sides of a vise,
Squeezing it into a slice of both.
Forgetting supports my ship,
Floats my soaring spirit toward the moon,

Anomalously conspicuous, against the azure,
In morning's northernmost corner.
Unconsciously, with sextant and astrolabe,
I take readings, satisfy my psyche
That the heading's correct for reaching Euphoria,

Then settle back into the wind's embrace
And wait for Satan's annealing ravishment
To subjugate my senses to endless gratification.
Only, the day lengthens inexorably,
Without temporal demarcations

Or suggestion that stars might appear,
To obliterate the monotony of so much freedom.
Suddenly, my sweet, opiate amnesia
Diminishes to cerebral pulsation.
Loneliness and guilt tie me to the mast,

As the hold takes on water
And the ship begins to list,
Disappearing, by half-lives, before my eyes.
In a last-ditch attempt to save myself,
I snap the bindings gyving my spirit,

Crying, repenting the obsession
That ever convinced me to leave home,
And leap into the maelstrom
Nightmare has caused to inundate sleep.
Rising through darkness, to the surface,

I reach for a spinning spar
Thrown free from the sinking vessel
And, holding on for dear, dear life,
Discover that it's my wife's slender arm,
Which her startled waking has cast in my direction.

9/10/79 — [1] (05653)

A Midwestern Cincinnatus at the Plow △

In this second autumn
Of my little son, Troika,
I'm stunned to numbness
By the amazing changes taking place.

Already, he's harvested a hundred words,
Tilled and reseeded his fields,
A thousand times, with new habits,
Concepts, coordinations between eyes,
Brain, nerves, muscles, and mind-designs.

In this season of epiphanies,
When the optic chiasma
Prefers seeing hopgrassers and flutterbies
To their inverted coevals

And the perceptual key to the moon's
Fragile visibility, day and night,
Is awareness perpetually heightened
Through the poetry of inner vision,
My boy matures under an abundant sun.

At the edge of his great climacteric,
My wife and I stand back and watch,
As he surveys the lay of the land,
And speculate on the success of his futures.

His is an innocence so sublime
We don't dare disturb the silence
By prophesying famine's seven lean eras,
Which wisdom whispers in our ears,
Rather rejoice as he stores up the years.

9/10/79 — [2] (01441)

The Runner

For Greg Goodmon

The legs pain with insane exhilaration,
As accumulating laps are recorded
In sweat beads exploding continuously
All over his straining body.
His heavy breathing is a sculptor's chisel
Hacking waste from a stratum around the heart,
Until it releases, from within, an Athenian
Pacing naked in his own Olympiad.

Fantasies pester him like flies,
In antic capriciousness, teasing, taunting,
*

Threatening to dissipate his concentration,
Break his stride, chase him off the track,
Where the day's jackals bark and growl.
Yet his dedication is too resolute
To be violated by common prostitutions.

One by one by one,
The ovals open before his running physique,
Then close in the dust, as he goes ahead,
Hoping that his lithe feet,
Like lips kissing the cinders, in rhythmic whispers,
Will wear away the rim of the urn
He envisions himself perpetually circumscribing.

In a final surge of speed, he turns
And converges on the predetermined finish line.
Purging every energized molecule from his blood,
He crashes through the barrier
Separating fatigue from gratification, and collapses,
As his palpitating shadow turns to twilight.
Only his winged soul lingers
To celebrate a victory over its bones.

9/10/79 — [3] (02147)

Unravished Bride of Quietude

Having entered the track, at different intervals,
From out of the vast, fathomless masses
And keeping a similar but spaced pace,
Like a voice being shadowed by its own echo,
We surrender to the oval's ceaseless embrace

And are assimilated by our very routines.
In between breaths, which, at first,
Come effortlessly, my imagination
Is given free run to exercise its gaze
On her lean, antelope legs, willowy body,

And brunette hair, haloed by the breeze.
The attractiveness of her lithe physique
Renders me weightless. Her graceful kinesis
Sets up before me a slipstream,
Into whose timeless persuasion I'm drawn

Without either advancing on her speeding shape
Or retreating a solitary step. Our motion
Is no mere rejection of stasis;
Rather, it's two moving shadows
Standing still in their immutable refusal

To break away from each other or be seduced
By fatigue. For the duration of the fantasy,
My dreaming locates this nameless beauty
And me in a fragile Keatsian reverie,
Until beads of accumulating sweat,

Conspiring to blur her design on the urn
We turn with each completion of the course,
Shatter my delusion of attaining immortal perfection.
Awareness of my growing deterioration
Forces me to abort visions of chaste lovers

Forever entranced by the nature of their chase.
In a final, gasping blast of pain,
I pass the lady who's sustained me
For twelve laps and collapse in the grass,
Without even a furtive glance from her.

9/12/79   (02549)

Interminable Journey

For three days, I've boated on Limbo,
Returned, each night, to a port
On one of its many anonymous shores,
To recollect what's left of my identity.

Only, nothing being familiar
Except my dirty socks and underwear,
Left strewn where I threw them off
As I raced to beat exhaustion to bed

The previous evening, I ponder the past
For trivia or sentimental images
To resurrect from forgetting, that I might rest
For a few moments, catch my breath,

Remind myself that solitude is finite
And loneliness a mere figmental mirage
*

That dissolves in sleep's dark dreams.
Memory refuses to prostitute herself

By relinquishing her prized visions
Without recompense, and my bankrupt soul
Knows that it's too late for old charms
And dissimulations that once functioned

To assist it in fabricating self-justifications
For leaving home with such frequency
And for staying away so inexcusably long.
Soon, I'll resume the interminable rowing motion

That has kept my momentum flowing
These last seven years,
Despite the absence of navigation instruments
Or an updated set of maps to follow.

My destination, although perfectly clear
Through the obfuscating daily fogs
And heat inversions my brain endures,
Grows less plausible, almost irretrievable,

As the glistening surface that bears my weight,
Like disappearing ink on a cosmic blotter,
Spreads mercilessly over the remaining islets
I once relied on as refuge from storms.

Just now, I hesitate to exit my room,
Turn in the key, settle my bill, leave
Without at least phoning home.
Only, in limbo, the circuits are always busy.

9/13/79   (05654)

A Bovine Fog $^\Delta$

Everywhere, bilious corn
Awaits, with desiccated impatience,
Its transmogrification
Into silage, trough feed, feces,
And fertilizer for the neighboring earth.

A hazy, vaporous fog
Grazes over the landscape
In bucolic, Inness-like solitude,
*

This autumnal dawn,
Numbly munching the brittle stalks.

Over hills, around every curve,
I encounter herd after herd,
Whose ubiquitous existence
Forces me to modify my speed,
Reevaluate the need for being punctual.

Each tentative confrontation I make
Elicits a corresponding retreat.
Even my headlights, like electric prods,
Refuse to clear a path through the confusion,
For my vision to take. Soon, the mooing fog

Is bellowing. I try to outrace my fear
Of being trampled underfoot
By the stampeding fantasy I've let escape
The unmended fences of my imagination.
Only, it nudges me off the road.

9/18/79 (05418)

An Early-Morning Journey in Late September

Dead ahead,
Incredible shafts of fog-fused sun
Funnel into the paved valley
Through whose convolutions
My solitudinous quest projects me.

I gaze into its vaporous moil,
Deluded into seeking
A trace of my former self-portrait
Still etched on its wet plate,
Yet forgetting has misplaced the image.

Only its autumnal edges,
Curling in on vision,
From each side of the highway,
Retain a faint outline
Of my once-recognizable features.

Meanwhile, the miles in between
Metamorphose into ghosts,
Whose bones I pulverize,
*

As the motion of this final drive
Lulls me slowly, slowly home.

9/25/79 (05655)

Antiphons Sung Among the Dead ^Δ

Once again, in slow abnegation,
The photosynthetic sugars coalesce,
Spurn growth, sacrifice their souls
To brief, prismatic ecstasy
Consisting of metamorphosing cells
Exploding in October's collective resurrection.

Tenuous and fragile,
Each leaf comes ungyved
From its desiccated twig, limb, tree
And tumbles even as it rises,
Whose downward spiral
Describes nature's ancient ritual of agony.

All the while, from my nervous vantage
Located midway between the eyes
And ears, I sense God's presence
Appearing in the material world,
Am aware of apotheosis on the air,
Epiphanies of russet, umber, mustard, and burgundy.

Yet I also know
That this magnificent climacteric
Is actually a vast, passionate crescendo
To the coda of a rhapsody composed not for me
But for those who've died
And savor hopes of returning again.

10/1/79 (05656)

Beyond the Shadow of a Doubt

Seated among old oak, mahogany,
And walnut pieces — hall trees,
Graphophones, pier mirrors, and chiffoniers —
His spirit begins to disappear.

The very aura of antiquity and dust
Rustles, like a prairie wind
Winnowing through an isolate Kansas night,
Within his mesmerized mind-eyes.

Subtle transmutations
Reincarnate his heart. It stutters,
As though desirous of speaking,
Before lapsing into silence, with its secret.

He's borne, into death,
On the jet stream his breath leaves behind,
As heat seeps from his pores
And his invisible essence penetrates oblivion.

Suddenly, vague music intercepts his escape.
It severs forgetting, like scissors,
Changing Scripture into twin forevers.
He remembers his name, his purpose and destination.

His return occurs in a solitary eye-blink,
An imperceptible twitch. Life is his wife,
Slender as a lambent candle,
Naked and wet, whispering him to love's bed.

Entranced, he anxiously obliges her shadow,
Follows through endless penumbras,
Until, inside her writhing primal designs,
His flown spirit revives in fevered climax.

Finally, the entire hallucination
(If, in truth, his delusion is such)
Disintegrates. He awakens, among brass,
Slag glass, and marble-topped filigree,

To a midnight illumination from a moon
Never before seen in such lucid gibbousness.
Beside him, still nude as a statue,
Lies the outline of his wife's shadow.

By dawn, even her silhouette
Will have dissolved, and in its place
Will shimmer the last traces of the dream
That made him believe his phoenix might rise.

10/4/79 (00690)

The Drift of Things △

Nature's patience has run its course.
Gravity demands prismatic sacrifice,
To keep its appetite satisfied.
In dazzling sarabands the leaves descend.
All along West Columbia Street,
Swaying patriarchs,
Like slings flinging winged shot,
Release their weights to the breeze.

My wincing eyes cannot quite accommodate
To such stinging ecstasy,
Nor the ears differentiate death's groan
From the singing of flown, transcendent things.
Instead, like an attendant pallbearer,
Stranded in this middle zone
Composed of brittle husks, stunted grass, and shadows,
I bury the passing season, without complaint.

Suddenly, a lingering butterfly,
Clinging precipitously to a weathered cider press
And to the edge of its own waning existence,
Beneath this cool, too-blue sky,
Ignites my senses to shame, as it soars
And mingles among the fluttering leaves,
Proclaiming its birthright,
Asserting, with grace and beauty, its delicate independence.

10/6/79 (00142)

Deathbed

The sheets of the etherized patient dissolve,
Leaving gray-naked morning
Resting questionably in night's deathbed.
Her cold pallor and acrid odor,
Redolent of smoky, smoldering leaves
And bodies bulldozed into hungry maws,
Congest my nose. My inner eyes are lachrymose
From the frost memory has broadcast,
In her blind fury, to eradicate the past
And insure the new season
Against threats from the heart's intrusion.

Slowly, I awaken to a vague awareness
Of my location and why I've come
All this way to pay my last respects,
Veil my maladroit condolences
In benedictions to the nonexistent future:
It's my soul, not October,
That has beckoned me to its side.
It, not the leaves or grass or sun,
Is fading ineluctably. In fear,
My imagination recoils from the grotesque vision
Of its own body withering into silence.

10/12/79 — [1] (05657)

Infestation

Like termites, they surface
From the Missouri woodwork,
To escape dry confinement
Their minds have actively sought
Without realizing a thirst for knowledge
Must eventually bring them down to earth.

Now, it's too late
To replace the old stone mansions
And decayed gingerbread filigree
Of Steamboat Gothic facades.
They congregate to take a vote
On how to efficaciously cut their losses,

Start from the basement up.
Someone suggests making the children
Guinea pigs, scapegoats, drones,
To build new foundations
For educating the soul in the ways of gentleness,
Seeing, loving, dreaming, devotion to friends.

Only, the kids are drugged, comatose,
Stuck to each other, like dogs
After copulation, in antic stages of fucking
For its own sake alone.
Not one offers his hand, her lips,
As a symbol of accepting the challenge of leadership,

And the stately pleasure domes collapse,
In a cascade of shattered glass and sawdust.
Soon, winter's funereal chill
Will scatter their heaped ashes,
Whose debris can barely be seen, now,
For cows and sheep grazing in solitude.

10/12/79 — [2]   (05658)

Stay of Execution

Ah, sweet, sweet October,
You delicate, agile ballerina!
How diaphanous and fragile you are,
Pirouetting across my twin stages.

Your moves form a series of beatitudes
Leaping from ecstasy to epiphany,
In a mystical synapse of sensa,
Whose brilliant fire defies Scripture.

Ah, dear lady, you are the hour
My life owns, this ephemeral moment,
The preternatural forever
My heart dreams before each beat.

Alone in this vast amphitheater,
You and I, dancer and poet,
Conspire to transcend our great mother,
Petitioning God for a stay of execution,

That our creations might persist
Despite our demise. With exultation,
I inscribe you in my unwritten lines,
While your undanced steps entrance my mind.

10/17/79 — [1]   (05659)

A Taste for Life ᐃ

Why can't they just die in silence,
Like ancient Indians and Eskimos
Offering themselves, in sacrifice to solitude,
*

In an abandoned wilderness-clearing away from the tribe
Or on an isolated ice floe?

What could be the importunate mandate
For calling attention to themselves
With such paradoxical, brilliant hues,
Making such evanescent claims
On my expectations, reawakening me

To the mystical nature of natural things?
Where else in all God's kingdom
Is there manifested a vibrancy so profound,
Just prior to death,
That time, neglecting, in sheer dazzlement,

To have itself rewound,
Bows, without shame or jealousy,
To its haughty scions, for an indefinite hour?
Is it perhaps an ineffable gesture,
A cosmic prophecy, an amen gently spoken?

Whatever their arrogant imperative
To be heard above the dry dying
And regardless of their reason for speaking out
In preposterous peacock-obviousness,
The October leaves have succeeded at persuading me

To forget petty death fetishes
I've allowed to accrete, over the years.
Desperately, I seize a leaf from a tree
And stuff it in my mouth,
To taste the fragrance of its flaming burgundy.

10/17/79 — [2] (05660)

The Road Peddler's Lament

Through dark recesses, I reach
And touch my wife's breathing aura.
Discovering her twitching lids,
My fingertips memorize visions
Swimming too near the surface of her dreams.

Even now, three hours south,
I can hear her rapid eye movements
*

Washing sleep's shores,
Where she lies naked and alone,
Hoping to awaken with me at her side.

Only, an insatiable rain
Keeps hallucination from fusing with truth,
Constrains my desires to retreat,
Return home before dawn
Confirms her premonitions of my gone spirit.

Circumscribed by a sad, silent grayness,
My soul's flown vehicle
Presses blindly ahead.
Softly she gets up and dresses,
Considerate not to disturb our separation.

10/22/79 — [1] (03585)

In absentia

> *To the memory*
> *of Al Martin,*
> *who ruled Tipton*

The windshield wipers
Keep an inessential beat
My eyes follow through the assailed glass,
Into lightning-charged ennui,

While, on the other side of the blades' half-moons,
The old man I so loved
For his anecdotes about the rag business
Waits to be lowered
And covered over with his own echo.

When I consider why my driving
Continuously takes me
Further and more irreversibly away
From his consecration, I'm stymied,

Unable to resurrect a justification
For my waywardness.
Certainly, forgetfulness is not the cause
Of my neglect. Perhaps the desire
To see him as he was in life,

Not as a disreputable effigy,
Motivates my flight
In an altogether different direction.
Maybe it's merely fear

Of seeing him disappear in the earth
That is discouraging me
From being there, in person,
Or the realization that our friendship has terminated
Keeping me from turning around.

The windshield wipers'
Furious sweep
Seems to clear my mind, by blurring the truth
Of his long-overdue demise.

I look through the half-moons
Their inessential beat describes,
For guidance, tune my ears
To it, but tears
Keep obscuring my vision.

10/22/79 — [2] (05661)

From Tiny Acorns, Poets Sometimes Grow ^Δ

For Troika's second birthday

My little boy, Troika,
Tries so hard to be a man,
By emulating every gesture, nuance, syllable
His big sister, Trilogy, postulates
In her grown-up, grandiloquent manner.

Each word he pronounces
Has special parameters and inflections
Suggestive of a Shakespearean actor.
At two, he's even mastered,
With some hesitation, "pepperoni pizza."

Nor is he inattentive
When Mr. Sneelock leaps from my lips,
Into a sponge held by Circus McGurkus,
Dick Whittington's cat
Dashes through Trilogy's imagination,

Or Cinderella's coach metamorphoses
Into a fat pumpkin,
Halfway through my animated readings,
Just before both children
Batten their hatches against sleep-demons.

In fact, he rather enjoys his status
As junior envoy and diplomat
From the state of Childish Antics and Fantasy.
He's still the tyro. His failures and accomplishments
Can be classified as conscious accidents

In an effort to control his cosmos.
Too soon, my little boy, Troika,
Will vacate his room, its space, that moment
In which his growing has been a pearl
Suspended in the gentle alembic of parental affection.

He'll enter oceanic adventures
That quickly tarnish the most lustrous gems.
Only then will he discover
Whether he possesses the gentle strength
That renders poets of mere exceptional men.

10/22/79 — [3] (01442)

Purveyor of Dead Sea Scrolls

Ah, when I consider
How nearly half my waking days
Have been spent, within this space,
Like a gravid Buddha
Interlacing aging visions of eternity
With pedestrian concerns,

And when I ponder
The sedentary nature of my contemplations,
The way they get translated,
Through word-chimes and images
Seeded in the uterine imagination
And arisen from airy, literary birth,

Into poems instead of actions
Capable of instigating others to action,
Shame changes my blood to flames
*

That tingle the ears, singe my eyes,
While feet and fingers freeze.
A valetudinarian odor invades my pores,

Forcing me to pull off the road
And cease my frenetic scribbling,
To scream at invisible demons,
Who, in apparent humorless arrogance,
Have found my doom, of having to compose
While driving, diverting and ludicrous.

In moments like these,
My composure suffers a sea change.
Psychic energy that powered my creativity
Dissolves, taking with it life-lies,
Resolves on which I depend
To keep from exposing my identity

While yet pretending
To be the Moses Maimonides of poets,
A seer, a man for all seasons.
In moments like these,
When I'm rendered immobile and empty,
I know there's no hope for success.

I recognize the tempestuous years passed
As mere satirical travesties
Of the future's insignificant morality plays,
In whose continuing role
Of wordmonger, obscurantist, ethical bastard
I'll be typecast.

It's in moments like these,
When the sad fact of my pusillanimity
Surfaces and I discover myself
Incapable of either breaking the pen
Or admitting I'm only a road peddler
Hawking flawed clothing,

That the pain and the frustration
Of trying to locate myself
Remind me I'm a scion of ragmen,
Rabbis, and Deuteronomic scribes,
A survivor of the ten tribes of Jacob
Lost as a dried-up ocean.

11/1/79 (02404)

The Doom

The earth has tilted too far
To one side, today,
For the raging sun,
Despite its blinding brightness,
To penetrate layers of November chill
That mummify my body
As I sit outside,
Hunched over a wrought-iron table,
Weaving silence into silent sounds.

Whether from unpredictable swirlings
Nurtured by quick, fickle breezes
Or squirrels scampering, in hasty jubilation,
Through scratchy shadows,
The dead leaves speak derisively of their fate.
Why, I question,
Do I have to be at their beck,
Submit to their deathbed confessions,
And suggest reasons for their collective deposition?

I am no Christ, no Nietzsche;
No dazzling rhetorician or theologian am I.
Why have my eyes been designated
Morticians, gravediggers, and pallbearers
For these sad, disreputable waifs?
Why am I supposed to compose odes,
Propose tracts on epistemology
And the mystical existence of reincarnation
Of spirits patently incorporeal,
Create verse worthy of Milton's "Lycidas"?

Can't the genius of creation and change
Be its own simple justification?
And is it being too presumptuous to proclaim
My own basic disinclination
To be seer, creator, and recorder of deeds?
Just once, let me enter the world
Without having to describe it.
Let me sit and grow cold, in silence,
While trees defoliate. Let silence thrive.

11/3/79 (05662)

A Justification for Living

Doubtless, regret for the passing season
Has brought me outdoors,
This afternoon, to see for myself
The metamorphosis at hand

And to speculate on its progress.
Possibly I have hesitated,
In venturing an appraisal, from trepidation,
Suspecting an irreversible fate,

Whose mandate requires complete subservience
By rendering the intellect impotent
And inessential in the face of change.
Perhaps I've remained disengaged,

Until now, for reasons unexplainable
Except to the imagination,
Which, somehow, can cope with finalities
When left to its investigations.

Fear, regret, sheer contrariness,
When forced to accept endings gracefully,
Have all conspired
To connect me with November's shadows,

Bring me in touch with undomesticated spirits
Who bear no grudges,
Harbor no malignities, evidence a dignity
Worthy of sainted souls, even in death.

They make me respect this spartan way
For which my heart has striven,
This blind acceptance of the call
That has given my glutted senses

The messianic goal of one day achieving
Total liberation from air and water,
To thrive in silent, unmetaphored isolation,
Like a monk devoted to otherworldliness.

Yet once outside, I realize
Why I've been assailed by failure
To abide with this attitude of insignificance
Inanimate things have toward existence:

It's the poet in me
Who, with vehement abnegation,
Refuses to be sundered or subjugated
By physical limitations,

Who prefers to pity the leaves
Their pervasive decay, the trees
Their bereavement, the season its demise;
And it's the poet in me

Who desires to celebrate his own tenuousness
In relation to nature
By inspiring in others
A reverence of tragedy paltry and great.

11/4/79   (02148)

Millenniums*

Sweet memories
Dance around our heads
Like radiant fall leaves
Swirling in the wind.

Then time ceases.

We settle to the ground,
In dead forgetting.
Another season,
Another generation decay.

[Poem written with Jan Brodsky]

11/5/79   (02132)

Cold Spill

A gray, arctic tincture
Slowly leaks across the sky,
As though a careless god
Knocked a cosmic bottle of winter
Off its shelf.

The spill spreads inexorably,
Congeals, at intervals,
*

On the horizon, as cloud-clots
That dot the eyes with holes,
Shadow the heart

With chiaroscuroed sadness,
Cause summer's easy breathing
To lapse, erratically,
Into rapid, painful gasps,
Until the chill fills the atmosphere.

Beneath the turgid, murky surface,
Lives squirm
Inside air pockets in the ice;
Spirits yearn for freedom
To exercise, burn with desire

To break out, take flight,
Walk on water.
But the stiff joints click,
In arthritic cadences;
Flaccid ligaments cramp.

The arctic mantle refuses to give
At its ubiquitous edges and center,
While those trapped by the floe
Transmogrify. The god
Doesn't even notice the broken vial.

11/6/79   (02133)

Cohabitation

When Forgetting stops, Memory begins.
— Thomas Hobbes

His trammeled psyche exits sleep,
In the tortured shape of one raw yawn
Attenuated to tensile breaking.

Night's dross settles to the sheets,
Like chalk dust,
While cold fingers erase his eyes.

Ideas of order materialize,
As the bones rise — twin specters
Nimbused by a similar human franchise.

Socks, shoes, wrist watch
Begin to move exclusive of his body.
The air assumes his will,

Fills the room with invisible presentiments
That a nude ghost
Is about to leave its tomb.

An unexpected sun
Explodes his numb brains.
They flow through the lymph nodes,

Like grapeshot, metastasizing.
His startled skeleton
Discovers its shadow scattered across the grass.

He has had an awakening, a revelation,
And now, in a solitary glimpse,
The ancient impasse dissolves.

He recognizes the black stranger,
The Ethiop of his bad dreams,
As the back half of his imagination,

That fraction of his mentality
That dictates the felonious actions
Of demons and serpents and fiendish creatures

Who writhe and coil behind his pupils.
Suddenly, the Prince of Lies
Disappears inside a cloud of doubt.

Forgetting is the disguise
By which he nets his better image,
Who calls himself poet, teacher, scribe.

11/13/79   (05663)

Spider and Flier

Once again,
I'm temporarily brought up short
By metaphors,
Forced to contemplate my surroundings.

This time,
Track lights, anodized air ducts
*

The size of whale intestines,
Plush rugs, tinted-glass windows,

And hidden, distant voices
Fix me like a pinned insect
In a display case.
My suspicious eyes twitch,

Focus on a "System Route Map"
Fastened to a room divider.
They're mesmerized,
Caught in its mazy net of looping lines

Connecting dots framed by names.
Caracas, Maracaibo,
Jackson, St. Louis, San Diego
Tangle and frustrate my imagination,

Sunder me with wanderlust
I can't possibly consummate,
For the routine schedule of my flight.
The mind-spider claims its victim.

11/15/79 — [1] (05664)

Taking Leave

The winged vessel surges ahead,
Enters the winds,
Singing an ancient evocation of dreams.

Like an ode's invocation to the Muse,
It lifts, soars free
Of earth-shackling gravities,

And casts a shadow
That telescopes continuously inward,
As it nears destiny's altitude.

Powered by its own momentum,
Floating on inspiration alone,
It disappears in a nimbus

Exempt from quotidian geometries,
Moves among deities,
Outside existential lines of force.

Eidolons, like northern lights,
Arrive, shimmer for a while, expire,
And are supplanted by newer dimensions,

Until the fires wane
And, in a daring leap of creativity,
Engines discharge their final thrust.

The plane climaxes into silence,
At runway's end.
Poet and poem are home safe.

11/15/79 — [2] (05665)

Positive and Negative

Last-minute leaves and birds
Scurry through November's winds,
Sinuous, nervous, and worried
That, without a minute's warning,
Winter will reverse its spurious warm polarity
And obliterate them.

                    I also wait
For the shock to short-circuit my current,
Turn my juices to acid,
Burn the veins to chars,
Ulcerate the brain's arteries,
Snap the synapses, like twigs in a storm.

Meanwhile, the cerebral machinery
Works flawlessly,
And my anatomy's intricate apparatus
Experiences no disruptions
To its network's main trunks,
Substations, and low-voltage conduits.

Even the sleeping grass
Seems to throb with greenness.
Trees despoiled by a draconian autumn
Glow with an incandescent halo,
Under the sun's abundance.
Nature's dynamo is in scintillant phase.

Whether this interlude lasts,
By passing beyond absolute fact,
*

To poetic truth,
Or passes into lasting disrepute,
By attaching itself to formulaic science,
Remains to be decided.

           For the hour, anyhow,
Fears of being stranded by shifting blizzards,
Having our power abruptly cut,
Witnessing our own freezing,
Electrify our skepticism,
Inveigh against an easy acceptance of design.

11/19/79 (05666)

The Drowning

The ship I sail, tonight,
Is white silence.
My solitude
Is raging Ahab's solitary confinement.

Baleful and demonic, I'm driven
Past the moon's edge, then back,
To traffic among foaming ghosts
Vomited by an epileptic ocean.

Loneliness is a saw-toothed fish
Of colossal design,
A finned set of fears
Circling interminably in my mind's wake,

Waiting for the first mistake
To occur in my rigging
Or navigation by dead reckoning,
Before striking, mutilating my tiny spirit.

The narrow bunk, hung from beams
Connecting the gunwales,
Creaks with each pitch and recovery,
Sunders sleep,

Keeps the numb libido awake
To fantasies its depravity has sustained.
But staying awake
Is just one more form of death,

As is dreaming,
For the person chased by demons
Breathing Hiroshimaed defeats,
Spitting arsenic-tipped apocalypses,

And death, at best,
Is merely the least monumental excuse
For prolonging the solitude
That accompanies uprootedness.

Suddenly, the vessel lurches
As if it has hit a drifting iceberg.
The shudder shivers my bones.
My lungs fill with brine.

The listing begins.
My *Flying Enterprise* is gripped in futility,
As the mast to which I'm tied
Slips out of sight,

Beneath the moon's reflection on my eyes,
And disappears in white silence.
Soon, the surface is whole again,
Implacably passive, at peace with creation.

11/20/79   (05667)

Willy's First Call of the Day

His disreputable station wagon
Sags like a swayback nag
Navigating the same old pasture
From clump to clump.

Once again, his load surrounds him.
He is a minuscule face
In a medieval fresco,
Arrested in sempiternal pain,

Whose halo and robes
Are made of flawed clothing
He must dispose of today
If he's to break even against draw.

The market's soft, he grieves,
And beneath his breath,
*

He bemoans the gods
Who've left him to fend for himself

And cope with a mere fistful
Of ragtags and bobtails —
Mistakes made by ladies
Sewing wrinkles into their years,

Machines gone crazy
Without anyone noticing them,
Computers silently miscalculating
Skewed human input.

Ultimately, it all sifts
Through inspectors' couponed scrutiny
And collects like sediment
At the base of a cesspool he drains

Twice each month to survive
The rising costs of dying alive.
Suddenly, despite a bright sun,
He shivers inside his heaving vehicle

As though a breath of stale death
Had blown over his neck.
His peripheral vision locates interlopers,
Dressed in his reject garments,

Jeering and chiding as, undeterred,
He nears his destination,
Just across the river,
Directly under Phlegethon bridge.

11/30/79 (02403)

Sun-dered

My leaving coincides with,
And is marked by, twilit auguries:
The ticking ubiquity of a kitchen clock;
Dusk-to-dawn mercury-vapor lamps
Flickering into eerie dissolve;
A community's vacant streets
Repeating, in each of their dioramas,
The shape of a peeping, sleazy voyeur
Prying on ancestral emptiness.

Why these three talismans
Have piqued my prescience,
Allowed me to single them out
For recognition
(As if concrete description,
Mixed with a tinge of the metaphorical,
Might somehow release mystical secrets)
Is inscrutable, yet death
Is their common denominator.

And as I drive this highway,
That same primal sun,
Risen, now, from its cave, finds me
Trying to escape my premonitions.
Evasive actions can't stave off
Its blinding single-mindedness.
The remainder of my journey
Is an endless burning,
Sempiternal punishment for a failure of courage.

12/7/79 (05668)

A Road Peddler's Lament ^Δ

Only now,
After I've driven two hours,
By dead reckoning,
Through night's dense dimensionlessness,
Do my eyes grudgingly accommodate to dawn.

Memories of yesterday's child-play —
Our histrionic backyard gamboling,
Capers, and antic verbalizations —
Fade into the obscurity
My momentum rapidly outdistances.

Only my shadow
Is catapulted through roseate space,
Toward forgetting and resignation,
To a more pragmatic articulation
Of quotidian nonpoetics.

Hastily I take a last glance back,
To regather the scattered sparks.
*

Their glow forms dust motes,
Effervescent bubbles
Running over from the sun's tilted cup.

In their shimmering parallax,
Evocations of your golden faces,
Troika, Trilogy, and Jan,
Are haloed Ghiberti-children
Repousséed on the chalice from which my intellect sips.

Thirst, this early morning,
Seizes my eyes insatiably.
They reach for a goblet of God's sweet Chablis
And linger in its bouquet.
Intoxicated with thoughts of you three —

My family, waiting,
Waiting for me, the savior of your aspirations,
To return home safe —
I taste your melancholia all day,
While my frangible spirit wrangles with fate.

12/10/79 — [1] (01443)

Starry, Starry Night

For Atlantis —
Bob and Irene Volpe

This night through which I travel
Is diamond-flecked.
It shimmers with scintillating lambency,
As if every asteroid
And moon-jeweled planet
Had achieved ignition at the same moment.

My eyes penetrate the density,
With easy equanimity.
I am the only ghost on the road
At this godly hour.
Memory works its own meteor shower
On my silent contemplations.

Evocations of Tipton's Masonic cemetery
Telescope time etched in sandstone,
*

Crumbling inexorably. I am all the dead
Who've ever turned to moss
On the shaded sides of gravestones,
Beneath snow and slow-blown rain.

I am their dust
Compressed into fine nothingness
And forgetting. My mere breathing
Reiterates their fleet arrivals
And retreats. My impassioned verse
Imitates their passage from the stars,

Through ephemerality, flesh, dreams
Of outlasting death,
Back to that wholly mystical quiescence
Which transcends rational silence.
It seems that my own clay
Has been shaped by the hands of everyman.

And yet these abstract platitudes
I conjure with such fluid self-assurance
Fail to assuage the palpable fact
That a dear friend lies there
While I fly free,
Lies there instead of me, flying

While I remain here,
Driving away from his fresh-cut stone,
Knowing that just a slight aberration
Might have crowned my head, instead,
With night's studded diadem,
Draped my shoulders with its gossamer robes.

12/10/79 — [2] (01342)

In Quest of Wombs

I

Adrift,
I cling vertiginously
To the lip of a wineglass
Tingly and frigid with singularly shimmering rosé.

Fear
Of floating out alone,
On a sea composed of ambiguities
And blurred visions, surges through my arteries,

Intoxicating my spirit,
Filling me with hesitation.
I sip its delicious deliquescence cautiously,
Suspicious of its sensuous venom,

Knowing from past entrancements
That its talismanic philters
Work fantastic magic on my rational senses,
Dismantle truth,

Transmute all my profound ambitiousness
Into mushrooms and music
And stained-glass orgasmic hallucinogens
Synesthetically confused.

II

Yet the temptation is too great to resist.
I indulge in nectars
Ancestral and totemically fermented,
Whose primal triggers discharge my madness,

Free the demons
I've spent so many desperate inhibitions
And sublimations containing,
Throughout nine-to-five millenniums.

Now, brilliance dissolves
In the superego's most guilt-free
Letting-go of tensions
It's ever known. My bones go limp;

They rise, weightless, to the surface
Of a salt ocean,
Disengaged from their fleshly incarceration.
I am the wine, the fear, the drift,

Circling, circling, circling
Interminably
In a whirlpool swirling, from its edges inward,
Toward the source of silence.

III

As in a series of endlessly reflecting mirrors,
I enter my ever-changing image
And disappear from sight.
The yellow lights flicker and dim

Like manifold suns,
Stranding my shadow on a sandless beach
At the glass's dry bottom,
While night invites me to taste

Sleep's sweet, concupiscent delights.
Again, I hesitate.
Only, the interval between serious contemplation
And resolve is fleet

And absolutely finite. I surrender
The remnants of my intellect
To inebriation, resign my lonely soul
To oblivion, devoid of remorse,

And await the first gentle tongue
Willing to transport my solitude toward morning,
Without fornicating with me
Or resorting to mothering the child I've become.

12/11/79   (02548)

In absentia: A Panegyric ^Δ

*For blessed Janny,
this Christmas gift*

Although our separations
Grow consistently more protracted
And increasingly frequent,
We need not be concerned.

They strengthen our resolution
To cherish interludes,
Share their heritage of moments and glances
That entrance the spirit

Regardless how evanescent
And frangible. No amount of hours
*

Or years spent in the cloisters
Of mere familiarity

Or in the convent's silent cubicles,
As conjugal bed partners
Indentured to a matrimony
Consisting of lip-service rituals,

Can approximate the intensity
Generated by a solitary kiss
We give each other
When returning from our worlds apart.

Indeed, blessed mistress and wife,
By these extended interruptions,
You and I may be making
Sage preparations

For best confronting and surviving
Death's bereaving us of our physical selves.
Eternity might require of us
Loving that must leap eons and galaxies.

12/12/79   (00108)

Rising to the Surface ^Δ

Shroud or godly nimbus
Is impossible to differentiate,
This bitterly frigid December morning.

No matter, its ubiquitous presence,
Hovering over the brittle land,
Is a presentiment

I can't afford to disregard or accept
Without careful clarification
Suggested by my intellect.

It might be an enchanter's spell,
A breathing reminder
Of evil agents that would blind me,

Force my unwitting spirit
Into a psychic Bermuda Triangle,
Then leave me stranded.

On the other hand,
This pervasive gray could be manna
Not quite ripe,

In embryonic gestation yet,
Which, at any moment,
Might break open into golden flakes.

Regardless, I drive south,
As if without choice of quitting
Or continuing ahead.

The commitment seems foreordained,
Irrefragable, unequivocal.
No decision has ever really existed.

Unannounced, a cardinal
Darts precipitously through my vision,
Smearing it with crimson.

An energetic Appaloosa,
In a field contiguous to the highway,
Bolts in antic frenzy,

Leaps a fence, charges the air,
With its sweaty freedom. Charolais,
In a herd, converge on my thoughts.

Startled by all these colors
In dizzy motion, patterns
Coalescing and dissolving in and out of focus,

I suddenly realize my whereabouts,
The geography of the dream
Separating sleep from wakefulness.

I rise. The windows beyond my eyes
Open onto a new day.
The rest of my life lies just ahead.

12/13/79   (05669)

In the Hall of the Mountain King

The machine lifts free of earth,
Screams unheard, invisibly,
*

As it threads the sky's needle-eye
And surges headlong into turbulence.

This early morning,
The Mountain King's roar
Shivers and shudders bones, structure,
Flesh, and sinews, with horrific reports

That resonate along the empty corridor,
Flicker plastic light-lids
To an eerie luminosity,
And bend the rigid core, in which we soar,

With vicious and nonchalant obliviousness.
Our breathing is a series
Of short screeches. We are Valkyries,
Huddling in helpless arrest,

At the mercy of merciless elements
Our collective destiny has left us
To parcel out as fantasies and paranoias.
Lifeless in fear-trees,

Perched on the peripheries of our seats,
Squat, cataleptic,
We wait for a variation
In the winds aloft, the murky stratosphere,

To relieve us of responsibility
For being ourselves
And for having to endure mortality,
With all its grave inevitabilities.

We wait, even as we pass Atlantis,
Drowsing, in oceanic repose,
Below us, hope we might crash
Safely into its shadowy depths

And be apotheosized by a great sea change,
Transmuted into gods
Capable of outlasting fate, consciousness,
And the memory of Creation.

But the plane resists its adversaries,
Overcomes aliens, to deliver us,
Pristine and bereft of gratitude
For having survived death's throes.

Only our baggage, ragged and disheveled
As street urchins, shows traces
Of having experienced a cataclysm.
Each piece is conveyed, out of the bowels,

With broken grips, ripped zippers,
Violent abrasions and scuffs,
As though to remind us bellicose Odin
Chose to hold his temper.

12/22 & 12/24/79   (05670)

Christmas on Sanibel

This Christmas season,
A quick, crisp Floridian mistral,
Reminiscent of Wisconsin summers,
Breathes its *joie de vivre*
Over Sanibel, its shell-stippled beaches,
And the transient spirits
Who attend them, each evening and dawn,
Like devoted holy people
Questing ancestral relics and echoes
To confirm their earthly estates.

Although possessing only a secular poetics,
I also partake of a higher mysticism
Of purposes breaching offshore,
Against morning's crimson conflagration,
And three-mile runs
Along a stretch broadcast with exotica
Disgorged from a satiated Gulf:
Desiccated fish, horseshoe crabs,
Portentous stingrays,
Conchs, whelks, wing and pen shells.

My joy is immeasurable,
Despite feckless condominiums
That have proliferated, unchecked, for a decade,
Effacing pristine seascape and land
(Wilderness bordering wilderness),
Over which men went, in boats, to fish
Or traipsed, all day, in white sand,
*

Just for the sake of exercising their eyes and feet.
Mine is a fantastic appreciation,
Albeit tempered by the treason of reality.

Fragments of truth and beauty
Are all that one can seize
From among conceivable possibilities.
I know this, and yet
Intimations I've apprehended
Are of no less essential dimension and design
Than objects collected by those chosen
To God's certain election.
In fact, mine may be more miraculous,
For being independent of homogenized faith.

12/27/79 (05671)

The Vital Silence

I

My immediate sense of isolation
And the silence that encapsulates it
Are singularly exhilarating.
I've not known such quietude for days.

This morning, I've succeeded
In escaping my extended family
And wife and children
By hiring a baby-sitter, while the rest

Dabble at tennis, discover the beach, sleep.
I sit alone, writing,
In this "interval ownership" apartment,
Contemplating its inoffensive Oriental decor,

Ordered up by corporate landlords,
Through absentee vassals,
To satisfy, with adequate sumptuousness,
The aesthetics of nomadic Snopeses.

II

Inspired, my eyes witness empty lines
Come alive with intended correspondences
*

Between my body
And this apartment, in which it presently resides.

Each is a refuge within the din,
A temple and brothel,
Bowery and towered university,
Landfill and citadel of altruistic pursuits.

Both are completely furnished shelters
Leased, from unseen owners, for a week, a life,
With first and last payments,
Birth and death, guaranteed in advance.

I'm reminded that my intellect alone
Needs no roof, no flesh
To protect its poetics from elements
That would silence its vital silence.

12/28 & 12/30/79 (05672)

1/1/80

1/1/80 —
Its placement at the apex of this page
And its vague familiarity
Evoke hieroglyphic ciphers
From the next decade's Rosetta stone.

Only ubiquitously strewn confetti,
Shaped in triangles, circles, and trapezoids,
Haphazardly tossed over euphoria's edges,
Echoes the evanescent revelry
That separates yesterday from the messianic unknown.

To anchor its intrinsic existence
In time's tangible, fluxing sands,
My intellect needn't recite
History's litany of contretemps,
Reproaches, and most recent accomplishments;

It need simply manifest hope
That contradictory and anomalous people
Will achieve peace, through self-love
And faith in an omnipotent being,
By common assertions of their own puniness.

Instead of relegating me to blind complacency,
These beliefs root me,
With steadfast optimism, to my generation.
My family tree flourishes in earth
No ordinary storms can threaten with erosion.

On this new day's dawning
Of the future's first decade, I stop
To contemplate resolutions waiting to be made
And hesitate, hoping to isolate
Fate's singular metaphor for universal joy.

1/1/80
Resonates through my bones like music
Rising, inside bubbles, from the base
Of a clear blue spring. I dive
Into its sound, leaving my skin behind,

And immerse myself in diaphanous silence
Surrounding its shimmering image.
Suddenly, I'm time's child,
A fetus floating in womb after womb,
Growing in endless seclusion — a poet for the ages.

1/1/80   (05673)

[Now, only Gate 8] †

Now, only Gate 8
Connects/separates my life
To/from earth/sky,
Land/air, sand/glare.

Its modernistic nexus
Welcomes/resists immigrants,
Voyagers

1/2/80 — [1]   (07724)

Kaleidoscopic Effects △

The plane's thin, double-pane window
Is a kaleidoscope's oculus,
*

Beyond which a wide sky
And endlessly desolate Everglades rotate.

The machine controlling my vision
Tilts, dips, soars, and sweeps forward,
Leaving intuition, alone,
To sort and order fragmented memories

Of lives gone out of focus.
Squinting into the sun-tunnel,
My eyes are singed to tears,
By scintillating glints of persons left behind.

In the cloudless mist, beads of light
Metamorphose into wife,
Five-year-old Trilogy, and Troika,
The little boy with euphoria for a smile.

I would recognize their faces anywhere,
Even as coruscations
Prismed through space. I'd know their profiles
Silhouetted in total darkness.

Their precious, delicate features
Shimmer, in colorful coalescence,
On my mind's screen, as I sit here, dreaming
Of our days together at the beach,

Playing, luxuriating, bathing
In perfectly peaceful innocence.
Now, however, my insights
Can't speak. Their happy laughter is mute,

As I spectate from this distant pinnacle,
Peering through a minuscule porthole
Illuminating six-miles-high,
Stretching liquescently sideways forever.

Homing in on its destination,
The plane slowly changes elevations.
It assumes new headings so subtly
My senses fail to notice the elements

Rearranging themselves for a final time,
Until touchdown arrests them,
In circular ecstasy, on the intellect's retina
And I awaken to my shadow on the pavement.

1/2/80 — [2] (01444)

The Divine Afflatus: On Reading "Centerfold" Poems, by Frederick Seidel, in the *American Poetry Review*

Force the issue, you son-of-a-bitch!
Expose your suspect intellect
To scrutiny and criticism from skeptics
Who would have your head and entrails
Spattered, like a Jackson Pollock abstract,
Against this generation's john walls!

Show your guts are made of fecal smut,
O courageless wonder from Yale Divinity,
Harvard Law, and Heidelberg, with a Ph.D.
In semiotics and philology! Show them
Your poetics are genuine Dead Sea Scrolls verse
Spoken through Elohim's terse lips!

Speak, you prurient, pseudointellectual cocksucker!
Inform me about *Zabriskie Point*,
Juliet of the Spirits, and *Modern Times*
In one hyperbolic regurgitation!
Explain the scientific ramifications of relativity
And the DNA double helix,

To satisfy a layman's comprehension of symbols!
Feed the reading public's voracious appetite
For arcane and far-gone conclusions
About life on Mars and moons around Jupiter!
Spew, bastard, spew your beliefs in theology
And views on macrobiotic breathing and nudity!

My ears await the jolt of your electrifying ideas!
Your feckless speculations spark my penis
To sustained erection! Even those clichéd allusions
To dust motes, muses, and French pedants
Of the seventeenth century shiver my bones to an ecstasy
Capable of exploding my brains, from sheer amazement!

Go then, babe! What's holding you back?
Redline your intellect and imagination,
Until the gross anatomy can no longer hold out
Against the pressure of your summa cum laude blood!
Don't deprive us of your Ahab tale
Or your *Notes from the Underground*! We await your mantra,

Your personal insider's view of the Kennedys,
Robert Lowell, and the Ayatollah Khomeini!
Oh, and don't dare forget the tapes,
Those elusive eighteen minutes you exacted,
By special deposition, from Rosemary Woods, to be replayed
In the double Christmas issue of *Playboy*!

We shiver in frenzied distraction, while you primp
Offstage, before the start of your reading!
Spare us the agony we experience, anticipating your brilliance!
Show now, son of the seller of coal
And his lobotomized wife, Jay and Thelma's
Precious little crucified high-school valedictorian!

Bring your entire forty-three years
To this podium, prepared to absorb eggs and tomatoes
In the face and on your ruffle-and-lace tuxedo shirt!
Read on, blind Tiresias! Earn your inflated honorarium,
While we count double double runs and peg
Toward a skunk on our cribbage boards!

Be our guest! You won't disturb us at all,
Wordmonger! Only, remember this one stipulation:
Please be sure to wash your hands
After defecating and micturating! God don't 'llow
No skin-flute players 'round here! God don't 'llow
No satyrs masturbating their own lute strings!

1/2/80 — [3] (05674)

Cat-alepsy

The shock is cosmic. Coming home,
From Christmas in Florida,
To thirty-degree snow the texture of cinders
Is difficult to reconcile or accept
On purely emotional grounds. My eyes
And cheeks are raw and bloody
From its tiny white paws'
Scratching and clawing. Cat-alepsy

Subdues my desire to resume the routine
I carefully tied in a neat series of knots
*

Before leaving. I can't even undo
The string-ball wound loosely
With my least profound future ambitions.
It's as though the feline snow
Has unwoven and fused it closed
With frenetic confusion.

A feckless lethargy overwhelms me.
Coffee by the pot fails to thaw
My withdrawn spirit. All I can dream
Is retreat, while beyond the frosted window,
The wind purrs, and myriad furry flakes
Pace back and forth,
In the shifting currents, stalking me
From their cage, making escape inconceivable.

1/3/80   (05675)

Snake Charmer

I

His words are outraged snakes
Scurrying from the cave
At the base of his ophidian face.

Whether from real threats
Or fear of demons and specters
Invading the brain-nest,

Where they rest when unperturbed,
Their panic-frantic escape
Manifests an irrefutable discontent.

Possibly, psychic pain
Has energized these viperish expressions,
Exiting in haste. Perhaps a spark

Illuminating the dark wall
On which sleeping shadows
Awaken like cracking limestone

Has caused the strange stampede
Of snakes from their hibernal repose.
A flash of new insight

Into unfinished business
Or destiny not yet fully accomplished
Might be responsible for the exodus.

II

Now, they slither across the space
Separating imaginary adversaries
From enemies at large.

Their direction is determined by inflection
And histrionic stance. Blindly
They bite the air. Vitriol drips from fangs.

Somewhere, an innocent victim writhes,
Dries up, and dies,
Without knowing why he was sacrificed

To such vituperative, arbitrary cynicism,
What he did to deserve
So misanthropic a personal condemnation.

The words go out of control,
Crazed, frustrated. Suddenly,
They turn on themselves in a frenzy

And begin consuming each other whole,
Until, in one choking inhalation,
They dissolve. The cave closes.

Silence camouflages the entrance.
People passing would never imagine
Such hissing and seething within.

1/4/80   (05676)

Winter Pilgrimage

Three days have elapsed,
And the pendulant censer still smolders.
Spirits emboldened by prospects of riches
And leisure, no matter how specious,
Float in a stratum of voluble braggadocio
And frontier exaggeration. The faces
Pulsate in anticipation of receiving communion,
Whose wafers are swatch cards.

Continuous coffee cups complete the eucharist
These road peddlers celebrate
As they prepare to take their suitcases
From the house of earthly worship,
Into heathenish Golgothas.

Meanwhile, their priests speak, in litany,
Antiphons and responsive readings,
Phrasing the redeeming features of their gospel
For easy assimilation and regurgitation,
Through rote memory, by obsequious disciples,

Who chant and mime and repeat aloud,
In raucous euphoria, "Gorge, hymo,
Hacking flap, and bellows patch pockets,
Side and center vents, suppression, slope."
Men's soft-shouldered sportscoats
Carry the day, in rarefied apotheosis,
As each rep leaves for his own lonely wilderness,
To sell pieces of Jesus' original robe.

1/5/80 (02402)

Struck by Lightning

The basement stairs he ascends
Form jagged extensions
Of a lightning bolt
Flashing through his waking brain.
Scar tissue the length of sleep's trunk
Renders once supple dream-leaves
Shriveled as desiccated locust husks.

Rising, he staggers with each step,
As though shouldering a hod —
A crucifix of bricks.
The ballistic shock to his system
Shivers his bones. His blue skin
Smolders from the electricity
His cells and nerve fibers have absorbed.

While morning's bloody shaft lifts,
Multiplies, and fans into a splitting headache,
*

He sits at the kitchen table, anorectic
As a lab rat, sipping caffeinated silence,
Waiting for the stinking odor,
Which his breathing spews and spits, to subside,
Before venturing outside.

1/9/80 — [1] (05677)

Belial and Me

Belial preens behind the screen
My pernicious intoxication
Places between me and responsibility.
He struts in pompous and vulgar obliviousness,
As though he were somehow dissociated from me
Rather than obligated, spirit and soul,
To my impoverished existence,
Which, without volition, has evoked him,
In meager hope of abolishing loneliness.

His bestial image doubles and trebles,
With fantastic lack of focus.
His dance-of-death sequences
Produce a medieval funereal cast
That sprays skeletal shadows over my eyes,
Bathes me in anonymity and shame.
Immediately, I see my wife and children
Reposing beneath a starry cross —
Loved ones lost in sleep, without their messiah

To guide them past the hoary shoals
Where night's demons nest
In restive slithering and sodomy.
I weep. My crying enters the wine
My lips imbibe. I taste my own brine,
Whose chemistry has preserved my cowardice,
All these years, while those closest to me
Have endured contumely and scorn.
At my tongue's draconian command,

Belial laughs and gloats. His mimetic gestures
Suggest the cloven-hoofed, horned creature
Whose features resemble mine in every detail.
Suddenly, I leave my slow inebriation
*

And unavoidably stumble on my own reflection
In a mirror shoved inconveniently in my path,
By the devil's surrogate. I shudder
On meeting myself behind the screen,
Where only the dead are allowed to trespass.

1/9/80 — [2] (02551)

Ozymandias Revisited

Yesterday, I met an antique traveler
From the land of Samothrace,
Whose bleached face
Was a sandstone cenotaph,
Its chiseled inscriptions totally erased
By voracious winds inexorably gnawing away
At everything in time's radius.

Only his bedraggled robe,
Like an eight-year-old's security blanket
No longer recognizable as a whole cloth,
Remained of a once sumptuous toga.
No one, least of all I,
A latecomer to this generation of Homers,
Would have known he was a king's son

Or guessed that his numb gaze,
Gaunt trunk, and grisly stick-legs
Were not starvation's legacies
But the result of a grave depression
Brought on, millenniums before,
By a plague of human deceit and greed,
A bigotry against believers in change,

Entered into by the brain and the heart
Of every citizen and senator
From Samothrace, during his father's reign.
To his chagrin and contumacious outrage,
They charged him with radical heresies
And continued worshiping the present,
Neglecting to fortify their walls against rain,

Sun, snow, wind, fire.
They even forgot to husband their abundance
*

In anticipation of chance and accident and
Circumstance, which, like orbiting planets,
Would someday be drawn
Into their gravitational field, by universal mutability,
To usher in famine, drought, pestilence, and

War.
Forced indoors, to spend his days
Teaching scriptural laws, decorum, and poetry
To his society's old and useless citizens,
Those too arthritic for conscription and farming,
He finally stole away, one night,
When the moon was completely dark in phase,

And headed for the mountains
Bordering this town, where I've lived
Forty years without ever hearing
Voices in that desolation or seeing
A solitary stranger come down to bathe
In our warm pools, obtain stuffs,
Gambol and converse with other humans,

Until yesterday, that is,
When this wizened descendant of ancient kings
Appeared at what apparently he had guessed
Was death's most proximate edge,
To confess his identity and address the future.
The city elders dismissed him as a fraud.
I alone stayed to listen and bury his bones.

1/10/80 — [1] (05678)

Madonna and Child

For Charlotte Malter

Slowly at first, gaining courage and wisdom
In the interval, then with momentum
Youth alone knows
And abandonment to reckless ecstasy,
He grew away from Creation's core,
The uterine source
That had bathed him in an alembic
Floated with serene, warm, breathing music.

Blueprinted, womb-forged, liberated,
He voyaged from the maternal estuary,
Into a saw-toothed ocean
Swarming with obstacles and cosmic monsters.
Prevailing,
He circumnavigated the peripheries of his psyche
And arrived at the land beyond birth,
Where naked maidens waited

To cut his umbilicus, dismantle his virginity
In a series of soft, sweet, sad passions.
Yet for all the euphoria he smoked,
The supple scuppernong intoxication
That rendered him unmotivated,
He never forgot his mother's touch,
Her unselfishness. She was with him
When he was not and when he was

Out of his mind, oblivious to himself
And to the world's possibilities and to time.
Her gentle visage persisted
Whenever his spaced intellect,
Laced with poppy seeds and poetry,
Soared above the Straits of Astarte.
She was ever his echo's reflection,
The stichometry of his rhythmic feet,

His heartbeat's wet nurse,
Progenitress of his genius and degeneracy,
Defender of his devilish slips
And omissions in the face of his Father,
YHWH.
He was her womb's harvest,
Her child of light, prince of truth,
Regardless of crimes against decency.

Now, she ages in ageless beauty.
Her slow-glowing eyes are rose windows
Radiating soft-hued shafts
That form a warm halo,
In which he kneels and prays for verse
To awaken and redeem him from loneliness.
To her, he will dedicate
Each little birth his words create.

1/10 — [2] & 1/12/80 — [1] (02545)

Intimations of Milton

All I know for certain
Is that blind Milton dictated to his dutiful daughters
Myriad verses, comprising *Paradise Lost*,
Before I was born, let alone
Conceived of his irrefragable genius.

He endured the profound disappointment
His failing eyesight presented,
Despite his growing awareness that he possessed
An extraordinary prescience,
A vivid, living insight

Into God's reprieves and indictments
For transgressions against His Word,
Deeds conceived in the name
Of a sacrilegious Elohim, a false idol
Erected in the Temple, to mislead true believers,

Confound the true religion,
Confuse the meaning of his own *Aeropagitica*
And elegiac "Lycidas." I ask myself
What I'm doing being a poet
For the 1980s — a prophetic deception —

Creating word after word on word
For those who would have eternity grow
From the most convenient mushroom
Or achieve transmogrification
From the nearest rock or stranded seashell.

The heavens drop no cogent responses,
And I continue to effervesce
Without formal training or schooled reason
To boast. With wineglass raised high,
I toast my own lonely existence,

Knowing that poetry is my goal
And my most sacred ambition. I shiver
With purblind recognition of the doom
That is mine, the curse of unrhymed verse
I'm obliged to create and record in my cursive scrawl.

Suddenly, the words pale in the gloom,
And I begin to identify with the ancient bard
Who could exhume Beelzebub and Belial
With the flick of his tongue and banish them
To sempiternal dungeons of Momus and Gorgon

With the slightest inflection or manual gesture.
I cringe. Delusions of achieving
His degree of imagination consume me
With disbelief. I write lines
My mind has never even approximated,

Constructing entire cosmoses
Replete with angels and demons
Capable of consummating lust and love.
I dictate, while my own daughter types
Notes transcribed from God, quotes from my soul.

1/10/80 — [3] (02638)

Two Stars △

My two growing children,
Trilogy and Troika,
Have become not daughter and son,
Rather figments,
Heavenly orbs chasing each other,
In inexorably widening, heliocentric ellipses,
Around my affection and love.

They reflect my warmth,
In miraculously refracting parallaxes,
Whose rays are engaging smiles,
Laughter, and verbalizations of divinity
That illuminate my sphere
Like rose windows lighting the spirit's gloom.
I consume them and am consumed,

In our mutual communion.
The constant tugging of our loving
Swells oceanic space
That occasionally separates our physical selves
By days. Yet even then,
A common tide washes distant shores.
One timeless ebb unites us in its sands.

Someday,
When my scintillations have banked
Or, in marriages by heavenly consent,
They have mounted the zenith,
To shower their own constellations with girandoles,
*

I will gaze skyward,
From the silence beneath my grave,

And see my little boy, Troika,
Rocking his horse,
Piecing his blocks into engines and cars,
And my wood nymph, Trilogy,
Wrestling with me, on our attic carpet,
To free herself from my rib —
Two stars, my eternal heart's single flame.

1/12/80 — [2] (01445)

Perning in the Gyre ᐃ

They turn in a fire,
Neither gyrfalcons loosed, on the air,
By a crazed Yeats
Hoping to see words mate,
Give birth to brilliant trilling,
Nor phoenixes able to lift the spirit
On feathered intellection

But, rather, my two precious children,
Whose twin scintillas
Form a graceful, soaring shape
Against a shimmering sun.
They are the falcons
And the phoenixes who ignite my brain
With inspiration. I am their fire.

1/25 & 1/29/80 — [2] (00242)

Ossuary ᐃ

Outside, the falling snow is frozen rain
Slowed to the pace of souls
Tracing their own echo home through space.

It no longer smells wet or glistens
As it did a month ago,
Rather partakes of a momentary permanence

I suspect is the whiteness of ghost-dust
Sifting to earth
From disappearing spirits. A foreboding,

An odorlessness redolent of present-day
Bergen-Belsen,
A necromancer's spell suspending the land

In feckless slow motion, compels me
To question myself,
My motives for living, my notions of dying.

Suddenly, an image of death shaving old bones
Into scrimshaw slivers,
To give as gifts to his mistresses and pimps,

Sends shivers through my sensibility.
I cringe at the possibility
That this first snow might indeed be me,

My own atoms flaking off an imagination
That has dared invent
Such grotesquery by focusing outside itself.

1/28/80   (00085)

False Gods ^Δ

Convinced of their superiority,
They joined a quilting bee,
To weave their radiant bigotries
Into a seal of Solomon,
Beneath which they would thrive inviolate.

Trapped in their tapestry
Of rumor, contumely, and calumny,
They worshiped the day when death
Would free them from pettiness,
But they survived their trial by suffocation.

1/29/80 — [1]   (02206)

Thanatopsis

In memory of Wit Ledbetter,
whose abrupt passing
has outraged me to death

Some nights, queasy uneasiness
Becomes upheaval, defeats sleep,
*

Pompeiis it under molten premonitions
That the city of dreams is being sieged
By demons. Frightened, I awaken beneath rubble,
Slip naked from my sheets,
And enter midnight's silent streets,
To reconnoiter the enemy. He hides
Like a squall, seen all the way
Across a lake, not yet arrived.
He's there, in the wind's invisibility.
His presence is my suspiciousness,
But we pass each other,
In a thin, mirrored corridor,
Without recognizing we share identical skins,
Wear the same faces and hair.

Last evening, an abrupt eruption
Showered my sleep with hot rocks,
Flaming lava, drove me from my home,
Into the cold, unknown hours,
Where displaced and homeless vagrants
Roamed alleys for thrown-out scraps
And bottles glistening with heeltaps.
Alone, I encountered my own shadow
Trailing and leading the silhouette I'd assumed
Between both dislocating shapes.
Suddenly, the enemy of many stalemates
Began to squeeze me from both sides,
As we tried to reach opposite exits
Of the mirrored passageway. Death and I
Wrangled and grappled, until, at last,
We entered each other, in a suffocating gasp.

1/31/80 — [1] (02023)

An Elegy

*For Anne,
beloved wife of Wit Ledbetter,
a gentle and loving man*

His presence is with us yet.
Forever will we be in his spirit's debt,
Who knew him from the next court,
Across the net, or through his newsprint,
Filled with pithy, syllogistic wisdom.

His gentle and discerning eye
Registered a down-to-earth concern for politics
Worthy of thanes and stable hands,
Chimney sweeps, heads of state, and aldermen.

A deeply modest keeper was he
For those of us who, even now, reside
Where, only days ago, he lifted us unknowingly
On his agonized brow. Tiny Farmington
Is diminished mightily by his going out.

Each family is deprived of the integrity
He strived for, in public life and private,
By taking time to listen, learn, endure.
Each one of us is less secure,

For his having left behind, so unexpectedly,
The thankless task of making suggestions
For changing ancient ways
Of doing things and growing old.
We are checkmated in life's game of chess,

Not Wit, who flies, with Godspeed,
Toward the city of sempiternal redemption.
Lest we forget his mortal legacy,
Let us bless those closest to us and weep.

1/31/80 — [2] (02022)

A Country Boy's Summer-Afternoon Idyll △

> For Joan Williams;
> from The Wintering
> this evocation arose.

Muscadine grows crosswise
And skyward. Its juicy, tumescent redolence,
A godly suspension
Entwined with ripe scuppernong clusters
Vining along the clapboard siding,
Festoons my drowsy eyes, suffocates me
In languorous scents of Mississippi.

I submit to its aromatic aphrodisiac,
A virgin easily surfeited,
Desiring sweet inebriation
And the reeling feeling of escaping the seasons
*

By violating hymen-daydreams
With psychic semen. But my seeds
Fertilize only fallen grapes.

2/7/80   (00050)

The Watery Parts

Undulations of thin winter sunshine
Nudge my intellect across time
As if it were a crystalline isthmus
In a medieval cartographer's mind,
Distant, remote, on which floats my intuition,
A whisperous bark on a mission of self-discovery.

Images and premonitions and superstitions
Splay my tiny vessel's gunwales,
Sunder its coarse sails,
Batter its hull like Etruscan hammers
Fashioning gold into sumptuous frills
For odalisques and plump empresses to flaunt.

As I travel alone in this concrete sea lane,
Solitude follows my wake like albatrosses
And saurian pelicans
Circling hysterically, in foul, imperturbable gestures
Of grotesque predation, waiting for my soul
To dump overboard its psychic detritus.

And I am drawn further away
From home, the universe, my sanity, each day,
As though a current above,
Not beneath, my fleet motion
Were conveying me to the fulminating lip
Of a vast, cataclysmic Niagara.

Suddenly, the endless ocean relents,
Closes myriad invisible openings
That have promoted my passage.
But its placid passivity
Unnerves me, turns invention and hope
To skeptical dismay. A heated breeze,

Impregnated with sweet cinnamon and cloves,
Insinuates my pores, dissolves bones,
*

Flesh, and tissue. The breeze metamorphoses
Into a satanic physiognomy
Shaped to accommodate my dust.
I, Ahab, succumb to nothingness.

2/13/80 — [1] (05679)

Away for the Holidays

Every year, for the last ten,
Whenever Valentine's,
Which arrives, again, tomorrow,
Or his children's and wife's birthdays
Or his anniversary recurs,
Willy's been away from home,
On the road, peddling men's clothing,
Sportswear, and expensive dress trousers.

Never once has she complained,
Though he's heard her weep
In towns remote as Tipton and Helena,
Where he's stayed the night,
Entertaining, at his own precious expense,
The graceless, uneducated people
Who enter and leave his life,
In random transitoriness,

Exchanging their "order" for his psyche,
Taking his advice on promotion items,
In return for free drinks,
Meals, relying on him to "steer them right"
Each new season. He's seen her crying
Alone in their bed, on special nights,
When they might have shared
Their mutual isolation from the universe

And gained comforting solace
From their common alliance against interlopers,
Exploiters, rapists, demons, and thieves.
In besieged dreams,
He's envisioned his boy and girl asleep,
Innocent of their daddy's deep remorse
And inordinate guilt for being gone. Their breathing
Has reached his moteled quarantines.

And all the miles and meals,
The days, occasions, moments alone,
The unconsummated memories
And half-lit dreams, are figments,
Stillborn babies, tapestries never woven
From elaborate cartoons they designed
In youth's studios — irretrievable trappings,
Accouterment, pleasures gone as a sigh.

This evening, he promises himself,
He'll phone long-distance, reassure them
He's their unswerving suitor/knight,
That they're his heart's blessed desire.
As usual, he'll conclude with apologies
And a promise to drive safely,
Before slipping back into exile,
One motel room closer to the next.

2/13/80 — [2] (02401)

Witches' Den

Its walls strewn with replica mirrors
Reverse-painted and gold-leafed with beer ads
From turn-of-the-century America,
The room reeks of cigarette smoke
And fetid jukebox music and obscenities
Spewed from mid-Southern dudes
Corpulent and garrulous as bulls
Guarding a harem of supple sea lions.

Only, no ladies are present
Except the two unfortunate waitresses,
Who cut through the stench and profanity
Like soldiers flailing machetes
To gain the upper hand on a bamboo forest.
They succumb to the pseudofriendly
Amenities of down-home gentlemen
Off on a manly jag and, thus, excused

For their slightly off-color propositionings
And ass-grab posturings, as they stare
Indefinitely into the mysterious cleavage
*

Made conveniently accessible to their lust.
In this smoky witches' den,
Demons disembodied and spectral
Conspire to ravage their heads and bodies
With potent, toxic brews and ghastly potions.

In a corner beyond the fascinator's pale,
I hide beneath my self-generating silence,
Hoping to eventually escape
With my eyes, ears, and breathing apparatus
Intact, capable of functioning again,
When the mists lift into morning's light,
Hoping, ultimately, to merely navigate
The passage back through the bamboo forest,

Past the seal mating-ground and the hall of mirrors,
Out of the den, to the spurious door
My curiosity opened while my tired soul
Was slowly counting the steps back to its room
In this limboed motel. Now, doubts multiply,
As the space rumbles with Vesuvian intensity.
Abruptly, I run into an endless corridor
Punctuated by numbered, unrelated doors,

Wondering which bristling key
Belonging to my exiled identity
Will unlock the Chinese puzzle box
Housing my fumbling imagination this evening.
Once inside, midnight, two,
Five o'clock transpire on schedule,
While I keep sentinel, from my parapet,
For shadows, sounds, odors, ghostly interlopers.

2/13/80 — [3] (02400)

Valentine

Jan,
my princess of peace

On this day, this sacred day,
I confess my love, in silence,
Pledge my fidelity to you,
And commit myself anew
To the celebration of our marriage vows
*

THE COMPLETE POEMS OF LOUIS DANIEL BRODSKY

And to the true spirit of a duty
Given us, in mutual trust,
To mother and father God's progeny.

My blessed lady, sacred love,
Embrace me with your eyes, your touch,
And let me know,
Though we be distant, we're close as whispers
Slipping from the lips of god
And goddess kissing, kissing inextricably,
Close as wind and water and sky
Drawn into the eye of a hurricane.

Press your breasts against the mattress
Where usually I sleep,
And they will remember me by my fragrance,
By my subtle indentations,
And by the weightlessness your chest will feel
As it inflates with gentle lust,
From the spell my incantations cast
Despite the vastness of our separation.

Tonight, alone, we two, together,
Will share the stillness,
Compare pulse rates, eye blinks,
Nightmarish paranoias, and redeeming dreams
Of seeing Trilogy and Troika growing old.
You and I, my blessed princess,
Will speed the fugitive hours, until we meet,
Then make them cease forever.

2/14/80 — [1] (02126)

Space and Time △

Space and time are the mythic components
Of loneliness. They thrive on psyches
Separated, accidentally or on purpose,
By miles, hours, misunderstandings and by vows
Broken or forgotten. They fester in the mind,
Like overripe tomatoes grown top-heavy,
Fallen to the ground, until, as measurements
Of one's identity and location and relative age,
They become mere anomalies,
Dead weights for the life-bearing boat.

Far from home, in this nameless bar,
With college jocks swilling beer
And Temple Drakes twirling verbal batons,
Smoking "gold" dope, on a lark,
I sit, a victim of clock-block
And place-stasis, a monument to nonmomentum,
A wrong note plucked, Ozymandias
With his shattered visage scattered among the sands,
An unoxygenated fire gasping for breath,
A baby contracting back into the womb.

Where and *when* descend the mind's stairs,
To its basement, and are placed in storage bags
By the Keeper of Ineffectual Adverbs.
Fastidiously, she labels each obsolete piece
Of every facet of my dismantled sensibility,
Before locking the boxes in which she'll keep me
For an indeterminate statute of limitations.
Meanwhile, chilled rosé, frequently poured,
Unwinds my taut-wound springs.
My numb skeleton dissolves into the din,

While the flesh remains inflated
Above its wine-swollen arteries and veins.
Suddenly, the music stops. Such abrupt
Lack of distraction cracks the cast bell
Whose clangor, for the last few hours,
Has drowned out all ratiocination.
The absence of sound returns me to myself.
My own body flows back to my touch.
A voice from the past recognizes me, begs me
Join. Ecstatically, I accept my own invitation.

2/14/80 — [2] (00038)

Jeremy

Two people, neither old nor youthful,
Are superimposed on each other, in the mirror.
Both peer at him,
With identical eyes and leering smiles —
One porcine, corpulent, obese,
The other gaunt, almost skeletal —
*

Registering complete recognition
Of the other's kindred features,
Without showing signs of knowing him.

He stares at himself with disbelief
That what he's seeing
Is really his own most recent reflection.
He suspects an inexplicable mystic force
Of intruding itself on his usually scrupulous vision,
Causing him to be lost in between
Two distinct perceptions, delayed eye-blinks,
A visitor knocking at his own door,
Waiting for himself to answer his rap.

Standing in the bathroom, shaving,
Disconcerted by the way his razor
Refuses to transform stubble to smoothness,
He suddenly notices both visages bleeding.
Hesitating, he saturates a washrag
And places it over his entire face,
To slow the flow long enough
To administer a styptic pencil.
Yet when he removes the cloth, it's white as soap

And the mirror is totally clear,
As though it were a blackboard
Someone just erased. The strange likenesses,
Disappeared without a trace, dematerialized,
Have bereaved him, left him alone
In a nowhere zone, free to forget
The past and neglect the ubiquitous future.
Groping for clothing, he dresses and leaves in haste,
Hoping to merge with crowds and be seen.

2/16/80   (05680)

Epithalamion

> *For Dale and Bob Brooks;*
> *may their stars forever align*
> *and the heavens ever celebrate*
> *their convergence.*

Two specks converge, enlarge,
Illumine the darkness with their incandescence —
Bold stars, novas not previously charted.

They pass through the atmosphere,
With dazzling lambency, crisscross,
Weaving themselves into night's fabric,

Then, entwined in their own inventions,
Knot the sky's loose ends,
To keep the secret of their design from unraveling.

2/22/80   (02127)

The Sky's Lorelei

In broad daylight,
The naked, dilatory moon
Parades with bawdy and shameless haughtiness.
She tantalizes the sky with a fragrance
Earthly eyes synthesize
By recreating vicarious climaxes
The mind's appetite might savor.

But the gossamer lady
Refuses penetration
Even by imaginations pulsating and burning
With fantastical carnal desire.
She chooses to remain chaste,
Outside the lushy gates of Hesperides,
While Tithonus insanely masturbates.

2/27/80 — [1]   (05681)

Procreation

The children devise frustrated schemes
Aimed at disclosing the budding rose
Growing in lush furrows of female gardens,

While season after abundant season,
Their parents seed and harvest, plow under
And reseed the family plot,

Until, one day, the passion ceases,
The rose starts spotting, its petals wither,
Decay, and its fragrance fades away

Just as the children reach the age
When they'll plant. Determined, a new generation
Hurries to the fields to grow its flowers.

2/27/80 — [2] (05682)

We Are the People We Deemed So Sad

Those we left behind at the Y in the road,
The proverbial fork, the other side
Of the tracks, just yesterday,
Are ghosts rushing back, of late,
On our disfranchised memories. We recall
Their faces or their names but can't focus both
Simultaneously. The road to utopia
We had taken early on in our careers
Somehow evaporated before we could consummate
A blissful marriage of our university dreams
With future exigencies. Wine-sipping nights,
Before a quiet fire, became diapers
And screaming and violences erupting between us
For no justifiable reasons other than fatigue,
Exasperation, frustrated lovemaking,
Insensitivity under relentless stress.

Now, ancient friends, relegated to reliquaries
Lining the mind's catacombs, haunt us,
Revive their former guises briefly,
While we sit by ourselves in restaurants
Or pass through airports or stroll
Along museum corridors. They assail us,
These young faces, vibrant as stained glass
Shimmering under a steady sun,
Reminders of time halcyon and untainted,
When our hearts were all poet and painter
And our eyes could sculpt millefiori china
From crude clay. They assail us
With their anarchic innocence, their vital naiveté.
Dear God, even to this day,
We realize they are us. Why can't we
Inherit their most recent incarnation?

2/27/80 — [3] (02128)

Changing

Awakening into myself,
From out of night's merciful stasis,
Is the fated, long-awaited blow
To my psyche. I had so hoped
Dreaming might interminably postpone
The aloneness that accompanies this endless sojourn
My heart calls home.

                                                                Now,

I must get my house in order,
Close yesterday's accounts,
Put a hold on anticipated communiqués
From the outside, open my doors,
As before,
To prospective renters of my foreclosed shell-ter.
It's time to change again.

2/28/80 — [1] (05683)

Sleeping Spider ᐃ

In this prolonged winter,
The mad, hungry spider grows thin
With discontentedness, eviscerated within
Its shivering fibrous net. Old letting-goes,
Free falls along invisible silk,
Five feet at a leap,
Winnow through its innocent sleep
Like a prairie wind shimmering wheat.

No cold drafts or freezing rain or snow
Penetrate its insulation, yet it knows
The time for liberation has not arrived
And that the inhospitable outside
Would embrace nothing more eagerly
Than its premature escape from exile.
Intuition informs its conditioned mechanisms
That continuance depends on cycles

Ordained by nature and selective evolution,
Guided by even higher divinations.
*

Impatiently, it remains in its makeshift shelter,
Contemplating inevitable conquests
And predatory gains, without the aid of intellection
Or memory. Like a tight-budded rose,
It edges closer to the moment when its explosion
Will cause the cosmos to briefly stop,

Take notice of its quintessential presence,
And admit its thorny perfection into a universe
Equally perverse, every bit as barbarous
And impersonal in its malevolent beauty.
Suddenly, the cottony egg opens.
Legs stab the air, with tentative gestures,
And April is once again bloodied
By species bent on reaching survival's winter retreats.

2/28/80 — [2] (02552)

Crazy Al

For "Funky" — Al Pethtel

I sit here, in Columbia, sipping wine,
Where first we heard each other's voices
And rhymed our sounds with excited tokes
Of Colombian gold and spoke ridiculous puns
Until they grew old and silly and smoky.

I sit here, disconsolate, dislocated, and alone,
Knowing that you are somewhere in Canada,
Stroking your bass guitar as though its chords
Were evoked from the earth's own clitoris,
Thumbed with perfectly sensual gentleness.

I sit here inebriated, guilty that I told you
I'd phone, then chose to leave my motel
Without showing you the courtesy
Owed the least business client, let alone
A friend so simpatico and close to my head

As you, my blessed buddy, "Crazy Al" Pethtel.
And now, instead of calling, I write,
Realizing that there's no way, tonight,
You might hear me screaming to you
My outrageous plaint for camaraderie,

That ribald laughter of yours, from the gut,
The ceaseless alcohol, the precious hashish,
And ubiquitous music. My regret is outsize,
My plight solitudinous and unrectifiable.
I so wish we'd been able to speak tonight,

But I sit here, sipping wine,
Guilt-filled, knowing only that all the voices
In this lounge, spuming and spewing their confessions
To the nearest listener with goat-bristled ears,
Aren't worth, together, the few encounters we've shared

Or the closeness we've known, though strangers
Born under confused and ambiguous signs.
So tonight, you play your bass guitar
On a foreign stage; I write my eccentric poems
In a room alien to my sensibility.

And apart, our hearts start pulsing at beats
Similar, preposterously urgent and fleet.
I see you doing karate maneuvers; you hear me
Repeating Miltonic and Shakespearean meters,
Until the space separating us decreases

And our sympathetic thoughts coalesce, ignite
In a singular burning urge to reunite.
Dear Funky, please hear me, tonight,
And be reminded that although we're alone,
We've never been closer. My tightness binds us.

2/28/80 — [3] (02655)

A Storm Forces the Captain Below Deck

All along the highway,
Striated drifts, like fingers of the aurora borealis
Streaking across a far-northern sky,
Sift over the concrete before me,
As though trying to elude
Something pursuing them, frighteningly malign
And unrelenting. I wince,
As if expecting each slithering cascade
To perforate my eyelids with frigid grits
Or turn vision into a blizzard.

Yet this vessel, dipping and rolling
Like a tiny caravel in perilous seas,
Persists. It slices through ivory interstices,
Oblivious to catastrophe or apocalypse,
While fear trims its sails,
Adrenaline steers its veering shape,
And intuition and providence conspire
To resist shipwreck on invisible shoals.
Beneath deck, I scribble, in my log,
My last known heading, my name, the date.

3/1/80   (05684)

On the Origin of Mordecai Darwin △

He awakens with a start,
Involuntarily debates the dialectic
Of breakfast versus dressing for work,

Ponders the existential notion
Of shaving his face, brushing teeth
And hair, resuming his daily despair,

Symbolized by the texturized polyester
Designer Collection suit he wears
To conceal his simian ethics. Lingering

In his womb-warm bathroom,
Gazing at himself in the mirror,
He deliberates on his amazing state of grace,

Reflects how evolutionary agents
Have flung him from change
To change, up out of rain forest

And jungle, onto the plains of civilization,
To perpetuate a higher order
Of negative capability and suspended disbelief.

Soon, he will be engaged in the battle
For survival. Rush hour
Will take its toll on impatient strains,

Whose inexorable gnawing away
At enfeebled psyches will inevitably lead
To certain species' extinction,

To which his strand, man,
Is most apocalyptically susceptible.
Now, he leaves his house,

Dragging a bag of private doubts —
His trusty attaché case —
Outdoors, and heads toward his car

And pauses beside a low-limbed oak,
Whose branches, like wands,
Entrance his spirit. Transfixed, he stoops,

Almost bending at the center of his being,
Then begins to locomote on all fours,
Tottering, gaining equilibrium,

Going sideways, straight, climbing
With the aid of opposable thumbs
And invisible prehensile tail.

Suddenly, in morning's sunlight,
He discovers the euphoria of arboreal soaring
And knows, in a flash,

He'll never concern himself again with shaving,
Craving meat, paring his toenails,
Or consulting the Douay or King James Bible.

3/4/80 (00115)

Five-Star City

Intellectual asphyxia is a constant mist
That has settled, each day,
For fifty years, over this city,
Whose silhouette shimmers irresistibly,
From the main-traveled highway,
Like Mont-Saint-Michel suspended in the distance.

Passersby remark its compelling quaintness,
Relegate it to a gossamer state
Of peaceful lassitude and quiet evenings
Etched with birdsong and whisperous jets
Heading easterly and westward —
A town, of the middle border, that time forgot.

Physical neglect is a collective birthmark
Its inhabitants wear. None sees
The other's affliction, for its pervasive sameness,
And outsiders mistake its preposterous
Annihilation of syntax and grammar
As a kind of apotheosis of Greek drama.

They confuse its obesity and slovenly dress
With unrepressed self-honesty,
The obscenities comprising its street speech
With double agents of hypocrisy.
Visitors are immediately impressed
By its relentless deification of the ordinary,

And yet those with their Baedekers,
Michelin Green Guides,
And SOS Directories don't stay
Beyond A&W or Pizza Hut
Lunch on the run, once they've bought gas,
Written checks for factory-outlet slacks,

In fact rush back
To the sprawl of castellated shopping malls
And the subdivided privacy of their own "loans,"
Just in time to shower, change,
Prepare the grill for steaks, and welcome bosses
And their wives with shoptalk and daiquiris.

3/6/80   (00200)

[I have watched my children] [†]

I have watched my children
And listened to their expanding demotic

3/8/80 — [1]   (03758)

Media Meteorologists

The heated breezes hung on,
All afternoon and evening.
March disappointed her projectors,
*

Embarrassed chauvinistic prognosticators,
Whose reputations are made
And sustained by accurately predicting
Her capricious female ways.

We at the station guffawed,
Taking a bellyful of pleasure
In calling attention to such blatant mistakes.
Complete miscalculations
Always make us look better,
Who never pass a day, at the controls,
Without miscues or technical difficulties.

Somewhere around 1 a.m.,
A sudden thunderclap
Shot through sleep, recalled dreams
From their past and future philanderings,
And escorted, from out the abysmal unknown,
An entire demonology of cold rain
And ocherous flashes of electricity.

Its outrage, loud as locomotives
Accomplishing a steep grade,
Awakened us to the presumptuousness we'd displayed
In quantifying and manipulating passion
Just to sate numb curiosities.
Abruptly as it had begun, the storm
Transformed itself into a sultry courtesan.

3/8/80 — [2] (00199)

[Let us touch, taste, take time]

Let us touch, taste, take time
To waste less than we expect,
By placing a quietus on our hasty
Lovemaking. May you contemplate
The flowing motion of the planets
Orbiting, gracefully as condors,
In my skyward eyes,
While I accompany the clitoral whispering
Your lips emit
Whenever I strum them to ecstasy
With my gently singing fingers.

Remember, the nemesis awaits,
Who gains his greatest pleasure
From others' sensual intemperance.
Let us banish intransigent death,
By protracting our kisses,
And force him to show his impatience,
Miss an appointment with fate,
By refusing to surrender to the glands.
And let us cherish our voices,
Soliloquizing, inside a mutual sigh,
The dialogue of our love.

3/11/80   (00269)

An Anomalous Snow

This mid-March morning
Is a hive with crystalline ice-bees
Buzzing precipitously around it, out-
Side.

It's a cyclotron,
Whose spiraling atoms, flying
At an ever-maddening pace, col-
Lide

In midair, this mid-March,
As they try to escape extinction,
By landing intact, in-
Side,

Just below the freezing zone.
Slowly, the hive increases in size
And density, until it no longer im-
Plies

Its former thriving design,
Rather shares the shape
Of Egyptian deities whose mummi-
Fication

Was accomplished by endless application
Of wet-gauze wrappings.
By degrees, the cyclotron shows mani-
Festations

Of violating all safe speeds.
Its unwieldy spinning
Unhinges stable particles, whose disin-
Tegration

Causes the apparatus to explode
Like a cosmic body, while the astounded day
Futilely witnesses its own transmogri-
Fication.

3/12/80   (00198)

Higher Education

Isolated in a booth, musing in silence,
In the local café,
Where he sits nursing coffee
And toast he's let go cold,
He rubs the opaque crust,
Deposited by defunct dreams
And fleet insights, from the lunar surface
Surrounding his unflinching eyes,

And for the first time, he notices others
Congregated around tables,
Glued to a background of animated sounds.
Although he's lived in this town
A decade, their faces might just as easily
Belong to an amusement-park scene
By Reginald Marsh, instead of neighbors
Who call him by his first name.

Unsuccessfully, he surveys the room
For a solitary recognition, a trace
Of an idiosyncratic feature, to awaken him
To an explanation for his pariahhood,
Make him burn with curiosity
To learn what alien force
Might have sighted his existence and reported it
To higher authorities, causing his obliteration.

He shrinks back into time's parentheses,
A victim of the process, a prisoner of a war
He reenlisted in on four different occasions,
*

Before being classified as "missing in action."
And all he recalls prior to getting lost
Just after his last graduation
Is his father itemizing the cost of his education
In dollars per day and his mother crying.

3/13/80 (00197)

On the Pursuit of Human Perfection

From parturition to hydriotaphia,
Whether volitionlessly, with eager consent, or by accident,
We each contribute to the perpetuation
Of misinformation, mendacious effronteries,
Calumniation of the body and the spirit of others
Engaged daily in similar occupations.

None of us is exempt from the endless pursuit
Known in some quarters as
Preservation of one's innocence, in others as
Self-defense; some even refer to it,
With euphemistic wit, as divine retribution,
To rid themselves of personal responsibility

For having provoked the legal deities
With lay cases of questionable civility,
For a fee. The selling of the soul
Comes easily to those who've faced the Sanhedrin
And seen firsthand the seething wrath
Of God's most anorectic and intractable fiduciaries.

Compassion, good conscience, and right reason
Flourish in the abstract. They're bandied
At the beach, in singles' bars, massage parlors,
On the confettied floor of the stock exchange,
Like so much "righteous indignation"
Spouting from the blowhole of a breaching pope,

Spewed in the McGuffy-like columns
Of Lewis Lapham and Hugh-man Hefner,
Set loose in State of the Union messages
Read, to a glutted nation, from TelePrompTers
Fed by malapropian Brobdingnagians
And drug-using Lilliputians

Bent on uncensored triplethink,
Reckless abandon to catch-as-catch-cant,
Flying-by-the-seat-of-pants economics,
And the push/pull-comes-to-shove/kick theory
Of international cosmopolitics. The collective effort
To set standards of classic behavior thrives

Despite unoccasional felonies and deviations,
By "decent" citizens, from prescribed righteous paths
Laid out, in official guidelines, like plats
For subdivisions, clearly identifying streets, curbs,
Gutters, drains, and rights of way
Allowed the brain and its crowded imagination.

Yet for our setbacks, we continue passing
Referendums and enacting amendments
That reaffirm our mutual, unbending belief
In the Manifest Destiny of absolute perfection.
With all lack of modesty, responsibility, and humility,
We congratulate ourselves on our lasting peace with dignity.

3/16/80   (05685)

Tiffany Lamp

For Jan,
on her thirty-sixth birthday

Tiffany spider webs, wisterias,
Dragonflies, and lotus leaves
Sift and drip into an arrested forever,
Through a leaded network
Connecting my eyes to the artifice of eternity.

Somewhere beneath the lacy tracery,
I glimpse your slender figure
Rising to the surface of a Favrile lake,
Hair streaming sinuously back,
In a slow-flowing Art Nouveau motion

Whose uterine sensuality takes me under.
I drown in your essence,
Forget my precious complexities
And shrill egocentric ecstasies
Long enough to feel your real beauty,

Taste the inky dissolve of your pigments,
Swimming, in shimmering translucence,
Between glass, my imagination, and the lake.
I revel in your mastery over objects
Make-believe, antique, and new.

All creatures worship you,
Gaze in amazement as you change colors
With the phasing moon. I grow dizzy,
Desiring to touch your dazzling shape
And be touched. How much more can I take?

3/22/80   (02129)

An Old Man's Midlife Crisis

Only eight days away,
Yet already my cultivation
And domesticated other-directedness
Have begun to deteriorate.

Forgetting is gelatin setting,
As the brain cools
To a smooth translucence, beneath breezes
In air-conditioned Eden, where excess,

Indolence, and greed
Turn sleep, eating, sexual fantasies
Into a trinity of perverse, solifidian worship
And divinity is the son of earthly appetites.

Each morning,
I've awakened in naked innocence — Adam
Indulging his long-awaited independence —
And taken to the tar-strewn beaches,

In reckless ecstasy,
Questing youthful flesh to rescue me
From the spirit's restless oppressiveness.
Each evening, I've surrendered my virginity anew.

Too soon,
I'll have to eschew my freedoms, resume life
With Eve and my polyglot issue,
Begotten of Socratic logic and a "fifties" belief

In the primacy of virtue,
Self-worth, and the Protestant gospel
Of ethical purposefulness. For now, anyhow,
I'd like these last few days

Of my recuperation from a doleful countenance
And endless guilt
To be spent in pursuit of excess, indolence, and greed —
My final repudiation of aging and death.

3/24/80 (05686)

An Untimely Opening in the Territory

Suddenly, two hours had elapsed.
They lay strewn along the highway,
With beer cans, cigarette packs,
The indistinguishable carcasses of cats and dogs —
Accidents of gratuitous passages,
Whose spirits momentarily had belonged to me.

In futile dissolve, I lamented their loss.
The grave beside whose edge I shivered
Was an incommunicable silence
Widening even as I drove south,
Threatening, each mile, to bury me
In my own anonymity.

At Sikeston, then Hayti and Blytheville,
I stopped for coffee. Persistent urinating
Quenched the bladder's conflagration
While destroying evidence
Of my former existence, cleansing and flushing toxins,
Antibodies, cells, my self,

Until the recluse who finally arrived
At his arbitrary destination
Was a mere effacement of the man
Inside of whom I'd left home,
Kissed my wife adieu,
And whispered sillinesses to my children.

I'd been expunged by the waning sun,
Become time's hapless surrogate,
*

Dislocated in a land of tarpits
And desolated ossuaries, a shade
Among fossils and skeletons and flesh
Freshly rescued from the living,

A disembodied soul, bereft of its vessel
And without hope of finding direction
Back through the vast, black warp
I penetrated unknowingly,
Sometime this afternoon,
On my routine visit to the home office.

3/26/80   (02399)

Shall Inherit △

Traversing easterly from Helena,
Across the primordial Delta,
Calls me to my smallness,
By exposing my dormant sensibilities
To black tenants' shacks
Indistinguishable from their junkyard gestalt,
Whose perpetually hung-out wash
Forms a patchwork quilt
That catches and distracts the eye,
Momentarily,
From such abject squalor and poverty.

If I were Dreiser,
Chance and circumstance
Would become determining factors
In my doomsayer's conclusion
That fate has cursed this land
And these people, with an irreversible plague.
My instincts rebel against explanations
So complaisant and facile,
Search for more compelling metaphors
By which to foretell the Delta's future
In relation to its ageless past.

I imagine myself plowing these fields,
On mulish tractors, sleeping on mats,
Eating collard greens, turnips, hominy grits,
*

Feeling dust and mud
Sifting and oozing through my toes.
The pulsing sun tans my skin to a hue
Permanent as charred scar tissue.
Suddenly, the answer manifests itself:
These anomalies are divinity,
Whose tribulations are imbued with mercy.
God's chosen hover closest to the earth.

3/27/80 — [1] (00032)

[The rains complain; they groan.] ‡ △

The rains complain; they groan.
Their low moaning pervades the evening
Like a slow threnody
Chanted over the grave of an old friend,
While, indoors, William Styron
And Willie Morris stroke the Muse's lute,
Take decorum to new heights
Of art and charm. The townspeople shimmer
In such august midst, preen
And trip over unpracticed pretensions
To literary insight and intuition.
Meanwhile, I maintain a low profile,
Considering myself an outsider
Invited by a simple slip of the tongue
Whispered by the lissome host, in passing,
Earlier this afternoon.
I know all these people by name,
Yet they

3/27/80 — [2] & (10/23/85 or 11/5/85 [?]) (00473)

College Town, Friday Night △

For Thomas Verich

As I sit here on this enclosed patio
Of Oxford's most animated watering hole,
I'm assailed by an agonizing desire to know
Who in hell invented higher learning,
*

The pursuit of degrees, tenure, celebrity
Through publication of treatises and novels,
And how this self-perpetuating invention
Evolved into such a complex phenomenon,
Out of its humble and innocent beginnings.

Strangers to this sophisticated moment in history
Might never guess these children,
Dressed in frivolity and timeless irresponsibility,
Are descendants of scions begotten by lovers
Copulating beyond latitudes bordering the Hesperides.
A certain totemistic freedom persists.
They tip their wineglasses to the winds and sip
As if oblivion would drip irresistibly
To their lips. They whisper to low-flying Artemis,

Hoping to persuade her handmaidens to abet
Their basest venalities, grant their wishes
To fuck God's own personal mistress.
She disregards such gross obscenities
As adolescent indiscretions, at once ludicrous
And humorously absurd, attempts at emulating
The original lotus-eaters, progenitors of their tribe.
Meanwhile, the music strokes their clitoral minds
To irreversible heights of inebriated night-glitter,

Where goats and "slithy toves" and satyrs
Roam, with uncontrollable abandon,
In desperate search of forever-after princesses
Obsessed with symbolic fornication,
Writhing in sweaty sleep, wetting their sheets
With semen-seeds conceived by priapic fantasies
Shepherding fleecy dreams in sleazy valleys
Beyond nightmare's reach. They climb mountains
Rising out of volcanic desire, to satisfy the glands.

Suddenly, I don't seem to be quite as constrained
By the convergence of wasted souls in this place,
Where spirits flow ceaselessly from rosé fountains.
I speak, in passing, with lassitudinous ladies
And boys. We tell each other that happiness
And being honest with each other's fragile feelings
Is "where it's at." I sign my autograph
On their receptive ears, as though I were a poet
Releasing odes, in the air, like beautiful balloons,

Scribbling elegies across their sensual cells,
In the gentlest metered graffiti. We converse,
Strangers until this poignant moment,
When meeting disassembles the human drywall
Separating well-insulated rooms we lease
From a common landlord. Suddenly, I know
Who in hell invented higher learning and why:
God bequeathed us this retreat
In which to languish and revel before dying into life.

3/28/80 — [1] (00973)

Buzzed Confession

I scribble my paltry vocables in the dark,
Hoping my children might read me
Posthumously,
Learn about their deceased daddy
From the verse he created while driving,
Drinking wine in college towns,
And thinking in irregularly measured feet
When sleeping through board meetings.
This aesthete's pathetic record
Exists above infinite blue lines
Containing the sum of one man's
Exaggerated imagination. I weep
For the sweet, sentimental souls
Whom I've seen standing in line
For the late show and known
As passing phantasms and chimeras
On the street. I grieve for my generation,
Which still finds Dylan's music
The apotheosis of radicalism and chic.
I pray for those who've now divorced
Their high-school sweethearts
In favor of Miss Campus Queen of 19
Blank-blank. I genuflect
To the time that spawned us with good intentions
And innocence, which never conceived us
As hedonistic demons bent on gratification
And instant satisfaction of the sensory glands.
Narcissism lurks beneath the dark surface,
*

A familiar face in the crowd, a shadow
Coming unbound from its mass.
We pass, recognize each other, stop,
And enter the procession marching toward oblivion.

3/28/80 — [2] (05687)

Enchantment △

Yesterday afternoon,
Just as a reluctant southern sun set
Into slumbrous blue-pine hills
Beyond Oxford, I was unexpectedly bespelled
By a shimmering semblance of Temple Drake,
The governor's golden coed.

She entered through my eyes,
Penetrated my senses like cool, nubile wine,
Entranced the sentries standing guard
Outside my somnolent conscience,
And danced naked on the stage
My dreams had made for sublimated lovers.

This occurred while I gazed at her
From a distance of years, without words,
A convergence of lusty spirits
Speaking in whispers, reaching to touch
Before lights, music, voices,
Amplified by inebriation, destroyed the philter

Connecting us with shadows the sun cast
Like a spider crosshatching a web.
Briefly we meshed, released seeds, unclung.
Suddenly, she was running from my fantasy,
Into the arms of a mere friend,
With whom she'd get drunk and fuck, that night.

3/29/80 (00053)

Turndown Day △

This early-April day,
So innocent, immaculate, pristine,
*

So warm and clean
And sunny, with forsythias exploding,
Like girandoles from skyrockets,
Against my image-making apparatus,

Contrasts starkly
To the dark and dour, glowering face
Of saturnine Trilogy,
Sucking her thumb,
Cauterized in numbness, head buried
Between her knees,

As we repeat the ritual of empty streets,
Leading to kindergarten, in silence.
She is a slowly imploding volcano,
Whose only release
Comes from screwing her features
Into grotesque death masks,

Refusing to do the simplest tasks we ask
For her sake, cursing us
With hissing sibilances reminiscent of speech
Spoken in Pandemonium.
I stand at her quaking base,
Wondering if her eyes will cease twitching.

4/2/80   (00193)

The Commuter

He has no idea
Whether concrete and countryside
Over and through which he drives
Are what they appear to be
Or even if he's actually alive, this morning.

His eyes refuse to comment,
While mind-parasites remain silent.
Logic and philosophical speculation
Deny him access to wisdom's inner sanctum.
Blind faith doesn't suffice.

Unleaved trees, striated shale bluffs,
Tawny tall grasses, green signs
*

Flash past his peripheries,
In irrevocable retrograde,
And are replaced incessantly by identical scenes,

As though he were standing at the dead center
Of a spinning Praxinoscope
Instead of pressing ever forward,
Toward a definite destination. He winces
From this continuous bombardment of his vision.

In the compartment his mass occupies,
He scrutinizes, with quizzical distancing,
His hands on the wheel. They complete
A crude Rube Goldberg tool
Made to aid an absurdly daffy creature

He fails to recognize as himself.
Curiously, the hairy pair
Is capable of coordinating his safety,
Keeping his existence intact —
Preternaturally or mesmerically he's not certain.

Time rushes at him and away,
In integers and ciphers
Disguised as trucks and cars,
Blurred shapes hurtling in and out,
Phantasms, chimeras, apparitions, mares.

Time sucks him into its draft
Just before he crashes through numbness
And disappears. Startled, he steps from his car
(Parked in the dark garage beneath his office),
Mindful of his bodily salvation.

4/3/80 — [1] (05688)

The Magnolias

A ferocious wind blows the twin magnolias
With such vicious commotion,
They metamorphose, before my poet-eyes,
Into two Medusas,
Whose fractious leaves are spastic tongues
Spitting curses back at the breeze.

Suddenly, a lull transforms my focus
Back into trees.
Their waxy leaves and stiff limbs
Intertwine in docile and obedient harmony.
I remember them as seedlings
We planted when I was barely sixteen.

Again, the incorrigible wind intervenes.
My brief reverie is caught and shredded
In their lashing branches, chewed up
And spewed out like useless confetti.
Forgetting consumes all time
Between youth and this present moment,

In which I sit staring at companions
Who've paralleled my mature span of years
Without ever having spoken to me.
Now, the air empties itself temporarily.
We share this solitude, alone, lonely,
Knowing the earth owns us,

Holds our clay in its shaping embrace,
And that one day, as in the beginning it obtained,
We will enter each other
As sisters and brothers of consanguineous origin.
For now, the quixotic wind
Elicits and mixes our disparate existences.

4/3/80 — [2] (05689)

Easter-Egg Hunt in the Square △

Yesterday morning, at eleven sharp,
I witnessed not a crucifixion in a literal sense
But a symbolic denouement
Of pre-Easter festivities, set in the town square.

All week, the children dreamed of the Bunny,
Though none could know
He'd arrive in a white Volkswagen convertible,
Throwing wrapped candies like grass seed,

Or that, at his sacred advent,
All hell would break loose, clotheslines
*

Holding back different age groups
From plots strewn with Brach's chocolate eggs

Would give way to surging masses
Anxious to overflow baskets,
Grocery bags, and makeshift reliquaries
With the rabbit's droppings, his mystical remains.

For a moment, I saw the shimmering promise
Of an entire city on the plains
Take shape in a ritualistic passion play
Enacted against a backdrop of smiling faces,

Then watched it dissolve as evanescently,
Leaving, in its wake, cellophane and silence
For Saturday shoppers to caustically remark
And the wind to stuff in its pockets and carry off.

4/6/80   (01447)

Musing on Campaign '80

Dialectical rhetoric, polemics, and cant,
Political debate, arbitration
Between labor and recalcitrant management,
And clandestine shuttle diplomacy
With Egypt, Iran,
Lebanon, Greece, and Israel
Are acanthus leaves
Tightly entwined above the coffin
Containing my dispirited intellect.

They form an intricate funeral spray
That drapes my breathless remains
With resignation and stagnant despair
That the hereafter, where redemption
Awaits my beleaguered soul,
Might merely be a newer Albion,
The newest Jerusalem in a progression
Of macrofacsimilies. I shudder to think
That death could be such a letdown.

4/9/80   (00196)

The Artisan

On this sultry, rainy April morning,
At the disreputable hour of 8 a.m.,
When, already, my subdued spirit
Should have driven Pat Lyon to his forge,
To sweat, in blind devotion,
Over mass-produced horseshoes
For carnival-game prizes
And Shriners' souvenirs stamped "Good Luck,"

I malinger, in an undefendable funk,
Over coffee, refusing to move
Or fabricate excuses for my disinclination
To phone in sick.
I order eggs and toast,
To postpone the moment when guilt
Will force me to emigrate
From this no-man's-retreat, into daylight.

Strange voices oscillating about me
Create an aura of fear. Paranoia
Thrusts me into the epicenter of their noise.
I weary, deciphering disconnected phrases
That skitter past my ears and disappear
Inside my derisive suspicion
That all of them are condemning me
For my presence here.

The judgment of outpatients
From the state hospital,
City officials voting in the new day,
Chronically unemployed carpenters, farmers,
Car salesmen, barbers, and tree cutters
Weighs self-consciously on my sensibility.
It strips away my clothing.
I sit naked as a potential rape victim,

Waiting to be violated,
Dispossessed of my few remaining privacies,
Before being thrown into the zone
Where those going from dole to dole,
In dizzying, dehumanized spirals,
Wear out their soulless days
*

As silent pariahs
In unnegotiable damnation.

I succumb to lethargy's addiction,
Sit in numb suspension,
A catatonic slug shriveled into itself,
Ambitionless except for a determination
Never to return to my forge,
To fashion gewgaws and implements of war
In a country where there are no horses
To be shod anymore.

4/11/80   (00195)

Mid-April Devastation

For almost two weeks,
We'd been reveling in spring's coming,
Her luxuriant fecundity,
Indulging sensual and intellectual appetites
With our naming, touching, looking,
And seeing through objects,
To their naked truth.

First, crocuses penetrated the earth,
In various shaded groves,
Surfaced, in our spiritual preserves,
As harbingers of all things green and gold.
Close behind, in two isolated beds
Lining our front walk,
Came bold, unbloomed tulips, in profusion,

Then jonquils and brilliant forsythias,
Shimmering in their own yellow auras
Like spinnakers billowing in a bay breeze.
Finally, to this premature season,
Magnolias, dressed in lavender-purple robes —
Elegant courtesans — exposed themselves,
To be had, to be sure, for the moment only.

We accepted this notion,
Knowing from past seasons not to expect
Much more than evanescence,
Pleasures dissolving into sere summer
*

Soon enough; we'd experienced vicissitudes
Brought on by cold spells
A time or two, winter refusing to quit.

Yet none of us ever would have suspected
That such voluptuousness
Could be arrested so abruptly,
With an absoluteness of executions,
As it was by a soggy snow
Falling unannounced all night —
An apocalypse for flowers and budding boughs.

4/14/80 (02131)

On the Nature of Birthdays

Simultaneous with spring's arrival
Is my singular ritual,
That time and day and hour,
Memorialized with spontaneous celebration,
When haughty April
Bows down, in solifidian obeisance,
To its momentary emperor, L.D.

Whoever decreed this season
Unreasonably cruel
Knew not the true nature
And meaning of curse,
From Plato, through Frazer, to Eliot.
Don't the puissant crocuses and jonquils
Exemplify redemption?

My birthday marks another passage
Through scattered ashes
That once were dreams and ambitions,
Kisses, smiles, disappointments,
Abstractions approached, unclothed,
And redressed with answers
Formulated by my perpetual imagination.

This occasion awakens me
To my present destination and places occidental,
Not yet mapped. I sit
In the backwash of past tenses,
*

Letting ancient voices
Have their say before I go forward,
On the future's fluid translation,

In quest of Rosetta stones.
Aging is a figment,
An incomplete vision of wisdom and truth,
Which exists in human vacuums
Perfectly accessible to the human intellect.
Today, I begin my fortieth year —
A baby growing in the eye of God.

4/16/80 (00194)

Love-Fetters

Once again, I've come unfastened
From the fragile hasp
That holds both halves of me together.
I'm an apparition, escaping
That part which keeps us in wraps,
Resisting excessive sedentariness.

My shadow passes through a space
In the focus my gaze
Closely aims as it penetrates your face
And imperceptibly sad eyes
And enters the sky above us,
Aboard a star-borne argosy soaring,

Soaring, toward a warp in history
Where lovers like us
Discover time is a series of openings
Connected by empty souls
Waiting for us to occupy them briefly
As our spirits fly into the sun.

4/17/80 (01023)

A Lighthouse Keeper's Lonely Night △

Even the simplest images,
Not to mention the fanciest vessels,
Elude my beacon's sweep tonight.

They resist being silhouetted,
Cast in shadowy, cursive lines,
Discovered floating in sublime silence.

No matter how substantial
My fulgent beam might seem,
They refuse to be illuminated.

(Being defined by surrendering their essence
To my light is a fate
Whose mandate has rarely exposed them.)

Rather, they hide in recesses,
Willing to brave the inscrutable,
For fear of being recognized, boarded,

Exploited, and compromised by pirates
Of the intellect. After a time,
My urge to safeguard visions subsides.

I sit idly by, discouraged,
While my searchlight pans a horizon
Void of ships to guide into port.

4/24/80   (05690)

Tyrian Purple

Each redbud is a preening peacock,
Whose extravagant purples
Scream out, from crowded coverts,
To be seen, to be heard, to be.

In this soft, supple, seething season,
My own sensual juices
Begin to flow, in prophetic sympathy
With lilac and lavender hues.

My blood is renewed. The bones
Grow restless, with prospects
Of being blessed, baptized, dressed
In smooth, fleshy robes.

My eyes wander off by themselves,
Snap twigs of forsythias,
Spireas, magnolias, and pink dogwoods,
From summer's shimmering prism,

Which they gather in their woven baskets
And lay before me
To sort through — ecstasies evanescent
Yet perpetual as retinal visions

Memorized from pre-Edenic times.
Childhood retrieves me,
Calls me into its nameless preserve,
Where colors and smells break loose

From their reciprocal elements
Like balloons drifting into the air
And forgetting assumes the shape
Of a naked muse waiting to take me,

From daily consternations and despair,
Home, to innocence and naiveté —
Womb-waters where my heart bathed,
The eternal/maternal alembic of youth.

For this one immutable moment,
My maniacal ego is sundered,
Subjugated to God's dominant omniscience,
A bug trapped on its back.

It is the senses' hour to regale,
To flower and dance, then perish
Without a trace of derision,
Before insects victimize the entire forest

And the sun scorches the spirit
To a crisp. In this greening presence,
The essence of redbud
Tinges me with the Tyrian elegance of divinity.

4/30/80 — [1] (05691)

Lament for Paul Gauguin, Who Died in the Marquesas, Bereft[*]

My grief is a frothing chimera,
Whose rabid bites
Leave me bleeding invisible fluid
Across the back of my neck and legs.

The senses' flesh wounds fester.
Their stench suggests death,
Despite life-throbs igniting the arteries,
Shuddering the dust bags,

Tightening gut strings and muscle bindings.
My grief is a nightmare
Multiplying incubi, ceaselessly,
From the psyche's hallucinating vagina,

As though I were an orphanage
For wayward brain-children,
A mistaken manifestation
Of a refuge for useless ideas,

Instead of a repository for promises
Unconsummated and forgotten.
My grief is my daughter, Trilogy.
It's neither visionary nor imagistic,

Rather as physical as her lingering frown,
Drawn down on my screen,
Early this morning,
When I confided to her my leaving.

My grief is her quivering lips,
Her tears, her futile litany
Of "Why?"s and "Do you really have to?"s.
My grief is the lonely soul's suicide.

---

* Gauguin loved his daughter Aline so strongly. He begged her to understand and keep faith in his strange and overwhelming need to isolate himself in hope of achieving the creation of his visions. Her death devastated him, in Tahiti, caused him to attempt suicide, then retreat further into his private isolation, to the Marquesas Islands. Six years after her death, from pneumonia, he died alone and consumed by grief, syphilis, and TB.

4/30/80 — [2] (00689)

Businessman and Poet

Still shrouded in mist,
The dappled hills entrenching Columbia
Beckon me approach and enter
Their ever-diminishing mystical distance.

I go against the noxious grain
Of this main-traveled highway
Carrying the discontented and bored
To their morning Gethsemanes,

Encouraged by the lack of phantoms
Going in my direction, not concerned
With the treasonable consequences
Of being wayward, nonconformist,

Guided by inner dictates,
Whose driving forces are self-reliance
And an innate fear of being forced into a herd
Of sheep or single-minded felines

Stampeded by a savannah fire.
Somewhere beyond the next hour,
My occupation waits
To let me penetrate its hallowed gates,

Practice its easy precepts
Of peace at any cost,
Prosperity maintained by experience,
Not monetary gain,

And perpetuation of customer response,
Through politeness, courtesy,
And service tendered with a personal touch.
Soon, my workday will commence.

My registers will produce tapes,
Whose cryptic numerations
And abbreviations suggest themes.
Words and verses will fill the tills

With accumulating booty
Exchanged for psychic energy,
The merchandise of my waking operation,
While I'll renew my stock,

From opening to late afternoon,
With imagination's surpluses.
Finally, I'll tally the receipts, reconcile them
With proceeds calibrated in lines

Accented, metered, internally rhymed,
Departments formed by stanzas,
Whose total will be another poem
Deposited and credited to my accruing balance.

Just ahead, the emporium looms,
A bustling thieves' market
Owned and run solely by me,
For purposes of serving my community of one.

5/1/80 — [1] (05692)

Manny Chevitz, Bail Bondsman △

Unabashedly disgusted,
He gnashes his teeth, scratches his genitals
With simian unself-consciousness,
And blasphemes chance and circumstance
(Bastard brothers who inhabit his fantasies)
For having shoved him headlong
Into this abyss, below Phlegethon Bridge,
Where his desk sits
In bald juxtaposition to a series of stalls
Equipped with sophisticated bidets
For the exclusive use of Satan's night-ladies.

For more than two decades,
He's conducted his petty chicaneries,
Base, politically motivated collusions and loans,
Bullied and browbeaten downtrodden,
Disfranchised schlemiels,
Jerkwaters, hicks, rubes, and schlimazels
Who've come to him desperate
For bail bonds, neighborhood favors, hits
On cuckolders, accidental intruders,
Heirs apparent, at fourteen, to a daughter,
Mistress, first-name-basis courtesan.

And for lucrative remuneration
(Biarritz with vinyl top, sunroof,
And Continental kit, a retreat in the hills,
Replete with tennis court, swimming pool,
Myriad phone jacks, Kotex dispensers,
His own dialysis machine, Jacuzzi,
In-house experts in onanism and feathers,
Consultants in S-and-M concatenations),
He's persisted in his shenanigans.
Having whetted his appetite for life's perversions
And tasted extravagantly,

He's lately become aware of his aversion
For the daring, a steady disinclination
To engage in others' devastations.
A pervasive going-through-the-motions
Has spirited him in and out of lower courts,
Back offices of local politicos
And inauthentic dagos-turned-godfathers,
With increasing boredom. Every scene
Is, for him, a déjà vu, a "sloppy second,"
History repeating itself, with only the names
Changed to protect the guilty, the guilty

Who've congregated, for twenty years,
In his sleazy office beneath Hell's Bridge,
To debate the merits of their degenerate cases.
Now, he senses fatigue, ennui,
The anomie his infected spirit has incubated,
Realizes good times are giving way
To the lean. He must escape
Before it's too late, but his age
Is a handicap, and the nicotine stains
In his mustache, on his fingertips and eyelids,
Single him out as a bad risk

To young ladies ambitious to become celebrities.
He has no choice other than to persist
In his daily inveigling, those imbroglios
Requiring his incomplete law education.
In his empty office, to a chorus
Of spraying bidets, he grieves over his condition,
Weeps, knowing the alternatives
For extricating himself are nonexistent.
Abruptly, he feels for his penis, squeezes it.
The pain makes him faint. When he awakens,
Death is waiting for his sage consultation.

5/1/80 — [2] (02553)

Confessions of a Young University Instructor

He's just a fucking lemming in disguise,
Not the sophisticated instructor
They've mistakenly attributed to his controlled presence
*

Each time he enters the classroom,
Assumes the lectern, and begins pontificating
On the nature of true grace
In seventeenth-century England, sixteenth-century Spain,
Or Dankmar Adler's protégé, Frank Lloyd Wright.

If they only knew, those young chicks
In tight jeans and Danskin tops,
That he frequents the local bistros
Every other night and leaves inebriated,
On chilled rosé or strawberry daiquiris,
They'd quit their embarrassed crushes,
Rush him after class, with their lush cunts
On platters, cut off their tits on a whim.

But he conceals his dissolute habits,
Never misses a lecture,
Despite the fact that his preparations are scant.
Each morning, he wings it, flings shit
At the screen whenever Fallingwater
Or the Guggenheim Museum requires exegesis.
They take notes assiduously,
As though he were transcribing Dead Sea scriptures

Instead of trivia retained from graduate school.
He maintains decorum despite the blood
Flooding his cock each time he glimpses
The petite blond in the front-row seat
Nearest the aisle, whom he vows to corner after class.
Intuiting his desire, she lingers one day.
He passes, retreats, invites her to review
His final exam. Politely, she acquiesces,

Retires with him to Bogart's, Bullwinkle's,
Katy Station, Harvest Moon,
Marries him before the next semester resumes,
And settles, with her modest wardrobe,
Books, cooking utensils, into his room,
On the second floor of the boardinghouse by the zoo.
For some inexplicable reason, his next courses
Dwell on Pompeian art and Hindu eroticism;

They focus on the Kama Sutra.
Abruptly, he ceases frequenting the local bistros,
Remains at home, discovering the mysteries
*

Inherent in fundamental Occidental sex.
Together, they formulate his syllabuses,
His texts, the content of his lectures,
As he settles into the complacent habitude
Of connubial bliss, forgetting his loneliness forever.

5/1/80 — [3] (02554)

Tonya

The wasted souls in this place
Remind me that my devastated spirit
Is languishing, alone and empty,
In this space devoid of wife and children.

I can't stand the disgrace, the contumely,
The fantastical desolation
That surround this stained-glass bar,
With its sedentary zombies and deadbeats,

Its after-midnight waifs,
Who've gravitated, like moths to light,
Around this oasis. I grope for familiarity,
Realize that nothing, not the people

Or the players or the fixtures, recognizes me
From former times in other towns.
I shrink into my drink, inebriated,
So that focus becomes a strange sensation

In which the cross section of cells
Overcomes me in its immediacy.
The female bartender lisps. Her harelip
Slips into my drunken brain. She speaks

A language of silent sex I can't refuse.
Her breasts leap from her dress,
Into my waiting eyes. I dive
Toward the distant surface of her libido,

Hoping to reach night's end,
Where she sleeps in anonymity's embrace.
But the wine is absorbed into my system.
Soon, I miss her frequent shape

Pacing back and forth behind her stage
Lined with glasses and whiskey bottles.
She escapes my gaze. I retreat
Into the music, its captive, entranced

By chords and harmonies. I surrender,
This dateless evening, to the sounds
Emanating from the stage. Neither Lorelei
Nor Medusa can bespell my dull brain.

I am suspended like a wandering Jew
Planted in a hanging pot, draped,
In haphazard braids, in thin, invisible air.
My psyche surrenders to its coeval,

Death, hovering in the recesses of this room,
Arrested in funereal resurrection.
When I look up, everyone has disappeared
Except the buxom bartender.

She stands naked, her nipples erect,
Stroking her erogenous folds
As though, any moment, she might climax
All over her plastic-spouted bottles.

Her thin body captivates me. I freeze
On her Attic pose, my ego fragmenting
With each step she takes. Suddenly, I die
In my seat, fatigued and unconsummated,

While the music dissipates into the stale air
And the lady in skintight Halenca,
Serving scotch — Helen of Troy, Wisconsin —
Dissolves in my ears and lascivious eyes.

5/1/80 — [4] (01348)

A Letter to My Mother

For C.M.B.,
Mother's Day 1980

Dear Mother,

I sit here contemplating all those days
When I'd fake out of school
*

And you'd eagerly write elaborate excuses
For my "perfectly legitimate" absences,

To keep me from squandering afternoons
I might spend in splendid isolation,
Hinging postage stamps into empty spaces,
Sorting through mail-order packets,

Anticipating a fortuitous rarity
In the shape of an inverted airmail
Or British Guiana one-cent magenta,
And how you'd buy my excitement on the sly,

Both of us knowing we were co-conspirators
In a scam to deceive Dad,
Whose irrefutable business acumen
Would instantly expose us as romantics.

I remember, less far back,
When Lionel tracks connected my adolescence
To the future, via spectacular passages
From the basement of our house,

Through youth's enthusiastic imagination,
To stations where friends paused
To learn ballroom dancing
And date and make erotic discoveries

In the backseats of their parents' cars.
Always, for birthdays and on occasions
Construable as gift-worthy,
You'd contribute yet another figment

To the cosmic picture: a passenger car,
Silver and lit from within,
Miscellaneous rolling stock, trestles,
Bridges — whatever I'd request

At that specific moment along the journey.
I recall how you'd help guard
The sanctity of my private meanderings,
By holding phone calls, canceling curfews,

Bringing meals on a tray, snacks, sodas,
To keep me from suspending operations.
You were ever sympathetic
To accomplishments seemingly inscrutable to you.

Now that I'm thirty-nine,
Although the need has not abated,
The means of escape have been grossly revised,
To accommodate my demons inside:

Legal documents, holographs,
And inscribed copies of books by Faulkner,
Received from his family members and friends
And dealers, consume my "other" time.

Although the questing is consistent
Regardless of its differences in kind,
Something has diminished
As the distance I've traveled into manhood

Has widened. I've been cut off physically
From your personal concern,
Your peering over my shoulder
As, once, I put each new stamp

Into its ordered place, with a sticky hinge,
Your spontaneous desire
To know why a GG-1 derailed,
The reason a switch failed to activate.

I yearn for your doting, empathic worry
Over my peace of mind, my well-being,
Without binding me to repay favors
Of compassion and love. I cringe,

Knowing I'm adrift, without anyone
To scribble excuses for missing work,
When sickness descends
Or depression rises to the surface.

Today, composing this elegiac letter
Seems my only way of saying I miss you
And wish you all my love,
My devoted adoration, my appreciation,

For your having given to my childhood, my life,
As, even today, they survive,
A measure of decency, gentleness,
Poetry, hope, and a trust of others.

5/8 & 5/10/80 (00189)

Zeitgeist

The days grow rife, age
To a blood-rust putrescence,
Like raw meat left out overnight.
Political strife and public unrest
Fester in the collective psyche.
From society's private sector,
Nixonian henchmen and press agents
Write exposés and "true-life stories,"
To reaffirm righteousness,
The ways of God to man,
And perpetuate the "rags to riches" myth.

Even poets and Arrowsmiths,
Steeped in their own ethers,
Are chattel, beef cattle
Grazing on multinational-conglomerate lands
Or in unfenced pastures
Endowed by institutions, for institutional use
Among institutes for higher obfuscation.
Daily they're brought to market
And bought, by the treatise or reading,
In one vast commodities exchange
For anonymous cartels and military juntas.

Fear is the flesh people wear,
The air they sully, the food consumed
In haste, to evacuate hazardous waste
Contained in every artificial bite
And savory appetite-teaser lobbied past
The FDA, XYZ.
Fear's surrogates, anxiety and paranoia,
Are canned laughter and advertisements,
Released, like nerve gas,
By neurotic disc jockeys and TV wizards
Pandering to the erotic cravings of a dazed civilization.

Back in an unmapped canyon,
A man and his lady, nameless and naked, hide.
The silent amity and sensual understanding
They share in this isolated ambience,
Stripped of violence, graft, warfare, scrap,
Keep their spirit for survival alive.
*

They plant and urinate, eat, sleep, copulate,
In plain sight of God. At night,
They pray for children to take their places
And multiply and bring hope to a dying race.
Each dawn, they bury their stillborn dreams.

5/14/80 — [1] (05693)

Losing a Train of Thought

He purchased his ticket for the right idea,
Then boarded the wrong train,
Whose destination was just backwards.
By the time a conductor could notify him
And the dispatcher show him the right track,
The *Limited* was out of the yard,
Rolling away, in mystic transportation,
On its own momentum, out of sight.

Having missed connections, he now sits,
Bored to death, in a vacant station,
Disgusted and frustrated about having to wait
For the next train, especially
Since the one he always takes
Is unscheduled and never arrives on time.

5/14/80 — [2] (05694)

Writer in Flight ^Δ

This morning, into which my startled spirit slips
Like shivering wind, past weather stripping,
Into a warm room, is gloomy and humid,
A doomed Mississippi a.m.
Consuming my vision with dim specters
Of Percy Grimm and the ancient snake
And a dispossessed pariah, Ike McCaslin.

Why I continue to be haunted and cursed
By such chimeras baffles me.
Yet these insidious demons persist
In pitting my stomach lining with painful abrasions,
*

Spitting acidic epithets in my face,
Castrating my hope to achieve safe passage
As I travel this alien terrain north, toward home.

Just up 55, Memphis looms,
A huge human ameba endlessly extending.
I can't avoid its suffocating grasp,
No matter how peripheral and ephemeral
Is my contact. Momentarily, its arterial system
Sends me coursing through the outer extremities
Of its slimy skin. Suddenly, I cringe,

Praying I'll reach the river and escape
Into a contiguous land of relative solemnity.
Reluctantly, the cypress bayous and pines
Fall away in my rearview fear,
As a sign declaring the Tennessee state line
Materializes. New Jerusalem welcomes me.
Soon, Missouri will reclaim its prodigal-Jew son.

For now, only Arkansas and two hundred miles
Separate my fate from the greater fate
Ordaining the rotation of all bodies
Terrestrial, galactic, and ethereal. I sigh,
Realizing time has hung me from its life-tree,
Suspended my four-wheel chrysalis
In a perfectly regulated elliptical orbiting

About the unknown sum of years bequeathed me
In which to accomplish my passage.
I drive on, no longer envisioning grotesqueries,
Mind-chimeras, psychic parasites.
My ego has, once more, gained suzerainty.
Driving home, I write my apostrophes to immortality.
Arriving is forever up ahead, just out of sight.

5/17/80   (00047)

One of the Kafka Group

I am a fly
Trapped in my own hapless frenzy.
My flights are exercises in repetition.
Back and forth, side to side,
*

I weave an invisible cover below the sky,
Leaving behind debris,
Detritus that once had meaning for me:
Friends, antiques, my children and wife,
A thousand and eighty-three poems
(No, one more, now — "and eighty-four")
I wrote to use as decorations
To cover isolation's walls.

Suddenly, my buzzing overtakes me,
Confounds orientation,
Scrambles the brain's radio reception,
Dismantles its severe concentration.
Cable connections to elevators and ailerons,
Tender membranes that keep my tiny machine
In straight and level flight,
Snap and shatter, setting up a chatter
So profoundly painful
I'm forced to abort my predetermined pattern,
Caught, by the wings, between fate's
Thumb and forefinger, too fatigued to resist.

5/19/80   (05695)

Uncle Sam Brodsky ^Δ

At ninety-three,
With a memory so keen and lucid
He could travel backward,
From this anomalous present,
Through an expanse of dimensionless tenses,
To his birth, in 1887, and easily return,

Conjuring, with his mind's wand,
Faces, facades, events from history
And his private life,
Like a magician changing night into eyes,

Uncle Sam,
Patriarch and lone survivor
From a generation of gentle merchants,
Slender, white-haired, dignified
Within the sphere of his shuffling ambulations,
Aphoristic wisdom, advice-giving, and love,

Has finally let go,
Whose hold vexed medical science,
Man's most respected authority,
Even outlasted God's expectation.

But he has not died today.
We've merely delivered him
Of his cumbersome integument and bones.
He's flown back to the fields
In which our own frangible ancestors,
Dia-spores blown out of Jehovah's palm,

First were scattered, then settled
And grew into perennials beautiful and sad.
Even now, we see him shimmering,
In lingering suspension, above our loving grief.

6/1/80   (02124)

After *Les demoiselles d'Avignon*

His visions depicted man's visage
In the shape of a painted bedsheet
Or shroud spread over dreams
Disembodied, demonized, unrealized,
Tattered violently in shreds,
As though each complete creation
Had been exposed to a tornado's rage
And changed in shattering cataclysm.

He'd known psychic dislocation
Firsthand. Depression was the worm
Attached to his imagination,
Feeding on his need to arrest essences,
Find a way to retain the sense
Of a person's reverberations on flat canvas,
A means of photographing the soul
Without resorting to lenses, shutters, negatives.

His fragmentations of cubes
And his swooping curves running backward
From viewers' expectations
Spoke a vocabulary so starkly new
And tantalizing that he became a messiah,
*

Whose ephemeral ladies and wives
Only heightened his mystifying existence,
Until fame was its own momentum.

Through the years, no one
Really understood what drove him
To touch, produce, incorporate his living
In pigmented transliterations.
Droves merely genuflected, gaped
In blind and mindless obeisance.
Only Pablo Ruiz Picasso
Knew he'd recorded God's visitations.

6/3/80   (00187)

On the Origin of Imagination

Giant staghorns,
Orchid plants profuse with dewy blooms,
Bamboo shoots thick as grass
Fastened to the sky,
And striped unicorns
Churning the horizon's gold hue to pewter
Remind me that phantasms and chimeras
Can appear, disappear, and reappear,
Any morning, without warning,
Just because the eyes
Require occasional baptizing
By the spirit of all sight visionary and divine.

Right now, the seething rain forest
Through which I drive,
Atop the dry, broad, bony back of a rhino,
Is not June-humid Missouri,
Polluted by speeding vehicles spewing fumes,
Rather one frame momentarily arrested
In an irreversible sequence
Of ever-perpetuating eye-blinks
Focusing, through a kaleidoscope's opening,
On a cross section of a mind-cell,
In whose blueprint swims evolution,
Potential invention for a whole new universe.

6/5/80   (05696)

The Man Who Knew Too Much Too Soon

The years I've lived most recently
Are Pyrrhic victories,
Mere illusions and shimmering mirages
That disappear, on nearing.

Momentum and youthful exuberance
No longer outweigh stasis,
Whose corporeal wasteland engulfs me
In somnolent, chalky, polluted hues

Death chooses to use in isolating
Its most imminent resisters.
I am a torpid anarchist,
Fearful of submitting to nonexistence

Yet disgracefully inept
At escaping the sinister shadow
That has trapped me in its cage,
With reprobates named pain,

Cynicism, resignation, and despair.
They keep me awake at night,
With their hysterical harangues and debates.
All day, I sleep while they exercise,

Out in the common yard,
With myriad inmates of similar persuasion.
I weary from an enlarged heart,
Scarred by deceits and repeated gullibilities.

Even my eyes refuse to distinguish
Daylight from darkness.
Both are murky, oceanic spaces
Floated with bloated, grotesque faces

Resembling persons I knew once,
Whom memory left stranded
On one of a hundred atolls
I sailed past, on my odyssey home.

Now, Pyrrhic trophies, silver and gold,
The years have given me,
To standing ovations from former peers,
Disintegrate, tarnish,

Gather dust, like hallowed reliquaries
Or hydriotaphian urns,
On shelves that line my padded cell.
Where my thumbs have coursed

Back and forth over their engravings
(They've served as touchstones),
Even my name is faint,
The dates vague, the events irrelevant

To my present disenchantment.
Some days, I pray for a conclusion
To this tedious prolongation of truth.
I'm thirty-nine; my decline is no illusion.

6/9/80 — [1] (05697)

The Distance Between Entropy and Attrition

As I head home,
The miles slide by in silence,
Like rank-and-file protestors,
In an endless picket line,
Petitioning their disfranchisement.

I sympathize with their plight,
Realizing that any chance
To ameliorate the conditions of my flight,
By slowing to accord them respect,
Is out of the question.

Destiny impels me at speeds
That obliterate focus,
Make positive identifications
Of faces in oncoming vehicles impossible,
Overwhelm my sense of direction,

And yet the miles
Are not my greatest enemies
Or even alien foes
Suspended in a Cold War nexus,
Rather simple recorded symbols

For a more endemic manifestation
Of intransigent time,
*

Time calibrated in distances between
Two destinations,
Death and breath,

As I drive home from being born,
Knowing only that what lies ahead
Is necessarily less
Than what's been left behind.
The miles bear witness to my passing cortège.

6/9/80 — [2] (05698)

[Greed, perfidy, capriciousness, and despair]

Greed, perfidy, capriciousness, and despair
Rush from me, like demons
Abandoning a pestilential land,
With the first shock wave from the bomb
Detonated just above rational belief.

I proclaim my individuality,
From beneath the rubble of an entire city
Decimated and irretrievable —
A sentimentalist too gullible to realize
That interlopers have taken over the fortress

In which I've sat reading and writing poetry,
These last twenty years,
Under the delusion that what I've had to say
Might change men's treasons
To sanctifications, their inhumanities to hopes

For reason and compassion and dreams
That fascism, fetishism,
And totemism of the soul will perish
From the globe, that polemical rhetoric
Like mine will give way to love,

Whose simple kissing and tender touching
Might supplant all the gross pornography
Oui, Playboy, Miller, and Burroughs
Could stir in the cauldron.
I speak of correspondences

Between the head and the heart,
The fusion of the heron and the wren,
Saints and demons, martyrs and satyrs,
"-Yrs"s that are so disparate as to sound alike
When spoken in the silence of typewriters

Regurgitating words, recording impulses
From vagrant fingers set loose
Against alien keyboards loaded, like dynamite,
With individual fuses
Waiting to be ignited, waiting to explode.

I regret that Dean Swift isn't here
To make pronouncements against vasectomies
And *Good Morning America* —
Hype American-style,
Which still decrees might is right

And reason is a dead issue when compared
To the *Donahue* show.
I refuse to prostitute my simple goals
To the great god Mammon,
Daddy Warbucks, geetus, "bread," gelt.

Famine is too close, just beyond sight,
Fornicating in the Quarter,
Where red lights flicker and whores saunter
With perfect equanimity
And dread of the Depression is a goat's game.

Soon, my own imprecise life will wane,
Reaching its climax like drunks
Wasting away in alleyways,
Masturbating the smooth green necks of bottles
Emptied of self-pity.

My post-office profile
Will be placed in the open-case drawer.
Myriad Rockfords will debate
Before taking a two-hundred-dollar-a-day fee
To locate me in some sleazy motel,

Shacked up with Lois Lane,
Doing a randy sadomasochistic number
On her perfectly suburban brain —
*

Clark Kent's archenemy,
Caught in the act of iconoclastic misogyny.

In the *New York Times* obit column,
They will eulogize my passing
As a sad moment in the chronicle of poets:
"His life marks the end of an era
In which truth once ruled supreme."

6/9 — [3] & 6/12/80 — [2] (00470)

Universal Formulations

Imagine if our conception
Of the movement of stars and moons,
Their massive cosmological attractions to
And repulsions from each other,
Were still based on a Ptolemaic
Renaissance misperception
Postulated by the Danish astronomer Brahe,
Who believed that our entire system,
Rather than being heliocentric by nature,
Is regulated by the tiny planet
Earth and that man,
With his reasoning, imagining, and abstracting,
Sits in the seat from which all decisions,
Psychological, physical, and theological, can be made.

How, then, might we explain away
Lightning, typhoons, earthquakes, famines
As mere natural phenomena
With solutions, if not causes,
Beyond our control? I, for one,
Am satisfied being a cipher,
Casting an ephemeral, infinitesimal shadow
On a Newtonian mind-scape
Located at the edge of a vortex
On the surface of the galactic ocean
Reductio ad Absurdum.
I celebrate my fate, dreaming of the day
When, exiting through the great cloaca,
My soul will be one incarnation closer to home.

6/12/80 — [1] (00260)

In the Ancient Lineage of Kings I

For my father, Saul

Less than ten days have elapsed
Since we furrowed the earth with our grief
And planted Uncle Sam
In our family's perennial memories.

Now, you alone, dear Dad,
Hold suzerainty over our devotion and love.
We come to you, this day,
To proclaim our heart's celebration

And elect you, by fortuitous decision,
Spiritual ruler
Over our tiny, far-flung enclave
Of poet, lawyer, merchant, housewife,

Schoolboy, and blessed matriarch, Charlotte.
You, with your voracious thirst
For knowledge firsthand
And through the printed word, have mastered

Vicissitudes and pitfalls of commerce,
With acumen, diplomacy,
And a bear-trap mind for figures and facts.
As members of this protectorate,

We anoint you with our voices,
Singing in joyous roundelay,
By unanimous choice, virtuous and sound,
Guardian in perpetuity,

Until the day when, by your silence,
I, through primogeniture,
With frightened, hesitant step, will rise
To assume your throne,

Realizing, even as I enter the ether,
You and patriarchal Sam
And our entire meek line,
Tracing back to the land of Isaac and Abraham,

Will be watching and waiting for me
To cover myself in your mantle
Of wisdom and kindness.
Blessed father, I shiver with ecstasy,

Dreaming of that responsibility
I'll one day inherit. For now,
We bow in quiet obeisance,
To praise your mild and mighty presence.

6/13/80 — [1]   (02208)

In the Ancient Lineage of Kings II

For my father, Saul,
6/15/80

Less than ten days have elapsed
Since we furrowed the earth with our grief
And planted Uncle Sam
In our family's perennial memories.

Now, Dad, you alone
Hold suzerainty over our devotion and love.
We come to you, today,
To proclaim our hearts' celebration

And name you, by unanimous decision,
Spiritual leader
For our tiny, far-flung enclave
Of poet, lawyer, merchant, housewife,

Schoolboy, and gentle matriarch, Charlotte.
You, who've thirsted for education
Firsthand, knowledge
Through printed words, and have mastered

Vicissitudes and pitfalls of commerce,
With acumen, diplomacy,
And a bear-trap mind for figures and facts,
Will accept election with humility and grace.

Singing in joyous roundelay,
We anoint you keeper of the scrolls,
Guardian of our fortress,
Our souls' progenitor, virtuous and sound.

In quiet obeisance, we bow,
Blessed father,
To praise your mild and mighty presence,
And pray this day shall never dissolve.

6/13–14/80 — [2] on 6/13   (02117)

Off the Beam

Just this minute,
All traces of the radio station
I've been receiving cease.

After a half-hour's increasing static,
The waves have disintegrated,
Leaving a cacophonous vacuum,

A den of hissing snakes.
This sudden, vexatious interruption
Awakens me to my isolation,

The total severing with familiarities:
Sounds, mind-sights, harmonies —
Channel markers in the changing stream.

I fumble for alternative vectors,
Without success. Finally,
The knob makes contact with silence,

As I sit back, twitching,
Utterly switched off,
Lost in this nether zone

Of open ocean separating Memphis
From Farmington, a peripatetic
Whose malfunctioning gyro

Has forced him to press ahead,
On dead reckoning, alone as Moses,
In the nexus of his own blessed skepticism.

6/16/80 — [1] (05699)

The Town Crazy ^Δ

His unobtrusively disclosed obituary
In the local paper
Concluded, all too figuratively,
He'd been a writer in the prime of his vision,
Sensitive to the nuances and influence of words,
Intoxicated by their shapes,
Whose sounds bespelled him to death.

Of course, almost nobody in his hometown
Saw the tiny notice,
*

And those few who did
Intuited it to be specious and unscientific,
Doubtless couched by him years prior.
His coffee drinking and nail biting were legendary.
Obviously, an aneurysm had sundered him.

Only after the AP
And UPI wire services
Picked up and packaged his funeral
Did the townspeople realize their obligation
To pay public homage, close their doors
For fifteen minutes, that afternoon,
As strangers from New York and Paris

Formed the procession that carried his coffin
To the nondenominational cemetery,
Where, on his headstone,
In hastily incised Gothic letters,
Read the following epitaph:
"Poetry was his mother tongue,
The earth his fatherland."

Now, the sleazy complacency
Among which he lived and wrote his poems
Has closed over his brief notoriety,
Resuming the pervasive sameness of religion.
In their drugged manifestations of divinity,
Even the children exaggerate and slander
The eccentricities of his behavior,

Unaware that his cryptic voice
Emanated from inspiration untainted
And compassionate despair, not hedonism, like theirs.
Only outlanders visit his grave,
Revere his oeuvre, quote his soul at will.
Recently, McDonald's installed
A wall-length portrait of the town's distinguished son.

6/16/80 — [2] (05465)

Breakdown

This morning,
My pen is the rigid end
*

Of a fidgeting needle on a graph
Recording variations in dendrite energy.

Sleep drips yet,
Like sap from a blooming redbud or mimosa,
Off my eyelids. Nightmares
Still scurry and slither for nearest cover,

Beyond my awakened mind.
All that I abandoned yesterday afternoon,
Unfinished, short-circuited,
Damaged irreparably, awaits my commands.

But something malign
Keeps me from God's obvious designs:
An essence of death-whiffs,
Blowing against my face, at gale force,

From an invisible source,
Or indistinct vision of hostile aborigines
Tying down my beached body,
Washed up out of sea-dreams,

Has obliterated my motivation to cast off sheets
And rush, ambitiously,
Into a transcendent dawn. Fear
Shackles my sedgy head to this bed,

Refuses me passage. The hours rotate
On their axis, their digital transformations
Seemingly calibrated to my blinking,
So that time and my breathing become fused

With the inexorably eroding present.
Soon, noon intrudes.
Klaxons, tornado warnings, police
And ambulance sirens converge

In a shrill, surging blast so crimson
The air coffining my prostrate body
Turns to liquid. Their knell
Reminds me my moment to rise is at hand

And that malingering is no longer the answer
To the insupportable question of my purpose.
From nowhere,
Attendants in black and white convene,

To escort me through the door
(My nakedness is not important to them),
Guide me toward the machine
That records variations in dendrite energy,

Where, once more,
Others will accurately determine the course
My convalescence is taking
And whether I'm making progress toward recovery.

6/17/80 — [1] (05700)

Aborted Metamorphosis

For Dottie Abbott

Suddenly, I'm possessed by the same demons
That subverted and transmogrified Kafka's psyche,
Perverted his equanimity, then changed him,
Via Gregor Samsa, into an insidious, repugnant bug.

I peer at shadows, made by facsimiles of me,
Looming in plate glass,
Shaving and rearview mirrors, staring out
Through slits in my own life-mask,

Asking myself repeatedly to identify features
Belonging to the original. All answers
Are stiff plates that form Gregor's hard shell,
As he lies on his back, contemplating a ceiling fan

Spinning with the nightmarish silence of planets
Coursing orderly, inexorably, in space.
The questions contain their own non sequiturs,
Yet I pursue them to their inconclusions,

Hoping to postulate a new notion of immortality
Compatible with my arrogant self-expectations.
Helplessly, my legs flail the air.
I'm unable to turn over, get going,

Make a solitary forward motion
Resembling progress toward the greater good.
All my aggressive energy is diffused
Amidst the confusion lifting, mistlike, from my solitude.

If only one damned, doomed soul
Would happen along,
To give this dumb husk of mine a shove,
I'd be appreciative, indebted to him or her forever

Or at least until I got back on my feet,
Functioning again
With my old sense of independence and free will.
But no one even comes to my door

Anymore
Or remembers the slightly timid, silent Samsa
Who tried to write, reach out
To one uptight lady after another,

Without touching the appropriate chord,
Break down religious prejudices,
To discover the true humanistic correspondence
Between people of every disparate persuasion.

In this fortuitous internment, I starve.
Consumption dissolves my entrails,
As night achieves permanent twilight in my eyes,
Whose glassy abysses collect all images

And refuse to allow the retinas
Their opportunity to make brain-translations.
Soon, too soon, the end begins.
In an instant, I recognize death in his disguise.

Without ceremony, he kicks me over,
Insists I get the shit out of this room,
Shouting, as I run for my life,
"Not yet, you feeble son-of-a-bitch!

"I don't take cowards, on principle.
Supply obviously makes me a choosy bastard.
Scat, sissy! Come back on your back,
After you've made a clean break with fear.

"I don't need another pusillanimous fruit
Like you, Gregor — bust their asses
Out there and then petition me to remove you
From the fray. For now, become yourself again.

"Singe your hands in the sun's tongues!
Fuck the moon's pussy to pieces!
*

Memorize the conventional wisdom,
Then forget all but its Rosetta signs!

"I reject you! Go back home!
When you're ready to die, I'll know."
Suddenly, the demons release their hold
Over my psyche. I awaken from my comatose state

In time for dinner with my parents,
Who gently remark my slight tardiness
With tacit glances and then ask for my hand
In prayer. Together, we solemnize life,

Exhort the Lord to watch over us,
Grant us peace and usefulness to His cause.
Secretly, I vow to seek a means
For enlisting God's aid in defeating Satan,

Realizing that the only way to avoid his thralldom
Is by annihilating the Prince of Lies.
Finishing dinner, I enter the *Strasse*,
In search of a good piece of ass to violate.

6/17/80 — [2] (05701)

The Saxophone's Erogenous Zone

In this anomalous two-horse town,
A day's ride from home,
Saxophone sounds, tuned in tandem duet,
Silhouette dusk, weave me
Into their musical stichomythia. I enter
And am captivated by their Lorelei riffs.
My tired spirit is set adrift
On tepid wine-red waves. My senses
Suspend thinking, send the imagination
On a wild chase after mind-geese
And wind-centaurs cruising above night,
Whose uninterrupted flight
Is freedom of the highest order,
The most dreadful kind of soaring
To which creative humans can aspire.

Soon, I am invisible, incorporeal,
Consumed by the music's susurrant spell.
*

The womb in which my being dwells,
Fastened to the fundus of a palpitant crowd,
Assumes a new, exclusive life of its own.
What emerges, by contracting degrees,
At moments grudgingly painful and labored,
Often smooth as running sap,
Are reverse lines of force, magnetic and true,
Drawing the brain's verse-children
Down from their word-horde in the ether.
Now, without willed effort,
They dance before me, waken me
To my most recent creation, this poem,
Begot by choice and chance and fancy. I rejoice!

6/18/80 — [1] (03491)

A Strange Plant

Now, dusk has assumed the absolute absence
Of all color except melancholia.
Its oversweet honeysuckle essence
Pervades my lonely musing
As though I were a swollen plant
Growing out of control. Beauty wilts
In this too-humid solitude.
Roots reach desperately along the earth,
Searching for purchase,
Without finding suitable room or nutriments.
Blooms are blind frogs
Swimming in a cave pool,
Colorless, mutant, sequestered in nature,
Deprived, forever, of seeing daylight.

Tonight, I am anonymity's child.
Neither self-pity nor desperation
Has taken hold, yet breathing
Seems a matter of my bench-pressing hippos,
With each wine-soggy suspiration.
I'm a victim of civil amnesia and spiritual rape
By intransigent academicians,
Of paid political assignations
Arranged by friends pushing reality,
Pimping vitamins, jogging,
*

Glandular ERA,
And euthanasia of all OPEC nations.
Off in the corner, by myself, I loom,
A potted cactus doomed to thrive in the desert.

6/18/80 — [2] (03490)

Mea culpa

Were I relegated to darkness,
Submerged under watery volumes,
Naked, tied to a stake aflame,
My flesh slowly crisping to vapors,
Or lobotomized from the nose upward,
By reason of Dantesque culpability,

I would grope in blindness,
Rise breathless to the murky surface,
Break my bonds
Despite permanent third-degree burns,
And graft a recently deceased brain
To the bleeding base of my skull,

Just to satisfy a need to write verse
So cursedly manifest
That to miss such perverse ecstasy,
Even one moment, when the urge
Takes hold of my bones,
Would be tantamount to an admission of original guilt.

6/18/80 — [3] (05702)

The Pageant Wagons

For some sinister reason, this morning,
The four-lane highway I follow
Has taken on a malevolence
Associated with war or sinister tornadoes.

For the last two hours,
My eyes have been assailed
By ambulances rushing head-on
Across the grassy median, blinking hysterically,

Missing me by a matter of refractions,
As I go north,
At speeds exceeding seventy. My car
Approaches unknowingly, almost collides with,

Then slides by myriad vault trucks,
Weighted with their eerie freight,
That seem to crowd the road
With more than coincidental frequency,

As though the entire scene
Were a surreal medieval turnpike
Dotted with pageant wagons
Going both ways, to and from a festival

Celebrating a recent death,
Wagons filled with harlequins and mimes,
Jongleurs and troubadours,
Wearing the same mask: my white face.

6/19/80 (03570)

Impenetrable Essences

As the scrub grass
Rushes by my bloodshot eyes,
Swollen from a night inside a wine bottle,
Antennae dotting my mind's highway
Come grudgingly alive,
Whose spontaneous erections
Have nothing to do with physiology,
Rather second-guessing, intuition, silence.

They sense something hovering outside,
Beyond their scope —
A vision, a shimmering image,
A crystallized truth-chip, echo of divinity.
But today, the median's high grass
Refuses my blurred focus insight.
Unimagined distraction
Accompanies me to the City of Poetry and back.

6/21/80 (05703)

Mainstreaming Out of the Mainstream

The hopeful, mediocre poets come and go
Like Eliotic echoes,
While those who show promise
Consult their Ouija boards for direction,
Insight into Rosicrucianism,
Rocks and bones,
Surreal or occult symbols of aloneness
And psychic enlightenment.

Both publish fanatically
Their chromosomal strands,
Give public readings for inflated fees
That fluctuate, monthly,
With a cost-of-living index
Calibrated not to the GNP
But the number of times
The poet died giving birth to creation.

I listen only to the wind,
Whose susurrant whispering is divinity,
And quote, from my soul,
Infinity's stirring voices.
My heart knows what vocabulary to use
For singing, sadness, and epiphanies.
Its rhythm informs my verse with music —
Earth-blood circulating through the years.

6/23/80 — [1] (05704)

Telecommunications Satellite

The sun barks and snarls at him
Like a spewing volcano.
Streaming photons
Drive him uncontrollably through space,
Force him into the hard, dark vacuum
Edging his mind's ionosphere,
Where silence blinds
And sight strips membranous skin
From the pain-wrenched tympanums.

In this phantasmagorical, oceanic void,
He is an omniscient speck,
A silicon chip scintillant and spinning,
Whose continuously activated receptors
Distill and transform solar radiation
Into a buzzing, touching shimmer,
A glinting body crossing galaxies
Without slowing to refuel
Or confirm the efficacy of his transmissions.

Back in earthly data-gathering centers,
Names and faces of friends
He knew in his construction stage
Watch with chaste amazement,
As his messages begin to arrive from space.
Molecular pieces of the universal poem
Are recorded and stored away,
For translation by future soothsayers.
They realize he'll never return the same.

6/23/80 — [2] (05705)

Moped ᐃ

At this fog-shrouded hour,
A baker's dozen of them gather
In the Crystal Café, to rehash the recent fire
That gutted the furniture store
Downtown. They praise the alacrity
Of Otterville, Syracuse, Sedalia, and Versailles,
In sending in men and units,
Saving Tipton from total Armageddon.
Soon, the Chevy dealer enters.
They chew his jovial ass,
For filling his showroom with mopeds.
"Let the good times roll!" they chant.
"They went broke at GMC,
So I decided to get into two-wheel drive,"
He retorts, smiling slyly.
And from the far end of the table:
"You gonna sell snowmobiles
When winter comes?"
"Now, I just might look into that."

The air in the converted filling station
Turns crispy as burnt toast.
They refuse to desist.
Someone taunts, "Mopy, mopo,
Mopy Dick." They snort and chortle,
Speculate on miles per gallon.
"You bastard," someone intones,
"You're gonna make it hot
On those poor A-rabs."
"Yeah," the cop adds, "one chicken
Can make enough shit in a year
To get you to Paris and back."
"It's cheap transportation,"
He retorts, in pseudoseriousness.
"You sell forty-dollar helmets for it?"
"Sure . . . but they're safe . . .
They're not exactly motorcycles."
"They ain't exactly tractors either."
"Hey, boys, give me a break!"

"I wonder where you put the city sticker."
(This after five minutes
In heated discussion, over farming, ceases.)
"Let the good times roll!"
"Motor awhile, peddle a stretch!"
"Hey, maybe you could wear the sticker
On your helmet." "Hey, Embry,
Does a customer get his special shoes
From you, too?" One by one,
These broad-shouldered, cigarette-smoking,
Seed-capped Tiptonians respond to the sun
Dissolving the fog, until only the dealer,
The last to have arrived, remains,
Like a baked turkey stewing in its juices.
In painful silence, he sits musing.
Visions of imported motorbikes
Clotting city streets and countryside,
Ubiquitous as butterflies, dot his eyes.
He has the future in his grasp.

But in his inner ear, he still hears
Their jeering: "Hey, Embry,
Did you get the pope's blessing
*

On that shipment?" "Hey, Embry,
If you'd just get T-otas now,
You'd have it made!" "Tipton presents
Embry's International Trade Center!"
"Bastards," he smiles, squirming over coffee,
Knowing better than most
How prevailing attitudes are hard to form,
Let alone change, and that, for the present,
The future may be too far away.

6/24/80 — [1] (00594)

The Lovers

Even at this hour,
When ladies and men sip cool wine,
Slip into easy cantering,
As they ride each other through meadows
Dappled with love-spill,

My damn pen commands my hand follow
As it fashions new combinations
Out of words waiting to be liberated
From thin air and arrested on paper.
There seems to be no surcease

To this cursed verse-making,
Whose sensual, enigmatic music haunts me
At work, while exercising, eating.
She trespasses over sleep's lawns,
Invading the innermost house of my dreams.

Her continual distraction
Is an ineradicable bomb ticking in my ears,
A quick, rhythmic swishing of tropical fish
In the eyes' bowls, coalescence of disparate images.
Yet I'm addicted to her brief ecstasies,

Victim of her selfish lovemaking,
Patronizing conceits, and empty flatteries.
Despite the fact that I've been warned
By Keats and Roethke, Trakl, Plath, and Darío,
I insist on genuflecting to my naked muse,

Who, in exchange for her acquiescences
To my palpitant desires
To stimulate her clitoral imagination
With my pen and make her writhe with delight,
Has exacted from me my sociability.

Long ago, in her unrelenting possessiveness,
She cast me into this isolation.
For years, now, I've remained her drone,
She my obliging regina.
Together, we've made a strange pair,

She the exquisite stimulator of intellects,
I the lonely poet of promise,
Who've eagerly slept together in the bed of roses
We've grown in our own Carcassonne —
Source and sorcerer, rhyming a deaf world.

6/24/80 — [2] (02555)

Scroll Maker

Although my puny voice screams out frequently,
The elements refuse to assimilate me.
Anonymity is my father, rejection my mother,
Who's suckled me on resignation
And despair. I exist for my creations,
Yet they grow to term
Only to result in stillbirths and deformities.

No matter how pleasurable and genuine
My encounters with the muse,
Our offspring seem to result in misunderstandings,
Flawed closures, incomplete metaphors,
Whose rhymes and content defy explanation —
Meanings abstruse and hermetic —
And I refuse to make myself naked

Except for those few who sense my direction
And introspective intent: the moon . . .
Ah, she's known what I've been up to
All these years. We've conversed
Late at night, alone, on my ultimate purpose
In rhyming words and making poetry
Conform to the music of my simple, dreaming heart.

I sit here, sipping wine,
Wondering why an intellect such as mine
Was doomed to recreate its visions,
A verse at a time, in ruled notebooks
To be stuffed away in closets,
Where only worm eyes might revel,
In greedy intemperance, on my tiny, fine lines

And consume the insights placed there
By one hopeful poet,
Who never rose above the applause of silence,
Attending him at every epiphany he experienced.
Perhaps the answer was inherent
All the while: I was one of God's scribes,
Assigned to copy His Scriptures over and over.

6/24/80 — [3] (02556)

The Children of the Children

In a long-ago afternoon,
When youth, as a final apostrophe to love,
Conceived two children with our names,
Then dissolved into the humid void
Where all years-ever-after
Fuse indistinguishably and are forgotten,

We vowed, "Ours is a sacred privilege,"
Referring to YHWH's bequest
In the form of flesh begot of our flesh.
We rejoiced in our creations,
Reveled in His earthly manifestation,
The human apotheosis to godliness,

Before settling, inexorably,
Into the unpoetic, Sisyphean necessities
Required by helpless nestlings for mere survival.
Now, they've both grown, flown,
Whose independence has left us bereft,
Together, in the strangest, immitigable silence,

With little to communicate, less to do or share,
Unlike in afternoons long ago,
When, supple, slender, passionate, and uncompromised,
We entwined our dreams and fantasies,
*

Danced like a solitary lightning bolt
Arcing between two charged poles.

Today, we scrutinize each other
Like observers from two neutral nations
Forming, recording, reporting back to superiors
Their objective views on the ruins
Of an ancient fortress devastated by war.
We sift and trip through memory's rubble,

Occasionally reminiscing, with apocryphal imprecision,
About the children, gentle interludes
In their breakneck, headlong progression
Toward adolescence and coming-of-age.
Lately, in inebriated weariness,
We've hymned ourselves to sleep,

Two used-up, sentimental people,
Who once knew youth
So intimately that when we spoke slowly,
Poetry flowed from our mellifluous lips,
Instead of erotica . . . two obsolete lovers,
Whose marriage, having reached impasse,

Has lapsed into unimpassioned collapse.
Now, out of self-preservation,
We cling to each other, to our past,
To that sacred privilege we were bequeathed
Through childbirth. Once again,
We entreat God for an alternative to our emptiness.

6/25/80 — [1] (02557)

Roanoke: The Lost Colony and Its Colonizer

At one time or another,
Always in solitude, my eyes have eagerly scanned
Verses penned by poets suspended in space,
Who've been forced to address
The vast nothingness of anonymity and disparagement,
Who've been willing to commit suicide,
Adultery, euthanasia, for the fulfillment of their visions.

Eagerly, I've read their cursive music,
Hoping to discover an easier route
*

To the Spice Islands,
A more convenient ocean lane to follow,
That I might arrive at aboriginal shores,
With my poetry, and show others the way to my heart,
So that uncharted storms won't sunder their passage.

But nothing I've assimilated has sufficed
To assist me in recording my imagistic cartography,
That other, younger conquistadors might know
I've staked my claim to landscapes
Inhabited by sky and rocks, noisy streams,
And recognize my hasty graffiti,
Incised on the majestic cliffs of Innisfree.

I go from rock-strewn cove to cove,
Hoping to find a friendly, permanent place
In which to anchor and go ashore,
Without ever knowing which poem
Might be titled "New Albion" or "America,"
Which voice rising from which persona
Might return home in a bottle, proclaiming my suzerainty.

6/25/80 — [2] (02558)

Death-Moth ^Δ

His resemblance to a moth
Homing in on, circling, incessantly, the mind's light,
Is scintillating and uncanny.

The poet soars, on cursive thermals,
Above night, slowing, descending,
Spreading reflections between the stars,

As he chooses an appropriate metaphor
To convert into a landing strip.
Down, in an inexorable sussurance, he flies,

Never quite settling or quiet
As long as the intellect's continuous glint
Hypnotizes him, holds him fast

While he passes, in erratic, elliptical orbit,
The conspicuous, speaking beacon
Silence flashes through creation.

Ultimately, dawn slides into twilight.
The sun rises along its horizon.
The moth reaches sleepy climax,

Seeks to hide beyond day's conception,
Knowing, even in its going,
Something's been left behind —

The slightest record of a disturbance
In the universe, wing-dust
Illuminating the psyche's darkest surface.

6/25/80 — [3] (01349)

Sportscoat Presentation ^Δ

For Erv Weiner

"The secret to the underpressing process
And our willingness to strive for quality
Despite added expense are the keys to our success.
We necessarily neglect not *one* step
In the essential fabrication of our garments.

"This coat has a definite slope to its shoulder,
A tangent resulting from our own
Sewn-in floating chest piece.
It has suppression, expression, not boxy.
We use one comfortable body,

"No matter how many refinements
We make to dress the silhouette up or down.
Blazers, so tremendously popular,
With patch or flap pocket,
Sewn with mercerized, topstitched thread,

"To harmonize with our fabrics,
Will appear in our Clayton and Clyde models,
For high fashion — center vent,
Three open patch pockets,
Simulated hand-stitched felling.

"Guys, there's sheer music here:
Polyester, combed cotton, rayon, and flax,
Blended into gingham, hopsack,
*

Chambray, Army twill, plaids, madras.
Say it! Sing it! Rejoice! Rejoice!

"Go, fellas! Sell the shit out if it!
Go and celebrate our great values,
Our make! Take our coats to the unpossessed!"

6/27/80   (02398)

"Lions Meet Here" ^Δ

It's not even 7:15 a.m.,
And yet the mid-Missouri heat
Is amassing, just beneath the macadam,
To mount an offensive against sensibilities
Already debilitated by birthright
And franchise — scions of scions of miners,
Farm hands, day laborers,
State hospital patients etherized and free,
Who hover just above the town,
Like buzzards, with an eerie resemblance to ghosts.

Behind me, past the closed door
In this café where I've come
To gather courage, through inebriation
From the sacred brown elixir,
To assault the great enemy, humidity,
A rented movie is playing
To a packed leonine audience
Intent on cementing their patriotic humanism.
Periodically, cries and shouts rise,
As the men applaud a victorious Popeye or Mighty Mouse,

Then lapse back in mesmerized silence,
While lumps of muffins,
German-fried potatoes, sausages, ham, and toast
Leap from cliffs, in useless suicide,
And dive to swollen abysses.
When I look up,
Their solemn faces are filing past me
Like war machines crossing a desert
To rendezvous with creatures of certain defeat.
My eyes recognize the Goyaesque features

Of these men, who are neither specters,
Avatars, nor dandelion spores
Floating in the imagination. They're babies,
Seraphic, roseate, naked, not attorneys
Dressed in three-piece pinstriped
Nazi uniforms sewn with human thread,
First Free Will Baptist preachers
Robed in holier-than-thou rhetoric,
Or prize-bull toilers of the earth,
Seething with hatred for investors from the city.

Strangely, each seems to know me.
Their individual salutations,
As they leave the café, make me aware
They've been alerted to my staring,
Have penetrated my pleasant outward appearance,
To the glaring concern my eyes wear.
Suddenly, I realize why I'm here:
I've been assigned to unleash the lions from their cages
And let them invade the coliseum,
Where the town waits to be eaten alive.

7/1/80   (00262)

Cargo Pilot

This stifling heat
And humid, looming cloud cover
Have conspired to keep my straining machine
Hovering close to the concrete,
Negating takeoff,
Immobilizing all glide capabilities
It might otherwise have utilized in flight,
From Farmington to New Athens.

Under normal conditions,
I would already have achieved elevation,
Reached maximum speed
Above this heat-shimmering troposphere,
Through which I seem to be going
As though taxiing over an endless runway,
Ceaselessly revving up, checking gyros.
Even my cruise control refuses to hold steady,

As I move ahead,
Vectoring toward afternoon's destination,
With a load of used clothing destined to be sold
As surplus thirds, firsts
From four seasons ago, stylish seconds.
On haze-heavy days like this one,
I dream of those old heroic pilots
Who flew the Burma run in "gooney birds"

Or dropped graffitied eggs,
From the shackles and bomb-bay anuses
Of Flying Forts, over Düsseldorf,
Wondering what in hell I'm doing here,
Coaxing this stubborn tub
On a hope and a prayer, only to turn around
And repair to home, for a similar load —
Another mission flown and logged in my book.

7/2/80 (02397)

Severe Thunderstorms and Flash Flooding

All night, the sky was alive
With flicking violet tongues and slithering bodies —
A nest of coiled vipers striking my eyes,
Keeping somnolent succubi and incubi awake,
Alert to possibilities of my being bitten,
Going blind from an accidental injection
Of electrical venom, becoming deaf
From quick, crisp, crackling hisses
Of the serpents, thunderously lunging out of the pit.

What had we done to outrage those snakes,
Force them out of their lair,
Make them turn on us, in grotesque revolt?
Even now, the following morning,
This city is under siege.
Angry fangs click and bang on my roof
And windshield, as I flee their attack,
Suspicious this storm could be the Pharaonic plague
Previously canceled for lack of rain.

7/3/80 (05706)

High-Wire Artist

Once again, he flies away
From all his comfortable domestic fetters,
To taunt the twin evils, Scylla and Charybdis,
Walks the tightrope drawn taut
Between Anywhere and Everywhere,
Daring to part the precarious air —
A bird in passage, a Moses-poet, acrobat,
A man alone, balancing his dreams
At both ends of the pen he grips for balance.

Invisibly, he etches the space
Through which he floats, soars, steps
Tiptoe, slowly, with invisible strokes,
Describing, at moments, ellipses, half-moons,
Erratic parabolas —
Poems scribbled with random inventiveness,
To keep him from falling into the netless abyss
Of hissing demons, circus clowns, freaks,
Beneath the intellect's main ring.

Now, with the tent's pure-blue roof
Above his head and earthly crowds below,
He stops to assay the distance traveled
And decide, in an instant,
Whether the design he originally intended,
When setting out, still fits
The conditions of his constantly changing existence
Or if, in order to safely proceed,
He must alter his vision of immortality.

7/7/80   (05707)

The Tenth Anniversary

For my flower child, Jan

In a new, juvenescent gesture
As purely romantic as that first, fast passage,
That last, shared, spontaneous, leaping lapse
Through cornflowers and hydrangeas,
Above the long-defunct Sutro Baths,
Where we wove strands of San Francisco and July
Into our dancing lives, ten years ago,

We've come to our other garden, Manhattan,
With its special flower, the Plaza,
That vast, gleaming gardenia
Whose alabaster and brass petals,
Surmounted by a sea-green mansard calyx,
Dazzle the senses, with irregular stateliness.
We've come back to be reenchanted,

Bespelled by deities and necromancers,
To celebrate our second efflorescing of vows,
Postulate another beginning, not a denouement,
And consecrate our planting, that it might bring forth
Our next decade's floral growth.
Neither cornflowers, gardenias, nor hydrangeas
Do we seek to harvest, this next season,

But sweetheart roses, tiny and tight,
A profusion of Trilogy and Troika,
Whose slow, unbudding textures will yield
The tender, gentle, deliquescent scents of children
Reposing in a bed of mild hours.
No matter how far we travel from now,
Their garden will flourish; it's rooted in our hearts.

7/8/80   (04186)

The Tourists ^Δ

Across from us, five Japanese sit
Eating eggs Benedict, ham, and sausage,
In the prestigious Palm Court.
Just behind an oversize Chinese vase
Potted with variegated fronds,
An Iranian, wearing dark glasses,
As though doing so
Might complete the "ostrich syndrome"
And keep him from the seething enmity
Emanating from the predominantly American motley
Here to be seen and recorded
By *WWD*,
Shimmers in his pure-silk veils and robes.
We absorb the ambience, in silence,
Imbibing coffee, crunching English muffins,
*

Without the slightest realization
That life is thriving outside, on the streets
Circumscribing the Plaza,
Or that, soon, we'll be forced to immerse ourselves
And be carried along in the millrace
Of endless sidewalks leading to destinations
Decidedly vertical in their desolated connections
With earth, borne hurriedly
Toward one of a hundred possible edges,
Like two empty skiffs, on a river,
Come accidentally untied,
Until we arbitrarily decide to fall over,
Into another gallery or jewelry shop,
Or simply stop long enough to glimpse mannequins
Clothed in someone's conceptions of latest taste,
Before once again being taken up
By the tenacious current surging, surging,
Merging momentarily, at corners,
To purge certain elements of the fluid debris,
Flowing once more,
With the two of us, hand in hand, dazed,
Going volitionlessly into the spinning wheel,
Which will shoot us, suddenly,
Between grindstones pulverizing the bones.
But we'll revolve freely,
Then enter the Plaza's air-conditioned lobby,
Home safe, for the moment anyway.

7/9/80   (01022)

Outside the Picasso Exhibit ^Δ

If the old prolific goat,
Who dabbled and doodled to defeat death
At its own deft designs,
In all its dissolute disguises,
Could see these queues, wriggling,
Like segmented worms, outside the sanctified gates
Of this museum, he'd squeal and bleat
With monumental ecstasy . . . queues pushing
To gain admittance at designated sequences
Spaced a half-hour apart . . .
*

Queues exposed to international hype
And local sidewalk sellers of T-shirts,
Tastee-Freezes, pretzels, snow cones,
Sodas, and roasted chestnuts . . .
Queues enduring the oblivious entreaties
Of a player of steel drums, a body,
Whole from the waist up, on a rolling board,
Offering derision, instead of pencils, for a dole . . .
Queues reminiscent of Jews
Huddling naked before the showers at Auschwitz.

If only the wiry Andalusian goat,
So ubiquitous in his pervasive absence,
Could witness this massive crush of people
Pressing restlessly to view, in numb herds,
The reliquaries and sacramental bone-strokes
Of his divertissement, his stays against boredom,
He'd baa and baa, not with cynicism
But out of pity for all these spirits,
These unobsessed, professedly empty souls
Dispossessed of his gifts, his desire
To fill every space on his psyche's walls.
He would decline an invitation
To the opening of his own retrospective exhibit,
Opting for a few precious moments
By himself, in which to contemplate a canvas
Based on the queues coalescing daily,
From ten until four, to view,
Genuflect to, and hymn his irrefragable genius,
A painting he might execute in two minutes
And title *Shepherd Tending His Flock*.

7/10/80   (02264)

Escaping the Castle's Dungeon

Free me from myself, O Lord!
Liberate my confining ego
From its duties as dungeon master of my body,
That I might roam, unencumbered, over the plains,
Toward the farthest forest,
Where being lost is the beginning of finding an identity,
*

Comfortable as healthy flesh,
At an affordable cost the soul can accept
Without repression or guilt that it sold out
Or accommodated to the most convenient alternative.

Let me discover the land behind the mirror,
Through whose transpiercing, silvered back
My peering eyes fly each time
They look to the past for guidance and comfort,
That territory where silence is color
And twilight the sounds of hummingbirds mating
In shimmering, argentiferous shapelessness.
The looking glass containing my present perspective
Is a profile elongated, articulate, and intense,
Reflecting the future, with insightful invisibility.

Its elliptical shape circumscribes the sum of days
Done and gone in the furious exhalation
Of lungs pumping to keep my organism alive.
In a naked instant, I recognize my own features
Sculpted into the landscape, begging me enter.
Headlong, my acquiescent fancy submits,
Relinquishes its arrogant, stubborn former esteem,
And penetrates the wild regions beyond the plains.
Having left memory behind, I wander blind,
Turning everything I touch back to primal wonder.

7/11/80 — [1]   (05708)

Triumphal Return

Five days ago,
The Trojan Horse we rode, or flew,
In which we comfortably hid,
To enter the city, in subterfuge, elusive, together,
Had wings and roaring engines —
A silvery Pegasus, perhaps a hippogriff.

In penumbral shadow, we penetrated,
Made our entrance undetected,
Settled into a plush blue room at the Plaza,
Began plotting our overthrow
Of the existing regime. We discussed our plans
Over half carafes of Chablis, in the Palm Court,

Then disappeared into the incandescent dissolve
Haloing Manhattan, our successful infiltration
Tinged, that first night of sleep, with ivory dreams.
Next day and the proceeding four,
We reconnoitered museums, in search of clues
To secret labyrinthine passageways

That Pablo Ruiz y Picasso and others
Reposing at the Modern, Whitney, and the Met
Cut into the face of the twentieth century,
That we might rifle and pillage
All the spoils of the past hundred years
And transport their precious visions safely

To Farmington. Or was it Argos or Ilium
Or some ilex-dotted Aegean isle
Shimmering on our enchanted minds' twilit horizon?
No matter, we gathered in the relics
Scattered about the city, gathered them assiduously,
Knowing we might never return

Or that, if so, the climate of these restive times
Might have worked its awful, inexorable alchemy,
Causing canvases and bronzes,
Pigments and papers to dissolve back to particles
Floating in a pernicious atomic slipstream
Initiated at the dyspeptic whims of disparate politicians.

Now, with our brains full of incredible cargo,
The giant flying silver-winged horse
Strains to break its earthen bonds and rise
And soar, with both of us inside,
Riding, or flying, with our prizes, excited to arrive home,
To begin a new dynasty in our Arcadian retreat.

7/11/80 — [2] (04185)

I Am the Egg Man △

For Jenny,
herself a metaphor
that soars

In this tiny room,
This nest, where each egg
Fertilized by the bemused union
*

Of imagination and intellect
Comes to rest on my brain, on paper,
I brood, hatching the future
In which my progeny will pace,
Prance like dancing guinea hens
And peacocks, and strut, fuguelike,
Through crepuscular études,
Crowing cock-a-doodle-doo poetics to the moon.

I envision my offspring taking wing,
Soaring above the roost
Where they were first conceived,
Slanting into the wind,
Rising over my restless fancy,
Into the thinner air
Where metaphors mate like unicorns.
In this tiny room,
Incubating with the typewriter's heat,
My pecking fingers
Persistently break out of their shells.

7/14/80   (00104)

July 17, Forever

*For my mother's birthday,
her sixty-fifth, this gift*

This life I live I love
So outrageously much
That no celebration, regardless how great,
Makes me greedy, giddy, or complacent
About showing an excess of emotion.

Every day is a gingerbread cookie;
Nights are pineapple upside-down pastries.
The seasons are marzipan ceremonies,
Ephemeral yet self-contained
And evocative as Proustian teacakes.

Even occasional pain and frequent melancholy
Fail to disengage my spirit
From its tasks of dissecting visions
And exercising options on free time,
Whose dividends are poetry,

Dreaming, dozing, daring to goad silence
Into revealing its springs
Spewing watercress elegies and odes.
Although my disposition inclines autumnally,
I rejoice in being alive

And in expressing my appreciation to you
For this miraculous gift,
My physical existence, by composing lines
Such as these conduits, Mom,
Connected from you, through me, to God.

7/17/80 (02112)

Stieglitzian Steerage

My thoughts are cramped in steerage,
As one destination gives way to the next,
Refusing to admit my restless spirit,
Give my wayward desires berth,
Accommodate my weary, wandering soul
With a convenient slip,
Where, for a season or two, at least,
The surcease might allow me opportunity
To advertise for a new crew,
Replace abused and jury-rigged parts,
Scrape rust and barnacles
Off brain-plates
Too long exposed to the despoliation
Of psychospheric sunspots,
Salt-spray, and cranial wave-seizures.

Feckless, peripatetic, without registration
In any country of origin,
My ship, like a Melvillean *Rachel*,
Churns ocean lanes endlessly —
A spectral shape, fleshy flotsam.
Wait! Just ahead I spy an atoll.
Triangulation identifies it as Death's Cove.
Neatly dressed dockhands secure my lines.
Safe at last, I kneel and kiss the land.

7/18/80 (05709)

The Daydream Tree ^Δ

By lascivious, fluttering pulsations,
Myriad nameless butterflies
Hover within their own wing-palettes,
Brushing the air yellow,
Partaking of delicate petals,
Pink, with sweet labial perfumes.

With singular fascination, my stunned eyes
Fix on their oblivious gathering in.
As I stare, hundreds materialize
Out of the dense, sensual overhang
That networks my imagination
Like cloisonné decorating a Ming vase.

The gentle folding and unfolding
That suspends each in one location
Long enough to empty that space of its spice
Reminds me of a naked lady
Slowly opening and closing her thighs
Over my lusty tree of everlasting desire.

Beneath this leafy delusion,
Lying in the supple-tufted grass
Strewn with afternoon shadows,
I surrender to solitude's undoing of hallucination,
Lamenting I can't be a mimosa bloom
Doomed to so gossamer a ravishment.

7/22/80 (05464)

[What, at twenty,]

What, at twenty,
Commenced, out of unquestionable necessity,
As a job, ended, today, at seventy-one,
As the embodiment of one man's perseverance
And determination to achieve
An orderly progress toward progressive success,
By an act of volition
In which an unbroken chain,
Fifty-one links golden,
*

Was unlatched, relinquished,
And passed over to a younger man,
To sustain, perpetuate, and, we hope, never taint
With personal ambition,
A domineering sneer, or the arrogance
That waits, like dormant fungus spores,
For the right conditions,
To manifest itself and multiply.

Sitting here, listening to him reminisce,
Elicits a vision of the man
Rising, paradoxically, out of 1929,
Into a career crisscrossed with disappointments,
Ebullience, and that ubiquitous conviction
That sincerity, perspicaciousness, and discipline
Were the capstones in a universe
Through which his shadow would have to pass
If ever he might transcend anonymity
And arrive at the promontory
Of his God-given capacity for self-fulfillment.
Sitting beneath his echoing good-byes,
Diffident in the presence of his disappearing act,
I shimmer with pride and love, and cry,
Not so much as a devoted employee at his retirement
But as his son, knowing that my growing up
Has come to its denouement, that I'm finally on my own.

7/24 & 7/28/80 — [2] (05710)

Part-Time Poet

Sestinas and villanelles,
Swirling through argentiferous dust motes
Floating before my drowsy eyes
Like galaxies lost in galaxies
Flourishing a thousand years from now,
Awaken my ears to the new day.

This celebration of gentle rhymes
Suffused with lyric-smooth, fluid passion
Reminds my resurrected spirit
That tragedy and nightmarish depravity,
Violence, degradation, and sloth
Don't necessarily dominate the stage

We pace with such deliberation
And unsophisticated ambitiousness,
Rather coexist with anagogic music,
Altruistic gifts motivated by love
Or friendship alone, echoes of divinity
Arrested for no reason except inspiration.

Suddenly, I'm a dove rising from its nest,
Soaring to full speed and height
In a matter of blinks, entering the sunlight,
Like a mica chip.
I'm a voice trained to translate word-chimes
Kissing in a scintillant wind

And return to earth for vespers and late wine.
Right now, dressed in suit and tie,
I light behind my desk downtown,
To investigate risk-free commodities,
Death insurance, welfare tax,
And a relaxation of Nixonian diplomacy in Congress.

7/28/80 — [1] (05711)

Willy Makes His Rounds

Once again, this morning,
The road absorbs me corporally.
Neither victim nor sacrificial gift,
My existence succumbs nonetheless to up-
                                    Rootedness,
That lonely abyss spectered with death-demons
Of my own eccentric invention,
In which I drive ever westward,
No matter the actual direction.

As I go home, this day,
Presaging neither doom nor celebration,
My psyche senses, in its isolation,
A vision hovering above the visor,
Just out of earshot and eyesight.
The ineffable voice of an ancient cantor
Standing on the horizon, keening,
Commiserates with the wailing miles,
In a silence I recognize as my own echo.

Suddenly, all forward motion ceases,
Metamorphoses into verticality,
As this ribbon riding the earth's surface
Decomposes into dense, dank dirt,
Through which I pass,
Lower and deeper with each succeeding mile,
Until I've arrived at my house,
Neither alive nor immortal, bereft of breath
Yet no longer destinationless either.

Not guest, visitor, or host
Of this vaguely familiar mansion am I,
But an itinerant merchant
Peddling relics of my recent incarnation.
I knock at the door and enter,
On the invitation of my former self,
To sell him notions: surplus time, mercy
Slightly flawed, salvation canceled for bad credit.
Cautiously, he paws over my line, then declines.

7/29/80   (02396)

Of Garbage Collectors and Refuse

A wobbly, shrouded 6 a.m. sun
Accompanies me out of drowsy doldrums,
Peers, voyeurlike, through the window,
As I grope for last night's clothes
And dress in solitude's soiled robes
Before performing, in robot motions,
The awkward complexities of making coffee trickle
From the automatic machine
That squats, like a fat, nesting hen, on the countertop,
In a kitchen that knows me
Only from the sounds of belching and mastication,
Which identify me as a frequent habitué.

Even before my fetal shadow
Has had time to unencumber itself from night's mares
And leave the air-conditioned darkness,
In which it's come to term with the inevitabilities of birth,
The postponement of its comatose tranquillity
In a sea of sleep, my body bolts,
*

Enters the humid outdoors, and, gasping for purpose,
Suffocates. For hours, it lies there
In the driveway, by the car, under the sun,
Which licks it like a frothing dog,
Until a garbage man, dumping my cans,
Distinguishes my prostrate shape from the bags of waste

And runs to the front yard, to get advice
From his boss, busy backing the truck
Over my lawn. Suddenly, I waken
To scratching cacophony emanating from Hades
And find myself trapped in the massive compactor,
Sullied with oozing dung-juices and odors
Too bilious and hot to survive, floating in an ocean
Crowded with maggots, horseflies, vermin, and lice.
As the jaws contract, my hallucination shatters.
The office in which I process Blue Cross claims
Reasserts its domination. Self-consciously, I look around,
Trying to mask the stench rising from my dissatisfaction.

7/31/80 (05712)

Jongleur: Initiation Rites ^Δ

Slowly, the membranous closure
Succumbs to flute notes
Her first lover's tongue blows
With its fricative motion. She whimpers
As the painful ecstasy of being penetrated
By that original, ephemeral exhalation,
Forever setting the valve ajar,
Quavers her spine, her toes,
Her swollen areolas and tumescent breasts.

He rests his tempestuous curls on her chest
And listens to her untried pumps
Thumping primal pulses
Like a blood-flood cresting in undulations
Elongated, inexorable, and irreversible.
She touches his waxed mustache,
Runs one finger around the mouthpiece
Beneath which silent poems await release,
As though to rouse one from drowsiness,

That she might be reassured,
In repose as in her victorious entry
Into the dominion of relinquished virginity,
That her supple and barely tainted maidenhood
Still elicits the voluptuous music
Stored in glands and time capsules
Inviolable except by desire,
Then readies herself for the coda he's chosen
By which to compose their epithalamion.

8/3/80   (03604)

Belinda, Lady of Fiesole ^Δ

Once again, empty self-centeredness,
In the form of silence so wide
Day and night are indistinguishable,
Violates me, vitiates all ties with today,
Rendering yesterday irredeemable
As an expired pass to the gates of Hippocrene.
Transmogrification is imminent.

Your gentle visage rises before me,
Mile after mile,
In sinuous, Beardsleyesque reiteration,
Plaintive, voiceless, yet murmurous
As seeds stirring beneath seething earth,
Waiting to burst and speak out,
In austere serenity, the virgin's first and final lament.

But my eyes are blind to your keening,
And the ears perceive a vague silhouette
On afternoon's shimmering scrim curtain,
Until nothing is certain
Except that you are continuously receding
Despite my reaching ever ahead,
To connect with your dissipating echo.

Abruptly, illusory mirages cease.
Neither of us exists; we never have.
For that matter, hallucinations,
Weighted with possibilities of sharing and touching
Someone whose future you possess,
*

Refuse to relinquish the secret of their clairvoyance.
Like a tidal wave unleashed in Hades,

The widening silence sideswipes my vessel.
Heaved overboard,
I float facedown, unable to breathe,
Yielding, by slow, comatose degrees, to sleep.
Suddenly, through the viscid liquid,
You swim into my eyes,
Guiding me back to dreaming's origins, to hope, and to love.

8/10/80 (03606)

Guilt-Throes ^Δ

And now, all that anticipation fragments,
Splinters into filaments of wonder and bafflement
Over how and why time
Can cast its caliginous shadows
Across shades we claim as our own
In the sacred cause of love, change, and wisdom
And alchemize twilight into its base obscurity.

Ah, the lament, that perpetual, immutable plaint
Writ by Marvell and the bard,
By Keats, myriad minor laureates, and me
Whenever questing anew the vessel
In which to bury an old grief or recent sorrow.
Each poem caskets the ashes and bones
We consecrate to blind and illusory immortality,

Designing, scheming how to outwit,
With mere syllables and rhymed sounds, obliteration.
Yet none has ever discovered,
Not even through necromancy, demonology, the occult,
How to materialize, jinnlike,
Whenever lovers rub the vessel gently
With recitations suffused with empathy and awe.

And so, having waited such a long time
Before sacrificing my integrity, dear lady,
Submitting myself physically to someone
Too smooth and youthful and bemused by the newness
Of possessing bodily an unfantasized man
*

To suspect the Devil of conspiring with ephemerality,
I finally know the shape of empty space.

8/15/80 — [1] (00160)

Mystic Twisting

He flees the city like a hurtling top
Wobbling beyond its locus,
Whose destination remains questionable
As a medieval knight's quest for his sacred Grail.

All he's been able to ascertain for certain
Is that his container is driven
By forces not so much beyond his control
As foretold by futures not yet dominant,

Meant, nonetheless, for his soul's resting place.
He follows the magically etched path,
Enraptured and bemused, watches the land
Fuse into endless stalks, whose grandeur

Draws him into its stark simplicity,
Distracts his narcissistic thoughts
Long enough to render him abandoned and alone,
Vulnerable to the slightest sentimentality.

Suddenly, he's lying naked beneath the sky,
Euphoric as a soaring cormorant,
In his desire to enter a pantheistic cosmos
And be swallowed alive by history,

Then restored to the twilight horizon
As a flying sound so mystical
As to combine prismatic lavenders and pinks
With the chaste moon's moans of maidenhood.

How he got here is conjecture's dominion.
This singular tree,
Fastened to the earth at the seeming center
Of endless density, protects his tender flesh

From the fulgent sun. He drowses,
Dreaming of reincarnations
Writ large in his fantasies, witnessing himself
Unfold in time-lapse sequences:

Abraham and Moses, Dante's rose,
Carcassonne's castle keeper's cat,
Sweet Caddy of the muddy drawers,
Ageless poet — O great word-maker!

On waking, he slips free from dream
And becomes invisible inside the dark evening,
At one with nocturne and eternality,
A creation conceived and shaped out of nothingness,

Adam and Jesus tied to each other
In a shared, agelessly self-perpetuating body,
Like a top wobbling over the earth's surface,
Like a dreidel spinning in the brain.

8/15/80 — [2] (05713)

A Temporal Redemption

Ah, merciful Jesus! From this nexus,
In which, for more than fourteen nights,
I've stayed fathomlessly inebriated,
I exit, extemporaneously,
Through a thousand urgent words
Splaying themselves, naked, across paper
Whose lined whiteness gives way
To my meditative ejaculations. I come

Like a priest meeting the smooth-white fantasy
He's secretively kept dehumanized
And fleshless beneath the tremulous rhetoric
Of his memorized homiletics,
Finally laying her out back of his church,
In the weeds, with stars
And murmurous crickets his only witnesses.
Ah, so sweetly am I possessed

By this nascent freedom to express loneliness,
I almost forget,
Under the subtle pressure of such anesthetizing,
How evanescent is euphoria
Derived from word-ichor, how fleet
Is its hypnotic spell on reality's demons.
Yet for the hour, I'm held speechless,
Spellbound, welcome in godly precincts

Where Milton and Keats and Calderón
Resonate the cloistral ceilings
With their whisperous voices. I listen
As my own flowing words fill the air
With prismatic trilling,
Soaring, hovering, fluttering bird-light,
On whose soft flights I migrate
West from my fragile soul's earthly nest,

Past the Land of Consternation,
Beyond ancient cities at Death's edges:
Depression, Desolation, Despondency.
Oh, that this cursive transportation might last
And waking be mere hiatus
In whose bemused grasp I might thrive
In anticipation of words to reconceive me
Perpetually in the universal past!

8/20/80 — [1]   (02242)

Dockhands

Under a hundred tons of unremitting sun,
We unload clothes,
Inventing obscenities to commemorate the curse
Of having to crawl on our bellies,
Work, by virtue of brow-sweat,
From dawn to obscurity, without surcease.

We disentangle hangered coats and suits,
Snagged on themselves
Like flood debris in murky backwaters,
And place them on standing pipe-racks.
We stack soiled wool slacks
In arbitrary piles to be sorted later,

Then withdraw into the air-conditioning,
To deactivate pernicious fever
Threatening dizziness and fainting spells.
"Hey, you dumb bastards,
Where in the hell are the belts and ties
Listed on this shitting shipping ticket?"

Once more, we enter the outside,
Inside the steaming, dark forty-foot
*

Transport trailer's anus,
Suffocating like bugs in a sealed container,
And stumble over tires and car parts,
Groping for two elusive Lilliputian boxes,

For a half-hour, before quitting in disgust.
"Well," the foreman screams,
"What the fuck! We ain't got all day!"
"It ain't there," we say in unison.
"Bullshit!" he spits in our faces,
As if we were pieces of wet excrement,

And we exit in time to catch the second bell
Herding factory hands back,
From afternoon's ten-minute break,
To tasks too oppressive, in this heat,
To allow them success against piece rates.
We slouch in the corner, out of energy,

Dreaming of drowning in ten feet
Of ice cubes floated with whiskey sours,
Where, for the next two and a half hours,
We might defy time, by malingering
In the sweetest double-time high,
Instead of resuming loading-dock duties

Or refusing in the name of human cruelty,
At the risk of losing our jobs. Slowly, we rise,
As fumes from another diesel, like Zyklon B,
Fill the zone my eyes inhabit,
Distorting vision. The truck's back door reads
"Bergen-Belsen Lines." I dread unloading its cargo.

8/20/80 — [2] (02209)

Save the Whales △

For my dear friend,
the Fisher King of Half Moon Bay,
Mike Köepf

The tedium of dreaming beached whales
Dying on the shores of nightmare
Increases with each passing season.

Why I've been isolated, out of millions,
To tend these nocturnal leviathans,
Provide an audience for their death rites,

Their lugubrious moaning, I don't know,
Lest it be a kind of expiation
For daily cruelties I perpetrate

In my selfish intransigence and profligacy.
Yet why would I be visited
By such preposterous symbols of vulnerability,

If all of us suffer, to some degree,
From hedonism and narcissistic tendencies?
Why me? I'm only a lonely poet,

Whose pretensions toward immortality,
Though great, can't hold a candle
To politicians' and shaggy mathematicians'.

Why should I have been doomed
To endure these sad and sorry obsequies
Rising from mere awkward whales

Too stupid to keep away from the shoals
Jutting out from my imagination?
Why must I stay awake in their suffering,

When others slumber like mimosa trees
Closing their leaves to the oblivious moon?
Because I write! That's it, isn't it?

You've chosen me to witness their obliteration
Over and over and over,
In tedious reiteration,

As though these sea denizens
Were only minnows
Instead of colossal mammals falling asleep

For eternity. I almost begin to know
The motivation behind this curse.
It has something to do with writing verse

And with self-discovery, almost as though
The sheer recognition of death,
Whether monstrous or minuscule, is moot,

In that creatures pass regardless
And, ultimately, their existence
Must be apprehended before the end converges,

Intervenes on the life process, dominates.
So, now, I believe I suspect
Why the dying whales disturb my peace,

My sleep, my dreams. They float in
Fouling solitude, with their final exhalations,
To remind me that I am alive, sentient,

And that, as such, I have an indebtedness
To myself, to thrive on symbols
Beached and dying. They are my poems in embryo.

8/20/80 — [3] (02662)

A Call to All Poets and Other Laity and Gentymen

How many of you bastards
Who call yourselves poets — the oldish Nemerov,
Homosexual Jim, W. S. Drunk-in-the-Furnace,
Phil Levine (prophetic Jew cum Hasidic beard),
And crazy-house Hayden Carruth,
Whose verse I adore (oh, and don't forget
Dear, sad Sivvy, whose images were orgiastic) . . .

How many of you bastards ever sat alone
And lonely as white Melvillean fear itself,
Contemplating anonymity, as, now, I do,
In this college-town singles bar?
Which of you has ever really known fear,
Other than Sylvia, who's no longer with us
To answer this rather academic inquiry?

Furthermore, which of you has ever had to grovel
With rejection slips daily,
Because you never had connections,
Suffered from a debilitated, questionable reputation?
I put it to you, court jesters, academy pets:
Have you had to write as if oblivion
Were ready to lower you, on pulleys, into the poem?

I have! I do constantly, despite the assurance
That *Southern Review* and *American Scholar*
Have tapped me for their exclusive fraternity.
I write as though tomorrow died yesterday,
Forever, and today were mere speculation
Made by a Peter Sellers Inspector Clouseau
More infatuated by his own voice than verisimilitude.

I can tell you only this simple truth:
The poetic vision has very little to do with truth;
Rather, it consists of orient moon-fruit
Planted by imaginative space travelers
Going in search of sky-orchards grown profuse
With Buddha-trees, and by rabbis and popes,
Who know nothing at all about everything

And anything except how to teach touching
To the very young, among societies
Just coming to fruition, the few gurus
Who have chosen to take, on their soft shoulders,
The omnipresent burden of perpetuating
What belongs naturally to all of us
Who pursue verse, make words conform

To conventions approximating mystical narration
And lyrical persuasion — truth. I beg you,
Laity and gentymen
Who consider yourselves sensitive and poetic
And genuine, seek your heart-murmurs.
They speak the only real feelings.
The universe throbs in your cosmic palpitations.

8/20/80 — [4] (02661)

Trapped in His Own Admonition

At this very moment,
Words fail me. Being assailed
By cliché leaves no room,
In a writer's workshop, for failure
By virtue of mistaken identities
Or ways by which reason might escape
In the caves of invention,
Situated beneath the imagination's root system.
They fail me,
For fear of being ridiculed
As blatant, unsophisticated, impersonal,
And lacking elemental compassion,
Knowing, as they do, my tools,
The words, the distinctions between idiom
And overburdened cliché.

Just now, they refuse
To go on public display or be used
As classroom exemplars of how
Not to convey beauty and truth,
Those classical twin Gorgons,
With verisimilitude. They balk,
Stand off my flicking tongue,
Fighting to render them numb and pliant,
Like the fabled mongoose and cobra.
Silence gains the upper hand
On my intellect, whose apparatus,
Lacking sufficient fuel, ceases operation.
What might have been
Another "Ode on a Grecian Urn"
Smolders in the brain's banked metaforge.

8/21/80 — [1] (02015)

Thus Spake Kilroy

Grudgingly, my tired psyche submits to captivity
By amber intoxicating vapors
Late afternoon has loosed on the air.

Surrender is its own best enemy,
In whose protection forgetfulness and reverie
Come to full term before the sentence gets served.

Incarceration forces diffident admissions of innocence
And culpability to consciousness.
I listen to all my inmates confess their sins,

Rap and scrape their bars with sharp obscenities,
Without being able to assuage their grievances.
In this adversarial milieu, we all suffer

From a fear of sharing compassion and sincerity.
Tranquillity, gentleness, and charity
Remain abstractions lifted intact from the Pentateuch,

Without adequate exegesis. We fear man
In his periwig and judicial robes,
The lawyer (that most parasitic of fishes),

Whose very ambitiousness threatens ethics,
Abrogates verities of the heart, and the politician,
Whose promises are ghosts rattling in the closet.

Ah, why am I beleaguered with these concerns?
Nothing I might say or do in our defense
Can exonerate us or commute this indeterminate sentence.

Doom is the name of this penitentiary cell,
In which each of my separate selves
Is locked away for its finite years of existence.

It matters not whether I escape
Or stay in this vaporous amber refuge.
The limits for my crime were set incarnations ago.

Only a miracle could free this dead soul
From its breathing anomie.
Only a leap of faith in words and phrases

Scrawled, scratched, gnawed, with dull teeth,
On the cold, dank, dark walls of oblivion
Might liberate me from time's inquisition.

Slowly, I peer through the translucent glass
Containing my reflection. My features
Enter the liquid, shimmering in limitless dissolve,

And are replaced by surrogates spelling out
My name on the retinas,
Where, not long before, my face was, saying,

"Here was a man, a dreamer, a poet,
Who never wrote, for fear of excoriation by authorities.
Mark ye these words, and persevere."

8/21/80 — [2] (02660)

Celestial Assignation ^Δ

Where are you, muse,
When I'm doomed to lose myself to solitude
Or break up on the lonely, treacherous shoals of genius,
Just outside creation's protective reefs?

Where are you, lady,
Into whose tender, gentle care
*

I surrender all my innocent vulnerability
Whenever I lose my way home,

Forget the street on which I reside,
My parents' names, my phone number,
And the sound of my own voice
Shouting epithets at the starry, starry skies,

Instead of crying for my irreversible mortality,
When hiding from the moon
Becomes impossible to justify
In light of its stark, scrutinizing illuminations?

Where are you, this very moment,
As throbbing music fuses with cool Chablis
To seduce my sensual mentality,
Arrest my will to remain chaste and tranquil

Beyond the sun-kissed confines of this prism,
In which twilight filters in streams,
Through stained-glass cigarette vapors and conversation,
Into my poetic gaze?

Lady, I pray you're witnessing me
From some distant station of the star-cross,
Watching me write my tangential, slightly crazed,
Exhortative verses to you, listening to their chimes

Dream you alive beside me,
Line by line by tiny, finely scribbled line,
And that, before this night declines,
You might save me from my lonely vigil

Over the word-pyre I alone consecrate
Above the dead, fired remains
Of one more poem left unto my keeping
To dispose of in the most appropriate way.

Now that I've concluded, I recognize you
Rising from my gauzy stupor,
Out of the inky record I've left behind,
Above the music and the thinking and the rhymes,

A fusion of waves forming a single tide
Touching my solitary shore,
Persuading all former imperfections to wash smooth.
I enter your irresistibly soothing suck.

8/21/80 — [3] (02659)

Charting Heavenly Orbs

Down wobbles the sun,
Done and sundered in its protean funneling
Earthward. I sense it tumbling
Into the invisible, baptismal ocean
The horizon hides from all but acolytes
Pursuing a holy vocation of abstinence and piety.

Soon, it will have completely disappeared from sight,
Its absence from the sky's vastness
Unimaginable, while the shy, modest moon,
For all its feminine ways,
Whom one might hardly expect to reign,
Will take its place in the welkin.

From where I sit, witnessing the light
In its predictable diminution,
Nothing could be more orderly or appropriate
Than this metamorphosis,
But it's obvious from the lingering light
That Helios is reluctant

To relinquish his position of dominance
To such a delicate and chaste creature.
How absurd and totally chauvinistic, I think,
How preposterous that God,
In His infinite conventional wisdom,
Would have arrogated to His sun such arrogance.

Yet another full hour transpires
Before the light-sponge is squeezed dry
And the daystar has passed into absolute quiescence.
Now, I walk outside, wineglass in hand,
To toast a full and supple alabaster Luna
For having vanquished, so naturally, day's suzerain.

When I confront her, standing under
The full aura of her nocturnal halo,
She seems struck dumb,
As though the battle for ultimate supremacy
Has exacted too much of her energy for her to respond
To my negligible terrestrial gesturings.

In stately taciturnity, she gazes down on me.
I wait for a sign
*

That might suggest she's recognized me
Wishing her a safe passage. Nothing comes
Except the normal lambencies and fluctuations
One would expect from her ubiquitous presence.

For another hour, I celebrate her ascendancy,
Until sleep overshadows me,
Subdues my infatuation, replaces it with repose
For an intellect much too fascinated
With the extravagances of sun and moon,
Those two fools forever chasing each other.

When I awaken, the sun,
Somewhat humbled for having to overcome
A thick fog, has begun to assume its place
In the kingdom of the living. I rise,
Stumble outside, to watch a dull silhouette
Break from the clouds and take its rightful throne,

Knowing that I have been privileged to witness
A universal climacteric, hoping that, one day,
I too will be able to hurtle
And perpetuate myself, like these heavenly orbs,
With verse capable of illuminating hemispheres
Which guide humans from day to day, through night.

8/21/80 — [4] (02658)

Tillers of the Earth

My pen bends under the strenuous burden
Of plowing fields never turned,
Breaking earthly plots
Dotted with gnarled roots and rotting bones
And rocks irregular as gravestones.

I follow behind its vibrating shaft,
Watching knotted clots,
Metaphors in their primal shapes,
Fly off the sharp-cutting sparking point,
Until, gazing over my recent labors,

I see rows, containing my seeds, materialize,
Verse paralleling furrowed verse,
Whose harvest awaits the alchemy of creation,
*

To bring forth food
That, in lean days, when planting ceases,
Will nourish my thoughts and feed my dreams.

8/22/80 — [1] (02657)

Prismatic Teleology

In this distant, open-ended prism,
Through which I pass at the speed of dreams,
Charisma and hubris conspire
To fire my imagination to extraordinary deeds.

I emerge from twilight's open-hearth furnace
As a burning ingot
Tingling with inspiration, anxious to fly
Through space, toward my life's destination,

And become the cornerstone
Of an edifice housing my first artifacts,
The singular thoughts
Cognition depends on to suspend its disbelief

In forged images artistic and unseen.
I am both source and object
Of my own creativity, poet and poem,
At home in the same inextinguishable soul,

Whose cauldron bubbles insatiably
With light and sound, rhythm and rhyme,
The moon's timeless inviolability,
The sun's goat-hoofed cunnilingus.

Myth and image vie with allegory and symbol,
For my attention. Both die
When I'm seduced by the nubile muse,
Who distracts me with veiled metaphor,

The intellect's most celebrated whore,
Who, on short notice, will metamorphose
From alluring courtesan into flower child
Bathing naked in the River Lethe.

Forgetting compromises me occasionally,
While amnesia poppies dream-streets I drive
*

Toward the City of Ancient Verse,
When contriving ways of reaching her heart.

The muse is unyielding in her chastity,
Forcing me to rely on ladies
Who knock on my door after midnight,
Begging me to read to them from the Rig-Veda,

Kama Sutra, and *I Ching*.
No matter how fatigued,
Disenchanted, and inclined toward sleep,
I oblige them for the pleasure of their flesh.

Yet as I've grown older, wiser,
More sedate and mellow, I've learned
The essential importance of impatience
And immoderation, that dreams are conceived

Not by practice and critical discipline,
Whose tolerances are severe,
Rather by accident and gratuitous act.
I advertise myself as a poet

Willing to read my secrets to the public
For nothing more than applause
When I'm done and awe-filled silence
At the outset, before I've begun

To ignite inside the prism
Through which I funnel in passing
From one place to another, in soaring
Above cities on the plain, toward dominions

Rooted in the ears of Milton and Donne,
Shakespeare, Swift, Carlyle, and lyrical Tennyson.
Slowly, I change from light to aura
To dusty halo shimmering on the horizon,

Not mystic or weird pariah or theologian
But mere maker of modest poetry,
Mind-blown and space-flown and terribly alone,
Recorder of inessential and fleet debris

Traveling across our collective psyche
Like dust from a meteor shower
Cascading into hazy illuminations
In a phantasmagoria the mind perpetuates

Whenever it attempts to locate its ancestry
Among the stars and galactic particles
Floating above afternoon's dissolving glow.
Slowly, I return to my base elements,

Neglected, absolved of any need
To prove my manhood or earthly purpose,
A writer, inventor of quintessential truths
Buried in wellsprings, beneath rocks, in the stars,

A person who's spent his entire adulthood
Justifying the intangible essences,
Shaped in their own unpremeditated vessels,
Embodying artifice and magic.

I return, by degrees, to the original light
From which my seed arose
And inundated the earth, return
To genes, double helix, atoms, dust,

As the prism shatters, scattering rays
Through space, past time,
Toward eternity. I reunite with God,
Disappear in a solitary gasp,

As words, syllables, and breath quit their soaring,
Collect in swirling motes, dissipate,
And enter the coursing life-force, pulsing,
Shorn of their primordial possibilities,

Until I am lost in the cosmic exhaust
Sifting into endless spheres —
A mere thought pressed between years,
Drifting off beyond sense and reminiscence.

8/22/80 — [2] (02656)

Ushering in Night's Final Sounds

Music stretches my elastic fascination.
My senses succumb
To the numbing echoes of guitar and tongue.
Tremolos, vibratos, and glissandi
Flow over frequencies my ears receive.

I rise, fly on lifting riffs,
Then swoop low, over harmonious notes
Gathering along the ground
Like poets miming songs
To admiring audiences of deaf-mutes.

When the players cease their strumming,
Nothing is left, except emptiness,
On which to concentrate.
Reverberations dissolve like bone
And flesh, in silence. I envision demons

Peering through the quietude
Of this room, from which all but I
Have disappeared. I sit here,
Whispering to myself an eerie motif,
Hoping to resurrect the music, from death,

Without conquering solitude.
Suddenly, the lights dim my silhouette
Into the shimmering shape
Of an incubus hovering above night,
Insinuating itself into sleep's sweet vagina.

8/22/80 — [3] (01304)

Smart Machines

The highways I travel
Comprise a series of integrated circuits
On a macrocosmic microchip.

My mainframe apparatus and mechanicals
Contain memory
Capable of recreating, from scratch,

Every last capital and comma
In all of Shakespeare's plays,
The facial features

Of each angel in Michelangelo's
Painted Vatican ceiling, all flats and sharps
In Tchaikovsky's *Pathétique* symphony.

Yet for all my sophisticated technology,
I keep forgetting
Intended destinations.

My readouts are curiously cryptic,
Inscrutable, whose accuracy,
Though irrefutable, seems inappropriate

Given my true heading.
Soon, I must either learn to communicate
With my machinery, speak computerese,

Or desist from these peripatetics,
For fear of being keyed off the screen
On which my digits fidget and pace.

8/23/80   (02243)

Recorder of Deeds Pro Tem

Outside my window, the mimosa tree shivers.
Its shimmering green patina
Blurs in the drizzle, runs down the glass,
Like sperm swimming toward redemption
Within the channels connecting inspiration
With creative release.

      Winds coercing a black storm
Lash its limbs in a miasmic swirl.
Fronds and ruffled seed pods
Flail away at the air,
Like swarming bees
Attacking, with outrageous ferocity, a dumb dog
Accidentally strayed into their path.

      Viewing the transmuted shape
Before me, beyond my reach
                  (a matter of
Vision having submitted to metaphor),
I ask myself what relationship sperm and bees
Might possibly have to each other
And both to the design of my poetic needs.

Suddenly, an upstaged sun breaks through.
The breeze dies.
Rain ceases its myriad streaked penetrations.
When again I gaze,
The tree is crazed with honeybees
Detained in frenzied pollination,
Singing the celebration of seasonal redemption,

And glazed with silver beads
Lingering on each frond
Like sperm arrived at their assigned seeds.
I'm reminded that a brief climacteric,
A minuscule alteration in universal status quo,
Has occurred just outside my focus

And that, soon,
Even tree, window, and poet
Will have dematerialized,
Leaving whatever newer means destiny might devise
By which to chronicle
The creative potentialities of all things
Green and golden, ocherous, cold, and about to be.

9/1/80   (02239)

Troika Starts In △

If ever curiosity could wand itself alive,
Surely it would take the shape
Of our little two-and-a-half-year-old,
Troika the Boy,
Better known to himself as "Benjy
The Dog" — excuse me, "Brown Benjy,"
If you please — who, on entering preschool
For the first time, this Tuesday,
Rather than finding himself sundered
In Babylonian captivity,
Sensed, at once, a newer freedom
Than ever he'd previously discovered.

His intellect dashed from image to object
Faster than his eyes could pass their batons,
Sprinting from golden, swimming fish,
Shimmering in a prismatic bowl,
To the shell a hasty turtle had forgotten
To take with him, past a twig
Laced with whisperous dried grass
Fashioned into a nest for baby birds.
Finally, he arrived at a bathtub,
Majestically lined with anomalous rug,
And slid quietly over the soft lip,
To its magical bottom,

Where, in continuous ablution,
He might bathe in the godly process
Of learning to assimilate the universe
By fusing likes and antinomies,
Seeing in all things
Linkages poetic, appropriate, and enchanting.
Thus, with silent, awe-struck,
Invisible tears did we set our child
Gently down in paradise,
To let his hide-and-seek curiosity
Begin finding titles for unwritten rhymes
And riddles to answers already devised.

9/4/80 (02240)

Condemned Tenement

One day, quite unexpectedly,
His oldest and best tenant, intellect,
Gave notice that at month's close,
He would be relinquishing his rented rooms,
Moving to more modest lodging.

Perplexed by the prospect of lost income
And empty chambers, boredom,
He hastily interviewed a hundred applicants,
Before deciding that senescence
Seemed to possess the most stable qualifications

For his constraints on the mind,
His brain's highly confining requirements:
Stolid self-righteousness, solitude,
And a studious disregard for politics and history.
Within a week, without the slightest confusion,

His new renter settled in.
The transformation was accomplished handily,
Since the transient brought with him
Little else than the base essentials
Demanded by protozoan survival.

As time transpired, the landlord
Noticed how his boarder rarely came to meals,
*

Prepared by thought's seasoned chefs,
Never attended memory's fetes,
Refused fancy's capricious overtures to him

To join in celebration,
With other friendly residents of the tenement,
Of their mutual pleasures and discontents,
Through mental exercise:
Debate, song, confabulation, reading, and dreams.

So infrequently would the lessee participate
That finally, his absence manifested itself
In a pervasive malaise
Within all the tenants' daily routines.
By degrees, each retired to his compartment,

Until silence, like a thick, quick odor
Of burning wires, infiltrated the environment,
Rendering its corridors and curtains,
Rugs, tables, wallpaper, bedding, and windows
Permanently tainted, contaminated, quarantined.

Now, with nothing to do
But count accumulating cracks in the plaster,
Unscrew blown-out incandescents
Without replacing them, and patiently wait
To notify the ambulance service

Of another passing, he sits alone,
Within dim chiaroscuro,
Musing, in penumbral solitude, on his future,
Until he enters a hallucination of eternity
And is forevermore absorbed by his delusion.

9/10/80 — [1] (05714)

The Veil of Maya

Divine design beckons me to her ear,
To hear me whisper dreams and expectations
I've devised for my destiny.

Drawing near, I try mightily to concentrate
On my fine, high-minded intentions,
But her naked body drugs me,

Perverts memory into a forgetful minah bird,
Numbs the tongue to dumbness,
Until it becomes a catatonic insomniac

Wanting to escape the desperation
Its own self-inflicted silence mandates,
Without being able to erase its babbling past.

I succumb to her lissome contours,
Whose smooth flesh seduces all intimations
Of immortality that once possessed me,

Arrests me in a momentary nexus,
From whose womb-warm pleasure vacuum
No one ever exits intact,

Rather languishes for the rest of his existence,
At which juncture divine design
Relinquishes her dominance

As a spider its prey's desiccated carcass.
Soon, I penetrate her hymeneal veil,
Taste, bathe in, the stream

That gushes from the earth's loins,
Until my groin aches
And fatigue draws me back from hallucination,

Through my daydreaming gaze, to reality,
Where with you, dear muse,
I sit agitatedly praising our liaison,

Speculating on how much longer
We might survive in a society that fails to redeem
High-minded dreamers and Keatses in embryo.

9/10/80 — [2] (05715)

Dying in Love, Shakespearean Style

Hurtling through wobbly trajectories,
Bending subtly along curves shaped by fate,
To avoid merging with the past,
In repetitious déjà vu,
My body, neither celestial nor cosmic,
Changing each changeless day,
Edges closer, sooner, to the universal precipice,
Where present and future cease

And eternity looms, palpably accessible,
Like a lady haloed by satin sheets,
Lying, legs drawn back,
In immemorial anticipation of being penetrated.
With gentle tentativeness, I enter time's vagina,
Hoping life's climax won't be premature.

9/12–13/80 — [1] on 9/13   (05716)

Secret Sharers

The close, cold air inside this car
Engenders hypnosis.
I can't imagine why the driver
Suspects me of knowing where or why he's going,
When only my bodily silhouette
Is fitted behind the wheel,
Not his mind's home-oriented will to survive.

Whether I gaze, in wild, crazed abstraction,
From his eyes or he peers from mine
Is mere trompe l'oeil sensation.
Either way, neither of us
Recognizes the land passing in rapid retrograde
Or is able to concentrate on the pavement, for long,
Without drowsing or shaking violently awake

Just prior to landing upside down,
Inside out, above the ground.
Like two blind amebas in a dish,
We finally sense each other's presence
And, with energies too feeble to excite thought,
Unite in stupid, useless blinking —
Ghosts going in and out of their own focus.

9/13/80 — [2]   (05717)

Los desesperados

Anymore, our lives criss and cross
With such quixotic unpredictability,
We never quite seem to know
Whether we've just finished
Or not begun an overture or its coda.

Waking and sleeping
Make up the parentheses for the continuum
We continuously pace
Without ever meeting each other
Along hope's sagging tightrope.

Even when we do spend a moment
In tentative reminiscence
Or restlessly digress to indulge our fantasies
In what-ifs, nothing palpable materializes —
Flattery, kiss, or unself-conscious laughter.

For the longest while,
No one noticed our painful estrangement,
Not friends, parents, or children,
Least of all us two,
Who were blinded by passion's laser rays,

Until the day we both left
And never returned to the nest
We'd made to protect and soothe each other
When the tempestuous world
Would press to separate and tattoo our mutuality.

Now, mistrust, envy, jealousy, and vindictiveness
Hold sway. We find it more bearable
To stay fastidiously out of sight,
Hiding beneath silences,
Conversations unrelayed, forgotten goodnights.

Although we passed away years ago,
We die a little less gracefully
Each day. Actually, only our shades
Survive the holocaust
Our misshapen souls still perpetuate.

9/13/80 — [3] (04184)

Voyager

I hurtle ahead relentlessly,
Entering and penetrating formidable oceans,
Whose waves are undulating paved highways
That seduce me, vertiginously,
With invisible, persuasively changing currents.

I surrender to the lure of places
Never fitted for clockworks
Or calipered, by the cartographer,
With orderly curiosity. My inclinations
Are best served by unpredictability and nervous energy,

Not reason. It's the freedom
Inherent in motion unimpeded by destination
That Virgils me through worlds
Accessible to the imagination, in flight, only when
The life-tree can come totally unrooted

Without dying or being blown away
By the mind's creative hurricane.
I live for these microcosmic deaths,
Voyages of the spirit, visions,
Achieved only when conditions are perfect

For sailing, soaring, driving through,
Above, wholly within, the psyche's clear alembic.
I die each time arrival occurs
And time's spider descends, suspends me,
Until the next urge severs the threads,
Hurtling my vessel ahead again, relentlessly.

9/13/80 — [4] (05718)

Hint of Winter

This bright, cool mid-September day,
Afternoon late, the sky is alive
With heliocentric butterflies —
Dreamy somnambulists
Cruising in bouquetlike profusion —
Splayed against infinity's ramparts
Far above the Monet-ed trees,
Beneath which I stand mesmerized
By Icarus a thousand times multiplied,
Listening to inaudible whispering of wings
Singing elegies to a gibbous moon
Prematurely suspended,
Looking at their swooping color-shapes
Exchanging spaces kaleidoscopically.

I gasp as they hover and copulate,
With incandescent ecstasy,
Realizing, of a sudden, the reason and design
Behind this ritualistic pastiche.
Furiously, they're speaking to me season's end,
Reenacting primal sacrifices,
That perhaps, in connecting with an imagination
As wayward yet tumescent as mine,
They might husband their fragile essence
Against impending winter quiescence
And be unlocked again,
In heliocentric ascendancy, when spring
Invites us to share the air closer to earth,
Redeemed briefly from these dreamy doom-heights.

9/18/80 — [1] (05719)

The Poet Admonishes Himself △

After the gravid heat
June, July, even September's first half,
Devised to shame everything earthly
Into surrendering instincts by which survival
Might otherwise survive, the days cool.
Relief reawakens the battered spirit,
Renews the subdued soul
To a primal delight in elemental essences:
Trees, streams, houses being painted,
People taking evening walks,
Children rushing to and from school,
Celebrating the creative spark
Unleashed by having curiosity, intellect,
And memory tightly wound.

With such immediate jubilation,
Who has time or prescience to heed premonitions
Dropped from gnawing squirrels' clutches,
Twisting inexorably from limbs, into brittleness,
Fluttering groundward
From wing tips bound south out of time?
And who was meant to sequester himself,
Brooding over such autumnalities,
*

When the few-and-far-between days of fall
Make themselves so accessible to us all,
Just by our calling out their names?
Even the most devoted poet
Should be ashamed to waste energy indoors,
Seducing a too accommodating muse.

"Fool!" I admonish myself. "Forget your despondency.
Exchange your grievances and fatigue,
For a swim in the quick-running arteries."
Ah, what a rush, to be floated, alive,
Toward the core
From whose auricular promontory they soar,
Who crave that free-falling feeling
Of leaving the head through the heart.

9/18/80 — [2] (00130)

Ear Infection

The sheer nearness of the ear
To the earth yields the heart's weeping,
The sun's detonations, footfalls of wandering Jews,
Creative sparks flying off grinding wheels
Artists operate to sharpen the objects
Of their solipsistic sell-ebrations.
I stop at the crossing where two days
Intersect a solitary night and listen
And ruminate on the heart's irregular beating,
Trying to isolate the etiology of loneliness,
Listening to the frictioned wheeling
Planets and other cosmic bodies describe in space.
My ears detect volcanoes erupting in Siberia,
Bowery drunks snoring in roaring crescendos
While asleep, and diesels and jet engines.
They also hear electric can openers, hair dryers,
And CAT scanners buzzing incessantly as bees
Defrocking mimosa blooms — conveniences
Whose existence prematurely obsoletes resourcefulness,
Accelerates the demise of dominant traits
In a species that has survived by its resilience.
My ears burn like sides of beef on spits
*

Turning above a barbecue pit
Whose fires are Kafka's penal needles
Inexorably killing them, with self-awareness
And shame for their duplicity, in a kind of genocide
That allows its victims to stay alive
In a Dantesque labyrinth. The ears sear,
Until audition diminishes to an indiscriminate howl,

In which chimeras and demigorgons
Appear before their openings, spewing and vomiting
News that the entire world is at war.
Now, I try to lift myself up off the ground,
Where, for hours, under a funereal moon,
I've lain with my face pressed sideways,
Absorbing, through a universal stethoscope,
Premonitory tremulations suggesting hope at hand
For all of us who've grown hard of listening.
But I can't move, and as I lie glued
To my brief stretch of history's express track,
I become conscious, one last time,
Of painfully definable sounds filling my Eustachian tubes
With fright-filled reverberations — those of a train
Bearing down on my tightly fastened head,
My neck actually snapping, and death laughing.

9/25/80 — [1] (05720)

Itinerant Limner

Driving daily from station to station,
Braving accidental collisions with fate,
Or converging on his own Doppelgänger
Returning from an ancient incarnation
To assume a newer form,
The poet writes his hieroglyphic script
In a notebook he keeps atop an attaché
He balances on the seat beside him,
Confiding, to invisible eavesdroppers, intimacies,
Metaphorical tours de force, and scorn,
Line by free-associated line.

Sometimes, while he's recording his verse,
Words he's never seen
*

Describe voices he's never heard
In configurations so distinct that on rereading his work
After completing a drive, he knows
Poltergeists have taken over command,
Subverted the cerebral machinery
That manufactures his lyrical tone poems.
Arriving home signals a time for recuperation,
Finding answers or justifiable explanations
For sequences redeemed from nonexistence.

Wine, occasional spontaneous sensualities
Shared among a harem of nymphomaniacal ladies,
And sleep all fail to dissipate the pressure
Generated by his creative urgency.
In fact, each avocation heightens anxiety,
Transports him past exhaustion,
To amnesic despair, fits of despondency
In which he's threatened to cut off an ear,
Commit his naked body to outer space,
Via lunar flights burning pure poppy vapors.
Nothing except utter forgetting
Finally leaves his dazed spirit free to relax,

Until the next day materializes,
Reminding him of his obligation to compose poems
Capable of informing generations to come
That at least one primitive limner
Tried to celebrate his seismic, silent self
By capturing, firsthand, each and every
Variation in lighting within the landscape
Containing his travel-weary spirit,
That one puny word-painter dared arrest
Atmospheres of jubilation and unrest simultaneously,
In the Land of Transients, where briefly he was stranded.

9/25/80 — [2] (05721)

A Morning Valedictory ᐃ

From an invisible source high up in the oak
That splays shadow-dapple across our yard,
Gnawed shards of nuts
Cascade, like sawdust, through a hundred feet
Of fifty degrees, this end of September.

Furious sounds of the tiny creature,
Hidden in the slightly melancholy folds
Of tree and leaf and green essence,
Sift down to my sleepy ears,
Here where I sit outdoors, freezing,

For the sheer sake of embracing the day
On its own terms. Contemplation is savory
When it contains no artificial sweeteners,
Depends, for its sustenance, on engaging the senses
Directly, to apprehend elements unadulterated.
My running nose, watery eyes,

Shivering fingers and toes and chest
Attest to this singular truth.
Poet and his entire circumambience
Become one. I am swallowed whole,
As though my dissolving into cricket and birdsong,
Shimmering shadow, frigid whispering of limbs

Were a celestial death not robbing me of vitality,
Rather restoring me to my natural ethic,
Reawakening me to the inevitability at hand,
That all things, having been gently admonished,
Will soon be expected to enter quiescence
In order to live again. I welcome my disappearance.

9/26/80   (05722)

The Heart's Autumnal

Today, the clichés* are 180 degrees
Out of synchronization.
It's me, not my vocabulary,
That's painfully inadequate at expression.
I fail my words pitifully,
Remaining disengaged
From autumn's immense presence,
Unable to translate, into personal rhythms,
Each dense tree's exploding ego,
Which splays the horizon
With impastos spoken by the Genius
Who paints infinity on the eyes' pinheads.

Jesus, how I see and sense!
Yet perception refuses liquefaction.
My cold soul won't free emotions
Long enough for mind-signs
To revivify them *in utero cerebro*,
Where the alchemization of vision
Coerces millions of leaves
To exchange their pied essences, for verse.
Despite nature's riot,
I am apart from the poem my heart has arrested.
Desiccation, I suspect,
Must have set in long before now.

* "No words can adequately express . . ."
   "Words fail me."
   "I'm at a complete loss for words."

10/9/80   (02006)

The Pied Kingdom

Thank God for pied things:
Shires ignited by fall leaves,
Trees tinged in miraculous conflagration —
Quixotic matchsticks
Flashing against the litmus horizon
Like whispers sifting from erotic lips.

Thank God for thingdoms pied
In psyche's cascading color-riot,
This climactic October,
Desiring decent burial in my imagination,
Whose slow, melodious catalyst
Changes touch to taste, sight to sound.

Thank God for pied kings
Who defy history and description,
By refusing transmutation. Their diadems
And scepters, decorated red, orange, gold,
Are older and nobler in moribundity
Than any traditions poetry might reflect.

Thank God for kingdoms pied
In mystical fixatives we perpetuate
*

Whenever we stop to watch forests on fire,
Dreams turning color overnight,
And phoenixes, resurrected from oblivion,
Flying, like leaves, toward Kenilworth.

10/12/80   (02238)

Another Day, Another Dollar

Sometimes
When I position myself
Behind my desk at the pants factory,
I'm a farmer mounting his tractor,
A cross-country truck driver
Ensconced in the cab of an eighteen-wheeler,
A jet pilot checking cockpit gauges,
In preparation for takeoff.

Sometimes,
In moments of pernicious absent-mindedness,
I even forget the net,
Woven of exposed conduits and steampipes,
Girders, joists, and fluorescent tubes
Undulating, like eels,
In oceans of sewing-room dust,
That keeps me snared in this office chair

And dream of becoming someone,
A poet, perhaps a vagabond
Or romantic bohemian composer,
Climbing convenient Matterhorns,
Crossing landlocked continents, on foot,
For the sake of entertaining ladies
Giddy with wit and sensuality,
Pleasured easily by my villanelles and elegies.

Sometimes,
Most often, to be certain,
No such surcease from routine occurs.
I revert to what I do best:
Checking production charts, absentee records
Of questionable workers,
Issuing warning slips,
Neglecting potentially expensive grievances,

And interviewing new prospects
To operate machines and hot-head presses
Being vacated constantly
By people able to earn higher wages
Than what we pay,
By claiming unemployment benefits,
Filing for food stamps,
Medicines, and aid to dependent children.

Sometimes,
About once every ten years,
A spirit approximating the demonic
Possesses me, makes me undress
Before the mirror reflecting my past,
And forces me to identify myself
Out of the crowd of strangers
That clouds my gaze.

It's then, when recognition takes hold,
That I phone in sick,
Requesting of my irate boss
The day off, to recuperate
From whatever has laid me bare.
Today, I've stayed in bed,
Hoping, this time,
Death might accept my application.

10/16/80   (02005)

The Refusal

*After an early-morning image
Trilogy envisioned*

For the very same reasons
We're not made privy to why or when
Or from what inscrutable source it emanates,

We have no idea what decides
Its going out. We simply know
When its presence is absent, flown, accomplished

And that what arrives must depart
Regardless of intellect, sensitivity, godly mien.
The leaves, for instance, this autumn,

Form curiously hued incunabula,
Yet we can't read them,
Decipher clues to their collective demise,

Or even intuit the design of their chronicle,
Much less hope to comprehend
Why all things earthly end,

Decay, suffer sea changes of shape.
Aren't we capable of survival?
I desire stasis, abjure transformations!

Can't the mind find a safe route
To the Spice Islands, where invention and memory
Are exempt from corporeal emphemeralities

And the soul, suspended in an alembic
Of poetry, music, and golden illuminations,
Can transcend the mandate for resurrection?

What might it take to arrest the leaves,
Preserve their greenness forever,
Allow my vital body and ideas to thrive

Endless generations? Who determined
That finite is absolute, that there's no way
To amend or abrogate natural laws?

I take exception! I refuse to accept
Such basic equations,
Be they animistic, pantheistic, or traditional!

I demand answers of the Commander in Chief,
Whose ukases I decline to obey
From this moment forth. For now,

I'll pick the green leaves still on trees,
Not brilliant colors covering the ground,
And collect them in a box.

10/18/80 (02007)

[God, how my eyes are listening,] †

God, how my eyes are listening,
This crisp, clear October afternoon,
To the colors. I never realized
*

That the speeds of light and sound
Are so inextricably identical
Or that waves and frequencies

10/19/80 — [1] (04358)

Runaway Child △

Today is autumn's apotheosis,
Indian summer's child
Running wild, in reckless ecstasy,
High through skittish maples,
Sweet gums, dogwoods, oaks
She flecks randomly
With dazzle-dapple and magical salves.

Occasionally, she stops
To play with butterflies and grasshoppers
Who've reveled too long,
Leaping and soaring on their backs,
Partaking of their giddy tontine
Without sensing the precariousness
Of her own purchase on air and earth.

And as she skips past,
Breezes her fleet feet unleash
Turn the horizon's clear blue bowl
Into a tornado of leaves
Twisting, spiraling,
Diving through invisible funnels
Until grasped by grass, captured.

She laughs at the birds' chatterings,
Whose urgent persiflage
Contains, in its prolix articulations,
A singular admonition,
That time, their silent partner,
Is indeed breathing down her neck.
She cares not for such trivialities.

Yet as the sun diminishes,
Fracturing into sharp penumbras,
She wearies from running,
Begins to wonder where she'll stay
*

Under cover of night,
Whether she'll ever find her way home,
Knowing in her heart she's strayed too far.

10/19/80 — [2] (02173)

The Little Bird's Last Flight

For dear Ernie

Recently, someone suggested to me
The leaves' fantastical color spray,
Which already has lasted three weeks,
In a sequence of seven-day passions,
Might be a direct result
Of this past summer's inordinate heat.

Focusing on such screaming ecstasy,
It's difficult for me to unravel
Or fathom the inherent paradox
By which one dry spell
Gives rise to such vibrancy
Just prior to another season's demise.

Yet as I drive toward the city
Beyond which I've lived in voluntary exile,
My mind refuses to cease drawing conclusions
About truth and apocrypha
Or deny possibilities
That nature's confusion is of godly design.

Precisely because such anomalies exist,
I persist in self-criticism,
Allow my inquisitiveness free run
To investigate correlative phenomena,
Such as the self-inflicted death
That calls me haltingly back, today,

Grieving in piteous disbelief
And compassionate stupefaction.
Sometimes, mere speculation
Assuages the pain bafflement causes.
Most likely, Joel's suicide was the autumn
Of a beautiful soul seeking apotheosis in flight.

10/20/80 — [1] (02175)

Joel Is Safe and Sound

For Jane and David

Now, having reluctantly departed
With bits of my sullen heart and soul
Scattered, like cigarette ashes,
About the immaculate house of mourners
And having started my vehicle,
In preparation for the return journey
To the Land of Solitude,
I dismantle myself one piece of attire
At a time — suit coat, vest,
Checkered tie, lustrous boots, flesh.
My bones step out of their silhouette,
Assume a new attitude
With respect to the living dead
And those who, having surrendered breath,
Finally have been liberated.

I fly home,
Naked as lightning slicing the sky,
Soaring untrammeled, barely able to see
My sweet mother, dear brothers,
David and Mark, so far below,
Slowly dissolving,
Until sight and memory, becoming one,
Are jettisoned and left behind,
Like delicate sprays weighting a coffin.
Ah, blessed resurrection!
Oh, how I've dreamed of such release!
Although moon-berries and star-fruits
Distract me, I hasten to get back,
That those I left will know I'm home,
Alone, tonight, safe and sound, at peace.

10/20/80 — [2] (02174)

Learning the King's English ᐃ

The little fella,
Fast approaching three,
Revels gleefully, squeals with ecstasy
*

Uncommon to his species,
Whenever his dad
Accidentally, on purpose, gets confused,
Commits a spoonerism,
Or trips humorously into a Freudian slip
And pretends to be chagrined,
Fit to be tied in his own faux pas,
While little fella,
With complete pride-filled satisfaction
That elevates him to a stately plane,
Corrects the mispronunciation with haste,
Admonishes his victim/culprit,
In hope that this most recent mistake
Will never again be perpetrated.

"Troika, look what I caught
In my moose trip, this morning!"
"No, silly, it's *mousetrap*!"
"Oh, yes, thank you, thank you.
Now, quit staring
And drink your worn moose."
"Duuuude, it's *orange juice*!
You always get confused."
"I guess I do, boy,
But you sure know right away
When I get conmoosed.
I appreciate being set straight.
Finish your cinnamon and speese."
"It's *spice*, cinnamon and *spice*!"
"Oh, yes, that's right, boy."
"I love you, Dude."
                    "I love you too, Treeka!"

10/22/80 (01448)

The First Snow ^Δ

I enter a morning brightly bedizened
In autumn's first frost.
It glints with diamond flecks
Thrown off a colossal wheel
*

Grinding the shiny horizon to dust,
Trapped in a dazzling earthly suspension,
Whose facets blind me to the freeze.

Arrested in brief cerebral anesthesia,
Beneath a tree, while the child
I drive to school each day
Lingers indoors,
I spend a moment being gently touched
By myriad leaves brushing past me,
On flutter-flumes, to the sea.

Slowly, they become butterflies
Neither completely green nor yellow,
For the premature frost
That has caused the letting-go to accelerate.
They sift continuously,
In floating irreversibility,
Collecting, like nibbling minnows, about my feet.

My ears intuit their whispering minims,
Courageous, last-minute wisdoms,
Regrets, confessions,
Adventitious prayers to the living,
Without being able to translate, into images
Capable of sustaining my faith in change,
Their sweet, fleet farewells.

Suddenly, my little girl
Penetrates my gaze, bursting the daydream
Containing my strayed thoughts.
"Look, Dad, it's snowing!"
When I focus again,
The sunny, leaf-dappled sky
Is a tapestry of swirling flakes.

10/30/80   (02262)

Halloween

Ah, just yesterday afternoon,
With what assiduous glee we worked,
Playing at decorating the porch
*

Of our absolutely Gothic Halloween house,
Until we'd fashioned its formidable entrance
Into a foreboding cave-mouth
With shimmering bats
And shadowy crepe-paper stalactites
Pierced by haphazard spiders
Dangling from invisible twine,
Redolent of Druids hidden somewhere deep within.

Oh, my sweet children, my caring wife,
How serious were our preparations,
The perpetuation of mythopoeic ritual,
Our extravagant anticipation
Of hobgoblins, "ampires," witches and wenches,
Ghosts, "skeledons," and creatures weird,
Too "spokey," eerie, and diabolic to mention.
How wondrous were the confrontations,
When, cloaked and masked,
Our neighborhood came petitioning alms
And left noisy images on our joyous eyes.

Now, I question how all my recollections,
Sufficiently vivid in focus,
As though seemingly derived
From an excited last-night occurrence,
Could possibly have changed shape,
Like witches taking flight,
And entered the thin, inessential air,
Where dementia engenders senescence,
Or why, each chilly October ending,
I'm still haunted by ghosts in this rest home,
If not for some abiding, incomprehensible love for you.

11/1/80 — [1] (02559)

Goebbels, Poet Laureate of the Third Reich

Let the words fall where they may.
Always, they have controlled my sensibility,
With their persuasive rhythms and lyricism,
I admit. I submit to their sway,
Complete slave to their totalitarian domination.

They scream rhetorical mandates,
Like pontiffs or Hitlerian commanders in chief,
Demanding total subservience to their wills,
From the balcony, below which I genuflect,
Complying by virtue of my faith,

Without questioning the ethics or innate morality
They insist derives from the Bible.
My loyalty is absolutely above suspicion.
Despite the fact that I am victim
Of my own self-inflicted remorse,

Guilt that surfaces each time
I desire to release hostilities
By writing graffiti in museum-restroom stalls,
I remain the prestigious poet-in-residence,
State's laureate, weaver of spells

By which monarchs and potentates and presidents
Convince themselves that all is well
In their kingdoms. I prostitute the intellect,
Of whose legacy I am recipient,
Down the drowning generations — the teller of dreams,

Who keeps rulers in check,
Assures them that too much questioning
Is a useless avocation.
They swoon under the word-spell I create
Whenever I read poetry

Fashioned for whatever cause they request —
War, political propaganda,
Birth control, the dissemination of information
Regarding crop rotation,
The controversy between church and state, resurrection.

Yet there are cold, starless nights
When, unable to perform other than reflection,
Feeble at making verse
Capable of moving an entire people to vandalism,
I recoil before the mirror,

In whose wordless prophecy I shrink
To the size of my least effective rhyme,
And cry, knowing in my heart
That dying is so damn simple
That no mystical incantation can change my mind

When once I've decided to quit the game,
Submit to polemics and hysterical rhetoric
Politicians and dictators, who make a habit
Of subterfuge, require. So the words fall in place
Like disgraceful obscenities, and I can only apologize.

11/1/80 — [2] (02636)

The Eavesdropper

I sit here, on a volatile Saturday night,
Eavesdropping on horny professors
And lawyers and C.P.A.'s,
With their *Vogue*-tailored-to-a-T mistresses
And wives,
In Katy Station, Columbia, Missouri,
U.S. of A.,
Nineteen hundred and eighty,
Pretending to be writing poetry,
While, in blatant actuality, overhearing them
Spew topicalities, legalities, sensualities,
And downright macho obscenities
Calculated to nudge their female seals into bed
Just as conveniently soon
As Hannibal ever moved his sheds
Up to the front lines
(Quam celerrime vineas agere),
In the outrageously named Pubic Wars.

I sit listening to serious discussions
On the virtue of birth control,
Spontaneous copulation,
Trouncing shit out of the Big Eight
Champion,
And the significance of the Mann Act
In modern court proceedings,
Wondering if, born in nineteen hundred
And forty-one,
I even have any right to question
The relevancy of still lusting to get laid,
When computers and walking on the moon
*

And laser imaginations
Have superseded Eisenhower's Atoms for Peace
And Johnson's Great Society.
Suddenly, I discover my wine has spilled
Over the page, made my ink run,
So that no one can decipher my heretical inquiries.

11/1/80 — [3] (02635)

Purchasing Agent ^Δ

I am, admittedly,
The buyer of toilet paper
And sanitary napkins and roll towels.
How you found me out, you bastard,
I'll never know,
Unless something about my kinky hair
Or slightly aquiline nose
Disclosed the truth of my Hebraic ancestry.

I must confess I've had experience
In fluorescents, cardboard cartons, gusseted bags
Either printed or plain.
I proclaim I'm no parvenu
When it comes to nonasphaltic tape
With printed warning message,
#8 tampons,
And Rochester Romp-On Maintainer.

Yet I believe it's a bit presumptuous
For you to assume, unequivocally,
That I can obtain for you
Prophylactics at wholesale,
Or *hole*sale, or, for that matter,
At below cost,
Just because I have the reputation
Of being a wheeler-dealer.

In fact, though I purchase TP
In quantity,
There's no reason to believe
I would ever be a co-conspirator
*

In your profligacy,
Let alone contribute to the degree of degeneracy
You cause by asking young ladies
To wipe my penis after I've climaxed with them.

11/1/80 — [4] (02634)

One for the Road

The simple electrical music,
Energized by gentle fingers
Slipping over keys easily satisfied,
Fills my ears with naked ladies
Slowly sliding over edges
Buttressed by the imagination.
I envision caryatids shimmering
Inside Santa Maria Cathedral.
I can't stand the leisure
In which my drowsing intellect revels.
It bows to the sounds,
Knowing that it can climax anytime
Except for the present,
In which it scribbles its little odes
On the vacuous air,
Hoping to come, while the waitress goes,
Bee-busy, from table to table,
Until it eradicates its anonymity,
Connecting, out of all this noisy silence,
Touching one supple human body,
Whose flesh echoes
A thousand times more provocatively
Than whores drumming up business
Along the Via Veneto.
I surrender to the wine-ripe music,
Leap onto the strutting lady
Delivering drinks to various stations,
Consummating the natural order
By which this place operates:
Dog is eaten only by dog;
No interlopers are allowed,
When it comes to canines coming.
*

I procrastinate, then raise my hand,
To place my order
For one barmaid with whom to fornicate
Before going to bed, with a thud.

11/1/80 — [5] (01350)

Not Quite So Mighty as the Sword

I tentatively touch pen to paper
And wait
For what will materialize,
Following the cursive script with my eyes,

Trying to translate the enigmas
Forming sequentially,
Coalescing, in words, as phrases
Breaking open slowly, like mimosa blooms,

Asking to be taken for their face value,
Without compromise —
Plants sprouting out of the imagination,
Brain-flowers growing

In plain air, naked as Naiads
Drowsing by pools surrounded by lantanas
And lilacs. The pen scurries
As though chased by worried demons

Aching to achieve release
From within my confessional verse.
It stutters, refuses to touch the truth
With its twitching fingertips,

Restless, yet cautious as Hell's dogs,
To bite my flesh
Just to discover what lies deep
Beneath my psyche's surface.

As night advances, the air thins.
Even the electricity
Begins to diminish. Sounds calm down.
The paper dissolves. The pen forgets its urgency.

11/1/80 — [6] (01351)

The Incredible Disappearing Man

One of the most remorseful awarenesses
The aging spirit
Can possibly have is that, on learning
The flesh is wizening,
It finds itself shrinking commensurately,
Like lettuce left out overnight
Or an apple, its meat exposed,
Slowly browning from neglect.

I know, because, having endured life
Thirty-nine years,
Producing, in my haughty stead,
Two children,
And having outlasted a dissatisfied wife,
I've run head-on into the enemy,
Boredom, who's demanded of me
Identification papers substantiating my existence.

And I've been found wanting,
In need of making futile excuses
As to why no amount of corroborating evidence
Can connect my fingerprints
With my spurious face. I touch myself
In the motel mirror and discover
My skin consists of subtle smudges
That, with a solitary swipe, are easily erased.

Unadroitly, I reach into the air,
To draw down a passing planet,
That I might climb aboard
And escape the dilemma
My mentality so palpably presents me.
But in my exasperation,
I grasp at a comet declining
And follow it earthward,
Into silent extinction, suicidal as a lemming.

Now, scattered like volcanic ash,
I return to atomic waste,
Half-life after half-life,
Until all that remains of my shadow
Is diplodocus dung
*

Waiting to be transmogrified,
Hoping to be utilized, exploded in an engine
Capable of powering my vehicle to the stars.

11/1/80 — [7] (01352)

Sunrise

I anticipate the sun's ascendancy,
This Lord's morning,
When sporadic stars, a quarter moon,
And tinges of orange
Spark my torpid mind to fantasy.

The sky is a womb,
The moon a lustrous ovum,
And the three stars closest to my focus
Spermatozoa
Moving slowly toward fruitful union.

Eventually, sweaty dawn
Delivers one last exhausted contraction.
The sun's glowing head
Shows just above the horizon's
Fully dilated opening.

Birth occurs.
I bear jubilant witness
To day's nativity —
A proud parent, slightly amazed
By the child I've helped create.

11/2/80 (05723)

No More Covenants for Noah Schwartzbaum △

Now, Mount Ararat fades
Like a graveside face
Shrinking back into a shroud.

My tiny ark
Slides further away from shore,
With the tidal sway.

The past has trapped me below deck,
In its mummy wrappings —
Just another chunk of ballast.

Cast off, perpetually lost
In miasmic waters,
I count rats

That scurry through my hallucinations,
Gnaw at my paranoia,
To stave off madness and desperation,

Hoping, one day, perhaps,
By gratuitous accident,
I might awaken to discover myself

Becalmed, stable, permanently anchored
At the base of a rainbow,
Free to begin dismantling my ship.

11/4/80 — [1] (00866)

Accountability

In between allusions to fiscal targets
For sales volumes, gross margins
Of profit, earnings, booked orders,
My dreamy eyes,
Straying from this high vantage,
Fix on Eads Bridge,
Shimmering in the green-tinted distance.

An illusive image of freedom
Needles away at motifs
Centering on deferrals of delivery,
Increased G&A, shipping,
Selling and interest expenses,
Diminishing control of flow of goods.
I see it restraining me in Egypt.

Sadly, the bridge separating my desperation
From the outside, beyond, grows wider,
Refuses to invite passage,
As the hour draws near
*

For me to present my detailed balance sheet
With another negative prophecy:
The river is an impassable sea.

11/4/80 — [2] (02395)

Election Day

I take to the road,
Leave downtown precipitously,
On my return journey home,
To exercise my seismic vote.

As fate's attaché in charge of change
For all things small
And inessentially great, I am ordained
To make my voice manifest.

Failure to express my choice publicly
Would result in arrest
And eventual death of freedom
To revel in self-delusion

Regarding the spirit's innate capability
To ascertain and correct deviations
From magnetic headings
Or connect lines of force with their true sources.

My psyche refuses to admit
That what it has to say
Makes no difference in the way atoms
Split or gravity shatters

Whenever its imagination soars,
Leaving, in its wake,
Weightless, shimmering metaphors,
Picassoed brush strokes, Chopinesque études.

Knowing, in my own heart,
It's not the candidate but the vote
That ultimately matters, I prepare
To cast my ballot in trochees and iambs.

11/4/80 — [3] (05724)

Empiricism

I can't fathom
How recombinant mind-spores
Effloresce into metaphors full-fledged,
Capable of translating tutelary ethers
Into tiny dinosaurs
Reincarnated as vehicular fuel,

Nor am I able to speculate
What changes clear pools to mirrors
Clouded by narcissistic silver
Or alters telephone poles
Into cruciforms growing, weedlike,
In local Golgothas.

All I know for certain
Is that I've never seen the universe
Wearing the same disguise twice
Or heard it repeat a single cliché,
Nor have any of its scientists
Ever explained me by isolating my poetry.

11/6/80   (05725)

Fall Starlings ^Δ

Even as the trees unload their debris,
Midway into November,
They yet seem almost full,
For three raucous hours
Each evening, prior to and through dusk,
Whose leaves are black starlings
Congregating, in clamorous, demented silhouette,
Prior to migrating en masse.

Abruptly they scatter,
Like a rack of pool balls broken
With incredible thrust. They tear the air,
Thousands, in arrhythmic crisscross,
Before resuming their maniacal chatter
High inside their own cacophony.
Oblivious to those below,
They play at aviary musical chairs,

While we're bewitched into docile immobility,
Aghast at their boisterous roistering,
Afraid that at any moment,
They might decide to strafe us,
Like vestigial saurians,
And bloody our most dominant fantasies.
Uneasy, we watch these leaves,
Hoping soon they'll drop from sight.

11/7/80   (05463)

Making a Settlement

I'm both appraiser and claims adjuster,
Sent out by the injured heart
To survey the extent of damage sustained.

I start out canvassing our backyard,
Trying to calculate, by color and species,
The exact number of dead leaves,

That my data might be accurate
For those who read reports
On natural disasters and the passing of civilizations.

My feet disturb the recently departed,
Sepulchered yet in this colossal necropolis,
While searching for a place to stop

And rest. The sheer quantity depresses me;
I anguish with tame squirrels
And torpid hares scavenging through the debris.

My bulky shape doesn't deter them,
As once, in May, it might have.
They sense we're all survivors,

Sharing the distinction of being named
Equal beneficiaries
Of nature's fully paid policy.

As day fades, we go our disparate ways,
Knowing we've been eclipsed
Despite being the recipients of additional life.

11/8/80   (05726)

In the Last Stages ^Δ

Acrid smoke,
Thick as chicken livers
Twitching in a scorching skillet,
Fills this sleazy café,
Early this glistening, honey-glazed
Monday morning,
Through whose brief chill
I've just bristled,
To order breakfast before work
And listen to "ain't"s,
"Smack-dab"s, and "hot-damn" politics
Scratch down the blackboard
Of my barely awake imagination.

Buick dealer and newly elected sheriff,
Undertaker, city attorney,
Various assorted farmers
And local owners of Ben Franklin
Sonic   Western Auto
Pizza Hut   MFA
Nick's Liquor's   IGA
Invoke rain, snow, tornado,
Or holocaust, to decide measures
Necessary for restraining free trade,
Through deceptive advertising,
Price fixing —
Their insular brand of laissez faire.

Cigars and filtered cigarettes
Foul the thick air
Inside this forum building
As cars, stalled by an accident,
On a freeway, do.
My pained eyes complain,
Squinting a headache into existence,
As they gaze straight ahead,
Through the flaking painted letters,
            "Capital Café,"
Precariously affixed to plate glass.
Slowly, four fluted columns
Of the courthouse come into focus.

Something in the smoke
Disposes me to skeptical preoccupation
With that imitation Helenic temple,
Surmounted by eaglelike pigeons,
Stuck to downtown's dead center.
Suddenly, it is a mausoleum.
I recognize all these plebeians
Surrounding me. Once,
They labored under my employ,
In the gardens of Ahenobarbus,
Which adorned my sumptuous estate.
Now, they rarely patronize
My shop, Nero's Heros & Deli.

11/10/80   (02267)

Jan's Panegyric △

This glorious morning
Is perfect for exploring euphoria,
Investigating prescience,
Planing the psyche's warped doors
And opening them to fresh insights,
Praising painted turtles
As they sun in prismatic bowls,
Hailing schism, dogma, YHWH,
Metaphors soaring above rhetoric,
And, most important, you —
Celebrating you, my blessed lady.

Without your fidelity
To my oblique ways of reciprocating love,
Changing gold into pyrite,
Letting sweet Chablis vinegar my tongue,
And lacking your patience
With promises made
In the heat of poetical creation,
Disavowed by forgetfulness
Once the spell dissolves,
I would see death and life
As two mere breaths anxious to be taken.

11/11/80   (00125)

Loose Connection

I'm locked in this speeding capsule.
My beleaguered ears block,
Pop, go closed again,
Then unclog, open without notice,
As though in a flying machine
Climbing, diving, pulling out
Precipitously,
Without allowing the mind's gyros
Time to regain their balance.

Even the quadraphonic speakers
Begin alternating
Like spark plugs, in a V-8,
Firing in sequence.
I don't know why these aberrations
Have chosen me for a host.
Possibly, someone above
Or behind the radio
Is playing a joke on my expectations,

Manipulating my patience
To see how much distraction
I can take before cracking.
Possibly, certain grotesque physiologies
Are actually at work,
Pressing on my brain,
Constricting blood flow,
Precipitating palpitations and dizziness.
Maybe I hear myself dying.

11/13/80 — [1] (05727)

From Little Acorns

In this wilderness
Through which I drive, going home,
Visions of children kiss me
Lightly on my eyelids.
Daydreaming redeems me from boredom,
Invites my straying gaze
To enter cinnamon-and-spice playgrounds,
*

Where they prance, do cartwheels,
Handstands, dance ballets
Redolent of splendid unendingness.

For an hour or so,
I indulge in Coleridgian suspensions,
To celebrate innocence and exuberance,
As though hypnotic evocation
Might disclose clues
To my future or a new way home.
As I slowly refocus on the road,
My thoughts pause
To kiss the lost little brooding boy
I never completely outgrew.

11/13/80 — [2] (05728)

As the Crow Flies ∆

There are no crows flying, today,
Only my loneliness,
Soaring south, toward a destination
Intuition alone knows.

And as I go, the whiteness dematerializes,
As though yesterday's blizzard
Were a cosmic joke,
Devised by a necromancer,

Instead of high- and low-pressure zones
Blown over November's shoulders
By converging wayward fates —
A joke without a punch line,

Unless, of course,
One considers black humor appropriate
To natural phenomena,
Interprets the snow

As God's class-action suit
Against this part of the state,
For exacerbating discrimination
And public calumniation of Negroes.

Up ahead, the entire gray horizon
Is streaked with saffron light-shafts —
*

A fusillade aimed at me,
Illuminating the design of my flight:

I'm a Northern apologist,
Scion of the original tribe of oppression,
An abolitionist preaching civil rights,
An anti–Jim Crow poet

Traveling, straight as an arrow,
Toward a podium located at Ole Miss,
From which I'll protest
Snow, loneliness, and necromantic jokers.

11/18/80   (00034)

[The perfection of disease] †

The perfection of disease
Infects the psyche with disorder.
Never has the brain had to quarter
Or contend with senescence, narcolepsy,
Superfetation

11/20/80 — [1]   (01385)

Scheduled for 8 P.M.

Confronting a silent, empty auditorium,
Uncertain whether his voice will work
Or remain withdrawn in its shell,
He scans the naked, waiting pages
Containing his poetries,
Hoping eyes and tongue will coordinate,
As they've been trained to do for years,
Bringing forth, oracularly,
In crisp, clear inflection,
Profound liturgies he's scribbled,
That he might arrive,
One fine night like tonight,
At this pinnacle, from which recitation
Will achieve ineffable profundity,
Express his deepest, innermost need
To be released from anonymity's grip.

But so far, no one has arrived.
It's minutes past 8:00;
They're late.
Suddenly, he feels his lips moving.
Preemptory words escape volitionlessly,
In articulate cadences,
And he realizes that, though sparse,
His audience is engaged, mesmerized.
Soon, he'll have invisible ears
Eating out of his hand,
Figmental devotees
Kneeling to catch every whisperous phrase.
He seems pleased, at ease, euphoric.
He's read to himself,
To a standing ovation,
On at least a thousand occasions before.

11/20–21/80 — [2] on 11/20 & [1] on 11/21   (03571)

Held Fast to the Past ^Δ

Although I've driven urgently
For at least two hours,
A persistence of imagery
Has kept my memory machine
Locked in neutral. Kudzu,
Long changed from lascivious green
To mere ineffectual coils
Hanging, like Piranesian *carceri* chains,
In midair, nowhere attached,
Still fills the tangled space
My dull gaze through the windshield
Continuously scans
Without being able to penetrate.
The tendrils linger portentously.

Whether these reptilian manifestations
Sully my imagination
From innate pusillanimity
Or superstitiousness,
I can't say with absolute certainty.
Yet their existence infests ratiocination.
*

I hear their lubricous slithering
Just above my eyes,
As though they might be nesting
In my spongy hemispheres
Or consuming themselves in crazed mating.
Possibly, these leafless vines
Intend to render me supine, useless,
Before I arrive home.

The highway begins to sway
Like a rope bridge in a rude wind.
Hallucinations overtake my slowing vehicle,
Enveloping fear in density
So stifling,
Suffocation almost might be more desirable.
Skidding to a halt on the shoulder,
I wait for the tremor to abate
And try to establish why
The damn kudzu has been stalking me,
Literally, through the eyes,
Gnawing on my thoughts.
Suddenly, their discovery dawns on me —
It's my fertile mentality they crave.

11/21/80 — [2] (00048)

Of Archaeological Discoveries ^Δ

After a week's absence from home,
Traveling to such exotic outposts
As Soudan, Luxor, New Athens, and Cairo,
I'm emphatically back.

Perched, pigeonlike, over a plate
Of Capital Café scrambled eggs,
Pecking at them with dazed abstraction,
As though trying to excavate bones

From an ancient civilization
Along whose banks I might divert my river
Or reroute my next life cycle,
I realize Monday morning is my Nile;

My pyramids are blunt yellow lumps
Clustered in the chipped-china cradle before me;
*

I am a sphinx
Whose location escapes history's eye-blink.

11/24/80   (00593)

"Caboose in Front of the Locomotive" ^Δ

Suddenly, from upstairs,
Down to the front hall,
Through the music room, into the kitchen,
An echoing shuffle comes running,
Just above which he floats,
In shimmering motion,
Spinning in his own excitement,
On meeting a new day head-on
And being greeted by both parents
Simultaneously.

He's morning's minstrel,
Bringing with him timeless villanelles
And roundelays and ballads,
Singing mystical verses,
To enchant our drowsy spirits,
Awaken our ears to mercurial reverberation.
"The worms go in, the worms
Go out, the worms play pinochle
On your snout!" he explodes with glee,
Though he's recited it ceaselessly for weeks.

"Hickory, dickory, dock!
The moose went up the clock.
The clock struck one, and down
Came the mouse, to wash the spider out,
While the little dog laughed
To see such sport.
The worms play pinochle on your snort."
My inspired intricacies
Tickle him, whose newfound lyricism
Reteaches us the need for improvisation.

Within seconds,
His sonorous chorus drifts off
And dissipates into thoughts
*

Of more important design.
Defining goals for his day and evening
Occupies his dreaming. He proclaims
A singularly inscrutable magical strain,
Calculated to grant him all conceivable wishes.
In rapid demotic, he chants,
"Caboose in front of the locomotive."

We require no explanation
For his gnomic catechism, this litany
Containing, at its core,
The quintessential universal symbol
For all things out of order
And humorously confused.
For a boy of three
To imagine a toy train
With its last car attached elsewhere
Is tantamount to papal heresy,

Yet the sheer possibility
Of such absurdity
Motivates his vagary-oriented mind
To demand immediate play. Our promise
To set up the trains tonight,
After supper, satisfies him restively,
As he concentrates on "breskus,"
Expressing his desire, *right now*,
For "eygs cream with chocolate spray,"
Without the slightest hesitation.

11/25/80 (01449)

Shoptalk

In class, last night,
Our extended discussion of creative writing
Touched on such fugitive insights
As honesty and inhibition,
Notions of making irrefragably naked
One's tame, timorous soul,
Taking out and laying on the table
All false eyeballs and lashes,
*

Toupees, teeth, prostheses, and pacemakers,
That a reader might see each imperfection
And appreciate the creator's alchemy,
Crucial to transmuting energy into feelings
Waiting, in limbo, for sweet release.

Yet as we talked,
Extruding garrulity, like nylon thread,
Through the collective orifice
Our animated eyes and heads provided,
Whatever wayward muses
Might have been flying in the vicinity
At night's start fled.
Evidently, as guardians of their fortress,
We had compromised secret designs,
Doomed our disclosures to hidden fissures.
Suddenly, the enemy, disguised as yawns,
Reduced us to students again,
Hoping attendance alone would determine our grades.

12/2/80 (05729)

Forever After

This eighteen-degree morning
Keeps my breath pressed painfully
Against the lungs.
Stomach muscles, contracting and relaxing,
Are frictioned shafts
On an out-of-time apparatus
Driving twin pumps in sinister cacophony.

Now, my visible exhalations
Congeal, foglike,
Blind me to the desolate square.
Dizziness disorients inner vision.
Pangaea coalesces in my mind;
Steamy swamps
Become fantasy's geography.

I exist before man's appearance
On a planet not yet violated by spasms,
Scarred by quakes with Himalayan excrescences
*

And volcanoes spewing magma,
Or divided by oceans,
At arbitrary tectonic-plate demarcations,
Like paper haphazardly torn by a child.

My transmogrification
Locates me, in pretime,
As an entity or portentous force,
A spore with endlessly permutable possibilities
For surviving the unconceived millenniums.
Shapeless, nameless, unbrained,
My spirit begins to spin and shimmer in the miasma,

Expanding, accreting cellular complexity,
Learning and unlearning myriad skins,
Membranes, vocabularies, and motions.
The ages swell, propelling me ahead,
Recede like waves consuming themselves,
Each time leaving my spirit behind
To outlive forgetting.

Suddenly, breathing heavily yet relieved,
I quit the hallucinatory freeze
And enter the Capital Café, for coffee and eggs.
Crowded with simian visages and voices,
It's a rain forest I've seen before.
Guarding my secret, I lift the cup
And celebrate the creation of another new universe.

12/3/80   (05730)

High Stakes: Reflections on the Nativity

Like Snopeses growing uncontrollably
Where, only moments ago,
Not even a crossroads existed,
Glowing lights materialize on trees,
Rim house eaves,
Illuminate myriad nowheres
With a Christmas spirit
Reminiscent of circus game-of-chance booths.

Myth in the making
Is again at hand. The celebration of miracles
*

Is imminent as Bible stories
Packaged in parables and fed to children,
For afternoon snacks. Ritual
Is the bewhiskered sweep with fat belly,
Leaping down chimneys
That vent the imagination's crackling fires.

Incantatory dream-stroking
Momentarily relieves pressures
To which sexual pleasures subject the flesh.
One desire is sublimated to another.
Drives are diverted,
Hopes postponed, in the lemmings' rush
Toward transitory gratification,
In the land of Every Man a King.

Brimming inventories are viscid water
Disappearing, in vortices, through tub drains —
A strange form of baptism
For such superstitious parishioners.
Yet cleanliness is its own virtue
And prophetic reward.
Empty store shelves
Are manifestations of the Lord's good works.

Soon, the immaculate day of days,
Cradled in a crèche
Made of cardboard and plastic, will arrive,
Wearing swaddling clothes
Of giftwrapping, ribbons, and cellophane,
And each of us will be expected to share
Parenthood for a birth
Nurtured at twice the cost of an arm and a leg.

12/8/80   (05731)

The Fool on the Hill △

For Yoko Ono and Sean

So stark and grizzly and swift
Was the disappearance of his physical spirit
That all who witnessed the killing
*

Purposely confused his last passing
With a godly, cosmic eye blink
And the flashing ambulance,
Transporting his perforated body to the useless hospital,
With a mystical apparition
Redolent not of visions apocalyptic,
Rather sparks blown back
From a vast flaming asteroid slashing the atmosphere,

While the rest of us,
Nationwide, universally,
Who, just moments prior,
Might have been drowsing, in dumb numbness,
Before *Monday Night Football*
Or asleep beneath trapunto blankets
Stuffed with comforting innocence and dream-down,
Awakened to the funereal gloom
That insinuated our rooms
With cyanide traces of tragedy's vapors
And united us, momentarily, in fear of the violent unknown.

Now, the volcanic hours have undulated and bubbled
Down night's mountainside,
To morning's base,
Where we lay comatose,
Dead to the truth of a new day,
Sundered by humanity's collective disgrace
In having once again crucified
The best and most vital among its species.
Yet we sense, who watched his ascendancy,
That the eyes in his head
Still see us and the world spinning 'round.

12/9/80   (02149)

Second-Generation Son of Immigrant Peddlers

This peripatetic morning,
As I set out for terra incognita,
With my bare essentials
(A spare set of clothes, high desires,
Dreams, notebook and pen,
And a billfold thin as sliced beef),

I realize that some necessities
Have been sacrificed,
Left behind,
Not so much in haste
As through discrimination and frugality,
To make room for cargo

Jammed into this spacious station wagon,
Which transports me,
In corporeal abandon,
Past temporal distraction,
Beyond forgetting, toward resourcefulness,
Where shore and horizon kiss

Behind opaque mists
That absorb me in thought,
Exchange ideas for metaphors,
And cause my eyes
To synthesize visions, from raw images,
Capable of sustaining my momentum.

Yet as I press ahead,
Getting, every second, closer in focus
To my prime destination,
Vague suggestions of intellectual inadequacy
Set up a resonating hum
My head at first mistakes for ratiocination,

Then later discovers
Is numbing pain emanating from the brain's base.
Suddenly, I know why my cargo
Is more important than supplies
Like dictionary and thesaurus,
Which I jettisoned last night,

When deciding what items to take
And which I might chance
Not bringing along for the ride.
At least my load of merchandise
(Flawed clothes, broken toys,
Damaged cans of vegetables and fruits)

Might provide for my survival
If I'm stranded in this no-man's-land
I'm traversing right now,
*

Whereas poetry I compose while driving
Wouldn't earn me two nickels
For a phone call or protect my flesh from the cold.

12/10/80 — [1] (02394)

In-sight

Slowly, the sky closes down.
My eyes are blinded by minute flakes
Shifting, in fine currents, sideways,
Like a million slithering pit vipers
Edging out of danger's way.

The vaporous, opaque cascades
Confound vision,
With their haphazard zigzagging.
My sense of direction
Becomes inexorably vexed.

Reflections of my perplexed face
Materialize inside,
On the windshield's screen,
As it changes from glass to mirror,
Due to crystallization on its back,

Causing me to pause momentarily
And actually gaze
On my own totally disoriented visage,
Whose intuition contains the key
To my destination, this blustery day.

Suddenly, the defroster
That instinct automatically engaged
Begins to coax the highway back
Into navigable focus. I lean forward,
Hoping to track my disappearing image home.

12/10/80 — [2] (05732)

The Writer Sees the Light

Soothing amber lights,
Swimming through my Chablis-filled wineglass
*

Like invisible schools of smooth-fluting fish,
Gently nibble my eyes,
Invite my tired mind to dive in,
Take a ride on their undulating tides.

Hesitant at first,
For fear of drowning, too near shore,
Before the free feeling of floating
Can buoy my cloyed, torpid body,
I refuse to lift the pool's edge to my lips
And tip it sufficiently to admit desire,

Then acquiesce, letting the liquid
Spill down an impromptu sluice I've built,
To a mill wheel waiting to spin my brain
Full tilt and grind day's chaff
To innocuous dust, its grain to dreams
Capable of sating sleep with their sweet taste.

Like spilled ink, the dim, fluid light
Spreads inside my body,
Exposing cells, psyche, dormant demons
Drowsing between seasons in Hell
To the sudden prismatic illumination of truth:
Their master can't think without a drink.

12/10/80 — [3] (02633)

Katy's Seduction

How it is that on certain brief occasions,
We make lasting impressions
On strangers, I can't adequately explain.

All I know for certain is that, once again,
The spirit named Katy
Has materialized out of the vast scatter,

To remind me we once converged.
Furthermore, she's remembered me
As the man who had fantastic words to compose

Regardless of the incongruous place
Or seemingly inappropriate hour, while I,
Looking into her urgent, smiling eyes,

Recognize that same gentle innocence
Which introduced her to me once before,
When my mind was too occupied

To inquire as to her sacred availability.
Now, we meet in accident's temple,
Strangers united by a strange desire

To know more about the nature of fate,
Possibly to remove a mutual layer
Of loneliness and discover the fragrance of love

No matter how evanescent
Or destined to imperfection. For now, I await
Ten o'clock's hands to signal our tryst,

Expecting nothing greater than incantation
Nor anything less than an invitation
To kiss lips until this moment dispossessed.

12/10/80 — [4] (01353)

Setting Traps ^Δ

My words are surreptitious mice
Sneaking cautiously out of holes
Gnawed in the brain's baseboards.

I wait until they are fully exposed
Before baiting my traps
With poetic cheese and messages,

Metaphors calculated to attract
Even the most skeptical devotees
Among their sneaky tribe.

Once they've smelled my enticements,
It's difficult to avoid capture
Or circumvent public display

In my frequently published verse.
Yet they continue trying
To grab hold of each new idea

And carry it away
Without anyone being made aware
Of their presence or its existence

In the mainstream of imagery
Being evoked and created
For the purpose of catching essences.

Every once in a great while,
A few of their species
Even succeed at stealing a whole poem

And transporting it behind the baseboards,
Where the rest nibble it, voraciously,
To an adequate, pragmatic death.

12/10/80 — [5] (02632)

Brodsky's *Life of Brodsky*

Why was I chosen to be
My own Boswell,
Recording, in ritualistic Sanskrit,
Occasionally minute by minute,
My most fastidious insights and visions?

Couldn't some other poor bastard
Or bored aesthete
Volunteer to be my amanuensis
When God takes time out
To ponder the teleological details of my existence?

The sacrifice required to recreate me,
Asleep and awake,
Demands such energy and dedication,
I often wonder what keeps me going
When no poetry discloses itself

And my loneliest undertakings,
Grave travesties of romance and the occult,
Only remind me that blood won't flow
From a fractured psyche
Or turnips grow in collapsed arteries.

Yet I fulfill my vocation
As though the will's will were divine,
Forgetting how reason once possessed me,
Nearly led me into a profession
Dignified by being wholly materialistic,

Sad that the Philistines failed to distract me,
Buy off my soul
In exchange for domestic comforts, a chic wife,
And myriad faddish gadgets
By which the "good life" is measured.

Had I succumbed, relinquished my questionable talent
To Mammon's treasures,
I might, right now, be sitting here,
In this animated Friday-night bar,
Wearing a three-piece vested suit,

Laughing my dead ass off,
Surrounded by sycophants and courtesans
Anxious to make my acquaintance
And take me into their confidences, ply me
With empty adulation and fraudulent awe,

Instead of listing into somnolent inebriation
While writing. Yet from my inception,
I've been forced to report my pilgrim's progress,
Sketch mortal self-portraits
For later generations to discover and appreciate.

What possibly could God have designed
When He commanded me to make poetry
Of my least poetic idiosyncrasies,
Fashion lasting metaphors
From my most iconoclastic and warring ambiguities?

Shit if I know!
All I can determine for certain
Is that, listening to inner voices,
My fidgeting fingers make the pen quiver
And spit a continuous history of my quizzical intellect.

12/12/80 — [1] (02631)

Entering the Buffer Zone

Sitting alone in this close restaurant,
Totally bereft,
I overhear, against my better wishes,
Sibilant whispering.

A specific word,
"Charlotte,"
Whose appropriate origins and fortunes
I can't begin to fathom, surfaces,

Eliciting, out of all my emotional core,
A very special response,
Being my own mother's name.
Intently, I listen,

As the vagrant conversation
In the booth adjacent to my own
Progresses in meaningless detail,
With the single exception

That, every so often, they repeat
My dear mother's name —
"Charlotte . . . Charlotte . . . Charlotte" —
Without knowing they've moved me,

Awakened my lonely soul
To an awareness of its own dislocation.
Slowly, I try to decode
Their garbled, cryptic transmissions,

Realizing there's no connection
Between our disparate lives,
Knowing we share only space
And this chance evocation.

And yet they've touched me
With their casual discussion.
I'm grateful for this circumstance
That has returned me to the universe.

12/12/80 — [2] (02630)

Mrs. Ebert

Today, I've seen the arthritic hands
Close in slow pain,
Witnessed the blank, glassy gaze
Of dead retinas, eyes blinking
With asynchronous dreams of seeing, again,
That which, for many years,
Has been mere blunt, indistinguishable figures
Swimming in murky fishtanks.

And now, after an entire afternoon
Has lapsed since my visit
To her one-room senior-citizen universe,
In which she passes her days,
Who, not so long back,
Was the intractable, indomitable harridan
Who ran an entire slacks outlet,
I still see that collapsed visage,

Wondering what it is about genes
And chemicals and hormones
That, in vast contrast to the will,
Trespasses on and devastates apparatus
And bodily functions, destroys one's ability
To squeeze and stand,
Amazed at realizing how dependent she now is
On another to bring her meals,

Clean her carpet, change her sheets,
Wash her clothes,
Draw her baths, buy groceries,
And write her checks. I shudder in pity,
Having, this very day,
Dropped by, in order to wish her
Merry Christmas,
Taking her a floral gift she couldn't see.

I weep for blessed Mrs. Ebert,
Who never would have dreamed
Of inconveniencing another human being
And, even in total dependency,
Never has. I worship her precious spirit,
Which, whether living or dead,
Will ever remind me how dedicated she was
To the sacred precept of self-reliance.

12/12/80 — [3] (02629)

Post-Postgraduate

Tonight, while I imbibe,
The students are hiding behind anxiety
That, with slight misfortune,
*

They might fail impending final exams,
Excommunicate themselves
From school involuntarily,
Violate all parental desires for their success,

Knowing that it all depends
On the awkward twist of the spinner,
Whose questions confound
Or invite brilliant regurgitation
Of material guessed as essential
And memorized. While I sip Chablis
And decode the mind's poetic Rosetta stone,

They try, in frustrating discussions,
To isolate all meaningful themes
Present in Piano Concerto no. 2
By Rachmaninoff, compare and contrast
Paintings by Tintoretto and Correggio,
Michelangelo, Bronzino, and Tiziano,
Distinguish between ameba and euglenophyte.

My envy of them, women and men alike,
Is minimal. My dues are paid
For the next two millenniums.
All that now remains,
While the younger generation hesitates,
Is for me to create, out of this precious solitude,
Another, newer Upanishad or *I Ching*

Before they manage to succeed,
Come away from their university training
Unscathed, their originality intact,
Their desire to encroach on madness maniacal.
I realize this interlude is mine alone.
My name is scribbled across the future,
But will what I write pass time's test?

12/12/80 — [4] (02628)

Mystical Sailing Ships

Cryptic reiterations
And crystal ships disappear,
Then materialize in the field I create
*

With mystical intuition
Powered by hemispherical silicon chips
Plugged into the right side
Of sinister inclinations, to inhibit mystery
And engender serious writing.

I sit back and scan the horizon,
On which weird noises
And phantom sampans and fireboats,
Launched by the Devil, float,
In silent procession, toward the mainland.
Slowly, the ocean drains,
Breaching vessels, of every flag,
On the dry top of the bottom of the wet sky.

I watch from my perch
In this makeshift crow's-nest
High above Hollywood,
Where Harold Lloyd still swings precariously
From oblivion's hour and minute hands,
Wondering what the fuck all those boats
Are doing sinking in the Beverly Hills Hotel pool,
While I am trying to set sail for Laputa.

Suddenly, day's light dissolves,
And I am caught inside the pollution
Rising from unfiltered stacks in Anaheim
And Palo Alto, knowing only
That the Love Canal is filling, again,
With dioxin
Instead of federal aid. Night descends,
Whose moon illuminates the boats,

Backed up in horrific quarantine.
I alone decide which are admitted
And which fail to pass my stiff inspection.
Those allowed to dock
Begin unloading their cargo of rats and opium,
Scabby geisha girls, tarantulas,
And banana snakes. Their abrupt invasion
Dislocates me, changes my notion

To devote my whole life to the pursuit of lust
And its ancillary tangents,
Passion and perversity. I decide,
*

With strict Baptist-fundamentalist emphasis,
To dedicate my life, from this point forward,
Toward capturing the essence of Christ.
Without a sign, the ships sever their lines,
Head for high seas,

While I return to my original concern
Of trying to define my purpose for writing
When weird vessels materialize
And oceans go dry as Israeli deserts.
Christ soon looms much less impressive
Than the mystical flying fish
That rise in phosphorescent halos
As I sink, inexorably, into my disappearing drink.

12/12/80 — [5] (01354)

Unable to Get in Touch ᐃ

The wide sky,
Striated with gray-blue-white strata,
Attracts my eyes to its vastness,
As I pass, in rapid transit,
Over this highway below.

It asks me to concentrate,
Define the nature of cloud configurations,
Isolate symbols
Hiding in its changing chaos,
And extrapolate ideas from its designs.

For miles, I lift my gaze
From road to *cielo* repeatedly,
In vexatious quest
After even the most basic traces
Of recognizable shapes

By which my literature's texture
Might gain in originality
And wit: a snake, perhaps,
Or an El Greco castle,
Faces, animals, mechanical apparatus.

No images coalesce out of the welter,
As I edge closer to home,
*

Convinced of my creative impotence,
Disgusted by having failed to touch God's eyes,
This glorious morning, with my own.

12/13/80   (05733)

Living on Memories ^Δ

Whenever I travel to time's outposts,
My wandering psyche reminds me
How the essence of memory
Not only revolves around my children
And blessed wife
But evolves out of discontent
Over being separated, set adrift,
From such elemental figments
Of my survival and well-being.

My heart weeps metaphors,
Moans in poetical cadences, images, and visions,
Whose shapes and fragrances resemble roses
Named Trilogy, Troika, and Jan.
It knows how all those moments,
Growing close in adoration,
Are so precariously juxtaposed to loneliness,
Just as death and breath
Are diametric sides of the same moon.

It senses potential tragedy
Inherent in each taking to the highway
I make, praying no ogres
Will intercept me and demand road tolls
Too grievous to pay.
My sad heart hears its own echo
Beating in phase
With fate's pulsating auricles,
Listens intently for the slightest fibrillation.

For now at least,
This day or hour, this minute
Anyway, my memories are safe
From instantaneous extinction.
With cautious jubilation,
Neither haughtily nor with false modesty,
*

I revel in my precious intellect's capacity
To float my speeding vessel, intact,
From one edge of death to the other, and back.

12/16/80 — [1] (00688)

Down and Out at Forty

These same few way stations,
Out of all this desolation
Through which I frequently pass,
Attract me as if I'm one more insect
Drawn to an acrid spot
On flypaper hung in a greasy kitchen.

I am memorized to them by convenience
And the imperatives creature comforts
Make on the sedentary spirit.
No matter their transitoriness,
The buffets, beds, men's rooms
Provide respite from the endless peripatetics,

Whose master and victim I am
And have been, this past decade,
Not against my will, rather as hapless thrall
To all that scratching out an existence
By the seat of one's pants implies
For survivors in the Land of Transients.

The euphony of my official title,
"Special agent," belies a location
Somewhere below "sales rep,"
"Registered territorial broker,"
"Road peddler," "drummer,"
"Door-to-door whore." It matters little,

In contrast to the reputation I've made
With waitresses, bartenders,
Motel clerks and receptionists,
Faceless late-night ladies,
And wayward college-town habitués of bars.
I'm known by sight,

Not by what I do for a living.
My money is better than good credit,
*

Readily accepted
In all the best places and palms.
Who I am or might have been
Is irrelevant to what I can do,

Right now, for whoever happens
To converge on my shadow
And get lost in the baffles
Of my desperate request for company.
Somewhere, the one lady lives
Who can redeem my dreams

From this bleary desolation.
I've seen her just once in person,
Little Sister Death,
Pursuing a dear friend of mine
And lover, my wife,
Deceiving her with martyrdom, in childbirth.

Often, I've thought how perfectly
I might adapt to traveling
Through eternity, if only I knew
My family would be waiting
For me to return
From the outer regions of oblivion.

12/16/80 — [2] (03572)

Handmade Gifts

For Mom and Dad,
Christmas 1980

Unredeemably stymied
After trying repeatedly
To buy you each a Christmas gift,
I've finally decided to sign my name
On every line of this page,
Rather than at the base of a check,
And convert my signature into a voice
Capable of purchasing exotica
Just by being words,
Writing bought at the cost of thought,
Pleasure gained at pain's expense.

My present, this simple wish,
Of every blessed one
I might have chosen from nothingness,
Is for you, my precious mother,
Charlotte, and you, dear Saul,
Father of my earthly kingdom,
To know, beyond shadows
Of my echoing poem, that all my gifts —
Intellect, sensibility, gentleness —
Belong to you already.
Only my endless love is original.

12/16/80 — [3] (00265)

Arriving by the Back Door

That hapless, lackluster bastard
Who introduced himself and signed his name
As "William McGonagall,
Poet and Tragedian,"
Without the least self-consciousness
Or doubt as to the propriety
Of his outsize titular nobility,
Sloshes around in my coffee,
This fine morning.

Lingering phrases from last night's reading
Assault me with imbecilic rapacity and vengeance,
As if specific lines of his verse,
Lifted, from context, onto the mind's tachistoscope,
Might reconcile my discomfiture
Or assuage my disapprobation
Of his idiotic vipers' pit
Of dissonant, contorted, and hissing attempts
At end-rhyming poetry.

They only serve to heighten my awareness
Of the vilification, calumniation, and ridicule
He must have suffered, unwittingly,
To satisfy his compulsive need
For creating and delivering words publicly,
Regardless of the occasion,
*

Always to the dismay of everyone but himself.
I shudder to think that such purblindness
Could have flourished undiscovered by him.

Yet William McGonagall died a genius
To the end, in his own mind,
Whom irony has since vindicated and magnified
By reprinting his books endlessly,
Until his celebrity has far outstripped
That of Lord Tennyson,
Recognized laureate of their day.
It matters little that our interest is fired
By inordinate fascination with the perverse

Or, worse, that fashion and taste,
Like Charybdis and Scylla,
Originate as manifestations of a secret desire
For self-annihilation of the psyche and spirit
Whenever we draw too near true inspiration.
Nor is it the door one uses to the mansion
Or outhouse, back or front, that's important;
Rather, it's the brashness
With which one slams it in the landlord's face.

12/17/80 — [1] (05734)

Return of the Conquering Hero

For Lady Jan

Oh, for a crystal-cold glass
Of aphrodisiacal wine, candles, and a passionate kiss,
With which to relax and find solace
In nighttime's inviolable confines.

To relinquish my arms and armor,
Disrobe to my vincible bones,
Forget, for the while, all strategies and tactics
Would be such sweet, naked repose.

My fast metabolism would cease
Driving me fanatically to create
And create and create anew
Crucial designs by which my life

Continues to pursue the same conclusion,
With myriad improvisation.
Eating and sleeping would become unnecessary.
My writing could breathe fresh air.

You and I, mistress, muse, and wife,
In this hypothetical paradise
Bounded by silence
Except for occasional noises

Rising, in concupiscent jubilation,
From the extravagant commingling of our voices
And bodies, celebrating their union,
Might discover each other for the first time

Since the last days of the Roman Empire,
When we lay together
In the lush, voluptuous gardens of Ahenobarbus,
Tasting forbidden moon-fruit

And amber love-apples
Dropping, in slow, wet profusion, from the sun,
As morning awakened us to our shadows
Running away from their oneness, into isolation.

Tonight, then, dear bride of quietude,
When I arrive home,
Let us devise a fitting ritual
Consisting of kisses, flickering candles, and wine

And, acquiescing without inhibitions,
Try to find, within its shimmering glow,
That passion which will sustain us
Even after our ashes have blown away.

12/17/80 — [2] (04183)

Disciple ^Δ

Although, during my unvigiled night,
I had no intimation that, this morning,
I might experience a great awakening

Or be possessed by oracular divinations,
Let alone be chosen, by God,
To be born, once more,

In a strange manger
Located in the corner of a warm dream
Forming the source of a poem,

It seems that this is indeed my lot
And that merciful Providence
Has isolated me from people and past,

Taken hold of my unsuspecting spirit,
And squeezed me alive.
I tingle, thinking these lines into being,

Amazed, dazed by the wonderment
Of word-splay
Perforating the pristine whiteness of my paper.

In this grip, I am the celebrated one,
The celebration itself.
All else falls away, for the moment,

As I proclaim to the uninitiated
That poetry saves,
Redeems the overloaded intellect from emptiness,

Resurrects its devoted novitiates
From earthly notions. At least, for me,
It has given dignity and purpose to my anonymity.

12/18/80   (05735)

Captain Martin

For Cindi and Amy and their Danny

This slightly white morning
Assails me with an irony, a paradox,
And a procession of prayers
Endlessly stippling vision
With grief and unspeakable consternation.
One at a time,
Like Orient men bearing gifts of wisdom
And insight, the intellect's trinity
Kneels at imagination's cradle.

Irony reminds me
How agonizingly coincidental
*

With the fabled birth
That we worship this exultant season
Our recent loss is
And how absolutely final
Is his sad passing,
As we prepare to celebrate not death,
Rather life everlasting.

Paradox begs me question
The way, the shape, the manifestation
In which his dying occurred,
Who, more than anything,
Lived for and loved flying.
That he should have departed
Roaring earthward
In his beautiful soaring machine
Somehow defies the gravity of fate and reason.

No gift seems fitting,
This Christmas Eve day,
Yet prayers for his sweet earthly repose,
His safe passage home
In the sleek ship his spirit describes,
Shimmering across memory's sky,
And his peaceful enshrinement
Urge me to retrieve his eternal optimism
And wear it like a Jesus robe.

12/24/80   (02151)

His First Set of Electric Trains Δ

Now, Christmas has fused,
Been opened, fascinated and mused over,
Left in the corner, neglected.
Soon, it, too,
Will be relegated to history's debris —
Detritus for Lethe.

Only one vast image persists,
To which I've kept returning,
These past few days,
Like a scriptwriter reviewing takes
*

For final inclusion
In a movie three years in the making:

That of a golden-haired little boy,
Seated in the lap of his daddy,
On the hardwood living-room floor,
Ecstatic, euphoric, gone,
Both surrendered to the streamlined diesel,
Tracking along the oval,

Roaring by their rapt eyes
Every few seconds,
With freight cars and a lighted caboose
The little fella names
Like God laying claim to all things
Small and great in His Creation.

Always before,
The possibility of colossal cliché
Bespelling me effectively
Was an alternative too outrageous
To distract me from preoccupation
With sophistication, intellectuality, aesthetics,

Yet listening to my little boy
Tonguing ululations
Imitative of real trains
Screaming through crossing gates,
Past operating stations,
Whistling down straightaways,

And seeing his face still entranced
Three days later,
Convinces me of my short-sightedness.
Reality is enchantment
Illumined by two dancing moons,
Reflective eyes, orbiting our human universe.

12/29/80   (01450)

Crystal Gazing ᐃ

The wisdom of Troika's innocence
Is a fine crystal goblet
*

Struck so delicately on its rim
That the mind's tines
Shimmer with whispering opiates.

Although visions of experience
Easily see through
Its stately translucent shape,
Both vessel, exempt from fissures,
And viewer remain inviolate,

While the resonating intellect
Enters the air as rainbow-halos
Hovering, then disappears,
Waiting to be raised, again,
By innocence toasting growth.

12/30/80   (01451)

New Year's Premonitions

Clavichords, lyres, and medieval recorders
Provide background cacophony —
The furious screeching of train wheels
Refusing to relinquish speed's heated stroking —
For this evening of ribaldry and debauchery,

On which we celebrate progression and death,
The feckless procession of days
And hours that enslave us,
Keep us in a state of chaos and flux,
Powerless to break free,

Exist apart, in space, from the galaxy
That defines time
Not in light-years illuminated by quasars
But mere decades, sheer years.
I hear the anomalous instruments

Moaning through laughter
And snatches of wit, cynicism, and gossip
From unfamiliar mouths
Gesticulating masklike, grotesquely, eerily.
My senses assimilate their distant whisperings,

As if, somehow, they were hissing voices
Wrenching me awake,
Provoking me to such discomfiture
That I can't mistake this occasion:
Satan's demons conspiring to invade paradise.

12/31/80   (05736)

INDEX OF TITLES

BIOGRAPHICAL NOTE

Louis Daniel Brodsky was born in St. Louis, Missouri, in 1941, where he attended St. Louis Country Day School. After earning a B.A., magna cum laude, at Yale University in 1963, he received an M.A. in English from Washington University in 1967 and an M.A. in Creative Writing from San Francisco State University the following year.

From 1968 to 1987, while continuing to write poetry, he assisted in managing a 350-person men's-clothing factory in Farmington, Missouri, and started one of the Midwest's first factory-outlet apparel chains. From 1980 to 1991, he taught English and creative writing at Mineral Area College, in nearby Flat River. Since 1987, he has lived in St. Louis and devoted himself to composing poems and short fictions. He has a daughter and a son.

Brodsky is the author of fifty-one volumes of poetry (five of which have been published in French by Éditions Gallimard) and twenty-two volumes of prose, including nine books of scholarship on William Faulkner and six books of short fictions. His poems and essays have appeared in *Harper's, The Faulkner Review, Southern Review, Texas Quarterly, National Forum, American Scholar, Studies in Bibliography, Kansas Quarterly,* Ball State University's *Forum, Cimarron Review,* and *Literary Review,* as well as in *Ariel, Acumen, Orbis, New Welsh Review, Dalhousie Review,* and other journals. His work has also been printed in five editions of the *Anthology of Magazine Verse and Yearbook of American Poetry.* The Center for Great Lakes Culture, at Michigan State University, selected *You Can't Go Back, Exactly* for its 2004 award for best book of poetry.

Other poetry and short fictions available from TIME BEING BOOKS

YAKOV AZRIEL
Threads from a Coat of Many Colors: Poems on Genesis

EDWARD BOCCIA
No Matter How Good the Light Is: Poems by a Painter

LOUIS DANIEL BRODSKY
You Can't Go Back, Exactly
The Thorough Earth
Four and Twenty Blackbirds Soaring
Mississippi Vistas: Volume One of *A Mississippi Trilogy*
Falling from Heaven: Holocaust Poems of a Jew and a Gentile *(Brodsky and Heyen)*
Forever, for Now: Poems for a Later Love
Mistress Mississippi: Volume Three of *A Mississippi Trilogy*
A Gleam in the Eye: Poems for a First Baby
Gestapo Crows: Holocaust Poems
The Capital Café: Poems of Redneck, U.S.A.
Disappearing in Mississippi Latitudes: Volume Two of *A Mississippi Trilogy*
Paper-Whites for Lady Jane: Poems of a Midlife Love Affair
The Complete Poems of Louis Daniel Brodsky: Volume One, 1963–1967
Three Early Books of Poems by Louis Daniel Brodsky, 1967–1969: *The Easy Philosopher, "A Hard Coming of It" and Other Poems,* and *The Foul Rag-and-Bone Shop*
The Eleventh Lost Tribe: Poems of the Holocaust
Toward the Torah, Soaring: Poems of the Renascence of Faith
Yellow Bricks *(short fictions)*
Catchin' the Drift o' the Draft *(short fictions)*
This Here's a Merica *(short fictions)*
Voice Within the Void: Poems of *Homo supinus*
Leaky Tubs *(short fictions)*
Shadow War: A Poetic Chronicle of September 11 and Beyond, Volume One
The Complete Poems of Louis Daniel Brodsky: Volume Two, 1967–1976
Shadow War: A Poetic Chronicle of September 11 and Beyond, Volume Two
Shadow War: A Poetic Chronicle of September 11 and Beyond, Volume Three
Shadow War: A Poetic Chronicle of September 11 and Beyond, Volume Four
Shadow War: A Poetic Chronicle of September 11 and Beyond, Volume Five
Rated Xmas *(short fictions)*
Nuts to You! *(short fictions)*

HARRY JAMES CARGAS *(editor)*
Telling the Tale: A Tribute to Elie Wiesel on the Occasion of His 65th Birthday —
Essays, Reflections, and Poems

866-840-4334
http://www.timebeing.com

JUDITH CHALMER
Out of History's Junk Jar: Poems of a Mixed Inheritance

GERALD EARLY
How the War in the Streets Is Won: Poems on the Quest of Love and Faith

GARY FINCKE
Blood Ties: Working-Class Poems

ALBERT GOLDBARTH
A Lineage of Ragpickers, Songpluckers, Elegiasts & Jewelers: Selected Poems of
  Jewish Family Life, 1973–1995

ROBERT HAMBLIN
From the Ground Up: Poems of One Southerner's Passage to Adulthood

WILLIAM HEYEN
Erika: Poems of the Holocaust
Falling from Heaven: Holocaust Poems of a Jew and a Gentile *(Brodsky and Heyen)*
Pterodactyl Rose: Poems of Ecology
Ribbons: The Gulf War — A Poem
The Host: Selected Poems, 1965–1990

TED HIRSCHFIELD
German Requiem: Poems of the War and the Atonement of a Third Reich Child

VIRGINIA V. JAMES HLAVSA
Waking October Leaves: Reanimations by a Small-Town Girl

RODGER KAMENETZ
The Missing Jew: New and Selected Poems
Stuck: Poems Midlife

NORBERT KRAPF
Somewhere in Southern Indiana: Poems of Midwestern Origins
Blue-Eyed Grass: Poems of Germany

ADRIAN C. LOUIS
Blood Thirsty Savages

LEO LUKE MARCELLO
Nothing Grows in One Place Forever: Poems of a Sicilian American

866-840-4334
http://www.timebeing.com

GARDNER McFALL
The Pilot's Daughter

JOSEPH MEREDITH
Hunter's Moon: Poems from Boyhood to Manhood

BEN MILDER
The Good Book Says . . . : Light Verse to Illuminate the Old Testament
The Good Book Also Says . . . : Numerous Humorous Poems Inspired by
the New Testament
Love Is Funny, Love Is Sad
The Zoo You Never Gnu: A Mad Menagerie of Bizarre Beasts and Birds

CHARLES MUÑOZ
Fragments of a Myth: Modern Poems on Ancient Themes

MICHAEL O'SIADHAIL
The Gossamer Wall: Poems in Witness to the Holocaust

JOSEPH STANTON
Imaginary Museum: Poems on Art